# THE
# MULTINATIONAL
# EMPIRE

*IN TWO VOLUMES*

# THE
# MULTINATIONAL
# EMPIRE

Nationalism and

National Reform in the

Habsburg Monarchy

1848-1918

*by ROBERT A. KANN*

*VOLUME I*

*Empire and Nationalities*

1 9 6 4
OCTAGON BOOKS. INC.
NEW YORK

*Reprinted 1964*
*by special arrangement with Columbia University Press*

## OCTAGON BOOKS, INC.
175 FIFTH AVENUE
NEW YORK, N. Y. 10010

LIBRARY OF CONGRESS CATALOG CARD NUMBER: 64-16383

*Printed in U.S.A. by*
NOBLE OFFSET PRINTERS, INC.
NEW YORK 3, N. Y.

*To Mariedl*

# ACKNOWLEDGMENTS

IT IS A PLEASANT DUTY to express my thanks to those who in various ways have furthered the pursuit of this study.

Professor emeritus Sidney B. Fay, of Harvard University, Professor Hans Kohn, of City College, New York, and President Walter C. Langsam, of Wagner College, have reviewed the outline of this study and have read the first draft of the manuscript either in part or in full. Their encouragement and friendly opinion of my study have greatly helped to make the publication possible.

To Professor Carlton J. H. Hayes, of Columbia University, in whose seminar I participated in 1941/42, I feel greatly indebted for his concern with my work ever since and in particular for having stimulated my interest in the field of nationalism.

As to the second volume of my study, in particular I owe a very real debt of gratitude to Professor John H. Wuorinen, of Columbia University, for his most helpful and tireless advice regarding the presentation of a difficult subject, as well as for his friendly interest in my academic career in general. Valuable suggestions have been made to me also by Professor Salo Baron, of Columbia University, and President Charles W. Cole, of Amherst College.

I am indebted to Professor Robert W. Seton-Watson, of Oxford University, for generous permission to quote from his works. In the same way Mrs. Gertrud Redlich, widow of Professor Joseph Redlich, formerly of the University of Vienna and Harvard University, has helped my work. Any student of the Austrian national problems in general and of this study in particular will realize that I owe far more to these two great scholars than this formal acknowledgment can convey.

Permission to quote from the following books is herewith gratefully acknowledged: Constable and Company, Ltd., London, R. W. Seton-Watson, *The Southern Slav Question*, p. 35; Jarrolds Ltd., London,

M. Hodža, *Federation in Central Europe,* pp. 58–59, Cambridge University Press, Cambridge, England and Macmillan Company, New York, the *Cambridge Modern History,* Vol. XII, Chapter VII by L. Eisenmann, pp. 176, 205, 206; Staples Press Ltd., London, O. Jászi, *Revolution and Counter-Revolution in Central Europe,* pp. 6, 7.

I greatly appreciate the truly constructive help in the editing of the manuscript given by Mrs. Mabel Erdmann, Princeton, N.J., Miss Helen Jantunen, of the Columbia University Press, and Mrs. Hattie Kennedy, New Haven, Conn.

My thanks are due to Mr. Vaughn S. Gray of the New York *Times* Art Department for preparation and revision of the maps. Dr. Alfred Berlstein, of the Slavonic Division of the New York Public Library, was very helpful in advising me on questions of spelling in Slavonic languages.

I feel greatly indebted to the Institute of Advanced Study in Princeton, N.J., and its director emeritus, Dr. Frank Aydelotte, for having given me the privilege of membership from 1943–1945. In writing a very substantial part of this study during that period I tried to make good use of the valuable opportunity thus offered to me.

I feel greatly indebted to the Research Council of Rutgers University for a generous grant for aid in publication of this study.

Furthermore the helpful services of Firestone Library, Princeton University and of many other collections too numerous to be listed here, are gratefully acknowledged.

Different from all the above listed sincere acknowledgments, but most deeply felt, is the gratitude which I owe to the late Max M. Warburg. His unwavering interest in the completion of this work was part of a generous friendship. Yet, beyond it, the study of the limited problem discussed in these volumes meant to him some contribution toward the achievement of a peaceful societal order, in which he put his hope and trust. His kind eyes, wide open to the world and its human problems, were not destined to see its dawn.

ROBERT A. KANN

*Princeton, N.J.*
*October, 1949*

# CONTENTS

VOLUME II

# MAPS

# INTRODUCTION TO VOLUME I

THIS STUDY deals with the development of the national problem within the multinational Austrian empire during the last century of its existence. This task is undertaken in a twofold way.

In the first volume the growth of nationalism among the empire's nationalities is sketched in broad outlines. The interrelations of the national claims of Austria's peoples are discussed.

The second volume analyzes proposals, as developed during almost a century, for reforms which should have solved the empire's national problem and thereby have preserved its existence. It represents the history of the conflict between national interests and this multinational state's claim for survival.[1] Thus, the supranational approach to the national problem, as developed in the second volume, supplements the national approach of the first volume. Both combined show the idea of nationalism operating in the field of political action.

It was intended to begin this study with the year 1848, one of the most important and ideologically most fertile in Austria's history. Yet, great as the influence of the Revolution of 1848 was on the further development of central European history, it by no means introduced the nationality problem into the history of the empire. The full development of the nationality problem can easily be traced to the second half of the eighteenth century, in important aspects to the seventeenth and even to the sixteenth century. Yet, the year 1848 gave the Austrian peoples for the first time the opportunity comprehensively to make their national claims in the political arena. The revolution meant the transition from ideological to political nationalism.

Though this study is concerned with fully conscious political manifestations of the national problem, the understanding of these problems is dependent on some knowledge of this period's cultural and ideological background. For this reason it was necessary to survey briefly the national cultural evolution within the empire prior to 1848. This appears particularly desirable, since the political life of the empire's national groups, even after 1848, was in varying degree still fettered both by the absolutist political regime and by the consequences of a feudal social order which had shackled their national culture for many centuries.

In other words, the manifestations of cultural nationalism in Austria prior to the Revolution of 1848 and for some time afterwards did not merely represent the foundations of political nationalism, they were also its means of expression.

It may not be obvious that a study concerned with the Austrian nationality problem should end with the dissolution of the empire itself in 1918. After all, this complex question was not only the problem of a state but also of a geographical area, and in that sense it is still a very living reality. Yet, one of the chief peculiarities of the Austrian nationality problem was the fact that the empire's political frontiers cut across ethnic frontiers of national groups. Thus Austria did not contain national groups, with the exception of Czechs, Slovaks, and Magyars, but fragmentary national groups. Therein rests one of the chief intricacies of the problem, an intricacy which has been largely, though by no means fully, removed by the peace treaties of 1919. Analysis of the nationality problem in the Danube area after 1918 involves problems perhaps equally difficult, yet in some points widely different, from those existing prior to 1918. Thus it is defensible to end this study in 1918, not because at that time the empire broke asunder, and certainly not because its nationality problem as such was solved in 1919, but because the specific form of the problem which confronted Austria ceased to exist in 1918.

This chronological problem of the study has its counterpart in a topical one. The following survey of the interrelations of the eleven main national groups within the empire discusses the national problems of Germans, Magyars, Czechs, and Croats at far greater length than those of the other national groups. This does not imply, however, that the national problems of these four groups are of greater importance. This study is not concerned with evaluating the specific significance of any national group. The decisive reason for this method is that the history of these particular groups contributes more to the understanding of the general pattern of the Austrian nationality problem than does that of the others. The Germans and the Magyars were dominant in the empire; their history was of greatest influence on other national groups. The history of the Czechs presents in a nut-shell nearly all the institutional reform proposals which the multi-national state has developed to solve its national problems. The Croatian problem illustrates in a particularly characteristic form, as, indeed, does the whole southern Slav problem, the influence of the evolution of cultural nationalism in the political field. It shows, further, the complex nature of the interrelationships of kindred ethnic groups within and beyond the borders of the empire.

Obviously, it should be remembered that the same conditions generally caused different reactions in every one of the empire's national groups. Consequently, they should be surveyed from different angles, with ever-varying stress on external facts of historic development. To illustrate this point: regarding the evolution of political nationalism among the empire's southern Slav peoples—Croats, Serbs, and Slovenes—the renaissance of cultural nationalism prior to 1848 should be particularly stressed. In the same period national conflict among the Poles and Ruthenians was primarily influenced by the tense socioeconomic situation in Galicia. In view of the belated rise of political nationalism among the empire's Rumanian subjects, the era after 1867 will be the focal point of the discussion of their national problems. Thus this study must be guided by the obvious fact that not all historic periods and events are equally important to all peoples.

This stringent concentration on the most decisive factors promoting the national development of every group of people is all the more necessary, since it is obviously impossible in a relatively brief historical area study on nationalism to review all the conflicting socio-economic, religious, and psychological factors connected with it. Nevertheless, though it is necessary to give preferential treatment to the politico-ideological aspects of the nationality problem, it is most important to keep in mind its intrinsic connection with the above factors.

This should help to answer a general objection which may be raised in regard to the purpose of the study beyond its possible significance as historical analysis. It may be charged that, since the study deals with bygone problems, the national claims and supra-national plans discussed subsequently are outdated and antiquated.

Yet the Austrian national problem, though it has ceased to exist as a state problem, will in changed form continue to exist as an area problem. The peoples living in these regions will have to meet issues in some ways similar to those which imperial Austria attempted to solve. Furthermore, the value of the Austrian experience is not confined to the situation in the Danube area. Its lessons may well be applied to territories where this experience is not charged with the bitterly contested memories of a relatively recent past.

And while it is obvious that none of the reform plans discussed in the following formulated projects could be applied as they stand to conditions in the world of today, scarcely one of them is unrelated to ideological forces valid today. A number of them appear more alive today in their basic principles than they ever were in the Austrian past. After all, this study deals primarily with ideas whose setting may appear old-fashioned but whose contents stand the test of time better than many forms of more recent human action.

Another argument is even more obvious. This study has been written in the United States of America, where large numbers of the descendants of south, central, and eastern European nationality groups not only live peacefully together, but in the course often of a single generation have become a part of the new nation. Why, it may be asked, could what has been done in the new world not be done in the old? If it has not been done, is it worth while to study the sterile problem of the alleged mishandling of the nationality problem in any part of Europe? The answer is, obviously, that it could not be done there and probably will not be done there in the near future. This is due not only to the fact that the age-old diverse affiliations of the European peoples with soil, history, culture, and language prevented such a process of amalgamation. This impossibility rests also on the lack of a common political philosophy and, beginning with the nineteenth century, the loosening of common cultural ties which could have been the basis of a "melting-pot" process for the Danube people. The existence of such bonds has made the American way successful. The existence of even the single tie of a common political philosophy, gained in an age-old joint historic struggle, has made the Swiss solution possible. The fact that neither solution was effective in eastern central Europe in the era of rising nationalism made them inapplicable for the Danube peoples. Whether these conditions will ever prevail in this region is a matter of speculation; that they do not exist today is a fact. Thus the eastern central European nationality problem cannot be disposed of by recourse to more fortunate conditions anywhere else which could not and cannot be introduced at the present time in central Europe.

Yet the final and most effective argument against the possible practical results of a study of this kind goes farther though certainly not deeper than the objections analyzed. It promotes "easy," direct, and comprehensive solutions of the nationality problem by means of wholesale population transfers, unjustified beyond the strictest possibly warranted limits of a few relatively narrow area problems.[2] Thereby this ideology intends to exorcise a totalitarian evil by ever increasingly totalitarian means.

To a point this opinion is perfectly correct, though. The general adoption of such ideology and procedure as applied behind the "Iron Curtain" eliminates the necessity of bothering any further about more humane ways of dealing with the nationality problem. Such programs and the principles on which they rest cannot be refuted by discussion, but only by strong moral dissent. The moral foundations of such dissent are embodied in the words of the great Magyar Eötvös, "Nationality is, like religion, a matter of the spirit and so belongs to those affairs which cannot finally be decided by the commands of a majority but only through mutual understanding."[3]

# EMPIRE AND NATIONALITIES

# CHAPTER I

# AUSTRIA: THE NAME

"Der Österreicher hat ein Vaterland
Und liebt's und hat auch Ursach, es zu lieben."

"The Austrian has a fatherland and loves it and
has reason to love it."
Schiller, *Wallenstein's Tod,* Act 1, Scene 5.

Austria is a purely imaginary name, which means neither a distinct people
nor a land or nation. It is a conventional name for a complex of clearly dif-
ferentiated nationalities. . . . There are Italians, Germans, Slavs, Hungarians, who together constitute the Austrian Empire. But there exists no
Austria, no Austrian, no Austrian nationality, and, except for a span of
land around Vienna, there never did. There are no attachments, no
memories of centuries-old unity and greatness, no historical ties which knit
the various peoples of one and the same state together—the history of
Austria is, all in all, small and sparse in factual material. None of these
peoples is so much superior to any other in numbers, intelligence, or pre-
ponderant influence and wealth as to make it possible for any one to absorb
the others in time.

National feeling, national pride, a vigorous, exalted consciousness of his
own strength is strange to the Austrian . . . and has to be.[1]
Andrian-Werburg, *Österreich und dessen Zukunft.*

INTERPRETATION of Austrian history wavers between these two opinions,[2] either one representative of countless others of the same spirit
—the one asserting the existence of an Austrian state, nationalism,
and patriotism, the other denying them outright. Obviously the historical approach to any study of Austria must first establish whether
the object of its investigation has been in existence at all.

What was Austria? Any answer to that question must analyze the
structure, function, and limits of a state, and, beyond that, the ap-
propriateness of the term "state" for Austria, indeed, the appro-
priateness of the name "Austria."

### THE HEREDITARY LANDS OF AUSTRIA

Broadly speaking, the so-called *Erblande,* or hereditary lands, are the Alpine domains from the spurs of the Alps in the north to the shores of the Adriatic in the south, from the Bavarian frontier in the west to the Hungarian plains in the east, predominantly German, but of Slav character in the south. After the downfall of the Bohemian king Otakar II, in the battle of Dürnkrut in 1278, Rudolph I (1273-91), the first Habsburg ruler of the Holy Roman Empire, conferred on his sons in 1282 the bulk of these territories, comprising what is known today as Upper and Lower Austria and a large part of the lands of Styria, Carinthia, and Carniola. In the course of the next generations, the Tyrol and Gorizia were added to the Habsburg fiefs.

Five centuries before the ascendancy of the Habsburg, the northeastern tip of this whole area was known as the Bavarian *Ostmark,* and two centuries later, around 1000, as the *Markgravate* of Austria. In the twelfth century it was raised to a duchy, and in the fourteenth century to an "archduchy," the latter term being created specifically for the Habsburg territories within the frame of the Holy Roman Empire. The name "Austria," however, was confined in the strictly legal sense to the Danube fiefs of Upper and Lower Austria. But for the Danube peoples in the eastern Alpine area, the term archduchy applied to the wider areas of the Habsburg Erblande, the core of the *Hausmacht* of the dynasty. Though the name "Austria" was at least intermittently applied in the following centuries to far wider areas of central Europe, it has survived as a permanent historic and geographic concept in the Erblande. It has been maintained there in the republic of Austria even after the disintegrating storms of the First World War.

### THE LANDS UNDER THE RULE OF THE HOUSE OF AUSTRIA

The accession of the Habsburgs to the rule of Bohemia and Hungary in 1526 and of Croatia in 1527 marks a turning point in the history of the idea of statehood in the Western world. These new acquisitions of the Habsburg scepter differed from any of their former gains in land and people, indeed in some respects differed from the aggrandizement of any other secular power heretofore known in the Western world.

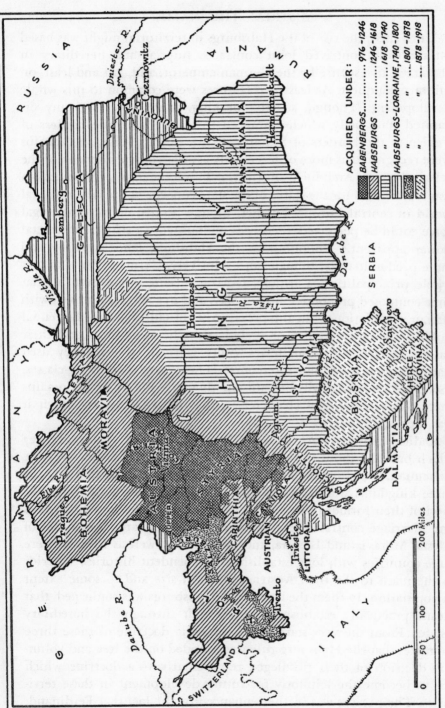

**AUSTRIA-HUNGARY, HISTORICAL DEVELOPMENT**

Only changes within the boundaries from 1878–1918, including the occupied and in 1908 annexed territory of Bosnia-Hercegovina, are shown on this map.

ACQUIRED UNDER:

BABENBERGS............976–1246
HABSBURGS............1246–1618
" ............1618–1740
HABSBURGS-LORRAINE, 1740–1801
" " 1801–1878
" " 1878–1918

RUSSIA

GALICIA

Lemberg

Vistula R.

Dniester R.

Czernowitz

BUKOVINA

RUMANIA

Hermannstadt

TRANSYLVANIA

HUNGARY

Budapest

Tisza R.

SERBIA

Danube R.

SLAVONIA

Drave R.

Agram

Save R.

Sava R.

BOSNIA

Sarajevo

HERCE-
GOVINA

DALMATIA

AUSTRIAN LITTORAL

Trieste

CARNIOLA

CARINTHIA

STYRIA

AUSTRIA

UPPER

Trento

TYROL

SALZBURG

SILESIA

MORAVIA

BOHEMIA

Prague

Elbe R.

Danube R.

GERMANY

SWITZERLAND

ITALY

200 Miles

0  50  100

Until then, the rise of the Habsburgs in territorial might was based on skillfully contrived joint contracts, nuptial and hereditary in character, investiture by the German emperor, and, last and least, on military conquest. At least two features were common to this whole development. Though, strictly speaking, there never was any organized state body which embraced the lands from the borders of Venice to the borders of Saxony, all the various Austrian domains were recognized as more or less closely associated dependencies of the relatively small Archduchy of Austria. This loose form of organization was typical only for the status of the state concept in the late medieval world in central Europe. Further, though no distinctive centrifugal force could be perceived, there was undoubtedly a strong centripetal power apparent.[3] Undoubtedly, the Habsburg lands were by and large predominantly, though not exclusively, German. Parts, in fact whole principalities—Carniola, Gorizia, Friaul—were even at that time composed preponderantly of Slav, and in some areas mixed with Italian, populations. But the protagonists of cultural life, the feudal nobility, whether secular or ecclesiastic—the liege lords and their vassals, church and monasteries—were German, though they used Latin frequently in their intercourse. These were the literate classes, though by no means fully literate, and they gave the Austrian domains their German national character in the limited sense in which it was then understood.

Radical changes were wrought by the events of 1526 and 1527 which brought about the extension of the Habsburg power over the Bohemian, the Hungarian, and the Croatian kingdoms. In a way the three kingdoms were subordinated under the Habsburg sway, like most of their former possessions, by the intricacies of hereditary laws and marriage contracts. But Bohemia, with her large accessories of Silesia, Moravia and Lusatia, and Hungary, as well as Croatia, were large countries with long-established independent histories, superior in the main to the then Austrian lands in size and to some extent in population. In them the rule of the Habsburgs was confirmed, that meant practically established, by election through the hereditary Estates. From the very start it was the basic doctrine of these three countries that the Habsburg rule was founded on the free and voluntary decision of their privileged representatives—a doctrine which was to become the leitmotiv for future development in these territories. Their status was further enhanced by the fact that Ferdinand, the first Habsburg ruler over these kingdoms, was not at that time German emperor (as such 1558–64).[4] As long as the archduke of Austria, ruler over some relatively insignificant Alpine principalities, did not wear the imperial mantle, there was no possibility that Bohemia, Hungary, and Croatia would ever be considered legally, politically, or morally as parts of the then known Austria.

The Habsburg accession to the throne of stronger, more homogeneous countries which culturally were, if not superior, at least equal, linked a chain of territories together in what may be called one of the earlier forms of dynastic of personal union.[5] Legally the union was based on the dynasty only, and such a loose tie with Habsburg rule interfered little with the independence of these lands. This was true at least until the first years of the Thirty Years' War, when the outcome of the battle of the White Mountain (1620) deprived the Bohemian lands of their claim to statehood. The later turn of events, which placed the rule of these diverse countries under the scepter of an almost uninterrupted succession of German emperors, resulted in some common interests. And this denominator of common political interests, accentuated by the fact that these rulers bore the German crown, raised their standard of power considerably.

Politically speaking, one must acknowledge that, with the year 1526, a new and strange Great European Power had emerged. There are numerous examples in history of a political Power existing on paper and not in reality. Here the opposite became true. A real Great Power was shaping up, but it had no name and few common institutions. Yet its armies were fighting decisive battles in many lands and its representatives, whether in the formal garb of officials of the German Empire, the Erblande, or the Hungarian or Bohemian kingdom, were conducting policies, in particular a foreign policy, which represented none of them directly, but rather the Habsburg Power itself.

Nevertheless, there could be no doubt of the existence of distinctive national features in every one of the newly acquired domains. The Austrian Erblande, despite their national incongruity, were lands of prevalent German character; the rich lands now joined under the Habsburg scepter were decidedly not, though the kingdom of Bohemia and its dependencies contained a high proportion of German population. Present in most of these lands were all or most of the upper-class elements of society which in the childhood of nationalism form the national character—a national nobility, an independent class of burghers, and, as far as Bohemia goes, an independent ecclesiastical culture. The national concept became inseparably interwoven in a cultural, political, and, to some extent, ethnic sense with the idea of independent statehood.

It is not necessary to go into the early history of the diversions between the concepts of state and nation to perceive clearly that the Habsburg rule taken as a whole thus lost its predominant German character in the ethnographic and cultural, though not yet in the political, sphere and assumed the multinational character of its combined domains. The first, still veiled, appearance of the gigantic problem of the Austrian multinational empire of later centuries came at a time when in western Europe just the opposite movement, the rise of the national state, was in full swing. From a purely political standpoint the Habsburg lands here began to lose step with the development of the Western world, and were never to regain it.

As long as in the sixteenth and seventeenth centuries the Habsburg rulers pursued two general aims, which, far beyond the interests of their *Hausmacht* policy,[6] were leading ideas of European policy in general—first, the struggle against the Protestant Reformation, and, secondly, the defensive and later offensive wars against the Infidels, the Turks—this development was not clearly recognized. It took almost two centuries to settle both issues. At the end of that period, in the early eighteenth century, Habsburg power had increased and its rank as a World Power was now unchallenged. The wars against the Turks ended in decisive victory and extended the frontiers of the Habsburg lands far to the east. Seen beyond the boundaries of the Habsburg domains from a world political standpoint, the other great struggle, the fight for the Counter Reformation, was by no means a clear victory for the Catholic cause, with which the dynasty will always be identified. But, judged from the viewpoint of the Habsburg *Hausmacht,* the outcome of this world struggle strengthened the power and the rule of the dynasty even more than the Turkish wars. It placed the Habsburg lands definitely as the first Power in the Holy Roman German Empire and showed that this position was dependent, not on the weakness of a decaying *Reich,* but on the strength and ever more rigidly enforced rule of the Habsburg *Hausmacht.*

The second decade of the eighteenth century brought the Habsburg rule to the apex of its power. With the outcome of the War of the Spanish Succession, it had acquired the Spanish Netherlands and the best part of the rich Italian territories. The Peace of Passarowitz with the Turks in 1718 confirmed the Habsburg rule in practically all the lands of the Hungarian crown in addition to parts of Serbia and Bosnia. This date marks, indeed, the decisive downfall of the Ottoman Empire, the great eastern rival of the Habsburgs. The end of this great struggle between Cross and Crescent meant the practical disappearance of the last important ideological unifying force in central Europe. If a new unity was to be achieved, it was of vital necessity to bind the Habsburg lands in some form of state organization. Thus, Charles VI, German emperor (from 1711 to 1740) and head of the Habsburg dynasty, realized this loss of spiritual unity and recognized the need for a common organization of his lands. He was aware that, because of their historic and geographic diversity, any such tie necessarily must be a loose one. In harmony with the valid concepts of this period, such a unifying force could consist only in the common allegiance of all his lands and peoples to the sovereign. Consequently, a chart of organization under this common affiliation could only be a hereditary law, a common order of succession of the dynasty, in short, the famous "Pragmatic Sanction." [7]

In a way the actual content of this state act, or rather collection of state acts, known as the Pragmatic Sanction is less important than the fact that such an order of succession was actually issued and particularly, the manner of its issuance. Five declarations comprise what is understood today as one important feature of policy: [8] (1) a resolution by the Estates of Croatia-Slavonia recognizing a common order of succession in 1712; (2) the so-called main declaration of April 19, 1713, made to the notables of the Holy Roman Empire in Vienna; (3) further resolutions by the Estates of the Free City of Fiume in 1720, (4) of the Estates of Transylvania in 1722, and, (5) particularly important, of the Estates of Hungary in 1722 and 1723.

There was one decisive difference between the Declaration of 1713 and the others mentioned. All of them established the same order of succession—male descendants before female descendants, the imperial line before the other lines, and so forth, and, most significant, that all the lands under the scepter of the Habsburgs should be ruled by the same sovereign.[9] But the imperial declaration of 1713, read to the notables and dignitaries of the lands under the Habsburg rule, was a "unilateral," one-sided declaration of the arbitrary will of the sovereign; it established a so-called *Hausgesetz*, that is, a statute for the dynasty. This sufficed for the "Austrian hereditary lands" and for Bohemia, which was still deprived of the ancient liberties she had lost in 1620. The declaration, however, was not adequate for such other lands of former independent history and constitutional tradition as the lands of the Holy Hungarian Crown of St. Stephen.[10] Here the emperor felt that only recognition by the legitimate constitutional power of the Estates could secure the establishment of his will in the form of law. But the sovereign was to get this recognition at high cost. He had to concede to all these lands, particularly to the Hungarian kingdom, all their ancient privileges; he had to confirm their territorial integrity, their constitutional setup, and, with particular reference to Hungary, their autonomous status as well.

From this period until 1918, Austro-Hungarian relations have been focused on the rights which were established, accepted, or claimed because of the Hungarian form of recognition of the Pragmatic Sanction. To be sure, the hotly contested legal dispute was here only the outward emanation and symbol of a political issue of far-reaching importance—first primarily of state conflict, and subsequently of national conflict as well.

Yet even the roots of the issue did not go back merely to the loose tie of common succession to all the Habsburg lands and the price paid by the dynasty for this unity. They were based on more far-reaching provisions contained in the state acts from 1712 to 1723. The documents comprising the Pragmatic Sanction in the Habsburg lands provided the explicit obligation to uphold the provisions of these pacts by armed force if necessary; in the case of Hungary a pact of mutual military assistance was set up between the lands of the Crown of St. Stephen and the other lands of the emperor. Thus, one of the most important branches of the state apparatus of the Habsburg lands, the armed forces, became common to all of them. The *de facto* existing Personal Union of 1526, based in principle only on the allegiance of the Habsburg lands to the same sovereign, was legally established, but its character was extended to an even closer union—the Real Union [11] of the lands—as solemnly stated in the Pragmatic Sanction—under the rule of the House of Austria.

As shall be seen in the course of this study, the ever-changing constitutional setups of the Habsburg lands, particularly of the non-

nds, and that
istinctions in
ongruity and
es, the Prag-
onstitutional
limits of its

only variations of this concept of
of two or more states under one
of the essential functions and in-
ion.[12]

ed, why do these documents refer
the House of Habsburg, the ancient
I? The answer is that the Prag-
a constitutional act of more far-
a family statute of the ruling house.
d, not merely under a scion of the
in his capacity as sovereign in Aus-
blande). It was, of course, inherent
Habsburg and Austria are, in a way,
rg would always rule over the Aus-
it was assumed that as long as the
dynasty of the Habsburgs, the Prag-
n force and all the Habsburg lands
ne ruler. The Habsburg dynasty, as
it, was the "constitutive" factor in
this legal political tie between the
tup of the Great Power ruled by it is
nanent factors throughout the history
re on the subject, however, it is some-
t justification made a testing point of
. This is probably one reason why the
Sanction has been often and unjustly

Sanction of
nich the first
firm ring it
ower of this

lands ruled
cept of the
t European

ic Sanction
s branches
, the Court
Chamber
or another,
the acces-
under the
imes when
ne time as

er of these
orm,[15] was
where the
nn recog-
, she suc-
the Hun-
her eldest
ever, dis-
stitution,
this case,
ght. His

ascribed to Prince Eugene of Savoy
hest of money and a well-trained army
kinds of solemn guarantees to respect
this statement Prince Eugene referred
d bargained for by foreign Powers, not
rrelations of the Habsburg lands them-
e is the consideration that the Magna
Power deals, by and large, only with
oncerned with the constitutional privi-
all concerned with the liberties of the
correct if measured by a higher stand-
ment. But, after all, the Pragmatic Sanc-

tion was a kind of Magna Charta for the Habsburg l
in itself was no small achievement. In spite of all the
historic rights and privileges so characteristic of the in
diversity of evolution of the central European count
matic Sanction brought about a transformation by
means and served constitutional ends according to th
time.

As Redlich expresses it so well, "Indeed the Pragma
the House of Austria is the solid legal fundament on
Continental Great Power of Europe was based. Like
has bound together the oldest supranational Great
continent for two centuries up to the sudden end." [13]

To use the words of these venerable documents, "T
by the House of Austria" are the second historical (
word "Austria" and embrace within their scope the lai
territory outside of Russia.[14]

### THE AUSTRIAN EMPIRE OF 1804

The era from 1526 to the promulgation of the Pragi
was by no means devoid of common agencies in va
of government, such as the Secret Council of the Empe
Chancellery, the Court War Council, and the Co
(treasury). Each of these agencies existed at one tin
from the time of Ferdinand I in the sixteenth centur
sion of Maria Theresa in 1740 as sovereign of the "la
rule of the House of Austria." But although there we
all of them were coexistent, they never all functioned
common agencies for all the Habsburg lands.

Under Maria Theresa (1740–80) the permanent cha
institutions, though in markedly revised and readjust
established in all the Habsburg lands except Hung;
"Queen of Hungary and Bohemia" [16] had to give
nition of a wide degree of Hungarian independence.
ceeded in making substantial centralistic reforms wi
garian territories. The more radical efforts in this respe
son and successor, Joseph II (as Emperor 1765–90),
regarded the sacred privileges of the royal Hungaria
despite its frequent confirmation by previous rulers. B
his endeavors, as so many of his other schemes, came

brother Leopold II (1790–92) restored the broad principles of the more moderate administrative reforms of Maria Theresa with relatively slight modifications, though he favored cautious gradual decentralization. With some reservations it may be said that this historic stage remained basically unchanged for a full century, until the Revolution of 1848, and, after that eventful interlude, again until 1860.

During the flourishing period of centralism in the Habsburg realm, the central government, under various forms represented by the State Council, was responsible solely to the sovereign. Its functioning, though often slow and cumbersome, due in part to the "collegial" [17] organization, was firmly based on the principles of a clear and on the whole well-constructed administrative system. With the exception of Hungary, an exception much modified in foreign and military affairs, the centralized system was never seriously challenged in this whole period from Leopold II to the Revolution of 1848. At one time or another a separate internal administration existed for some of the Habsburg lands, for example, in Bohemia in the first half of Maria Theresa's reign, in the newly acquired Galicia for a few years in the second half, and intermittently in the Italian possessions under the reign of her grandson, Emperor Francis (1792–1835). In the latter period in particular, Hungarian self-administration was confined to purely internal affairs and in military matters to the grant of a varying quota of recruits by the Estates. Institutions such as the old Hereditary Estates in each crownland were severely curtailed in their ancient rights to levy taxes, but these rights were never actually abolished, and, formally, the right of traditional representations of secular and ecclesiastic lords, knights, and town representatives was extended even to include the newly gained Galician territory.

But these rights in no way served to counterbalance the strong system of administrative centralism, though distinct features of other counterbalancing factors were visible in an elementary stage. The first was the combined influence of long-established and never fully discarded state rights of the various Habsburg lands and the rising trend of national feeling then chiefly evident in the form of ancient, legal claims to restoration of autonomous statelike organization. Because of their national feelings, the peoples under Habsburg rule began to view the traditional German character of the central administration with misgivings, though it rested primarily on technical administrative expediency and not as yet on conscious national interests.[18]

A second factor, the impact of the institutions of the crownlands,[19] bears a close relation to the first. The term "crownland," as used in English as well as in Continental European history, referred originally to the direct possession of a territory by the sovereign or by the ruling dynasty in the person of the sovereign. The meaning of the term crownland has been gradually extended from the private estate of the king to include state land, as used in the sense of the "crown colony." In the history of the Habsburg lands, however, this concept has a somewhat more specific, though never legally established, meaning. Here the term has never been extended to signify state land in general, but is confined to the specific relations of a certain territory to the crown: that is, a crownland is not just a domain devised by reasons of administrative expediency. Such a notion of mere administrative units has never existed in Austrian lands for any period of time.[20] Until 1918 a "crownland" was in name, legal title, geographic size, and, to some extent, population, the true image of the original fief, principality, or kingdom added to the Habsburg rule in the course of over six centuries. True enough, during the continuing growth and rule of the centralistic system the status of these crownlands was reduced to that of provinces and, as a matter of fact, often to that of provinces of inferior political constitutional standing as compared to provinces in Western countries. Still, the crownlands, preserved in their historic entity even in the Austrian republic of 1918 and in Czechoslovakia, stand as seemingly indestructible forms of an independent historic tradition.

The crownlands, the products of national traditionalism, feudalism, and crown rights, were, indeed, pillars of the Habsburg rule. At the same time they were chief impediments to a successful conversion of the Habsburg lands either to complete centralism or to a federalist setup on ethnic lines.

As to the prevailing modified centralist system, it is notable that the Habsburg lands were at the peak of administrative centralistic efficiency at the time of the rule of Maria Theresa, when the constitutional bond of the state organism rested solely on the loose bond of the Pragmatic Sanction. On the other hand, when Habsburg centralism was at last put on a firmer legal basis under Emperor Francis in 1804, the working of the state machine became seriously impaired.

This discrepancy between a rigid centralistic form and diverse national political trends from the liberal Left to the feudal Right became even more obvious in the era of what is usually called "Neo-Absolutism"—from 1849, after the suppression of the revolution, to 1859 and 1860, when new constitutional experiments were introduced. It would be rather superficial to say that the functioning of centralism in the Habsburg lands was contingent on the condition that it would be practiced, but never established as a permanent constitutional principle.[21] Nevertheless, it is true that the functioning of administrative centralism was possible in Austria as long as it did not definitely and permanently collide with the historic tradition of the country. This idea was aptly expressed by an Austrian parliamentarian, "The most permanent state of affairs in Austria is the provisional." With due reservations, it could well be argued that, in a state system as complex as the Austrian, this provisional "state of affairs" was, in a way, the safest one.

The political reasons for the creation of the hereditary Empire of Austria on August 11, 1804 by Emperor Francis [22] are obvious. Primary factors leading to this development were Napoleon's acceptance of the title of emperor only three months before, and the justified fear of the Habsburg Power that it would be driven out of Germany completely. The consequent establishment of a legally recognized Austrian Great Power was to a certain degree a successful move to preserve for the Habsburg lands at least the outward semblance of the status of a Great Power during the trying years of the ascendancy of the French emperor. The influence of this legal-political move on the internal conditions in the Habsburg lands and on their relation to German affairs was more problematic.

Again, it is Redlich who finds apt and succinct words to formulate the intrinsic meaning of the change.

The new Austrian imperial crown was only the solemn outward expression of the long-established fact that the position of the House of Habsburg as European Great Power rested exclusively on the solid structure of this empire as a whole (*Gesamtreich*), not on the election as the head of the Holy Roman Empire of the German Nation by the German electors.[23]

This interpretation goes beyond the transitory aspects of the two closely connected state acts—creation of the Austrian imperial title and renunciation of the German Imperial Crown. Though necessitated by the prompting of a superior foreign Power, it is nevertheless true that the creation of the Austrian Empire and the subsequent forced withdrawal from German affairs were only the last in a chain of conclusive historical events. These were, above all, the rise of the rivaling second Great German Power, Prussia, and the gravitation of the House of Austria throughout the greater part of the eighteenth century toward the east, to territories beyond the boundaries of the Holy Roman Empire of the German Nation.[24] It is, perhaps, the best proof of the logical necessity of this development of a shift, not so much in power as in the center of gravitation of power, that the great European peace settlement of 1814 and 1815 did not restore the German imperial power to the Habsburgs, though it gave to Austria the position of the presiding Power in the new German Confederation.[25]

In regard to the internal affairs of the Habsburg lands, the creation of the hereditary empire, the *Erbkaisertum,* represented technically no change of fundamental nature. The Pragmatic Sanction had established a common permanent tie between the Habsburg lands; the creation of the Austrian Empire established little but a new title for the sovereign and the lands ruled by him. No change in the administration and organization of the Habsburg lands accompanied either the imperial promotion or the demotion in regard to German affairs two years later. Above all, no change was effected concerning the relation of the Habsburg lands to each other. The Pragmatic Sanction was a carefully contrived scheme which was put into effect with scrupulous consideration of the established rights and principles of the various lands and with the consent of their Estates. The bond which it established was certainly not too strong, but firm and tenacious. The Declaration of 1804, however, was a mere unilateral declaration of the sovereign, prompted by political developments in foreign affairs and with little concern for the historic rights of the Habsburg lands or for the unhistoric "unconstitutional" method by which it was established. Primarily because of the unilateral character of this declaration and the failure to make its general acceptance dependent on the consent of the Estates of the various lands, its chief issue remained bitterly contested. This issue was: Does the new empire comprise all the Habsburg lands? Is, therefore, the new emperor of Austria, whose identity with the sovereigns of the various kingdoms and lands under Habsburg sway rests on the Pragmatic Sanction, superior to these fictitious rulers? Were they coordinated with or subordinated to him?

In all the Habsburg lands except Hungary, this question was not difficult to answer. Bohemia's right to independent statehood had been forfeited since the battle of the White Mountain, and it appeared of little practical consequence that the Czech peoples refused to recognize this fact. Croatia, as early as the eleventh century, had entered a rather unequal union with Hungary; the claims of all the other Habsburg lands for equal standing within the new empire stood on still weaker foundations. Imperial supremacy could hardly be challenged by any of them.

With Hungary, the matter was somewhat different. Seemingly in quite unequivocal terms the imperial declaration stated, "In the inseparable possession of our independent kingdoms and states, we have resolved on our and our successors' behalf to accept the title and mantle of a hereditary emperor of Austria." [26] Yet, the same declaration, in a clause as well as in a separate rescript directed to the Hungarian Estates, reasserted that Hungary's ancient rights and privileges should remain unimpaired by the new state act. Indeed, these rights, as formulated in the Pragmatic Sanction and as reasserted in 1790–91, implied clearly that Hungary was subordinated to no other and to no higher authority than the king of Hungary. It is a fact, however, that the Hungarian Estates did not raise the issue in regard to the contradictory state acts of 1804 until the Magyar Revolution of 1848–49. The suppression of the Magyar Revolution, which led to the complete forfeiture of Hungary's constitutional rights, made this question purely academic. These constitutional rights were restored again not, on the basis of the Declaration of 1804, but on the basis of the Compromise of 1867.

To summarize: For the period from 1804 to 1867 it is admissible to use the brief term "Austrian Empire" in place of the long-winded term "the lands under the rule of the House of Austria." The question whether Hungary was understood to be a part of this Austrian Empire or not remained contested in its theoretical aspects. In actual state practice, especially in foreign affairs, it can be answered in the affirmative.[27] In terms of power politics, and in interrelations with foreign states, the term "Austria" was generally understood to comprise all the Habsburg lands as they have been recognized since the Habsburg power of the *Hausmacht* outgrew the might and the authority of the crown of the Holy Roman Empire.

### AUSTRIA-HUNGARY UNDER THE COMPROMISE OF 1867

In a sense, the concept "Austria" underwent several radical changes from 1849 to the Compromise of 1867, and, from a strictly legal standpoint, the formulation of a fifth or even sixth and seventh phase in the history of its evolution could be justified. Yet, the so-called March constitution of 1849, the first representative though decreed constitution intended for all the Habsburg lands,[28] was never put into practice and, in fact, was formally abolished with the Sylvester Patent of December 31, 1851. Nor were the October Diploma of 1860 and the February Patent of 1861 ever truly operative as originally conceived, namely, as schemes of organization for the *Gesamtstaat*. These constitutional reform measures from 1849 to 1867 certainly were significant in the history of the Austrian reform movement, but, unlike the stages of development previously discussed and the Compromise of 1867, they do not form decisive phases in the history of the Austrian state concept itself.

All the more important in this respect is the period of Austro-Hungarian dualism of 1867 which was in force until the disintegration of the Habsburg monarchy in 1918. The reformers from 1848 to 1867 did not fail to find means of compromising between the universal Austrian Empire concept and Hungarian separatism, but they failed to effect its actual realization. On the other hand, the solution finally put into practice in 1867 proved to be the main stumbling block for any satisfactory readjustment in subsequent years. Thus, all the schemes with which one has to deal here are largely focused on the problem, before 1867 seeking to establish a permanent solution, after 1867 attempting either to override the effected solution or to eliminate it as the first premise for the organization of the multinational states system.

Indeed, most of the plans concerned with the constitutional, and, above all, national reforms of the empire are focused on this twofold problem.[29] Consequently, it is necessary to review the basic legal institutional facts on which this compromise was founded before the political premises and repercussions of its establishment can be discussed.

The facts are founded on the principle of the dualistic concept— two sovereign states united by a common ruler—two states having not only the ruler but also certain important state functions in common.[30] That is, their joint affairs do emanate from the sovereign rights of either state, not from a collective power (*Gesamtstaat*) superior to them. On the other hand, the relations between Austria and Hungary resting on the community of important functions of government, not merely on the personal identity of the sovereign in either state, are classified, not as a mere Personal Union, but as a Real Union.[31] If there ever was a comprehensive empire organization prior to the compromise, legally it has ceased to exist. The union of the dual states took its place.[32]

Common affairs of the two states are, first of all, foreign affairs and the disposition of the armed forces, the latter, however, only with important reservations providing that the grant of the quota of recruits, legislation concerning compulsory military service, transfer and provision of the armed forces, and regulation of the civic, nonmilitary affairs of members of the armed forces should belong to the functions of each of the two states separately. The third branch of common affairs was the matter of finances, but restricted exclusively to the budget of their joint functions. The joint ministry of finance expanded its activities, although most of the other joint agenda, through state practice and ordinances prompted by Hungary, were increasingly curtailed in their scope over the years. The administration of Bosnia and Hercegovina, occupied in 1878 and annexed formally in 1908, was, however, transferred to this ministry of finance.

Expenditures with regard to these common governmental functions were to be determined by agreement between the parliaments of the two countries, such expenses to be sanctioned by the sovereign in accordance with a fixed quota to be determined every ten years. If no agreement were reached on this point, the sovereign could fix this quota, but only for a period of one year.[33] This ten-year arrangement had the unfortunate effect of creating a severe crisis at regular intervals in addition to the irregular, but frequent crises in Austro-Hungarian relations. It undermined each time the foundations of the union and restricted the freedom of action of the monarchy in domestic as well as in foreign affairs. This was all the more serious, as the ten-year settlement—the periodic compromise within the compromise—included important problems of an economic nature such as those concerning currency, railroads, common public debts, and, above all, the question of the further continuance of the customs union.[34] The whole cumbersome procedure was blanketed

## AUSTRIA-HUNGARY, POLITICAL ORGANIZATION

Names of crownland capitals and one-time capitals of historicopolitical units
within Hungary and Bosnia-Hercegovina are underlined.

under the clumsy concept of the "affairs, not under common administration, but administered according to common principles to be agreed
upon from time to time."

／ Still stranger was the provision concerning the parliamentary responsibility of the ministers of common affairs of the two states. These
officials were responsible to the so-called "delegations" (apart from the
notorious Polish *Reichstag* with its *liberum veto* institution, perhaps
one of the most unusual parliamentary bodies which ever existed).
The delegations consisted of two sections, comprising sixty members
of the Austrian and sixty of the Hungarian parliament, in each case
forty members of the lower and twenty of the upper house. These
delegations convened each year as separate bodies, alternately in
Vienna and in Budapest, generally communicating with each other
only in writing. This provision was nothing but the logical consequence of the irrational principle that, due to Magyar pressure, the
established sovereignty of the two states could not endure the existence of a joint parliament or of any body superior to the Austrian and
Hungarian parliaments. The strain of such separatism within the
dualistic system was great, since it outruled the setup of joint parliamentary committees in case of all too frequent discord between the
Austrian and Hungarian sections. Consequently, the original dead-
lock remained unbroken in most cases.[35]

The Hungarian and the Austrian versions of the compromise, except for minor points, were identical as far as the actual provisions
concerning common affairs and procedure go; they were markedly
different with regard to the basic principles on which the compromise
was built. The Austrian version in the new Austrian constitutional
laws of 1867, unlike the Hungarian, was not rooted in a tradition of
constitutional liberties and privileges. The Hungarian constitutional
law, Article XII, which contains the compromise, reasserts in its
preamble the constitutional liberties of Hungary as developed in an
ancient and proud constitutional tradition. Above all, the validity
of the compromise in Hungary was reaffirmed as resting on the one
and only bond recognized by Hungary in regard to the other Habsburg lands—the Pragmatic Sanction. However, one new condition
is added, on which Hungarian adherence to the Pragmatic Sanction
was based, that is the continued existence of constitutional representative government in the non-Hungarian part of the empire. As in their

interpretation of other provisions of the compromise, the Hungarian claims, the so-called *Gravamina*, have stretched this point, too, and argued that the further validity of the compromise rested on the existence not of *a* constitution, but of *the* new Austrian constitution of 1867.[36] In fact, the announcement of radical constitutional changes in Austria, made under dire necessity by the last emperor, Charles, in October, 1918, in spite of the reassurance to respect the integrity of the lands of the Hungarian crown, gave the Hungarian parliament the legally highly questionable pretext for severing the Real Union with Austria.[37]

The ruling Magyar regime had weighty, though not uniformly "good," reasons for insisting on an adjustment of the Austrian constitution to the provisions of the compromise. The artificial balance between the western and eastern part of the Habsburg monarchy could not be preserved if one country were to be ruled according to autocratic and the other—at least potentially—according to parliamentary principles. Hungary was not afraid of the powers of a multinational, disparate, disunited Austrian parliament, it *was* afraid of the power of an absolute ruler in the more populous, industrially and economically more advanced western part of the monarchy. Yet, for better or for worse, there undoubtedly were strong reasons other than those of pure expediency. The short-lived, but truly great, tradition of Magyar liberalism—kindled with the spirit of the fateful and heroic Hungarian Revolution of 1848 and 1849 and continued in the political activities of such worthy political successors and standard-bearers as Deák, Eötvös, and the older Andrássy—was a strong factor in the resolve never to join a union with a country under autocratic rule which might threaten Hungarian constitutional liberties. However, the most decisive reasons of the Magyar ruling class, that is, the feudal nobility and gentry already sprinkled with the interests of big business, were less lofty. The rule of a Magyar minority in the Hungarian lands, based on the fiction that Hungary was not a multinational state, as Austria was, but, rather, a Magyar national state, was politically tenable only if Austria, too, did not grant autonomous rights to her nationalities. In this respect the Magyar rulers cared little for the fact that all these nationalities, with the exception of Poles, Italians, and Slovenes, were also represented in relatively large numbers and had generally settled on contiguous territories in Hungary,[38] and by and large were separated from their Austrian kin only by the Austro-Hungarian border line of the narrow Leitha River.[39]

Yet in their own way the Magyar rulers were keenly aware that the national question might endanger their own rule. They perceived that Magyar preponderance in Hungary could be upheld only if Austria was built up basically on centralistic foundations. Austria should not further any organized national movement which might spread to the other bank of the Leitha. But if Austria was to be preserved as a centralistic state, this could hardly be done on a multilingual, multinational basis; it could only be accomplished by conferring on one nationality group a dominant position approximate to the Magyar position in Hungary. For reasons of geographic and ethnographic position and size as well as of historic tradition and culture, such a group in Austria could only be the Austro-Germans, the one and only national group which, then backed by the German *Hinterland* and later by a recognized German Great Power, was strong enough to keep such a centralistic system in force. An Austrian centralized constitutional state based on German predominance, struggling with a national problem, but without organization on national lines, was the premise on which the Magyar Tory rule in Hungary rested and was, therefore, the premise of the compromise. To make it permanent, it was further necessary to tie the interests of Austria's predominant German national group to the preservation of the Dualist Union.

The community of German Austrian and Magyar interests in this respect was, indeed, the basis of the compromise and its rigid inflexibility.[40] It has often been asserted, particularly from the liberal point of view, that these key supports to the Austro-Hungarian Union were at the same time responsible for its destruction, that, having barred the way to a thorough political reform of the Habsburg Empire, they courted political disaster.[41] It appears, however, highly questionable whether political reforms alone could have saved the old Habsburg Great Power after the Austro-Prussian War of 1866. Yet it is certain that the underlying idea of the compromise—the sovereign equality of the two states, the one ruled by the Magyars, the other directed by the Austro-Germans—represented the key problem of the last two generations of the bygone Great Power.[42]

Turning back to the technical, but in implication far more than technical, development of the legal concept of this Power in the period from the compromise to 1918, another strange phenomenon becomes apparent. The Hungarian version of the compromise, that is, Article XII of the Hungarian constitutional law, refers to the union and relations between the lands of the Hungarian crown and "the other lands and provinces of his Majesty." The Austrian constitutional law of 1867, as well as the Austrian version of the compromise, names Austria the "kingdoms and lands represented in the *Reichsrat* ("die im Reichsrat vertretenen Königreiche und Länder")." Nowhere is the term "Austria" used, in spite of the imperial Declaration of 1804 creating the Austrian Empire. This somewhat derogatory nomenclature of the "other lands and provinces" would not be surprising if used solely by the Hungarian state. In fact, Magyar Hungarian constitutional theory—from the standpoint of historic tradition, with some right—never considered the "other lands and provinces" as a unit comparable in homogeneity of any kind with the Hungarian kingdom. This, however, does not explain Austrian usage of similar legal terminology, which so openly makes the non-Hungarian lands appear as the weaker and lesser part of the union.[43]

As has often happened in Austrian political history, two very different, even opposed, ideologies agreed here on a provisional, though poor, solution, in order to avoid a permanent and definite commitment to one or the other viewpoint. Well-established forces in Austria stressing the traditional autonomous character of the crownlands, as well as of larger historical units, particularly the vital and growing tradition of the rights of the Bohemian crown, stanchly opposed the threat of extinction of their name implied under the general leveling concept of "Austria." An old historic tradition and a new ethnic trend, both of strong federalistic tendencies, united here in joint endeavor to preserve or obtain their individual status in the new concept of Austria.

Still, an ideology of entirely opposite, strongly centralistic, character which deplored the dualistic split in the Empire was not unwilling to yield on that point—though most probably for very different reasons.

Here it should be remembered that the majority of the peoples in the lands under the sway of the Habsburg dynasty did not think of Austria according to the dualistic interpretation of 1867. Both friends and foes of the imperial idea—Magyars by no means fully excluded

—considered Austria not as the legal concept of the "hereditary lands" or as any other composition of historic units, least of all, perhaps, as the lifeless construction of 1804. They understood Austria as a living political reality, represented in the common allegiance of all the Habsburg lands to the sovereign. They conceived it, further, as the Great Central European Power which, irrespective of the fact that its legal character had been contested for the greater part of four centuries, in a very real way had remained in the forefront of European history. If this broad concept of Austria was willingly accepted by all the peoples of the monarchy, it was ardently supported by the force of German Austrian centralism and the social groups, irrespective of nationality, sustaining this system.[44] During the decades immediately preceding the First World War, the concept was taken up by the federalist conservative movement which rallied around the heir presumptive, Archduke Francis Ferdinand, in support of, a "Great Austria" which would replace the dualistic construction of 1867.[45] It was perfectly natural that the champions of an Austrian imperial concept comprising all the Habsburg lands, including Hungary, considered with considerable misgivings an Austrian state concept confined to the lands west of the Leitha. Waiting for the day when their comprehensive empire concept would become a legal, as well as a political, reality, they put up with the official monster term, of "the kingdoms and lands represented in the *Reichsrat,* rather than concede the existence of a less comprehensive Austria falling so far short of tradition, hopes, and expectations.

Nevertheless, political considerations could not obviate established political facts. It is true that the political concept of the great imperial Austria remained alive to the days of Austria's breakdown in 1918. At the same time, the narrower concept of an Austria confined to the lands west of the Leitha—Austria-Cisleithania—(as counterpart) the Hungarian lands east of the Leitha—Austria-Transleithania or just Transleithania—except in strictly official usage had been accepted as workable.

As far as mere technical expediency goes, an imperial ordinance in the form of a letter to Count Beust as "Reichschancellor," [46] November 11, 1868, clarified this terminology, at least in regard to the usage of bureaucratic officials. Here the sovereign rules that the Habsburg lands, and this refers particularly to intercourse in foreign affairs, should be called either "Austro-Hungarian monarchy" or "Austro-Hungarian Empire." The former term, which again conflicted with the Magyar sensibility in regard to unimpaired sovereignty, was soon to be dropped, but even the latter gave offense to the Magyars as an alleged indication that the sovereign ruled in the same capacity in both states, not as king in one and emperor in another.[47] It was therefore replaced by the more innocent and briefer "Austria-Hungary," the final official label under which the Habsburg Great Power was known in history. This designation preserved, if not a great imperial tradition, at least the name of a "hyphenated" Austria.

In line with colloquial usage and traditional political practice, the term "Austria" will be used in the further course of this study to designate the non-Hungarian Habsburg lands. Inasmuch as the problem of the dualistic division of the empire preceded the ill-fated Compromise of 1867 by centuries, it is permissible to use this term in reference to events prior to the Compromise of 1867 as well.[48]

The decision regarding the use of a standardized terminology for the combined Habsburg lands is more difficult. Beyond doubt, the legal concept of an Austrian Empire did not exist before 1804. On the other hand, as pointed out before, even after 1804 the term "Austrian Empire" is equivocal. However, it is essential to find an adequate term to define the concept of the political power of all the Habsburg lands without going into the issue of constitutional conflict each time the term is used. The English language offers such a possibility in its meaning of the term "empire"—an empire refers to a "supreme and extensive political dominion." [49] Undoubtedly, the use of this sweeping term "empire" best designates the concept of power analyzed in this study. The empire or the Austrian Empire stands for the whole Great Central European Power in a political, social, and ideological sense, notwithstanding Magyar claims that the physical sovereignty of one ruler was legally divided in two.

In conclusion, the term "empire" will be used for all the Habsburg lands alternately with "monarchy" or "Austro-Hungarian monarchy" or "Austria-Hungary" for the period after 1867. Only in cases where the context makes it unmistakably clear—this refers largely to quotations and references to foreign policy—will the word "Austria" be used in reference to the empire as a whole. Otherwise, the term "Austria" alone—Bosnia-Hercegovina excepted—must be used for the non-Hungarian lands under Habsburg rule, whether before or after the enactment of the compromise.[50]

This is nothing more than an expedient, though a well-substantiated one. For, after all, the whole history of the Austrian Empire, in the sense outlined before, is in a way the history of the application of expedients instead of solutions. In this chain the terminological question of the Austrian name in itself is, perhaps, not one of foremost importance. But apart from its symbolic significance in relation to the complexity, contradictions, and yet strict traditionalism of Austrian development, it is linked inseparably with so many problems of foremost importance that to use it as an introduction to this study should prove relevant.

# CHAPTER II

# PATTERN OF THE NATIONAL PROBLEM IN AUSTRIA

THE GENERAL CONCEPTS of the national problem as they have developed in Europe since the eighteenth century apply to Austria as well as to any other state.[1] Yet in Austria, more than in any other state, ethnic, cultural, political, and historic aspects of this problem are inextricably interwoven. A survey of the pattern of Austria's national problem thus represents the application of a general terminology to a specific and, indeed, unique historic problem.

## NATIONALITIES AND NATIONAL MINORITIES

There are two possible ways to designate the ethnically and culturally different peoples of one composite state or union of states, such as Austria was before 1918. Either one may speak of the various nations, or of the various nationalities, in such a state organization. Neither term is fully satisfactory, nor, indeed, is scarcely any definition of the concept of nation. Most definitions conceive a nation in more or less vague terms as a social group bound together by several of the following main factors: common language, religion, institutions, traditions, customs, descent, and territory. Such a community of people frequently live in their majority under the same government, thus forming a state nation, as distinguished from the cultural nation where either no union under a common government exists or where the union extends beyond that of a common government. Thus, state and nation are—as rather generally agreed—related and sometimes overlapping, but by no means identical terms.

With regard to the specific problems of this study, the main objection to the use of the term "nation" is that, in spite of all theoretical distinctions, this term as frequently discussed is used, indiscriminately, but widely, to mean "state."[2]

The Austrian national problem, however, is based on the conflict between the national claims of the various peoples versus the demands of the empire, the state. This issue reappears within the sphere of specific national groups, that is, in the conflict between historic tradition and ethnic claims. Often these claims are wider, though sometimes even narrower, than the historic state concepts of specific Habsburg domains, of which Bohemia, Hungary, and Croatia serve as outstanding examples. Thus, it is essential to employ a terminology which distinguishes clearly among the main forces directing the Austrian national problem, namely, the supranational central power of the state, the diverse ethnic groups, and the historic units of kingdoms and lands in which the national culture and claims of these ethnic groups, "the nationalities," were developed.

Still, the use of the term "nationality," though not easily confounded with "state," is not entirely satisfactory, either. It designates the status of a national group, as well as that of an individual. Nevertheless, its use here is recommended for two main reasons: first, the distinction between the national status of an individual and the designation of a national group is easily discernible in the proper context. Secondly, the term "nationality" conveys a specific meaning closer to the concept of the Austrian national groups than either the sweeping term "people" or the somewhat archaic "tribe."

The term nationality, as employed to indicate the collective status of a group, is complex and, since national groups are the product of the living forces of history, fluctuating. Hans Kohn brings out this point well. After listing the factors which usually determine such a nationality concept (common descent, language, territory, political entity, customs and tradition, and religion), he adds, "None of them [that is, in itself] is essential to the existence or definition of nationality." [3] True, but combinations of some of them are essential in order to give the term its meaning. Though in reality it is most likely that one or some of these factors may be absent, the general notion itself will still be recognizable.

Indeed, this concept of nationality rarely appears in "complete" form. Frequently, some important factors, as those of political entity (as Kohn calls it) and very often also of territory (that is, nationally homogeneous territories), are lacking. It is just the more distinctive lack or rudimentary character of one or several of such factors that, by degree implies one of the basic differences between the grander concept of "nation" and the more modest one of "nationalities." [4] This less than perfect condition of nationality is shown very well in the English language. According to the *Oxford Dictionary,* nationality is "a nation; frequently, a people, potentially but not actually a nation." [5] Definitions in other languages—in the case of Austria, the German language would be the most important—agree with this.[6] No other term has the same connotation of an ethnic group striving to be recognized as state or state nation, that is, as the national majority group in a state. No other term expresses or circumscribes so well the peculiar status of the Austrian peoples, who, by some limited degree of state recognition, were something more than mere ethnic groups and considerably less than real nations.[7]

Finally, the concept of the Austrian nationalities must be distinguished from the concept of national minorities. It is scarcely less difficult to define than the notions of nations and nationalities. This holds true particularly for the state of affairs before 1919, that is, before the treaties drafted at Versailles established a definite legal meaning for this term.[8]

Generally, a national minority is perceived as an ethnic group distinctly conscious of its national and cultural character—to be determined by one [9] or more of the previously listed main factors constituting a nation—living, however, in a state inhabited by a majority of different national character.[10] Such a minority usually wants to preserve its distinctive group character permanently.

Minorities are usually classified in various subdivisions, such as genuine and nongenuine, natural and artificial, relative and absolute, conditional and unconditional. Only the first classification is universally accepted. It has a particularly important bearing on the topic of this study. Genuine minorities are those minorities which are settled in the interior of a country—not necessarily in contiguous territories—and whose minority status is static and permanent. The Volga Germans in Russia are considered a classic type of such minorities. Nongenuine minorities are rather different. They are created if a part of a nationally homogeneous territory is dominated by a neighbor state, the majority of the population of which is of different national character. Those minorities owe their existence usually to determined political actions such as war and interstate treaties, and not to a peaceful organic development of emigration. Naturally, they are of a less permanent character than genuine minorities. To cite one example out of many, the Poles in the eastern part of royal Prussia were considered this type of nongenuine national minority.

These and other controversial national minority concepts have one basic assumption in common, namely, that the existence of such a minority is dependent on the existence of a national majority. This basic premise did not exist in regard to the national groups in the Austrian Empire. As far as the history of the nationality census in Austria proved, none of the nationalities, not even the Germans, ever held an absolute majority. As for Hungary, if Croatia is included, even the Magyars in their exorbitant national claims have not gone so far as to assert that they formed an absolute majority.[11] Consequently, the national groups within the borders of the empire were not minorities in their interrelations; none of them was numerically equal, let alone superior, in size and in numbers to the other groups combined.[12]

This does not mean that Austria contained no national minorities and that the national minority problem in the empire should be disregarded. First of all, from a purely geographical point of view, a number of genuine permanent minorities of long standing inhabited territories surrounded entirely by members of a majority national group, and were cut off from their own fellow nations. These included the German Swabians in the Hungarian Banat, the German Saxons in Transylvania, and the Czechs in Vienna. Indeed, if one does not consider the various national groups as a whole, but turns to a regional analysis, there were substantial minorities in most of the Austrian crownlands.[13] Among the seventeen Cisleithanian crownlands [14] there were several in which no nationality formed an absolute majority,[15] and there were only six in which, during the whole period from 1848 to 1918, more than 90 percent of the population spoke the same mother tongue.[16] Within certain districts and communities there existed minority problems, even if the crownlands possessed no absolute national majorities of population.

Nevertheless, the national groups taken as a whole, including various merely regional minorities of the same national character, fall under the concept of nationalities. In some cases problems of a regional minority in this or that community or district have attracted more attention than at times the seemingly academic question of the position of a nationality as a whole. But in the long run, the plans for a solution of the national problem, either in the whole empire or in Cisleithania and Transleithania separately, were focused on the more comprehensive concept of nationality problems.

Indeed, the principles of national minority protection, whether appearing in the internationally recognized form developed after 1918 or in the provisions generally shaped in state law throughout the nineteenth century, could never do justice to the specific national problems of the multinational state having no absolute national majority. Minority protection derives its *raison d'être* from the existence of majority rule. Where, technically speaking, a national majority is nonexistent, one must avoid the use of a terminology solely confined to the problem of majority—minority interrelation.[17] It is even more important to realize that the unequal, unsatisfactory, and sometimes even desperate, status of certain national groups in the multinational state is caused by phenomena of a more complex nature than those summarized in the cliché term of the minority problem, namely, national discrimination.

The solution of the main problem involved in the organization of the multinational state is not focused on tolerance or protection of any specific rights of minorities, though their adjustment should be taken as a matter of course. It is focused on the far more comprehensive problem of the equal coordination of all the national groups in the organization of the whole state according to the national principle.[18]

### THE AUSTRIAN HISTORICOPOLITICAL ENTITIES

The gradual evolution of nationalism to a clearly discernible political movement is usually associated by historians with the eighteenth century, its rise to one of the most dynamic and most powerful forces in history, with the nineteenth century. It is also widely agreed that before nationalism became a clearly recognized force of its own, its antecedents, or rather, important aspects of its antecedents and earlier manifestations, are closely connected with the development of the territorial state and its historic tradition.

The development of the nationality problem in the Austrian Empire is no exception to these conclusions. But this analogy is true only up to a certain point in the course of history. The rise of the national state—and here the nationally homogeneous state is meant—has generally led to a complete fusion of the concepts of nation and state, of nationalism and patriotism. In the nationally heterogeneous state, the multinational state, and the state containing large minorities this fusion has never taken place, and there the concept of nationalism was almost completely transformed to an ethnic and racial one.

Austria decidedly belongs to the nationally heterogeneous states, and yet the development of the idea of nationalism here differed considerably from that in other states belonging to this category. The nationalism of the Austrian nationalities in the course of the nineteenth century contained such widely accepted ethnic racial concepts as Pan-German, Pan-Slav, South Slav, and All Polish movements. At the same time, the traditions of the old territorial states, the sovereign entities out of which the Habsburg Power was developed in the course of so many centuries, have been kept alive in Austria. They have been basically preserved, reorganized, and promoted as full-fledged national movements, partly overlapping, partly running parallel to, and partly conflicting with the ethnic racial trends of the nineteenth century. These historical units, commonly referred to as the historicopolitical entities (*historisch politische Individualitäten*) were backed up and revived by national forces distinctly different from those promoting ethnic programs. No similar concepts exist otherwise in the history of eastern central Europe.

To be sure, many another small eastern European nation nursed its dreams of a glorious past and kindled its national ambitions on the fire of such tradition. The traditions of a short-lived Serbian empire, a Great Bulgaria, and a Poland from the Baltic to the Black Sea are obvious examples. In those cases, the aim of the national legend was to foment nationalism in general. Nineteenth-century political nationalism, though backing up specific territorial demands by the appeal to history, no longer identified its interests with the claims of a medieval past.

In the Habsburg lands, traditional historic nationalism worked with marked difference. Promoted by conservative forces, it was not much concerned with adjusting the borders of the empire in conformity with the dreams the various nationality groups had of past national glories. But it was very seriously concerned with upholding, regaining, and adjusting the rights, the privileges, and the social structure of the historical entities, "kingdom or lands," which, in the course of time, had joined the association of the Habsburg lands. Unlike the familiar notions of "traditional nationalism,"[19] historic national claims in Austria did not form merely the background of an ethnic nationalist movement; they stood for a very real program of their own, frequently shaped and organized in the form of an actual party program.

The term historicopolitical entity is not a strictly legal one, but it has been used frequently in Austrian parliamentary debates [20] and came particularly into vogue in the period from the Austro-Sardinian war in 1859 to the conclusion of the Compromise in 1867. Particularly during that period of Austrian constitutional experiments,[21] the attempt was made to substitute the limited recognition of the historicopolitical units for the fulfillment of genuine national claims.

As Anton, Count Szécsen, a leading statesman and promoter of this concept, expressed it in 1860:

The historicopolitical entity of the different lands of the monarchy is exactly the expression and the reunion of the whole development and all the activities of the diverse parts of the monarchy in a national historic and political sense; this concept comprises not only a kingdom of Hungary, a Danube, Tisza, Carpathian district, but also, instead of a district of Troppau or Salzburg, a land of Salzburg, a land of Silesia; no district of the Moldawa or the Adriatic, but a city of Trieste and a kingdom of Bohemia. But in varying degrees the attachment to the historicopolitical entity exists throughout the whole monarchy.[22]

Eisenmann analyzes the function of this concept thus:

These living historicopolitical entities were meant to have become the foundations of the Austrian monarchy. It was their task to conciliate the demands of the present time with the just traditions of the past. It was their task to strengthen the modern institutions by attaching them to those historically developed in the various lands. The principles of the . . . system are: Recognition of the historicopolitical entity of the various lands; . . . equality between the various lands of the monarchy, their administrative and legislative autonomy to the widest possible extent . . . full guarantee of the rights and privileges of the crown, respect for the ancient historic institutions, except for the modifications necessitated by the recent political and social transformations; constitutional modifications in the interest of the power of the monarchy, but only where a true political necessity demanded it.[23]

A prominent contemporary of Szécsen and an ardent adherent of the concept of historicopolitical entities and its use as building material for the reformation of the empire was the leader of the Czech feudal nobility, Heinrich, Count Clam-Martinic. He declared that the nationality problem could be solved only by preserving these historicopolitical entities in the crownlands. The modern theory of nationalism—modern from the standpoint of 1860—

which consistently wants to draw the frontiers of the lands according to the language frontiers is erroneous. Thereby the frontiers of the empire would be blasted just as well as the frontiers of the individual lands of which it is composed. In all the lands, not just in Hungary, peoples are striving as far as possible for autonomy of the lands.[24]

Credit for the classic theoretical formulation of this notion goes to the great Magyar Liberal leader Joseph von Eötvös. In his *Die Garantien der Macht und Einheit Österreichs,* he asserts:

Austria owes its existence and its present greatness neither to its national homogeneity nor to its geographic frontiers, but it is to be conceived solely as a product of its history.[25]

In another context he says:

The Austrian monarchy has an unchallenged historic right to by far the best part of its provinces. . . . At the same time the monarchy as a whole is, in its present appearance, a product of modern times. . . . Just because the right of the monarchy in the single provinces is legitimate, because it is based on historic foundations, just because it has preceded the present organization of the monarchy and is therefore independent of it, just therefore must the concept of the legitimate rights of the dynasty remain closely connected with the historic rights in force in its individual parts.[26]

At this point it is necessary to differentiate, as far as possible, between this newly introduced concept and that of the crownlands, as these concepts are largely overlapping. Several crownlands, due to their historic tradition, formed historicopolitical entities of their own. In others, in the course of time, an independent historic tradition lost much of its practical significance, largely due to administrative boundary revisions. Often, however, the crownlands were historicopolitical entities themselves and, at the same time, parts of larger historic units, such as the lands of the Bohemian crown,[27] the Erblande, and so on. Yet, none of the Austrian crownlands formed a mere administrative unit entirely lacking a distinctive historic cultural tradition of its own. In the nineteenth century, this tradition was far more alive in some of them than it was in others.

Thus, the distinction between a historicopolitical unit and a crownland is theoretically a sweeping one, and yet not difficult to determine, when practically viewed in the proper context of historic and geographical conditions and political claims. The true significance of this concept of the historicopolitical entities within the Austrian nationality problem is based on the specific nature of the conservative social forces behind it.

Well into the second half of the nineteenth century, these forces were distinctly under the leadership of the aristocracy in the outlying crownlands who were opposed to the centralistic tendencies of the German-directed administration. But it would be erroneous to assume that the cause of the traditional historic claims was supported only by this small upper class, anxious to restore and to regain its privileges. Actually, the stage of the national struggle, from the pre-revolutionary period well into the third quarter of the nineteenth century, was largely dominated by this concept of traditional nationalism, and, consequently, broad strata of the nationally conscious bourgeoisie, the intelligentsia, and the peasants, sympathized with this idea. Undoubtedly, a great shift to the forces of ethnic and, to some extent, even racial [28] nationalism occurred during the second half of the nineteenth century; but the national idea, incorporated in the concept of the historicopolitical entity, never fully succumbed to these forces.

One might perceive the interplay of conservatism and traditional nationalism as follows: From the standpoint of direct group interests, the claim for the restoration of the ancient historicopolitical entities was dominated by small units of the landed nobility of the various national groups. Wherever existent,[29] they were anxious to preserve and to restore their privileged position in the old crownland Estates. National feelings of a large part of this territorial nobility were not to be questioned, but in a way these feelings were a mere by-product of their social group interests. In any case, the fact that the nobles, for centuries the unchallenged leaders of the nationalities, championed the cause of traditional nationalism swelled the ranks of their followers throughout the main strata of the population, with the exception of the slowly rising industrial labor class.

This broadening of the popular base of the historicopolitical entity concept strongly encouraged the rise of nationalism in general. Yet, no nationalism of wide popular appeal could remain within the narrow confines of the historicopolitical domain idea. Inevitably, ideas developed of a more up to date and seemingly more democratic ethnic nationalism. Thus, beginning with the late 1860s, the nationalist forces were pretty much split, and from then on the concept of the historicopolitical entities gradually became the clearly limited issue of a strictly conservative movement. The main stream of nationalism no longer flowed in the direction of the old historic schemes.

The masses had become aware that the motivating force behind the historicopolitical entities was basically the conservative program tinged with nationalism.

## THE ORGANIZATION OF THE NATIONAL GROUPS

Preceding the survey of the ethnic and historic claims of each national group, an attempt will be made to place the various nationalities in appropriate groups. Thereby, more insight into the chief features which unite as well as distinguish them from each other will be gained. Various methods suggest themselves.

The status of the following national groups (listed alphabetically) will be analyzed: Croat, Czech, German, Italian, Magyar, Pole, Rumanian, Ruthenian, Serb, Slovak, and Slovene. These nationalities were empirically, though not by the letter of a truly comprehensive nationality legislation, recognized as the principal Austro-Hungarian national groups.[30]

This enumeration does not entirely correspond with that generally given in the literature on the subject, since Serbs and Croats are usually listed together as Serbo-Croats,[31] Czechs and Slovaks frequently as Czecho-Slovaks. Though Serbs and Croats are of the same racial stock and speak the same language, they are, nevertheless, distinguished by several features of considerable historic significance. It is sufficient to refer here to the use of the Cyrillic, Greco-Slav alphabet among the Serbs and of the Latin alphabet among the Croats; and even more important, the adherence of the overwhelming majority of the Croats to the Roman Catholic church and of the Serbs to the Greek Orthodox church. Thus, one finds a Roman, Latin, Western tradition among the former and a Greek-Byzantine tradition among the latter. These distinctions, traceable in a history of Serb-Croat political conflict, justify a separate treatment of these two nationalities. Regarding Czechs and Slovaks, the fact that the Czechs were concentrated in Cisleithania and the Slovaks in Transleithania made their history run such different courses in the monarchy that a joint treatment would seem rather unrealistic.

The above list could be further expanded. Apart from insignificant minorities of Raetho-Romans in Tirol, numbering some few thousands, the question comes up whether some of the "genuine minorities" do not form national groups of their own. This would apply, for instance, to Rumanians in the Littoral, to Croats in German-speaking parts of western Hungary, and to Germans in the Hungarian Banat of Temesvár. It would apply, above all, to the Szekels, or Szeklers, and Saxons in Transylvania. The former are closely related to the Magyars, while the latter are of German stock, but both settled for centuries in the same areas, both for centuries were invested with certain national rights and had unmistakably distinct, collective characteristics. Yet they cannot be treated as separate national groups, since their distinctive national character is only regionally, not universally, recognized.

To a certain extent this is also true of the Jews. Controversial as the question of the separate national character of the Jews is in general, a point could be made that a Jewish nationality was recognized, in a very limited political sphere before the 1860s—that is, before full emancipation was universally and permanently established all over the empire. Furthermore, it could be said that the Jewish national movement rising in the 1880s, partially succeeded in securing the recognition of a Jewish nationality status, this time on the basis of equality, at least in Bukovina and Bosnia-Hercegovina. But such nationality status was never universally recognized in Austria,[32] and not at all in Hungary.

A crude systematic grouping of the eleven nationalities listed above would be, of course, by division into national groups in Cisleithania and in Transleithania. Since, however, the majority of the nationalities were represented in both of the dual states, a topical treatment which intends to analyze the problems of each national group as a whole could not conform with this division.[33] A related method might place the dominant nationalities in Austria and in Hungary— the Germans and the Magyars—in one group, and all the other nationalities in another. This scheme could be elaborated by joining to the two politically leading nationalities, those of somewhat privileged semiautonomous or autonomous status, at least in relation to the status of other national groups. This would apply to the Croats in Hungary and to the Poles in Austria.

Another scheme, which likewise stresses factors of political significance, is the division into national groups settled wholly within the empire and those others whose conationals were largely subjects of neighbor states outside the empire. If the concept of genuine and

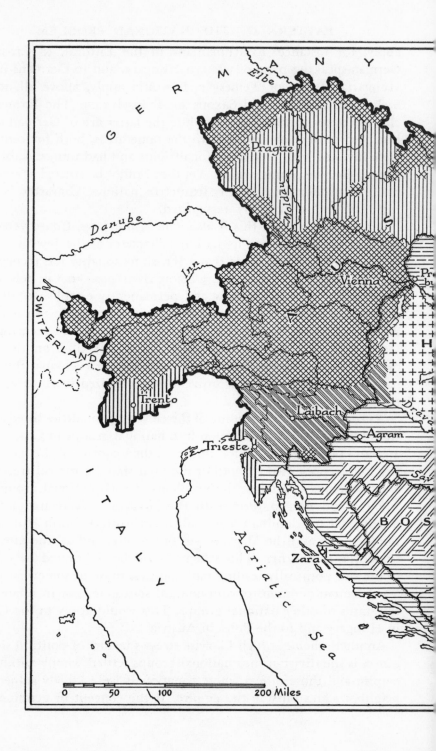

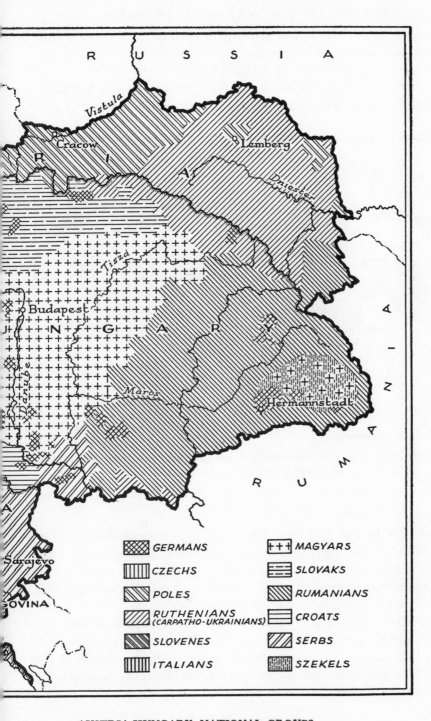

**AUSTRIA-HUNGARY, NATIONAL GROUPS**

nly national groups representing more than 50 percent of the population in a given area are shown on this map.

nongenuine minorities were extended to nationalities, there would
be some justification in referring to genuine and nongenuine nationalities in the monarchy. A division following this pattern would
include in one group Germans, Poles, Ruthenians, Italians, Serbs and
Rumanians, and in the other, Magyars, Czechs, Slovaks, Slovenes, and

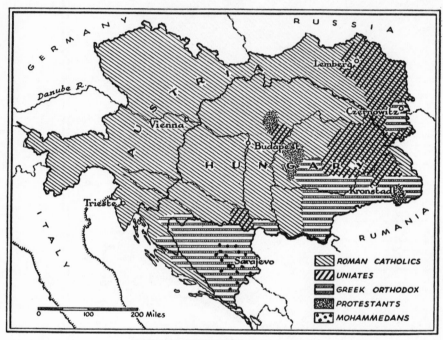

**AUSTRIA-HUNGARY, RELIGIONS**

Only religious groups representing more than 50 percent of the population in a given area
are shown on this map.

Croats.[34] Yet the fact that these last five groups were confined within
the borders of the empire was, in the nineteenth century, a determining factor only for Czech, Magyar, and Slovak policy; it could not
block the union movement of the other two nationalities belonging
to the same group—Croats and Slovenes—with the Serbs.

An analysis according to ethnic factors would appear to be more
obvious and simple than any of the above-mentioned schemes. Following this method, one might break up the total population of the
empire into four major ethnic groups: the Germans, the Magyars, the
Slavs, and the Latins.

| Germans | Magyars | Slavs | Latins |
|---------|---------|-------|--------|
| | | Northern Slavs: | Italians |
| | | Czechs | Rumanians [35] |
| | | Slovaks | |
| | | Poles | |
| | | Ruthenians | |
| | | Southern Slavs: | |
| | | Slovenes | |
| | | Croats | |
| | | Serbs | |

The adoption of such a classification, however, might lead to the erroneous assumption of general political and historic affinities where sometimes only those of ethnographical nature existed.[36]

Even though these ethnic relationships were to become important as the basis of empire reorganization plans, the Habsburg monarchy developed, in the main, out of the union not of ethnic, but of historicopolitical, units. Therefore, an attempt should be made to organize the nationalities along historic patterns, since such a classification bids well to provide additional insight into the national problem.

The idea of distinguishing between nations or nationalities which have or do not have a distinct independent national history of their own is Marxian, though it has also been adopted in modified form by non-Socialist historians. The original idea as advanced by Marx and Engels, which will be dealt with in connection with the national revolutionary movements of 1848–49, was crude.[37] It distinguished between national groups which were strong enough to exist as independent nations and those which either never reached this status, due to their alleged cultural backwardness, or lost it, due to their political weakness. In this respect Marx went further than Engels by denying rights to an independent national life to practically all the Austrian nationalities except the Germans.[38] Engels, however, extends the rights to national existence to the Magyars and the Poles, the only ones among the Austrian nationalities who were "the bearers of progress." [39]

Thereby, the issue of the historic tradition of any national group as a basis for the restoration or acquisition of its national rights becomes dependent upon an entirely subjective partisan qualification, namely, the contribution of such a national group to the fight for human freedom, as Marx and Engels perceived it.

Otto Bauer, almost two generations later, eliminated this subjective factor and showed the connection between the development of nationalism and historic tradition in general, irrespective of revolutionary national merits. Bauer started from the Marxian idea of the "nations without history" but changed it as follows:

We do want to retain this concept, but it does not mean that a nation never had a history, nor even, as Friedrich Engels believed in 1848, that such nations would be incapable of regaining historic life. This opinion is finally refuted by the history of the nineteenth century. We call these nations, "without history" for the one reason alone, that their national culture had no history and no further development in the era when only the ruling classes were carriers of such culture.[40]

Referring to the particular Austrian nationality groups, Bauer observed:

Austria contained at the beginning of the nineteenth century—Hungary omitted for the time being—three historic nations: the Germans and Italians, who had nobility and bourgeoisie, further, the Poles, who by way of their nobility had the character of a historic nation. Czechs, Ruthenians, Slovenes, and Serbs were still to be considered as nations without history in the sense familiar to us. In Hungary only the Magyars and Croats, due to their nobility, and the Germans, due to their bourgeoisie, were historic nations. On the other hand, Slovaks, Serbs, Ruthenians, and Rumanians had no share in the ruling classes of society; they were, culturally, nations without history and politically without any constitutional rights. The Slovak nobility had become Magyar, just as much as the Czech had become German, the Ruthenian, Polish.

Bauer attributed the cause of the national awakening of the nations without history from the end of the eighteenth century to the development of capitalism.[41]

This latter line of thought has often been contested. Still, Bauer's main thesis of the nations or nationalities without history and the recognition of national nobility and bourgeoisie as a preliminary condition of national culture has been widely confirmed by historic experience. Conversely, the existence of social groups with no independent politico-national history of their own in the early formative stages of their development has been widely accepted. Here, however, the term "independent" is by no means meant to be identical with "sovereign." It does not mean that a national group with history necessarily formed, for some time, a sovereign state of its own. Yet it does mean that such a national group for some time formed not only a clearly marked ethnic unit, but a politico-national unit as well. The general correctness of Bauer's thesis is not impaired by disagreement of this study on specific points, such as his designation of the Czechs, even at the beginning of the nineteenth century, as a nation without history and of the Hungarian Germans as a nation with history in the sense qualified above.

The sound basic idea itself has been further elaborated in Harold Steinacker's concept of "the so-called historic nations." [42] According to this, one group is here represented by Magyars, Czechs, and Poles,

who remember their former independent statehood. . . . They all reject an empire centralism, but they are striving for, if possible, an even stronger crownland centralism. And the essence of this crownland centralism was not the equality of the peoples, but the rule of the Magyar, Czech, Polish political nations [that is, the majority peoples in those lands] over alien minorities.

In a second group belong the nonhistoric peoples, as defined above, and the Croats.

Wholly different was the attitude of the smaller nationalities. To them the historic lands and their constitutional law meant nothing. What they wanted was to administer a homogeneous territory as "land" in their own language or to obtain within a historic land a national territory, a "nation's university" [43] with a certain degree of autonomy.[44]

In regard to Croatia, Steinacker refers to the conflict between the historic concept of the Croatian kingdom and the great ethnic unification plans of the southern Slavs in general, opposing trends which ran parallel for a longer period than similar ones in any other national group.

According to Steinacker, the Austro-Germans are not in the same category with any of the other national groups. They are the only ones of the national groups "with history" who stand neither for a traditional-historic concept of a German political entity within the monarchy nor for an ethnic union of the Austro-Germans in a state-like organization. As Steinacker puts it, they stood "for the decentralized parliamentarian centralistic state" (*Einheitsstaat*) with autonomous municipalities under the supervision of autonomous and nationally homogeneous *Kreise* invested with some legislative functions.[45] Though Steinacker's reference to consistent German parliamentarian tendencies, partly of a decentralizing character, even after 1848, is debatable, he is indeed right on the essential point in this context: the Austro-Germans formed a national group "with history" of a very specific type. They did not strive primarily for the recognition of their historicopolitical entity as a state unit within the empire, but for the recognition of a German-dominated empire based on the alleged superiority of their historic cultural and social tradition.[46]

Thus, nationalities with history, that is, independent national political history, within the territorial frame of the Habsburg Empire are the Germans, the Magyars, the Czechs, the Italians, the Poles, and the Croats. The fact that some of these national groups went through this historic experience even before their incorporation into the orbit of the empire is of no consequence here, since they remained on their own soil and transferred their tradition and their well-stratified social structure into the Habsburg monarchy. The nationalities without history, that is, those without independent national political history in the early formative stages of their development, are the Ruthenians, the Rumanians, the Slovaks, the Slovenes, and the Serbs. Either designation, nationalities with or nationalities without history, is applied in this study only to the status of these groups within the territorial frame of the empire.[47]

Within the first main group discussed here, the nationalities with independent national political history, the problems of the Germans and the Magyars will be treated first, as those having had the greatest influence on the political fate of the empire. In particular, the survey of the German group as carrier of the centralistic empire tradition will give the connecting link of historic facts which are of significance for the following chapters as well. A chapter on the Magyar problem will follow. Then the Czech problem which, regarding historicopolitical tradition, shows some similarity to the Magyar topic, will be surveyed. The analysis of the Polish and the Croat position will follow. Both nationalities, as compared to most other national groups, enjoyed a relatively privileged status, the former in Austria, the latter in Hungary. The Italian status will be surveyed last, since it was, from the standpoint of internal policies, the least significant in its influence on the Austrian national problem in this category of national groups "with history."

In regard to the survey of the nationalities without independent national political history in the early formative stages of their development, the classic case of the Slovaks, as a national group without even a political sister nation beyond the borders of the empire, will be discussed first. A survey of the status of the Serbs, whose interrelations with the Croats are in some ways similar to those between Slovaks and Czechs, will follow. It is logical to take up next the case of the Slovenes who, together with the Serbs, formed the Yugoslav (Serbo-Croatian-Slovene) union movement. This survey will be concluded with the review of the position of the Rumanians and the Ruthenians on the easternmost periphery of the Austrian nationalities.

# THE NATIONAL GROUPS WITH INDEPENDENT NATIONAL POLITICAL HISTORY

# CHAPTER III

# THE GERMANS

## THE AUSTRO-GERMAN STATE CONCEPT

IN A REFLECTION on the peculiar Austro-German position [1] in the empire Friedrich von Wieser, the famous Austrian economist and sociologist, wrote in 1905 as follows:

In Austria the term nationalities some decades ago referred, in fact, only to the non-German peoples, but today it must also be extended to the German people.[2] Finally they, too, were drawn into the national movement. The German Austrian in our grandfather's time was German, because he was an Austrian and for him the terms "Austria" and "German" were inseparable. In the general interest of the state, which was close to his heart, he opposed national movements. He opposed the damage done to the central organization of the state, the breaks in the unity of jurisdiction, in the firm organization of bureaucracy, in the preparedness of the army. The Germans developed national sensitiveness only gradually and slowly. They began to consider the concessions to the alien nationalities as a lowering of their national status. Finally, they arrived at the doctrine of national assets,[3] which they had to defend. They were pushed forward one step further in Bohemia, where they saw themselves curtailed as a minority. Here they changed from a policy of mere defense to one of raising demands of their own to restore the balance which had been disturbed to their disadvantage. They asked for assurance of their equality in all national affairs. By a peculiar reaction, as frequently happens in evolutionary development, the most radical among the Germans returned almost to their historic starting point. After they had first put national and state interest in opposition to each other, they finally returned to the viewpoint of upholding the state and thereby acting for their nationality. They asked for the German state language;[4] they asked for a German-led Austria as historic development had created it in the period from the awakening of the national spirit onward. They asked for it now in regard to the accomplished self-assurance of the alien nationalities as a German national claim.[5]

This statement, made by a stanch Austro-German liberal of the old, orthodox school, contains a good deal of truth. More than that, it conveys much of the atmosphere of the national problem as conceived by the moderate German Liberal whose loyalty to the monarchy was above suspicion. These Liberals were, indeed, loyal to the state, but—by implication—only because Austria was a German state and only for as long as it remained a German state. As long as this condition existed there was no need on their part for blatant nationalism, which was somewhat contemptuously to be left to "alien" nationalities and not yet to German nationalists of all shades. The problem of the organization of the multinational state on the basis of ethnic equality did not exactly run counter to that old German Liberal ideology, yet well into the second half of the nineteenth century, the ideology remained rather indifferent to reform.

What kind of German Austria did men such as Wieser, of high moral and intellectual quality, and yet shortsighted, picture when they deplored its decline in the whirlpool of the national movement? How did it develop, how did it work? Redlich answers this question succinctly.

This creation of Maria Theresa, the Habsburg monarchy, and within it the Austrian state, was chiefly the work of the political and general culture of the Germans in Austria. Right from the beginning its character, therefore, was thoroughly German. Chiefly members of the high nobility of the hereditary lands and the German Empire and commoners as learned officials of German nationality were the advisers of the empress as well as the executors of her work. But the language and customs of the non-German peoples inside the monarchy were tolerated as far as possible: important laws and ordinances were to be published not only in German but in the languages of the crownlands, too. But political knowledge, general and learned culture, could be communicated only in the German language in the Austria of that time; German was the language of almost all the bourgeoisie, even in the towns of the Slavonic lands and of Hungary. . . . Only among the masses of peasants living in serfdom was a different vernacular language used: in Austria, western and southern Slav languages; in Hungary, besides the Magyar language, the Slovakian, the Serbo-Croatian, and the Rumanian. Therefore, the new state administration, this creation of the Empress Maria Theresa, in spite of its thorough German character, was considered by the masses of population as not at all unjust, as the functioning of the new government agencies for the most part were set to alleviate, protect, and promote the conditions of the middle and lower strata of society.[6]

It is well worth while to follow Redlich's line of reasoning further, into the reign of Joseph II in Austria (1780–90) after the death of Maria

Theresa, in many ways the center from which the forces of Austrian nationalism radiated into later periods.

By declaring the German language the only state and administrative language in Austria and Hungary,[7] Joseph II created the first impulses of resistance and aversion against the German nationality by the non-German peoples of the monarchy. . . . The awakening of Magyar national feeling as such, and thereby of Magyar language consciousness in the Hungarian nobility, strengthened the always existing stubborn self-reliance and tenacious sense of independence against "Vienna and the German foreign country" (*Deutsches Ausland*).

In many important points this development thus can

be traced back directly to the policy of Joseph II. . . . The bureaucratic and German-administered empire of Austria, the creation of which was the lifelong thought of Joseph II, disappeared with him: but the idea of this centralized empire remained alive in the ruling bureaucracy, and two generations later it became effective again in ominous force.[8]

Clearly, the forces which molded Austria into a German, or, more correctly a German-directed state organization (at least on the surface), were anything but nationalistic. Just because the foundations of German culture were so firmly established, no contributing cause such as those which were soon enough brought to the fore by the other nationalities, existed for the development of a German nationalism on traditional historic lines. Joseph II was not a nationalist, but a rationalist of the dangerously consistent type, who sacrificed tradition, individuality, long-established loyalties, and, paradoxically, even a measure of common sense, to rigidly fixed and essentially unhistoric concepts. Yet, as Redlich rightly points out, the influence of Joseph II, or, perhaps more correctly, the reforms of Maria Theresa as understood and revised by her successor, survived in important aspects even until the collapse of the empire in 1918.

The fact that the Germanism of Joseph II was firmly rooted in the political and social philosophy of the Enlightenment made possible the transformation of "Josephinism" into a well-established governmental liberalism of a rather peculiar Austrian brand. It had very little in common with the classic concepts developed in the Anglo-Saxon world. It was based, above all, on the firm concept of centralized government which, well into the second half of the nineteenth century, implied in Austria the reduction of the influence and power of the hereditary high nobility in the crownlands. It thereby helped to pave the way for the great agricultural reform of the 1850s, cul-

minating in the abolition of the last vestiges of serfdom. This strange
Josephinian "liberalism," further, stood for almost unlimited *pouvoir*
for the bureaucracy, with wide interference in what would be called
today the private affairs of the individual. Yet, it must not be forgotten
that this governmental interference did not enter a sphere in which,
up to then, the individual had been free; rather, it substituted the
power of a more remote, more abstract central government for the
power of the feudal lords, which was more arbitrary, closer, more
direct, and, with some exceptions, more ruthless and oppressive.
Furthermore, this administrative centralism gave the commoner, or
at least the gentry and the lower nobility, a chance to rise to the top
positions in the state. The Austria from Maria Theresa to Francis
Joseph is usually associated with the aristocratic names of the leaders
of foreign affairs, the prime ministers and commanders of the army,
above all such representatives of the nobility as the princes Kaunitz,
Metternich, and Schwarzenberg, and the counts Colloredo and Kolowrat. But the main reformers of the administration, the top civil
servants outside the realm of the army and diplomacy, were very often
men who had risen from the ranks, or learned commoners called from
abroad, both groups as exemplified by such less conspicuous, but in
many ways more significant, men as Bartenstein, Sonnenfels, Gentz,
Adam Müller, and Bach.[9]

Finally, Josephinism implied a strong principle of noninterference
by the Catholic church in the most important affairs of the state and,
on the other hand, a strict control of church activities by the state. The
first part of this policy, noninterference of the church in state affairs,
was strongly rooted in Austrian administrative history. It should be
noted, however, that this principle had little to do with what is commonly called anticlericalism. Members of the Austrian dynasty and
leading statesmen, all of strictest religious observance often exposed
to the reproach of bigotry, clung tenaciously to this policy of noninterference by the church. Except for the major part of the first two
decades of the rule of Francis Joseph, this was and remained a settled
principle of Austrian governmental policy, despite the great influence
of political Catholicism in the parliamentary activities of later periods.

Centralism, antifeudalism, and noninterference of the church in
state affairs—the pillars of the Josephinian tradition—developed at
a time when Austro-German governmental influence was not only
prevalent but almost omnipresent. True enough, the government

sometimes steered a rather different course. But all the time these principles were part of a vigorous, living tradition in Austria, and all the time they were closely connected with the Germanism of the Josephinian brand. The strong, positive elements implied in this concept explain to a large degree how and why this tradition could outlast the empire.[10]

It was equally significant that the preservation of these principles, by tradition, by expediency, and, not least important, by a rather understandable governmental opportunism, was based on a German foundation. It is absolutely credible that, as long as this German character of the empire was uncontested, the Austrian Germans were not even aware that their much praised loyalty to the empire and their status as allegedly the best of Austria's sons were conditioned, as well as determined, by their unchallenged privileged position. The fact for which they were to blame, however, is that most of the German political forces continued to cling to the concept of exclusive Austrian-German identity of interests when and where it finally was justly contested. On this inability, equaled only by their unwillingness to adjust themselves to the changed conditions of an era of rising liberal nationalism, rests a main cause of the insolvability of the Austrian nationality problem.[11]

Similar ideas are again well summarized by Redlich.

In Vienna and in the circles of the German bourgeoisie in general there had developed a vigorous, but not politically clear, concept of the *Gesamtstaat*. One became accustomed to the Great Power idea of the monarchy. . . . When the revolution, like a volcano, brought the tremendous power of the national idea to the fore, the Germans faced the other peoples as strangers with no understanding of their national ambitions. But they themselves began at that very time to turn vigorously their old cultural national feeling to the political sphere. That was perhaps just the reason why they considered the same phenomenon in other peoples as an inimical power which threatened them. . . . Even if this "state," due to its absolutist character, was strongly repulsive to the bourgeois class of the Germans in Austria and their young political "world of ideas," they were soon reconciled to it by considering that the authority in this state represented a national asset to them, the expression of their old national master position in this empire.[12]

It would be erroneous to assume that the entire complex of German nationalism would fit into the pattern of this Josephinian centralism. Prompted particularly by the dramatic developments of

European political history from the French Revolution to the end of the Napoleonic era and their profound effect on Austrian history, a more vigorous, expansive, and emotional kind of nationalism increasingly supplemented and penetrated the austere concept of Josephinian Germandom.[13] But above all, with particular regard to the subject of this study, the Germans played a hand, and had interests at stake, not only on the high level of the central administration of the empire but also in the regional units of the crownlands and the historicopolitical entities. In other words, the Germans appeared at the same time not only in the role of the leading national group of the centralized state, but also, on a lower level, they were a competing national group among other national groups in various territories of the empire.

True enough, in many of these territories where the Germans mixed with other nationalities, national consciousness of these other nationalities was, prior to the revolution of 1848, seemingly not yet developed to a degree seriously to challenge the supremacy of the German *Staatsvolk*, which was identified so closely with the works and aims of the central government. This undoubtedly holds true for the interrelations of Germans and the southern Slav peoples, above all the Slovenes who mixed with the Germans in the southern Alpine lands of Styria, Carinthia, and Carniola. It does not apply to the peoples clinging to the concept of the old historicopolitical entities having a vital political-cultural tradition of their own.

Such nationally conscious peoples included, particularly, those who had been united under the old Bohemian crown: Moravia, Silesia, and, above all, Bohemia. German-Czech interrelations in the nineteenth century formed by far the most complex and the most instructive and fertile field of study of the struggle, compromise, and experiment in Austrian inter-nationality relations. These interrelations, however, represented the crucial problem of the Czech people in Austria, whereas they formed only one important part of the German problem in Austria as a whole. Therefore, it seems advisable to discuss these questions, at least in their general outlines, in connection with the Czech rather than with the German status.[14]

At this point, it is sufficient to say that the rise of the political nationalism of the Austro-Germans as just one nationality, though a privileged one, among other nationalities is closely connected with the rise of the national struggle in Bohemia. The German problem, coinciding with the Revolution of 1848 and strongly influenced by it, not just originating from it, must increasingly be faced on these two levels: The Germans fight for the preservation of their role as the *Staatsvolk*, the pillar and main beneficiary of Austrian centralism, and, at the same time, they fight, on the lower provincial level of the crownland administration, as a political *primus inter pares* to gain ascendancy in the crownlands. As to the first aim, German supremacy was not at all seriously challenged by the Revolution of 1848; as to the second, by and since the revolution, the Germans were fully drawn into the regional national struggle.

Sosnosky's comment on the rise of political nationalism among the Austro-Germans is typical of many similar views:

If the Germans in this country [that is, Austria] had preserved a little judgment and insight, they would have seen that this propagation of the national idea must have the unavoidable consequence of ending, or at least curtailing, their supremacy in Austria. Naturally, the other nationalities would then claim the same rights, and these nationalities could throw the weight of their greater number into the scales.[15]

Naturally, indeed! But Sosnosky was wrong if he assumed that the Austrian Germans voluntarily abandoned a policy of "splendid" isolation. Much as the Germans were to blame in the following decades for their intransigence in refusing to face the nationality problem as equals among equal nationalities, it is nevertheless true that they were drawn into the national struggle by the compulsive force of the rising nationalism among the other nationalities, above all the Czechs. This course was more or less forced upon them; not that they followed it was their chief fault, but that they did not know, and did not want to know how to deal with it.

It is true that Austro-German claims for the organization of a German member state in a federalized Austria became increasingly prominent as early as 1848 and continued to be prominent until 1918. Nevertheless, such federal concepts never dominated the Austrian brand of German nationalism and its gradual rise. Though the German contributions to federal schemes are varied and significant, the premises to these ideas did not grow on German ground, where national federalization appeared identical with impairment of the German position all over Austria. German-directed centralism, but never German-directed federalism, had a chance to run the multinational state.

The main currents of early racialism in German Austria, to which National Socialism justly confessed so deep an obligation, well recognized this obvious fact. In its doctrines of state, Pan-German racialism in Austria was entirely a cruelly distorted product of Josephinian centralism. It did not stand for national organization of the empire, but for a ruthless German supremacy in a centralized state.

In conclusion, Austro-German centralism and political German nationalism in the crownlands represented the main trends of German national policy, the former based on the governmental systems of Maria Theresa and of Joseph II, the latter resulting from the national conflict of the non-German nationalities with the Germans in nationally mixed territories. In a way, both had the same ultimate goal of policy, preservation of the supremacy of the German course in Austria's system of government. Josephinian tradition, however distorted, directed the policy. Provincial nationalism cemented the very foundation of German centralism by securing a strong foothold in the crownlands.

CENTRALISM AND ESTATES: REFORM IDEAS, 1835–48

The development of politically conscious nationalism of the major Austrian national groups can be traced at least to the first years of the nineteenth century, if not to earlier times.[16] Political reform literature, however, dealing with the empire's national problem as a whole, in the "pre-March period," from the death of Francis I in 1835 to the Revolution of 1848,[17] is not only confined almost exclusively to the German language, but was largely written by individuals of German nationality as well. This fact is not due to an intrinsic superiority of German political philosophy, or to more mature national consciousness at that time, but, probably, is chiefly the result of what may be called national or nationality power politics and positions.

The scope of Czech, Polish, Italian, Croatian, and even Magyar nationalism was, to some extent, confined to the advancement of unrecognized, or at least not duly recognized, national claims within the empire. Largely due to the mixed blessings of Josephinian centralism, the privileged German national position was, at least in the western part of the empire, still widely recognized. Because of their almost uncontested position, the Germans were able to assert their specific national interests within a wider frame than the other nationalities.

German nationalism in the pre-March period did not need to be concerned primarily with the demands of a German historicopolitical entity; its attention could be focused on the preservation and organization of a German-directed empire as a whole. Obviously, in a period not as yet advanced to the curse of integral nationalism, this fact also had wide ideological repercussions on the national developments of all the other nationalities, whose specific interests unwittingly were represented to no small extent by prerevolutionary German nationalism.

This applies, above all, to the basic conflict between the philosophy of Josephinian centralism and the medieval Estates institutions [18] of the empire's crownlands and larger historicopolitical entities. It is the social conflict of the group interests of aristocracy and gentry, of high ecclesiastic dignitaries, bishops, and monasteries, and, to a limited degree, of the upper strata of the burghers in the chartered townships, with the demands of the centralized state. To be sure, this state administration, built on the premises of the enlightened absolutism of the eighteenth century, did not subscribe in principle to a social order different from that promoted by the Estates. In practice, however, it was not only more efficient but more apt to attend to much-needed administrative and technical reforms. In a way, it was also, from the socioeconomic angle more inclined to consider the interests of the state as a whole. Even though these interests were largely considered identical with those of the upper classes of society, this was surely a more comprehensive aim than the narrow group privileges represented in the Estates.

Undoubtedly, socioeconomic progress, though in a devious and limited way, aided the cause of the central government against the Estates.

An intricate political problem of the era was that, on the other hand, the development of conscious political nationalism was to a large extent tied to the cause of the historicopolitical entities and the crownland Estates. Fighting for their prerogatives as the principles on which the social order of the historicopolitical entities was based, the Estates, at the same same, stood for the maintenance of the historicopolitical entities themselves. Thus they promoted in the Habsburg lands the old concept of nationalism there, that of traditional historic nationalism.

This contradictory interplay of rising nationalism—revolutionary and at the same time socially conservative—with administrative centralism—absolutist and at the same time socially progressive—resembles in many ways the conflict between the traditional historic nationalism of the aristocracy and the rising bourgeois nationalism among the Czechs and Croats.[19] Yet, in the case of the politically underprivileged nationalism of these Slav peoples, this clash was more or less confined to the affairs of specific national groups.

In regard to the Germans, similar tensions tended to influence the organization of the empire as a whole. Here the student of the history of nationalism is not only confronted with the concept of a German-directed absolutist centralism and a conservative territorial Estates "particularism," but with a liberal movement based on the Estates idea as well.

In the Estates concept, this rather peculiar German trend recognized elements which potentially could be developed into truly comprehensive, representative institutions in a political and national sense. This is the starting point for the most significant traits of national political reformism in the pre-March era.

Equally influenced by the tradition of German centralism and his own affiliation with the Estates system as a former member of the Tirolian Estates, Victor von Andrian-Werburg (1813–58) appears as a characteristic representative of such ideas. He firmly stood for the recognition of the ancient crownland Estates rights, above all, right of assembly and petition, direct communication with the emperor, special jurisdiction, approval of tax legislation, and advice in provincial legislation. These rights, severely curtailed since the reforms of Maria Theresa, ought to be fully restored [20] and even strengthened.[21] While this implied a long step backward from the far more efficient administrative setup introduced by the centralism of Maria Theresa and Joseph II, Andrian proposed at the same time to modernize the Estates institutions in the direction of a fairer representation of the towns and the admission of peasant representatives. The most important reform proposal, and here the centralistic element came in, was the planned convocation of representatives of the crownlands Estates in an imperial Estates assembly (Reichsstände) in Vienna. This new assembly was to be entrusted with a control of government expenditure, a limited right to grant taxes, and an advisory function in legislative matters in general.[22]

To be sure, none of these proposals reflected directly on the national reform which, a few years later, was limited to the Estates reform plans of the artillery captain Karl Möring, an ideological friend of Andrian and a fellow member in the Frankfurt assembly of 1848–49. Möring stated quite clearly, "The provincial Estates are the first link in the state chain . . . that is, the national principle. The last chains are the *Reichsstände* [imperial Estates] . . . They are the unifying principle in the monarchy." [23]

Yet, Möring only put into words what had been clearly implied in Andrian's previous plans. The crownland Estates were to maintain and to develop the national claims of the Austrian peoples, firmly checked by the inherent conservative character of these ancient institutions. At the same time, the machinery of the German-directed centralized state was to be controlled on the highest level of administration by representatives of the national Estates assembled in the *Reichsstände*. However limited this control might have been, it would have represented a first break with the principles of German Josephinian bureaucracy.

Actually this program, if realized, would have, in a way, furthered the cause of nationalism. Yet, by and large it would have been chiefly the nationalism of the national groups "with history," and even here only the nationalism of the bearers of historic tradition, aristocracy, high ecclesiastic dignitaries, and patrician burghers. It is obvious that a newly accepted peasant class could not have played any important role in such "Estates nationalism" of old, unless, at the same time, the institutions of serfdom and patrimonial jurisdiction of the lords were eliminated. Still, Andrian expressly objected to such social reforms.[24] Thus, traditional historic national claims could have been met only at the cost of the restoration of the badly working double-track administration, Estates rule in the crownlands and central administration in Vienna.

When, two generations before, the reforms of Maria Theresa and Joseph II had, for all practical purposes, eliminated this form of administration, something more had been accomplished than the mere streamlining of the government organization. To some extent, these two rulers had lifted Austria to the socioeconomic standard of western European civilization and, what was more important, they had cleared away one of the most cumbersome obstacles to potential progress.

Such an evaluation does not make light of the most serious shortcomings of this governmental philosophy: its inherent absolutist character and, particularly since Joseph II, its complete disregard of the rising national problem. Although it appears doubtful that these deficiencies could ever have been eliminated in an evolutionary way, the record of ample historic experience makes it fairly certain that the Estates institutions offered no way to transform enlightened absolutism to constitutional government, ready to recognize civil and national liberties. The powerful conservative tradition of the privileged groups sustaining the historicopolitical entities might well have been able to support a slowly decaying form of traditional historic nationalism, yet their ideological inheritance and their narrow social base prevented a development to truly representative institutions and to the evolution of liberal nationalism.

It will be shown in subsequent chapters that many reform trends in Austria started with the intention to revive and modernize the Estates as means and safeguards of civic and national liberties. Yet all these movements wittingly or unwittingly contributed to exactly the opposite result, that of strangling socioeconomic and political reforms and sidetracking national claims into the blind alley of medieval state concepts.

Why, then, did men such as Andrian and Möring, with undoubtedly enlightened, if not liberal, aims, cling to the preservation and restoration of what was even at that time as outdated a concept as the Estates in their ancient form? After all, both supported self-governed municipal organizations and evolutionary reforms in regard to the patrimonial rural administration; both opposed pressure of political censorship—to list only a few significant points in their program. Why did they in their writings make the most of assailing an oppressive central bureaucracy, which seemed to them not only evil means but evil ends,[25] though the introduction of central bureaucracy in feudal Austria, in spite of all its shortcomings, was a great step forward in itself?

The most likely explanation seems to rest in the lack of political experience and training among Austrian intellectuals of that period. Probably, this was not due primarily to the oppressive system of the police state in general, nor to censorship in particular [26] which, after the decrees of Karlsbad in 1818, affected almost all of Germany in the same way, though with not exactly the same results. Neither did lack of theoretical knowledge blur the outlook of men such as Andrian,[27] for, in this respect, Austrian intellectuals were not inferior to those of Western countries. It is, rather, the fact that of all the great countries west of Russia, Austria was the only one where the direct ideological repercussions of the French Revolution, with few exceptions, had not become clearly evident in the form of actual administrative measures.[28] It must be remembered that for nearly a full decade during the Napoleonic period the greater part of Germany was under actual—though in southern Germany more or less veiled—French occupation, and that a good part of the French institutional innovations were brought back to the German people. Even in Prussia in the era of the Stein-Hardenberg reforms, they were not entirely unheeded. On the other hand, the Austrians, whose practical acquaintance with French reforms in general was far less thorough and of far shorter duration, in their overwhelming majority never enjoyed the benefit of these object lessons. The notion that the institution of the crownland Estates could form the pattern for truly representative government could develop only in a country such as Austria, where, until 1848, no realistic conception existed of the working and meaning of the philosophy of representative government. In realizing this fact, one gains some insight not only into the motives of Andrian and his friends but also into a significant feature of the coming revolution itself.

Thus, Andrian's and Möring's prerevolutionary ideas, much as they contribute to the understanding of the national reform movement, did little to further the actual solution of the national problem. In this respect, a far more positive contribution came from the radical liberal camp, obviously less influenced by traditional associations than the Estates member Andrian and the imperial officer Möring.

Here, the ideas of Francis Schuselka (1811–86), one of the most interesting among the Austrian political writers from the pre-March period to the era of the Compromise of 1867, deserve particular attention. The German Bohemian Schuselka's background was very different from Andrian's. In all his education and career a self-made man, he was always radical and uncompromising in the expression of his views, yet most susceptible to new ideas, changing his own concepts frequently, though never sailing in the wake of political opportunism. One finds proof of this in his strange religious conversions. Reared as a Catholic, converted in 1845 to "German Catholicism," and in 1849, at the height of the Austrian reactionary period, to

Protestantism, in his old age he became again a faithful and even devout Catholic.[29]

The change in his political views was no less radical than that in his religious beliefs. At the start of his political career, however, his basic principles were not too different from those of Andrian, though right from the beginning his far keener insight led him to think of the real problems of Austria as those of the multinational state. Nevertheless, he, too, accepted the premise of her German character, "The empire of Austria as such can be only German, any other course means a deviation from its historic origin and loss of its only possible aim and purpose." [30]

According to Schuselka, this held true particularly for his own fatherland, Bohemia. He proudly asserted:

The culture of Bohemia is German, there is no other in this country. This is not of yesterday, but a matter of a thousand years.[31]

Yet he perceived German preponderancy as a justified claim rather than as an established fact, and he was fully aware of the magnitude of the national problem. In 1847, he exclaims:

Nationality inspires to great resolves, but it reduces at the same time to petty and pernicious absurdities. It is the battle horse, but at the same time the hobby horse of our times.[32] . . . The empire of Austria has been selected by fate to become one of the most unruly, one of the most threatened theaters in this threefold national struggle.

Schuselka, referring here in particular to the national strife between Germans, Slavs, and Italians, asserted:

A miracle is necessary to preserve the peaceful character of this struggle and to avoid the demolition of the empire.[33]

As for the Magyars, Schuselka contradicted the opinion of the majority of his contemporaries, who saw the chief issue of the Austrian state problem in the conflict between the Magyar-dominated Hungarian kingdom and the empire.

The Magyars are far too small a people and, after all, they live far too much mixed with Germans and Slavs to succeed in working themselves up to a permanently ruling nation. Too much consideration for the Magyars would hurt the Slav interests and would drive them into the arms of Russia, Austria's worst foe.[34]

Regarding the Slavs, among whom he considers the Czechs the most promising group, he sees their political and cultural level as inferior to that of the other European peoples, because the Slavs—in their overwhelming majority, peasants—have no bourgeoisie, consequently, according to Schuselka, no nation can crystallize among them.[35]

Nevertheless, Schuselka was not blind to the phenomenon of rising Czech nationalism which, as a true liberal, he saw entirely as a political problem. According to him, the Czechs were by no means adverse to German education and culture. Behind Czech nationalism there was really nothing else but enmity against the Austrian political system of Metternich's police state, which could find its only outlet in raising the national claims.[36]

At that time, Schuselka was more occupied with an analysis of the Austrian national problem than with its solution. In his concern for the German position, he proposed that Austria should give up Galicia and, by implication, Bukovina, thereby reducing the Austrian population to approximately numerical parity with Germans and Slavs. He declared, however, that this strengthening of the German element must not lead to an oppressive national policy.[37]

Literally taken, nothing in Schuselka's views of that time openly contradicts the existence of the German-dominated centralistic state, although he violently attacked its autocratic ruling forces. Nevertheless, Schuselka's very insight into the magnitude and urgency of the national problem strongly indicated that no solution on the rigid basis of the *Einheitsstaat* was considered possible. Certainly, the mere abandonment of Galicia, promoted in changed form by the Pan-Germans a generation later, would at neither time have offered a solution of the nationality problem in itself.[38] Even in this proposal, however, the idea of the desired national equilibrium, much discussed since 1848, is already clearly visible.

Schuselka's prediction concerning the impossibility of Magyar rule in Hungary, as events turned, proved wrong. But, from the standpoint of 1847, he had some reason for his thesis. Few non-Magyars would not agree with him today that one—if not the chief—stumbling block to the solution of the Austrian national problem was the oppressive and intransigent Magyar policy against the other nationalities in Hungary. It is frequently argued that the intricacies of the Austrian political status in internal, as well as in external, political affairs made a change of this situation impossible after the Compromise of 1867. This is as it may be, but it is undoubtedly true that in 1847 no intelligent political observer had reason to doubt that this problem could be solved, and in a way, the events in 1848 and 1849 supported Schuselka's views in that respect.

More difficult to comprehend is Schuselka's opinion that Czech nationalism was only an outlet for political opposition. No doubt such a belief viewed the Czech national problem along too simple lines. Important roots of nationalism, as it appears to observers of today, anticipate by far any issue of possible political conflict anywhere. But, unquestionably, strong interrelations exist among other roots of nationalism and political conflict, and those certainly are to be found in the collision between Czech nationalism and German centralism. Today, when the concept of nationalism seems so much more complex than it did in Schuselka's time, an attempt to establish a system of priorities for political and national conflict seems to be academic. Still, it must be conceded that Schuselka has approached here one of the most important issues of political nationalism, important far beyond the specific issue of the German-Czech conflict. Indeed, he can claim in more than one respect to have been among the first of the German Austrians to understand and set forth in his writings the problem of the multinational state.

Schuselka goes beyond Andrian and Möring in that he comprehended the national problem, not in its full, but certainly in its somewhat more realistic, implications. Two anonymous publications, in all probability written by Austro-Germans, can lay claim to have gone one important step farther, by approaching on the basis of national equality the problem of a national federal solution. The unknown author of *Politische Memorabilien aus Österreichs Neuzeit,* published in Leipzig, 1844, is still vague, when he prophesies:

Austria will create a new era in her history and inoculate the virile force of youth in her senile limbs, if she no longer blocks and jealously guards the free and independent development of her various nationalities rallied under one scepter, but if she will support and further them with all her might.[39]

More specific is *Vier Fragen eines Österreichers,* also published in Leipzig in 1844. The author appealed for the creation of a true Austrian patriotism, above and beyond the national affiliations of the Austrian nationalities.[40] But he realized that national feeling among these nationalities was too far advanced to create an Austria on the basis of Austro-German centralism.

Particularly the Slav lands have tenaciously and consistently resisted all attempts for Germanization undertaken at various times. It would be foolish to hope today for any success in following further this course as leading to a fusion with the Austro-German element. And just as little as the Czech nation and the other Slavs would the Magyars, Italians, and others, be persuaded by any means to sacrifice their nationality and to make any concessions to the Germans in this respect.[41]

The modern age follows a different course, which is diametrically opposed

to the previous one. It perceives in the free development of the . . . Austrian nationalities the basis, the guarantee, for national unity in the Austrian Empire.[42]

To be sure, this free development of the Austrian nationalities is still understood on the basis of the historicopolitical entities, primarily the German hereditary lands—Bohemia, Galicia, the Italian possessions, and Hungary. Demands for liberal reform, foremost among them for a liberal, representative Austrian constitution, continue to be based on the vain hope of modernizing the Austrian Estates system, particularly by means of introducing a central Estates assembly.[43]

Nevertheless, these demands convey a rather different connotation than similar proposals advanced by Andrian and Möring. Special emphasis is not put on the preservation of the prevailing system by means of limited reforms, but on the establishment of an entirely different constitutional federal empire, which could initiate the transformation of existing institutions. This new state, clearly and unmistakably, is to be the federal democratic union of the Austrian nationalities.

All of them will mutually respect and support each other, due to the fact that the distinction between rulers and ruled, between the privileged and the peoples discriminated against will disappear, and the Austrian Empire, firm in itself and through itself, will be an inseparable confederation of free nationalities capable of advancing to the highest development.[44]

Literally, this program still recognizes historicopolitical entities and Estates, the pillars of the old order. Actually, the demands for a liberal constitution, for national equality, for the elimination of distinctions between privileged and nonprivileged peoples raised claims which never could be obtained within the frame of this old order.

Thus, this program strikes a truly new and, in Austrian-German lands, particularly strange tune. It introduces the principles of national liberalism and national federalism [45] into the history of the Austrian national problem, thereby helping to set the ideological stage for the national revolution of 1848.

## THE AUSTRO-GERMAN UNION PROBLEM IN THE REVOLUTIONARY PERIOD, 1848–49

The ideological union between the centralism of Joseph II and the leading political position of Germandom lasted until the end of the empire itself. Nevertheless, in the long run, its momentum certainly decreased after 1848, that is, after the political rise of the Austrian nationalities in the Revolution of 1848.[46] If it ever was before, it certainly is no longer possible, from that period onward, to confound the history of Austria with that of the Germans in Austria, though the setting of Austrian history was still largely that of German centralism and the language of its actors remained predominantly German. Consequently, the specific history of German nationalism must be distinguished from the general course of revolutionary and post-revolutionary history and therefore must be surveyed in the same way as that of other national groups. In particular, the most important contributions of the revolution to the solution of the national problem (the work of the constitutional assembly at Kremsier) no longer belong exclusively in the German orbit, but in a supranational sphere.

Geographically, though, the revolution, from the downfall of Metternich in March, 1848, until the suppression of the October Revolution in Vienna by the armies of Windischgrätz and Jelačić, was focused largely on events in German territories, particularly in Vienna. Yet, the influence of the national question on the happenings in the German center of the empire was far less dominant than it was on the revolutionary developments in the non-German crownlands and above all, in Hungary. There the national factor, the redemption of the national demands of the peoples within the framework of a liberal constitution, is the main issue, while here in German Austria, in the camp of German centralism, the national factor was of importance chiefly as mere reaction to the impairment of the field of German centralism by the rising demands of the nationalities. On the other hand, the general liberal aspects of the revolution, the significance of which should not be minimized in any of the outlying territories, occupy the field in German Austria, at least in the spring of 1848.

THE AUSTRIAN EMPIRE AND THE GERMAN CONFEDERATION
1815–1866

Furthermore, though the national character of the German revolution in Austria is relatively unimportant in relation to the fight against the absolutist central government, it is of great importance regarding the struggle with the other nationalities to keep up the privileged German position. Consequently, this part of the actions of German nationalism will be reviewed in connection with the survey of those national movements in which inordinate German power appeared an all-important problem.

*St. Paul's Church Assembly in Frankfurt*

Beyond these problems of the mutual relationships of the Germans with the other nationalities, a fuller vista on the comprehensive position of German nationalism during the revolution opens up in connection with the activities of the National Assembly at St. Paul's Church in Frankfurt in 1848 and 1849. Its scope is the democratic union of the German people, beyond and within the Austrian borders; its consequences are the rise of Germandom in Austria to fuller national consciousness.

From the wealth of material dealing with Austrian affairs at Frankfurt, it is necessary to eliminate, first, that part which deals primarily with the analysis of Austria's considerable share in the development of the German Revolution beyond the borders, and, secondly, that concerning German influence outside of the Habsburg lands on Austrian affairs. What remains is the analysis of the Frankfurt proceedings in as far as they deal with Austria as a prospective major part of a potential German federal organization and have a direct bearing on the development of the national problem within Austria herself.[47]

In connection with the Frankfurt Assembly, it is necessary to realize not only that the revolution followed a very different pace in Vienna, in the various Austrian crownlands, and in Hungary, but also that the revolutionary timetables in Germany again were entirely at variance with those in Austria. The main assembly in Frankfurt had been in session since May, 1848. Technically, the Austrian representatives participated in its councils until March, 1849, when they were formally recalled by the Schwarzenberg ministry, some three weeks after Prince Schwarzenberg had dissolved the Austrian *Reichstag* at Kremsier, thereby crushing for good the revolution in Austria itself. This happened five months before the "day of Világos," when the Magyar revolutionary army surrendered and the new absolutist regime had free reign in all the Habsburg lands for another decade.

But the Austrian Revolution did not actually receive its deathblow at the hands of Schwarzenberg in March, 1849—his actions at that time only sealed an already fairly well-established fact. The dynamics, the soul, of any revolutionary movement was destroyed as early as June, 1848, with the dissolution of the Slav Congress in Prague and the establishment of Windischgrätz's military dictatorship there. Though the activities of the *Reichstag* of Vienna, and later of Kremsier, from the summer of 1848 to the spring of 1849, were full of meaning for the development of the Austrian national problem, they present an evolutionary, rather than a revolutionary, development crushed in its bloom through the power of counterrevolutionary absolutism.

It is true that a somewhat similar process can be recognized in the revolution in some German states, particularly in Prussia, but this similarity does not hold good for the great movement of German unification in Frankfurt. Caused, in a way, only by the increasing reaction in Austria, Bavaria, and Prussia, this movement gained a wider popular appeal well into the spring of 1849, until the ill-fated and ill-received attempt to elect the king of Prussia to the dignity of a German emperor. These facts have a very important influence on Austrian affairs. At a time when the revolutionary force was receding in Austria proper, exclusive of Hungary (except for the tragic flare-up of the October Revolution in Vienna), the German imperial idea had its heyday in Frankfurt. On the very days when the majority of the Frankfurt Assembly voted Austria practically out of a prospective German empire, thereby documenting its wish for a firmer German imperial organization, Windischgrätz smashed the October Revolution in Vienna with fire and sword. The course of the Austrian and Prussian revolution was running out, but the German empire idea still flourished.

Three main ideas connected with the work of the Frankfurt assembly have a direct and immediate bearing on the Austrian problem in relation to German affairs. The first is the fight for the creation of a democratic German federal organization as against princely absolutism, an issue which stands, in a way, above all further questions of internal organization. How and why this great struggle was lost is a question which, obviously, has a vital influence on the German future as well as on future Austrian development. The failure to establish democratic government at Frankfurt and the failure at Kremsier are closely related in this respect.

Of even greater specific importance is the second problem, the conflict between Austria and Prussia focused on the issue of supremacy in Germany. In terms of plain power politics, this struggle is, in many ways, the basis of the Austrian-German conflict at the Frankfurt Convention in general. Yet, in the light of intellectual history, this probably is the least intricate part of the Frankfurt problem. "The fight for the supremacy in Germany," to use Heinrich Friedjung's famous phrase, was, in the revolutionary period and long afterwards, more a conflict of state politics and cabinets than of nationalist forces. Therefore, this conflict was the only one of the great Frankfurt problems that was subject to a clear-cut solution in 1866.

Inseparably connected with the question of Austro-Prussian rivalry, though with an essentially different meaning of its own, evolves the third and most complex problem, how to join an Austrian empire having a predominantly non-German population, to a German federation. Such a concept implied the creation of a great German empire without concern for Austria's multinational composition, but with great concern for complete Austrian sovereign integrity within this "German" federal union.

It was an even more difficult proposition to preserve the German character of such a federal organization while joining to it the Habsburg lands, vastly superior in territory and resources and even in numbers of population, especially since the majority of this population was a different national character. Yet this, briefly stated, is the theoretical problem of Austria's part in the German future dreamed of so nobly in St. Paul's Church.

It is true, though, that Austria, according to the *Bundesakte* of 1815, was a member of the *Deutsche Bund* only with her German lands. Thus, about two thirds of her territories (the lands of the Hungarian crown, including Croatia-Slavonia, the Military Frontiers, Galicia, Istria, and the Lombardo-Venetian kingdom) never formed a part of the *Bund* of 1815. Nevertheless, even the concept of the Austrian German lands within the *Bund,* by comprising the hereditary lands and those of the "dismantled" Bohemian crown, included the whole Czech and the major part of the Slovene national group. But whether Austria should become the member of a German federal union only with her "German" lands, in fact German-Czech-Slovene and—partly—Italian lands, her other territories being excluded or only very loosely affiliated, it was clear enough that these "German Austrian lands" were to stand under the conflicting loyalties of a loose German federal organization, on the one hand, and a historically far more firmly established Habsburg Great Power on the other. Furthermore, there was no legal way of getting around the political problem that the genuine German Austrian lands, by way of their association with the other Habsburg lands, would exercise an inordinate influence within a German federal organization.

This whole array of hopelessly difficult problems must be viewed in the very real setting of the Austro-Prussian political conflict, which, even if matters and theory had not been as intricate as they were, would be weighty enough to explain the failure of any great national solution at Frankfurt. On the other hand, however, balancing the issue of theoretical difficulties with the Austrian-Prussian game of power politics, the equally real fact emerges that a German and German Austrian national liberalism sincerely endeavored somehow to break through all these theoretical barriers to the desired national unification. That is the contradictory form in which the issue —*Grossdeutsch-kleindeutsch*—a German political organization inclusive or exclusive of Austria—appears at Frankfurt, dominated by national emotions yet replete with conflicting interests.[48] But, all in all, it was generally handled there on a high intellectual level, free from the degradation and deviations which these ideas suffered in later times.

Technically, the Frankfurt problem in committee as well as in the decisive vote taken in the assembly in October, 1848, is focused on the fight about Articles 2 and 3 of the draft for a German constitution which, in the form finally adopted by an overwhelming majority, ran as follows:

*Article 2:* No part of the German Empire must be incorporated with non-German lands into one state.

*Article 3:* If a German land and a non-German land have the same head of state, the relation between both countries is to be adjusted according to the principles of Personal Union.

It was obvious to everybody that the acceptance of these decisive provisions by the majority of the German deputies (the Austrian delegation being split on the issue) [49] ruled out any possibility of Austria joining a *Grossdeutsche* federal organization. The Habsburg Power would never agree to practically commit political suicide as an empire by reducing the ties between its German and non-German lands to the loose form of a mere Personal Union.

This decision accentuated the nature of the Austrian parliamentarians' failure at Frankfurt, resulting from the deep emotional conflict

that by them, their *Österreichertum* [Austriandom] as the essence of their love for their native country, their attitude to the whole history of their nationality and their nearly 600 years old dynasty, was felt just as deeply as the feeling of the inseparable union of the German Austrian peoples with the whole of the German cultural nation.[50]

Though this failure to achieve national unification may appear, to the interpreter of today, as a foregone conclusion, it most certainly did not appear so to the Frankfurt Assembly and to the heirs of the German liberal idea of 1848. True enough,

it was to be of decisive importance for the position of Austria in Germany that she belonged only with a third of her lands to the German *Bund* and that these territories were not fully German, but interspersed with other nationalities.[51]

It should be noted that, though 1848 represents an era of a suddenly increased rise of the national idea, it by no means represented the culmination of this idea. The distinction between political and national affiliation, though long recognized in political theory, was not universally accepted in political practice. The conviction of many a good German Austrian centralist voiced at Frankfurt, that political and national affiliation were identical and that the German *Bund* (including Austria from Bohemia to Trieste) was German indeed, was undoubtedly of good faith, and it needed strong Slav opposition to destroy the myths of such allegedly true German confederation.[52]

The Czech national leader Palacký deserves lasting credit for having exposed the fallacy in this artificial concept of a German Austria and, even more important, for having publicly asserted that her welding to a great German confederation would end the hope of developing the Austrian Empire into a truly multinational federation. Moreover, aside from the most important Slav veto, voiced from outside the assembly by Palacký,[53] the Frankfurt convention itself was by no means entirely blind and adverse to a fair and sober consideration of the Austrian nationality problem. After all, the assembly carried the motion of the Austrian deputy Marek, asking for protection of the legal inviolability of all nationalities on German soil, meaning, more correctly, German-dominated soil.[54]

Certainly this bill was drafted and carried in the spirit of national tolerance, embedded in the history of German centralism, but, as a good part of the Austrian delegation already realized at Frankfurt, mere tolerance was not a substitute for national equality.

In political practice, furthermore, the tradition of a well-established German Austrian centralism within the Habsburg lands, in spite of all its shortcomings, provided a relatively more solid guarantee for the preservation of a limited degree of nationality rights than did the somewhat hazy liberalism of Frankfurt. Its visionary idealism obviously could not count on the backing of the real ruling forces of German society.

It would be deceptive, nevertheless, to think that the shortcomings of the Marek bill, the resistance of the Austrian liberal delegates to a solution of the German problem endangering the structure of the Austrian empire, or, lastly, the opposition of the Slav world voiced by Palacký, were chiefly responsible for the failure at Frankfurt. Months before the Austrian prime minister, Prince Felix Schwarzenberg, formally recalled the Austrian representatives from Frankfurt, in March, 1849, his aggressive and independent policy, concerned exclusively with Austria's interests as a Great Power, tied the hands of the Austrian delegates. The prime minister gradually turned from strict insistence on Austria's absolutely unlimited sovereignty within the German union to the demand that all of German and non-German Austria should become an unqualified, and thereby all-powerful, member of the whole confederation. Obviously, he could not and did not expect unconditional acceptance of such a policy by a truly German national convention.[55] Indeed, Schwarzenberg's policy, resolute in concept, clear-cut and ruthless in execution, colliding with stubborn Prussian resistance, was largely responsible for the failure of the *Grossdeutsche* solution in Frankfurt in general.

Recognition of the fact that the national course of the German Austrian representatives at Frankfurt was largely hamstrung by the supranational imperialistic policy of their own government does not detract from the interesting contribution of some of these deputies to the idea of the multinational state. In general, one may distinguish very roughly among three main approaches to the Austrian problem at the convention. These were the *Grossdeutsche* solution, not basically adverse to the preservation of the Habsburg Empire; the *Kleindeutsche* approach, partly supported by Prussian political ambitions, though partly truly democratic, conceiving a German confederation without Austria as only a concept born out of necessity; lastly there was the notion of the radical Left supporting the idea of the homogeneous German national state.[56] This Left wing, bitterly opposed to Habsburg absolutism, was chiefly concerned with the incorporation of the truly German Austrian lands into the confederation, and would have been well satisfied if the rest, actually the major part of the Habsburg lands, had fallen asunder.[57] At the same time, the Left wing dreaded the possible emergence of a Slav or Magyar federation out of the non-German remainder of the empire.

The parliamentary practice of Frankfurt, a practice with little experience in the techniques of parliamentary life, however, did not approach the Austrian problem along strict party lines, with the partial exception of the Left. This applied to *Grossdeutsche* and *Kleindeutsche* alike. Nevertheless, it is possible to classify the most interesting ideas of prominent Austrian representatives at Frankfurt according to their general political position. Such a classification shows a predominant influence of the Right and Center as well as a comprehensive trend toward the *Grossdeutsche* idea from the Right to the Left. That is to say, the overwhelming majority of the Austrian representatives basically favored an Austrian affiliation with Germany closer than a mere alliance. The differences consist chiefly in disagreement on the form of this affiliation and on the form of organization of the Habsburg Empire, which would make such an affiliation feasible.[58]

Eugen (Megerle) von Mühlfeld (1810–68), a radical Right-wing representative in Frankfurt and, on the threshold of the constitutional era in Austria in the 1860s, a German Liberal leader, represented the *Grossdeutsche* solution as far as it was compatible with an unimpaired Austrian sovereignty. This he conceived in the frame of a federalized Austria granting her nationalities complete equality.[59] He was supported in this respect by a fellow Conservative, Unterrichter, who stated clearly, "A constitution for the Austrian monarchy would be possible only if every single nation (*Volksstaat*) were to be organized as an autonomous entity according to the principle of old-established nationality." [60]

Andrian, also of the Right, though more moderate than Mühlfeld, and of great influence as vice-chairman of the constitutional committee, stressed the need for the preservation of Austria's sovereign integrity even more strongly and more consistently than the former. Ready, rather, to sacrifice the *Grossdeutsche* union than to compromise Austria's sovereignty to the slightest degree, he championed the concept of a kind of comprehensive Austrian nationality—the nationality concept of German Austrian centralism.[61] This radical Austrian standpoint was closely related to the viewpoint of the *Reichsverweser*, Archduke Johann (1782–1859), whose direction of German affairs at Frankfurt markedly supported the German Austrian centralists.

Closest to Andrian's views among his fellow deputies was Count Friedrich Deym, an enlightened Conservative like Andrian, a representative of Austrian crownland Estates. He strongly promoted the idea of an Austrian *Gesamtnationalität*, to him a fully political and not at all ethnic concept. Deym perceived nationality as "the self-assertion of an independent organic body, whose independence and power permit the individualization and self-determination of a people." [62] He believed that a powerful empire may well weld the various ethnic groups of a state into one state-nation. According to him, the Austrian lands ought to remain united in a *Realunion* which should conclude a close alliance with a German federation.[63]

A center group in itself, listed here from approximately the Right to the Left, was represented foremost by Carl Möring (54), the author of the *Sybillinische Bücher,* and by Anton von Schmerling (1805–93), the future champion of Austro-German centralism, whose difficult task it was to exercise and to reconcile the mutually conflicting positions of deputy, representative of the Austrian cabinet and minister of the *Grossdeutsche* Frankfurt shadow ministry.[64] Also in this group were Schmerling's adviser, the brilliant Hans Perthaler, Carl Giskra, the Liberal leader and minister of the "burgher" ministry of 1867, and Joseph von Würth, likewise close to Schmerling. Whatever may be said against the oppressive force of Austrian conservatism, participation in the convention on the whole has not adversely affected the later career of the Austrian protagonists on that stage.[65]

At Frankfurt, Möring, progressing considerably from views he had held previously, came out for a federalized Austrian empire, including Hungary as part of the great German confederation which should consider in her organization ethnic as well as crownland frontiers— undoubtedly a most difficult proposition. To Möring, this Great Austrian federalized empire appeared not merely as part of a German confederation, but as part of a great multinational and federalized central European super-Power.[66] In short, he appeared as forerunner of the idea of "Middle Europe," as formulated and followed by such eminent men in the convention as Julian Schmidt, Joseph von Würth, Friedrich Fröbel, to some extent Franz von Sommaruga, and, above all, the brilliant economic statesman of the neo-absolutist era, C. L. von Bruck.

In a way, Schmerling's attitude at the convention was more complex than that of any other chief protagonist there. It derived from his ambiguous position as a moderately liberal personality in national and constitutional questions who was forced to act as a mouthpiece of Prince Schwarzenberg's aggressive policy of reactionary expediency. Judged by his own political individuality, Schmerling appeared a stanch supporter of the comprehensive German confederation including a sovereign Austria. In his opinion (and this is in line with his eminent future as the "classic" representative of Austro-German centralism), Schmerling favored only the incorporation of the "German" part of Austria into the confederation, which should suffice to secure the Austrian supremacy which he desired so earnestly. A great German confederation under German Austrian supremacy, and in turn German Austrian supremacy within the Habsburg lands, was his political concept. The idea of the Great Austrian federation promoted so earnestly by men like Möring and Mühlfeld left him rather cold.[67]

Carl Giskra was the advocate of the idea of the personal concept of nationality at the convention, implying that national consciousness of people creates nationality. Accordingly, in the era of rising nationalism, he promoted the federalization of Austria on the basis of such a national principle. German Austria should become a part of the German federation, all the Habsburg lands a part of a broader confederation comprising German as well as non-German lands. Such a union should afford mutual protection to all its members, all of them under one supreme head, all of them sharing a common army and a common tariff policy. At this point, Giskra's view was similar to the central European program as proposed by Möring and Würth.[68]

The democratic idea was put before any other by Johann Nepomuk Berger (1816–70) and by the poet Moritz Hartmann (1821–72), who in his poetical writings was profoundly sympathetic to the basic doctrines of the Czech revolutionizing national tradition of Žižka and Hus. If the Slavs could guarantee the establishment and preservation of democracy, Berger would come out in support of a Slav state. As matters actually appeared to him, Berger, the chief representative of the Left, did not believe in a Slav democracy. He was violently opposed to the idea of a "Slav Austrian federation" which would separate Austria from Germany. Strongly renouncing the *Kleindeutsche* solution, he wanted Austrians to become Germans, not

Prussians. In his opposition to an assumed impairment of the German future by the Slav world, he was joined by Schmerling's brilliant partisan Hans Perthaler, who, far to the Right of Berger, came out for a German-directed central European policy.[69]

In the beginnings of their political career at Frankfurt all these men, and this holds good for those on the Right as well as those on the Left, are distinguished rather by the definite historic concepts they present than by original contributions to the national problem. The ideas of Franz von Sommaruga, a moderate Conservative member of the Austrian delegation, are an exception to that statement. Neither as representative of a program of wide political appeal nor through his limited political influence, but strictly on the merits of his individual ideas, Sommaruga appears as the most significant and original Austrian analyst of the national problem at Frankfurt.[70]

Sommaruga's *"Österreichs Zukunft" und dessen Stellung zu Deutschland* (Stuttgart, 1848) was written under the impact of the acceptance of Articles 2 and 3 of the German constitution drafted by the convention in October, which practically excluded Austria from the planned German confederation. He discusses succinctly in this treatise how and why an Austria complying with these articles could not be preserved, and would necessarily disintegrate. Yet, he explains,

Never can the German national assembly have a better right to found Germany than the Austrian peoples' assembly to preserve Austria.[71]

Sommaruga proposes the creation of a narrower federation and a wider confederation, the former to be joined by Austria's German territory, the latter by her remaining lands.[72]

The Austrian constitutional structure must comprise all the parts in their entirety which are destined to cooperate strongly with each other and which are dominated by a great comprehensive political idea. . . . This idea cannot be anything else but the idea of a federation in which full justice is done to the peculiar traits of each single heterogeneous part, and yet the union of the whole great dominion must remain intact.[73]

Sommaruga envisioned an Austrian federal government whose executive branch should be confined, in the main, to the ministries of foreign affairs, defense, finance, commerce, and public works. The legislative branch of government should consist of two chambers, the lower one elected directly by the people and an upper one (senate) consisting of representatives of the diets. Sommaruga, remarkably progressive in this respect, does away with property qualifications for eligibility to election and proposes, instead, educational qualifications, chiefly—and here the German centralistic tradition comes to the fore—knowledge of the German official state language.

Sommaruga supported the federal partition of the empire into five main groups. Such proposals for division into five groups will be found again and again in the history of the Austrian nationality reform movement, advanced by such diametrically opposed men as, among others, the feudal adherent of the concept of the historico-political entities, Count Richard Belcredi, in the 1860s, and, in the First World War period, the Magyar representative of an ethnic federal solution, Oskar Jaszi.[74] Though the units suggested in such plans are not always identical, obviously the idea of the five predominant historicopolitical entities in Austria was the basis of all these proposals. Exactly the same concept was also the premise of Sommaruga's scheme. He divided Austria into:

1. Those lands which have formed a part of the German *Bund* up to then, comprising, in addition to the Germans, Austria's entire Czech, and the best part of her Slovene, population
2. Galicia, then still including Bukovina, to be separated completely from the hereditary lands [75]
3. The Lombardo-Venetian kingdom
4. Hungary
5. Illyria, comprising Croatia-Slavonia, the (southeastern) military frontier, and the part of Hungary populated by Serbs and Dalmatia

Objectionable as this plan was from the standpoint of ethnic justice, it was, in a way, well reasoned. The reason for lumping together the Czechs and Germans (that is, the nonrecognition of the historic entity of the lands of the Bohemian crown) was to strengthen the already threatened German political leadership in Bohemia. Even more important, as with the proposed separation of Galicia from the hereditary lands, it was thus Sommaruga's intention to obstruct permanently the formation of a comprehensive Slav bloc in Austria potentially outstripping the Germans in political and economic power.

Sommaruga's establishment of a separate Italian unit appeared obviously necessary for historic, political, and national reasons. More original was the concept of an Illyrian (southern Slav) unit. Here Sommaruga went beyond the schematic approach in terms of Aus-

trian and Hungarian lands, by including in the same territorial complex the Croat lands, the Military Frontiers, and the Serbian domains
in Hungary proper and Austrian-administered Dalmatia. Yet, while
promoting the union of the empire's Serb and Croat population, Sommaruga ignored completely the Slovene problem, a fact not fully
explained by the modest role which this nationality played in the
political life of the empire until the revolution. The justified claims
of this group could hardly have been unknown to a man with Sommaruga's political acumen. Very probably, however, he feared that
any consideration of Slovene national aspirations in Styria, Carinthia,
and Carniola would again have impaired the German position in
favor of the Slav world.

Perhaps most interesting is Sommaruga's attitude toward the national problem where principal German interests were not directly
involved, that is, in regard to Hungary. Here he intentionally left the
question of Transylvania open, to be decided according to the will
of her population. He considered, however, the various possibilities
of an autonomous Transylvania, a Transylvanian autonomy within
Hungary, or a partition, according to which the Magyar-speaking
"Szekels" might be joined to Hungary, and possibly the German
"Saxons," as well as the nationally not yet recognized, so-called
Vlachs (Rumanians), to Illyria. Obviously, the fact that Sommaruga
considered the Rumanian problem at all was of greater significance
than his actual suggestion concerning it, which shows little regard
for, and probably little knowledge of, the specific ethnic character
of the Rumanians. Yet, even this proposal to join the largely Slavicized
Rumanian national group to a southern Slav Illyria, rather than to a
Magyar Hungary, represented a relative advance in the direction
of ethnic nationalism.

Furthermore, it was to Sommaruga's credit that he faced openly
the then rather inconspicuous problems of the Ruthenians and the
Slovaks within Hungary. It was recommended that local autonomy
and diets of their own be granted to these national groups. This idea
conformed to his general proposals to set up not only general comprehensive diets in the five main units (often referred to as *General-
landtage*) but, subordinated to them, crownland and provincial diets.

This concept of diets of a higher, more comprehensive, and a lower,
more specific, order reappeared several times in different stages in the
history of the Austrian national reform movement. It had been de-

veloped most clearly and in conservative form in the medieval concept of the "Bohemian *Staatsrecht*," according to which the representatives of the lands of the Bohemian crown were to assemble in the general diet of all the Bohemian lands—Bohemia, Moravia, and Silesia—while these three crownlands, as smaller historicopolitical entities, would maintain their own provincial diets.

Sommaruga, in a rather unsystematic way, introduced a new ethnic element into this traditional historic concept. According to him, the general diets were to represent, partly, ethnic units such as the Lombardo-Venetian kingdom or Illyria, and also to some extent historicopolitical entities, for instance, Hungary. The lower "provincial diets" were to be set up in ethnic units such as Hungarian-Slovak, and Hungarian-Ruthenian territories, to function in the same way as those already established in the historic Austrian crownland units. Almost two generations later, Karl Renner took up and transformed this idea to the planned organization of general as well as lower regional diets, both on an ethnic basis.[76]

In spite of all their obvious weakness, resulting equally from the prejudices of a German centralistic tradition, which presupposes German leadership in an Austrian federation, and a still insufficient knowledge of the ethnic conditions of the Austrian nationalities, Sommaruga's ideas are nonetheless an important initial contribution to the reform of the Austrian nationality movement. They work for the reconciliation of the concept of the historicopolitical entities with the ethnic national claims.

His proposals also show, for their time, a rather extraordinary understanding of the Hungarian nationality problems. Still, like many of the German Austrian political theorists and statesmen, often biased far less by nature than by the impact of a historic tradition which had favored their own national group so conspicuously, Sommaruga failed most glaringly to evaluate fairly the German problem in Austria. This failure primarily determines his place in the history of the nationality problem in the empire, and his work, in spite of the wide range of its ideas, does not belong in the same class with that of men who were able to subordinate their national affiliation more fully to supranational concepts. But, not so much in their conclusions as in their evaluation of the national problem, Sommaruga's ideas still hold a superior rank in the German dream world of Frankfurt.

This very atmosphere of political unrealism, so characteristic of the convention of St. Paul's Church, makes it difficult to evaluate the significance of the entire contribution of the Austro-German representatives to the solution of the Austrian national problem. Redlich perceived as the common platform on which all the various Austrian opinions practically agreed

that Austria in a narrower sense must be preserved as the essence of the German and the German Slav hereditary lands in the form of a German-administered, centralist, unified state. The national-federal organization of the whole monarchy, as Palacký and, in his wake, the whole intellegentsia of the Austrian western and southern Slavs asked in all their manifestations, is unanimously rejected by all German Austrians as the grave danger of a "Slav" federation.[77]

However, the assertion that the German Austrian deputies unconditionally opposed the establishment of a multinational federation cannot be fully upheld in the light even of the incomplete evidence submitted here. The idea of Austria's federalization, though never fully and clearly separated from the structure of German centralism, was honestly, and even ardently, promoted at St. Paul's Church by Giskra, Mühlfeld, Sommaruga, Unterrichter, and others. That the national influence on these reform plans, nevertheless, was far stronger in the environment of Frankfurt than in the truly multinational atmosphere of Kremsier is, of course, evident.[78]

Much can be said for Redlich's further thesis that the development of "two basic formations of German Austrian thinking" can be traced back to Frankfurt,—one placing the idea of the Habsburg Empire above the desire for German national unity, the other not believing in the preservation of the multinational state, but holding fast to the idea of the German and German Austrian union above any other loyalty.[79] Though this observation is certainly correct, it does not cover the whole ground. The rift between the German Austrian centralism, loyal to the monarchy until the end, and German Austrian nationalism, craving a kind of *Anschluss,* though not originating in the Frankfurt convention, certainly became stronger after 1848. Undoubtedly, the *Anschluss* ideology, though sometimes seemingly dormant for long intervals of time, was advanced by the Frankfurt events. Undoubtedly, also, the idea of German Austrian centralism as the leading German force even beyond the borders of the monarchy, though apparently triumphant in the counter- and immediate postrevolutionary period, later began to lose ground as a result of the "more conscious" nationalism of Frankfurt.

However, in this connection another concept also became dimly visible at Frankfurt. It is the idea, not of a German nationalism in Austria seeking union with Germany or claiming the role of a state nation in an unequal federation as *primus inter impares,* but of the nationalism of an Austrian-German nationality group wishing to be equal among equal national groups in an Austrian federation. In short, it is the leading idea of Kremsier. However, the work of Kremsier, though much superior in its understanding of the national problem, was in development of political thought inseparably connected with the work of the Frankfurt convention. Though chronologically the activities of both assemblies largely overlap, a definite chronological sequence is plainly visible in the work on the organization of the Austrian national problem.

In the main, the insolvability of the Austrian national problem within a German confederation was obvious by the end of October, 1848. The constitutional committee at Kremsier commenced its activities in January, 1849. If the politically enlightened intellegentsia of German Austria had not gone through the widely publicized experience of Frankfurt, through all the scheming concerning a rather imperfect Austrian federalism, it would not have advanced at Kremsier to cooperation with its fellow nationalities in the spirit of true national equality. The results of Kremsier, blighted only by the force of an uncompromising and, in general, nationally indifferent absolutism, are comprehensible only if one realizes that at least the most enlightened Austrian representatives at Frankfurt were honestly battling their way through from German-dominated semifederalism to true cooperation among the national groups.

### THE GERMANS FROM THE SUPPRESSION OF THE REVOLUTION TO THE COMPROMISE OF 1867

#### The Neo-Absolutist Period, 1849–60

The decade from March, 1849, that is, from the dissolution of the *Reichstag* of Kremsier to the reforms introduced in March, 1860, as a consequence of the defeat in the Austro-French Piedmontese War in 1859, was a period of stagnation as far as action concerning the national question in Austria was concerned.[80] This, however, does not mean any minimization of the significance of the period of neo-absolutism for the further intellectual evolution of the Austrian nationality problem, nor does it imply any weakening of the German position within the empire. In a way, exactly the opposite of both these assumptions is true. In spite of the suppression of any traces of representative government or of any national activities, theoretical work initiated during the neo-absolutist period ranks among the most fertile in the history of the idea of multinational organization. Obviously, theoretical planning—largely ignored by the administration—was baffled relatively little by the ideological concepts of an absolutism whose elimination in the near future somehow was to be expected. It actually became more seriously disturbed in the following period by the necessity of compromising with the government's feeble and contradictory reform attempts.

Regarding the specific German position in the neo-absolutist period, it might well be said that, since the days of Joseph II's frantic attempts to Germanize the empire, the range of the German language and of German administration had never been so wide, nor its penetration so deep, as during that decade. German centralism in 1849 was of course different from the centralism of the eras of Maria Theresa and Joseph II. The tune of the revolutionary experience remained always audible in any manifestations of the following decade. In different keys, it appeared just as distinctly in the German Austrian central European concept of Schwarzenberg and Bruck, in the revised corporate schemes of Andrian, and in the exiled Kossuth's plan for a Danube federation.

All these concepts have one feature in common, widely as they differ and whether developed in the government offices of Stadion, Kübeck, Schwarzenberg, or Bruck, in the quiet study of the theorists, Andrian and Eötvös, or by Fröbel and Kossuth under the hardships of political exile. All of them were drafted by men necessarily more or less out of touch with the thwarted public opinion of the day. Whatever broad principles they represent, for whatever national groups they speak, representative institutions and national groups are not subjects, but mere objects, of their planning. Neither the people, nor public opinion in general, nor an ever so narrow selection of representative government had any direct influence in the evolution of these concepts.

It will be apparent that the status of the German national group presents the most striking illustration of the complete stagnation of officially recognized national life, if one realizes the fact that the widest range of the activities of German centralism and the narrowest scope of German national activities fall into exactly the same neo-absolutist period. What makes the German position during that period so singularly unfortunate in its consequences is not the fact of political oppression itself. The Austro-Germans, due to their old advanced cultural, and privileged legal, position, were understandably more sensitive in that respect than some of the smaller eastern nationalities, yet objectively they were certainly not worse off than any of the other national groups. The German Austrian tragedy rests rather in the reserve of the advantages deriving from their privileged position. All nationalities charged to the German account either the indiscriminate, unwise, and ruthless enforcement of a German administration on a suppressed postrevolutionary Hungary or the betrayal of the national aspirations of the "loyal" non-Magyar national groups in Hungary and in Austria, which exchanged Magyar and Polish feudal oppression for the German bureaucracy of the absolutist regime. It was of little avail that this regime, though perhaps equally exacting, was at least more efficient and better organized than the previous rule of the feudals of the Magyar and Polish master nationalities. What mattered chiefly was the fact that the "Bach regime" and the "Bach Hussars" [81] appeared even more strange and distasteful to the people than did their perhaps more brutal conational oppressors of long standing, to whose unjust rule they had been accustomed for centuries. Probably of even greater psychological importance was the fact that the Austrian people, who had gone through the revolutionary experience, were not willing to consider whether the absolutism of the 1850s was better or worse than that of the 1840s; they merely compared the new absolutism with the short-lived hopes of the revolution, and the new regime certainly could not stand up under this comparison.

Naturally enough, the non-German nationalities, united at least in their hatred of this regime, confounded completely the issue of German centralism with that of German nationalism. Yet, the German people in Austria not only failed to benefit directly from the forced extension of the rule of a German bureaucracy, but the *spiritus rector* of this system, Alexander Bach, was hated by the Germans as much as by any other national group, and almost equally from Left to Right. To the Liberals, Alexander Bach was not only the very soul of the absolutist regime, he was above all the Liberal renegade of the revolution who, in public opinion, had sold his great gifts to the reaction, allegedly for merely opportunistic reasons. To many Conservatives, on the other hand, he was merely the tool whose invaluable service they rather unwillingly, and with the contempt which the political convert must face, accepted.[82]

In any case, the enhancement of the position of an absolutist German centralism had reversed the auspicious beginnings of Kremsier, when the Germans, then willing to sacrifice many of their national privileges, were ready to fall in line with the other nationalities. Now the Germans, wrongly, though understandably enough from the point of view of the non-German national groups, identified with the policy of the government, were separated from the other nationalities by a psychologically wider and deeper rift than ever before.

However, the German national position can be fully defended only in the era of unmitigated absolutism itself. It was the tragedy of the major trends of German Austrian political opinion that, as soon as the grip of the absolutist regime was slowly loosened, they did not avail themselves of the opportunity to revert as far as possible to the national policy of the revolution. The unjustified criticism heaped against the Germans in the neo-absolutist period became increasingly justified from the era of constitutional experiments (1860) onward.

### The Era of Constitutional Experiments, 1860–67

The entire era of legal political transformation from 1860 to 1867, the national reform ideas of which will be discussed in the second volume, may be divided into three main sections.[83]

1. The period under the ministry of Rechberg-Goluchowski, which was appointed immediately after the unfortunate outcome of the Austro-French-Piedmontese War and remained in office from the summer of 1859 to December, 1860. It is characterized by the attempts, with as few concessions to representative government as possible, to proceed from the hated German centralist absolutism to a kind of still authoritative, but mildly representative, federalism under the leadership of territorial aristocracy. The convocation of the *Verstärkte Reichsrat* in March, 1860, and the introduction of the half-federal Estates constitution of October, 1860, by imperial decree, are the milestones of that regime; the initiation of attempts for reconciliation with the Magyars, its only achievement.

2. Far more significant is the second period, from Schmerling's appointment as minister of the interior in December, 1860, until his fall in July, 1865. Schmerling's main achievement (if it can be called an achievement), in the ministry headed formally by Archduke Rainer was the promulgation of the constitution of 1861, the February Patent, which had the distinct purpose of re-establishing and perpetuating the rule of German centralism, sprinkled with a slightly stronger spray of representative institutions than the October Diploma. In its Hungarian policy this German centralistic government was far more unfortunate than its predecessors, a factor which finally led to its downfall. The following Conservative ministry, under Count Belcredi, from July, 1865, to February, 1867, the cabinet under whose tenure of office the German question as an aspect of the European question was finally decided against Austria in the Seven Weeks' War of 1866, has perhaps too abruptly been called the *Sistierungsministerium,* that is, the ministry which abolished the unfortunate constitution of 1865. Yet, the distinctive character of this cabinet was due not merely to the abolition of the constitution but to a new attempt for the federalization of Austria along the lines of a strangely modified concept of the historicopolitical entities.

3. Lastly, in 1867, under the ministry of the Saxon diplomat Count Beust, momentous changes took place which were marked far more by the conclusion of the compromise with Hungary than by the grant of the parliamentary constitution for Austria-Cisleithania in December of that year. It has been pointed out that the basic principles of the new Cisleithanian constitution, the legal embodiment of German centralism guarded by the privileged German national group, were largely the consequence of Magyar demands. In spite of his decorative title as imperial chancellor, his functions then comprising the direction of foreign affairs of the empire as well as the leading position in the Cisleithanian government,[84] Beust was not, except in merely the formal sense, the father of the Austrian constitution. Its sponsors in a far more real sense were the Magyar leaders Deák and Andrássy.

It is precisely here, in this submission to Magyar claims on the one hand and the acceptance of a privileged position on the other, that German political responsibility rested during that whole period from 1860 to 1867. Austro-German opposition, within its extremely limited possibilities, was slight during the first period, from 1859 to 1861, which was characterized by the attempt to break away from centralism. Yet, even then, the brilliant writings of the minister of finance, Bruck, and Perthaler, Schmerling's theoretical adviser, stand out strongly against a political course endangering the potential German predominance in the empire.

This opposition became far more conspicuous in the second German centralistic period, under Schmerling's leadership. In this era of limited, but after all existing, parliamentary activities, the "alibi" of nonresponsibility for the actions of the government does not hold good for a German policy then unquestionably supported by major trends of public opinion. This policy, largely directed and influenced by the old guard of Frankfurt and Kremsier, Lasser, Perthaler, Mühlfeld, and including Fröbel at the radical Left, may be summarized thus: The Schmerling government, with limited reservations in regard to non-German national rights, attempted by constitutional means to re-establish and perpetuate the ill-begotten and unjust Germanization of Austria established by the absolutist regime under Bach. However, the character of this policy of Germanization was changed completely in this attempt. The German predominance, which had been the rather accidental by-product of bureaucratic absolutism, was to become slowly, but surely, the determined product of German presumption and national intolerance. The process had seemingly been stopped during the two brief years of Belcredi's renewed return to a "paper federalism." It was revived and accentuated in the Beust era, when, in a tragic bargain, the political leadership of German Austria submitted to the Magyar master role in Hungary and, in a way, in the whole empire. While thus perpetuating their precarious supremacy in Cisleithanian Austria the Austro-German statesmanship barred forever the monarchy's return to the great tradition of Kremsier, to the true organization of the multinational state.

THE GERMANS IN THE CONSTITUTIONAL ERA SINCE 1867

The parliament whose predetermined task was to adopt the December constitution of 1867 [85] contained 118 German Liberal deputies, that is, 118 members promoting the cause of German centralism and German predominance in Cisleithanian Austria, fifty-seven Federalists, with few exceptions non-German Conservatives and Conservative Agrarians, and eight Clericals who were close to the Federalists.[86] German Liberals, consequently, held the majority not only among the German parties but also among all parties of all nationalities combined.

## The Liberals

The parliamentary supremacy of the German Liberals outlasted by far their position as the principal government party.[87] Except for the intermission of the last peacetime Federalist interlude in the history of Austrian government, 1870–71, the Liberal governments held office from 1867 until 1879, being even until that time, significantly enough, under the leadership of the enlightened aristocrats, the two princely brothers Auersperg. Since that time no Liberal government —"liberal" used in the technical parliamentary sense—held office in Austria, though for relatively brief periods Liberal *ressort* ministers were still represented in various cabinets. Yet, the influence of the party, though never entirely in line with its parliamentary strength, was considerable for a long time after 1879. Even after the fall of the long-ruling Taaffe ministry (1879–93), the German Liberals continued to be twice as strong as all the other German parties combined, though by that time a very marked trend existed within the Liberal party toward the German Nationals and Clericals. However, in the elections of 1897, the German Nationals and the Catholic parties already were twice as strong as the Liberals, and similar shifts away from liberalism were to be registered in the Czech political development and, to some degree also, among the Serbs and the Croats. Even before the election of 1900, the German Right was nearly four times as strongly represented in parliament as the Liberals, and the rise of labor as a political force from then on made just as many inroads on the Liberal residue from the Left as the Clericals and Nationals made on it from the Right. After still another twenty years in the elections of the young German Austrian republic, the Liberals lost their last parliamentary representative among Austro-Germans.

The history of the downfall of German parliamentary liberalism is reflected in the contradictory concept of its policy. Any student of German liberalism in Austria in the constitutional era is confused by the ambiguity of the term in Austrian parliamentary history. Ludwig Gumplowicz, the well-known authority on Austrian constitutional law, refers to the Liberal party terminology bitingly, but with little exaggeration, as follows.

Whereas the term "German Liberal" party is very misleading, particularly since party names change frequently in Austria, I have to explain more clearly how I understand its meaning. It is the party which called itself the Left at the very time when it was to the Right of Schmerling (in the 1860s). When the party became disloyal to the constitution of 1867, which it had created itself . . . it called itself the "loyally constitutional" (*Verfassung-streue*) party (in the 1870s). At the time when, heavily disunited, it disintegrated into a number of factions fighting each other, it called itself the United Left (in the 1880s). Finally, when it was exposed as the reactionary guard of capitalism, it called itself German Progressive (in the 1890s).[88]

To be sure, the most important reasons explaining this twilight of parliamentary German liberalism lay technically beyond the field of the national problem. Even in its heyday, this once huge parliamentary party was as disproportionately great from the standpoint of proportional representation as it was unrepresentative of the broad social-economic interests of the German-Austrian peoples. The fact that the party increasingly fell out of step with the social development of the times probably contributed more to its decline than the evolution of the national spirit in the last quarter of the nineteenth century. The German Liberals in Austria after 1867 were essentially the representatives of the upper bourgeoisie, finance, commerce, and industry, academic intelligentsia and professional classes. The interests of agriculture and labor and, worst for the destiny of the party, those of the lower urban middle classes were scarcely represented in its council at all. Even Liberal representation of the interests of big business was not too successful. The German Liberals, whose power was for the first time forcibly shaken in the great crash of 1873, were characterized, rather, by a kind of dogmatic laissez-faire inertia in economic and national questions.

Nevertheless, heavy inroads were made from every angle into their field of activities. In the economic sphere the struggle between growing expansion of industry and the small artisan and business class turned broad strata of commercial and industrial lower middle classes, traders, and artisans away from the Liberals to the camp of the rising Christian Social [89] movement. In the cultural field, the evolution of nationalism gaining momentum in the era of Nietzsche, Gobineau, and LaGarde swayed what might be called the economically weaker part of the intellectual and professional classes, the lower state officials, the high school teachers, and others, into the Pan-German camp. And, at the time when the tide of Pan-Germanism seemingly was ebbing as an active political, though by no means ideological, force, the rising German Social Democrat party made further inroads on the Left of the already much reduced Liberal intellectual forces.

But even if the German Liberals had shown more understanding in economic questions, stronger resistance to the forces of integral nationalism, and, above all, had grasped the true nature of the Austrian nationality problem, it is doubtful whether in the end they could have been more successful. Because of the sociohistoric tradition and structure of the Austrian Empire, it was less feasible than in any Western state that the industrial and commercial upper classes in urban areas and the upper strata of the intellegentisia could be the main bearers of the state idea. After all, socially the empire stood halfway between the industrialized Western states and feudal agricultural Russia. Obviously, political power would shift from aristocracy and gentry— representing army, clergy, and, to some extent, bureaucracy—and, for generations, leading agriculture, to the urban and rural lower middle classes, rather than to the small stratum of the bourgeoisie whose power was embedded neither in the historic tradition of feudalism nor in the economic and ideological interests of the urban majority.

Furthermore, no bourgeois party, just and fair-minded in national questions, could rely on popular appeal unless it was willing to abandon its anticlerical attitude. If, as the Liberals, such a party did not want to do so, it had to make political success somehow by compromising with the unholy forces of national imperialism and, even more important, of racialism. That the Liberals remained unyielding in the religious question was deeply embedded in their political tradition, that they refused to compromise with Pan-Germanism on their basic principles was to their credit. Both reasons, however, were equally responsible for their decay. Finally, in the social field no party could hope to stem the rising influence of labor as organized in the Socialist camp if it were unwilling to leave the tracks of a still widely unlimited Manchester liberalism and to meet at least halfway the economic interests of the lower middle classes and of agriculture.

None of the issues mentioned above concerned, technically, the failure of the German Liberals in the handling of the nationality question. Yet all of them combined alienated the middle-class and lower middle-class groups, the principal bearers of the national idea.

If one checks the political merits of this Liberal regime at the height of its power, its decisive support for the establishment of permanent representative institutions in principle, its sincere loyalty to the Austrian Great Power, and its unchallenged merits in matters of educational and juridical reforms, one is struck by a far-reaching similarity to the actions and ultimate fate of democracy in Germany after the Peace of Versailles. Both regimes, in various ways and degrees, were burdened with the political weight of defeat, particularly if one rightly comprehends the Austro-Prussian War of 1866 as a conflict fought primarily over the German question. Both had to go through a most difficult struggle for survival of the states they represented as Great Powers. Finally, both regimes were superseded by strong conservative and reactionary forces at the very time when they had at least partially succeeded in restoring the political positions lost, not by their own faults, but by those of their politically bankrupt reactionary predecessors. In the case of Germany, this came true with the ascent to power of the Junker regimes of Papen and Schleicher in 1932; in nineteenth-century Austria, with the rise to power of the conservative regime of Taaffe, in 1879.

As with German democracy in 1932, immediately after the Liberals in Austria and in Hungary had succeeded in regaining a political position for Austria, which led to the diplomatic comeback at the Congress of Berlin in 1878 and to the conclusion of the seemingly auspicious alliance with Germany in 1879, they were thrown out of power. Thus, Austria's liberalism was offered the chance to come to power because Austria's European position was most unfavorable in 1867, and it was overthrown largely because her position had markedly improved by 1879 and the conservative forces saw their chance to harvest the credit for this development. The analogy with the unfortunate history of the Weimar Republic does not end here. Only a weak, unpopular government, disunited in itself, could be driven from power in 1932; only a similarly decaying regime could experience a similar, though certainly far less cruel, fate in 1879.

This downfall over a basic question of foreign policy, namely, strong opposition to the empire's acquisition of Bosnia-Hercegovina,[90] that is, to the initiation of Austria's more expansive Balkan policy, culminating in the fateful events of 1914, appears, in the light of today, as a remarkable sign of political foresight, as a bright spot in the record of the Liberals. Under the entirely different conditions of 1878, however, such an interpretation is somewhat misleading. German opposition to the occupation was motivated primarily by the fear that a further increase of territories with non-German population would gravely impair the dominant position of German centralism. Although this was undoubtedly true, it was not at all obvious that Austria's Balkan policy of that time, if accompanied by a constitutional reform of the empire along federal lines, was inevitably heading for trouble. The political constellation among the southern Slavs within and without the empire, at the time of final and complete Serbian liberation from the Turkish tutelage, in a way would have boded well for a comprehensive solution of the southern Slav problem, including all Serbs and Croats, and possibly Slovenes too, as a separate unit within the empire. Again, it was chiefly the curse of the Magyar-German Compromise of 1867 that blocked the way of one of the last chances of solving successfully this great problem of future European peace.

Thus, even if the German Liberals had wanted such a federal solution, as they most certainly did not, it would have meant an uphill fight to put through such far-reaching changes in the political structure of the empire. However, they made not even the slightest attempt to that end. Indeed, the Liberal position in the crisis of 1878 serves well as an illustration of a policy led by considerations of narrow German centralism. And this policy of 1878 was only the logical consequence of the Liberals' policy of 1871, when they wrecked the admittedly imperfect plan for a solution of the Czech problem along federal lines. Such a policy, although it had driven the Czechs from the parliament in protest, had failed completely to "appease'" the broader demands of the more active wing of the German liberal party—a rather typical political phenomenon.[91]

Clinging to the doctrinaire principles of a rigid centralism had alienated other nationalities not only further from the German Liberals, but, and this was more fateful, largely from liberalism itself. Submission to the wishes of the German nationalists, on the other hand, far from appeasing them, had only increased their demands and paved the way for the disintegration of the party. Thus, in spite of merits in the cultural field, primarily in the matters of educational and juridical reforms, merits which in their results outlasted the empire, the Liberals as a political party organization had failed in every major field to consolidate the empire, and they had failed permanently.[92]

*The Liberal Inheritance, 1879–1918*

The year 1879 is decisive in German Austrian history. It marks the conclusion of the Austro-German alliance, which, in a way truly unpredictable at that time, led to the empire's disintegration at the side of Germany in the First World War. If it had not been for this alliance, the downfall of the German Liberal regime in Austria in the same year might conceivably have finally terminated the German centralistic course in Austrian internal policy. The alliance, however, prevented such a lessening of the German status in Austria. The monarchy's dependence on Germany's support made it increasingly necessary to remain loyal to a system which alone safeguarded the alliance. This meant, of course, the dualistic empire organization under German-Magyar leadership, directed by the two peoples who were expected to be loyal to Germany against Slav opposition. Though Magyar dominance in Hungary was never seriously challenged until 1918, the result was, in particular, that political changes in Cisleithanian Austria could, at the utmost, modify the government's course there, but could never reverse it in an anti-German direction. In the long run, German centralistic leadership in Austria thus appeared better protected after 1879 than at any time after the termination of neo-absolutism.[93]

In 1879, this did not appear obvious. The German regime was replaced by an ever-varying sequence of combinations of Conservative, Clerical, bureaucratic governments, frequently with a strong Slav (particularly Polish), even Czech, tinge. Representation of German parliamentarians, Liberals, moderate German Nationals, and Christian Socials, though not entirely lacking in the later constitutional era, was seldom very significant. However, the influence of German centralism in some of these cabinets was considerable, particularly in the cabinets from 1900 to 1907 (Körber, Gautsch, Hohenlohe, Beck), all of them supporters of a German centralism of a relatively liberal brand. Yet, this was more or less the contradictory liberalism of enlightened, modified, and matured Josephinism, tolerating the institutions of increasingly tattered and paralyzed Austrian parliamentarianism as well as it could; it was not a liberalism led by the representatives of the peoples in the spirit of Western democracy.

More conspicuously, the period immediately following 1879 was characterized by the fact that since then, largely because of the Liberal decay, the three leading future forces of German-Austrian political life emerged more clearly: Pan-Germanism, the Christian Social movement, and the political organization of labor in the form of Social Democracy.

The general setting for this important development was largely formed in the era of Count Taaffe's administration (1879–93).[94] During that period, a coalition, predominantly of Slav Conservatives but including a fair share of Germans, for the most part of Federalist inclinations, ruled against an increasingly feeble Liberal German opposition. The Taaffe regime has been frequently called in German historiography the rule of the "iron ring," meaning the coalition which intended to encircle and smother German liberalism and, indeed, Austrian Germandom's position as a whole. Such an exaggerated interpretation is contradicted by the frequently quoted characterization of the regime by the cynical Count Taaffe himself, who called his policy one of *fortwursteln,* an untranslatable, yet most illuminating, slang word which implies trotting along from day to day, compromising on every point, and never attempting to disturb the balance by an effort to put through far-reaching reform plans. Indeed, this policy of *fortwursteln,* agreeing with that other basic doctrine of Austrian governmental policy that provisional arrangements are the only lasting ones, helps to explain how Taaffe's regime could manage to remain in power for fourteen full years.

Not even trying, in the constitutionally prescribed legislative way, to reform Austria's national organization, the prime minister managed skillfully to evade trouble with the central parliament by mere administrative measures as much as possible. Thereby, he compromised with the non-German nationalities and appeased their national claims on a day-to-day basis with small concessions. Certainly, the "iron ring" of this policy was very malleable. In many ways, if seen at short range, it was a policy of correct evaluation of the national forces, though at long range it was not only ineffective in its means, but executed with the aid of men without popular support, the Feudal Conservatives. Significantly for the fate of Austrian statesmen, Taaffe was overthrown when, after fourteen years of reactionary policy, he wanted to take a courageous forward step forward by the presentation of a new electoral law which approached the introduction of general equal franchise. Uniting against Taaffe on this issue of extended franchise were, significantly enough, not only his former feudal supporters but also the socially unrepresentative German Liberals.

## The Pan-German Idea

Of the three great German ideological party movements evolving after 1879, the Pan-Germans broke away first from the Liberal mother tree.[95] The fact that liberalism was the branch from which future Pan-German, Christian Social, and Social Democratic party leaders split off in that chronological order, one shortly after the other, emerged impressively enough in the Linz party program of September 1, 1882, drafted by the more active, progressive, and nationally more conscious younger members of the German Liberal party organization. The content of this officially still liberal program stood for stronger centralization of Austria under German leadership to be brought about by complete separation of two outlying Slav territories, Galicia and Dalmatia, from the bulk of the Cisleithanian lands, whose alleged German character should thereby be strengthened. Furthermore, the program advocated closer cultural and economic cooperation with Germany, even favoring a customs union with the new *Reich*. Social legislation and extension of the franchise by considerable lowering of the still stiff property qualifications was likewise demanded. Only two years after the drafting of this program, with the addition of one more provision demanding the elimination of Jewish influence, it was adopted as the new program of the *Deutschnationale Verein*, that is, as the first political Pan-German organization in Austria, under Georg von Schönerer's leadership.

Even more illuminating is the personal history of the chief collaborators in the original "liberal" draft of Linz: Georg von Schönerer, the leader of the Pan-German movement in Austria, glorified in Hitler's *Mein Kampf* as the most important forerunner of National Socialism in the political sense, Robert Pattai, subsequently a radical leader of the Christian Social movement; Victor Adler, the future founder and active leader of the Austrian Social Democratic party; and Adler's political friend Engelbert Pernerstorfer, later the chief representative of the German trend in that party. Lastly, there was the famous historian Heinrich Friedjung, the only one of the abovementioned collaborators of Linz who remained faithful to the Liberal fold. Consequently, of the men of Linz, he was the only one who was not destined to play the role of a leader in his future political life.[96]

To be sure, this common Liberal connection of German Nationalist, Catholic, and Socialist leaders meant in no way that their specific ideologies were derived from the Liberal program. Yet, all three movements were influenced by the Liberal inheritance in at least one point: the common adherence to a German national idea in its broadest sense. In regard to Pan-German and Socialists, a further Liberal ideological influence on their religious policy was conspicuously obvious.

Furthermore, it would be erroneous to conclude from the participation of future prominent Socialist and Catholic leaders in the formulation of the Linz program that Socialism and political Catholicism were, in the future, to be directly influenced by German national or even by Pan-German ideas. The agreement of Linz, conceived in answer to the more clearly recognized deficiencies of the Liberal position in social and national questions, proved to be quite different. It showed that as the widely divergent Pan-German, Christian Social, and Socialist movements developed, each of them approached the social and national problem in a way more in line with the developments of the day than had the Liberals. All three of them attempted in different ways to represent broader and economically weaker strata of interests than were represented by the Liberals; each of them, in greatly varying degrees, moved away from the academic form of German centralism to emotionally more accentuated, socially more pronounced concepts of nationalism. Although no common platform whatsoever united the offspring of the Liberal party movement—Pan-Germans, Christian Socials, and Social Democrats—the development of all three of them, apart from the specific premises of their doctrines, was strongly influenced by the dominant trends of modern times, which liberalism had fully ignored.

As far as the Austrian Pan-German movement was concerned, it is not necessary to dwell on its tremendous ideological influence on the ideas of German integral nationalism in general and National Socialism in particular. The extent to which these powerful currents, emerging first in the form of various national associations after 1882, have drawn on Schönerer's gospel was freely acknowledged by Hitler.[97] In striking contradiction to this overwhelming ideological influence of the movement were its poor forms of organization in odd national competitive organizations, generally fighting each other violently. Consequently, in spite of the extensive and expanding influence of the movement on the development of German nationalism in Austria, its power to intervene directly in the national organization of the empire remained limited.[98]

The reason the Pan-German program failed specifically to exert direct influence on the course of actual legislation can be concluded easily from a brief survey of some of its main points. It stood for the direct subordination of Austria to Germany in the form of a customs union, permanent parliamentary enactment of the alliance with Germany, complete administrative Germanization of Austria, reduction of the Real Union with Hungary to a mere Personal Union,[99] and, of course, abolition of legal equality in regard to Jews on a racial basis. Probably of even greater public significance was the violent campaign against the Catholic church and its alleged political influence, summed up in the widely popularized slogan: "Without Juda, without Rome, We shall build the German dome!"

Yet, in only thinly veiled form, the program went even further. It promoted the break-up of Austria, the union of German Austria with Germany, and German sovereignty over the Slav and Magyar bulk of the remainder of the empire. While these plans could not be publicly voiced in the monarchy—though literature of this kind was to be published copiously in Germany—even the more official plans of the movement had no chance to be adopted in Cisleithanian Austria, a country containing a Slav majority of population and still preserving parliamentary institutions. Even by means of a *Putsch* such objectives had not the slightest chance of being achieved in the face of a European civilization still ruled, at least on the surface, by the basic concepts of liberalism. Nor were these plans seriously meant to be put into immediate political practice; they were voiced chiefly as a means of political propaganda to radicalize German nationalism for the time to come, that is, for the still very indefinite and still rather uncertain event of the break-up of the empire. In the meantime, while the plans had no chance of actual materialization, the main aim was to stiffen the national attitude of the more moderate German parties and to prevent by all means a fulfillment of the demands of the non-German nationalities for a federalization of the empire along ethnic national lines. As long as such comprehensive pacification was not achieved, Pan-Germanism's ultimate aims still stood a chance in the future. Most other claims of the Pan-Germans in regard to local national issues and anti-Semitic and antireligious campaigns, and so forth, much rabble rousing as they caused, were only secondary aims, advanced largely for propagandistic reasons.[100]

An analysis of the effect of this political strategy of the Pan-Germans is very simple. As far as actual legislative achievement of their publicly voiced claims went, its effect was practically nil. As far as achievement of their underlying, further reaching, ideological objectives went, its success was much greater. Their policy of national raving, charging any moderate national policy with betrayal of the cause of the German people, led to a generally stiffening, more uncompromising, and more intolerant attitude on the part of relatively moderate nationalists, who anxiously, and in the end unsuccessfully, tried to accommodate their national program to a great extent to the Pan-German program.

It is a rather typical precept of political empirism that if a moderate party, instead of taking a firm stand on basic differences, tries to partially copy the program of a radical one, thereby hoping to take the wind out of the latter's sails, it will in the end, lose to the radical movement. This might not apply, in a parliamentary technical sense, to the policy of the moderate German Nationals of Liberal inheritance. Particularly after the elections of 1907, they outnumbered by far the demagogues of openly confessed Pan-German convictions. Ideologically, however, it proved almost completely to be true. Pan-German integral nationalism influenced predominantly—if it did not dominate—the policy of the moderate national groups.

This is not to say that these German Nationalists or National Liberals actively propagated the ultimate Pan-German aims. Neither did such a policy seem expedient to the majority of them, nor did this majority share, even surreptitiously, the Irredentist Pan-German convictions. But it did mean that, true to the Pan-German slogans of the betrayal of the German fatherland, they were firmly and obstinately opposed to a federalization of the Austrian Empire along national lines. In their way, they rigidly continued to advocate the preservation of the German centralist state, a German centralism of a far more intolerant brand than that transmitted by the tradition of Josephinian centralism. Though largely unconsciously, they worked hand in glove with Pan-Germanism and its speculation on the twilight of Austria, and therefore they, too, must be listed among the gravediggers of the empire.[101]

## The Christian Socials

As far as its organizational roots (not its ideological character) are concerned, the Christian Social movement was an offspring of the German Liberal party movement.[102] Technically it emanated, however, from the German national associations which seceded from the Liberal fold after the early 1880s.[103]

Three main reasons are of outstanding importance in explaining how and why the Christian Social movement thus broke away from radical German nationalism only a few years after the latter's official establishment in Austria, in 1882. The same reasons will explain why, measured in terms of popular support, the Christian Social organization outgrew the Pan-German movement almost equally fast. First, the Schönerer movement, ideologically led largely by the economically lower strata of the intellegentsia, including large numbers of university students and petty state officials, paid scant attention to the economic interests of the lower urban middle class, particularly the small business, artisan, and trade groups. Secondly, the Christian Socials were separated from the Liberals as well as from the Pan-Germans by their positive attitude toward the Catholic religion, toward which the Liberals were coolly negative and the Pan-Germans, in spite of occasional merely propagandistic extolling of a distorted "Christian-German spirit," openly hostile. The third reason was closely connected with the second. Their religious principles were undoubtedly one of the reasons for the appeal of the Christian Socials to broad masses who were ignorant of and at the same time hostile to the dreary rationalism of the Liberals and confused by the national idolatry of the Pan-Germans. At the same time the strongly Catholic position of the Christian Socials was in itself a weighty reason for supporting the idea of a Catholic Austrian empire. Therefore, aided by religious, social [104] and political reasons combined, the Christian Social movement stood in clear and strong opposition to the national Irredenta policy of the Pan-Germans, whether camouflaged or not.

These issues have seemed to many observers somewhat confused. After all, the reasons which promoted the brilliant leader and organizer of the Christian Social party, Karl Lueger (1844–1910),[105] to break away from the Liberal fold were, to a wide degree, identical with those promoted by Schönerer—dissatisfaction with the economic indeterminism of the Liberals and strong anti-Semitism, though of a social not racial, brand. Also similar in their beginning were the radical and violent forms of popular and parliamentary tactics of both movements. Yet essentially, the Pan-German movement was basically a destructive centrifugal force in its effect on the organism of the empire. The Christian Social party, on the other hand, became ever increasingly, in its merits as well as in its shortcomings, a powerful centripetal force.

It should not be concluded from the above that nationality problems stood foremost in the councils of the Christian Social party, which has been since 1907 the strongest party in the Austrian parliament. In a way, its geographic radius of political action remained limited. Until 1918 it drew its main strength from the Viennese soil and, secondly, from the urban and increasingly, also, from the rural communities in German Austria's Alpine provinces. The story of its political success is largely focused in Lueger's fight for the Viennese mayoralty—at one time probably the most important elective position in German Austria—and the annihilation of the Liberal regime in the city. Further, it is largely the story of a fight for the interests of the small businessman against high finance and big business, on the one hand, and rising socialism, on the other. It is, lastly, the story of the fight against "Jewish-liberal intellectualism." Least of all, except in regard to the religious issue, it is an account of activities in the service of a comprehensive national program.

Of all the major German Austrian parties, the Christian Social party was least concerned after the decay of German parliamentary liberalism, with such broad programmatic issues. For a long time, conspicuously in the great Austrian parliamentary crisis of 1897, which led to the downfall of the Badeni cabinet's endeavors for a Czech-German compromise, the party, as did the Liberals, still trailed in national questions in the wake of the German National Radicals. In the following decade a close association of the party with the heir apparent, Francis Ferdinand, made the Christian Socials apparently more friendly toward rather vague federal reform plans which were destined never to materialize.[106] More striking was the party's firm rejection of Magyar presumptions in Hungary's relation to Austria and a consequent friendly attitude toward the justified claims of the

Hungarian nationalities.[107] However, the practical results of this benevolent approach were entirely insignificant. Few specific Christian Social proposals concerning the problem of Austria's national federalization exist. Prior to 1918 none of them received the official blessings of the party.[108]

Of the theoretical contributions to the nationality problem from the Catholic camp, chiefly those of Wenzel Frind (1843–?) and later, above all Heinrich Lammasch (1853–1920) and Ignaz Seipel (1876–1932), the former, Austria's last prime minister, the latter, a member of his cabinet, were of real significance.[109] Yet, neither Lammasch nor Seipel were party men in old Austria's political life, though Seipel was destined to become chairman of the party and, as such, federal chancellor in the republic of Austria. Neither of these interesting personalities in old Austria confined their ideological concepts to party history. Nevertheless, in outlining the common basis of Catholic social philosophy and Catholic political doctrine, their ideas shed some light on the national policy of the Christian Social party. In this respect there can be no doubt that, fundamentally, political Catholicism had a keener perception of the premises, limits, and consequences of ethnic nationalism than the German liberalism of the latter part of the nineteenth century.

In spite of this fact, the direct contribution of the Christian Social party to the national problem in Austria remained limited. Yet stress should be laid on the word "direct." The Christian Socials were the heirs of the decaying Liberals to the extent that they stood unconditionally for the maintenance of the empire, with the main difference that their policy was based on a broad popular support, which the Liberals, who owed their parliamentary strength to the franchise restrictions of the 1870s and 1880s, had never really possessed. The question may well be asked whether the empire could have survived as long as it actually did if the major German bourgeois party in the twentieth century had not supported the empire idea.

*The Social Democrats*

An attempt to determine the effect of the national policy of the major German parties in the constitutional era leads to the following result. The Pan-German ideology, irrespective of the specific organization in which it was raised, was the most widely publicized, and its concepts from the empire's point of view were entirely of a destructive nature. The Catholic philosophy in regard to the national problems was the least doctrinaire and the least conspicuous, yet probably the most influential in the last fifteen to twenty years of the empire's existence. The plans of the Socialists, the third major group since the beginning of the twentieth century, presented the most comprehensive, the most "planned," and the most doctrinaire approach to the subject; yet, at the same time, the actual influence of this party ideology on Austria's public affairs was far more limited than the influence of either the national or the Catholic ideology.[110]

The history of the extremely intense Socialist interest in the Austrian nationality problem does not begin in the constitutional era. Marx and Engels devoted a great deal of attention and critical comment to the experiences to be drawn from the Austrian national revolution. Reference to their crude approach to the problem has already been made and will have to be elaborated further in connection with the history of the Revolution of 1848.[111] In regard to the specific problems of Austrian internal policy, however, their activities were those of outsiders. In this respect the early history of the Austrian Socialist movement as an active political force had very little connection with their theoretical work. The struggle within the labor movement in Austria between the *étatist* approach, developed under Lassale's influence, and the trade unionism inspired by Schultze-Delitzsch was also not greatly concerned with broader aspects of the national problems. Even in the 1870s and the 1880s the typical conflicts between trade unionism, syndicalism, and anarchism were still the questions of the day,[112] and it was only after the end of the 1880s that the Socialist movement, as bitterly opposed by the Liberals as it was by the "Feudo"-Clericals under Taaffe, gained a comprehensive political organization. The party convention of December-January, 1888–89, at Hainfeld, in Lower Austria, uniting the Czech and Austro-German Socialist labor movement, resulted in the actual birth of the Austrian Social Democratic party. At the same time, it marks the only example in Austrian internal history, of the emergence of a major party which spread beyond national frontiers. It is, furthermore, the only significant case where a major party was organized primarily along the pattern of common socioeconomic interests rather than along national or combined national ideological lines.[113]

The influence of this new political organization was, and remained in imperial Austria, rather limited. A weighty, yet insufficient explanation for this is offered by the fact that the Socialists, representing the economically lowest strata of the population, until 1907, were more than other parties retarded in their growth as a parliamentary group by the property qualifications of the Austrian franchise. It is true that, because of the introduction of general franchise in Austria in 1907, the Socialists, in the last decade of the empire's existence, became a true mass organization competing with the Christian Socials for the first position among the Austrian parties; yet their political influence, except in questions of social legislation, did not increase proportionately. The fact that no Socialist was ever represented in an imperial Austrian cabinet seemed rather natural in Europe before the First World War. But even the idea that the Socialists could be counted upon as a cohesive centripetal force of the empire seemed absurd to a large part of the ruling classes, who still considered democratic socialism a weird force of absolute terror. The announcement that with the party convention of Brünn in 1899, Austrian socialism had entered a new stage in its history, breaking away from the old slogan of "the peoples' jail, Austria"—*Der Völkerkerker Österreich* —and strongly supporting the empire idea was greeted with ignorant incredulity and derision.

The program of Brünn and the previous and particularly the subsequent works on the nationality problem above all by the party's theoreticians, Karl Renner and Otto Bauer, introduced, indeed, a penetrating new chapter in the theory—though not in the practice— of multinational state organization. In this nationality program, from the time of its proclamation almost until the end of the First World War, the Social Democrats promoted a policy which, wholly unfettered from the Marxian revolutionary doctrine, stood strongly and unconditionally for the preservation of a reformed Austrian empire. Their program, in its basic idea of the conversion of the empire into a federation of national member states along ethnic lines, was obviously only the continuation of a line of thought which might be called the intellectual inheritance of Kremsier. The essentially new features adopted in the Socialist position in the early twentieth century are twofold.

First, Social Democracy had overcome the concept of the national revolution at any place and at almost any price, not so much for the sake of national aspirations, but as a preliminary and transitional step in the struggle for the social revolution. The official party program as adopted at Brünn as well as the pioneer work by Renner—Bauer's theory was in some ways closer to the older doctrinaire Marxian concepts—no longer proceeded from this tie between social and national revolution. The new Social Democratic national program was conceived as an unconditional affirmation of the multinational empire, whose preservation and conversion was considered in many ways as a precondition of social reformism, but not of social revolution.

Secondly, the Socialist program, of all the concepts which in the course of two generations had ever advocated some kind of ethnic federalization of Austria, came closest theoretically to reconciliation with the centralistic empire idea. It limited the sphere of jurisdiction of the national member states roughly to the fields of primary national interests, that is, the cultural sphere. It preserved the central empire power not only in the sphere of military defense and foreign affairs but, faithful to the Socialist theory, in the wide field of economics. Furthermore, its concept of national autonomy—a notion fully developed by this Socialist doctrine—was far more concerned with the organizational problem of interrelations among the various nationalities than any other federal program had been.

According to its basic doctrines, the Socialist program was not a German program. Greatest care had been taken by the party to emphasize its supranational character, joining together individuals of the same socioeconomic interests among all the nationalities. Yet, from the angle of political reality the Socialist nationality policy was not only welded essentially by German Austrians (Adler, Bauer, Pernerstorfer, Renner, and others) but the ideology of the party contained also, irrespective of the more radical or more moderate character of their intellectual leaders, a good deal of German national centralistic ideology. This trend went straight back to Marx and Engels and was possibly enhanced by the fact that two of the chief intellectual leaders of the party, Pernerstorfer and, more significantly also, Victor Adler, came from the national wing of the Liberals to the Socialist movement.[114]

Actually, the German tendencies in the party, greatly accentuated by the patriotic emotions aroused at the outbreak of the First World War, were in permanent and increasing conflict with the strong, nationally influenced Socialist party branches among the Slavs, above all the strongly nationalist Czech Socialist party. The cumbersome structure of Brünn finally could not withstand the opposition of this virile young nationalism of the Czech Socialists, who clearly placed nationalism above their Socialist affiliations. After considerable friction, the Czech Social Democrats, who advocated a much looser form of Austrian federation than did the Germans and, above all, were against any program of national partition in Bohemia, set up their own independent party organization in 1911.[115]

The issue at this point is not the theoretical problem involved in this split, but the very fact of the conflict itself, steadily increasing in the course of the First World War. At the end of the war, the Slav Socialist parties openly stood for the organization of their newly won national states. The Austro-German Socialist movement was, in a way, divided between tendencies to support Slav separatism and a desire to remain faithful to the idea of the federalized empire until the end.[116]

On the other hand, two theoretically opposed trends, the Liberal right wing, still influenced by the idea of German centralism, and the Left, primarily interested in the existence of great states whose socialization should prove easier than that of small ones, found a common platform of action. It was, thus, natural that, with the final collapse of the empire, the German Social Democratic party of Austria, though not agreeing on motives, agreed with other German parties to the union with the great national state Germany. The *Anschluss policy* [117] was not only in line with the national revolutionary Liberal tradition of 1848 but it also agreed with a socialist notion of furthering socialization through formation of the large state.

On the whole, however, the Socialists were not successful in uniting the adherents of their doctrine in a common nationality policy. This failure in political practice undoubtedly impaired to some extent the value of their nationality program, fluctuating as it was for generations between what may be called a German revolutionary and a central European federal approach.[118] Yet, from whatever angle the Social Democratic nationality program is looked upon, it was a grave omission on the part of official Austria to ignore it, instead of making comprehensive use of some of its ideas and, even more important, of the pro-Austrian ideology of those of its supporters who were willing to give the empire, unconditionally, what belonged to the empire.

One of the many tragic paradoxes of the First World War was that the German ideology, which had failed most dismally in Austria's internal policy came out successfully in the end. What had seemingly triumphed was the German national doctrine which had blocked the roads to reform and salvation until the end, either consciously or unconsciously. Ridiculously blind to the realities of the day, it had solemnly voted for the creation of a new German county court in Bohemia at a time, when the Slav deputies proclaimed the separation of their peoples from the empire.[119] These German nationalists gained the support of the other parties for the desired union with Germany and, even though this aim could not be achieved, they gained the national German Austrian state, however short its frontiers fell of their sweeping aspirations.

The most tragic disappointment undoubtedly was experienced by the Christian Socials, the party most unconditionally faithful to the idea of the empire as it was. Yet their responsibility actually rested in this rigid, uncritical form of allegiance. If this true state party of old Austria's last generation had shown in national questions the same independent policy as it had in religious and to some extent in social issues, if the party, instead of haltingly following the track of German centralism, had joined hands with the democratic federalist forces all over the empire—it might have been able, more than any other party, to help in the preservation of the empire. The tragic error of their passive rather than active support of the empire idea finally demanded from the Christian Socials in the probating of the empire's inheritance and in the unwilling submission to the *Anschluss* ideology, a *sacrificum intellectus* which the other parties were spared.

The difficult task of Austrian Socialism was to act in accordance with the conclusions drawn from the deceptive success of nationalism and the inconclusive defeat of clericalism.

CHAPTER IV

# THE MAGYARS

THE FOLLOWING STATEMENT may well serve as leitmotiv for an analysis of the Hungarian nationality problem, with all its tragic implications.[1]

While other peoples may determine a course of action on the basis of the true merits of a cause, little concerned with its source or form, the Magyar wants to garb everything, great or small, in Magyar dress. Anything which is not so garbed is an object of suspicion to him. I for one know of no real Magyar who, though his hair may have grayed and experience and worldly wisdom may have furrowed his brow, would not, as a lunatic whose *idée fixe* has been touched, disregard doctrines of fairness and even of justice when the affairs of our language and nationality are touched upon. On such occasions the most cool-headed becomes ecstatic, the most perspicacious, stricken with blindness, and the fairest and most just, ready to forget the first of the unalterable rules of eternal truth . . . : Do unto no one what thou would'st not have them do unto thee![2]

These are not the words of any of the opponents of Magyar national aspirations among the Austrian nationalities or of a Magyar radical leftist. They were spoken in 1842 by Count Stephen Széchenyi, the Liberal Magyar reformer, on whom Magyar historiography usually confers the title "Greatest of the Magyars."

## THE NATIONAL CONCEPT OF MAGYARISM

In a way, the causes of this rather specific brand of nationalism can be understood more clearly and can be seen in better proportion by noting some of their effects at a later time, particularly in the period immediately preceding the First World War. In 1910, Hungary had a fully functioning parliamentary system. It rested, however, on a truly extraordinary franchise law. The right to vote, by open ballot to be sure, was the privilege of only 6.1 percent of the population, that is, 27.6 percent of all men over twenty-one years of age. The disfranchisement of nearly three quarters of the male population was largely the result of stiff property qualifications, which were based, not even on the amount of taxes paid, but on the value of the property.[3] This provision gave free rein to an arbitrary assessment of property in favor of big landed estates.

In the parliament elected on this basis the Magyars, who formed about 54 percent of the entire population of Hungary, or, if Croatia were included, a mere 45 percent, occupied 405 parliamentary seats. The remaining 45 percent of the population in Hungary proper had eight seats, five allotted to the Rumanians and three to the Slovaks.[4] This proportional relationship appears all the more striking in that the population percentages quoted above were based on official Magyar statistics, bitterly and in many ways justly contested by the non-Magyar Hungarian nationalities.

In the civil administration this "national equilibrium" worked in a manner suggested by the following figures: The Magyars supplied approximately 96 percent of all government employees, 92 percent of all high school teachers, and 93 percent of all university teachers. Some 800,000 students of the minority nationalities were instructed by, roughly, 5,000 teachers, a million Magyar students by some 26,000 teachers.[5]

This situation was just as much the product of social as of racial or national discrimination. The disfranchisement of nearly three quarters of the whole male population of the kingdom certainly was neither legally nor politically aimed directly at the suppression of the non-Magyar nationalities. It was largely based on a policy primarily concerned with preserving the privileges of a small class of feudal lords [6] in alliance with a landed gentry whose relatively modest means were quite disproportionate to their social prestige and national pride. Since the era of the compromise, these pillars of the old Magyar social order received ever-increasing support from a thriving business class. This relatively small, socially unhomogeneous, but economically united upper class remained in power partly because of the intricacies of the restricted Hungarian franchise laws and terroristic election practices at the polls. It was by no means representative of the Magyar people.

There can be no doubt that the so-called "Liberal party," which, but for a brief interval, governed Hungary from the 1870s to 1918 and also after the collapse of the empire, under the new label of "Party of National Unity," was elected by only a minority of the

Magyar peoples, let alone non-Magyar Hungarians. Its economic policy in every respect ran counter to the interests of the majority of the Magyar people—the small peasant class and later the slowly rising laboring class as well.[7] Nevertheless, the ruling classes received a certain share of popular support, particularly if they appealed to the glory of Magyar nationalism, and this for two main reasons. First, the Magyar rulers, and this means the proud Magyar aristocracy and gentry, rather than their business clientele, whose popular appeal was definitely limited, could appear before the people as the upholders and defenders of an ancient and proud national tradition, such as none of the neighboring peoples claimed with equal assurance. Secondly, the interests of these ruling classes were represented by people firmly united in their interests, well trained to rule, resolute and well prepared to fight, and open-minded in adjusting their feudal inclinations to the necessities—and benefits—of the industrial age of free capitalistic enterprise. This was not a decaying and soon-to-be-superseded aristocracy; it was a virile, daring, intelligent, and ruthless class with every trump card in its hands except that of justice.

None of these factors could appeal to the non-Magyar nationalities. Except for the Croats, whose relations with the Magyars must be treated separately, all national groups within Hungary, were nationalities without history, in the sense outlined above. Here the concept of national groups with neither a national aristocracy nor a bourgeoisie assumes full meaning. The interests of the poor peasant majority of the population, whether Slovak, Ruthenian, Rumanian, or Serb, were diametrically opposed to those of the Magyar rulers. The chasm separating them could not be bridged by appeal to a common glorious national tradition, which was nonexistent. To be sure, economic interests in common with the Magyar rulers might have reconciled the upper classes of the nationalities—nobility, intelligentsia, businessmen, and industrialists—if such classes had existed among them. But well into the second half of the nineteenth century there existed among these national groups no upper class strong and numerous enough either to organize their peoples along the Magyar pattern or to rally them to the cause of the Magyar upper classes. These national groups within the empire had no nationally conscious landed aristocracy, and only relatively insignificant industrial and commercial interests.[8]

Following the pre-March era, national intelligentsia came increasingly to the fore in these territories, and its effectiveness grew substantially in ensuing generations. But a national intelligentsia and national professional groups without complementary industrial and commercial classes could hardly be expected to join in an alliance with the Magyar Liberal party based on a true community of interests. One course, frequently chosen by such non-Magyar intelligentsia, lay in the direction of making peace with the Magyar ruling classes and in accepting Magyarization as quickly as was possible and profitable. The second alternative was to reject advantages deriving from national conversion and to join the national movement of their own peoples. By virtue of character, ability, and training, individuals of such type had a fair chance of becoming the spiritual leaders of their own kin. Indeed, they were to be found increasingly in the forefront of the national struggle among the suppressed nationalities. The status of their broad masses continued to be based on collective social discrimination, irrespective of the pro- or anti-Magyar attitude of their intellectual elite.

Thus, the Magyar upper classes could not possibly hope to reconcile the interests of the nationality groups with their own economic and social interests. On the contrary, they had to expect that any concessions to these nationalities would only help to create among these oppressed peoples a formidable opposition to their own economic and national policy. They also had reason to fear that the Magyar peasant population, whose economic situation was so similar to that of their fellow peasants among the other nationalities, would join them in their fight against the magnates and their business clientele. While a coalition of the Magyar upper classes and those of the nationalities was not feasible, this was not true of the overwhelmingly more numerous peasant class among all the Hungarian peoples. The threat of an agricultural reform, in the eyes of the Magyar Tories perceived as agricultural revolution, was by no means to be regarded lightly.

Still, it must not be forgotten that, even in the socioeconomic field, the suppression of Magyar and non-Magyar underprivileged classes was markedly different. While the Magyar peasant suffered from social discrimination, the non-Magyar peasant, in addition, suffered from national discrimination. This fact was of relatively small significance in the rigid feudal societal order of the pre-March period, but it became increasingly important in the semiliberal parliamentary system in force after the 1860s. From then on, in the era of rapidly increasing industrialization in Hungary, the Magyar peasant worker had an opportunity to raise his social standard, but the non-Magyar did not. Not unlike the relations of the British worker to the natives in the colonies under nineteenth-century conditions, the Magyar peasant and worker profited in a limited way socially, psychologically, and economically from the inferior position of his fellow peasant worker among the nationalities. The Magyar ruling classes had to preserve this socioeconomic distinction based on national discrimination, if the existing social system itself were to be preserved.

This was a main reason why these Magyar ruling classes could never consent to a policy of national justice and conciliation. It was also a main reason why they followed and propagandized a policy preserving and deepening the conflict between the "Magyar master race" (in fact, only a narrow stratum of the Magyar race) and the other nationalities. However, it was not the only reason.

Reference has already been made to the powerful impact of Magyar national tradition, which undoubtedly was partly due to the racial isolation of the Magyars, not only within the boundaries of the empire, where they were surrounded by Slavs and Germans, but all over Europe.[9]

The inspiring influence of this fact on the perseverance of Magyar nationalism has been best expressed in poetic form in the famous lines of Mihaly Vörösmarty (1800–55):

O Magyar, keep immoveably thy native country's trust,
For it has borne thee, and at death will consecrate thy dust!
No other spot in all the world can touch thy heart as home;
Let fortune bless or fortune curse, from hence thou shalt not roam.[10]

The legal and sociopolitical consequences of this attitude, acquired in the course of many generations, have been illustrated thus by Friedrich von Wieser.

In Hungary, rule fell to the Magyars. Because of an Estates tradition of longer standing, the self-administration of the *Comitats,* [counties] and the institutions of the revolutionary state of 1848, they enjoyed better political training. In their nationally conscious nobility, endowed with rich landed property and overwhelming influence even in the non-Magyar territories, they had a popular national ruling class; in the surviving warriors of 1848, they had politically picked troops, and the leaders of that time were still their recognized leaders. But, above all, the whole people was united by its national passion. . . . In any other respect—numbers of population, wealth, and educational background—they were inferior to the western part of the empire, but were they not, after all, politically the superior nation? They were capable of leading their state, of exploiting it in a way which increased their resources to an unexpected degree, of winning numerous citizens of other nationalities over to their own political idea, and even to their own nationality, and thereby of raising their culture and wealth.[11]

And Friedrich Tezner, though stanchly opposed to Hungary's aspirations to unlimited national independence, admits, in 1905:

No doubt, Hungary is culturally greatly superior to Austria, as far as the creation of general conditions for a modern state life are concerned. Austria was the much-abused center and is even today the hope of political and cultural reaction, while Hungary nearly three centuries ago . . . achieved the final victory of freedom of religion and conscience . . . and established a secure place for the freedom of expression vis-à-vis the crown. The Austrians, and that refers to all of them without distinction of nationality apart from the Poles, have in the more modern period of their history no appealing personality of epic greatness. In contrast to this, Hungarian History is a continuous heroic epos.[12]

And again it is Wieser who tries to find comprehensive and conclusive reasons for the historic fate which, in spite of grave setbacks, so markedly favored the Magyars among the Austro-Hungarian nationalities.

Turkey has destroyed the independent Hungarian state, she has cut off from European culture the part of the land conquered by her, and she has retarded the cultural development of the remaining territory. But . . . ultimately she preserved for the Hungarians a valuable asset of the people's property, which has almost been lost in the rest of Europe. Hungary owes to the Crescent the preservation of her medieval Estates rights and liberties; thereby she has saved her national independence as she enjoys it today [that is, after the Compromise of 1867]. . . . In the first two centuries of the modern era, while the military power of the princes had developed everywhere else and had destroyed rights and liberties of the Estates, in Hungary . . . the Estates institutions have been preserved. England in the far west has been preserved by her fortunate island position from being drawn so deeply into the continental wars that her kings could gain overpowering military might and could use it against their own subjects. The position of Hungary in the southeast was similar to that of England. She was not drawn into . . . the great wars of central Europe which have destroyed popular liberties, and she was saved from sharing the fate of Bohemia. She escaped the Counter-Reformation and could manage to transfer her religious and political liberties unharmed into a more peaceable period.[13]

These observations are not only notable for excellent presentation of salient features in the historic development of the Magyar national position. They are equally interesting because of the most typical fallacies which they present in other respects. Wieser and Tezner, like many lesser lights, though fully aware of the presumptuousness of Magyar claims, nevertheless could not avoid being caught in the trap of the impressive Magyar myths.[14] The assumption that the Magyars themselves were firmly united in their national claims is contradicted by the simple fact that, even in the flourishing period of Hungarian parliamentarism, the overwhelming majority of the Magyars, to say nothing of the nationalities, had no voice in their national affairs. It was not until the great Hungarian political crisis of 1905, which led to the dissolution of the parliament by armed force, that any doubt existed in Austria of the credo of Magyar national unity and strength. This myth of unity found a supposedly historical basis in the Bulla Aurea, a charter issued in 1222, only seven years after the British Magna Charta, and in Magyar eyes appearing indeed, equal in importance to the Magna Charta. It fostered the image of a Hungary enjoying parliamentary institutions and a bill of rights.[15]

While it is perfectly true that the Magyars had a clearer conception of the significance of their ancient Estates institutions than any other national group and any other historicopolitical entity within the Habsburg lands, it must not be assumed that these institutions implied the guarantee of popular liberties. Neither—and this is indeed the chief difference between the significance of the Magna Charta and the Bulla Aurea—did they develop in such a direction. As was the case with other medieval Estates rights, the Hungarian institutions remained chiefly a means of upholding the rights of the nobles against the crown. It is a controversial question whether Hungary, from the sixteenth to the nineteenth century, was administered more liberally than any other Habsburg land, since such an assumption is based on identification of a striving for national independence with a striving for liberal reforms. Yet it is certain that after 1867 Hungary's political system, relative to the other Habsburg lands, was in many ways more backward than it had been before 1848–49. In general, the famous words of the venerable Hungarian statute book of 1514, the main source for the study of the historical interpretation of Hungarian constitutional law, extended their influence beyond the life of the empire.

Under the name and designation of the people one comprehends here only
the bishops, the lords, the other aristocrats, and all the nobles, but not the
commoners. . . . Under the name of plebs only the commoners are comprehended.[16]

Renner's sardonic comment on the alleged glory of Magyar constitutionalism is largely to the point.

Indeed it had to be a miracle of a constitution which succeeded in creating
a parliamentary representation, but not a representation of the peoples.
It succeeded in basing the state on national consciousness but at the same
time in killing the national consciousness of five nationalities. It succeeded
in using all kinds of democratic devices against the court [crown], and yet
it considered the aristocracy an unlimited master. It succeeded in leading
freedom to triumph and yet managed to keep half of the population in
national, and nine tenths of it in social, bondage.[17]

However, one distinctive feature in the Hungarian constitutional
and administrative setup goes beyond the familiar features of the
Estates institutions and, in some respects, has influenced reform plans
beyond the Hungarian border. It is the medieval Hungarian *Comitat*,
or county organization, with its substantial degree of administrative
autonomy. No similar institutions existed until the nineteenth century in Cisleithanian Austria, except for some chartered towns.[18] To
be sure, even in Hungary the *Comitat*, or county system, meant chiefly
the extension of the Estates system into the local administrative sphere
and by no means implied a thoroughly democratic administration.
Until 1918 one half of the members of the *Comitat* councils consisted of the highest taxpayers of the citizens in the county, and the
other half, of citizens chosen by lot.[19] Still, in an important way the
Hungarian *Comitat* system opened the door to progress in the administrative sphere in the empire.

Reform proposals concerning the national problem in nationally
mixed territories from 1848 onwards increasingly promoted the idea
of autonomous territorial *Kreis* institutions. These were perceived as
higher in the administrative setup than townships and districts, but
lower than the crownlands.

Although autonomy on the level of small townships and districts
would have to be too restricted in administrative scope and too complex in national organization, the setup of the larger *Kreise*, corresponding in size approximately to the Hungarian *municipia* (that is,
*Comitats* and chartered townships) could have created territorial organizations small enough to be built up in a nationally fairly homo-

geneous way, yet large enough to be entrusted with fairly wide administrative functions. Equally important, the introduction of this *Kreis* system, either to be organized within the crownland system or, preferably, to replace it altogether, could have led to a democratization of the administration of the empire on every level.

To be sure, the Hungarian *Comitat* system was not only very far from such democratic organization, it was even further from a fair national organization. Still, the mere existence of the Hungarian *municipia* offered an example to fill their administrative frame with a justly organized national and democratic life, which, unfortunately, was never properly followed, either in Hungary or in Austria.[20]

Actually, the Magyar contribution to the advancement of Liberal reforms in the empire was by no means confined to the creation of a useful device in the administrative setup of the empire. Wieser and Tezner are right if they refer to the inspiration which liberalism has received from the Magyar cause. They should have made clear, however, that they refer, not to the Magyar party liberalism of the ruling system after 1867, but to the idea of the Hungarian Revolution of 1848 and 1849 and the reform period preceding it. After the death of the great leaders Deák and Eötvös, in 1876 and 1871, liberalism in Hungary, particularly from the 1870s on, was reduced to mere religious tolerance which, on the whole, was stronger in Hungary than in the denominationally unhomogeneous parts of Cisleithanian Austria. Apart from this aspect, there was little left but the name "Liberal," which in the new era of national unification of Germany and Italy, in the permanent introduction of the constitutional system in Austria, and in the rise of the Third French Republic had an undoubtedly popular appeal.

But, on the whole, Magyar liberalism drew its main strength from the identification in the mind of the people of a fight for national independence with a fight for human freedom. That such identification took place is not surprising. The memories of the Dutch, the American, and the Italian struggles for independence certainly were proof of the widespread concurrence of struggles for national and political freedom. These interrelations were far less recognizable in the process of German unification or in the establishment of the independent Balkan countries; they are simply nonexistent in the consistent Magyar endeavors after 1867 further to loosen the tenuous bond with Austria. Nevertheless, in the minds of the Magyar people, the continued bickering about the interpretation of the compromise was connected with the memory of the liberal national Magyar Revolution and its heroic and romantic leaders. Beyond Hungary, the concept of Magyar liberalism remains confined to the prerevolutionary and revolutionary era of 1848–49 and the Liberal revival in the 1860s. Even then, a strong accent must be put on the national prefix of this liberalism.

## THE "REFORM PERIOD" IN MAGYAR-HUNGARY, 1825–48

Viewed objectively, the merits of the social reforms introduced in Hungary between 1825 and 1848 outweigh the nationalist aberrations of that period of Magyar history.[21] Unfortunately, the repercussions of the latter were far greater than those of the former. Magyar policy from the Revolution of 1848–49 onward generally followed and accentuated the nationalist trend of the Magyar pre-March period, while it dropped the spirit of social reformism of that era.

Practically all the constructive work of this period is somehow connected with the ideas and endeavors of the great reformer Count Stephen Széchenyi (1791–1860). The plans, which never went beyond the paper stage or ended in failure, are linked with the strange genius of Louis Kossuth (1802–94). There are, indeed, few government activities for whose reforms Széchenyi did not wage a ceaseless fight during the two prerevolutionary decades. Important agricultural and municipal reforms, improvement of communication facilities, and the regulation of the waterways of the Danube and the Tisza formed only a part of his work. The foundation of the Hungarian Academy of Science as well as general educational reforms culminating in the substitution of the Magyar language for Latin—widely used among the upper classes and generally used in official business—were promoted by him. The subsequent development of the latter reform into a means of national oppression, instead of enlightenment, was violently contrary to the reformer's intent. Though not greatly concerned with the dynamics of politics, he was always a stanch and consistent liberal. Though he had little respect for the national myths and made light of the alleged, and so proudly boasted, similarities between English and Hungarian political institutions, he nevertheless promoted an adjustment toward the relatively far more advanced social standard of England. By 1840 he had successfully exerted his influence on the diet with respect to the serf-tenants who, as a result of his actions, became qualified to buy land and to gain personal independence. He failed, however, in his efforts to eliminate the odious law that exempted the nobility from all taxation. This exemption, which included the gentry, by far the most numerous group among the nobles, benefited not less than some 700,000 people.

Most of these reform proposals by Széchenyi and his political friends Deák, Wesselényi, G. Apponyi, and others, were not directly concerned with nationality and constitutional problems. Yet, just as the solution of the nationality problem in Hungary was inseparably connected with the solution of the economic problem, so was the rise of Hungary to a more independent position in relation to the empire dependent on the enactment of economic reforms. Only a Hungary with a free and prosperous citizenry, not a Hungary of destitute bondsmen ruled by a small aristocracy and a large gentry, could rise to the level of political independence which Széchenyi, no less than the leaders of the revolution, desired. Széchenyi realized that in Hungary economic reforms had to precede political reforms in regard to her relations to the empire; he was also aware that the economic issue was in itself the weightier one. On this political basis he joined the first parliamentary liberal reform ministry, formed by Count Louis Batthyány in April, 1848. Opposed to a two-front policy of simultaneous political and economic reforms which, as he foresaw, would inevitably lead to open conflict, he possibly might have resigned before the outbreak of such conflict with the empire. However, he was suddenly stricken with a mental illness before he had committed himself definitely.

Széchenyi had to face the twofold opposition of the Magyar aristocrats and the central government in Vienna, on the one hand,[22] and the radical liberal nationalists, on the other. Much as the Metternich government and the Magyar feudals were divided otherwise on the purely national issue, they were firmly united in their opposition to radical agricultural reforms which would ultimately lead to change in the Estates order and to the downfall of the feudal ruling classes. This, in turn, would also mean a dangerous step toward the abolition of the system of the police state, represented by the central government. Agreement between these two political forces on the basis of important common interests thus appeared by no means impossible.[23]

Opposition on the Right might have been overcome if the reformers around Széchenyi had secured the united support of the Liberal Left. Actually, the opposition from the Left proved to be not only more powerful, but also far more violent than that from the Right. The movement under Kossuth's leadership—a "young Hungary" following Mazzini's pattern—reversed Széchenyi's policy. Political reforms, focused on the ultimate, though not yet clearly formulated, goal of complete separation from the empire, stood well in the forefront of their political aims. Yet Kossuth, also, was fully aware of the necessity of social reforms. In the paper *Pesti Hirlap,* founded in 1841, he came out violently against the feudal system, the aristocratic privileges, and, in general, the existing inequality before the law, yet he pictured Austria and Austrian institutions as the root of all evil. In general, he regarded these reforms as dependent on the fulfillment of Hungary's constitutional aims. He never recognized that conditions of social misery and national discord in Hungary were major causes of the growing Magyar revolution and its ultimate failure.

Kossuth's genius, and a genius he was despite all his shortcomings, was, indeed, full of strange contradictions. In 1842 he opposed Austria's, and also Hungary's, entry into the German *Zollverein* as leading to isolation from western Europe and to subordination to German interests.[24] Yet at the same time he was shortsighted enough to oppose, largely for reasons of national prestige, a customs union between Hungary and Austria, in spite of their complementary economic interests. Far more ominous was Kossuth's inability to understand the Hungarian national question from any but a purely Magyar nationalist point of view. He undoubtedly considered himself a true nationalist and a true liberal, and he was equally sincere in his belief that this combination of Magyarism and liberalism would satisfy the interests of every Hungarian subject, Magyar and non-Magyar alike. Legal equality before the law, in his opinion, made a guarantee of national equality superfluous, a notion which consistently was opposed by the nationalities as insufficient protection of their rights. Obviously, however, this insufficient legal equality of the individual was not even enjoyed by the Magyar population, let alone by the other nationalities.[25]

Széchenyi and his friends Deák and Wesselényi, who were both destined to play an important and constructive part in Hungary after 1848, realized that national tolerance was of the utmost importance for Magyar policy and that it was wrong to assume that the forced spread of the Magyar language throughout the kingdom would necessarily convert all the nationalities to Magyar feeling.[26] Kossuth consistently and with grave consequences for the Magyar people opposed the recognition of any ethnic rights for the other nationalities. Count Michael Károlyi, the leader of the Magyar October Revolution of 1918, who tried to avoid Kossuth's errors in this respect, comments thus on Kossuth's nationalism.

It was a nationalist radicalism, the extreme expression of which was a sentimental exaggeration of the principle of Hungarian nationality. But there is another Kossuth, the Kossuth of the period of exile, who realized that the one great and probably crucial error in his revolutionary policy had been the antagonizing of the non-Magyar races in Hungary.[27]

Undoubtedly Kossuth had grown in political stature during his life in exile after the revolution; yet basically he never changed his concept of nationalism radically. In 1881, still sure of Magyar liberalism toward other nationalities, he had the following statement published.

Liberalism in relation to foreign races remained . . . to such a degree a leading principle of Hungarian policy, that there is no second example of such kind in the whole history of the world. Never before has a state-building race banished even the mere idea of an exclusiveness of its rights to its own disadvantages from the policy. Never before has it made the concept of citizen equally independent of the concept of race like the Magyars. . . . If this firm will and resolution press the stigma of the ruling race on our forehead, then I want to recognize this stigma as a letter of nobility for our race.[28]

Thus, according to this strange "liberal" nationalism, to be a Hungarian and a Magyar is one and the same thing. There is no nobler aim for anybody raised on Hungarian soil than to be recognized as a member of the "master race."

Accordingly, when, in 1848, a Hungarian-Serb delegation opposed this theory and asked for limited administrative autonomy for its people, Kossuth revealed the alternate course, "The sword will decide between us." [29] The tragic course of Magyar nationalism is well summed up in the remark made by another famous Magyar statesman, Count Stephan Tisza, with reference to the claims of a Serb-Bosnian delegation in 1918, "It may be that we [the Magyars] shall be ruined, but before then we shall have the power to crush you." [30]

To return to the prerevolutionary development, the Estates assembled in Bratislava (Pressburg, Pozsony) in November, 1847, were anxious to maintain and extend Hungary's home rule. To strengthen their cause within Hungary, they favored a liberalization of the constitution. The outbreak of the revolution in France in February of the following year and in Austria a few weeks later forced the king-emperor, somewhat beyond the hopes and expectations of the Estates, to consent to their decisions and, on April 10, 1848, to sanction them. This meant that for the first time in Hungarian history a ministry responsible to the nation through parliament—comprising the great names of Batthyány, Széchenyi, Deák, Kossuth, and Eötvös—took office.[31]

Thus, April 10, 1848, is the birthday of the first constitution in the Habsburg land, based, at least to some extent, on the principles of truly representative government. Though its sanction by the sovereign would have been inconceivable without the pressure of revolutionary events, the Magyars could rightly claim that the ideas, and even the actual content of their reformed constitutional laws, were wholly a product of the prerevolutionary period.[32] Replacing the Estates assembly, the new parliament was to consist of a lower house to be elected on the basis of property qualification, while the upper house was to represent chiefly the landed nobility as hereditary members. For all practical purposes, only the conduct of foreign affairs was left to the empire. Service of the army beyond the Hungarian frontiers was to require the consent of the cabinet, which in turn was responsible to parliament.

In regard to social reforms, the assembly, spurred on by the revolutionary atmosphere and under the very active support of Kossuth and his followers, voted for the abolition of serf labor and elimination of tax exemption for the nobility and tithes for the clergy. Franchise was extended, and the main demands of political liberalism—freedom of the press and of religious worship—were granted.[33]

The new Hungary was to be consolidated by the direct representation of Croatia-Slavonia in the modernized parliament. She was to be enlarged by the incorporation of a *Militärgrenze* (military frontier), that is, roughly the southern part of the frontier district between Drava and Sava.[34] Finally, she was to be subjected to a process of equalizing Magyarization—and on that point, in scope and in means, the reform policy failed lamentably.

In this case, the otherwise beneficial work of the *Reichstag* [35] was seriously impaired, if not altogether wrecked, chiefly by the nationalist intransigence of Kossuth and his followers. From the beginning of the reform period, a national language movement, tending to replace the supranational (Latin) language of the upper classes by

Magyar, had grown in force. It was violently rejected by the non-Magyars, though chiefly only the Croats, who were represented as a national group on the *Reichstag,* had an opportunity to voice this opposition.[36] Kossuth, in the protracted negotiations of the *Reichstag,* stubbornly prevented any major concessions to the non-Magyar Hungarians on the subject. He asserted that the Hungarian people whose native language was not Magyar did not form national groups. There could be no question that Magyar must be made the official, legal, and administrative language, by threat of force, if necessary. Where Magyar was not understood, Latin was to be used as the official language instead of the local vernacular, but only for a transitional period of six years.[37] The assembly, against the most violent opposition of the southern Slav representatives, adopted a language law incorporating these ideas. Furthermore, an even more radical law of colonization was passed, making the right to permanent settlement in all of Hungary dependent in the future on the command of the Magyar language. It is not too much to say that public reaction to these laws created a revolutionary situation in the south Slav territories of Hungary even before the outbreak of the open conflict with Austria.

It has sometimes been said that the real reason for the outbreak of the Hungarian Revolution was the attempt to silence the non-Magyar peoples in Hungary in order to Magyarize them all the more easily. As Francis Palacký put it, "The real cause of the revolution was the refusal of the Magyars to grant equal national rights to the Slavs, the Germans, and the Rumanians living in Hungary." [38] This offers, perhaps, too limited an explanation of the cause of the revolution, which, after all, was equally tied up with the political issue of revolutionary liberalism. But it is safe to say that the complete breakdown of the revolution, as in the case of any of the other great catastrophes of future Magyar history, was caused by the failure to comprehend the socionational problems of Hungary.

### THE MAGYARS IN THE REVOLUTIONARY PERIOD

In the entire history of Europe from the French Revolution of 1789 to the various revolutions of 1918, the Magyar struggle with the Habsburg centralist power in 1848–49 [39] was one of the most violent and most serious conflicts between the forces of supranational feudal absolutism and national liberalism. It was the tragedy of this revolution,[40] as indeed of the whole heroic history of the Magyar people, that its contribution to the emancipation of the Hungarian nationalities was entirely negative. In particular, in this great conflagration the role of the two conflicting powers on the national issue was nearly reversed. Habsburg centralist absolutism largely, though not entirely, for reasons of political expediency supported either the cause of the non-Magyar nationalities or at least promoted a nationally colorless imperial centralism. Magyar liberalism, for a brief period a vivid and powerful political force, at that time undoubtedly supported the idea of Magyarization of the Hungarian nationalities or, plainly speaking, national oppression.

These facts contributed to the undoing of the Magyar Revolution, and, in their wider implications, led to that future tragic course of Magyar policy which was in permanent conflict with the surrounding Slav nationalities and tied it to the orbit of German imperialism. This does not mean, as Magyar feudal pretensions wished to make it appear, that Magyar Hungary, except for the first post-revolutionary decade, was subjected to German Austrian domination. To be sure, Magyar-ruled Hungary after the Compromise of 1867 formed, if not the stronger, certainly the privileged, partner in the Dualistic Union. It does mean, however, that Austria-Hungary's dependence on Germany, welcomed by the Magyar rulers, made Hungary the battle-ground of the German-Russian conflict.

Neither does the statement that the defeat in the Civil War of 1848–49 was due to intransigent Magyar nationalism refer to the military outcome of the struggle. No combination of political circumstances could have given the Magyars a chance successfully to withstand the combined intervention of the imperial Austrian and Russian armies. On the other hand, a sane and moderate course of Magyar nationality policy might have avoided this intervention and might have succeeded in concluding in 1848 a compromise with the empire. Influenced by the revolutionary situation and by the strong liberal trends of the Hungarian reform period, such a compromise might have altered the course of the counterrevolution all over the empire. Certainly by conceding liberal terms to the non-Magyar nationalities, it would in the long run have served Magyar interests decisively.

Even Austrian military absolutism, not to speak of the conciliatory liberal, but powerless, imperial ministries of Pillersdorf and later of Wessenberg,[41] were still, in October, 1848, hesitant to open the battle against the popular Magyar revolutionary regime. Military considerations, which decreased in weight after Radetzky's victories in Italy, did not determine this hesitancy. Probably more important were the political fears that a fight for the destruction of the liberal, representative April constitution in Hungary might lead to a new revolutionary flare-up in the empire. These governmental fears were to some extent justified by the history of the radical October Revolution in Vienna, a movement largely led by the workers and very different from the liberal March Revolution. Conceivably, the spread of such a movement to Germany would have fully justified such fears. Indeed, at that time the fateful question, whether to come to peaceful terms with Hungary or to proceed with the dangerous plans for intervention, hung in the balance. Perhaps the chief factor promoting the policy of military intervention favored by the military and court circles was the consideration that imperial Austria could rely on the support of the troops from Croatia and the Military Frontiers under the leadership of the *Banus* of Croatia, General Joseph von Jelačić (1801–59), a leader of fair military, but superior political abilities.[42] Yet, Jelačić would neither have had the backing of Croat public opinion nor could he have made light of the revolutionary Magyar influence on his Croat troops, if Magyar oppression had not embittered the Hungarian nationalities against the revolutionary cause. In other words, the possibly favorable social influence of the Magyar Revolution on the nationalities was offset by a sorry record of national suppression.

Furthermore, without Jelačić's action, the radical course within the Hungarian government under Kossuth's leadership, against the wiser counsels of Deák, Eötvös, Batthyány, and, previously, Széchenyi, would not have succeeded in wrecking further negotiations with the crown and in leading the Magyar nation to an open fight against the imperial Power. Most probably, the Slovak and above all the Serb and the Wallachian (Rumanian) uprisings in Transylvania could not have taken place without the preceding flouting of the Serb claims for autonomy and the enforced union with Transylvania. The military implications of these revolts were considerable, though probably not as decisive as their political consequences.[43] These consequences were based largely on the fact that the revolutionary appeal of the Magyar liberal cause all over central Europe was paralyzed by its intolerant nationality policy.[44]

Generally, the Russian intervention is attributed to the policy of Czar Nicholas I, defending the principle of dynastic legitimacy all over Europe and specifically intending to forestall a new revolution in Poland. It is, however, open to question whether the intervention was not promoted by the further intention to crush a potentially dangerous anti-Slav power, that is, independent Hungary. In that respect the Czar succeeded, for the time being. With the Russian intervention, the fate of the Magyar Revolution was sealed, and Kossuth's frantic last-minute effort to compromise on the nationality issue in July, 1849, a few weeks prior to the final collapse, could not reverse the Magyar fate.[45]

## FROM SUPPRESSION TO FULL RESTORATION, 1849 TO 1868

Talleyrand's famous saying referring to the execution of the Duc d'Enghien, "It was more than criminal, it was stupid," could well be applied to the ruthless suppression of the Magyar Revolution, highlighted by the execution of its heroic military and political leaders, on the order of the Schwarzenberg government.[46] The subsequent history of the military and political partition of Hungary, under the regime of German centralistic absolutism directed by the minister of the interior Alexander Bach, contributed little to the evolution of the nationality problem in Hungary, and the Magyars themselves could not actively influence that evolution. The extent of the consideration of the centralist regime for the non-Magyar nationalities—even for the most privileged, the Croats—appears most succinctly expressed in the frequently repeated remark by a Magyar to a Croat, "What we received as a punishment was bestowed upon you as a reward," namely, the almost complete subordination to German Austrian centralism.

The administrative setup in the era of complete Magyar Hungarian subjection from 1849 to 1860 was as follows. Immediately after the suppression of the revolution, the country was divided into five principal territories, at first almost entirely under military control, and, from the autumn of 1850, gradually replaced by civil administration. These territories, contrary to plans soon dropped in Vienna,[47] did not correspond closely to the national organization of Hungary, a fact which already indicated that the complete dismemberment of Hungary and the reduction of its Magyar territory to mere provincial status was never seriously contemplated. Actually, the decreed March constitution of 1849 for the whole empire expressly recognized the continued existence of a constitution of the kingdom of Hungary (Paragraph 71), though its provisions were subject to change in accordance with the imperial constitution. "The equality of all nationalities and languages customary in the land in all matters of public and civic life was to be guaranteed by a separate statute." The autonomy of the Serb Voiwodina was promised, and the full independence of Croatia-Slavonia and Transylvania from Hungary was proclaimed (Paragraphs 72–74).[48] Thus, seriously as Hungary's legal status was infringed upon, and severely as the extent of her territories was cut by administrative orders,[49] the actual dismemberment of Hungary did not take place. The restoration of Hungary to its previous constitutional status was not recognized though until 1860, and even then not without reservations—first in a merely administrative way—but strengthened by the proclamation of the October Diploma of the same year. This process of formal recognition, first aimed merely at a restoration of the status held prior to 1848, but soon extended to meet farther-reaching demands, was completed only in the Austro-Hungarian Compromise of 1867 and the Hungarian-Croatian Compromise of 1868.

Viewed from a nonpolitical perspective, Magyar Hungary's status under imperial absolutism in the 1850s was by no means as desperate as Magyar nationalism proclaimed it to be. In fact, the rule of Bach's centralistic system, replacing many abuses of the old *Comitat* order under the sway of the local nobility, in many ways exerted a beneficial influence on the country, in particular in regard to judicial, financial, and agricultural reforms.[50] From the viewpoint of national psychology, it is interesting to note that Bach's efficient, socially rather progressive, civil administration, pursued in the spirit of Josephinism, was disliked by the Magyar Conservatives even more strongly than the preceding, frequently brutal, military regime. The opinion of even enlightened Conservatives—and only Conservatives had a chance to voice their opinion—was to the effect that any temporary military administration, even under the threat of martial law, was, from the national viewpoint, not as dangerous as an alien bureaucratic regime with a dangerous tendency to perpetuate itself. Furthermore, the rule of imperial officers who were, to a great extent, members of the nobility appealed to the Magyar gentry and aristocracy far more than the handling of affairs by German bureaucracy.[51] Probably this Conservative opinion would have had far less popular support if the

policy of German administrative centralism—confined, at the beginning of the Bach regime, to intercourse between local government
and central authorities—had not been gradually extended and, at the
same time, increasingly tightened in its application. On the other
hand, it is true that the central government's consideration for the
language rights of the non-Magyar nationalities,[52] extremely limited
as it was, aroused Magyar opposition no less than the policy of administrative Germanization.

Reviewing the currents of Magyar political opinion from the time
of complete suppression to the era of restoration, Dominic G. Kosáry
sets forth three principal platforms, "The first, conservative, was
based on the old constitution of 1847; the second, moderately liberal,
considered the April, 1848, legislation as its standard; and the third,
radical, accepted as its foundation the 1849 Declaration of Independence." [53]

Concerning the national problem, the third and most radical of
these platforms, the one represented by the political emigration of
1849, particularly by Kossuth, was undoubtedly the most interesting,
though, at the same time, it had the fewest immediate, practical implications. It will be dealt with in connection with the survey of federal reform projects in the second part of this study.[54] The first platform voiced the Old Conservative proposals—as prolix as frequently
sterile—for the restoration of the autonomous Estates order of prerevolutionary Hungary before 1848. The second platform, for a time
the program of a true liberalism under Deák's powerful leadership
and largely influenced by the theories of Eötvös, gained gradual
ascendancy in the 1850s until it trumphed with the Austro-Hungarian
Compromise of 1867. Yet, it also comprised in its scope an intra-
Hungarian compromise between conservatism and liberalism.

The memorandum of 1849 of the Conservative Count Emil Dessewffy, probably written during the last stages of the War of Independence, proves that this intra-Hungarian reconciliation was hardly
less difficult to achieve than the understanding with Austria. Dessewffy agreed wholeheartedly to the suppression of the Magyar
Revolution by the joint Austrian and Russian armies and, further,
welcomed a military dictatorship in Hungary until the last vestiges of
the Liberal revolutionary regime were eliminated. Yet, not only the
Magyar revolutionary regime, but also the national movements of the
non-Magyar Hungarian nationalities were to be suppressed. Absolute

exercise of royal power was to last "until in these (Hungarian) lands the desire becomes strong and general to be admitted within the constitutional mechanism of the whole of Austria and to . . . relinquish all memories of a previous privileged position once and for all." [55] In short, this program, by denouncing the Liberal revolution as well as the danger of similar occurrences among the non-Magyar nationalities, attempted to reconcile itself with the Habsburg Central Power on the basis of the defense of the joint Conservative interests. In return, as emerged more clearly in Dessewffy's second address of 1850 to the sovereign, signed by some thirty Magyar aristocrats, the Conservatives asked for a recognition and restoration of the old state organization and its national administration. [56]

The social solidarity of interest between the Conservatives in Austria and in Hungary was to guarantee that these privileges would not be misused again. Nevertheless, the intellectual leaders of the Magyar Conservatives—Jósika, Somssich, Dessewffy, and Szécsen, men of undoubted moderation in national questions—asked in vain for the restoration, even though they were willing to accept it as mere autonomy under a clearly recognized imperial authority. The Schwarzenberg ministry was determined to break the political power of the Magyar nobility, and resolved to convert it to a supranational imperial viewpoint. Therefore, it rejected the theory of restoration of the nation's historic rights, and upheld the opposite principle, that of forfeiture of national rights as punishment for the revolutionary uprising. However, the Austrian Conservatives themselves were split on this issue. The feudals in the crownlands—the Bohemian feudals foremost among them—strongly backed the idea of the historic rights, which offered to their own Estates order a status of great political significance. The court nobility around the emperor, on the other hand, largely supported the idea of absolutist centralism. The narrow-minded field marshal Prince Windischgrätz, the incapable military leader of the counterrevolution, was the leading exponent of the idea of the historic rights, centralist absolutism was directed by the superior political ability of the brilliant prime minister, Prince Schwarzenberg, the brother-in-law of Prince Windischgrätz. For the time, Schwarzenberg's far more efficient centralist policy remained successful, and only Austria's defeat in the Piedmontese War of 1859, seven years after his death, revived the idea of the historic rights as ardently proclaimed by the Magyar Conservatives. [57]

Far more frank and outspoken than the generally cautious policy of the Old Conservative set was the position of one of the signers of the second Dessewffy address, Count Paul von Somssich (1811–88), whose views may well be characterized as those of an enlightened Conservative. Somssich openly rejected the March constitution of 1849 as imposed by the imperial government, and asked for the restoration of Hungary's old liberties, but not of the prerevolutionary constitution, in which respect he differed from the demands of the Old Conservatives. While rejecting the Magyar Revolution itself, he asserted that the laws of the Hungarian *Reichstag* of April, 1848, passed before the break with Austria, were still valid, and that this in many respects liberal, and certainly socially progressive, reform work should be the foundation of Hungary's legal restoration. Concerning the national question, Somssich was still close to the ideas of his fellow peers, upholding, above all, the territorial integrity of the lands of the Hungarian crown and the historic rights, though they conflicted with the concept of equality among the Hungarian nationalities. But, at least within the limits of the historicopolitical units in Austria as well as in Hungary, he favored the recognition of national rights.[58]

Related to Somssich's views are those of Siegmund von Kemény (1814–75), who in his criticism of the national government of 1848–49 in general and of Kossuth in particular was more bitter than Somssich, yet at the same time more liberal in regard to the nationality question. If a federalization of the empire should not prove feasible, Kemény favored some kind of national autonomy.[59]

Both Somssich and Kemény were influenced in their political activities by the ideas of Joseph von Eötvös, the promoter of an all-Austrian compromise between federalism and centralism and, as minister of public instruction, technically the chief author of the Hungarian nationality legislation of 1868.[60] Somssich, Kemény, and Eötvös, though differing on many points, had this much in common: they did not regard a return to the old prerevolutionary order as possible, yet at the same time they denounced the revolution and, in particular, the final revolutionary aim of severing Hungary's ties with Austria. Consequently, they stood for the compromise between a reformed Hungary and Austrian centralism and in that respect they were the collaborators of Francis Deák (1803–76), who almost equaled Eötvös as a political theorist and surpassed him as a man of political action.

Deák's position as a leader was firmly established from the early

days after the revolution, when he remained the silent though un-
shakable pivot of passive national resistance to the centralistic reforms
of Bach and Schwarzenberg, as well as the intellectual focal point of
the movement for restoration. Yet, Deák's political stature is determined not merely by his combination of legal and popular acumen,
his sense of the political requirements of the day, which made him
appear firm and insistent in times of suppression and early constitutional experiments and moderate in the moment of supreme empire
crisis after the defeat of 1866. His well-deserved fame as one of the
greatest of Magyar statesmen rests also in the resurrection of Hungary
from the prostrate position of the defeat in 1849 to the new power as
one of the dual states of 1867. Yet this power at its best is not represented in the Austro-Hungarian Compromise, but in the endeavors of
the Magyar Liberal leaders, Deák and Eötvös for a just settlement of
the Hungarian nationality problem. If these endeavors had fully succeeded, a truly liberal Hungary would have formed the union with
Austria, the basic misconceptions of the compromise notwithstanding.[61]

Deák's endeavors for national conciliation in Hungary were all the
more creditable as he could be sure that the imperial government
would not have the compromise with Magyar Hungary and her ruling
classes wrecked for the sake of the non-Magyar Hungarian nationalities. In fact, the central government in 1860 readily withdrew Serb
autonomous rights within Hungary, tolerated the Croatian Compromise with the Magyars in 1868, which fell so far short of the
Croatian expectations of 1848, and consented to the reincorporation
of Transylvania into Hungary.[62] Nevertheless, even without external
pressure, Deák clearly wanted to avoid Kossuth's mistakes. He was
resolved that the dualistic system in Hungary should rest not only on
the will of the Magyars but on the support of the entire population
of the Hungarian lands. Deák was, indeed, able to gain this support,
and in this fact there is a good deal of tragic irony. The assumed basic
concurrence of the Hungarian nationalities to the restoration was
due almost exclusively to the confidence of all the Hungarian peoples
in the great leader and in his spirit of justice and moderation.[63] Only
the tremendous political prestige of the "great old man" of the Magyar nation, who, though holding only the public office of a deputy, was
the unchallenged leader of the people, can explain the passing, without marked opposition, of the laws of 1868 on the part of the na-

tionalities. As long as the interpretation and the execution of these laws, which were rather deficient on important issues, were dominated by Deák's liberal spirit, the nationalities remained assured of at least some legal protection of their rights. Unfortunately, the non-Magyars regarded as a permanent Magna Charta of their political liberties what actually was nothing but the creed and conviction of a few leaders of rare political skill and moderation.

Only by remembering these facts can the mistake be avoided of considering the creation of Magyar nationality legislation solely as a propaganda instrument born out of hypocrisy and kept on the statute book as a dead letter for the mere purpose of decoration.[64] The men who sponsored it did not take into account the ever-increasing spirit of integral nationalism of the Magyar ruling classes in the near future. Yet, in their attempts for national pacification they could not, even in their own time, go as far as they might have gone in a more tranquil national atmosphere than that of Magyar Hungary from the 1840s to the 1870s. The hero and martyr of this period was Kossuth, and his doctrine that alleged legal equality of the individual was identical with national equality still stood. In the light of these facts, one has to acknowledge the merits of the Hungarian nationality legislation and to excuse some of its obvious deficiencies. It is true, though, that the deficiencies of these laws, including the Hungarian-Croatian Compromise and the union act with Transylvania, which will be referred to presently, made their later intentional misinterpretation easy, indeed, and their repeal unnecessary. But it would be naïve indeed to believe that the Magyar administrations from the elder to the younger Tisza (that is, from 1875 to 1917) would have hesitated to ignore or to repeal more stringent and sweeping nationality laws, if they had deemed it opportune to do so.

Typical of the difference between the spirit and the letter of the nationality laws was the statute (XLIII of 1868) regulating the union with Transylvania. By abolishing the special privileges of the autonomous Transylvanian nationalities of old (Szekels, Magyars, and Saxons), the new law professed establishment of national equality. Yet the mere repeal of privileges remained meaningless in this respect as long as positive guarantees for true national equality were not given—undoubtedly against Deák's wishes. Thus, the neat, practical result of the whole legislation, in so far as it aimed at the abolishment of special nationality privileges in favor of the state, was the permanent establishment of Magyar predominance.[65]

The least assailable of the legislative works of the Deák period on the nationality problem was the compromise with Croatia.[66] Its acceptance, judged from the Croatian viewpoint, actually meant nothing but the choice between a seemingly greater evil and an evil which then seemed lesser, the former presented by the fresh memories of Bach's absolutist regime, the latter, after 1849, by the somewhat faded memories of imperious Magyar ambition. But it presented, also, a choice between reliance on the unsuccessful and inconsistent constitutional experiments of the Austrian reform cabinets from 1860 to 1867, wavering between centralism and feudal traditional absolutism, and the apparently straightforward liberalism of Deák and Eötvös. An additional powerful reason for coming to terms with the Magyars was the disastrous outcome of the War of 1866, which made it imperative for Austria to give Magyar Hungary practically free rein in the settlement of her affairs with Croatia.

The Hungarian-Croatian Compromise of 1868, according to prevalent non-Magyar political theory, was a (Real) Union between two states, which had their sovereign and certain functions of government in common. Yet, unlike the Austro-Hungarian Compromise, it represented a union, not between nominally equal, but between unequal partners, that is, the Croatian status was not coordinated with, but in important aspects subordinated to, that of Hungary, much as Finland's relation to czarist Russia or Iceland's to Denmark before 1918.[67] Basically, Croatia and Hungary were to form one state (*Staatsgemeinschaft*) in relation to the other Habsburg lands, as well as in regard to foreign affairs; in internal affairs, however, Croatia-Slavonia was "a political nation possessing a special territory, and a country which in its internal affairs possesses a legislature and government of its own." [68] In affairs common to Hungary and Austria Croatia was represented by a small number of members in the Hungarian delegation, in regard to affairs common to Hungary and Croatia, by a number of deputies in the Hungarian parliament at Budapest. The former representation, actually a mere token of Croatia's share of influence on Hungarian-Austrian common functions, in practice meant that, in foreign affairs and in questions of joint defense and finances, Croatia was subordinated to Hungary.

Matters considered as joint affairs of Hungary and Croatia—to mention only the most important ones—were taxation, laws relating to recruiting and military service, commercial treaties, maritime and commercial law, customs and trade, post office, and telegraph, railways, and so forth. In this whole, widely drawn sphere of administration, it was not the Croatian diet and the Hungarian parliament which decided, but the Hungarian parliament, increased by a Croatian delegation which could be outvoted at any time.

Croatian autonomy was confined mainly to the fields of general internal administration, education, and administration of justice, matters in which the use of the Croatian language was unrestricted. The chief bone of contention in regard to this autonomy, and at the same time the most severe fetter of this autonomy, was the position of the chief of the Croatian government, the *Banus*. As head of the government, he was responsible to the Croatian diet, yet his appointment by the king was dependent upon his nomination by the Hungarian, that is, the Magyar, prime minister. Obviously, the *Banus*, the chief executive of Croatia, became thereby a representative of Magyar, not of Croat, interests. He could easily evade the Croatian diet's control by proroguing and even dissolving it, a device which, indeed, the Magyar *Bani* frequently employed.

Nevertheless, the rise of the southern Slav political movement to increased political importance in Hungary, Austria, and, particularly, beyond the borders in Serbia, restrained the ruling Magyar classes at least from flouting openly the provisions of the compromise.[69] On the other hand, no similar scruples prevented subsequent Magyar governments from flagrantly violating Deák's and Eötvös's Hungarian nationality law of 1868 for the protection of the non-Magyar Hungarian nationalities exclusive of Croatia.[70]

The nationality law—in its theoretical concepts chiefly the work of Eötvös—represented a compromise between the claims of the nationalities that Hungary should be divided into distinct administrative territories on an ethnic basis [71] and the Magyar demands for a unified national state. Mainly conforming to the draft of a Hungarian parliamentary commission of 1861 under his ideological sponsorship,[72] Eötvös tried to compromise on the issue of cultural and administrative interests of the nationalities without impairing the political unity of the country.

In order to attain this aim the law of Eötvös provided that the nationalities should have their own elementary and middle [secondary] schools and a certain share in the higher education; that they should develop without restraint their ecclesiastical institutions; that the non-Magyar middle classes should have an adequate participation in the offices of the state; that the local administration in the counties, districts and villages should be carried on in the maternal language of the native population; and in general, that the development of their cultural and national life should be unimpeded. The whole conception was formed on the idea that the nationalities should not form distinct territorial units or nationally organized corporations, but as individuals should enjoy the same rights and opportunities as the Magyar citizens. According to the official doctrine, they became "equal members of the Hungarian nation" and this term "Hungarian" . . . meant now not only the Magyars but all the citizens of the country.[73]

Yet this was precisely the controversial point. As previously noted, in the Hungarian language in general, and particularly in its statute books, the same term is used for "Magyar" and "Hungarian." This fact, of deep psychological meaning beyond the aspects of legal technicalities, had a most important bearing on the interpretation of the nationality law. The preamble seemingly stated very clearly:

Since all citizens of Hungary, according to the principles of the constitution, from a political point of view form one nation—the indivisible unitary Hungarian nation—of which every citizen of the fatherland is a member, no matter to what nationality he belongs . . . the following rules will serve as standard.

From the nationalist point of view, however, the argument could well be brought forward that the term "Hungarian nation" actually referred only to the "Magyar nation," or, in other words, to the ruling national group in Hungary.[74]

Though it would be naïve to assume that Magyar nationalism, in its subsequent violations of the law, was dependent on the use of such advocatorial devices, the point proves rather well that the enforcement of the nationality law was entirely dependent on the spirit of the executive organs destined to enforce it. Again the fact becomes obvious that the Hungarian nationality law, in spite of its obvious shortcomings, could have done much to improve the individual status of Hungary's non-Magyar citizens if it had been applied in the neoliberal spirit ruling in Hungary for an all-too-short period after the delivery from Bach's centralist absolutist regime. Moreover, it could have done much to allay national tension and to prepare the ground for more comprehensive reforms.[75] As soon as this liberal spirit began to wane, no law, even if it had been far superior to the law of 1868, could have helped the non-Magyar nationalities in Hungary. It was entirely in the hands of a nationalist and antisocial, mock-liberal government, deriving its power from one of the most unjust, restricted, and arbitrary franchise laws in Europe to wield the provisions of this law according to its interests.

This is precisely what happened, and it is in the main, well expressed by Jaszi.

Since the death of Deák in 1876 [76] a new generation has occupied the political arena, a generation of the "gentry" which forgot the great lessons of 1848–49 and which regarded the situation of the country exclusively from the point of view of their momentary interests. The leader of this generation, Prime Minister of the country between 1875 and 1890, Koloman Tisza, came into power by cynically abandoning his principles. . . . The new ruling party, called the "Liberal party," a fusion between the parties of Deák and Tisza, had nothing liberal in its character (except its benevolent attitude towards Jewish finance and big business) [and, it must be added in fairness, in religious tolerance], but was simply an organization for the à tout prix maintenance of the Compromise and for the domination of the country by big landed interests. In this political atmosphere a new spirit was developed concerning the nationality problem, which, pushing back the meaning and the statement of the Nationality law, began to propagate . . . a policy of Magyarization, the necessity of the creation of an exclusive Nation State as a kind of a summum bonum for the realization of which Machiavellian principles were advocated.[77]

These principles combined a system of discrimination against non-Magyars with spoils, in the form of government jobs and favors, as the price for submission to Magyar ideology.

Yet, though the records of Deák and Eötvös, of their followers, and even of their predecessors, moderate Conservatives such as Somssich and Kemény, appear shining by comparison with those of the rulers of Hungary from the 1870s onward, they cannot be absolved from part of the responsibility for the development of the future. Neither can the centralist power of the Austrian state prior to 1867 be fully acquitted, as long as it had a say in Hungarian affairs.

The moderate nationalism of the Conservatives, more concerned with the restoration of the old social order than the old national order, might have tolerated a status of Hungary as a member in some form of imperial Austrian federation based on the historic rights of the nationalities. Such a solution, certainly not adequate in itself, would at least have left the door open for farther-reaching reforms on an ethnic federal basis, which the Dualistic Compromise closed for good. Yet the overbearing demands of absolutist Austrian centralism, linked to the narrow social concepts of the Magyar Conservatives, made a program sponsored by the Conservative adherents of the Estates idea unacceptable to the overwhelming majority of the Magyar and the non-Magyar populations in Hungary.

As for the Liberals, the views of Deák and Eötvös, undoubtedly more in line with the trend of the times, were, indeed, in general far more acceptable to the people. Nevertheless, they were founded on the dualistic premise, which excluded forever a comprehensive solution of the nationality problem. Their program, backed by similar interests of the German Liberals in Austria, was further founded on the dogma of the complete integrity of the old Hungarian kingdom and its in the main centralistic organization. This second premise barred the conversion of the monarchy into a federation along ethnic lines, which would do away with the state and crownland frontiers. Yet it also blocked more modest plans to transform the monarchy into a federation along traditional historic lines and even a federal organization within Hungary herself. The responsibility for the fatal course of 1867 rested with more than one party and more than one people.

## MAGYAR "LIBERALISM" IN POWER: FROM 1868 TO THE FIRST WORLD WAR

The last half-century of Hungary's history within the empire not only shows no progress in the handling of the national problem, but, ideologically, shows definite regression.[78] To be sure, in Cisleithanian Austria, also, the evolution of integral nationalism during that period made the nationality crisis ever more serious and strengthened the centrifugal forces of the empire. Yet in Austria nationalist forces became stronger not only in their emotions and convictions but in actual power as well. The fact that the organism of Austria was increasingly weakened by the nationality struggle does not mean that the understanding of the national problem there was inferior to that of previous generations. On the contrary, the attempts to solve the national problem in Cisleithanian Austria, though they fell short of perfection and success, on the whole became technically more efficient and increasingly progressive in social and cultural aspects. The trouble was that increasing awareness of the nationality problems could not catch up with the momentum of the social and political development within and beyond the empire.

Conditions were altogether different in Hungary. The rise of integral nationalism among the Magyar and the non-Magyar nationalities found outward expression only in the stiffening of Magyar nationalist intolerance and shortsightedness, but not at all in a rise of the political status of the non-Magyar Nationalities. That is to say, the rise of the non-Magyar peoples in national cultural consciousness was not supplemented by a corresponding rise in legal-political status.

While the process of Germanization in Austria proper had stopped and was on the decline, the process of Magyarization in Hungary, unheeding the signs of the times, was surging relentlessly ahead.[79] Perhaps the last historical chance to reverse this ominous development appeared in the eventful years of 1905 and 1906, when the all-powerful Liberal Government party was defeated by a coalition of the National Independence party, under the leadership of the younger Kossuth (the weak son of a great father), the dissidents from the Liberal fold (later the Constitutional party), under the leadership of the younger Andrássy, Count Apponyi's National party, and Count Zichy's Catholic People's party. These groups rallied around the Independence party, which denounced the Compromise of 1867 and unheld, at least in theory, the Declaration of Independence of 1849. The actual demands of these factions were not as radical as the theoretical platform of the leading Independence party. They stood firmly, however, for a revision of the Compromise of 1867 in the direction of further loosening of the ties between Austria and Hungary, and especially, for all practical purposes, for the partition of the joint army into separate Austrian and Hungarian forces.[80]

This time the king-emperor, in line with the wishes of the best part of the army itself and supported on this point by a fairly unified popular opinion in Austria,[81] was weary of further appeasement of Magyar constitutional presumptuousness. He decided to take a strong stand. As the new Magyar parliamentary majority was unwilling to desist from its demands and equally unwilling to pass the annual military quota, the king appointed as prime minister a military man in his personal confidence, General Fejérváry. Willing to take the most drastic step short of actual military intervention against the Magyar ruling class, he had a bill introduced in the Hungarian parliament requesting the adoption of general and equal franchise. Subsequently, he ordered the dissolution by military force, against the resisting deputies. Essential legislation which the parliament had refused to pass was decreed by the king-emperor.[82]

Contrary to expectations and fears by the sovereign's advisers, the country accepted quietly and without the slightest movement of popular resistance this energetic action against the sacred constitutional rights asserted so loudly by the Magyar nationalists. The assiduously planted myth that the Magyar regime represented the real wishes of the Magyar people, not merely of the ruling classes, the "Liberals," the Independents, and the Liberal dissidents, had been proved a bluff. The Magyar people had not sprung to arms to defend the privileges of their narrow class parliament. The way for peaceful changes of the national and social organization of feudal Hungary, to be initiated by a just franchise system, seemed to be open. This illusion, however, was destroyed soon enough.

Obviously, the introduction of general equal franchise in Hungary could have had two main purposes. The first would have been to give the suppressed nationalities, as well as the Magyar peasants and workers, an ordinate share in the rule of their country. Then it could be expected with reasonable certainty that the "liberated" nationalities, in recognition of the fact that Magyar suppression could be fought only in a union with Austria, would oppose the claims of the Magyar Independence party and its allies. Furthermore, under an equal franchise law, the majority of the Magyar people themselves, small peasants and workers, probably would have joined the nationalities in their fight against the socially oppressive Magyar rulers. The promised introduction of general equal franchise had a second meaning, also, which happened to be the ulterior motive behind the action of the crown. It could be foreseen that the "danger" of extensive social changes in Hungary, the specter of a radical change in the social-national setup of the country, might persuade the feuding groups of the ruling regime to modify their demands. In return for an at least *de facto* abandonment of their claims for extension of Magyar Hungarian independence, the crown might be willing to withdraw its general franchise bill.

And so it did. The powerful and electrifying force of general equal franchise was used in Hungary merely as a cunning device to bring the ruling parties to terms. Franchise reform and revision of the compromise were shelved, and the new coalition under the leadership of the Independence party, for the time being tamed in spirit, took office, only to make way in 1910 for a revised Liberal regime under the label of "Party of National Labor." Essentially this very party, unchanged in its spirit of national and social intolerance, was restored to power after the First World War. It led the country into the Second World War on the side of Hitler.

Considering the social structure of the monarchy, the turn of events stirred up by the introduction of the franchise bill, was not surprising. Except that for a time the Magyar "Liberal" rulers of long standing accentuated the interests of the feudals and of big business somewhat more, while the Independents stressed those of the gentry and the agricultural upper middle classes, there was no important social difference between the systems of the two parties. It was clear enough that a bloc of such social structure as represented by the forces rallied around the nucleus of the Independence party would much rather postpone or shelve their demands concerning revision of the Compromise of 1867 than submit to far-reaching social and national reforms. Concerning the position of the crown, it was equally clear that its precarious hold on the power in Hungary had rested so far on the cooperation and, to a wide degree, the community of interests between aristocracy, gentry, and the upper industrial and commercial classes in the dual states. The introduction of general and equal franchise in Hungary would have changed this situation radically. Small peasants and labor, particularly among the nationalities, would have come to the fore. It would have been necessary to buy their support with not only an entirely reversed nationality policy but with far-reaching social, especially argicultural reforms. Their introduction would have seriously embittered the economic upper classes, as illustrated by the introduction of general equal franchise in Austria in 1906–1907.[83]

Further, it was most likely that a fair nationality representation in Hungary, particularly of the southern Slavs, would have raised the issue of union with their conationals in Austria. Thus, the whole problem of the revision of the Dualistic Compromise and the conversion of the Habsburg lands into a federation on an ethnic basis would have become an urgent political issue. Again, such a conversion in the decade preceding the First World War could have succeeded only if the crown had been willing to secure the support of the

lower middle classes, the peasants, and the workers among the nationalities all over the empire in exchange for that of centralistic
bureaucracy, aristocracy, big business and industry, the officer class,
and, possibly the church.[84] In other words, the crown would have
had to decide whether to abandon the support of those classes which
for generations had been the pillars and foundation of its rise and
strength, in exchange for the cooperation of the masses, some of whose
national interests lay beyond the borders of the empire and whose
social and political aims might easily have transgressed beyond the
framework of the monarchic principle. Considering these alternatives,
it was natural, indeed, that the crown shrank from carrying through
the general franchise policy in Hungary, even though this policy
conceivably might have led in the end to the preservation of the empire in a federal form. That under such conditions, even if the
monarchic form of government could have been preserved, such an
empire would have had little in common with the historic age-old
phenomenon of the Habsburg Power, is clear. This very fact barred
the possibility of reform.

As frequently stated, every historic movement can complete its
course only according to the laws and conditions to which it owes its
existence. In the case of the Habsburg Power, these laws were carried
chiefly by a feudal system and later supported by the upper capitalist
classes. At the end of the empire's course, the support of the peasants
and the workers could scarcely have been substituted without shaking
the power of the crown and the ideas it stood for.

### THE FIRST WORLD WAR AND THE OCTOBER REVOLUTION
### OF 1918

The Hungarian state crisis of 1905–1906 offered the last, though
remote, possibility of tackling in a comprehensive way the Hungarian nationality problem within the empire. The following period,
until the downfall of the cabinet of the younger Tisza, in 1917, shows
a stiffening of the Magyar position in regard to the empire as well as to
the Hungarian nationalities.[85] Only the last year and a half of the
First World War produced some retarded and generally amateurish
efforts of the ruling Magyar regime to arrive at emergency solutions.
They no longer carried much practical significance. The course of
the war, the fall of czarism, and the rise of the Czechoslovak and
southern Slav political emigration abroad had bridged the gulf be-

tween pro- and anti-Austrian Slav forces. In 1917 Magyar-dominated Hungary's fate appeared thus practically sealed.

Magyarism's cooperation in the war effort, before it realized the defeat of its cause, was enthusiastic. It was inspired by the idea that a victorious outcome would break, once and for all, the danger of Slav ascendancy in the Hungarian plains, represented by Russia and her then alleged satellites, Serbia and, later, Semi-Slav-Rumania. At that time Hungary's specific contribution to the war effort of the Central Powers—apart from her manpower—consisted in her large agricultural food supply, on which Austria depended so much, often in vain. Politically, her record was "distinguished" by her ability to deal with Slav opposition far more effectively and ruthlessly than Austria. Thus, within the alliance of the Central Powers, Hungary continued to gain in political status. Various political schemes attempted to comply with these changes. Plans were advanced that, if "liberated" Poland should be joined to Austria, the Austrian southern Slav territories and Bosnia should be incorporated into Hungary. After the victorious Rumanian campaign in 1916–17, the annexation of Rumania by Hungary was considered feasible, as well. Even more sweeping was another scheme discussed in Austria. It suggested a reorganization of the empire which would make the Magyars, legally, its leading national group.[86] The Hungarian prime minister was to become imperial chancellor, Budapest was to be the empire's capital, and Magyar was to be the common language of the army. For the notion of suicide because of fear of death no better political illustration could, indeed, be found than the plan to fight the empire's chief disintegrating force, Magyar nationalism, by completely surrendering to it. Yet in court circles the idea found support that the empire which could not be held together by the traditional powerful force of German centralism with its wide hinterland, could be upheld by the hegemony of 10,000,000 Magyars. Another idea very much in vogue at the time, the central European scheme of Friedrich Naumann, assigned to Hungary an eminent role in eastern central Europe and expressly supported the idea of Magyarization of the nationalities in Hungary.[87]

Not all of these schemes, certainly not those striving for an imperial federation in any form, were supported by official Hungary. As a matter of fact, as stern as Count Tisza's Magyarization policy was within Hungary, he greatly hesitated to add new non-Magyar territories to the lands of the Hungarian crown. Yet, relatively cautious as his policy was in July, 1914, it finally yielded to the aims of the imperial and royal dignitaries who wanted to smash Serbia.

Undoubtedly, the situation in Hungary changed gradually with the unfavorable turn of political, and eventually of military, events. Less sure, not of the justness, but of the success of its cause, the Magyar regime began to toy with the idea of reforms. Such trends became accentuated with the accession of Charles I (in Hungary Charles IV) in November, 1916. The new sovereign, influenced by the ideas of the late heir presumptive, Francis Ferdinand, favored (in theory) a radical and fair solution of the Hungarian nationality problem. Yet, against the counsels of his, previously Francis Ferdinand's, advisers, he hesitated to introduce reforms before he had committed himself in his coronation oath to the preservation of the existing territorial and constitutional order of 1867.[88] But on Count Tisza's insistence he took the coronation oath before any reform plans, including the franchise reform, were even seriously considered.

It appears extremely doubtful whether the empire, during the supreme crisis of the war, could have weathered a Hungarian constitutional crisis evolving from a conflict between the Magyar upper classes, still loyal to the dynasty, and the nationalities, whose main spheres of interest already lay largely beyond the borders. However, it is definite that the feeble attempts for mere alleviation of the Hungarian nationality problem within the smothering frame of the compromise undertaken under Charles, were foredoomed to failure.

Several reform proposals submitted by confidants of the emperor must be judged in the light of these considerations. Inadequate as they were, they could be submitted only after Tisza, unwilling to introduce even a small electoral reform, had resigned from office in the spring of 1917.[89]

The diplomat Baron J. Szilassy, for some time a prospective candidate for the position of common minister of foreign affairs, drafted a memorandum in the fall of 1917, which even at this late stage offered no more helpful advice than suggestions for "peaceful [Magyar] penetration" of the nationalities instead of forceful Magyarization, ennoblement of distinguished non-Magyars in Hungary, and so forth. The necessity of general franchise was recognized in Szilassy's proposals, though he cautiously refrained from any further reference to the nature of this general franchise as really equal and secret.

Szilassy's proposals have an almost tragicomic touch where he gives vent to the hope that a Hungary of his dreams might become the center, "the federal district," of a new European federation, adding new splendor to her old privileges. Only in September, 1918, when a separate peace with the Allied Powers appeared a crying necessity for the monarchy, did the Baron agree to the setting up of an autonomous southern Slav "state-structure"—still not a state—which "if possible" should be connected in a loose way with Hungary. And he added, literally, "There is hope then that Serbia will join voluntarily" this state-structure.[90]

These proposals were made more than a year after the declaration of the Serb, Croatian, and Slovene representatives in Allied territory at Corfu in July, 1917, concerning the setup of a united, independent Yugoslavia. Nevertheless, the vastness of Szilassy's error rested, not in the belief in the preservation of the monarchy in reorganized form, but in the astounding supposition that such a reorganization would leave Magyar hegemony in Hungary unimpaired, and, indeed, practically increased. Nevertheless, he should be ranked among the more moderate Magyar statesmen of that period. His misconceptions were not due to individual shortsightedness, but to the collective inability of the Magyar ruling class to comprehend a political situation unfavorable to its interests.

The political outlook of Prince Ludwig Windischgrätz, Hungarian minister of food supplies in 1918 and one of the younger Magyar noble leaders, can best be judged by his evaluation of Szilassy's view in September, 1918.

The intelligent, pithy and, from a diplomatic point of view, masterly formulation of these propositions delighted me as much as the clear insight into the political, military and moral strength of the conflicting world complexes, and the forcible logic of his argumentation and demonstration.[91]

Windischgrätz was a man of considerably more influence than Szilassy. As a follower of the younger Andrássy, holding politically the middle course between Count Tisza's nationalist intransigence and Count Michael Károlyi's radicalism, he pledged himself, at least, to the introduction of general and equal, though not generally secret, franchise. He also favored rather vaguely defined agricultural reforms. Yet, in the national questions he remained considerably behind Szilassy's second program. He suggested a solution of the southern

Slav problem without union of the Austrian and the Hungarian southern Slavs, based merely on the grant of autonomy in either part of the monarchy.[92] Surely, the views of men like Szilassy and Windischgrätz, who in national questions were considerably more moderate than Tisza (though he held a so called center rather than an extreme position on these issues) can be judged only as illustrative of the political concepts of the Hungarian ruling classes, not because they had any intrinsic value.

Unquestionably, the theories of the leftist leaders of the Magyar October Revolution of 1918, particularly those of Count Michael Károlyi and Oskar Jaszi, the latter, one of the profoundest theorists of the empire's nationality problem, were on a rather different level and had wider popular support. Nevertheless, it is difficult to maintain Jaszi's contention that the

Károlyi government . . . [of late October, 1918] was being demanded with remarkable unanimity by every progressive element in public opinion. . . . Had the Károlyi government been appointed six, or even four, weeks earlier, events in Hungary would have taken a very different course.[93]

Such an opinion overrated the force of these Magyar Progressives. Actually, their backing consisted, first, in the support of various small groups of leftist Liberal intellectuals, seriously divided among themselves, without adequate political organization, yet spiritually the core of the October Revolution. Secondly, there was the Social Democratic party, infinitely weaker than its Austrian sister parties, raised primarily in trade-union ideas, and not yet equal to the pursuit of a radically reversed nationality policy.[94] The third and chief force kindling the revolution was Count Michael Károlyi himself, the leader of a small parliamentary group continuing in some ways the policy of the radical wing of the Independent party.

Károlyi, the aristocratic *frondeur,* the dissident of the Magyar ruling class, was undoubtedly a brilliant parliamentarian of social understanding. Yet neither in political stability, consistency, nor power of cool reasoning could and did he then and later hold, or justify, the confidence of the masses. Still it was difficult to foresee that the alleged victim of a Bolshevik *coup d'état* after the First World War would espouse that very cause after the Second World War. This explains the following interesting but, in retrospect, all too favorable evaluation of Károlyi's position, published by Bauer in 1923:

He was the last bearer of the tradition of Kossuth; his name and goal connected modern democracy with historic Hungary. His aim was the destruction of the Compromise of 1867, national independence. By means of a
democratic electoral reform and a democratic agricultural reform, he
wanted to mobilize the masses of the Magyar peasants to the fight . . . for
Hungary's independence. When, after the annexation of Bosnia, the
foreign policy of the ruling oligarchy became more and more dependent
on German imperialism, he, the heir of the Kuruczian and Kossuthian
tradition, put up Western orientation against German tradition. Before
the war he tried to establish relations with Western democracy and Russian liberalism. During the war he represented democratic pacifism as
opposed to German imperialism.[95]

Though Károlyi had little of Kossuth's tremendous popular appeal
and scarcely any of his spectacular, though transitory, successes, in his
failure he had much in common with Kossuth. Most of the promised
Károlyi reforms including the electoral and the agricultural, were
not carried out. Furthermore, the growing influence of the encroach-
ing Communist dictatorship to which Károlyi gave way all too easily
—but, as it seemed then, not voluntarily—forced the issues and
robbed them of their potentially tremendous popular appeal. His endeavors to solve the nationality problem necessarily came too late.
Thus, the only permanent achievement of his wretched regime was
the conclusion of the armistice under very severe terms. This in the
eyes of the nation placed the blame for the collapse on a leader less
responsible for the breakdown than were many of the "pillars" of the
previous ruling regime.

The phrase "less responsible" needs some explanation at this
point. Károlyi, as long as he was active in political life prior to the
collapse of 1918, was not an unequivocal adherent of a comprehensive ethnic-federal organization of the peoples in the Danube basin
on equal terms. He stood for the territorial integrity of Hungary,
though he was willing, long before 1918, to grant the non-Hungarian
nationalities a wide degree of national autonomy. Clearly, however,
no comprehensive solution of any of Hungary's national problems was
possible, even within such "Hungarian autonomy." Hodža, the Slovak leader and later Czechoslovakian prime minister who negotiated
with Károlyi in the fall of 1918, was right, indeed, when he said,

Count Károlyi was not able to free himself from the idea that Hungarian
political and geographic integrity had to be rebuilt, although his general
views of the new European order may have been quite liberal. . . . "Traitors" like Michael Károlyi might have been of some use to their country

forty years ago, in 1910, the year in which he entered politics—and in 1918 it was too late.[96]

Yet Károlyi's national concepts must not be judged only by the dismal failure of the October Revolution, that is, of the period when Magyar Hungary for a time ceased to exercise any further influence on the national order in the Danube basin. As head of the new government he was entirely the prisoner of the evil political inheritance of the Tisza regime. Prior to the fall of 1918 he had fought the nationalist prejudices of Magyar Conservatives and Liberals. He was then and later, however, under the spell of a lasting ideological tradition—that of Kossuth in exile. This implied the *leadership* of a truly liberal, socially progressive Magyar Hungary, in the area where a conservative Magyar regime which was intolerant in national questions had failed. That Hungary, on the basis of historic justice, let alone of her historic record, was not justified in demanding to join the free association of the Danube people, except as a cultural, social, and political equal, was not stated in unequivocal terms by Károlyi prior to the October Revolution.[97]

The same held true for Oskar Jaszi, minister of nationalities in the Károlyi government and, even before the war a courageous and brilliant champion of the rights of the Hungarian nationalities.[98] He promoted the idea "that a Hungary reorganized on the model of Switzerland, closely united in federal bonds with the neighbor states," would have been preferable to the solution of Trianon. He wanted, however, "to reserve the way for a future reconciliation and federation, assuring complete autonomy to each of the nations living within the Danube basin, where possible on a territorial basis, and where not, on the basis of the registration of inhabitants," thus combining the principles of territorial and personal autonomy.[99] Such a program still promoted a bond stronger than a merely economic bond between the Danube nationalities. Indeed, Jaszi admitted that the Károlyi ministry had insisted on the preservation of Hungary's territorial integrity, though he personally renounced the revolutionary illusion that any solution of the nationality problem could have preserved the postwar integrity of Hungary.[100]

In any case, it was scarcely surprising that the nationalities did not think that the fulfillment of their desire for ethnic unification would be assured in a program which still toyed with the idea of Hungarian "territorial integrity," even if allegedly confined to the economic sphere.[101] They were certainly justified in demanding that even a mere economic union could not be materialized within the historic frontiers of Hungary, but only within the ethnic union of the Danube peoples.

Their distrust, that even a progressive Hungary might not have dropped its old territorial claims altogether, may well have been based on other facts, too. Jaszi himself, at the beginning of the war, had supported the "Middle Europe" idea. While his concept of the great central European bloc certainly had a very different democratic connotation from the imperialism of its chief sponsor (Naumann), it still maintained fully the idea of the old historicopolitical entity of royal Hungary.[102]

Even as late as 1918, Jaszi had promoted a political concept in many ways out of line with the spirit of the October Revolution. Thus, less than a year prior to the collapse of the empire he supported publicly the idea of Austria's federal organization based on the historicopolitical entities of the "Big Five"—Germans, Magyars, Czechs, Poles, and Croats. Jaszi's plan, in some ways similar to Count Belcredi's conservative "Pentarchie" concept implying the national priority claims of the historicopolitical entities, chiefly regarded the five groups listed above as numerically and culturally capable of pursuing an independent national life. According to this proposal, the Hungarian nationalities, except for those in Croatia, were to remain in a territorially unchanged Hungary.[103]

It was fully in line with the Kossuth tradition, to which Jaszi subscribed as Károlyi had professed to subscribe, that straitened conditions led to radically changed programs, though not to radically changed national ideologies. Consequently, non-Magyar Hungary did not interpret Károlyi's and Jaszi's program in the sense they demanded. Reviewing his policy as minister of nationalities in the Károlyi cabinet, Jaszi asserts:

I regarded it as my first duty to prove to all the world that the imperialist proposals for the partition of Hungary were incapable of solving the problem of the nationalities and could only replace the old irredenta by a new one; and that the guarantees of a better and more stable order could only be found in the genuine autonomy of each nation, and in a union of these self-governing entities on a basis of equal rights for all.[104]

Do these noble words mean—as seems likely—the federal organization of prewar Hungary, or do they go further and imply the mere economic union of the fully independent Danube peoples within their ethnic frontiers? Do they deny or confirm the union of the Rumanians in the Rumanian kingdom with those in Transylvania, of the Slovaks in Hungary with the Czechs, of the Serbs in the Banat with their kin in Serbia, Bosnia, and Croatia? Jaszi's enunciation is not clear on this point. What is more important, his record, the record of socially progressive, nationally moderate Magyar Hungary in the empire, does not warrant the most liberal interpretation of that policy.

Much as Jaszi thus deserves respect for his courage and understanding of the Hungarian social national problem within the framework of the Magyar ruling system until the collapse, he, like Károlyi, cannot claim to have severed himself completely and unequivocally from one of the most important of this regime's tenets: the preservation of the historic entity of the lands of the Hungarian crown, which blocked the true union of the Danube peoples. As it appears in the light of today's experience, two ways lay open to secure "the equal rights for all" which Jaszi proclaimed. One was the formation of completely independent national states within their ethnic boundaries. The basic deficiencies of such solution, on which Jaszi had some good points to make, are strikingly apparent in the world of today. On the other hand, it is true, its good points have never been fully tested, since the treaty system of 1919 fell far short of the realization of ethnic boundaries.

The second basic solution, likewise founded on the ethnic organization of the Danube peoples, and likewise resting on the abolition of the historicopolitical entities of the Hungarian crown domains, was the formation of an eastern central European union of a merely economic character which would leave the Danube peoples independent politically. Magyar political thinking until 1918, even that of its most progressive exponent, has never clearly faced in its full democratic implications this never materialized alternative on which the future of the great Magyar people was and is so greatly dependent.

CHAPTER V

# THE CZECHS

THE SOCIALIST Otto Bauer, the more conservative F. G. Kleinwächter, and the Liberal Josef Redlich, have, each in his characteristic way, succinctly summarized the peculiarity and the special significance of the Czech problem within the Austrian nationality setup.[1] These supranational views on Czech-empire relations and Czech-German issues will precede the discussion of the specific Czech standpoint—largely based on Czech sources.

Bauer perceives the Czech problem as the interrelation of the position of a small western Slav people to the orbit of German power.

Palacký's statement that Austria would have had to be invented if she did not exist already was particularly relevant for the Czechs, as long as Germany was strong. Under such conditions the only possible existence which they could envisage for themselves was that of a Czech state within the Habsburg Empire. With the defeat of Germany and the dissolution of the Habsburg Empire, the danger no longer existed that the Sudeten provinces would fall to Germany. The Czech people then lost their interest in the Habsburg Empire and could think in terms of another statement of Palacký: We existed before Austria, and we will remain after Austria.[2]

Kleinwächter supplements the above estimate of shifts in political Power relations with a pointed reference to cultural competition between Czechs and Germans.

Two fifths of the people of Bohemia were Germans; three fifths, Czechs. The supremacy of the two fifths over the three fifths was possible only as long as this difference in numbers was made up by a difference in cultural standard. The very moment when the difference in cultural standard was no longer a balancing factor, German supremacy was lost.[3]

Redlich considered that the supreme importance of the Czech problem rested in its paradigmatic character for the study of the multinational area with its overlapping tendencies of ethnic, national, and traditional historic claims.

As far as Austria is concerned, the national conflict between Germans and Slavs first flamed into political battle in Bohemia. That took place in a country where the Germans from the very beginning as a minority, were in a defensive position and where the offensive of the Czechs seemed at once to have won for the Slav movement surprisingly great political successes. Bohemia then remained for seven decades—until the last hour of the monarchy—the classic battleground of the national struggle in Austria. Here for the first time (in their roots clearly since 1848) the forms and methods, the whole technique, psychology, and procedure of the modern national struggle of civilized nations were developed. Here the whole phenomenon of nationalism fully evolved for the first time in its boundless ideological and psychological effects.[4]

These three opinions combined briefly synthesize and elucidate the complexity of this specific, extremely interesting national problem. It is the problem of the most advanced of the Austrian Slav peoples, existing only within the Austrian borders and struggling, within its own historic territories, with a strong German national group whose kinsfolk held the supremacy not only in Austria proper but in central Europe as a whole. The German position was, therefore, as Bauer observes, the directing influence of Czech policy, and remained so at least until 1918. It is further true, as Kleinwächter comments, that the rise of the masses of the Czech people to a standard of cultural equality with the German minority made the national conflict unavoidable. It is not true, however, that this rise in itself made impossible the settlement of national conflict. Nor can the onus be placed primarily on the intricate conditions of mixed cultural, social, and ethnographical settlement in Moravia and especially in Bohemia. The reason for failure lay largely in the fact that behind the Germans in Bohemia stood the whole impact of the national power of the Germans, and behind the Czechs, the impact of Russian-directed Pan-Slavism—less conspicuous, less active and direct, but none the less powerful. In other words, the position of the only people in Cisleithanian Austria who ethnically did not extend beyond the Austrian frontiers was, politically speaking, clearly just as much a world problem as it was an Austrian problem, a fact evidenced by the history of both World Wars.

Nevertheless, in the whole period from 1848 to 1918 official German policy beyond the Austrian frontiers interfered only a few times, and then only secretly, in Bohemian affairs, though it permanently and effectively influenced the ideology of the Sudeten German leaders. On the other hand, the Slav movement drew strength from the stable, permanently attractive power of Russia, the "mother of the Slavs," rather than from the occasional, clumsy, and, until 1914, relatively insignificant efforts of active political agitation supported from the East.

### CZECH CULTURAL EVOLUTION IN THE PRE-MARCH PERIOD

There were more immediate and direct causes for the national struggles in the ancient lands of the crown of St. Wenceslav—Moravia, Austrian Silesia, and the Czech "heart land," Bohemia. In the foreground of the political battle were three alternatives—German centralistic supremacy, complete separation of the German and the Czech people, and Czech predominance within the framework of the old historic charter known as the "Bohemian *Staatsrecht.*" Ideological influences from abroad notwithstanding, these three conflicts all came into play exclusively within the Austrian problem.

The political starting point of the Czech national movement in nineteenth-century Austria was the revived claim of the old *Staatsrecht,* but the subsequent and more important development of the national issue rested in the revival of the Czech language. The Bohemian *Staatsrecht* originated at the time of the independence of the Bohemian crown, before the crown came under Habsburg sway in 1526. This incorporation resulted ultimately in the inevitable clash between the crown and the proud Bohemian Estates. Yet in a wider sense this conflict, which at the Battle of the White Mountain struck at Czech national life, was actually that between the centralistic forces of the Catholic Counter Reformation and the separatism inspired by the national religious ideology of Hus and Žižka. This disaster of 1620, though it paralyzed, did not kill the historic concept of the *Staatsrecht.* The government uprooted a large part of the Czech nobility, it rescinded the rights of the Estates, but the national tradition had already transcended far beyond the nobles. Yet the frame of the Estates order was not completely wrecked. A century after the national catastrophe of 1620, the Pragmatic Sanction was still formally submitted to the Bohemian Estates, and Maria Theresa, not more than a generation later, was again crowned queen of Bohemia. Thus, the foundation of the old institutions, on which a new structure could be erected at the opportune moment, was preserved. Its purpose was to revive and to preserve the historicopolitical entity of the lands of the Bohemian crown within the new union of the Habsburg lands created by the Pragmatic Sanction. Legally, this concept was defined as follows.

The Bohemian *Staatsrecht* was the public law of Bohemia before Maria Theresa, that is, the right of the Habsburg dynasty to the crown of Bohemia according to the law of succession established by the Pragmatic Sanction, the right of the legal representatives of the three Bohemian lands in case the dynasty should become extinct to elect a new king freely. It was the right to the indivisibility and union of the three lands and the right to unlimited independence of the lands of the Bohemian crown.[5]

The Bohemian *Staatsrecht,* the charter of the once independent lands of the crown of St. Wenceslav, was, indeed, the shelter in which Czech nationalism hibernated throughout the two centuries from the Thirty Years' War to the period after the Congress of Vienna.[6] National struggle during all this time was not, on the surface, easily traceable in the sporadic conflicts between German centralism and the territorial Bohemian nobility, who were the chief champions of the *Staatsrecht.*

A true revival of Czech nationalism, however, became possible only when these secular and ecclesiastic nobles were joined by powerful forces of a rejuvenated bourgeois national intelligentsia, who perceived the Bohemian *Staatsrecht,* not as a bulwark to maintain a feudal Estates order, but as a means of reviving the Czech national cause.

From German sources it has been repeatedly charged that this revival of Czech nationalism was not only a determined but also an entirely artificial move by a small group of intellectual rabble rousers who just did not want to admit to themselves that the Czech people were already practically extinct as a national group with history. How such a move could ever successfully restore not only a national movement but also a supposedly extinct people has never been sufficiently explained. The spirit of this kind of "interpretation" of history is, perhaps, best depicted in the frequently repeated anecdote which tells how Palacký, the father of modern Czech historiography, and Šafařík, one of the founders of the new science of Slavism, once, in the thirties or forties of the nineteenth century, found refuge from a violent thunderstorm in a shed somewhere in the Bohemian forests. Supposedly both had agreed, in this uncomfortable situation, that if the roof over their heads should collapse, the newly revived Czech nationality would die with them.

It is natural that this kind of cheap ideology was violently opposed in Czech historic literature. The whole evolution of Czech nationalism is represented in this literature as a completely evolutionary process which was only strengthened and accelerated by the intellectual leaders of the Czech people in the early nineteenth century. How great their influence actually was, is difficult to estimate. But certainly the fact that a nationally conscious intellectual leadership played a very significant part in this development neither contradicts the assumption of an organic growth of Czech nationalism nor does it detract from its significance. Indeed, in its wide scope, as well as in its intensity, in the extent to which intellectual endeavors became evident, the history of Czech nationalism in the early nineteenth century is one of the most fascinating fields of study.

The revolutionary force of Czech nationalism has not been minimized by all the contemporary writers of German or German Austrian nationality.[7] Charles Sealsfield, for one (known to Austrians by his original name, Karl Postl), gives, as early as 1826, a vivid picture of the intensity of national feeling among the Czechs; and, unlike many other authors of that time, he uses the term "Czechs" to refer to the entire population, not merely to the strata represented in the Estates.

One has only to mention the name of a free people and their [the Czechs'] features darken. One can hear how the Czechs gnash their teeth if one starts to praise British liberty. But they are filled with unmistakable sadness if their own country is mentioned, the battles which they have to fight for an alien cause, the armies for which they have to deliver recruits, and which actually serve as tools for their own oppression. They feel it is just as painful to be at the disposal of a dynasty which remained cold to their wishes in spite of their centuries-old rule and which, in its incapacity, wants only to keep the Bohemians subjected and to frustrate their national aims. An instinctive feeling of hatred against strangers in general and against the Germans in particular is peculiar to all Slav peoples.

Sealsfield distinguished sharply between the tense standard of national feeling in Bohemia and the far less strained situation in Moravia. Thus,

It is unlikely that there will be a general insurrection to gain the rights of the people with the sacrifice of blood. The provinces are too strictly controlled and their internal differences too great to make such an understanding possible. [But] the Bohemians would not hesitate to march against the Hungarians, the Poles against the Italians and the German Austrians, even today against all the above mentioned.[8]

This observation certainly takes full cognizance of the conscious, broad, national aspirations of the Czechs, particularly in regard to the Germans, and yet it is a fine point in Sealsfield's analysis that he stresses the democratic opposition against the government just as much as the national opposition against the Germans.[9]

The virility of the rising Czech opposition was fully recognized by Andrian in 1843: "Bohemia daily considers herself more and more destined to assert her own separate nationality, and with the feeling of this strength and unity the antagonism against foreign domination is growing." [10] Though the broad popular basis of Czech nationalism was an established fact, and was recognized even by enlightened and sincere German authorities, the myth of the artificial nature of Czech nationalism has survived even among conscientious authors for many decades.[11]

A principal reason suggests itself in explanation of this historic misinterpretation, wherever it does not appear as a conscious distortion of the facts. It is the unfortunate confusion of the traditional national program embedded in the Bohemian *Staatsrecht* with early nineteenth-century Czech nationalism. Transferred into social terms this means essentially the conflict between the claims of a powerful landed nobility of rather ambiguous national character and the thriving commercial, professional, and intellectual middle class.

As to this nobility (except for Magyars and Poles) the noblest, wealthiest, and most influential of the Austrian aristocratic families (such as the Schwarzenberg, Lobkowitz, Thun, Liechtenstein, Kinsky, Clam, Czernin, and Dietrichstein) had the greater part of their large estates in Bohemia and in Moravia. This feudal group, with important exceptions, was rather indifferent regarding the national question. They formed part of a largely denationalized social top set, and their affiliation was "imperial," that is, with the crown and everything it represented. Alluding to the colors of the Austrian (Cisleithanian) flag, this attitude was often called "black-yellow."

However, a large part of the aristocracy, particularly the landed territorial nobility in the outlying crownlands as distinguished from the court nobility in Vienna, were, by power of historic tradition and interests, greatly concerned with the preservation of their rights and interests inherent in the old Estates orders of the crownlands and the larger historicopolitical entities. In that sense the aristocracy in Bohemian lands identified its interests with those of the crownlands and larger historicopolitical entities, of which its ancient domains formed a part. Yet its interests and patriotic loyalties were primarily tied to the geographic notion of specific lands, not to a national cause. They considered themselves Bohemians or Moravians, not Germans or Czechs.[12]

It was altogether different with the Magyar and Polish aristocracy, who had not experienced the almost wholesale destruction of the truly national nobility, such as that in Bohemia after the battle of the White Mountain in 1620. There a truly national nobility existed until the end of the monarchy. On the other hand, in the Alpine Hereditary Lands, where court aristocracy and landed aristocracy were largely fused,[13] the German-speaking aristocracy was rather indifferent regarding the national issue.

Bohemian and Moravian nobility thus occupied a middle ground between the almost fully denationalized German Austrian aristocracy and the almost fully national Magyar and Polish nobles. This key situation within a feudal order agreeable to the crown gave the Bohemian aristocracy a strong position as controllers and alleged protectors of the rising Czech cultural national movement.

Kleinwächter, from the Right, and Bauer, from the Left, met in a correct appraisal of this situation. Kleinwächter asserted:

Policy has brought the democratic leaders into contact with the high nobility, which, though of German origin or Germanized for centuries, had suddenly discovered its Czech heart. But it did not come to a closer affiliation. They knew that the Czech high nobility did not care for the cultural and political rise of the Czech people, but for its own political and economic power, which, it believed, it could claim in an independent Bohemian state. . . . The part of the Czech nobility which had joined the Czech movement did so for the sole reason that it believed in the restoration of the old Estates order. Because of its immense landed property it hoped to gain the rule of Bohemia.[14]

And Bauer stresses the fact that the identification of the national interests of the Czech people with those of the Bohemian feudal class fatefully influenced the destiny of the Czech people. His observations point to the development after 1848, and especially to the ideological concepts of the postrevolutionary "Old Czech Party," who, as stanch Conservatives, defended the social and political idea of the Bohemian *Staatsrecht* in alliance with the aristocracy. But these concepts have a definite bearing on the prerevolutionary development as well, when Bauer succinctly states that the price for the support of the national cause by the landed aristocracy was submission to its economic and ideological interests.[15]

This line of political thought is, indeed, dominant in official Czech policy from Palacký's course in 1848 until the final failure of the Hohenwart cabinet in 1871 to materialize the idea of the Bohemian *Staatsrecht*. Yet in a way this concept was outworn even before the revolution, due to its principal shortcomings, which held good then as well as later. By shortcomings are meant here above all clinging to the socially untenable Estates institutions and disregarding a settlement of the German-Czech national questions within the desired union of the lands of the Bohemian crown (Bohemia, Moravia, and Silesia), on the one hand, and the Slovak problem in Hungary, on the other.[16] Political dependence on these Conservative concepts thus fettered and distorted the growth of Liberal Czech nationalism well into the postrevolutionary era.

One point, in particular, should be stressed regarding the other principal criticism of the broad popular foundations of Czech nationalism, the alleged artificial character of the literary renaissance movement in the early nineteenth century. A difference exists, depending on when, in a nation's history, the conscientious efforts for cultural national restoration are applied—whether they must go back to a semimythical past or whether, as in the case of the Czechs, the further development of a rich historic cultural tradition has been blocked by only two centuries of political oppression.

The "revivers," the great linguists and creators of the science of "Slavism," who were concerned with the study of Czech language and culture, are indeed to be compared to surgeons who restore to its natural function a limb which had been almost paralyzed, but not severed from the national body, by a crushing blow of political destiny. Albert E. Schäffle, minister of the cabinet of Count Hohenwart in 1871, was one of the few German statesmen who admitted his previous misunderstanding of this historical process.

I had formerly believed that Bohemia was already Germanized. And more than two hundred years of joint work by bureaucrats and Jesuits under the system of absolutism from the Battle of the White Mountain until the fourth decade of the nineteenth century had made it possible for the educated strata of the Czech population to talk German. But the people had not become German, and two decades were scarcely sufficient to weld the whole Czech-Bohemian population into any strong, new national feeling. This resurrection came so suddenly that it exceeded even the expectations of Francis Palacký (1798–1876) and Paul Šafařík (1795–1861).[17]

Indeed, the conscientious revivers of the language, history, and tradition of the Czech people—Šafařík, Joseph Dobrovský (1753–1829), and Joseph Jungmann (1773–1847) from the angle of philology, Palacký from the historical side—only followed a course set by the gradually crystallizing political demands of their people. This fact certainly does not diminish the credit which is due to their scholarship, their national consciousness, and their creative ability.

It is true that they themselves were, in a way, greatly indebted to the pioneer literary historic works of Germans such as F. A. von Schlözer (1735–1809) and, above all to J. G. von Herder's (1744–1803) *Ideen zur Geschichte der Menschheit* for their wealth of ideas in general, and particularly to Herder's estimate of the glorious future of the Slavs. Yet, the tremendous impact of Herder's ideas on the rise of humanitarian and liberal nationalism, the entire influence of the German historic school of Savigny and of German and French romanticism, have worked through the medium of ideas alone, which, in an intricate ideological process and by less worthy successors, have been transferred to the political field. But the rise of the idea of nationalism as a cultural and intellectual concept worked somewhat differently among the Slav peoples in Austria, principally among the Czechs. The division between political philosophy and political action is here almost nonexistent. The rejuvenators of the Czech nation acted in the dual role of scholars and men of politics; their scholarly work was directly influenced by political demands. Their efforts in either field are inseparable, and their scholarly achievements transmitted to us bear evidence of the fact that they were not hampered by their patriotic motives. Theirs was a political science in the truest and noblest sense of the word.[18]

In this respect, the revival of the language movement furthered a new approach to the problem of the Austrian Empire: the concept of the organization of the Austrian peoples along ethnic lines. This fact has been obscured by Conservative endeavors to revive Czech nationalism as a by-product of historic traditional claims for the restoration of the historicopolitical entity of the Bohemian lands. It has been further obscured by the fact that the Austrian central government under the influence of Metternich, and more especially of Kolowrat, favored the movement leading to the renaissance of the Slav and particularly of the Czech language. Emperor Francis graciously accepted Dobrovský's books as commendable works of scholarship, "essentially in the interest of the state." [19] Practically all the other Czech scholars were unchallenged in their government positions, as professors in colleges or universities, or as librarians. Šafařík, for a time, even was censor of Slav literature. This did not mean, however, that the government was ignorant of the possible influence of cultural nationalism on political separatism. Neither did the government's policy indicate a conciliatory move in the direction of political liberalism.

The Austrian government had good reason to believe that its position would be more secure if the landed nobility in Bohemia and in Moravia, rather than the German bureaucracy in Vienna, appeared, at least on the surface, as the dominant power in the lands of the Bohemian crown. Their support of the scheme of Bohemian crown rights as exercised by the Bohemian aristocracy did not appear very dangerous, and in almost any other respect the interests of this group concurred fully with the policy of the government. In order to enhance its position in a Czech environment, the feudal nobility would, in turn, naturally support or at least tolerate the strictly cultural activities of the intelligentsia and thus demonstrate that the hated policy of Germanization in Bohemia had been checked.

Perhaps even more important was the religious issue involved. In the Orthodox churches of the Slav nationalities in Austria, the so-called Old Slav liturgical language was used in the ritual and prayer book. This was fundamentally the language used in the Russian Orthodox church. Translation into the western Slav languages and Latin letters appeared to the Austrian police state as an important device to fight the political danger of a pro-Russian Pan-Slav movement.[20] True enough, the overwhelming majority of the Czechs were not members of any of the Eastern churches, but were either Roman Catholics or Protestants. Yet, it was probably correct to assume that the renaissance of any of the Slav languages would have its immediate effect on Slav ethnic-cultural consciousness in general. But as so often results from political reasoning that is too clever, an effect was achieved that was in direct opposition to the one intended. The revival of the Czech and the other western Slav languages was not an effective weapon against the Pan-Slav movement, but, on the contrary, strengthened it enormously. The influence of this fact on the Austrian state problem can scarcely be overrated.

Edvard Beneš distinguishes among three historic meanings of this concept of Pan-Slavism. Firstly, in its broadest sense it stands for the union of all the Slav peoples. Secondly, there are Russia's aspirations to draw the Balkan Slavs from the Austrian and the Turkish orbit into the Russian political sphere. The conquest of Istanbul, particularly the dreams of Catherine II of a Byzantine empire, belong to these schemes. The third concept was at first limited. It embraced cultural and intellectual cooperation rather than political union of the Slav peoples. Its foremost intellectual leader among the western Slav people was the great Slovak Jan Kollár (1793–1852).[21] This third concept was the first to influence Austria's national organization.

Beneš characterizes this last manifestation of Pan-Slavism, with its craving for spiritual union with the East and its unrealistic premise of a revival of an allegedly pre-existent Slav union, as follows:

Kollár is the father of western Slavism of romantic conception. . . . Russian Pan-Slavism and Pan-Russianism approached this concept and exploited it politically.

And, turning to the Czech political opposition against this mystic Slavicism,[22] he continues:

The fight started with the opposition of Palacký and Havlíček against Kollár, and it is still waged today. Essentially, it is the fight of the realistic Slavicism with the Slavicism of romantic conception. The war of 1914–18 has demonstrated again that the romantic conception of Slavicism following Kollár's pattern does not comply with the demands of practical policy.

The task of the Neo-Slavicism of the early twentieth century, following the ideas of Palacký and Havlíček and under Masaryk's guidance, has been to assume the leadership of the Czech cause.[23]

It is true, Kollár's mystic Pan-Slavism was not destined to lead the Czech people to national independence. Its attachment to Russia, the "mother of Slavs," implied, if not sympathy, at least neutrality toward the Russian sociopolitical system. Yet in many ways this system not only was more reactionary than Austria's, it even bolstered up the Austrian government's absolutist course. It certainly favored a policy directed against the popular national movements in principle. Thus, rising Czech nationalism could not consider the support forthcoming from the Russia of Nicholas I (1825–55) as an unmixed blessing. Nevertheless, the unqualified welcome which at least Russia's intellectual world gave to the Slav cause in Austria had a certain significance. It was based, not on support of the czarist government, but on the feeling of ethnic-cultural solidarity focused at and sponsored by the Pan-Slav Russian ideological center. In their common relationship to Russia the Austrian Slav peoples discovered the relationship with each other which gradually was to be transformed into the solidarity of some of the Austrian Slav people in the political field.

It should not be inferred that this growing understanding of the common interests of the Austrian Slav peoples led immediately to a change in the political scope of the Czech national movement. The old concept of the historicopolitical entity of the Bohemian crownlands still remained in the foreground of Czech political thinking. After a brief, but glorious, struggle, in which he fought for the ethnic union of the Czech people and for their peaceful separation from the Germans, even Francis Palacký, the great, universally recognized, political leader of the Czech people returned to the old social and political notions of the Bohemian *Staatsrecht*.[24] Even under as recent and gifted a national leader as Karel Kramář (1860–1937), the fusion between the concepts of the historicopolitical entity of the Bohemian crownlands and a Pan-Slavism oriented to czarist Russia handicapped the evolution of a democratic Czech national cause.

Nevertheless, the main achievements of the Czech cultural renaissance were not permanently affected by the political course of the Pan-Slavist movement. Two positive contributions of that great movement overshadowed all others. First, the rejuvenation of the Czech language had created the tools for further political activity of the Czech people and had, in the same process, trained a vigorous and promising intellectual class. Even more important, any policy based on the recognition of the ethnic, linguistic, and cultural relations of the Austrian Slav peoples had to appeal to the peoples as a whole.

Thus, the renaissance movement, despite the political affiliations of some of its leaders, made the Czech people politically conscious by an inevitable process. As the process was inevitable, so, too, was the final effect of this revived political consciousness. A liberal democratic Czech national movement developed, which transformed the old notions of Pan-Slavism and the Bohemian *Staatsrecht*.

Czech democracy has roots in the recognition of the ethnic affinity of the Slavs inspired by the image of Pan-Slavism. Through a political process of long standing initiated by the ideological appeal to the peoples in the pre-March period, democratic Czech nationalism gradually turned from the one-sided program for ethnic and spiritual fusion with absolutist Russia. With increasing success it attempted to reconcile its Pan-Slav ties with the intellectual demands of the Western world.

## CZECH POLITICAL EVOLUTION IN THE PRE-MARCH PERIOD

In the pre-March era political activism among the Czechs lagged somewhat behind the evolution in the cultural field. Its public manifestations had to be confined largely to Conservative claims for preservation and restoration of the ancient Estates rights of the notables living in the territories of the Bohemian crown and particularly in Bohemia, the main theater of the coming political struggle.

But even before the revolution the personality of Count Leo Thun (1811–88) had to a certain extent joined the political concept of the Bohemian nobility and the more liberal philosophy of the Young National movement. Thun's political ideas, from the time of the revolution onward, were largely determined by his responsibilities as a high government official, as president óf the *gubernium* in Prague during the revolution, and as imperial minister of public instruction and worship during the entire era of constitutional experiments (1849–1860).[25] His prerevolutionary political writings appear amazingly unrestricted by the impact of political censorship, very likely because of his eminent social position and his basically conservative conceptions. This observation refers equally to his writings on the Slovak pıoblem and the Czech problem,[26] the latter discussed first in his widely read essay, "Über den gegenwärtigen Stand der böhmischen Literatur und ihre Bedeutung." On the surface, this little book appears to be just another contribution to the renaissance language movement, though written by an author who freely admits his scanty knowledge of the Czech language. Nevertheless, this representative member of the landed Bohemian nobility openly sides with the Czech national cause. The Count, a sincere friend and admirer of the Czech cultural programs, denounces the Pan-Slav movement as merely a political dream. He considered the ethnic relationship between the Slav peoples too narrow a basis for a joint political program or political union. As to specific Czech claims, he demanded the wider recognition of the Czech language and asserted that Czech and German language claims in Bohemia do not have to conflict if the orbit of each in official intercourse is determined by the principle of political expediency. "Without petty, smallish considerations or motives to use in business without exception the language in which this business can be most quickly and efficiently perfected and furthered—that is the simple rule which always and everywhere will do away with all difficulties." [27]

Thun expanded these ideas in another study, *Betrachtungen über die Zeitverhältrisse insbesondere im Hinblick auf Böhmen,* written shortly after the revolution, in 1849. Strongly pressing the demand for equality of the Czech language, particularly in institutions of higher learning, he promoted the idea that every citizen of Bohemia should be trained at least to understand both national languages of the country and, if possible, to command both completely.[28] He stressed also the great unifying force of a political party system built, not on national affiliation, but on adherence to the same political ideas.[29] These suggestions embody basic features common to the great empire reform plans developed until 1918.

Indeed, the notion of bringing into play the practical factor of expediency, instead of exclusively mathematical parity in territories of mixed nationalities, has proved valuable. In Bohemia this meant recognition of the fact that, entirely independent of the proportional relation between Czechs and Germans, at least until 1918, a far larger percentage of the Czech population understood and spoke German than vice versa. This failure of the larger part of the German population of the Bohemian lands to command the language of the majority —due partly to the fact that it was difficult for them to learn a Slav language, but more so to their ill-fated national pride—could not be ignored in practical life as long as such a situation existed. Thun disapproved of the German demand to perpetuate the benefits accruing to them from their ignorance of the Czech language, namely, that the country should be administered permanently in German. But, though he took a vigorous stand in favor of a widening of the orbit of the Czech language, he realized that until this aim was accomplished by gradual reform, disregard of the existing privileged position of the German language might lead to administrative chaos.

Indeed, the error of imposing a language law, in itself not unfair, on Bohemia and Moravia without previously providing appropriate

linguistic and political education for the population led in 1897 to
the serious state crisis connected with the downfall of the Badeni ministry. Moreover, it is safe to say that from then on the fate of both, Austrian parliamentarianism and a mutually agreeable solution of the
German-Czech language conflict, was sealed.[30]

The proposal for the introduction of the principle of expediency
into the language conflict accounts for Thun's demand for the bilingual training of the population in mixed territories. Only by the
actual achievement of bilingual training could legal equality for both
Czechs and Germans be possible in practice. In that case, neither people would have suffered direct disadvantage from intercourse in a
second national language, and a great deal of technical and psychological tension would have been removed. A further consideration—probably as little realized by Thun as by the shortsighted German liberal
and nationalist leaders of the following two generations—was that in
the end the familiarity of the German central and crownland bureaucracy with the language of at least one of the other nationalities
would have strengthened the cause of German centralism tremendously.[31] Thereby the demand to replace the German bureaucracy by
a truly national Czech administration might have become less relevant
from the standpoint of practical necessity, or at least might have lost
much of its tense, emotional character. Indeed, it might have been
possible, up to a point, to reconcile the issue between reformed Jo-
sephian centralism and liberal nationalism among the nationalities,
and it certainly would have greatly helped to facilitate the functioning of the centralistic regime.

Most remarkable among Thun's ideas was the observation that the
conciliation of the Austrian national question should be based on the
substitution of the political party for the national one. In this respect,
the feudal leader of the Bohemian nobles, though rigidly clerical and
antiliberal,[32] realized that the solution of the Austrian nationality
problem, as, indeed, of the nationality problem of any multinational
group, depends primarily on one factor: to break up blocs of national
isolationism and to organize the various peoples according to their
comprehensive social, economic, and cultural interests. It probably
was not Thun's intention that any such regrouping of interests would
ultimately serve the cause of social and political progress against territorial feudalism and provincial nationalism. It stands to reason that
when he promoted the idea of political as against national affiliation

in 1849 he had in mind the rallying of all loyal imperial-minded
citizens against the cause of the revolution. But that does not change
the significance of his observation. One of the most characteristic features of the ideas exposed in this study is that their range and ultimate
goal are often far wider than at first assumed. They often lead into a
direction not foreseen by their original sponsors.

Certainly, the repercussions of the conservative ideas of Francis
Palacký (1798–1876) and the more liberal ones of Karel Havlíček
(1821–56) were more immediate than those of Thun's long-range views.
Palacký's weighty influence before 1848 was chiefly founded on his
work as national historian which, in its combination with political
action, represents a characteristic feature in the evolution of Czech
nationalism.[33]

All the great Czech leaders down to Beneš were in a sense disciples of Palacký. This was due equally to his great contribution to the
national renaissance of his people and to his repeated changes of opinion on basic political issues. As will be seen in the course of this
study, in some ways and at some time in his life he was related to
every one of the major political currents of Czech history, though
he actually belonged wholly to none.

The political starting point of Palacký's national policy becomes
clear if it is compared with and supplemented by Havlíček's program.
Havlíček's record [34] before and after the revolution, unlike that of
Palacký and of the great teachers of Slavicism, does not rest on scholarly
achievement. It is the work of a political journalist, the first of his
nation in every sense of the word. In the last years before the revolution, Havlíček (under a pseudonym) published regular accounts of
political conditions in Ireland and China in the journal *Pražské-
Noviny*, and the readers could easily recognize, in this rather obvious
disguise, the first public discussion of the future program of action of
the Czech people. Havlíček's theoretical program, originally based on
the historic views of the younger Palacký, may best be described as a
modernized and democratized edition of the old Bohemian *Staatsrecht*. The main constitutional postulates as outlined by Palacký and
first promoted actively by Havlíček, are masterfully summarized by
Beneš.

The Czechs claimed a certain independence on the basis of historic
rights (*droit historique d'état*), but they wanted independence from the
crown in accord with a united monarchy and consented to a fairly close

link with Austria on the condition that they could keep the old right of the autonomy of their country where they alone would be the masters of their destiny. They were ready to concede to the central government certain prerogatives in regard to Bohemia's inner affairs; their claims referred primarily to the equality of language, national status, public affairs, and a share with the Germans in the administration of the empire.

Complete independence, such as the Magyars tried to achieve in 1848, was a tempting but dangerous dream for Palacký, and its realization was scarcely desirable. . . . In 1848 Havlíček, too, expressed his opinion on the future of Bohemia and showed some pessimism in regard to the schemes for independence:

"Complete independence for the Czechs at this time, when only tremendous empires are being formed in Europe, would be very unfortunate. We could not be anything but a very weak state, dependent on other states, and our national existence would be constantly imperiled. On the other hand, in a close union with the other Slavs in Austria we would enjoy a large amount of independence for the Bohemian crown and, at the same time, considerable advantages from the association with a powerful state. All we can do is to cooperate frankly and sincerely in building and maintaining the Austrian empire."

Havlíček's words quoted above in a way express the program of all Slav nationalities in Austria and Hungary in 1848. They explain why the Slavs were so fervently in favor of a powerful Austria. They explain obstinate Czech resistance to the Frankfurt parliament, and they give the key to the constitutional projects of Palacký and his ideas of Austrian reorganization.[35]

Regarding the difference between Palacký and Havlíček in their actual approach to this program Masaryk says:

The union of the elder Palacký and the younger Havlíček [the latter was only twenty-seven years old in 1848] was very natural. It joined the past to the present. Havlíček accepted the program of Palacký—not only the words but its leading ideas and its spirit. He executed this program in detail, complemented it and expanded it later on the basis of his practical experience; he spread it and explained it, in the manner of a journalist. In this way Havlíček by the side of Palacký became our first political awakener. Palacký was, so to speak, the first ruler on the basis of representative government—Havlíček was the minister of the interior. . . . Where Palacký gave way, Havlíček fought alone for the policy of the Czech people.[36]

Redlich aptly perceives the ideological difference between the two great leaders as follows:

The national idea was the starting point and yet the ultimate goal, though Palacký, as a faithful pupil of the humanitarian philosophy, still gives precedence to the supranational idea of the union of the peoples as the universal principle before the purely national idea. This basic cosmopolite idea is dropped by Palacký's disciple and collaborator as an empty shell. All the more vigorous and impressive, the pure national idea then comes to the fore in the thoroughly popular, visual, and convincing language of this great popularizer of Palacký's ideas. From its very beginning this national idea received, through the original, typical Czech personality of Havlíček, the genuine democratic form, which alone conforms to the very nature of the western Slavs, to the psychology of their people—small peasants and petty bourgeois. But all the time Palacký remained the teacher, Havlíček the disciple. This becomes most obvious in the fact that Havlíček holds fast to the historic Bohemian state idea as formulated by Palacký. Consequently, in the further course of events he sees in the concept of federation the only form in which the national idea of the Czechs as well as of the southern Slavs can be materialized in a practical manner. National equality, democracy, and the dogma of the unforfeited right of the Bohemian people to its historic state, as the union of the lands of the Crown of St. Wenceslav, these are the three basic doctrines of the Czech national program of 1848, as formulated by Palacký and as popularized by Havlíček. On the basis of these principles, the former "preceptor" of his people endeavors, in the course of the movement of 1848, to build the specific "Austrian" program of the Czechs, that is, Austrian federalism.[37]

This last observation is relevant in regard to Palacký's revolutionary and postrevolutionary political philosophy, which will be discussed in another context.[38] At this point, however, it already becomes clear, following Carlton J. H. Hayes's terminology, that Palacký's work is chiefly the product of humanitarian and traditional nationalism, Havlíček's of liberal and partly Jacobin nationalism.

Havlíček's realism manifested itself in his unqualified renunciation of political pro-Russian Pan-Slavism as well as in his demand for the recognition of the Czechs as the real state nation in the envisaged union of the Bohemian lands. His concept of equality between Germans and Czechs resembled the ideas of the liberal promoters of minority protection in 1918 more than the notion held for a time by Palacký,[39] of the strictly binational Czech-German state.

A main difference between Palacký's and Havlíček's political creeds is the latter's more democratic approach to the cause of political liberalism. General suffrage on the basis of a very low property census, antifeudalism, and vigorous anticlericalism were main points in his program,[40] all of them certainly not endorsed by Palacký's prerevolutionary political philosophy.

Czech claims were, indeed, directed just as much against the system of political absolutism as against national oppression. Thus, it was not surprising that Havlíček, in spite of his more radical approach to the national problem, found a good deal of support among German Liberals in Bohemia. These Liberals were by no means adverse *in toto* to the concept of the undivided historicopolitical entity of the Bohemian crownlands. They were equally attracted by the progressive demands in Havlíček's program and by the fighting religious tradition of Žižka and Hus, culminating in the battle against the Catholic Counter Reformation. They understood this tradition as the common heritage of all the people in the Bohemian lands.[41]

The spirit of the times, particularly the example of the February Revolution in France, made it understandable that at the initial stage of the revolution the Liberal political claims overshadowed the national demands. At the famous meeting in the dingy hall of St. Wenceslav in Prague on March 11, 1848, Czechs and German Liberals were united in their demands for the restoration of the union of the lands of the Bohemian crown under a liberal regime. The motto of this assembly was "Čech a Němec jedno tělo,"—"The Bohemian [that is, the Czech] and the German form one body." [42]

The resolution adopted by this assembly, drafted by a committee under the able Czech Liberal lawyer Dr. Adolf Pinkas, later the eminent Czech representative at the constitutional assembly of Kremsier, was addressed to the emperor and was transmitted to the minister of state, Kolowrat, on March 20, 1848. It was the first publicly acclaimed and promoted political program of the Bohemian people for centuries. From the precipitate course of the following events it is easily understood that this program was soon to be regarded as a manifesto of Czech claims and interests. Its content is herewith presented in condensed form.

*Your Imperial, Royal Majesty:*
A great event in the west of Europe, like a threatening meteoric stone, shines upon us. Scarcely started, the powerful movement, which we believed far from us, sweeps the allied states of Germany with it; around Austrian borders there is a tremendous rise. Your Majesty's high allied sovereigns direct this movement by magnanimously taking its lead. They guide it hereby and preserve it from abyss. . . .
Two different national elements inhabit the blessed kingdom, the pearl in Your Majesty's sublime imperial crown: the one, the original one, which has the strongest right to the country and its king, was until now impeded

in its development to culture and legal equality by institutions which, without being inimical or of a denationalizing character, nevertheless by their very nature made the stripping off of the original nationality a condition of civic recognition.

Free development of both nationalities, the Bohemian as well as the German, by the resolve of destiny both united and interlaced, inhabit Bohemia, equal strife for . . . higher culture will establish, strengthen, conciliate, and fraternize the welfare of both of them.

That Bohemia of today has not yet reached the level which she ought to reach is one of the consequences of the existing schism and of the legal and administrative rule of the German element.

The following specific demands were raised:

1. Guarantee of the Bohemian nationality and complete equality of both languages in school and government agencies.
2. Up-to-date revision and expansion of the constitution of the Bohemian land [that is, the old Estates constitution] by guaranteeing to represent the interests of townships and landed property by freely elected deputies. The association of Bohemia, Moravia, and Silesia in a joint Estates assembly should be initiated.
3. Grant of independent charters for townships with freely elected representatives and mayors, full publicity for the meetings of the township councils, humanitarian up-to-date improvements in agricultural conditions.

[4-7. Demand court procedure in public, freedom of the press and freedom of worship for all denominations, and safeguards against unwarranted arrests.]
8. Filling of all public offices by men who command both languages of the country equally well.

[9-11. Deal with the introduction of general conscription, progressive tax reforms, and extension of educational facilities for both nationalities.] [43]

Except for the preamble, it is obvious that, in this program of action, the issue of political liberalism and social reforms takes precedence over the specific national claims, to which only two out of the nine demands refer directly (points 1 and 7). Formally, the program was still strictly based on the ancient concept of the historicopolitical entity of the lands of the Bohemian crown (point 2). Its real contradiction is clearly that the forces which stood for restoration of the medieval kingdom under the crown of St. Wenceslav could not consent to the demands for liberal reforms raised in this resolution, least of all if they became a binational issue, and thereby twice as "dangerous." And the Liberals of both national groups could see no political future in a union represented in an assembly of the "Estates" of the three lands under feudal, Conservative sponsorship. This conflict was not settled by the revolution or by the following era of neo-absolutism. It was revived in new force after the conclusion of the Compromise of 1867, which by-passed this problem. The demand for a democratic and socially just solution of the national problem of the lands of the Bohemian crown outlived the empire. That it was primarily made, though in a contradictory form, by the Czech peoples, then the democratic vanguard among the Austrian nationalities, is to their lasting credit.[44]

The Assembly of St. Wenceslav preceded by only two days the popular uprising in Vienna and the fall of Metternich, which usually is considered as the actual outbreak of the Austrian Revolution. Though the development in Vienna was so much more conspicuous in the eyes of Europe, the rich intellectual inheritance of the revolution was more decisively influenced by the events in Bohemia. Indeed, the fact that the uprising in Prague preceded the revolution in Vienna was of great portent.

### THE CZECH REVOLUTION

If the Czech revolutionary movement in Austria was the first to gain momentum and the first to gain seemingly real political results, it was also the first of all the major central European revolutionary uprisings to be suppressed by force.[45] The Czech Revolution actually lasted barely three months, from the draft of the first petition at the hall of St. Wenceslav in March, 1848, to the installation of Windischgrätz's military dictatorship in Prague by the middle of June, 1848. The eminent contributions of Czech deputies at Kremsier, some six months later, show little of the revolutionary spirit. They are not even fully representative of the major ideological trends of Czech nationalism, but rather of a supranational, comprehensive, Austrian political philosophy.

The history of the brief Czech Revolution and its effect on the position of the lands of the Bohemian crown within Austria must also be separated from the history of the Slav Congress assembled in Prague at the end of May, 1848, and dissolved by military intervention two weeks later. The far-reaching ideological influence of the congress was, of course, focused more strongly on the cause of the western Slav peoples in general than on any specific national group. Yet, of all the specific national groups, it was least concerned with the cause of the Czech people. The Czechs were the only one among the Austrian peoples who then seemed to have good reason to believe that their chief revolutionary demand, the recognition of the old Bohemian *Staatsrecht* (that is, the autonomy of the lands of the Bohemian crown, Bohemia, Moravia, and Silesia as one historicopolitical unit) was already fully assured as early as April, 1848.

Most illuminating on this point are the declarations exchanged directly or indirectly between the revolutionary Liberal representatives, who, in March, 1848, emerged as a political body from the Assembly of St. Wenceslav and for a few months overshadowed the Estates in political importance. This holds true particularly for the so-called second petition of the citizens of Prague on March 29, 1848. Two major political events, which had taken place since the first—afore quoted—declaration in St. Wenceslav's Hall on March 11, explain the decidedly more radical character of this new document. The first event was the imperial manifesto of March 15, promising the introduction of constitutional government and followed five days later by the appointment of the cabinet of Kolowrat-Pillersdorf, whose task it was to transform Austria into a constitutional monarchy. Of even greater importance were the repercussions of Emperor Ferdinand's "rescript" of March 17, issued in his capacity as king of Hungary and promising in principle the imperial acceptance of the demands of the diet of Pressburg. As will be remembered, this virtually meant a grant of responsible constitutional government to Hungary.

Indeed, the immediate causes of the constitutional reforms promised for Cisleithanian Austria were largely the result of poorly organized revolutionary uprisings on a relatively small scale in Prague, Vienna, Lemberg, and other major cities of the empire. The demands raised by the Magyar representatives at the diet of Bratislava (Pressburg), on the other hand, presented the well-planned claims of the legally recognized representative body of Hungarian constitutional life. Obviously, the Magyar standpoint, viewed from the vantage of the imperial pre-March administration, stood a good deal closer to realization than the revolutionary issues raised by any of the other national groups. Because the claims for the special rights of the Hungarian crown were successfully reasserted, similar demands inherent in the traditional brand of Czech nationalism were revived and strengthened.[46] The same relation between the Magyar cause and the Czech effects reappears in the ideological connection between the Austro-Magyar Compromise of 1867 and the "reaction" (in every sense of the word) to it by Czech feudalism in 1871.

The petition of March 29 technically still advocated the complete equality of Czechs and Germans as individuals in the lands of the Bohemian crown. However, the demand for the union of the lands of the Bohemian crown on the basis of historic, national, and geographic considerations left no doubt whatever that this program advocated the formation of a state of traditional Czech national character.[47] It was the unsolved crucial problem of Czech Conservative policy to reconcile the demands for national equality of the individual with the desired national Czech character of the Bohemian *Staatsrecht*. However, the open promotion of the concept of the Bohemian *Staatsrecht* implied not only Czech predominance over Germans in the Bohemian lands but to a greater extent, also, the victory of the Czech Conservative doctrine over democratic liberalism.

The publication of the imperial rescript of April 8, 1848, addressed to the minister of the interior, Francis von Pillersdorf (1786–1862), acceded almost unconditionally to the demands raised in the second March petition. Equality between the German and the "Bohemian nationality" was recognized; the convocation of a Bohemian diet on the basis of a rather democratic franchise law and, by implication, the organization of a general diet of all the Bohemian lands were approved. The establishment of a common administration for the three lands of the Bohemian crown—obviously the most important concession—was granted. Liberal reforms, such as abolition of patrimonial jurisdiction of the lords, autonomous democratic township organization, and freedom of the press and of assembly, were promised.[48]

German reaction was immediate and strong. In a petition drafted the next day, April 9, 1848, the status of the Bohemian crownlands as parts of the territories of the German *Bund* of 1815 was reaffirmed. Protests were launched against separation from the rest of the Austro-German lands and the impairment of the German national status in general. The specific objections raised on this point were highly illuminating for the sustained German position in the language conflict of coming generations. Particular objections were raised against the Czech demand that in nationally homogeneous territories, German as well as Czech, the second national language should be taught to a point where everyone could at least understand it. The introduction of the Czech language in the secondary schools of Bohemia was strongly opposed. Likewise, the German character of the only university in Bohemian lands at that time was to be preserved.[49] The Czech demand that only people born in the lands of the Bohemian crown were to be appointed officials in the administration of the three crownlands was rejected as incompatible with the centralist character of the empire.[50]

The Bohemian charter of April 8, with its almost complete recognition of the rights of the historicopolitical entity of the Bohemian crown, was not destined to be fulfilled. Due to speedy suppression of the revolution in Prague, its practical annulment was the first in a series of broken promises made by the imperial government to every nationality of the empire. Nevertheless, the promise contained in the "Bohemian Charter" was not formally rescinded but—a characteristic feature of Austrian governmental policy—its enforcement was merely held in abeyance indefinitely. The charter remained a pillar of the Czech historic state concept in the following generations, well into the era of Young Czech nationalism in the 1880s and 1890s, until the further-reaching concepts of Western democracy introduced by Masaryk made a clean sweep with a national policy built on a *privilegium Ferdinandi*.

Even more important than the provisions of this unredeemed charter of Czech liberties was the character of the social forces behind it and the national forces fighting it. The men of the first petition of St. Wenceslav Hall were the bourgeois Czech and partly the German radical intellectuals who rallied around Havliček. The grant of the second petition, apparently far more sweeping in character, resulted from the fact that the Czech high nobility wanted to take the edge off the revolutionary movement by supporting it in a limited way. This gained for them renewed influence in the directing of Bohemian affairs. The princes Lobkowitz, Schwarzenberg, Auersperg, and the counts Paar, Harrach, and Czernin, and others, representing the old Estates, could well afford to join in the demand for the charter, since two days after the publication of the imperial rescript a leading representative of their own clan, the brilliant Count Leo Thun, was appointed president of the *Gubernium*, that is, head of the administration of Bohemia.[51]

Henceforward the Bohemian feudal lords managed to take the lead in the national movement, thereby directing if away from the dangerous revolutionary sea into the safe harbor of the Bohemian *Staats-recht*.

This came out clearly in the nobles' reaction to the seizure of power by the troops of Field Marshal Prince Windischgrätz. Obviously, the street riots in Prague during the sessions of the Slav Congress were only a pretext for the military intervention which was to crush all vestiges of the liberal revolution in Bohemia. It is not clear whether Thun secretly supported Windischgrätz's counterrevolutionary course from the beginning. It is certain, however, that he fully approved of that policy, though he was careful to keep up appearances as a Bohemian patriot.[52] At the very time when the entire crownland was virtually under martial law, he proposed the convocation of the new diet, which he had deemed impossible before Windischgrätz's military coup. This diet, cleared of Liberal revolutionary elements and rendered almost completely a tool of the Bohemian feudal lords, was not acceptable to the new, enlightened Pillersdorf ministry in Vienna. The ministry prohibited its convocation and recalled Thun, for the time being, from public office. German liberal as well as centralistic tendencies, likewise opposed to autonomous territorial federalism and undue military power in civil affairs, played a major role in this decision.[53]

Thun's policy, so much more skillful in the suppression of the revolution than Windischgrätz's mailed-fist actions, was supported by Palacký and his son-in-law, Francis L. Rieger (1818–1903), likewise one of the most influential and popular bourgeois Czech leaders. Naturally enough, their attitude unwittingly confused and deceived the Liberal Czechs' perception of the political picture. These Liberals knew little about qualms of conscience within the weak, mildly liberal government in Vienna, but they had experienced the conflict between Windischgrätz's imperial troops and the forces rallied around the idea of the national kingdom of St. Wenceslav. Thus, the Bohemian aristocrats appeared to them as the defenders, and Windischgrätz's army as the ruthless destroyer, of their newly regained liberties. They had little or no opportunity to see through the ambiguous policy of the Bohemian nobles. They scarcely thought of the possibility that this group, if threatened in their interests from the Left, might at any time sacrifice the defense of the Bohemian *Staatsrecht* in favor of protecting the military power of absolutism.

The government in Vienna, however, was not yet committed to

this latter course. It was the tragedy of the Czech Revolution that, at the very time when the support of the central government in Vienna, which was still moderately liberal, might have helped to secure the national-liberal reform of the empire, it held steadfastly to the program of the antiliberal Bohemian Tories, thereby unwittingly strengthening the rising cause of the counterrevolution. And the further tragedy of Czech nationalism during the following generations was that it made peace with the central government only after the latter's liberal character had completely given way to a narrow conservatism.

This historic error was understandable, though. The power of the historic tradition of the Bohemian *Staatsrecht,* the fact that the achievements of the brief national renaissance had directly appealed to only a relatively small number of liberal intellectuals, as well as the national attitude of some of the aristocratic leaders—subjectively irreproachable and upright though it was—certainly contributed thus to the failure of the Czech Revolution.

Of great importance, also, was the presumptuous intolerance of many of the German national representatives in Bohemia, as exemplified by the German address of April 9. Had these German nationalists been willing to accede to the moderate Czech demands for national equality in the lands of the Bohemian crown, had they not peremptorily refused to deal with Czech nationals as equals, Czech nationalism might not necessarily have identified itself almost exclusively with the conservative Bohemian *Staatsrecht.* The cause of German liberalism, which was divided between the moderate centralists in Vienna and the radical vanguard of future Pan-Germanism in the national frontier territories, might not have succumbed to the absolutism of the Schwarzenberg era.[54]

### THE CZECHS AND THE GERMAN CONFEDERATION

German opposition to the promotion of the Bohemian *Staatsrecht* produced an immediate Czech reaction, shown especially in the Czech attitude toward the German confederation plans at Frankfurt. The Germans had launched their protest against the imperial rescript granting the autonomy of the Bohemian crown on April 9, 1848. On April 11 Palacký wrote his famous letter declining by implication, in the name of the Czech peoples, participation in the activities of the Frankfurt preliminary parliament (*Vorparlament*). Though the basic ideas in Palacký's famous answer certainly were not determined by events of the day, the rapidly growing national friction between Czechs and Germans probably influenced the form of his letter.

Palacký's refusal, the catechism of "Austro-Slavism" (Redlich), and, indeed, one of the most important documents in the history of the Austrian nationality problem, was based on three principal reasons. First, he contested the legitimacy of any arguments drawn from the legal connection between the bygone German Empire or its successor, the German *Bund*, and the Bohemian kingdom, which was, to him, the home of the legally, ethnically, and historically independent Czech people. He defied any plans which considered the land of the Czechs as part of a German union.

Palacký's second argument, particularly interesting to the reader of today, is as follows:

You know which Power rules in the whole vast east of our continent; you know that this power, grown now to immensity, . . . with every decade rises and becomes increasingly stronger. Such increase in power could not happen in the western countries. This power, in its interior nearly unassailable and inaccessible, has long adopted externally a threatening policy. Even if it is aggressive in the north, driven by natural instincts, it tries and will try to expand primarily to the south. Each step which this power could make forward on this scale threatens to create and to bring about a new universal empire [*Universalmonarchie*] . . . that is, an incalculable and unspeakable disaster, a boundless calamity. I, in my capacity as a Slav, in soul and body would deplore this in the interests of humanitarianism, even if this disaster would proclaim itself a predominantly Slav disaster. With the same injustice which calls me in Germany an enemy of the Germans, in Russia I am called and considered by many an enemy of the Russians. I declare, loudly and publicly, I am no enemy of the Russians: on the contrary, I watch at all times and with joyful sympathy, every step forward which this great people makes on the path of civilization. Yet, in spite of my ardent love for my people, I place the interests of humanity and science forever above those of nationality: the mere possibility of a Russian universal empire does not meet a more determined foe than myself; not because it would be a Russian empire, but because it would be a universal empire. . . .

The southeast of Europe along the borders of the Russian Empire is inhabited by several peoples distinctly different in origin, language, history, and customs—Slavs, Walachians, Magyars, and Germans, not to mention Greeks, Turks, and Skipetars. None of these is strong enough in itself to resist the overwhelmingly powerful eastern neighbor successfully. . . . They are able to do so only if a strong bond unites them all. The essential artery of this vital association of nations is the Danube. Its Central Power must not move away from this stream if it is to be at all effective. Indeed, if the Austrian imperial state had not existed for ages, it would be necessary to create such a state, in the interests of Europe and of humanity in general.

But why was this state, destined by nature and history to be Europe's bulwark against Asiatic elements of all kinds, rendered almost helpless when abandoned to any severe attack? Because in its fatal blindness it did not recognize, indeed repudiated, the legal and ethical foundations of its existence: the principle of complete equality and liberal treatment of all the nationalities and denominations united under its sway. . . . If the bond which joins several nations to one political entity is to be strong and lasting, then none of them must have reason to fear that it would lose any one of its dearest possessions through the union. On the contrary, every one of them must hold the firm conviction that the Central Power will protect it against any encroachments by its neighbors. Should such an emergency arise, the Central Power should be provided immediately with adequate power to exercise this protection effectively. I am convinced that it is not yet too late for Austria to proclaim this principle of justice . . . loudly and without reservation, and to support it practically everywhere. Yet time is running short.

As soon as I look beyond the frontiers of Bohemia, natural as well as historic reasons compel me not to look toward Frankfurt, but toward Vienna, to seek there the center which is likely and destined to secure and protect my people's peace, liberty, and right. Your tendency, gentlemen, seems to me to have the clear purpose not only to weaken this center . . . but even to destroy it, though I trust that its vigor and strength would be beneficial, not merely to Bohemia alone. . . . For the sake of Europe, Vienna must not sink to the role of a provincial town. But if there are people in Vienna who want your Frankfurt as their capital, one can only say to them: Lord forgive them, for they know not what they ask.

Finally, Palacký gives as his third reason for the rejection of the invitation to Frankfurt his disbelief that a union of principalities could organize Germany successfully. Here, salvation could only come from a German republic, yet in regard to Austria he strongly rejects the republican system which would only lead to the dismemberment of the empire in the interest of "a universal Russian empire." [55]

The significance of Palacký's letter can scarcely be exaggerated. Even before the Frankfurt parliament convened, the letter reduced to a myth the concept of the union of the two Great German Powers, of which the still dominant one, Austria, was only partly a German Power. The German *Bund*, whose existence was prolonged, against the wishes of the majority of the Austrian peoples, until 1866, henceforth lacked the aura of political reality which it had possessed in the Metternich era, at least as a bulwark against liberalism. It became increasingly obvious that the Austrian Slav people could be held in line with the exacting requirements of the Austrian governmental system only if they were spared the rule of a *Grossdeutsche* nationalism.

This does not mean that political leaders of Palacký's viewpoint considered impossible a compromise with the bureaucratic supranational ideology of German centralism. Palacký's letter and the draft of the May, 1848, constitution of the Bohemian lands imply that an understanding, on the basis of a limited degree of autonomy for the member states of an Austrian federation and a wide sphere of jurisdiction for the German-directed Central Power, was still possible. Palacký's evaluation of the Russian danger and his close tie to Western civilization, particularly in the form of the German philosophy of the Age of Enlightenment, leave little doubt that he and his followers would have been ready to meet the demands for German cultural and administrative priority halfway. Indeed, the enlightened Slav bourgeoisie in all parts of the empire, much as they wanted their own national groups recognized as federal member states of an Austrian federal union, were ready to put up with a modified rule of German centralism in Austria as long as the basic supranational character of the empire could be preserved. They were, however, violently and irreconcilably opposed to the rule of manifest German nationalism. The three great crises of 1867, 1871, and 1897, in which German nationalism shook and finally destroyed this supranational state doctrine, were the turning points in the history of Czech relations toward the empire.

### THE CZECHS FROM THE REVOLUTION TO THE HOHENWART REGIME IN 1871

The postrevolutionary development of the Czech national position was limited by the double barrier of the neo-absolutist regime in Austria and the re-entrenchment of the feudal nobility in Bohemia. Political activities were paralyzed during the decade of the absolutist regime in Bohemia, as in every other part of the empire. Havlíček, the most active leader of the radical Czech liberal movement, died in exile. Moderate "bourgeois" leaders, such as Rieger and Palacký, found it advisable to withdraw completely from politics during that period. Political life was reduced to the continued petty frictions of the language conflict which had come into the open since the revolutionary days. As Redlich observes,

the foundation was laid for the whole seven decades of hopeless struggle for the Austran language law in administrative intercourse [*Amtssprachenrecht*], a chapter of the more recent Austrian history which will permanently be judged as the strongest evidence of the political and legislative inability of the new Austrian authoritarian state. Concerning the official language of administration even in 1848, the very real contradictions of class interests between Czech and German bourgeoisie appear unmistakably: for nearly half a century these class interests were externally identified with the basic vital interests of the two peoples.[56]

But unlike the situation in other crownlands, further inroads of Bach's administrative Germanization policy were to some extent checked in Bohemia by the influence of the nobility, particularly of their outstanding leader, Count Leo Thun, who was imperial minister of education from 1849 to 1860. During his administration, instruction in the Czech language was introduced in the Bohemian secondary schools. In general, language regulations regarding intercourse between public and administration, particularly in the judicial branch, were slightly modified in favor of the Czech people, as compared to conditions before 1848.[57]

The share of the nobles in the Conservative transaction of affairs in Bohemia and in Moravia remained unimpaired in the early period of the era of constitutional experiments beginning in 1859. In the convocation of the conservative, pseudo-representative *Reichsrat* in 1860, men such as Count Heinrich Clam-Martinic and Thun himself had a great deal of influence on the drafting of the semi-Federalist constitution of October, 1860. This applied in particular to their promotion of the idea of the crownland autonomy to be exercised by the old historic Estates diets, actually only a modified version of the concept of the historicopolitical entities.[58]

Czech nationalism became more active the moment when, upon the appointment of the German centralist cabinet under Archduke Rainer and Schmerling, the centralistic February constitution of 1861 became effective and liberalism, in however diluted form, advanced markedly. Czech nationalism protested violently against this new constitution. The rift widened between the Czech middle-class nationals, who were aroused by the revival of German centralistic policy, and the Bohemian nobles, who had gained control of the reorganized crownland diet by way of dubious governmental devices.[59] Yet, at this very time, when liberalism all over the empire saw a new dim light, when it hoped to advance beyond the limits of the socially unrepresentative, semiliberal February constitution of 1861, Czech liberalism under Rieger's well-intentioned, but shortsighted, leadership again succumbed completely to the forces of crownland feudalism. In return for a more active support for the cause of the old Bohemian *Staatsrecht,* the Czech nationally conscious bourgeoisie readily submitted to a reactionary social and cultural policy.

This conservative-feudal-bourgeois coalition, known under the label of the Old Czech party, stood, not for the common claims of the nationalities discriminated against in Austria, but essentially for outdated social-group privileges clad in the framework of the historic traditions of the Bohemian crown. With no popular appeal whatsoever, this course represented, indeed, the low ebb of Czech national policy throughout the period from 1848 to 1918. This political surrender of Czech nationalism to the forces of social reaction worked greatly to the advantage of the imperial government. It is most unlikely that the Compromise of 1867, with its complete disregard for the claims of the Czech people, could have been put through so smoothly if the Czech people had at that time been represented by a force which was more democratic and progressive than the Old Czech party.[60]

Yet, though politically not immediately effective, Liberal Czech reaction to the official policy was not lacking. As early as 1863, a radical party movement, later known as the Young Czechs, was developing. In economic questions it was clearly more representative of the interests of the bourgeois industrial and commercial classes than the Old Czechs, who were under feudal-agrarian leadership. In regard to their national aims, the policy of the Young Czechs was in theory not very different from that of the Old Czechs. In practice, however, it was far more intransigent, far more influenced by the fervent national religious tradition of Žižka and Hus than it was by the legal arguments derived from the Bohemian *Staatsrecht.* An increasing tendency toward the new national movement [61] was shown by Czech active participation in the new Russian Pan-Slav Congress in Moscow in 1867, where even as close a friend of Western orientation of the Czechs as the Old Czech Rieger had to make a stand for Pan-Slav solidarity.

Nevertheless, Czech official policy of that time still was entirely negative in its feeble protest against the centralistic policy of the government, expressed in the intermittent demonstrative absentation of the Old Czechs from the central parliament and the Bohemian diet. However, it was by no means bare of potential influence.[62] As soon as the Compromise of 1867 was under cover, the crown looked for an opportunity to replace the German Liberal, centralistic cabinet by one of Slav Conservative-Federalist ideas. Neither antipathy for German centralism nor sympathy for Slav federalism motivated this new course, but, rather, a desire to substitute a Conservative for a Liberal regime.

When the Czech passive resistance against the German Liberal regime was finally taken up by the Poles, the Rumanians, the Slovenes, and even the Italians, the crown used this opportunity to appoint a semi-Federalist ministry under the Polish Count Alfred Potocki. Potocki tried to appease the Czechs with minor concessions, some administrative, though not legislative, autonomy for Bohemia, and a proposed coronation of the emperor with the royal crown of St. Wenceslav in Prague—dear to Czech traditionalism, yet in itself without practical significance.[63] When these attempts for national or, rather, feudal-conservative appeasement failed, the crown thought it advisable to make a more drastic attempt in the direction of federalist organization. The result of this consideration was the appointment of the Hohenwart cabinet, which was in office from February to October, 1871. Its history represents one of the most significant episodes in the records of the Austrian national question. Its failure reflects almost as unfavorably on the promoters of the federalization scheme as on its opponents, who thwarted its realization.

### HOHENWART'S FEDERALIST MISSION

In the winter of 1871 the chances for the success of a far-reaching attempt to federalize the Habsburg Empire were certainly slim, yet not entirely hopeless.[64] The Compromise of 1867 had blocked the way to a comprehensive solution of the national problem in the empire as a whole. On the other hand, the national claims of the two politically leading nationalities, the Germans and the Magyars, had for the time being been satisfied. The demands of two other leading national groups had at least been appeased by the Hungarian-Croatian Compromise of 1868 and the far-reaching administrative concessions which the Austrian government made to the Poles in Galicia at about the same time. If the new Austrian cabinet of Hohenwart, appointed in February, 1871, had succeeded in its endeavors to arrive at a Czech-German conciliation in Bohemia and in Moravia, the five major nationalities of the empire could have been rallied around the imperial idea. It could have been hoped, then, that these "Big Five"—enhanced in their national position—would have been ready to make at least minor concessions to the other national groups. If such an attempt for federal solution had been based chiefly on an understanding with the liberal commercial and industrial classes and the peasants, not primarily with the feudal representatives in the old Estates in Bohemia and in Galicia, it might have received broad popular support, notwithstanding opposition on the part of the German and Magyar ruling regime.

Count Hohenwart, the foremost leader of the Conservative Federalists in the following decades, in theory was not blind to the first aspect of the problem, that is, the necessity for a comprehensive federal solution, built not exclusively on special historic privileges for the nationalities with history, but on equality among all nationalities, at least in the Austrian part of the empire.[65] Hohenwart, however, was not ready to make any concessions regarding the social premises of a federal program. This right-wing Tory leader was called to office by the emperor and the court circles not so much for the sake of federalism in itself, but for the sake of federalism as a means of destroying the ruling German Liberal system. If he was to succeed in the task of securing a social and cultural order acceptable to the imperial will, he could not negotiate and compromise with the radical intelligentsia and the small peasants in the Slav crownlands. He had to rely on the support of the guarantors of the social order acceptable to the crown and himself, that is, the Polish and Bohemian nobles and their following.[66]

More complex and sophisticated than Hohenwart's views were those of his chief collaborator, Albert Schäffle, formerly professor of political economy at the University of Vienna and minister of commerce in the new Federalist cabinet. Schäffle's political activities were by no means confined to this technical post. As one of the outstanding social scientists of his time, he belonged to the group of German Protestant scholars who, since the days of Charles VI, had been called into Austria from time to time to perform some specific administrative or political reform mission. Some of these German administrative "missionaries" had to contend with a specific antagonism in official Austria. Undoubtedly the assignment of a not-too-tactful Swabian Protestant to the role of arbitrator in the delicate Czech-German language conflict impaired the success of his program from the beginning. On the other hand, however, if a man were to be selected on the merits of his theoretical comprehension of a difficult political situation, no abler person could have been chosen than Schäffle, who was aware equally of the national and the social implications of his task.

To Schäffle, the Federalist program which he attempted to put through by cumbersome negotiations with the Old Czech leaders in Bohemia was only the rudimentary beginning of a far more inclusive concept. He defined these wider aims rather well, as follows:

I never did homage to federalism either in Austria or in Germany in the sense in which federalism was understood in Austria at that time, that is, the incarnation of reactionary tendencies going back from the modern state to the old territorial empire [Territorienreich]. The federalism, which I strongly promoted before it was generally publicized, in my [treatise] Kapitalismus und Sozialismus—that is, the development of the cooperative society in contrast to the atomistic economic individualism— had nothing whatever to do with this Austrian federalism.[67]

This enmity against "atomistic . . . individualism" perhaps explains better than anything else why he was made a member of the Hohenwart cabinet. Schäffle, above all, was strongly antiliberal and, in a way, antinational as well. He opposed the rule of a "parliamentarian national [German] and class minority system." According to him, "this minority regime means, indeed, rule of big capitalism with the support of doctrinaire liberalism, lawyers, literary writers, and professors."[68]

Schäffle advocated the radical reform of the old Estates diets and their conversion into truly corporate representations which would reduce the inordinate influence of big landowners and would give agriculture, trades, and also, by implication, labor a share of responsibility equal to that of commerce and industry. Franchise was to be extended in order to break the rule of the German Liberal regime of the upper bourgeois, which was unrepresentative. Gradually, the reform was to proceed to the introduction of general equal franchise. Austria would benefit from the creation of comprehensive parties effective all over the empire and based on social interests as counterbalance against the centrifugal Nationalist forces.[69]

Schäffle further advocated comprehensive legislation concerning the rights of the various nationalities in all of Cisleithanian Austria. A Bohemian national compromise should represent only the first step in this respect. He did not intend to attack frontally the provisions of the new Dualistic Compromise of 1867. Yet Schäffle counted on the fact that the creation of national equilibrium in Austria would bear sufficient moral and ideological pressure on the Magyars to force them to national compromises with the non-Magyar peoples in Hungary, similar to the one to be proposed by him for Bohemia.[70] Schäffle implied that through Austrian reforms the absurdity of the dualistic organization of the empire would be clearly demonstrated in Hungary. Thus, without external compulsion a solution could be arrived at, according to which the empire would be reorganized on the basis of four or five historicopolitical units.

In view of these ideas it is difficult to comprehend how a scholar of Schäffle's vision—entirely free from narrow national prejudices [71]—could have seriously believed that the adoption of the Hohenwart program would actually represent a preliminary step toward the realization of his plans. That this belief turned out to be an error of great and fateful proportions is unquestionable. The Hohenwart program which, after a month of secret negotiations, was finally exposed to public derision, contempt, and opposition of the Magyar and the German Liberals, was indeed a poor product of statesmanship. It consisted chiefly of four documents: first, the imperial rescript of September 12, 1871, addressed to the Bohemian diet and inviting it to draft a constitutional charter in line with the specific "constitutional position of the Bohemian crown" and its "power and splendor," as well as with the obligations of the imperial crown to other parts of the realm, and above all, of course, obligations based on the Compromise of 1867. The second and main document, negotiated between Schäffle and the Old Czech leaders, and adopted unanimously by the Bohemian diet, was the constitutional charter itself, the so-called "fundamental articles" (*Fundamentalartikel*). Lastly, a "nationality bill" and a new franchise bill were accepted by the diet as corollaries to the Fundamental Articles.[72]

The Fundamental Articles recognized, at least formally, the validity of the Compromise of 1867, but they proposed changes of the constitutional position of the Bohemian lands which implied a reorganization of Cisleithanian Austria as a whole. Bohemia was no longer to send deputies to an Austrian parliament, but merely was to send representatives of the Bohemian diet to a congress of delegations of the various Austrian crownland diets, whose function was to be confined in the main to matters of commerce, communications, currency questions, and control of public debts. An Austrian senate, somewhat similar in composition to the existing house of lords, was to function in matters concerning state treaties, jurisdictional conflicts in the administrative and legislative sphere, and constitutional revisions. Otherwise, Bohemia's autonomy, to be established under a Bohemian court chancellery and coordinated with the Cisleithanian government in Vienna, was to correspond to that of Hungary according to the terms of the Compromise of 1867.

These constitutional changes were to be adopted by a joint Bohemian general diet consisting of the representatives of Bohemia, Moravia, and Silesia. Yet so clearly was the privileged Bohemian position established in the draft of the Fundamental Articles that the Moravian diet acceded to them only with important reservations, which stressed the legal equality of Bohemian and Moravian legislative and administrative institutions. The Silesian diet rejected outright the proposed establishment of a super-diet of all the Bohemian lands.[73]

This charter corrected scarcely any of the basic deficiencies of the Compromise of 1867. Instead, it added new ones by immensely complicating the Austrian constitutional setup and permeating it with the reactionary spirit of the traditional historic, semi-federal program. Far from endorsing a Bohemian diet reform following Schäffle's democratic principles, the new draft of a Bohemian franchise, though adjusting the national inequality between Czech and German status, did little to change the unjust social position of the old Estates order.

Admittedly, the third part of the Hohenwart legislation, the draft of a nationality law for Bohemia aiming at a conciliation of the Germans with the Fundamental Articles, was a far more liberal and sensible document. Its provisions actually honored the promise it made, namely, to put the members of the two Bohemian nationalities, as individuals, on a footing of complete equality. An administrative organization was proposed which would carve out administrative areas which would be nationally homogeneous, as far as possible, yet the use of the second national language was recognized in official public intercourse, if spoken as the native language by at least one fifth of the population. Complete equality of both languages was to be practiced by the government in any administrative functions concerning the entire crownland. Important and salutary was the provision that the appointment of judges and other officials with academic training should be made dependent upon their command of both national languages. The Bohemian diet itself was to be divided into two national curias. Separate budgets concerning cultural expenditures of both national groups were to be set up, in particular for educational institutions. Adequate arrangements were proposed in the order of procedure of the diet to prevent the complete overruling of the interests of the minority in national questions.

This bill made a concession to the Czech viewpoint in only one major point, the piecemeal introduction of the requirement of bilingual training for the civil service. Thus, the generally bilingual Czech intelligentsia obviously gained a chance to get a fairer share of representation within the overwhelmingly German bureaucracy, which was still steadfastly opposed to learning the Czech language. On the other hand, concessions made to the Germans were far-reaching. The setup of national budgets in cultural questions was to reduce considerably the financial burden of the economically stronger German population and correspondingly to increase the Czech obligations.[74] Even more advantageous to the Germans was the proposed separation of the diet into two national curias. This, indeed, appeared to be the first step toward achieving the basic German demand for administrative partition of Bohemia into a Czech and a German part, a claim bitterly opposed by the Czechs, who stood unanimously for the indivisibility of the territories of the Bohemian crown. It must be recognized as proof of the spirit of Czech national tolerance that the Bohemian as well as the Moravian diet unanimously passed this proposed nationality law with the other bills on the proposed Czech-German compromise.

Its acceptance, however, could not save the Hohenwart cabinet. Failure of the Old Czech party to reorganize the Bohemian lands within Austria, and with them Austria herself, on the basis of the conservative-corporate crownland federalism and failure on the part of the Liberal Germans to recognize the nationality bill as a basis for a compromise were equally responsible for the collapse of Hohenwart's policy. Yet they were not solely, and perhaps not even chiefly, responsible. In spite of all internal opposition within Austria, the prime minister's position was strong.

Count Hohenwart had dissolved the central parliament in Vienna, as well as eight crownland diets. By means of rather dubious devices, particularly the use of gentle influence on the big Estate owners in the crownlands and an extension of franchise in districts where an increase of votes supporting the government was to be expected, the prime minister had a good chance of bringing about the election of a parliament and diets with a federalist Conservative instead of a centralistic-bourgeois-Liberal majority.[75] Furthermore, and even more important, he was backed by the firm support of the influential court circles and, above all, of the crown itself. He certainly had no reason to fear the opposition of the German Liberals and the demonstrations of national rabble rousers in Vienna—usually with university students foremost among them. Full Czech support for the new order in Bohemia was gained by the tenth of October, 1871, and a parliamentary majority to back the program in the central parliament was secured. The emperor, with the promulgation of the September rescript, had practically pledged himself to support the program. Yet by October 20, he refused, in a new rescript, imperial sanction of the Fundamental Articles and a week later the federalistic cabinet was out of office.[76]

Two main reasons are usually given for this sudden and complete change in the imperial political course—strong German and Magyar objections, the former voiced by Count Beust, the minister of foreign affairs with the title of imperial chancellor, the latter by the Magyar prime minister, who was soon to be Beust's successor, Count Andrássy. Greater stress is usually laid on Andrássy's opposition, voiced in the imperial council of ministers, against those provisions of the Fundamental Articles which were incompatible with the Austro-Hungarian Compromise of 1867. Andrássy particularly objected to a changed procedure of electing the delegations, the transformation of the house of lords into a senate, the reduction of the status of the Austrian central parliament to a mere congress of delegations, in short, to a federalization of Austria in whatever form.[77]

There is no point here in going into the legal technicalities of Andrássy's argumentation, whether the Fundamental Articles violated the letter of the Compromise of 1867 based on the "indivisibility and inseparability" of the Cisleithanian lands.[78] It was obvious, anyway, that the Fundamental Articles clearly ran counter to the spirit of the compromise, which was based on German supremacy in Austria, as well as on Magyar supremacy in Hungary. Furthermore, it was clear that the real reason for Andrássy's objections was not the technical flaws in the Hohenwart proposals, but, from his standpoint, the not unjustified fear that any step toward federalization of Austria might lead to similar demands by the non-Magyar nationalities in Hungary. The view that Andrássy was chiefly responsible for the breakdown of the Hohenwart program was further supported by the fact that less than two weeks after the downfall of the Hohenwart cabinet the emperor dismissed Beust and made Andrássy, now entirely victorious, his successor.

Yet against such reasoning stands the fact that Howenwart, Schäffle, and the emperor could be reasonably certain, before they started on the federal course, that a federalization program introduced in any form in Austria probably would lead to conflict with the Hungarian cabinet. In fact, as previously pointed out, it was one of Schäffle's main aims, by means of the Fundamental Articles, to bypass the compromise and to force Hungary into a position where she would have to accede to a reorganization of the empire. It is unlikely that the emperor's cabinet would have yielded practically without a struggle to a Magyar attack they were prepared to meet.

It is fairly certain that the government took the weaker opposition of the Austro-German Liberals even more lightly. Yet it was German opposition, though opposition from beyond the frontiers, which in all probability brought the Hohenwart plan to naught. The chief support of this thesis rests in Count Beust's policy, succinctly expressed in his letter of October 13, 1871, to the emperor. The Saxon Beust, as the Swabian Schäffle, was strongly anti-Prussian in sympathy and basically antagonistic to the creation of the German empire of January, 1871, which he perceived as an enlarged Prussia. Thus, in the beginning of the pro-Slav Hohenwart regime, that is, before the conclusion of the Peace of Frankfurt of May 10, 1871, Beust was by no means opposed to the Austrian prime minister's program,[79] which fitted well into his own anti-Prussian and pro-French foreign policy. The unexpectedly complete victory of Prussia-Germany in the war of 1870–71, which ruled out forever the hope nourished in court

circles of a "revenge for Sadova," forced him to change his political
course gradually. He realized that, in view of the changed balance
of power in Europe, an anti-German policy was henceforth too dangerous, and he slowly adjusted his views in internal policies accordingly.

In the letter to the emperor, mentioned previously, Beust referred
first to the Magyar objections to the Hohenwart program, yet, continuing, he particularly stresses the danger involved in arousing angry
German opposition in Austria, and states in this context:

With a truly terrific speed has the constitutional party [the *Verfassungs-
partei,* that is, in the main the German Liberals] converted itself into a
German national party. The ties which join this party, through the feeling
of national, linguistic, and historic community to Germany-Prussia, daily
grow stronger. Even now a popular meeting recently held in Dresden has
proved that right next to our frontiers the national movements of the
Germans in Austria are followed with the closest attention. One is only too
ready to hear calls for help and support even before they are raised. It
must not be assumed that an authoritative character can be attributed to
these demonstrations. . . . They have to be taken no less seriously, nevertheless. They are only the precursors of a revolution which one is well ad-
vised to keep before one's eye.[80]

Beust's warning to heed the danger of possible German intervention probably impressed the emperor all the more since the new
German emperor, William I, in a meeting with Emperor Francis
Joseph in Ischl, had already administered a warning to him, couched
in diplomatic language, that he did not want to be embarrassed by the
"turning of the Germans in Austria" toward Germany.[81] Perhaps the
most convincing evidence that the emperor really heeded Beust's
warning is that he was dismissed after Hohenwart's fall as the former
initiator of an anti-German policy. Indeed since 1866 Beust had always been considered a definite, though inadequate, antagonist of
Bismarck's policy.

The same sentiments were even more clearly expressed in the
letters by the old Liberal statesman Ignaz von Plener, who, as early
as 1869, had voiced the opinion that the indignation of the Germans in
Bohemia would lead to the loss of the German Austrian crownlands to Prussia-Germany, whereas Czech sulking seemed to him far
less dangerous.[82]

It is, indeed, true that the actual Czech reaction to the betrayal of the September rescript, violent as it was, could not compare with the possibilities implied in a potential unloosing of a *furor Teutonicus* from the outside backed by a German irredenta within the country. The Czechs protested, abstained from further participation in the parliament until the Taaffe era, and Rieger declared that the Czechs had lost a great battle, implying in no uncertain terms that they were not only defeated by German nationalism but betrayed by the crown itself. Consequently, this political leader, who had so easily succumbed to Feudal-Conservative leadership and had involuntarily weakened the cause of the Slav nationalities in Austria for the sake of the narrow privileges of the Bohemian *Staatsrecht* [83] was not destined to lead in future the cause of Czech nationalism. The outcome of the Hohenwart experiment struck the death knell for the Old Czech cause and their outdated notion of the Czech national idea.

On the other hand, though government in Austria passed again to the German Liberals, they had no reason to be jubilant. Their narrow understanding of the Austrian national problem, their clinging to the Compromise of 1867, and their submission to Magyar wishes were long steps leading to the gradual disintegration of the empire, a disintegration which was, in its final outcome, more ominous to them than to any other national group. Yet even in its immediate aspects the only consequence of their policy was the rise of a far more intransigent Slav nationalism than the one they had to deal with previously. Not the Magyars and the Germans, but the Magyar ruling classes and the second German Empire were the real victors in this conflict, Germany to a far greater degree than Magyar Hungary. While the Magyars had only succeeded in warding off an attack against the compromise, imperial Germany had taken a long step toward bringing the Danube monarchy into her political orbit. She had clearly shown, though still with the reserve often employed in Bismarck's diplomacy, that a deviation of Austria from the dualistic course to the federalistic reorganization would be resisted not merely by Magyars but by the power of the *Reich*. Henceforth, to an Austria weakened by permanent national struggle within, Germany meant to be the "protector," the bulwark against Russian Pan-Slavism. Austria had moved closer to the future alliance of the First World War, concluded in 1879, but actually initiated in 1871.[84]

All things considered, the Hohenwart program, the last, deficient and incomplete federalization plan offered by an Austrian peacetime cabinet, failed as much because of its intentions to achieve national reconciliation as because of its shortcomings. However, the government cannot be absolved of a very great share of responsibility for these shortcomings. In this respect, Sieghart succinctly summarizes the basic reasons for the failure of 1871.

Austria could no longer stand a federalism based on the crownlands or groups of crownlands. The crownlands had grown too closely together and they were nationally not sufficiently homogeneous. The concept of the "political nation" had for a long time been replaced in the minds of the Austrian peoples by the concept of the "ethnic nation." The German in the Sudetenlands [that is Bohemia, Moravia, Silesia] no longer considered himself as Bohemian, and the feeling of common citizenship between the Germans in the Alpine and Sudetenlands was strong enough to prevent the "mediatization" of the nation through intermediate Powers, the historicopolitical entities. It was strong enough to prevent the dismemberment of the nation through crownland frontiers.

If the crownland federalism could have been enforced by an act of the crown—those were the wishes of the Czechs—it could not have lasted long anyway. It would not have been a real solution of the national problem. The Germans in the Sudetenlands, as well as the Ruthenians, the Yugoslavs, the Italians, and others, would have opposed it continually. This opposition would soon enough have had the Germans in the hereditary lands on their side, and thereby it would have gained a decisive majority. Therefore, federalism was not wrecked by the Hungarian veto alone.[85]

One may add, not even by the Magyar and Austro-German Liberal veto combined. Austria's reform policy had to pay the bill for the empire's defeat in the fight for supremacy in Germany.

### THE INSTITUTIONAL EVOLUTION OF THE NATIONAL CONFLICT

A review of the Czech national position within the Austrian Empire in the last hundred years of its existence as discussed thus far might lead to the following broad conclusion: The pre-March period and the brief revolutionary era, the times in which the Czech national renaissance reaped a brilliant cultural and ideological harvest, may easily be called the most fruitful period since the days of Comenius in the seventeenth century. The era from the suppression of the revolution to the downfall of Hohenwart represents a marked slump in the political, though not in the cultural, evolution of the Czech people. Yet in a way this period, characterized by the decay of the idea of the Bohemian *Staatsrecht* in its conservative social form, already paves the way for the deep democratic penetration of the whole Czech national body which evolved victoriously in 1918.

Far more in the limelight of the political issues of the day, far more discussed in political literature than the preceding periods combined, was the third, from 1871 leading to the First World War. Yet for some thirty years until the turn of the twentieth century and the rise of Masaryk's "Realist party," this era appeared to students of the national conflict as the most sterile in recent Czech history. It is the period when the Bohemian *Staatsrecht* as an exclusive political program was already dead, yet could not be formally abandoned for lack of a truly national democratic goal attainable within the framework of the empire. It is the era in which radical nationalism superseded the *Staatsrecht* program in its conservative form, largely by sheer force of greater emotional vigor rather than by new and keener perspectives of the Czech national destiny. Thus, the lack of a modern national program of comprehensive scope, far more than practical considerations of Czech and German nationalism, focused emotions on the narrow battleground of the language problem. Historians as hostile to the institutions of the empire as to the empire itself have considered this struggle completely sterile, if not destructive, and have disregarded its possible contribution to the multinational area problem.

It is true that none of the often fairly satisfactory provisions concerned with the settlement of the national-language issue contributed to the actual solution of the Czech-German conflict itself. In many ways, the language struggle was only a symptom of the deeply rooted enmity between Czech and German nationalism. Their conciliation would have made the settlement of the language problem, which seemed very intricate, a matter of secondary importance; their continued feud and the blocking of Czech political emancipation within the empire would have doomed a technically exemplary language law to political insignificance.

These facts, however, do not diminish the importance of the problem itself. The perpetuation of the dreary Czech-German language conflict was representative of the language conflicts of all the Austrian nationalities and, thus, of an important problem of Austrian history. Much practical experience, as well as theoretical insight into the handling of the problem of multinational areas in the future, was gained in this struggle, above all on the main battleground in Bohemia.[86]

From the 1870s onward, and especially from the beginnings of the Taaffe era (1879) and the subsequent return of the Czech deputies to the parliament in Vienna, the language question became the main issue of official Czech policy. Its discussion demands the analysis of a few basic technical concepts which were differently interpreted by the feuding German and Czech nationalities. The Czech doctrine was based rigidly on the indivisibility of the Bohemian lands as a separate unit in the Austrian Empire,[87] the German doctrine on complete, or at least far-reaching, administrative separation of the German from the Czech territories. Thus, the problem of binational administration would be confined to those very mixed districts where an administrative partition between Germans and Czechs proved to be impossible. Yet, as long as such an administrative partition could not be achieved, the Germans, holding to the letter of the Dualistic Compromise of 1867 and the Austrian constitution of the same year, maintained that Austria was a supranational entity, the national character of her crownlands not being recognized by law. Consequently, the central administration, not only of Austria but of any of her crownlands, was to act in the traditional spirit of centralism and to speak its traditional language, German.[88]

Technically, the Czech viewpoint represented a strictly traditional concept, too, that of the Bohemian *Staatsrecht*. Indeed, the basic differences between the Old and the Young Czech programs and even, to some extent, Masaryk's Realism do not consist in fundamental disagreement on the question of the indivisibility of the Bohemian lands as implied in the *Staatsrecht*. The basic differences between the older and the newer forces of Czech nationalism rest, above all, on the different approach to the social content of the constitutional order within the Bohemian lands, old Estates order here and democracy there. The gradual transformation from the one to the other dominates Czech national policy from Palacký to Masaryk, as illustrated in the language conflict.

## Autonomy

In theory and in practice the greatest significance of the language reform is the fact that two basic concepts of empire reform plans, the principles of territorial and of personal autonomy, evolve and clash here.

Both may well be subordinated to a general legal concept of autonomy as "the legal sufficiency of a social body and its actual independence," at least in certain fields of general administration.[89] Yet disagreement commences immediately in the political sphere. Redlich goes to the core of the problem, as far as it came up in the struggle between German centralism and Slav nationalism. To the Germans, autonomy meant the legal principle of self-administration itself, as exercised in *Kreis*, district, and municipal administration. To Czechs, Poles, and other Slav nationalities, it meant the right to statehood as embodied in the claims to the Bohemian *Staatsrecht*, the Polish national kingdom, and so on.[90] The fact that technically the German viewpoint was legally correct was considered somewhat beside the point in a chiefly political conflict.

Closely connected with this basic conflict on the autonomy principle itself is the controversy on the principal forms of autonomy relevant to the national problem, usually referred to as national autonomy. This national autonomy may amount to an almost complete form of self-administration or more often it may be confined to affairs of particular concern to national feelings. Such "cultural autonomy" usually comprises matters of education, general cultural activities, problems of taxation in all these fields, and language regulations in general.

In either form, national autonomy may appear as "territorial" or as "personal" autonomy. Territorial autonomy means the self-administration granted to a certain territory, whereby every individual residing there partakes of the privileges and rights deriving from such autonomous status. This type of national autonomy may work well, indeed, in areas which are nationally fairly homogeneous. If it is granted in affairs of particular national concern, such as cultural autonomy, the whole population of a nationally homogeneous territory will benefit equally from it. Yet, if this territorial autonomy is vested in a nationally unhomogeneous territory having a strong national minority without adequate minority protection, then only the national rights of the majority are safeguarded. According to Renner, territorial autonomy, if imposed upon a nationally unhomogeneous area, means, "if you live on my territory, then you are subjected to my rule, my law, and my language. It is the expression of domination, not of equality, the expression of force and not of right." [91]

Personal autonomy, due to its capacity to determine more accurately the status of the individual, is sometimes also called genuine or real autonomy. It is that form of autonomy in which, according to the personal or personality principle, the autonomous status applies to the individual as such, not to the territory. Thus, it does not refer indiscriminately to persons residing in a certain area, but in matters of specific national concern to those individuals whose national status makes them members of a recognized national corporate body. Such status is accorded to individuals in various ways, either on the basis of their own declaration in the form of national registration, government ordinances, or court decisions based on definite characteristics of native language, origin, place of birth, residence, and so forth. Several of these devices may be combined. Yet in all of them the determination of national status is based, not on the alleged or actual national character of an area, but on that of a person, hence the terms "personal" principle and "personal" autonomy.[92]

Obviously, the introduction of the principle of personal autonomy does greater justice to the rights of minorities in a nationally unhomogeneous area. It is equally obvious that the grant of cultural or of any more sweeping or narrower form of autonomy is applicable both to personal and to territorial autonomy. It is certain, however, that institutions of personal autonomy applying, not to a definite, narrowly limited area, but to all the often widely dispersed individuals of a national group within a province or even a state, are necessarily more complex than the institutions of territorial autonomy. It may well be said, though, that much more intricate as these institutions of personal autonomy are in the nationally unhomogeneous area than are those of territorial autonomy, they are more just from the purely national viewpoint.

The entire problem had a direct and most important effect on the Czech-German conflict in Bohemia. In terms of the concepts discussed above, the basic issue presented itself as follows.

Should territorial autonomy be introduced in the form compatible with the Czech doctrine of the Bohemian *Staatsrecht?* That meant local self-administration without national administrative partition. In accordance with German claims, should territorial autonomy grant and assure the rights of local majorities by means of administrative national partition? Should further German claims for national protection in mixed territories be complied with by means of personal autonomy? In other words, should a twofold German and Czech administration in cultural affairs be established on a per capita basis in these districts? [93] All these issues are again reflected in the national conflict focused on the language problem.

## The Languages of the Land

The interrelations between autonomy and the language problem are thus presented by Sieghart.

The legal regulation . . . of the language question may be based on different foundations—on the idea of the personality principle or on the idea of the territorial principle. Concerning the first principle, language rights are connected with the individual, and the use of the language is dependent on the association of the individual with either one of the two languages of the land. The premise concerning the other principle is that a language of the land is generally spoken in a strictly limited area of the land. Here the doctrine applies: *Locus regit actum.* [The place determines the law to be applied].[94]

These basic issues reflect specifically on the analysis of the terms *Landessprache* (language of the land) and *Landesübliche Sprache* (language customary in the land or spoken in the land by custom) as they appear in the meager Magna Charta of Austrian nationality rights, Article XIX of the constitutional law, No. 142, of December 21, 1867.[95]

Austrian Cisleithanian languages of the land, according to the general interpretation of this article, were Croat (Serbo-Croat), Czech, German, Italian, Polish, Rumanian, Ruthenian, and Slovene. These were the languages spoken by the recognized nationalities represented in substantial proportion in any crownland (as usually determined, by at least 20 percent of the population there). To be sure, German centralism frequently claimed successfully that German was the language of the land even in the crownlands, where the Germans represented only a very small percentage of the population.[96] In regard to Bohemia, Moravia, and Silesia, German claims for recognition of their language as *Landessprache* (language of the land) were, however, rightly uncontested.

According to the census of 1880, the first fully official nationality census taken in Austria, the ratio between Czechs and Germans was 63:37 in Bohemia and 70:30 in Moravia, where as in Silesia 48 percent of the population was German, some 28 percent, Polish, and nearly 23 percent, Czech. Thus, Czech and German were the only languages of the land (*Landessprachen*) in Bohemia and Moravia, while in Silesia, Polish was recognized as the third language.

In deciding which language should find official recognition in a certain district in intercourse with the administration, public education, cultural activities, and so forth, the second concept evolved —the *landesübliche Sprache,* or the language customary in the land. Although there never was any substantial disagreement among the conflicting nationalities on the meaning of the term "language of the land," the concept "language spoken in the land by custom" was vigorously contested. According to the Czech viewpoint, the language of the land and the language spoken in the land by custom were practically the same. The Germans argued that if the law used two different terms, this obviously meant two different concepts, and they were supported in that view by decisions of the highest courts. The language customary in the land, they argued, did not refer to whether a language was spoken by a substantial proportion of the population of the whole crownland. According to their claims, it applied to a language of the land in its qualification as the predominant language of a certain *Kreis,* district, or municipality. Consequently, Czech, though certainly the language of the land, obviously was not the language spoken by custom in every part of the land. It was not customary, not *landesüblich,* in all parts of the lands.

This distinction was of great practical significance. The Czech viewpoint held that the languages of the land were recognized as such in all parts of the land and therefore administrative partition of Bohemia, Moravia, and Silesia was unnecessary. This interpretation, therefore, strongly supported the doctrine of the indivisibility of the Bohemian lands on the basis of territorial autonomy. The German theory, on the other hand, ultimately worked for a partition along ethnic lines in national homogeneous areas and—by implication— for personal autonomy in nationally mixed districts.

The geographic conditions of Bohemia certainly did not favor a complete administrative partition, and political conditions practically forbade it. Thus, the Germans hoped for such a national division, at least in the lower administrative units of *Kreis,* districts, and municipalities. In itself, the German legal interpretation of the term *landesüblich* (customary in the land) was not unjustified. It must be admitted, also, that as long as no solution of the national problem in the empire in general, and in Bohemia specifically, could be achieved, there was much to be said for the German proposal to separate, as far as possible by means of law and administrative or-dinances, Czech and German districts and to confine the national struggle to the nationally mixed districts. Undoubtedly, however, the Germans would have had a far stronger moral position had they upheld the same principle in those crownlands which had a German majority and a considerable Slav minority—specifically, in Styria. Here, the Germans were strongly opposed to administrative parti-tion. They proved to be far more intolerant than the Czechs in Bo-hemia by strongly opposing the recognition of the Slovene language as the second language of the land throughout Styria.[97]

Irrespective of its legal merits, the Czech approach to the problem, that is, the complete equality of both languages in the indivisible lands of the Bohemian crown, was not illiberal in theory. However, the basically fair Czech approach to the language problem often strongly conflicted in practice with the claim for the recognition of the ancient Czech tradition and inherent nature of the Bohemian lands. Unless the empire as a whole were reorganized according to the principle of complete equality of all recognized nationalities and national languages in mixed as well as in nationally homogeneous territories, the Germans in Bohemia and Moravia would still have held the status of a mere minority, well protected, but, as a corporate body, still not equal to the Czechs.

Clearly, the way out of this dilemma was the introduction of cultural autonomy, preferably following the principle of personal autonomy, not only in the limited area where it worked exclusively to German advantage but in all parts of the empire, where the Ger-mans opposed extensive reforms more strongly than did any other nationality. To be sure, such policies of narrow national self-interest in a limited area, which disregarded national interrelations in the empire as a whole, were not confined to the Germans. Other national groups also employed different legal and moral codes in territories where they were national majorities than they did in territories where they were mere minorities. The point is, however, that by force of historic tradition and geographic distribution, no other nationality had as good an opportunity to employ these tactics as the Germans had.

It speaks as well for the degree of Czech national tolerance as it does for the merits of the institutions of cultural national autonomy that, in spite of all discriminating national politics, some progress toward a German-Czech understanding was made in the cultural field. Separate Czech and German boards of education were organized. Nationally separated agricultural advisory boards followed. The former were to be organized on a preliminary and incomplete basis in 1873; both types of nationally separated agencies were established permanently in 1890.[98] Furthermore, the ever-increasing development of Czech cultural life, leading to the foundation of the Czech University in Prague in 1882, followed by the organization of other Czech institutions for the pursuit of cultural activities, dealt in an effective way with important factors of national friction. Thus, national tension was somewhat modified. After all, it was realized that national demands regarding cultural affairs could to some extent be satisfied, or at least appeased, by the use of greater appropriations for national institutions of both nationalities. This held true particularly as long as it was economically possible to absorb all the Czech and German intelligentsia into the labor market.

The question of the language of administration was the permanent, unhealed wound of the national struggle, completely untouched by the salutary effects of state spending for national purposes. Unquestionably, an issue of actual power was involved here, the problem of whether the Czechs, the Germans, or the centralistic empire organization, that is, in a different way the Germans again, were to be masters in the Bohemian lands. But even more important than practical problems, which, after all, affected only a small number of the sphere of human activities, was the burning question of national prestige connected with that issue.

To comprehend this problem in its broadest aspects, it is necessary to examine the concept of the *Amtssprache*, that is, the language used by the government authorities. Three main subdivisions of the official language concept should be distinguished: first, the so-called external language, that is, the language in which the government communicated with the parties concerned and with the public in general; second, the internal official language, "the language used by the authorities for the handling of all affairs, not intended to be communicated to the parties, as well as the language in which

the officials of a government board communicate with each other";
and, third, the so-called innermost official language, or language of
official correspondence, that is, the language in which government
authorities communicate with other government boards, particularly
with the higher authorities, the supreme crownland administration,
and the central imperial government.[99]

The struggle over each of these language concepts presents a decidedly different aspect. The first one, the problem of communication between the government authority and the public, most urgently
demanded some kind of solution. Obviously, no government could
function if the people did not or, as was often the case in the multinational areas of Austria, pretended not to understand the language
used by the government. Two principal solutions were suggested:
the bilingual government board, on the one hand (the Czech viewpoint), and strictest division of the land into nationally homogeneous
administrative units, on the other (the German viewpoint). The second
and third concepts of the inner and innermost official language obviously touched a far deeper problem than the first, the solution of
which was largely a question of essential administrative expediency.

Preservation of German as the inner and innermost official language
in the whole administration of Cisleithanian Austria was one of the
basic features, perhaps the basic feature, of the centralistic system
itself.[100] The Czech demand to replace it, at least in Bohemia, by the
Czech language as the inner official language raised the problem of
required bilingual training of state officials. This practically meant
the training of Germans in the Czech language, since, as pointed out
previously, in contrast to the Czechs the majority of educated Germans in Bohemia did not know and refused to learn the second national language.[101] Beyond that, the Czech claim for recognition of
their language as the innermost official language raised the problem
of the continued existence of the centralistic system itself.

THE DEVELOPMENT OF THE LANGUAGE CONFLICT, 1879–1909

*From Taaffe to Badeni*

The first comprehensive regulation of the language question for
Bohemia and Moravia in the constitutional era was issued in 1880
under the Taaffe cabinet, a short time after the return of the Czech
deputies to the central parliament.[102] This so-called "Stremayr ordinance," named after the minister of justice in the Taaffe ministry,

recognized the Czech claim that both national languages were languages of the land, as well as languages customary in both lands. Consequently, it prescribed intercourse of the government authorities with the parties concerned in either language requested by them. The inner and innermost official language remained German. The following period, from 1880 to 1897, was characterized in many ways by a vigorous rise of Czech nationalism, which helped to strengthen the Czech national position within the empire. German attempts to solve the language problem once and for all by recognition of German as the official language of government authorities within the whole of Cisleithanian Austria and persistent claims for the national partition of Bohemia were rejected by Slav opposition in parliament.[103]

The stiffening of Czech nationalism was readily confirmed in political party life. In the elections of 1889 for the Bohemian diet, the Young Czechs for the first time outnumbered the Old Czech-Conservative coalition. In the parliamentary election of 1891, they already secured more than three times as many parliamentary seats as did the old party. The political death of the old Czechs—which represented a significant parallel to the supersession of the old Liberals by the more radical German groups in the same era [104]—was therewith sealed. It was one of the gravest blunders of Count Taaffe's policy that he not recognize this rather obvious political fact. In 1890 Taaffe succeeded in bringing Germans and Czechs together in a conference to again work on a language compromise. The progress of the conference and the final agreement appeared satisfactory beyond expectations. The previously mentioned partition of the boards of education and the agricultural advisory boards, the principal point of compromise ever to materialize, was agreed upon. It was further decided that a definite minimum quota of forty children of a national minority in any district was entitled to a national primary school of its own. National demarcations of the court districts were arranged, and the organization of national curias in the Bohemian diet was agreed upon. While the agreement met the Czech demands in specific points—constitution of a Czech chamber of commerce, Czech majority in the agricultural boards, and so forth—it also went far toward satisfying German wishes for national partition of the Crownland administration. Unquestionably, the pact of 1890 represented a true compromise.[105]

Indeed, it had only one, though cardinal, shortcoming. To make things easier, Taaffe had preferred to arrange the negotiations between the Germans and the decaying Old Czech party alone, rather than to invite the increasingly powerful Young Czech party also. The latter, not bound by the agreement, raised violent objections to the alleged national partition of Bohemia, and radical German nationalism on its part was pleased, too, to see the compromise wrecked. Each party accused the other of having gone back on its word; the compromise failed to pass the diet, and the national struggle continued with increased fury. Clashes between German and Czech nationalists forced the government in 1893, for the first time since Windischgrätz's days, to impose martial law on Prague.

The next major step in the language question proved to be decisive and fatal for the further course of Czech-German relations as, indeed, of Austrian parliamentary life in general. In 1895, a Polish aristocrat, Count Badeni, was appointed prime minister, and his cabinet of moderate Slav leaning, though not without substantial German representation, made a new attempt to solve the Bohemian and Moravian language problem. Badeni's language ordinances of 1897 made some significant concessions to the Czechs. For the first time Czech was introduced in Bohemia and in Moravia as the official "inner" and "innermost" language on an equal footing with German, though this extension of Czech language rights was still restricted to certain fields of administration under the control of the ministries of the interior, finance, commerce, agriculture, and justice. Furthermore, in accordance with Czech wishes, the Badeni decrees implied the administrative indivisibility of Bohemia and Moravia and strictly rejected any form of administrative national partition. As a logical consequence of these principles, Czech and German were considered languages of equal status in every part of Bohemia and Moravia. Accordingly, Badeni required any state official in these crownlands to prove his command of both national languages in speaking and in writing by the first of July, 1901; that meant within four years' time.

Basically, none of these provisions were unjust. Yet though the request for the use of Czech as the inner official language was fair in itself, it certainly was not entirely compatible with the administrative procedure of German centralism. Badeni, however, could have put forth a strong argument if he had asserted that the German centralistic system was not compatible with the preservation of the Austrian Empire and that if a comprehensive solution proved to be impossible he had to have recourse to regional solutions. More serious was the objection that a regulation as important as Badeni's language provisions should not have been issued merely as decrees, but in the form of a comprehensive language law subject to parliamentary approval. Yet undoubtedly, as the ordinances referred only to two crownlands, Badeni still acted technically within the limits of the law.

His grave mistake was that he permitted himself to be provoked by the blind fury of the German opposition. For six months, German obstruction raged in the parliament in Vienna, accompanied by noisy street demonstrations in the German parts of Bohemia. Pan-Germans and Liberals alike, not yet joined, however, by Christian Socials and Socialists, frustrated any attempt by the government to proceed with even the most essential legislative work. At this point Badeni succumbed to the inducement to achieve his justified aims by breaking the rules of parliamentary procedure. By undoubtedly dubious means, the Slav-Conservative majority passed a bill changing the standing order of the lower house of parliament, which enabled the speaker, at that time a member of the Polish *Szlachta*, to exclude members from the assembly on his own decision. Should a member decline to leave the house, the speaker was authorized to have him expelled by the police. The events that followed the passage of this revised standing order had no precedent anywhere in the history of Austrian parliamentarism. There were concerted attacks of the German Nationals and Liberals—joined now by Christian Socials and Socialists. Actual battles developed between Germans, Czechs, and Poles; the police marched into the house and violently dragged out resisting deputies. Mass demonstration occurred in the streets of Vienna and other German cities. The movement, led by the intelligentsia, particularly by nationalist university students, spread tremendously; the workers were aroused and assailed the regime, not as anti-German, but as antiparliamentarian. At the point when the opposition against Badeni fell little short of truly revolutionary proportions, the emperor, as in the case of Hohenwart's attempt, again yielded to the pressure of German opposition and dismissed Badeni. Thenceforward, German obstruction was replaced by Czech obstruction of a less violent, though far more permanent, character, lasting, in fact, until the end of the empire itself.[106]

These, however, were only the external consequences of Badeni's

failure. More serious than the symptoms were the causes of the ail-
ments. In the first place, it became evident how much more embittered
national feeling had become on both the German and the Czech
side. It became clear, also, how far beyond the bounds of reason national feeling had grown, if two language decrees, not unsound in
their main principles and practically of limited implications, could
create an almost revolutionary situation. Secondly, Badeni's fall
showed how weak and unstable the foundations of the Austrian constitutional system were. The government had proved its inability to
put through nationality legislation by way of regular parliamentary
procedure. The parliament, discredited in the eyes of the Austrian
public and of the world by the continuous national obstructions and
scandals, was unable to distinguish between comprehensive state and
national interests. Unable to agree on the national questions, it was
unwilling to agree on, or frequently even to enter into, a discussion
of vital economic and social affairs of the state. After Badeni's fall,
parliament was intermittently adjourned by successive ministries,
who ruled increasingly, and without great scruples, by administrative
ordinances.

The full seriousness of this development is illustrated by a comparison of Badeni's policy with that of Hohenwart twenty-six years
earlier. In both cases a Conservative statesman of federalist leanings
had failed to realize an idea sound in itself, the reorganization of the
German centralist system in favor of the Slavs. A basic reason for the
ultimate failure in both cases rested in the fact that Hohenwart, as
well as Badeni, tried to pursue a policy of national conciliation, in
general with the support of the Right, representing relatively small
curias of vested interests, whereas the deputies opposed to the government were elected by a majority of voters including the lowest in-
come groups.[107]

Badeni had the same basic inherent tendency as Hohenwart to introduce reforms from above rather than to go through the grind of
regular parliamentary procedure. Consequently, his high-handed way
of treating parliament proved to be his undoing. On the other hand,
his proposals, far more reasonable than Hohenwart's, could never
have been passed by an unenlightened parliament substituting nationalist obstruction for majority decision. On the whole, Badeni's
failure thus proved to be far more serious than Hohenwart's. The
latter's downfall exposed the fact that the Austrian conservative sys-

tem and the pressure of factors of foreign policy prevented a solution of the Austrian nationality problem. Badeni's failure did not disprove the continued existence of any of these reasons, yet it added another even more ominous one—the inability of Austrian parliamentarianism, torn by internal nationality strife, to solve the national problem.

## From Badeni to Masaryk

After Badeni's fall, hopes for a settlement of the Czech-German language conflict were doomed to failure. Czech-German antagonism had deepened so much that a further compromise on the language question, though not impossible, was unlikely in itself to dispel the deepening national friction.

Badeni's successor as prime minister, Baron Gautsch, had to change his course to revise the Badeni decrees. In his new ordinances of 1898 he initiated a territorial language policy, which provided different regulations for Czech, for nationally mixed, and for German territories and confined the operation of the Badeni ordinances in principle to the Czech and mixed districts. He also modified Badeni's directives regarding the bilingual training of state officials in Bohemia and in Moravia, by making the general linguistic requirements dependent on the requirements of specific government positions. Though the Gautsch ordinances actually changed the Badeni decrees only slightly, they presented a clear sign that the tide of the national conflict was turning again in favor of the Germans. In the following year, 1899, the aggressive German national Whitsuntide program was issued, and the new Clary cabinet obligingly met its demands to the extent of restoring the language regulations as they had existed prior to Badeni's regime, that is, from 1880 on.

In 1900 and again in 1903 the government, under the direction of the capable prime minister, von Körber, renewed the attempt for a national compromise. Körber elaborated the setup of three kinds of language territories—German, Czech, and mixed territories. Based on the principle of territorial autonomy, Bohemia and Moravia were to be divided into a number of widely autonomous *Kreise* of nationally homogeneous character. In the German *Kreise,* exclusively German, and in the Czech, exclusively Czech was to become the inner official language. According to Rudolf Sieghart, at the time of the publication of these decrees the prime minister's chief legal adviser and a strong advocate of territorial autonomy, "experience in numerous fields of administration, and above all in school and agricultural affairs, has taught that separation of national spheres was the only possible form of peaceful life between the two nationalities side by side. Here separation had unifying character." [108]

Again, the Körber proposals, maintaining a precarious balance between German and Czech demands, were in themselves sound. However, they necessarily had to try to cure the symptoms rather than the disease itself. It was obvious to every truly impartial observer at that time that terms such as "personal," or "territorial," principle, "external," or "inner," official language were only symbols concealing the real issue, federalization or centralism, even reorganization or dissolution of the empire. No solution which, following the requirements of the day, ignored these basic issues, had a chance to succeed. Obviously, neither the government nor party politics on either side dared to face this broader issue squarely. Consequently, the Körber proposals were rejected by both nationalities, the German holding fast to the principle of national partition, the Czech, to the doctrine of the indivisibility of the Bohemian lands. The last government draft on the problem preceding the First World War, submitted by the Bienerth cabinet in 1909, met the same fate.[109]

The Bienerth proposals were merely a modification of Körber's ideas, and their rejection, therefore, would scarcely have been disappointing had it not been for the fact that, in the interval between Körber's and Bienerth's administrations, general, equal franchise had been introduced in Austria (1907). The hopes of progressives of various parties had run high that this new, bright feature in Austria's constitutional history would lead to a broader, more farsighted approach to the national problem. The political miracle of national pacification was expected from the new parliament elected on a democratic basis in 1907. Viewed retrospectively, it seems only natural that, in an atmosphere of broadening national tension, a parliament fettered by the burden of the Compromise of 1867 and the ever-tightening grip of the Austro-German alliance was certainly not in any better position than the supposedly supranational goverment to tackle the tremendous problem of Austria's national pacification. The simple truth, fully recognized two generations previously at Kremsier, that general equal franchise could help only if introduced as part of a federal reorganization of the empire, remained unheeded.[110]

## THE MORAVIAN COMPROMISE

The only truly bright spot during that whole era of failure was the conclusion of the Moravian national compromise in 1906, which served as the pattern for a similar solution in the far eastern province of Bukovina in 1910. But for the outbreak of the First World War, it might have influenced future development in other crownlands as well.[111] Unfortunately, this compromise did not lessen the national conflict in the neighboring crownland of Bohemia. This state of affairs is explained by the increase of national tension for general as well as for local reasons.

The situation was different, however, in Moravia. Here the percentage of German population was considerably smaller than it was in Bohemia, roughly 29 percent in 1880 and 1890, and 28 percent in 1900, as compared to the average of 37 percent in Bohemia during that period. Furthermore, the historic-national tradition of Moravia, in the course of medieval and early modern times, was by no means as conspicious and as strong as that in Bohemia. Well into the present era, Moravia has preserved far more of its agricultural character than has Bohemia. The influence of the role which the radical nationalist intelligentsia played in the history of the land was more limited.[112]

The Moravian compromise, drafted by a diet committee, consisted of four separate bills: a new crownland constitution and franchise, language, and school laws. Essentially, the crownland representation, the reorganized diet, was still built upon the old Estates system, divided into curias of great landowners, towns, cities and chambers of trade and commerce, rural communities, and, lastly, a curia, comprising only 20 out of 151 seats, elected according to the principles of general equal franchise. From the viewpoint of democratic progress this composition certainly was disappointing.

Regarding the national question, however, the improvement was marked. Except for the curia of the great landowners, representing the aristocracy, who were rather indifferent regarding the national question, the three other curias, comprising four fifths of the diet, were to be divided into national sections with seats allocated to Czechs and Germans in a ratio of 73 to 40. The legislative functions of the diet were, however, not to be divided according to national affiliation. Only the election of the diet committees and, above all, of the

*Landesausschuss* (crownland executive board), the supreme executive agency besides the imperial governor (*Statthalter*), was to be performed by the national curias. The standing order of the diet provided for a two-thirds quorum of deputies for any changes in these provisions. The fact that the functions of the national curias were confined to matters of election aroused particular criticism on the part of the Germans. Yet the well-considered significance of the compromise undoubtedly was due to these provisions of a constitutional guarantee of fairer proportional representation of either nationality, particularly in regard to the important administrative functions of the *Landesausschuss,* but rejection of the German claim for national partition so unacceptable to the Czechs.

Truly original ideas dominated the new franchise law. The principle of national registration was introduced on the basis "of option of the individual. It was checked by official control procedure" [113] through the municipal authorities and subsequently through appeal to the crownland administration. Such corrections of the original registrations were, in principle, based on the language status of an individual. Ten years' experience with this system proved that arbitrary abuse of registration for obvious national political purposes could be effectively checked. Thus, without major friction, Czech and German voters exercised their voting rights exclusively for the representatives of that nationality group in whose list their names were properly registered.[114]

The new Moravian language law applied chiefly to the autonomous authorities, that is, the municipal councils. Here the law made the determination of the official, external language and the inner language dependent upon the decision of the municipalities themselves, while the intercourse between municipalities and higher administrative boards was to follow the official language of the lower agencies anyway. Official use of the second language (of the land) was to be made if it was spoken by at least one fifth of the population of any community. The crownland's board of education, as in Bohemia, was to be divided into national sections.

The deficiencies of this Moravian reform, especially the complexity of its procedure and the narrow social concept of the diet's composition, were obvious. It was equally clear that these flaws could have been eliminated in time. Then the new concepts of national diet organization and national registration, not only for election but in due course for national autonomous administration, might well have served as a pattern for a comprehensive new national organization of Austria. It was not due to lack of appropriate institutional devices that this chance was not offered to the empire.

*An Estimate of the Period Preceding the First World War*

The history of the last twenty years of the Czech national struggle in Austria is frequently perceived as merely the prelude to the collapse of 1918. The policy of the chief Czech protagonists of that era—as interpreted after the event—is often pictured as straightforward and determined working for the break-up of the empire. Yet among the outstanding Czech leaders of that time, Joseph Kaizl, Karel Kramář, and Thomas G. Masaryk had, prior to the First World War, professed their loyalty to a future reformed Austria in no uncertain terms. They were joined in this respect by the political novice Edvard Beneš. What is more, Kaizl, Kramář, and Masaryk had by their very actions proved this loyalty, which national historiography after 1918 was all too readily inclined to argue away.[115] Nevertheless, there was no need to fear that the heroic legend of the national revolution of 1918 might be blotted out if the prewar activities of the Czech leaders should appear very different from their war and revolutionary records. A basically pro-Austrian Czech national policy, as long as there was any reason to believe in an organic, peaceful reorganization of Austria, was logically not at variance with a revolutionary policy after any reasonable hopes for the preservation and reorganization of Austria had disappeared.

As a matter of fact, the point could well be made that there was no decisive change or reversal of progressive Czech policy between the foundation of Masaryk's Realist party in 1900 and the achievement of national independence in 1918. The true essence of Masaryk's Realism, its concept of a liberal and social democracy deeply conscious of religious values, was primarily dependent upon the ascendancy of his sociopolitical philosophy rather than on a definite state form.[116] When Masaryk, shortly after the beginning of the First World War, dropped the plans for the reconversion of Austria into a truly democratic confederation of nations and took up the cause of the independent Czech republic, he thus, in a way, changed only the forms in which his ideas were presented, not the ideas themselves. In theory his aims could be realized in an Austrian confederation as well as in a Czechoslovak republic. This comes out rather clearly in Masaryk's statement, written after the war:

In judging Austria morally as well as politically I differed from the Young Czech Party and subsequently from the Czech Radicals. My view of what was called "positive politics" differed also from theirs. I thought we should take part in the Government, not merely in order to reform the Constitution, but also to infuse a Czech spirit into administrative practice. I used to speak of "unpolitical politics" and always insisted on the moral and educational side of public affairs. Seats in Parliament and strictly "political politics" did not seem to make up the whole of real democracy. . . . My opponents thought me too Socialistic; and my religious ideas were repugnant to their Liberalism. For my part I could not agree with their German, Russian and Slav policies. My object was to de-Austrianize our people thoroughly while they were still in Austria. What our eventual form of government might be and to what foreign State we might ultimately be attached, seemed to me, as things then were, matters of secondary importance . . . I fought simultaneously on two fronts—against "Vienna" and against "Prague." [117]

Until 1914, Masaryk's outstanding contribution to the evolution of the Czech people within the empire and, in a way, to the empire idea itself did not consist of actual political leadership. Masaryk, who had entered practical politics as the head of the newly formed Leftist Realist party, one of the smallest in the Austrian parliament, exercised technically very little parliamentary influence.[118] Entirely out of proportion to this parliamentary position, his ever-increasing spiritual leadership was based on the tremendous impact of his personality, as philosopher, academic teacher, and scholar, on the young Czech and also, to a wide extent, on the young southern Slav intelligentsia.

Masaryk's parliamentary activities in Austria between 1900 and 1913 were primarily distinguished by their undoctrinaire and realistic approach to the national problem. His ideas were neither sweeping and utopian, nor were they ever limited to the narrow nationalism of a policy fighting for special national privileges. Masaryk proceeded from the thesis that the Czech cause did not rest on the historic privileges of the Bohemian *Staatsrecht,* but on the position of the Czech people as equal among equal Austrian nationalities. An autonomous and democratic Czech nationality group, so he asserted again and again, could only exist within the Austrian borders if the other nationalities enjoyed exactly the same degree of autonomous democracy. Prior to the outbreak of the First World War, his objective "to de-Austrianize" the Czech people implied probably nothing more and nothing less than such program of federalization.[119]

Concerning the specific question of the Czech-German conflict, Masaryk saw the language question against a wider background than did any Austrian party group except the Social Democrats. He started from the assumption that

the national idea in the course of the nineteenth century has developed to one of the most effective social, political, and general political forces. Therefore it is the task of the Austrian state as a whole to make use of this force in its own and in its peoples' interests.

He believed that

while the national struggle cannot be eliminated entirely, it might be possible to transform it to a means for cultural competitions.[120]

In a parliamentary debate in 1907, Masaryk declared:

The national question is not only the language question. It is at the same time an economic and social question. The Czech students . . . were older [than the Germans] because they had to learn Czech first. Therefore, the language question is a question of money, too. . . . If we want peace and order . . . only one solution is possible, to expand general franchise, that is, to introduce minority and proportional representation and separation. . . . We want home rule, that is, liberal self-government, representations of districts, municipalities, and so on. . . . The solution is that, not only in Bohemia but in the whole of Austria, freedom of democracy has to win the field. On this platform understanding is possible, but on no other.[121]

Thus, Masaryk's position approached the German demands for national separation. He recommended a compromise between the Czech and the German viewpoints, asking for recognition of the bilingual character of all government agencies in Bohemia, yet he was ready to drop the demand that all state officials have a command of both languages.

I believe I can sum up our Czech demands as follows: The Czech as well as the German has to be served by each government agency from the lowest to the highest, orally as well as in writing [that is, served in his own language]. The bilingual character of an administrative district can be determined according to a fixed percentage of the linguistic minority. . . . The linguistic and national separation can serve its purpose only if both people thereby gain opportunity to determine and to administer their national and cultural affairs themselves. . . . The slogan "centralization and autonomy" . . . means, therefore, merely that existing centralization and autonomy have been insufficient. An organic state cannot exist without centralization, it cannot exist without autonomy. . . . It has to be repeated again and again that the language question is primarily an administrative question for the state as a whole. The language reform can be realized only in the frame of an up-to-date administrative reform. From this viewpoint, the democratic principle applicable to elected and representative bodies of the Bohemian lands is derived: General franchise with proportional representation (protection of minorities).[122]

In passing from Masaryk's direct influence on Czech-German pre-war relations to the broader aspects of his intellectual influence on Czech policy, one does well to follow the brilliant analysis of Czech national evolution presented by his tragic disciple, Edvard Beneš.[123] In analyzing the intellectual evolution leading to Masaryk's intellectual leadership, Beneš asserted that the permanent Czech dilemma between the concept of the Bohemian *Staatsrecht* and national autonomy on an ethnic basis had been apparent since the days of Palacký and Havlíček. He perceived this conflict, finally, in the difference between autonomy on a territorial basis (the old Czech autonomy in the territories of the Bohemian lands) and personal autonomy as connected with ethnic principles. The latter idea appeared to Beneš to be most clearly expressed in the Socialist program.[124]

Beneš took issue with the historic development of this conflict. He severely criticized the Old Czech program. "It responds excellently to the wishes and dreams of the Czechs but has little practical and realistic value. One cannot seriously think of establishing a Czech state if one-third of the population of the country [that is, the Germans] is ready to fight it with all means." [125] The failure of the historic solution became most conspicuous in the Hohenwart attempt. Its disastrous consequence for the Czech's was the subsequent policy of national isolation which was only abandoned in 1879 by the Young Czechs, who, "due to their historic association with Havlíček, were a little more liberal and more radical than the old Czechs." [126] Yet, the Young Czechs destroyed the Compromise of 1890 and "soon followed in the steps of the Old Czechs, making opportunist national policy. They, too, considered the historic right of Bohemia as a holy right and as the final aim of Czech policy." According to Beneš, however, they realized at last that the Czech question would be brought closer to solution only by the solution of the entire Austrian problem, that is, by a comprehensive constitutional revision based on the federal principle. "In theory they [the young Czechs] are radical nationalists who fight for the *Staatsrecht;* in reality they are Federalists." [127] But, though the Young Czechs finally promoted a federal program, they did not recognize ethnic federalism. They never abandoned the demand for historic rights, "forgetting that in order to justify and obtain it, they needed material power, while the natural right is a moral force in itself. In this respect the Realists and the Socialists were far more logical." [128]

To be sure, the Young Czech program was markedly modernized in the first decade of the twentieth century, when the influence of the vigorous Karel Kramář became increasingly discernible, though not adequately acknowledged by Beneš.[129] After 1903 the Young Czechs unequivocally advocated the introduction of general and equal franchise not only in the central parliaments but in the diets as well, where they supported the idea of national curias. They wanted to change the Austrian house of lords into a federal senate. In general, the powers of the diets were to be enlarged, the power of the central parliament being curtailed correspondingly. But this federal program, conforming with the ideas of the Bohemian *Staatsrecht* and the theory of historic rights, still adhered to the old crownland frontiers; it preferred an Austrian federation of semiprovincial units to one of national groups.[130]

After the introduction of general equal franchise in Austria in 1907, the Young Czechs were outnumbered in parliamentary strength by other Czech parties and party groups, namely, the Agrarians, the Clericals, and, strongest of all, the Socialists. This party [131] was the only one, apart from Masaryk's own followers, the Realists, that broke with the idea of the Bohemian *Staatsrecht*. The Realists did not agree with the Socialist interpretation of the national problem as purely social. Though they concurred with the socialist demand for federation of the Austrian nationalities on an ethnic basis, they objected violently to the subsequent Socialist demand that such a federation should be built not on the foundation of territorial, but of personal, autonomy.[132]

Beneš severely criticized the enormous administrative complexity of a system based on personal autonomy, which in the same territory would have two and in many regions even three or more, national agencies entrusted with similar (cultural) functions. Running counter to the very idea of Marxism itself, the application of this principle would completely disregard geographic, territorial, and, thereby, economic interests. Setting up a separate budget for the different nationalities would lead to grave social injustices, particularly in the case of the Czech workers, who would pay for their own schools, while the German factory owners, enriched by the labor of these workers, would pay only to the German national fund.[133] Yet, according to Beneš, the chief objection to the Socialist program was the fact that it favored the Germans not only economically in specific areas but politically in general: "The Germans are spread out over the monarchy to an extent which makes it impossible to apply to their status the principle of territorial reorganization, while all the other nations form territorial blocks." [134]

This argument was even more strongly raised by Masaryk himself, who admitted that the Socialist system of personal autonomy, though it might in some cases improve the lot of minorities, would, in general, work against the interests of solid national blocs such as the Poles and the Czechs. In the end, Masaryk asserts that these projects work for the preservation of an artificial German-Magyar majority. He charges,

In that respect the program of the German Socialists Renner and Bauer does not differ in principle from the program of the Pan-Germans: Renner accepts Naumann's Central Europe; the national autonomy proposed by him is only a concession for the purpose of preserving Austria-Hungary and her German character.[135]

This highly partial evaluation of factual concepts, known and developed widely beyond the Socialist camp, makes it clear that Masaryk and Beneš were primarily concerned, not with the Socialist national program, but with an alleged new emanation of German nationalism clad in a Socialist robe. They took issue, not so much with the principles of Socialist national philosophy, but with the secondary, and sometimes rather accidental, facts that these principles were colored by the Liberal national and cultural affiliations and traditions of German socialism. Not the rejection of the Socialist national program itself, but the argumentation proves that even the enlightened program of "Political Realism" could not free itself entirely from the influence of intransigent nationalism.

The basic aspects of the program of "Political Realism," again following Beneš's presentation and adding his own contribution to its formulation, may be summarized as follows. The Realists denounced the Bohemian *Staatsrecht* and adhered to the program of a federation of the Austrian nationalities. In Beneš's own words, they put natural—that is, ethnic—before historic rights. Yet they were still influenced by the inheritance of the Czech policy after 1848. They not only rejected the idea of personal autonomy but they also recognized national autonomy in general—with modifications—only in the frame of the old crownlands of mixed nationality.

They want to solve the Austrian problem and the Czech question by decentralization, a constitutional revision in the federalist and autonomist sense. The different Austrian provinces, as they have developed historically, would be the autonomous units. . . . Finally, the Realists, in order to solve the unfortunate struggle between the Czechs and the Germans in the mixed territories, came back to the idea of *Kreise,* as already contained in the Kremsier constitutional draft.[136] In fact, a reconciliation of the two races in Bohemia is only possible if both of them have autonomy. They have to be separated from each other. It requires a long historical evolution to make it possible for two or three nationalities to live quietly together, as, for instance, in Switzerland. In Austria no such tradition had been developed, and where it existed everything had been done to destroy it. . . . Therefore, there is no other way but the institution of *Kreise.* It will never completely suppress national conflict, but many opportunities for conflict will be avoided.[137]

In matters of national separation within the still preserved crownland units, the Realists would be willing to accede to a division of the administrative and judiciary branches of government according to nationality. The Realists would further agree to national division of the administration of municipalities with mixed nationalities, and would recommend the introduction of national curias.

Beneš himself—following the suggestions of the Czech Socialist František Modráček—wanted to improve this system by setting up courts dealing solely with matters of national conflict concerning education, public employment, language questions, and so forth. As he observed in retrospect

in almost fantastic faith in the vigor and influence of democratic principles, I trusted that the introduction of general equal franchise in Austria would lead to a transformation and rejuvenation of Austria in the spirit of federalism and of the ideas of Palacký and Havliček.[138]

Not the slightest idea is traceable in Masaryk's or in Beneš's writings or actions before the First World War that this program of 1908 was written with any mental reservation.

*The First World War*

It is more difficult than it appears to determine the time when Czech nationalism definitely broke away from the empire idea. Patently, the notion that the collapse of the empire left no alternative but the pursuit of an independent national policy, although in the main a satisfactory explanation for the German Austrian national policy in 1918, does not fit the Czech case. Czech nationalism took a most active and determined part in its own delivery. Yet even a Czech policy openly and aggressively antidualistic and anti-Habsburg would still conceivably have been compatible with the aim to make use of the fortunes of war and its outcome to work for the transformation of the empire, to build up federal union on an ethnic basis. Scant as the chances for such a transformation were, there is no ready answer for the fact that on the part of the Czechs a major attempt to work for that objective was not made during wartime.

A tentative explanation lies in the unusual combination of circumstances: first, a war caused by conflict with a Slav country (Serbia); secondly, this war fought in alliance with Germany and against (third) the Western democracies as well as (fourth) against the "mother of Slavs," Russia. While the first two factors set the psychological background for Czech policy, the last two were decisive. Only a war fought by Austria against the two ideological main forces hailed by Czech nationalism, Western democracy supported by the humanitarian Realism of Masaryk and the pro-Russian conservative Pan-Slavism promoted by Kramář, could have united the Czech people against the empire. Czech identification with the two main ideological trends of the Entente of 1914 led to the fact that political emigration abroad, not patriots at home—not even "underground patriots"— took the lead in the formation of national policy. A course aimed at the dissolution rather than the reorganization of Austria was the natural, almost organic, consequence of this shift of the center of national policy to the countries of Austria's enemies. This fact seems rather odd, since the principal Allied Powers, well into the spring of 1918, were not committed to the dissolution of the Austrian Empire. Austrian inability to disentangle herself from the German alliance and the disintegrating influence of the Russian Revolution on the Austrian Empire were among the chief causes for the reversal of that policy of the Western Allies.[139]

These causes did not force the Czech political emigration to change its course. In fact, the course of Masaryk and his originally small groups of followers became increasingly clear as early as the winter of 1914–15; namely, that they were committed to the dissolution of the Austrian Empire and the subsequent creation of a Czechoslovak republic.[140]

Masaryk's estimate in the summer and fall of 1914 regarding the probable outcome of the war—the defeat of the Central Powers and Austria's impending doom—was amazingly accurate. It was perfectly clear to him that the Czech people had to work for the destruction of Austria within the framework of the Compromise of 1867.[141] However, it was by no means clear in itself that this fight would necessarily imply the complete destruction of Austria or that it would have to be waged primarily, not within Austria, but from the Allied camp abroad. That it so happened was due equally to the initiative of the great leader and to the force of circumstances. Masaryk realized that no successful war against the Austrian system could be waged within the empire, not so much due to the wartime suppression of civil liberties as to the ineptness of the outworn Czech political party array. Its Right wing was chained to the politically and socially faded concept of the Bohemian *Staatsrecht;* its Socialist Left wing, because of international and supranational (all-Austrian) commitments, was not free to pursue an independent national policy; bourgeois Czech nationalism in the Center appeared fascinated by the specter of the czarist Russian steamroller pushing forward into Slav territory. Even as astute a leader as Kramář welcomed a Czech state as a Russian dependency under a grand duke as sovereign.[142]

Masaryk realized that these parties, laden with the inheritance of the political defeats of 1848, 1871, and 1897, could not successfully lead the fight for Czech resurrection in Austria.[143] Events from 1914 to 1918 largely supported his views. Great as were the Czech sympathies for the Allies in the beginning of the war, particularly for the Russian cause, and great as were the individual sacrifices made for their support, independent Czech political leadership within Austria in general was not successful in the promotion of the cause of Czech nationalism. At times, it seriously hampered the activities of the political emigration abroad.[144]

To be sure, political party life in Austria was almost completely paralyzed until parliament reopened in the spring of 1917. Though political hardship under Austrian wartime absolutism was pale in comparison with Czech sufferings during the Second World War, there is no doubt that political persecutions during the first war years could not miss their effect on Czech political activism in Austria.

They do not fully explain, though, the vacillating position of Czech parliamentary policy in Austria [145] in 1917. It is, of course, possible to argue that the declaration of the Czech parliamentary club, May 30, 1917, demanding the organization of a Czechoslovak member state in an Austrian federation, represented only a necessarily camouflaged claim for independence.[146] Yet in view of Czech political tradition within Austria and the (in Austrian eyes) still undecisive war situation, such an interpretation is not convincing. Though the fall of Austria was rightly predicted by Masaryk at that time, it was not yet decided. Neither was the psychological warfare undertaken by the Austrian government against the emigration abroad completely ineffective. In this respect, Beneš and Masaryk themselves bear ample testimony to the fact that Czech anti-Austrian policy abroad was deeply disturbed by even the halfway measures introduced under the young Emperor Charles in 1917 to reconcile the Slav nationalities, such as the reopening of parliament and the general amnesty for those convicted of high treason, above all, the Czech leaders Kramář and Rašín.[147]

Thus, Czech policy in wartime Austria was in the main neither decisive in achieving independence nor particularly imaginative. Yet, unless measured by the yardstick of a heroic legend, it cannot be blamed for a cautious approach to a complex situation.

Indeed, only the declaration of the Czech deputies at Epiphany, 1918, in Prague changed this situation. Though again not completely without cautious reservations, it demanded self-determination for the Czech people, and thus came considerably closer to the course of the emigration.[148] Even then, except for several effective demonstrations, above all, the workers' strike in January, 1918, it was not possible to initiate a policy of active resistance. The proclamation, on October 28, 1918, of the Czech National Committee at Prague as the government of the new republic—the true birthday of the new state— actually followed, and did not precede, the military collapse of Austria.[149] The events of these last days of October ended not only the revolution of the Czechs in Prague but practically the revolution itself.

Thus, it was left to the emigration abroad to make the decisive contribution to Czech national independence. It could never have been successful, of course, without the equally active contributions, both strategical and psychological, of the Czech legions fighting on the Allied side or without the at least passive accord on the part of the patient Czech masses in Austria. Yet neither support would have been effective if directed by a less inspiring, determined, and cool-reasoning leadership than that provided by the emigration.

In conclusion, Masaryk's insight that the struggle for Czech political emancipation could be directed and organized only from abroad was certainly one of the outstanding features of his leadership. His action was equally determined by military and political expediency and necessity, as well as by the inadequacy of the leadership at home, which was burdened with a tradition of social and political ineffectiveness. Consequently, the decision to shift the center of gravity of political action to Austria's foes undoubtedly was absolutely rational. The motives of subsequent actions were probably somewhat different though again every one of them was entirely rational in itself. Czech resolution and action abroad to bring about the downfall of the empire might not necessarily have been as firm and as fast as it actually was. Yet it was clear that, as soon as it collaborated openly and officially with the Entente Powers, the power of decision was taken out of the hands of the Czech leaders. This is not contradicted by the fact that Masaryk was among the first of the major political leaders on the Allied side who had set his mind on the destruction of Austria. But even if he had wished differently, he could scarcely have checked a development which was inevitable by that time. His actions were primarily determined, not by his own antagonism toward Austria, but by the inevitable and irreconcilable course of the conflict between the Western democracies and German-dominated central Europe. As soon as Masaryk openly linked his movement of liberation with the cause of the Entente, the return route was blocked. According to the political conditions prevailing in the period of the First World War, the very fact that Czech armed forces opposed Austria, helped to make this decision irrevocable, despite Allied hesitation to agree to the dissolution of Austria.

It may well be argued that Masaryk's political philosophy did not exclude the Czech people's participation in a republican, democratic, Danube confederation. But if Masaryk had recommended such a course, it is unlikely that the Czech people would have followed it. If Czech nationalism had definitely adopted the ultimate goal of attaining equal partnership in an Austrian confederation of nationalities, this goal might conceivably have remained unchanged at the end of the war.

Yet as soon as Masaryk had proclaimed the doctrine of Austrian dissolution, every psychological and political experience pointed to the fact that it would have been impossible to reconvert Czech nationalism to the more limited aim once the wider was within reach. Again, the decision was out of the hands of Masaryk and his movement.

Well-reasoned criticism has often deplored the complete severance of the legal, political, and social ties between the Austrian nationalities and its consequences for the political order between the two world wars. This has been considered a result of false reasoning on the part of the political war leaders of the nationalities. Such criticism, however, can often be applied only to preliminary decisions of seemingly limited significance. Final consequences, such as the political emancipation of the Czech people, may have been caused, though not all the way intentionally, by such decisions. An acknowledgment of the unalterable and irrational trait involved in the triumph of the Czech national cause in 1918 certainly does not detract from its achievements in the period between the two world wars.

# CHAPTER VI

# THE POLES

THE POLES ranked with the Germans, the Magyars, and the Czechs among the four numerically largest national groups of the empire.[1] Yet their position within the empire was markedly different from every one of these other national groups "with history," in that the Poles—at least prior to the Compromise of 1867—did not exercise the same kind of influence on the organization of the empire.

This was, of course, partly a consequence of the late incorporation of Galicia, the crownland predominantly Polish in population, into the orbit of Austria (1772). Thus, the Poles, as the youngest members in the Habsburg empire among all Austrian nationalities,[2] naturally were connected more loosely with the main currents of Austria's political problems. This historic factor was related to one of physical and economic geography. The Carpathian crownlands, Galicia and Bukovina, on the northeastern fringe of the empire were separated by high mountain ranges from the other Habsburg lands. They were far from the focal lines of the empire's traffic—the great river systems of the Danube and the Elbe and the communication lines from the Adriatic, from the Italian and the Hungarian plains to the Alpine and Bohemian lands. In addition, as to common factors of economic geography, the Carpathian lands formed only a remote part, if any, of the Danube area. Historic interpretation which bases the growth of the Habsburg power on the natural economic interdependence of its domains has to make an exception in the cases of Galicia and Bukovina, with regard to both economic and to socio-cultural interdependence.

The Poles are unquestionably a historic national group of the purest kind, in the sense developed by Bauer. In regard to a tradition of independent statehood and national culture, they were second to none of the major Austrian national groups. In fact, the national tradition of none of the Austrian nationalities was as strongly and directly connected with recent memories of a fully sovereign, national statehood as that of the Polish people, who were deprived of the major remnants of this status scarcely a generation before the Revolution of 1848.

Unlike the nationalism of the other Slav peoples in Austria, Polish nationalism did not need to be revived by a cultural renaissance movement in the early nineteenth century. Language and literature, so recently deprived of its political focus, continued to form a natural and a very vivid issue, but Polish nationalism in the nineteenth century was unequivocally a political nationalism. Its ultimate aims were focused on the restoration of the independent statehood of the Greater Poland, whose major parts in territory, as well as in population, had been taken by Russia and Prussia.

Thus, no permanent solution of the Austro-Polish problem was ever to be expected within the empire, with the exception of the later phases of the First World War. Yet the hectic efforts from 1916 to 1918 to comprise a Greater Poland within a revised constitutional frame of the monarchy were doomed to failure from the very beginning because they did not take fully into account the discrepancy in political power between Austria and the Allied Powers, on one hand, and between Austria and her own far stronger ally, Germany, on the other. Disregarding this transitional period, it is safe to say that the actual handling of the Polish question in Austria was always undertaken under the implied premise of a temporary provisional arrangement.

It has been said jokingly, but with a good deal of truth, that the only definitive, permanent arrangements in Austria were those of a provisional nature. This saying applies fully to the Austro-Polish status. Austrian government and Polish leaders were implicitly agreed that this status would endure as long as, in principle, the power relations among the heirs of independent Poland, Austria, Russia, and Prussia (respectively, since 1871, the German Empire) remained basically unchanged. In the long run this was true from the Congress of Vienna in 1814 until the First World War, a full century later. In spite of the shortcomings of the Austrian nationality policy, it was no mean record that, but for a brief period in 1846, the "provisional" Austro-Polish interrelations remained undisturbed for a full century.

It is precisely the provisional nature of the Polish status in Austria that explains to a considerable degree why the Polish question was dealt with far more peacefully than most of the other great Austrian national problems. Any attempt at a radical solution of the Austro-Polish problem would have been futile unless the major problem of the Poles under Russian and Prussian domination could have been settled simultaneously. Such a settlement, however, could only have come as the consequence of a conflict between these Powers. Until that conflict, which Roman law defines as an "Event certain to happen at an uncertain time," the Poles had no reason to pursue a radical, separatist policy. They could refrain from a more active policy, that is, as long as their interim demand for home rule in Galicia was satisfied and as long as their position did not compare unfavorably with that of their unredeemed brethren beyond the German and the Russian borders.

Because these interim demands appeared to be met, at least in the period from the Compromise of 1867 until the time of the First World War, the Polish problem, except for the local conflict between Poles and Ruthenians in Galicia, assumed a static character. It was rather dynamic, however, at the point at which this analysis starts, the events leading to the Galician Peasant Revolution of 1846.

Two factors affecting the attitude of the Polish people in Austria in the first half of the nineteenth century must be considered: the socioeconomic conditions in Galicia and the political ideology of the Polish people beyond the borders, particularly in Russia. It is fairly generally agreed that the powerful Polish landed aristocracy and the numerous rather poor, but class-conscious, gentry contributed equally, in their political and social shortsightedness, to the destruction of the Polish state. When Austria took over Galicia she became to a certain extent heir to the hereditary evils of Polish mismanagement, evils aggravated by the fact that the territory allotted to Austria consisted largely of poorer strata of the former Polish kingdom.[3]

These conditions may be summarized roughly as follows. There existed in Galicia a social disparity between lords and serf tenants which was unequaled in degree in the other Austrian crownlands, due to the more severe system of agricultural exploitation and the purely "patrimonial" administration. Practically the whole local administration and jurisdiction, except on the provincial level itself, was exercised not by a civil-service system, but by the lords themselves. Practically no artisan or industrial labor class existed beyond those working under the bond system of the lords. Agricultural development was more primitive than it was in the other Austrian lands, and the whole socioeconomic status of the province was far below that of Hungary, which hitherto had represented the purest form of economic feudalism anywhere in the Habsburg realm.[4]

Historic misinterpretation is often due to the fact that an evaluation of social factors which is correct for one definite period is applied indiscriminately to another. This holds true for the generally accepted belief that the position of the Austrian Poles was far more favorable than that of their kin either in Russia or in Prussia. While politically the status of the Polish people in Galicia after 1867 was definitely more favorable than was that of the Poles in either Russia or Prussia, the same was by no means true in regard to the economic and social conditions of the masses of the Polish people. In many ways these conditions were considered as oppressive as political control by the Austrian government certainly had been for most of the period from 1815 to 1848.[5]

Józef Feldman succinctly describes the attitude of the administration after 1815.

Of the three foreign governments ruling over Poland none was then so hard on the Poles as the Austrian. The leading ideas for the dependent countries were a bureaucratic police administration, with moderate "Josephinism" in church relations and the intention of Germanizing the Slavonic and Romance population. These principles were applied with particular intensity to the Polish element, which together with the Italian, was regarded as the most dangerous for the monarchy. Metternich expressed the opinion of the highest Vienna circles, when he said: "Polonism is only a formula, the sound of a word underneath which hides a revolution in its most glaring form: it is not a small part of a revolution, but revolution itself. Polonism does not declare war on the monarchies which possess Polish territory; it declares war on all existing institutions and proclaims the destruction of all the common foundations which form the basis of society." [6]

Indeed, the spirit of the Polish Revolution, symbolized by Tadeusz Kościuszko (1746–1817), the constant rebel and valiant fighter for Poland's freedom, was frightening to the autocratic empires of that period. Feldman rightly compares this governmental scare with Austria's fear of the *Risorgimento* in Italy. But, according to him, Austria used opposite methods in fighting these two movements. While the government tried to appease the spirit of rebellion in Italy by the introduction of sweeping economic reforms, it attempted, instead, to block the political rise of the Polish independence movement in Galicia by a determined economic destruction of the Polish nation. According to Feldman, only fear of growing Russian political influence among the Poles finally prompted the Austrian government to introduce economic and political reforms in Galicia.[7]

The charge that Austria plainly intended to strangle Galicia not only politically but economically can scarcely be substantiated. It is true, though, that the reforms introduced in Galicia were promoted far more by ulterior political reasons than they were by economic motives. Yet the few economic reforms instituted were not without effect. Moderate agricultural and commercial ameliorative measures were introduced, such as the founding of a state-controlled credit society, savings banks, and an economic society for the benefit of all the landed gentry. A technical academy was set up in Lwów.[8] A considerable number of promised reforms were not carried through, however. Above all, concessions to Polish nationalism were strictly barred, even in the mere form of cultivation of the Polish language. Feldman is right in his assertion that "offices were held mainly by Germans and Germanized Czechs; German colonization was fervently promoted, the German and Latin languages ruled in schools, court and administration." [9]

Nevertheless, the Austrian police-state system, by no means devoid of political skill, did not like to govern outright and exclusively by political suppression. As early as 1817 the government decided to revive the Galician Estates constitution of Maria Theresa (1775) in somewhat revised form. Accordingly, there was to be a diet of lords, gentry, and town representatives and an Estates board consisting of three lords and three knights (members of the gentry).[10] It could be safely assumed that a diet system of such composition would neither endanger the stability of the existing social system nor appeal to a potentially revolutionary national spirit of the population. The revival of this institution, innocuous in every way, was of great practical advantage to the government. By giving the powerful Polish lords a say in the rule of Galicia, the government took a long step forward in appeasing this powerful class.

Even more important was the fact that the resistance and the subsequent violent and bloody opposition of the Polish masses to a regime of economic exploitation was largely diverted from the government in Vienna and turned against the Polish lords and their followers, the gentry. These two groups, combined as a political force, became notorious under the name of the *Szlachta*.[11] In their stubborn adherence to the old socioeconomic order, these groups missed the opportunity to win over the poor peasant masses to the Polish national cause.[12] In their class egotism, combined with poor political judgment, they thus unconsciously played into the hands of the Viennese government.

The last main device which the central government employed in handling the Polish population was its policy toward the Ruthenians. The Ruthenian national group represented more than two fifths of the population of Galicia as a whole and the overwhelming majority of the population of eastern Galicia. It was in many ways the stepchild among all the Austrian nationalities, and, forming the lowest strata of the peasant population, it was unquestionably the underdog of the nationalities in Galicia. The Ruthenians were treated as a national group chiefly in so far as specific, socially discriminatory measures were directed against them.

The government in Vienna finally decided to alleviate somewhat the miserable social conditions of these people and even resolved, within limits, to meet their national claims. Thereupon, the Polish national leaders charged (and this charge was upheld to the end of the monarchy) that this was done only to stir up national trouble in Galicia, thereby weakening the Polish national cause. These Poles considered the Ruthenian nationality merely an invention of the Austrian provincial governor, Count Francis Stadion (1806–49). This was largely due to the fact that Stadion, in the immediate pre-March era had submitted, with the backing of Metternich, a program of economic, cultural, and administrative reforms, culminating in the administrative partition of Galicia into Polish (western) and Ruthenian (eastern) parts.[13]

These charges of the *Szlachta* were rather typical of the policy of an oppressive class regime which, by kindling national hatred against the Ruthenian minority, attempted to divert the opposition of the Polish masses from the abuse of economic power by their own upper classes. In a way, such tactics were understandable, since the imperial government had followed a similar policy when it used the *Szlachta* as an often willing tool for the execution of its own unpopular measures in Galicia. It was, thus, not at all surprising that the Poles, probably largely in good faith, considered the government's pro-Ruthenian policy as the exclusive product of a *divide et impera* policy in the interest of the absolutist power of the crown. To be sure, such ulterior motives were by no means beyond the political philosophy of the Metternich-Kolowrat government. Yet, whether or not these motives were primarily responsible for the government's policy, they did not refute the existence of an evil state of social and national oppression. Actually, the motivation of the government's policy was somewhat more complex.

Certainly, the able governor Count Stadion had not invented the Ruthenian problem.[14] The Ruthenians were as much a part of the native population of Galicia as the Poles. Furthermore, if the political Ruthenian problem had to be "invented" at all, it was invented by Maria Theresa and Joseph II, who, as early as 1775, only three years after the first partition of Poland, ordered a careful investigation of the Ruthenian question in Galicia. Some measures securing the freedom and future of the Ruthenian Uniat church were granted at that time. And these ecclesiastic reforms of Maria Theresa and Joseph II, introduced as the first concession to Ruthenian nationalism, had in a general way exactly the same aims as the reforms proposed by Stadion: to fight off Polish irredentism and political propaganda by the Russian kinfolk of the Ruthenians.[15] The difference between the reforms of Maria Theresa and the plans of the pre-March period was not so much the fact that the former were chiefly ecclesiastic, the latter secular, but that only the former were carried out. The latter, though agreed to in principle by the Emperor Ferdinand, Metternich, and Kolowrat, never went legally beyond the paper stage. Nevertheless, the practice of the imperial provincial administration showed an increased understanding of the needs of the Ruthenian peasants. Even these meager results of the government's reform policy before 1848 had profound repercussions on the Polish cause and therefore on the destiny and preservation of the Austrian centralistic police system.

One of the chief aims of the government's social, cultural, and national reform program was to prevent Galicia from becoming a hotbed of the All-Polish national revolutionary activities. This movement's liberal, revolutionary influence beyond the Prussian and Russian frontiers was dreaded in Vienna even more than were the Polish national claims themselves. The central authorities recognized that only force of arms could quell this danger once and for all. The necessity for armed intervention obviously had, in itself, little to do with any danger deriving from the Polish national movement in Austria. In view of the primitive cultural and social conditions of the crownland, the activities of the secret Mazzinian "Association of the Polish People" (Young Poland) [16] were necessarily no match for the Habsburg executive power. The revolutionary movement in the city republic of Cracow ("the heart of the Slavs," as it was called by Polish patriots), the central seat of the "Association of the Polish People," was far more influential, though the autonomy of the city republic had been increasingly restricted since 1833. The continued existence of this city republic was actually due only to the rivalry between the three "Protecting Powers," Austria, Prussia, and Russia.

A planned Polish insurrection in the Prussian province of Poznań in 1845, in the main frustrated before its outbreak, was perceived as only the first move in an organized All-Polish revolution, fomented and supported by the Polish intellectual emigration in Western countries and in Cracow. The spread of this movement beyond Austrian frontiers was—not entirely without justification—expected at any time. Events, however, took on a rather unexpected and decisive turn. Before the revolutionary activities of the Polish intelligentsia beyond the frontiers and the aristocracy and gentry in Galicia came to an open breach, the suppressed masses of the Polish peasants in western Galicia rose against the lords in February, 1846. This social, rather than national, revolutionary movement may justly be called a diminutive peasant war, following the pattern of the peasant revolutions in Germany and in Austria in the sixteenth and seventeenth centuries. Hordes of desperate peasants, ignorant of the nobles' national aims, but mindful of their own economic suppression, rose in full fury and struck, burning and killing, at the feudal lords in western Galicia. Thus, to a wide extent they quelled the predicted national revolution of the lords and the gentry at its very beginning.

This was in sharp contrast to the comparative quiet which prevailed in eastern Galicia. Here, the widely known loyalty of the Ruthenian peasants to the imperial government, on the one hand, and their equally well-known hatred of the Polish lords, on the other, acted as strongly restraining influences on Polish nationalism. Thus, no Polish insurrection was initiated in eastern Galicia, and, consequently, few peasant riots actually took place there. The full significance of the

Polish-Ruthenian conflict as a potentially decisive force in Galicia's political future thus became increasingly obvious.

For the time being, even more important, the unexpected Peasant Revolution in western Galicia, though on a small scale and quelled after a few days by Austrian troops, dimmed the flame of the expected national revolution. The later insurrection of the *Szlachta* in western Galicia almost appeared as a historic aftermath, doomed to failure from its beginning. Thus, in the last analysis the suppression of the Polish Revolution, culminating in the permanent occupation of the national center of Cracow by the imperial army,[17] was not primarily due to the conflict between Polish nationalism and imperial centralism. Instead, it was chiefly due to the narrow social base of a revolutionary movement confined to the upper classes. It was due, furthermore, to the opposition of the Ruthenian peasant masses, who submitted to the remote control of imperial absolutism rather than to the rule of the Polish lords, which was socially at least equally oppressive, but nationally more intolerant. The contemporary Conservative historian A. von Helfert was correct in the main point, when he commented:

The ill-fated insurrection of 1846 might have turned out altogether differently, in view of the fact that the Austrian government was unprepared and completely surprised, if the revolutionary leaders had not disregarded two important facts: the class hatred of the peasant population against their oppressors and the antipathy of the Ruthenian nationality toward everything Polish.[18]

Considering the fact that a successful outcome of the Polish revolt of 1846 might possibly have decisively weakened the position of the imperial government in 1848, its failure presaged far-reaching consequences, indeed. The events of 1846 actually resulted in a triumph of long-lasting effect for Metternich's Polish policy. By the mere announcement of agricultural reforms, abolition of patrimonial jurisdiction, and the initiation of very limited economic reform measures the government, with only trifling concessions to the peasants, had fully succeeded in turning the wrath of the Polish and Ruthenian masses against the feudal lords, who had to pay in the political sphere for their stubborn opposition to any change in the socioeconomic system of Galicia. Not the bayonets of the Austrian government, but the flails of Polish and Ruthenian peasants actually had blocked the planned national revolution of the *Szlachta*. The government's task now was to restore the social *status quo*. It had to avenge the harm done to its political, but not social, enemies by cruel action against their crude and now useless allies, the peasants.[19]

,Clearly, the government had not made such ingenious use of the fury of the wretched Polish and Ruthenian peasants just to spare its own troops in the fight against the Polish Revolution. A few battalions of Austrian infantry could have suppressed any revolutionary movement far more efficiently and with much less loss of life. This was proved, in fact, in the ensuing Austrian military intervention in Cracow. All evidence points to the fact that this brief, unrestrained release of the revolutionary peasant force was intended and used as a stern warning to the Polish lords and gentry. It meant that any current or planned national revolutionary attempt on the part of the ruling Polish upper classes would and could end only with the overturn of the Galician feudal system.[20] If the upper classes wanted to preserve the system, an objective which, with some modification, agreed with the government's intentions,[21] they were to abstain from further national revolutionary "All-Polish" activities.

This warning was well heeded. The short-lived Polish revolutionary movement in 1848, in the wake of the revolutionary events in Bohemia, Lower Austria, and Hungary, only faintly resembled the revolutionary ardor of two years earlier. And even these revolutionary activities on a relatively small scale were no longer led by the nobles, but were largely centered on the growing intellectual and professional middle class, which had been gaining in importance since the inclusion of Cracow in the provincial administration. The lords had learned their lesson well.[22] From 1848 on, it became increasingly clear to the Polish *Szlachta* in Galicia that national revolution in any part of the former Polish territories was inseparably tied to social revolution. The nobles realized that one was not possible without the other. They were, therefore, ready to tolerate existing conditions rather than to risk a double conflagration, which, even if ending in national victory, might well have led to their social destruction. They knew, further, that, in any attempt to force the Polish national issue, the Ruthenians, with the support of the central government, could and would certainly present their own national and social claims. This factor, too, had great weight in restraining action in the councils of the *Szlachta*.

Familiarity with these trends existing before 1848 is absolutely essential for an understanding of the Polish Austrian problem in general, and also helps one to comprehend the evolution of the Polish position in Austria well into the period of the First World War. From the suppression of the revolution, throughout the entire period of neo-absolutism (1849–60) and the period of constitutional experiments (1860–67), until the Compromise of 1867, this prerevolutionary experience was still vividly remembered by the Polish upper classes. During all that period national interrelations in Austria were in a state of precarious balance. No permanent, far-reaching changes upsetting the political and national *status quo* took place.

Failure of a renewed large-scale revolution in Congress Poland (Russian Poland) in 1863 furnished weighty and specific reasons to the *Szlachta* for not precipitating action. But the conclusion of the Compromise of 1867 with Hungary, which alienated the Czechs and the Croats, gave the Poles their chance. Badly in need of parliamentary support, the Austrian government under Count Beust then concluded the well-known deal with the *Szlachta* in 1868. Its broad principles involved the grant of administrative, though not legislative, home rule to Galicia. This meant, in effect, delivery of the provincial administration to the *Szlachta* regime and continued governmental disregard of the Ruthenian national problem as well as the Ruthenian and Polish social problem. In return, the ruling Conservative-party machine in Galicia gave loyal parliamentary support to the government and agreed to shelve the national question in its wider aspects for an indefinite period.[23]

This agreement was well kept. During the half-century preceding Austria's disintegration, the Poles, always under rather Conservative leadership and strongly organized in the Polish (parliamentary) Club, remained, but for a few brief intervals, the strongest pillar of the Austrian governmental system. Fully aware of their specific conservative-national interests, unconcerned with the problem of Slav political solidarity, "they were in the fortunate position to enjoy actually full autonomy, yet [in general] to have a weighty share in the affairs of Austria and to draw on the resources of the state."[24] The alliance between the "Polish Club" and the government, based on the solidarity of Conservative interests, remained basically undisturbed until 1918. The Polish political Left never became powerful enough to upset this political deal, which ultimately was canceled only by the precipitate events leading to the dissolution of the empire during the last stages of the First World War.[25]

Other factors, needless to say, helped to shape this peculiar Polish position in Austria. Thus, considerations of foreign policy played a weighty part when, after 1867, the government came to an understanding with the Poles rather than with the Czechs. That is to say, the government could afford to ignore the national claims of the Ruthenians in Galicia, but not of the "Sudeten" Germans in Bohemia, Moravia, and Silesia, who were backed by the political power of the German *Hinterland*. It dared to dislodge the rule of German centralism in remote and conservative Galicia rather than in radical Bohemia, which was so much closer to the arteries of the empire. Yet basically the deal with the Polish national Right, after 1867, and the subsequent Polish Austrian political status were influenced for almost five decades by the memory of the peasant insurrection of 1846. The Polish Right had postponed the national revolution, to prevent social revolution.

Only events of far greater importance, no longer focused on the development in Galicia, could change this state of affairs entirely. The restoration of a (Russian) Polish puppet government by the Central Powers in November, 1916, and the corresponding and subsequent rise of Polish nationalism to action in all Polish lands severed the Polish cause in Austria finally and irretrievably, from the coalition between the *Szlachta* and German centralism. But this final development, leading during a very limited period to active participation of all the Polish peoples of all classes in the service of the national cause, took place only after Austria's fall.

# CHAPTER VII

# THE CROATS

## CROATIA'S POSITION WITHIN THE SOUTHERN SLAV PROBLEM

THE LEGAL POLITICAL position of Croatia within Hungary from the 1860s until 1918 was in important ways similar to that of Galicia in Cisleithanian Austria.[1] Both the Croats in Hungary and the Poles in Austria were, except for the master nationalities in both states (Magyars and Germans) the most privileged nationalities or, perhaps more correctly, the ones who suffered least from national discrimination. Since 1868 the Poles had enjoyed an increasing administrative autonomy in Austria. In the same year, 1868, the Hungarian-Croatian Compromise was established on the legally even firmer basis of mutual constitutional charters.[2]

The similarity between the status of Croatia and Galicia extends, also, to ethnic composition. The Poles had to assert their privileged position against a substantial Ruthenian minority, while the Croats stood their ground against a Serb minority. In both cases the two master peoples, Poles and Croats, had to yield gradually to the rising national strength of two nationalities which were "without history" within the empire. But at the time of the break-up of the empire the Poles still maintained a precarious supremacy in Galicia, while the Croats in the monarchy had already lost southern Slav leadership to the Serbs.

In another even more important field Croat destiny ran an almost opposite course from that of the Poles. In the pre-March era the Polish question was one of the most serious national problems of the empire. Yet in the course of a generation, the Poles changed from a centrifugal to a centripetal force within the empire. Contrary to this Polish development, Croatian loyalty in the prerevolutionary and revolutionary times of 1848–49 was considered a main pillar of the empire's unity. After the revolution, however, and particularly from 1867 on, this situation was gradually, but radically, reversed. On the eve of the First World War the south Slav problem, and within it primarily the Serb-Croatian [3] national claims had become not only one of the major problems of the empire but, finally, the one deadly problem which defied any solution short of the empire's disintegration.

Obviously, decisive events in world policy played a most important part in bringing about this state of affairs. Definitely belonging in this context are the gradual disintegration of the Ottoman Empire, the rise of an independent Serbia, Austria's occupation and annexation of Bosnia-Hercegovina, the clash between Austrian and Russian Balkan interests, and the interplay of all these factors with the two great European alliance systems existing at the outbreak of the First World War. It is obviously necessary to evaluate these facts for an understanding of the Croatian question. Though in many ways they transcend the scope of this study, their influence on the development of the Austrian southern Slav problem must be kept firmly in mind.

The student of Croatia's historic national problems is faced at every point by the wider aspects of this southern Slav problem. Political and historic literature, as, indeed, history itself, has always considered the Croatian question a mere part of the empire's southern Slav problem, whose ethnic and prospective political nature was far wider. The fact that a major part of this unit lay within the realms of the Hungarian crown made it necessary to discuss important constitutional aspects of the Croatian problem in Chapter IV, dealing with the Magyars. It will be necessary to analyze equally important national aspects of the problem in Chapters X and XI, dealing with the Serbs and Slovenes.

The complex, comprehensive character of the Croatian problem leads to the justified conclusion that, in this field of regional nationalism, ethnic factors have a greater impact than historicopolitical ones. This became gradually apparent when an active, and increasingly united, southern Slav political movement came into the open with the famous joint declarations of Croat and Serb representatives of Austria and Hungary at Zara, in 1905.[4] Yet the full importance of these trends was not generally recognized until the First World War when in the Declaration of Corfu, in July, 1917, the Croatian and Slovene irredenta abroad joined their political fate irrevocably with that of the Serbs in a prospective southern Slav union stretching beyond the realms of the disintegrating empire.

The development leading to those events is clearly traceable to the pre-March era. This historic link has frequently been overlooked because of a double error made by superficial observers of that period. They altogether ignored Serb and Slovene national problems in the empire. They viewed the Croatian problem as consisting chiefly of century-old bickerings on the limits of Croatian autonomy between the Medieval Croatian *Sabor* (diet) and the Magyar Hungarian government, represented by the royal *Banus* (governor) in Zagreb (Agram).

To avoid similar mistakes it is necessary to separate two closely interrelated, yet essentially different, problems: Croatia's constitutional struggle with Hungary and Croatia's struggle as part of the southern Slav people with the empire as a whole. To be sure, these two aspects of the Croatian problem resolve themselves into the already familiar category: the twofold problem of a national group as a historicopolitical entity and as a national ethnic unit. However, one important new factor is involved. The ethnic and, in a way, even the historicopolitical concept of Croatian past and future was not restricted to one national group, but appeared as the common problem of the three southern Slav peoples in the empire: the Croats, the Serbs, and the Slovenes.[5]

By "Croats" is meant that part of the southern Slav peoples, overwhelmingly of Roman Catholic affiliation, who settled in the domain of the historicopolitical entity known for nearly one thousand years as the kingdom of Croatia. As stated before,[6] the Croats must be distinguished from their ethnic and linguistic kinsmen, the Serbs, who are of predominantly Greek Orthodox religious affiliation and Byzantine historic and cultural inheritance. Though these Serbs settled mainly in former Turkish territory,[7] they also formed substantial minorities in Croatia and in Hungary proper.

The Croats must further be distinguished from their Slovene neighbors to the north and west. The Slovenes, the most northwestern of the southern Slav peoples, are ethnically more distant kinsmen of the Croatians than are the Serbs. While the Serbs in the empire were chiefly represented in the lands of the Hungarian crown, the Slovenes were confined to Austria proper. The Slovenes share the Roman Catholic faith with the overwhelming majority of the Croats, but they do not speak the same language.[8] Their language, as in many ways, indeed, their entire tradition, forms the connecting link between the southern and the northern Slav languages. Thus, it is closely related to the language of the Slovaks, the most southern of the northern Slav peoples. Nevertheless, the cultural ties of the Slovenes are stronger with their neighbors in the south, the Croats, than with the Slav peoples in the north. Within the south, due to the common inheritance of western Latin culture, they appear far more closely related to the Croats than to the Serbs.

The majority of the Slovenes never formed a part of the Croatian kingdom. Nevertheless, Croatia's historic position within the imperial southern Slav orbit was always dominated by the fact that she held the central historicogeographic and political key position between their cultural kinspeople to the north and the west, the Slovenes, and their ethnic conationals, the Serbs, to the east and south.

Turning from the ethnic to the historicopolitical problem of Croatia, a good deal of the difficulty involved in its understanding is caused by the ambiguity of the meaning of the geographic and historic term "Croatia" throughout the last centuries. This ambiguity already appears in the official designation of the land of Croatia. Croatian state acts referred consistently to the "Triune kingdom of Croatia, Slavonia, and Dalmatia." The "Hungarian-Croatian Compromise of 1868," the basis of Croatian status within the empire until 1918, appears formally as a treaty concluded with the three kingdoms, of which one, Dalmatia, was actually under Austrian administration from 1814 on; the other, Slavonia, did not appear at all as a political reality at that time. Antiquated as these historic contradictions appear, they exercised, however, a very real influence on the development of nationalism—a typical phenomenon in Austrian history.

The kingdom of Croatia, at one time or another since its establishment in 924 A.D., had held sway over territories which subsequently came either under Austrian administration (Dalmatia), under direct Hungarian jurisdiction (partly Slavonia and Fiume),[9] or, a further bone of contention, under Turkish rule (Bosnia). On the other hand, in the second half of the nineteenth century Crotia gained territories by the incorporation of a major part of the Military Frontiers, which formerly had been under imperial jurisdiction.

With regard to the kingdom of Dalmatia, the ancient Roman province of the same name, Magyar Hungary, was anxious to bring this major part of the eastern Adriatic coastline under at least indirect control. Thus, she was only too ready to support the claims of her dependency, Croatia, for this land.[10] The request for the administrative incorporation of this semi-Austrian crownland into Hungary as part of Croatia dragged on unsettled until 1918. Hungarian opposition to sweeping Austrian reforms in Dalmatia greatly hampered the economic development of this beautiful land, so rich in historic tradition, and artificially supported Croatian national radicalism in Cisleithanian Austria.[11]

While Dalmatia as a living reality stood outside the Triune kingdom of Crotia, her third historic part, the kingdom of Slavonia (not to be confused with the Cisleithanian Austria lands of the Slovenes, that is, the Slovenia of today) existed in the nineteenth century only in name, in state documents.

At the time when the Croat peoples were joined under a Hungarian ruler, that is, at the end of the eleventh century, the term "Slavonia" referred to the greater part of the south Slav lands, including Bosnia and Serbia. When, in the sixteenth and seventeenth centuries, the major part of the Croatian lands was overrun by the Turks, the name became confined to the remainder of the Croatian lands which were free for a longer period than were other parts from Turkish rule in the south and east, and from Venetian domination in the west. In early modern times this Slavonia, then comprising roughly the lands between the Sava, the Drava, and the Danube, including the capital city of Zagreb, was indeed nearly identical geographically with the Croatia of today and enjoyed autonomy within the territories of the Hungarian crown. When, however, in the course of the early eighteenth century, the old Croatian territories were reconquered from the Turks, the term "Slavonia" was limited to the eastern parts of the old Croatian lands, and even these territories, in the course of the eighteenth and nineteenth centuries, were partitioned between Croatia proper (also called Upper Slavonia), and Hungary.

Actually, during the best part of the nineteenth century and throughout the twentieth century, the term "Slavonia" had only a geographic, not a legal political, meaning. Thus, it referred only to the eastern parts of Croatia, within the boundaries of 1868. Any allusion to the autonomous, political legal status of Slavonia, such as that found in Croatian state acts, refers to the times when Croatia and Slavonia were practically identical and when the term "Croatian autonomy" could be substituted for "Slavonian autonomy," and vice versa.[12]

Though technically obsolete, until 1918 the term "Slavonia" was still not devoid of a potential geographic and constitutional meaning, skillfully exploited by Croatian autonomists. Yet, the legal preservation of this outdated historical term stood for something more than a mere political dodge on the part of the Croatian autonomists. Its meaning was symbolic and representative not only of the designation of the Triune kingdom of Croatia but of the threefold, contradictory, and ambiguous aspirations of Croatian nationalism as well. Slavonia, as "land of the Slavs," stands for the sweeping idea of the ethnic unionism of the southern Slavs. It stands, further, for the even older idea of the full restoration of the Greater Croatian, or Greater Croatian-Slavonian kingdom, with claims to territories in either the Austrian or the Hungarian part of the empire. As such, the Greater Croatian political concept did not appeal so much to the ethnic affiliation of the southern Slav peoples, as to the historic tradition of Catholic Croatian supremacy in the Austrian southern Slav orbit. Finally, the geographic identity of the terms "Croatia" and "Slavonia" represented in the narrowest sense the claims for full-fledged autonomy within the lands of the Hungarian crown. Out of the conflict among these three concepts emerged Croatia's political future. Her political past, from medieval times until 1918, was, however, largely dominated by the narrowest of these three concepts, the claims for Croatian autonomy within Hungary.

## CROATIAN AUTONOMY WITHIN HUNGARY

Essentially, the Croatian Magyar problem, implying in legal terms the constitutional relations of the kingdom of Croatia to the Hungarian crown, was not only one of the oldest, but in many ways one of the most static, problems of the empire. The first union between Croatia and Hungary was formed as early as 1089, after the Croatian national dynasty had died out. In different forms, this union lasted until 1918, except for the Turkish wars in the sixteenth, seventeenth, and early eighteenth centuries and several other relatively short intermissions.[13] Throughout this period, Croatia was never a truly equal partner in this union; she was always a dependency of Hungary or, as Magyar constitutional law called it, *partes adnexae*, collateral lands of Hungary.[14]

Yet, on the other hand, Croatia, except for a brief period after the Peace of Carlowitz with the Turks, in 1699, never was just a province of Hungary. She always enjoyed an autonomous status, though the extent of this autonomy varied throughout a period of more than 700 years. Generally speaking, it might be said that until 1848 this autonomy comprised a civil administration under a royal Hungarian *Banus,* frequently of Croatian nationality and entrusted with wide powers. His adminstration was largely under the control of the Croatian Estates. However, legislative action taken by these Estates, which, through delegates, were also represented on the Hungarian *Reichstag,* had to comply with Hungarian statutes. Nevertheless, two of the most important state acts of Croatian history in modern times up to the Hungarian-Croatian Compromise in 1868—the election of a Habsburg as king of Croatia in 1527 and the adoption of the Pragmatic Sanction in 1712—were free acts of the Croatian Estates, and a clear manifestation of Croatia's status as a historicopolitical entity in relation to Hungary, as well as to the empire as a whole. Practically all unbiased historical evidence points to the fact that this interrelation of two nonequal Powers in one state organism, both dependent on a third power, the imperial one, was never free of friction. This appears only natural if the intricacies of the legal situation, as well as the rigid force of Magyar political organization, are taken into account. In fact, it was surprising that this system worked fairly well until the end of the eighteenth century.

After the profound, though temporary changes of the Napoleonic period, Croat-Magyar relations were marked by ever-increasing conflict, chiefly represented by the feuds of the medieval Croatian and Hungarian Estates, respectively, of the Croatian and Magyar representatives on the Hungarian *Reichstag.*[15]

The chief bone of contention in this struggle was seemingly the question of which language, Magyar or Latin, the Croat representatives were to use in the proceedings of the Hungarian *Reichstag.* This originally narrow language conflict assumed a far wider character at the Hungarian *Reichstage* of 1840, 1843, 1847, and 1848, where the Magyars, against the violent opposition of the Croat deputies, passed a law making immigration into the lands of the Hungarian crown, including Croatia, dependent on the command of the Magyar language. Furthermore, Magyar instead of Latin was to become the official language of Magyar-Croatian intercourse. The new Hungarian electoral law of 1848[16] provided that even the name of Croatia was no longer to be mentioned!

The wide implications of this Magyar law and the violent Croatian opposition to it made the language conflict the chief promoting factor, though not the ultimate cause, of Croatian anti-Magyar policy in the pre-March era. In the subsequent revolutionary period, this strongly contested legislation was undoubtedly a chief reason for Croatia's very active participation in the military intervention against Hungary.

The mere narrowness of this technical subject of conflict appears of great significance. Croat opposition was not directed against the suppression of their own language; practically no demand was made for its official application until 1847.[17] Before that time, the aims of Croatian autonomism were confined to the upholding of their right to use Latin, the erudite language of their ruling upper classes, instead of the national language of their overbearing Magyar neighbors and protectors.

Two facts evolve clearly from this conflict. First, only a very limited part of the Croatian and Magyar upper classes could have been directly concerned with the fight for the preservation of Latin as the representative language of Croatian autonomism. In this respect the medieval Estates system, which chiefly represented aristocracy, gentry, and the higher clergy, indicated rather clearly the group interests involved in this struggle. Secondly, the broad flow of Croatian and southern Slav nationalism in general could no longer be held within the confines of the petty bickerings of the conflicts on the interpretation of Croatian autonomy in general and the Latin-language question in particular.

Thus, because the subject matter of this conflict was so restricted, its broad causes and even broader consequences must not be disregarded. The language conflict originally set the scene for the dispute between Croatian Estates autonomism and Magyar Hungarian crown rights, and was very similar to the conflict between crown and territorial feudal nobility in Cisleithanian Austria. As soon as Magyar nationalism first transcended the well-trodden pattern of this age-old conflict and attempted, after 1790–91 and more definitely after 1840, to Magyarize not only the Estates proceedings but education and administration in Croatia as well, these broader issues became increasingly apparent.[18]

By unanimous consent, the Croatian Estates, in 1847, resolved to counteract the Magyar attack on their part by the substitution of the Croatian for the Latin language in government administration and the schools. The smoldering national conflict thus came into the open; not Croatian autonomism, but Croatian and southern Slav nationalism, became the order of the day. The consequences of this change were profound in the field of national evolution and equally important in the field of social evolution. Obviously, the introduction of the national language widened the range of group interests concerned with Croatian state affairs from the carriers of Latin culture—the nobles and the clergy—to the representatives of bourgeois culture—trade, commerce, and a growing professional class.

The question remains, why did the Croatian feudal system agree to a policy which certainly could be expected to impair, and finally to overthrow, its class rule? The answer is obvious. As soon as the Magyar regime refused to obey the rules of the old Estates struggle, and particularly after this conflict acquired a broader basis under the influence of Kossuth's dynamic national liberalism, Croatia was able to maintain her position only by following suit. The reason she was able to do so was because a sweeping southern Slav nationalism, paralleling similar movements among the Czechs and the Poles, was already in ascendancy among the Croatian middle classes, who had not been represented heretofore in the Estates system. The appearance of this new brand of nationalism on the political stage, in the form of the southern Slav union movement, gradually replaced Croatian autonomism. Thenceforward, one has to face not only the problem of autonomism but also that of nationalism; not only the conflict of the Estates but the conflict of the peoples as well.

### CROATIA AND SOUTHERN SLAV UNIONISM

The development of south Slav unionism has ample and wide interrelations with the rise of Pan-slavism in general and the national movements among the northern Slavs, above all the Czechs. Yet in modern times the south Slav national movement had to demonstrate a distinctive historic experience of its own, that is, the actual southern Slav unification in the period of the Napoleonic Wars. The kingdom of Illyria [19] was established by Napoleon after the Peace of Schönbrunn, in 1809, when Austria had to cede to France her coastal regions, all her Slovene, and most of her Croatian territory. The new kingdom, set up under a French viceroy as a springboard for Napoleon's expanding eastern ambitions, comprised the greater part of Carinthia, Carniola, Gorizia, Istria, Dalmatia, and Croatia.

Peoples annexed by force of arms of a foreign conqueror usually do not hold in affectionate regard any measures by the conquering regime, however efficient and technically beneficial they may be. The French Illyrian administration proved an exception to this general rule, because its efficiency in abolishing the feudal system was combined with extraordinary political skill.[20]

The achievement of the brief period of French administration in these territories, lasting in all less than five years, may essentially be summarized thus: the replacement of the old Austrian, feudal state organization by the system of the modern centralized police state. This was accomplished in a backward area which still suffered in many respects from the consequences of Turkish invasions. Of particular popular appeal in the history of this administration were such measures as the substitution of codified French law for the patrimonial law administered by the lords, a unified customs system for the many existing forms of inland duties, and the abolition of the economically restrictive guilds and corporations. The rural robot system was eliminated, and agricultural ameliorations were furthered, which vastly increased the orbit of arable lands. Finally, and perhaps most important, a system of public education following the French pattern was organized.

The effect of this regime on the rise of southern Slav nationalism was less direct, less radical, but far more lasting than that of the administrative economic reforms, which were abolished with the return of the old Austrian administration in 1814. Like the Czech national movement in the pre-March period, southern Slav "Illyrism" was at first largely a literary movement, and as such it was greatly strengthened by the French educational system. It replaced the limited and sporadic instruction (which had existed chiefly through the good services of the monasteries alone) with a general, free system of elementary instruction in the vernacular languages, Croatian and Slovene. In that respect much preparatory work was necessary to weld vernacular idioms into literary-language systems suitable for instruction. Again, as in the Czech case, the problem was not the creation of a literary language which already existed in venerable literary documents, it was that of linguistic organization, popularization, and standardization, of developing the grammatical skeleton from the literary treasures of the past.

There was a widespread conviction at that time that a somewhat mythical southern Slav, Illyrian "mother language" already existed [21] and had only to be excavated and restored. Scholars were actively engaged in reconstructing the grammar of this allegedly common southern Slav language. Modern philologists are wont to belittle these efforts. Yet, even though these attempts were highly questionable from the viewpoint of philology, they became of great significance to the rise of the ethnic, national movements among the southern Slavs.

A very real linguistic contribution stimulating the rise of Illyrism in the entire southern Slav world was made by the publication of the Grammar of the Slav Languages in Carniola, Carinthia, and Styria, by Bartholomäus Kopitar (1780–1844). Kopitar lifted the practical use of the Slovene language from a mere peasant idiom to its rightful place as a newly restored literary language. The broader efforts made on behalf of the excavation and restoration of the imaginary Illyrian language [22] found an even more friendly and interested reception among romantic scholars in Germany and in German Austria even before the political effect of these activities became apparent among the southern Slav masses themselves. Thus, from the period of the French administration onward, the southern Slav cultural renaissance and, even more, the southern Slav folklore and literary monuments of a romantic and heroic past were favored interests of literary Germany. As Wendel aptly puts it, "Illyrism was nursed at the breasts of German Romanticism." [23]

All this rapidly spreading cultural development was by no means in itself a direct product of the short-lived French Illyrian administration. French political expediency could make use of existing national trends and treasures; it could support them, but it could scarcely create or revive a national movement for its own sake. Nevertheless, the rapid pace of this cultural development was largely, if only in a curious and twisted way, the consequence of the socioeconomic contrast between the French administration and the following Austrian regime. Wendel summarizes this change as follows.

The Habsburgs, to whom the whole territory of the Illyrian provinces was awarded at the Congress of Vienna, with a great sponge erased everything that the French regime had instituted, as one would erase crayon strokes from a board. True, the Illyrian kingdom, apart from Dalmatia, which formed a separate administrative district, was still made up of the *Gubernia* of Trieste, Laibach, the territories of Carniola, Gorizia, Gradiska, the Littoral, and, up to 1822, of Croatia to the south of the Sava.[24] But nobility and clergy again proudly donned the now faded mantle of their old privileges and honored posts. The schools were delivered to the priests, the peasant was removed from the orbit of civic jurisdiction, and the nobility flourished again the whip of patrimonial jurisdiction over humbly prostrated subjects. In 1813 an imperial (Austrian) manifesto denied that the French had completely abolished the feudal system. At any rate, it was rapidly restored by the Austrians to its full extent. The shadows of the medieval ages again dimmed the eyes of the southern Slavs, which had been dazzled by the unaccustomed light of a new world.[25]

One does not have to agree fully with this glorification of the French system, marred as it was by the severe burden of taxation for alien and imperialist military purposes,[26] to realize the profound impact upon the population of the restoration of the Austrian governmental system. Still, in spite of natural resentment against foreign domination, it is an entirely conceivable reaction of human experience that a province of any state, finding its lot far better under the conquering power, may, if returned to its original status, sometimes direct its efforts toward reincorporation into the orbit of the foreign power whose administration had proved so beneficial.

Obviously, the French administration in Illyria could not create a similar effect. It appeared practically impossible that a French regime could ever be restored in the Illyrian southern Slav territories. Thus, the preservation and propagation of a French tradition could have little practical meaning for the Illyrian national groups. What, then, was most likely to be the basic impression of this short-lived administration on the peoples benefiting from its social, economic, and cultural advantages? Probably the Illyrian peoples perceived the basis of their brief prosperity not so much in the enlightened spirit of the reforms introduced by a foreign conqueror as in the fact that under the French regime they had been united for the first time in many centuries. It corresponds in every respect to the pattern of any national legend that the people considered the improvement of their political position the consequence of such unification. The idea became deeply rooted that any further rise in the fortunes of the southern Slavs would depend upon the restoration of an allegedly preexistent Illyrian union.

For weighty political, social, geographic, and linguistic reasons the union movement among the south Slavs developed far more strongly than that of the western and northern Slavs, who were separated from each other by a German territorial wedge. The least obvious, but certainly one of the most important reasons was the Illyrian response to the historical experience of the French administration from 1809 to 1813.

In addition to obvious geographic, historic, and political factors favoring the rise of ethnic-national regionalism in the agricultural areas between the Drava and the Sava, imperial Austria's patronage of early Illyrian nationalism is of outstanding importance.

The point has been stressed earlier that the Metternich-Kolowrat regime, in support of the territorial aristocracy in Bohemia and in awareness of the threat of Pan-Slav influence from Russia, was to a limited degree inclined to tolerate the cultural national activities of the Czechs. This tolerance changed to actual governmental support in the case of the cultural nationalism of the southern Slav peoples.[27]

The motivations of the southern Slav policy of the imperial government were similar, though not identical, to those prompting its Czech policy. Surely, Croatian aristocracy was not as powerful and influential a factor as Bohemian and Polish high nobility, yet in a way the threat of Russian Pan-Slavism appeared far more real in regard to the southern Slavs than in regard to the Czechs. Common cultural and religious ties between Russia and Serb orthodoxism, a closer linguistic relation between the Russians and the southern Slavs in general, and, above all, the greater distance of the southern Slav territories from the German center of the empire, were strong reasons for concern.[28] Even weightier was a distinctly political factor, the government's aim to play the Illyrian national renaissance movement, which seemed politically still innocent, against the long-established and powerful national separatism of the Magyars. Lastly, the human element came in. Early Illyrian cultural nationalism benefited from the extraordinary political skill and farsightedness of leaders who knew how to pursue their objectives in collaboration with an Austrian government, which was not fully aware of the potentialities of southern Slav national evolution.

Foremost among the leaders who helped to put the southern Slav claims into the front line of the Austrian national conflict was the

Croat Ljudevit Gaj (1809–71).[29] Gaj's literary life work presents a unique combination of the scholarly linguistic research of Jungman, Dobrovský, and Kopitar, the poetical flourish of Kollár, the historic traditionalism of the young Palacký, and the popular democratic journalism of Havlíček. Gaj, as a man of letters, was probably inferior to any one of these great champions of Slavism in their particular field of study, yet he was, in a way, superior to all of them in the broad undoctrinaire character of his method, the variety of his gifts, and particularly his political ability. His endeavors by no means began under wholly auspicious circumstances. He was still confronted with a political situation dominated by the Croatian Estates autonomists, who fought for their own privileges rather than for the peoples' national claims.[30] Furthermore, he had to face a typical situation in Croatian history in which the nobles, in so far as they did not make their peace with Magyar nationalism and become Magyarized themselves, turned to the empire for support. Yet the imperial administration in the territories bordering on Croatia, Dalmatia, the Military Frontiers, and the Austrian Slovene lands was under the rule of German centralism, as well as under German cultural influence. This influence, to which Croatian nobility readily submitted, did not stop short of the rising bourgeois intelligentsia.[31]

Gaj, a graduate of the Imperial University of Vienna, was in a sense a typical example of this German cultural indoctrination of the young Croatian intelligentsia. But, though influenced by German learning and culture, he kept free of the specific German romantic nationalism of the day. The directing influence of his national ideology remained thoroughly Slav and, at that, in the form of the romantic Pan-Slavism of Jan Kollár. The strength of this impulse geared him to the task of realizing Kollár's dream world in the southern Slav orbit. It was primarily his idea to give the new southern Slav ideology of Illyrism a common written language, "Illyrian." [32]

The way in which Gaj attempted to overcome the insurmountable difficulties of seemingly restoring, but actually creating, this language is typical of the curious blend of romantic traditionalism and enlightened rationalism apparent in the Slav cultural renaissance. He did not propose Croatian, his own language and that of the most numerous, historically most significant of the Austro-Slav peoples, as the basis of "Illyrian," but favored the primitive southern Dalmatian "Schto." [33] He held that this rather elementary idiom could serve as a better common denominator of Illyrian than more highly developed forms of the Croatian language. He considered, also, that the factor of national rivalry could thus be eliminated from the reform work. This well-meant national unselfishness, despite the ultimate failure of the Illyrian program as a language movement, is almost unique in the field of cultural nationalism. As proved by the history of the Croatian-Serb conflict of the following generations, this unselfishness could not be preserved after the political programs of southern Slav nationalism became prominent. Still, it indicates that national conflict could have been settled more easily with a nationalism of such well-reasoned restraint than with the narrow aspirations of Croatian autonomism.

Actually, though only up to a certain point, the imperial government in Vienna was ready to come to terms with "Illyrism." With the patronage of the minister of the interior, Count Kolowrat, Gaj succeeded (1833–34) in establishing an Illyrian national newspaper, and he was even permitted to set up his own printing press—an achievement unheard of during that period of Austrian administration. National reading circles and the organization of an Illyrian literary foundation, the famous *Matica Ilirska* (Illyrian book foundation), soon followed.

Against the opposition of the autonomist strata of society which denounced the allegedly scheming ethnic nationalism of the Illyrians, Gaj and his followers in the following years gradually emphasized the political aspects of their program. In 1837 the Illyrian leaders openly began to promote the idea of Illyrian unionism in their newly established journals.[34] Such a union was to include all the southern Slav peoples, including Serbs and Bulgarians under Turkish domination, in a Great Illyria. Furthermore, the romantic Pan-Slav ideology, stressing the affinity of the southern Slavs to the great Slav mother country, Russia, soon trespassed the bounds of mere cultural ties.[35] The Illyrian flag (white, red, blue) and the new Illyrian coat of arms were publicly displayed, and the resistance movement was stiffened against the Magyars on the Hungarian *Reichstag*.

Though this dynamic *Illyrismus* was a form of nationalism neither agreeable to nor compatible with the policy of the Croatian Estates, they were caught in the wake of the movement and made their own peculiar contribution to its success. This consisted of their increasingly stubborn insistence on the medieval concept of Croatian autonomy within Hungary, an insistence which no longer shrank from forcible resistance to the overbearing demands of the Hungarian Magyar *Reichstag*. Bloody riots between Magyars and Croats took place in Croatia as early as 1842, and in Magyar Hungary the radical national wing under Kossuth gained the upper hand. It was significant that there the people's candidate, the Liberal national leader Kossuth, realized at once that, irrespective of the immediate occasion of the clashes, Illyrism was potentially far more dangerous than Croatian autonomism, which, after all, was still in power in Croatia. Thus, while making rather light of the opposition of the Croatian autonomists, he painted in glowing colors the picture of the Pan-Slav danger threatening from the south and—of all things—even branded the imperial government's policy as basically neither pro-Croat nor anti-Magyar, but pro-Pan-Slav.[36]

At this point the imperial government in Vienna deemed it advisible to enter the picture in order to calm the brewing Magyar tempest. It did not intervene, though, in the politically rather innocent and not even unwelcome struggle of the Croatian Estates with the Hungarian *Reichstag*, and it did not directly suppress the southern Slav language movement in Croatia. It tried, however, to check the evolution of Illyrism to political nationalism.

Undoubtedly, the government in Vienna, from its standpoint, had taken the necessary measures with skill and caution. Nevertheless, it failed to defeat nationalism by means of diplomacy. It could appease the Croatian autonomists and the Magyar Conservatives, but it could neither reconcile the virulent nationalism of the Magyar Kossuth Liberals nor keep the Illyrian movement within the bounds of Croatian autonomism or of mere cultural aspirations. Political nationalism was on the march. Yet undoubtedly it had advanced much farther within the Magyar "master race", under the increasing influence of the dynamic Kossuth, than it had in the remote semi-medieval Croatian dependency under the leadership of the cautious Gaj.

Inevitably, and much against its own volition, the central government was forced into a position where it could no longer intervene between Magyar and Croation southern Slav aspirations, but had to take sides with those people among whom national separatism appeared less threatening, where the potentialities of social reform seemed more remote. These considerations determined in principle, though not always in practice, the policy of the Austrian government during the revolution and the first after-revolutionary decades.

To a great extent external factors enabled the imperial government to support and sustain a Conservative Croatian regime in the late pre-March era and in the revolutionary period of 1848–49. Nevertheless, the transformation of Croatian autonomism to southern Slav unionism inevitably led to a gradual social transformation of feudal Croatia. Realizing the political, as well as the prospective, social radicalization of Croatia, the imperial government again reversed its southern Slav policy in the 1860s. From then until 1918, it accepted a consistent pro-Magyar policy, following the apparently compelling reasons which had forced the conclusion of the Compromise of 1867.

Yet in the pre-March period sociopolitical radicalism in Croatia still seemed far off. Gaj, always anxious to remain on the best of terms with the imperial government, was not only a moderate nationalist in politics but also a definite conservative in the social field. He not only appeared disinterested in any changes of the ruling latifundia system in Croatia, he and his followers even actively opposed the grant of any political rights to the peasant nobility, the free peasants of Croatia.[37] Nevertheless, even before 1848 it appeared doubtful whether in the long run Illyrism could be maintained within the social limits approved, and the national objectives to some degree tolerated, by Vienna.

With much stronger justification the imperial government relied on the effectiveness of a defense against the Pan-Slav advance in the religious field. There was a definite danger that the common, Old Slavonic language of the Orthodox churches might serve as a springboard for a move from cultural to political affiliation between southern Slavs and Russia. In a way, Gaj's trip to Russia in 1840 could be interpreted as the first step in this direction. The very "real" dreams of the Empress Catherine II, scarcely two generations before, to set up a new Mediterranean Byzantine empire, were not yet forgotten. Their revival appeared a definite possibility after Russia's rise in political and ideological power following the end of the Napoleonic Wars.

Two ways were suggested to ward off this danger. One was to further a modern southern Slav language movement which would deliver the ecclesiastic and secular literature of the Austrian southern Slav peoples from the fetters of Old Slavonic and its Pan-Slav Russian affiliation.[38] By supporting Gáj's Illyrism, the imperial government had attempted to follow this policy, but it realized soon enough that this course was beset with the danger of cultivating, in the end, not an anti-Russian, but a separatist, anti-Austrian, southern Slav movement. Thus, southern Slav unionism obviously had failed as a means of upholding the existing order. The second course open to the government was again to support southern Slav national aspirations to a limited degree, this time not under the leadership of a vague ethnic unionism, but centered around the Catholic church, which was historically and ideologically the most powerful cohesive force in the empire. Catholic Croatia was to be the natural center and pivot of this policy; its aim was to unite the Austrian southern Slavs under the leadership of the Catholic Greater Croatian idea.

### THE GREATER CROATIAN IDEA AND THE TRIALIST CONCEPT

Just as the program of Illyrism was connected with the lifework of Ludevit Gaj, so was the Greater Croatian idea, the third major concept of Croatian nationalism, connected with the work of the Slovene Bartholomäus Kopitar (1780–1844).[39]

Kopitar, the great Slovene linguist, was far more a scholar and far less a man of practical politics than was Gaj. Nevertheless, his scholarly work formed the basis of an important trend in the political thinking of Austria. Four somewhat vague principles dominated his national program. First, unlike Gaj, he considered the Slovene language, the first western and southern Slav language into which the Holy Scriptures were translated, instead of a rather arbitrarily chosen idiom, as the basis of linguistic unionism. This idea, from the philological angle on much sounder foundations than Gaj's Illyrism,[40] already implied the recognition of western Slav cultural leadership in the Slav world. This premise emerged more clearly in his other broad political principles. Thus, secondly, Kopitar perceived Austria as predominantly a Slav power. Correspondingly, she should be the true center of a Slav culture opposed to barbaric Russian Pan-Slavism. In other words, according to Kopitar the Slav center should move from east to west, from barbaric Tartarian Russia to Austria the outpost of Western civilization. Thirdly, Austria should promote the idea of Western Catholicism among the Slavs, as opposed to Eastern orthodoxism. It is difficult to express Kopitar's fourth guiding principle in the form of a strict thesis. Yet, as a consequence of his previous ideas, the concept of an inseparable union of interests between the southern Slavs and the Catholic Habsburg empire emerged clearly. Thus, the Catholic Slavs under the Habsburg scepter should serve as the nucleus of an even greater southern Slav union also including the Slavs still under Turkish domination, and this union should be linked to Habsburg rule.

TRIPARTITE EMPIRE ORGANIZATION PLAN

Seemingly, this program in its final ethnic aims appeared not very different from the objectives of Illyrism or, later, of the Yugoslav movement. It was, however, profoundly different in its intermediate objectives and the means which it employed. To Illyrism, the union of the southern Slavs was the primary objective, and though in its beginning the movement was by no means anti-Austrian, it was little concerned with the question whether this union was finally achieved within Austria, within a completely independent state, or even within the sphere of Russian political influence.

This early political concept of the Yugoslav movement, which put the southern Slav union before loyalty to a specific state, was, indeed,

at the roots of its final turn against Austria. The conclusion of the
Austro-Hungarian Compromise of 1867 and the recognition of full
Serbian independence in 1878 made it increasingly clear, on the one
hand, that overwhelming obstacles prevented the realization of southern Slav union within the Austrian orbit and, on the other, established
an independent southern Slav "Piedmont" beyond her boarders.
Thus, inevitably the center of gravity of the Yugoslav movement
switched from Austria to Serbia, from Croatian Catholicism to Serbian Greek Orthodoxism, from indifference toward Austria to hostility.

It was altogther different with the political program, in its beginnings so profoundly influenced by Kopitar. In this concept the
union of the Austrian southern Slavs under the Catholic idea and
under Catholic-Croatian Slovene leadership was of primary importance; the inclusion of the Serbs, subsequently even of those still
under Turkish rule, was only a secondary aim. The political objectives of this program, though less broad than those of either Illyrism
or Yugoslav unionism, became far more concrete.

Kopitar actually introduced the idea of a tripartite Austrian-Hun-
garian-southern Slav empire organization, known as "Trialism," into
the political theory, and later the practice, of the Habsburg monarchy.
Thereby the way was paved for a state concept envisaging a union of
the Austrian and Hungarian southern Slavs under the leadership of
the Catholic Croats, the group within the empire that was strongest
in numbers and in historic tradition. According to widely held southern Slav (particularly Croat) intentions, such a tripartite or "trialistic" empire organization under German, Magyar, and Croat leadership should have replaced the dualistic monarchy of 1867.[41]

In a technical sense, the trialistic concept was thus formulated only
after the dualistic reform of the empire was under way, that is, after
1859. It was raised to a definite program of action only after the
Dualistic Compromise was finally concluded, in 1867. Actually, the
emergence of such a program was implied in the demands made since
the Revolution of 1848 and the Magyar War of Independence of
1848–49 [42] for the recognition of a united southern Slav state organization under Greater Croatian leadership. It was persistently asserted by Croats (southern Slavs) that no simple federal empire organization but the "trialistic" one could do justice to the preponderance of the combined southern Slav peoples in numbers, extent of

territory, and geographical position.[43] This, indeed, became one of the leitmotivs of southern Slav policy from 1848 to 1918.

The fact that such a program fitted into neither the state concept of German centralism, the dualism of 1867, nor the federal concepts developed from 1848 to 1918 helped to explain the irresolute approach of the imperial government to the Greater Croatian idea and the contradictory position of the Greater Croatian leaders themselves. The first stage of this conflicting policy is well illustrated by the appointment of Joseph von Jellačić (1801–59) as Croatian *Banus* in March, 1848, his declaration of Croatian independence from Hungary in June, his consequent ousting from office due to Magyar pressure, his reappointment by the emperor, and the Croatian invasion of Hungary in September of the same year. The second stage is represented by the imperial "paper" recognition of Croatian independence from Hungary in the March constitution of 1849, which met Croatia's territorial demands halfway, but ignored her political claims even in the form of local autonomy, as well as by the acceptance of this state of affairs by a leader such as Jellačić, in his conflicting position as Croatian patriot and imperial general. The unsuccessful endeavors in the period of constitutional experiments, from 1860 to 1867, formally for the restoration, actually for the creation of a Croatian kingdom as a full-fledged member within the Habsburg Empire organization, further proved the ideological ambiguity of Croatia's political evolution within the empire. It is true that at this stage of Croatian history the weakness of imperial Austria's position in foreign and domestic politics, impaired equally by two lost wars, made her abandonment of the Croatian cause almost a political necessity. Yet it cannot be said with the same certainty that a Croatia politically less divided among autonomist, southern Slav unionists, pro-Magyars, and imperialists might not have stood its ground far better against the Magyar claims, which finally were materialized in the Magyar-Croatian Compromise of 1868.[44]

However, the intrinsic connection of the Croatian national problem with the broader issues—on the one hand, Illyrism and Yugoslav unionism, and, on the other the Greater Croatian state concept and Trialism—remained. The representatives of all these ideas distinctly felt that any radical approach, even to the mere Croatian problem, meant the "release" of powerful and conflicting ethnic, religious, and political forces within and beyond the empire. To avoid a showdown on these issues on the part of Croatia, as well as the empire, at the price of submission to Magyar demands meant the postponement of threatening revolutionary consequences. Such consequences would have equally affected the empire as a whole as well as the leading position of Croatia within its southern Slav orbit. Conservative, pro-Habsburg Trialism wanted to prevent this clash; at the same time it wanted to increase the power of the southern Slav peoples within the empire by organizing them as the third member-state of the monarchy. Yet it was not prepared to forego the claim for Catholic Croatian leadership within a southern Slav national federation in the frame of the Austrian empire organization. It demanded a privileged position for Croatia within the planned southern Slav state and a privileged position for the southern Slav state within the empire itself.

It is understandable that such a concept found a divergent and on the whole negative reception, except for the strata of Croatian conservatism. Typical of the negative action of an opponent of the Habsburg Empire in general is Wendel's view.

As it [Trialism] had to raise the Catholics over the Orthodox, the Croatians over the Serbs, the trialistic concept was but a flowering of the *divide et impera* policy. Without definite shape, Trialism—which was to replace the dualism in force since 1867—oscillated between the poles of centralism and federalism.[45]

And Milan Hodža, the late prime minister of Czechoslovakia and one-time supporter of an Austrian nationality federation, declared:

It would have been futile to replace dualism, that is, domination by two races, by Trialism, which would have meant the privileged position of three groups in an empire where eight were fighting for equality.[46]

These two statements concisely express the opposition, ranging from the liberal Federalists to the Socialists. It goes without saying that for reasons of national self-interest this opposition, though certainly not its motives, was shared by German Austrian centralists and supporters of the ruling Magyar regime. Finally, Serb opposition beyond the empire, and during the last decades of its existence within the monarchy as well, turned out to be decisively important. This particularly held true after the formal annexation of Bosnia-Hercegovina (1908), where the Serbs outnumbered the Croats by two to one.[47] If Trialism were ever to be materialized, it could no longer be put into effect around a Croatian national nucleus, but needed a Serbian nucleus. Yet, if for no other weighty reasons of foreign and domestic politics, such a solution would have been impossible in an empire whose foundations rested so much more on a Catholic Western than on a Byzantine Eastern tradition.

Certainly, the champions of Trialism did not succeed in popularizing their cause beyond the strata of relatively narrow, group interests. The Conservative Croatian nationalists, in their Party of Right, under Antony Starčević and during the last decades of the monarchy's existence in the Party of Pure Right, under the leadership of Josip Frank, made it abundantly clear that to them Trialism meant, not the equal union of the southern Slav peoples, but the rule of the Croats.[48] They regarded the Serbs as only an Orthodox branch of the Croat people. Nor did the fact that at times the imperial government in Vienna and, more openly, an ultra-Conservative circle around the heir presumptive, Francis Ferdinand, encouraged the trialistic idea serve to give it popular appeal. Instead, it nourished southern Slav suspicion that just as imperial Austria before 1867 and 1868 had made use of the Croatian-Magyar conflict to foster her own rule, so she was now ready to back up Croatian against Serb claims for exactly the same purpose.[49]

What was possibly true in regard to certain trends in Austrian policy was certainly on the contrary far more true in regard to Magyar policy, which had widely ruled Croatia's destiny since 1868. Particularly during and after the banship of the Magyar Count Khuen-Héderváry (1883–1903),[50] the Magyar rulers in Budapest, for the sake of political expediency, consistently supported, often by insiduous and unconstitutional means, the Serb minority against the Croats. This is not to say that the Magyar regime in any way favored a southern Slav union program under Serb leadership, but only that this divide-and-rule policy, supporting anti-Croatian opposition in the interest of Magyar autocratic rule, fomented Croatian national intolerance. Thus, the idea of the trialistic union was thoroughly discredited in the eyes of the southern Slav world.

Nevertheless, it is true that the idea of Trialism, in spite of the disturbing consequences of the annexation of Bosnia-Hercegovina, seemingly did not entirely lack Serbian support. As late as 1911 a group of Liberal politicians in Serbia, under the leadership of Professor Zivojin Perić, possibly with the knowledge of the Serbian ministry of foreign affairs, intimated that Serbia would be ready to join a southern Slav union under the Habsburgs, provided such an Austrian-

Yugoslav member state would have equal constitutional standing with Cisleithanian Austria and Hungary. Austria, having rejected a somewhat similar, almost official, offer on the part of King Milan of Serbia in the 1880s, did not consider these new hints seriously in 1909.[51] Apart from the intrinsic opposition on the part of the Magyars and the Germans to a strengthening of the Slav element in the monarchy, there was general fear that proposals of this kind would mean only one thing: a Serbian Trojan-horse policy to undermine the monarchy from within, with no guarantee that such a new southern Slav state would not secede from the monarchy within a few years. Thus, the time had definitely passed, if there ever was such a time, when Trialism could have been introduced peacefully, with sincere Serbian consent.

With the ascendancy of Serb leadership in Austrian southern Slav affairs at the turn of the twentieth century, a revived Yugoslav unionism evolved. Soon enough it turned ever more markedly anti-Austrian. Its success was largely due to a political transformation of Croatian party life from the autonomist, Conservative Right to the socially underprivileged, unionist Left. Trialism definitely had lost its hold on the political course of Croatia, yet it still had a precarious political existence. It was cautiously encouraged by Vienna, frequently by the descendants of the imperial Military Frontier men, to whom Austria still represented the old occidental bulwark against a Turkish onslaught from the East. They were ready to accept the trialistic Greater Croatian solution under almost any condition, even in the odd form of the so-called *subtrialistic* solution, which conceived a southern Slav state either as semiautonomous condominium of Austria and Hungary or as a dependency of either of the dualistic states,[52] usually of Hungary.

Obviously, such plans had no future in an empire where national consciousness was relatively as far advanced as in early twentieth-century Austria. Yet Trialism had been recommended by as keen, brilliant, and discriminating a student of the southern Slav question as R. W. Seton-Watson [53] as well feasible for the solution of the southern Slav problem of the empire and as the first step toward its federalization on an ethnic basis. His conclusions are based on a curious mixture of correct and obviously erroneous arguments. In 1911 he considered the Pan-Serb solution very lightly as "altogether outside of the realm of practical politics." Wrong as this first conclusion was, his second unfortunately proved right, "Croato-Serb Unity outside the Habsburg monarchy can only be attained through universal war and a thorough revision of the map of Europe. The achievement of that unity inside the Habsburg monarchy is a far more practical policy." [54] Why so? Among the various reasons advanced by Seton-Watson, one brought forward in a different context was clearly of paramount importance. He believed strongly in the future of the empire. Thus, he asserted in 1907, "The present writer disbelieves not merely in the probability but even in the possibility of a break-up of Austria-Hungary," and as late as 1911 he stated "Servia-Montenegro can only watch and are helpless to hinder the process of evolution which is gradually making for Serbo-Croat unity under Habsburg sway." [55] To a political analyst who took Austria's political future as assured, the impact of Serbian influence as negligible, and, rightly, the realization of the Pan-Serbian solution as a cause of war, Trialism, indeed, had much to recommend it. Unfortunately, Seton-Watson's sympathy with the desirability of a trialistic solution led him to believe that it was also a feasible solution. Thus, he took it as a matter of course that Croats and Serbs would be ready to abandon any claims for the incorporation of the Austrian Slovene lands in the southern Slav state and that the Czechs would welcome Trialism as a step toward federalism.

Actually, the very term "Trialism" precluded a comprehensive federal solution of the empire problem. It recognized, not equality, but a privileged position of Germans, Magyars, and Croats or, at best, Germans and Magyars, together with the joint southern Slav peoples. Any farther-reaching, just, and equal solution of the Austrian nationality problem comprising all the national groups of the empire was directly contradicted by the terms of the trialist concept itself. Wherever representatives of other Slav nationalities in Austria supported the concept, they did so only because they aspired to a similar privileged status. This applied at times particularly to certain Conservative Czech and Polish groups. Obviously, the grant to other national groups of a status similar to that demanded by the Croatian trialists would have meant, not Trialism, but federalism in the traditional form of the historicopolitical entities.

Yet possibly the term "Trialism" should not be understood as literally implying the organization of the empire into three leading nationality groups. It could be perceived merely as the attempt to settle national conflict, not in a reform movement comprising all the nationalities at once, but gradually solving one specific national problem at the most appropriate time. On the basis of Austrian experience, the value of such a piecemeal approach may well be questioned, as materialized in the German-Magyar Compromise of 1867, the Magyar-Croatian Compromise of 1868, and as attempted in the Hohenwart plan for the reconciliation of the Czechs in 1871. Every one of these solutions or attempted solutions certainly had its own specific shortcomings; yet they all had one cardinal deficiency in common. They considered the national status of one national group and the national relationship of two or at best three national groups alone. But such was the intrinsic complexity of the Austrian nationality problem that the handling of any of these problems greatly interfered with that of all the others. Any revision of the Magyar position in Hungary touched upon the conditions of all the nationalities represented in Hungary and in Austria as well, as far as these nationalities stretched beyond the borders of the Leitha. The same held true in reverse for general and even merely regional national reforms in Cisleithanian Austria, as has been shown in connection with Hohenwart's plans.[56]

Thus, since Trialism greatly influenced the German and the Magyar position, it was not only the concern of the southern Slav groups but also of the other Austrian and Hungarian national groups. Their conflicting claims could be reconciled, if at all, only on the basis of general concessions and sacrifices, a comprehensive give and take, but certainly not by a mere mutual compromise between two parties. In this sense Trialism proved to be a failure, even in its wider combined meaning as a concept of southern Slav state organization and as a method to solve the Austrian nationality problems one by one. In the final analysis there existed, not many nationality problems in the Austrian Empire, but one problem, composed of diverse parts interrelated with the whole as much as with every other part.

To be sure, the peculiarity of the unsettled southern Slav question, from the viewpoint of the Croatian people, rested in the interplay of Croatian autonomism, the Greater-Croatian Catholic state program to be realized in the form of Trialism, and the program of the Croatian future, southern Slav unionism. But it also arose from Croatian-southern Slav interrelations with all the other national groups, the dualistic states, and the empire as a whole. The political superiority of Yugoslav unionism was based on the fact that it was able to eliminate at least some of these conflicting ties, those to the empire and to the dual states. Croatian autonomism and Trialism had struggled with them vainly for two generations. At the eve of the First World War, when unionism became the unchallenged carrier of the Yugoslav future, they no longer were political forces to be taken into account.

also information had bearing on the matter, the issue of these difficulties, complying... perhaps conceded... these... ties and to the actual... these... civilian... merely for two... justification be... other to be at least distinct forces to be the very strongest.

CHAPTER VIII

# THE ITALIANS

VIEWED from the ramparts of world history, the Italians have the longest and proudest historical tradition among all the Austrian national groups.[1] From the viewpoint of political history, the additional fact stands out that the Italian national problem was directly involved in the issues of the four major wars Austria had to fight after the Congress of Vienna.[2] Thus, Austria had to meet Italian attacks four times during the two generations from 1848 to 1915. United Italy's political aspirations were among the most important single, direct causes of the destruction of the empire in 1918. Nevertheless, the Italian question, though a major political problem, was not one of the empire's major national problems.

This became conspicuous when, with the loss of Lombardy in 1859 and of Venice in 1866, Austria's Italian population was reduced from some five millions to about 600,000, the smallest national group in the empire. However, it was true long before that time. From Piedmont's participation in the Crimean War, in 1854, on the side of the Western Allies, Italian nationalism could be reasonably sure that achievement of the centuries-old aim of national unification was imminent. Yet even the situation of 1848, before the process of political separation from Austria commenced, made the achievement of this goal likely. An Italian national cause supported by such ardent ambitions, not merely by passive sympathies of western Europe, saw little reason to work for intermediate solutions. Not national reform in Austria, but on the contrary national separation from Austria was its definite aim.

These facts were recognized by Austrian centralism as well as by Italian nationalism. Austrian political thinking,[3] though by no means ready to voluntarily abandon imperial rule in northern Italy, was fully aware that these "possessions," as historicopolitical entities of long standing, were only loosely tied to the empire. In fact, the

Lombardo-Venetian administration was entirely separated from that of all of the other Habsburg domains.[4]

This Austrian administration in Italy, which held a more than fair record in the economic and industrial field,[5] may certainly be blamed for various unjust and oppressive political measures. It cannot be reproached for never having seriously tried the obviously impossible, to satisfy the national aims of the population of these lands within Austria. No matter how divided and complicated the political setup of the Italian peninsula was until 1859, none but the most narrow-minded observer could have any doubt that the ascendancy of Western political thought would insist on nothing less than a comprehensive solution of the Italian question as a matter of primary European interest. The world-wide recognition of the problem of Italian unification as one of western European civilization made a comprehensive solution possible at a time when the Polish cause, less fortunate in its appeal to the West, had completely failed to achieve its national aims.

Obviously, the Polish national cause in the pre-March era, in many ways amazingly similar to the Italian, was subjected to stronger and more complex political forces. Its great cultural heritage was not endowed with the world-wide fame of the Italian tradition. Even more important, the Italian peoples were not torn by the same violent social conflict as the Poles. Italian national redemption did not irretrievably depend upon social revolution, as did the Polish national cause. This helps to explain how western Europe supported the Italian cause far more readily than it supported the Polish cause.

It also helps to depict the national position of those Italians who until 1918 remained under Austrian rule and whose settlements had for more than four centuries almost consistently formed a part of Austrian territory or sphere of influence: the Italians in far southern or "Welsch" (Italian) Tirol and their conationals in the Austrian Littoral (Trieste, Gorizia and Gradiska, Istria), Dalmatia, and (Hungarian) Fiume.[6] In Tirol they were, socially and economically, closely connected and on an equal footing with the German population. Their economic position and their cultural facilities in the Littoral were in many ways superior to those of the native Slovene and Croatian population. On the whole, their social status was favored by a relative degree of prosperity and security, which in some ways neutralized the otherwise invincible appeal of Italian nationalism beyond the frontiers.

To be sure, these Italians in Tirol and the Littoral, for centuries joined politically to peoples of other nationalities, had never formed a historicopolitical entity of their own within the Habsburg lands. Still, in Bauer's terms, they were to be considered, even within Austria, as a national group "with history." From medieval times, they were organized in a society in which the upper classes formed a national nobility and free burghers in towns and cities.

Nevertheless, there were marked differences between the status of the Italians in Tirol and those on the coast of the Adriatic, who were separated from each other by a stretch of German and Slovene land. The Italians in south Tirol lived in a territory separated from German Austrian lands by about the clearest language frontier existing in the empire. To the south they were directly connected with the bulk of the Italian people in the kingdom. The Italians in the Littoral—with the principal exception of some major towns, particularly the city-state of Trieste, which was to some degree autonomous,—constituted only a relative majority among the four nationality groups inhabiting these joint crownlands, and thus, in many districts, only a minority.[7]

All in all, nowhere in Austria did ethnic conditions appear more propitious for a clear-cut solution of the national problem than in Tirol, and in few crownlands did the solution seem as difficult as in the Littoral.[8] Although it is easy to understand why a fully satisfactory solution to the national medley on the shores of the Adriatic was never achieved, it is not so easy to comprehend why the government failed in Tirol to satisfy completely the Italian claims—that is, for the duration of Austrian rule, to be sure.

These Italians in Tirol, though unalterably opposed to this Austrian rule, knew how to adjust their policy to the force of circumstances. Before the unification of Italy was achieved in 1861, the aims of the unredeemed irredenta were expressed in the officially tolerated form of a desired union between the Italians in Tirol and those in the Lombardo-Venetian kingdom.[9] When Austria lost Venetia, in 1866, this slogan had to be dropped, since from then on it could no longer have camouflaged the aims of the irredenta.

From that time, the second interim aim of the Tirolese Italians (particularly of their moderate wing), the partition of Tirol into a German (northern) and an Italian (southern) part, became increasingly prominent. Yet this was not a new scheme, having been voiced by the Italian Tirolese representatives at the *Reichstag* of Kremsier in 1848–49, where deputies of the Lombardo-Venetian kingdom were not represented at all.[10]

While the Austrian government had always rejected the idea of union between the Tirolese and the Lombardo-Venetian Italians as an open move toward defection from the empire, it never rejected outright these secondary Italian-Tirolese aims. Neither did it ever fully accept them, not without reason from the standpoint of the administration.

In this case the fear that administrative partition would be the first step toward complete separation was not the only factor determining the government's position. Among all the Austrian crownlands of preponderantly German character, Tirol was most clearly a historicopolitical entity of its own, and its Estates honored a tradition which at times closely approached separatism.[11] Tirol was joined to the Habsburg domains as early as the fourteenth century, but well into the seventeenth century (1665) it was for long periods under the rule of collateral branches of the dynasty, thereby preserving a relatively high degree of independence.[12] Nowhere else in the monarchy was Catholicism more deeply rooted than in this crownland, frequently called the Holy Land of Tirol. Mighty monasteries and bishoprics held powerful positions, and one of the principal aims of Tirolian policy until 1861 was to prevent the legal introduction of Protestant public religious service throughout the land. Tirol not only considered itself the fortress of Catholicism in the empire and a separate historicopolitical entity of its own; it was also proud of its record as the most imperial, the most loyal of the imperial lands. This fact had been decisively proven in the heroic Peasant Revolution of 1809 against the French occupation. Thus, religious and historic tradition, more than direct national tendencies, opposed a partition of Tirol, whose stubborn, but in the end supremely loyal, support the Austrian government was most anxious to preserve.

Nevertheless, in the period from 1849 to 1861 the Italian Tirolese enjoyed a far-reaching degree of autonomous administration, though short of actual partition of the crownland. However, for weighty political reasons these concessions were withdrawn in 1861. The cession of Lombardy in 1859 had made Tirol a borderland on its western frontier toward Piedmont-Sardinia. The loss of Venetia in 1866 did the same on its eastern frontier toward the new Italian kingdom. The setup of a separate Italian crownland, or even a wide administrative autonomy, in a border territory whose population longed for delivery from Austrian rule and for union with Italy, appeared to the government increasingly dangerous.

It was one of the most unfortunate events in Austrian history that the militarily successful Austrian campaign against Italy in 1866 enhanced the government's determination not to yield more territory to Italy than demanded by the terms of the Prusso-Italian alliance. An Austrian foreign policy of vision should, at that time, voluntarily have satisfied the ethnically justified Italian demands for the cession of the Trentino. This probably could have been done without significant loss of political prestige and with practically no less of the empire's military security and economic interests.[13] It is likely that thereupon subsequent events might have taken an entirely different turn. Italy, satisfied in her principal national aspirations in Tirol, might possibly have compromised on her demands to acquire the multinational Littoral with Trieste, which was vitally important to Austria but, without *Hinterland*, of limited economic value to Italy herself. Instead of the mockery of the subsequent Tripartite alliance—as far as Austria and Italy were concerned an alliance of permanent enemies—stable and peaceful relations might have developed between both countries. As events actually turned out, unappeased Italian nationalism asked for and was promised by the Entente Powers in the Treaty of London in April, 1915, not only the Trentino but the entire Littoral and the northern part of Dalmatia as well. The acceptance of such sweeping terms would have made Austria practically landlocked. Obviously, this would have been, politically and economically, equally incompatible with her position as a Great Power. Today, it is recognized that insistence on the terms of the secret treaty of London largely wrecked the chances of a separate peace with Austria in 1917, and it may well be said that the existence of that treaty, far more than Italy's actual military contribution, ranks high among the immediate reasons for the destruction of the empire.[14]

In the last analysis such a course of events was caused to a great extent by the conservatism of Austrian statesmanship. Afraid of the shattering influence of a possible "precedent," it hesitated to settle in time the only Austrian national problem conceivably soluble by small territorial concessions to a neighboring country. The fact that in size and in geographic, historic, and political conditions the Italian question pointed toward different and in a way easier solutions than any of the other Austrian national problems was ignored by this doctrinaire way of political thinking. Until spring, 1915, Austria's attitude toward Italy was largely dominated by the fear that voluntary withdrawal from any advanced position was worse than war, worse even than a lost war; that it meant, in fact, the suicide of the monarchy.

The rigid orthodox application of this principle does not mean, however, that Austria was entirely blind to her destiny in this respect. Austrian statesmen were aware that the Italian question within Austria did not represent a major national, but a political problem dominated almost exclusively by the influence of foreign policy. Yet they moved in a vicious circle. Since the Austrian government was not ready to settle the Italian problem in time, at the price of reasonable concessions, its fear that major concessions to the Austro-Italians would pave the way for the final triumph of Irredentism was understandable.

Nevertheless, it would be wrong to assume that after 1866 Austria's policy toward her Italian subjects was particularly oppressive. Neither was the Italian reaction to governmental policy characterized exclusively by the activities of a vociferous political irredenta which without support from the neighbor state beyond the frontiers would scarcely have been significant.

In fact, almost the opposite was true. Austria's policy toward her Italian citizens after 1866, especially after the conclusion of the Tripartite alliance in 1882, was determined by one main idea, to mollify nationalist feelings in Italy by a liberal attitude toward their kin in the empire. Though unwilling to express this liberalism by way of territorial autonomy in strategically important frontier regions, Austria intended to prove her good will on the smaller scale of administrative practice. Thus, in many ways the Italian national position in due course became more favorable than that of almost any of the other smaller national groups.[15]

Italian language rights in school, court, diet, and administration were widely recognized. A separate section of the Tirolian board of education administered Italian school affairs. Not governmental opposition, but primarily local German chauvinism impeded and delayed the development of an Austro-Italian university system.[16] It is true, though, that in the Littoral the complexity of multinational conflict between Croat and Slovene southern Slavs, Italians, and even Germans led to oppressive police measures which at times rigidly curtailed the political activities of the population as a whole. Fom the national viewpoint, however, the Italian situation was definitely better than that of the Slovenes and the Croats. The latter's elementary rights as national groups in regard to language were recognized in the Littoral, in addition to already existing German and Italian language rights, only in 1849. Still, up to the period immediately preceding the First World War, the Italians received preferential treatment.[17] This trend of governmental policy was even more obvious in Dalmatia, where an insignificant Italian minority (some 3.5 percent in 1910) held, until 1909, an inordinately dominant position in regard to language rights and educational facilities.

Indeed, in the Littoral and in Dalmatia, Italian institutions and, even more markedly, Italian language rights enjoyed relative privileges which Austrian centralism otherwise was accustomed to reserve for the Germans. One might go even farther and state that after the introduction of general equal franchise in Austria in 1906–1907 the Italians became the most privileged of all national groups from the angle of "franchise arithmetic." This reform allegedly graded the size of electoral districts according to standards of cultural and economic maturity of the various national groups, but actually according to political expediency. In any case Italian representatives were to be elected by the smallest electoral districts, with the Germans and the Rumanians as runners-up.[18]

This "most favored nationality status" in the electoral reform was based partly on the German concept of a parliamentary majority coalition of the non-Slav national groups—Germans, Rumanians, and Italians—against a Slav parliamentary bloc. This scheme did not work, because Slav parliamentary representation finally turned out to be larger than originally estimated. Yet even under different conditions it would hardly have been practical, since the government was unwilling to foresake the parliamentary support of a major Slav group, the Poles. Still, the idea accurately depicts the peculiar Italian position in Austria, which resembled the Polish one.

Both groups, in their basic national aims, were more irreconcilable to the empire idea than was any other group in Cisleithanian Austria. But they were, not without reason, counted by the government among its temporary supporters. Waiting for the final day of national redemption, they struck, in the meantime, a mutually profitable bargain with the forces of German centralism.

In regard to the Italians, the basis of this bargain was support of the Austrian government in matters of general policy in return for a benevolent pro-Italian policy in the sphere of local administration.[19] At the same time, however, the activities of the Italian Irredentists, with their headquarters in Triente and Trieste, ran their course. Ignoring any tacit agreement on questions of internal policy, they kept the great Italian idea alive before the eyes of the young generation. They were firmly and rightly convinced that the future was theirs.

The analysis of the handling of the Italian problem in Austria particularly illustrates one of the most significant and most fateful illusions of Austrian policy: the idea that a benevolent and fair administrative policy could be substituted for a comprehensive solution going to the roots of the national problem. But mere administrative benevolence, however willingly accepted as a temporary expedient by any national group, could never persuade it to swerve from the course of national destiny—if and when its hour struck.

# THE NATIONAL GROUPS WITHOUT INDEPENDENT NATIONAL POLITICAL HISTORY

# CHAPTER IX

# THE SLOVAKS

IT WAS the lot of the Slovaks in the century from the Congress of Vienna to 1918 to be one of the national groups of the monarchy most severely suppressed in their cultural, national, and political development.[1] Four main reasons are evident for this unfortunate position.

First, there are the statistical geographic facts. The Slovaks rank among the smallest national groups of the empire, superior in numbers only to the Slovenes and the Italians.[2] As proven by the example of the Italians, the mere fact of a generally low population figure did not in itself lead to discriminatory treatment. However, the Slovaks were not only a small national group; the population also was thinly spread over poor and mountainous regions of the Tatra, the low Carpathians, and the northwestern part of the high Carpathian Mountains. Consequently, the combined effect of geographic factors, the small population, the character of settlements, soil conditions, and poor agricultural management worked to their disadvantage.

The second reason is that the Slovaks represented the type of nation without independent national political history, a factor which made their later rise all the more remarkable. After the fall of the Greater Moravian Empire which emerged at the turn of the eighth century and succumbed to Magyar aggression scarcely a century later, its Slovak offspring had always been suppressed in its cultural, social, and political development.[3] Yet the specific influence of this suppression on the development of Slovene nationalism has become fully evident only in modern times.

The very fact that the Slovaks had lived for over a thousand years under a specific form of Magyar domination [4] is the third influence on their destiny. Until the end of the eighteenth century, when "Hungarism began to change into Magyarism," [5] this domination made itself felt exclusively in the form of social discrimination. Until that time the discriminatory treatment of the Slovaks resulted chiefly from the fact that they formed a group consisting largely of agricultural serfs without a sizeable upper strata of society,[6] without a nationally conscious nobility, and with very small industrial and professional classes. Here, the influence of conscious Magyar and Slovak nationalism became distinct only after the beginning of the nineteenth century. Magyars and Slovaks to some extent unintentionally aroused each other's national feelings. From that time on, the discrimination against the Slovaks was no longer based merely on the structure of the Hungarian feudal system in general, but increasingly, in addition, on the claims of the supremacy of Magyar nationalism in particular. This trend, which continually grew in strength throughout the first half of the nineteenth century, received a mild setback with the ascent of the neo-absolutist centralist system in the empire after the suppression of the Magyar Revolution. But it became more firmly entrenched with the conclusion of the Compromise of 1867, which gave practically free rein to the Magyar rule over the Hungarian nationalities. It is fair to say that in modern times the political fortunes of the Slovak people were at their lowest ebb in the period from 1867 to 1918.

Yet, all these factors, ominously working together, also apply in varying degrees to other national groups in Hungary. Only with reference to the fourth factor—namely, the nonexistence of a foreign state of predominantly conational population—was the position of the Slovaks distinctly more unfavorable than that of the Rumanians and the Serbs in Hungary. It is true that this fourth and politically decisive disadvantage of the Slovak position was partly offset by the ethnic affiliation with one of the principal national groups in the western part of the empire, the Czechs. But the history of Czech-Slovak interrelations was beset with distinct difficulties. The Czech historic national group, in tradition, numbers, geographic, economic, and cultural conditions, was considered by far the stronger part in any conceivable form of association with a poor mountain people without history. Slovak fear that affiliation with the Czechs would mean, not union, but absorption, was and always has been understandable.

That does not necessarily mean that this fear was justified. The Czechs themselves were a people restricted in their national domains, though in the nineteenth and twentieth centuries certainly not to the same degree as the Hungarian Slovaks. Furthermore, the rise of Czech nationalism in Austria and Slovak nationalism in Hungary accentuated rather than eradicated the linguistic, social, religious, and political distinctions between the two peoples, and this development in a way impaired the full effectiveness of their close ethnic relationship.

Nevertheless, the mere existence of such a Czech-Slovak relationship represented the one and only factor which enabled the Slovaks in the nineteenth century to pursue at times something like a national policy. The rise of Slovak nationalism was the premise of any political future for the Slovak people. Their social conditions under Magyar rule conditioned its growth; the Slovak-Czech relationship was the redeeming factor which called it to action.

It is undoubtedly true that a low standard of culture and a very limited national consciousness in a group necessarily have a strongly negative effect upon political standing. From this commonplace truth is sometimes derived a commonplace falsehood referring to the reverse condition—namely, that continued political suppression inevitably leads to a lowering of national consciousness, and this irretrievably to the decay of national culture. Slovak history in the nineteenth century is an exemplary case proving that such a conclusion is not necessarily true. Slovak national consciousness and national character have been preserved throughout many a century not only of political suppression but of actual political nonexistence. Yet in the era of national awakening in Europe at the turn of the nineteenth century, Slovak nationalism, as evidenced by a rich harvest of national cultural activities, came to the fore within an incredibly short time. In its intensity of national emotion and fullness of cultural achievement, it was second to none of the other Slav nationalities in the empire. The stature of their political and cultural leaders, from the time of Kollár and Štúr to that of Štefánik and Masaryk, ranked among the first.

The complexity of this cultural national development profoundly affected the future course of Slovak political nationalism, particularly in regard to relations with the Czech people. Several authors, particularly S. H. Thomson and R. W. Seton-Watson, have stressed the point that Czech-Slovak interrelations were closely connected with the religious history of both peoples. Indeed, the most intimate affinity of cultural and linguistic relations, amounting, as far as the written language is concerned, to practical identity between Czech and Slovak, was reached with the spread of Lutheranism into Bohemia and Slovakia in the first half of the sixteenth century.

The Counter Reformation, a movement the influence of which in its consequences still continues to influence the Slovaks, attempted to stop this trend. Gravely concerned with the influence of Czech Hussite Protestant ideas on Slovakia,[7] Catholicism endeavored to block the development of Czech-Slovak interrelations from mere ethnic similarity to a strong cultural union. The intense Jesuit cultural activities in seventeenth-century Slovak territories, as, indeed, the whole lasting Protestant-Catholic conflict in the Czech-Slovak orbit, could not permanently quell a political union movement. But these activities certainly helped to preserve and to restore distinct national peculiarities in both peoples. This antagonism also influenced in no small way the shaping of definite and conflicting political objectives in nineteenth-century Slovakia; that is, the union with the Czechs, autonomy within Hungary, and, somewhat artificially, complete Slovak separatism. Thus, cultural and particularly literary and linguistic distinctions between Czechs and Slovaks conditioned the minds of the people to a nationalist political reaction to what once was a purely religious problem.

The Czech literary language (largely the language of the Reformation among the Slovaks) became identified in the minds of the people with Czech-Slovak cultural and political union. Beginning with the Counter Reformation, the local dialects used by the Jesuits for their missionary and educational work came to represent the language of submission to the Catholic empire. With the rise of the national idea, these dialects were identified with the rather different movement of autonomism within Hungary and of national separatism between the Czech and the Slovak peoples.[8]

As the course of Slovak history proves, every chance of Slovakia's ultimate redemption from Magyar suppression rested with the first alternative—the Czecho-Slovak cultural union, with the ultimate aim of a political union in the future. And yet, in spite of the historic association of Protestantism with unionism and of Catholicism with separatism, the former in a curious way helped just as much as the latter to widen the rift between Czech and Slovak culture.

To Catholic scholarship, in its endeavor to mold a literary language clearly separated from the Hussite spirit of Czech literature,[9] goes the credit for the first attempt to establish a Slovak grammar, the so-called *Grammatica Slavica* of 1790. Father Anton Bernolák (1762-1813), the chief representative of this movement, did not succeed in having his grammar generally accepted in Slovakia. His language adaptation corresponded so closely to the dialects of western Slovakia and the bordering lands of Bohemia and Moravia that it was hardly understood in central and eastern Slovakia.[10] Furthermore, the rejection of the Catholic background of this proposed language reform by the non-Catholic camp certainly was not helpful in its propagation.

It might have been expected that the Catholic attempt to create an independent Slovak literary language would have led to a linguistic countermovement stressing the linguistic union of the Czech and the Slovak literary languages. An inherent and autonomous trend in any movement of rising cultural nationalism, regardless of religious and political distinctions, indicates a different course. A strong demand came to the fore to build up a literary language more comprehensive and different from any other language or, in other words, a language that would be more "national" than the Catholic attempt. Hence, nationalism was fought with nationalism that was even more accentuated.

If this natural, though not quite rational, development is put in its proper setting—namely, the Slav cultural renaissance in the pre-March period—the nature of the Slovak national movement under the leadership of the Protestants L'udovít Štúr and Jan Kollár will be better understood.[11] The peculiar intellectual contribution of the Lutheran L'udovít Štúr (1783–1844) was his aim not merely to create a Slovak language, even at the price of alienating the Czechs, but also, by general adoption of his language reform, to reconcile the national religious conflict among the Slovaks, both Protestant and Catholic. Though he was bitterly opposed by his great conationals of pro-Czech and Pan-Slav leanings, his literary endeavors and those of his literary friends Joseph Hurban and Michael Hodža proved amazingly successful. In many ways the national revival initiated by Štúr under most difficult conditions proved as effective as the parallel movements among the Czechs and the Croats, discussed previously.

Štúr, like many of the foremost intellectual leaders of the Slavs, was educated at a German university. Also like many of his fellow-Slav leaders, he became a teacher and used the limited political potentialities entailed in a professorship at the Gymnasium of Bratislava (Pressburg) to build and further the Slovak national cause. The publication of a Slovak newspaper, *Slovenské Národné Noviny,* (the people's paper) in 1845, with a literary supplement, the *Tatranský Orol* (Tatra Eagle), followed familiar trends in the Slav renaissance movement. So did the new Slav grammar, published in 1846. Finally, the involuntary leisure of exile after the outbreak of the Magyar Revolution in 1848 gave this champion of the cultural linguistic claims of the Slovak people at the diet of Bratislava in 1847–48 the opportunity to collect Slav songs and fairy tales.

While Štúr's political activities preceded and overshadowed his literary achievements, the poetic and scholarly work of the romantic Jan Kollár (1793–1852) on the subject of Pan-Slav tendencies was the pivot of his lifework.[12]

Paul J. Šafařík (1795–1861), the great Slavist with Czech leanings, agreed with Kollár's basic ideas. He was opposed to cultural "isolationism" as implied by Štúr, Michael Hodža, Joseph Hurban, and, from the Catholic camp, by Jan Hollý. Thus, Czech-Slovak unionism, romantic cultural Pan-Slavism, and Protestant as well as Catholic cultural separatism each contributed in its own way to the fullness and variety of Slovak cultural and national life in the pre-March era.[13]

Like other Slav national movements, the Slovak national renaissance was fortunate enough to receive backing from external quarters in the beginning. As in the case of the Czechs, and particularly the Croats, the Austrian central government was concerned about the growing claims of Magyarism and was ready to tolerate and even to support within limits the Slovak aspirations. Ignoring violent Magyar objections, it authorized the Slovak literary activities previously outlined.

Of less actual, but probably greater potential, significance was the support from the pioneers of the Czech cultural renaissance. They acclaimed in particular the ideas of the two great Slovak literary men Šafařík and Kollár, who in their lifework belong, indeed, equally to the Slovak and the Czech causes.

Beyond these learned groups, the active and weighty support given by the leader of the Bohemian nobles, Count Leo Thun, must not be overlooked. Thun's correspondence with Kossuthist Francis Pulszky, upholding Slovak rights to a limited cultural autonomy within Hungary, and Pulszky's pseudo-Liberal failure to understand national liberty in any but the terms of Magyar Kossuthism, is particularly illuminating in this respect.[14] The position of liberalism (the striving for national liberty) and that of historic traditional conservatism (generally upholding the *status quo*) appear here to be strangely reversed. In this case Thun's Catholic Conservative program appears at least ready to recognize Slovak national rights *within* the framework of the Hungarian lands, while Pulszky's tense Liberal national philosophy proclaimed tenets little short of integral nationalism.[15]

Thun's activities on behalf of the Slovak cause, which form a consistent trend in his policy as a member of the Austrian cabinets after 1848, were decidedly the result of his pro-Czech attitude in general. And the Czech attitude toward the Slovak problem relied firmly and sometimes almost blindly on the indestructible ties of ethic and linguistic relationship between the two northwestern Slav peoples. The rise of a Slovak national movement that was directed not only against Magyar political oppression, but for an independent national culture of its own, had a greatly disillusioning effect on Czech nationalism.[16] This attitude, though changing with changed conditions, has in fact prevailed ever since.

Regarding the revolutionary development of 1848–49, it is scarcely surprising that Palacký's great empire reform plan, envisaging a Czech-Slovak member state of an Austrian federation, was not seriously considered by the Austrian government. Here, revolutionary reform was doomed to a twofold failure. First, the general counterrevolutionary reaction leading to the dissolution of the *Reichstag* of Kremsier in March, 1849, blocked the realization by democratic means of any further sweeping national reforms. Secondly and more specifically, even prior to the triumph of the counterrevolution it was politically impossible to put through Hungarian national reform plans while the Magyar War of Independence was in full swing.[17]

Nevertheless, it is noteworthy that Czech-Slovak union plans appealed little to the Hungarian Slovaks themselves. Neither the Slovak national revolutionary program, as formulated in the improvised national assembly of Liptovský Svätý Mikulás in May, 1848, nor the Slovak representation at the Slav Congress in Prague, led by Štúr, Hurban, and Hodža in the following month, struck a note which in any way exceeded the demands for a limited autonomy within Hungary.[18] As for the Slovak national program of Liptovský Svätý Mikuláš, except for opportune political demands, generally liberal in character, it stood for the convocation of a national parliament for all the national groups within Hungary. Furthermore, it demanded a convocation of provincial assemblies on an ethnic basis. The creation of a Slovak national guard and wide recognition of Slovak language rights in public life, especially in public instruction, were claimed.

It is difficult to determine whether a realization of the limits of actually obtainable political objectives was responsible for the relatively narrow scope of these demands or whether isolationism, fearing national self-dissolution in a union with the Czechs, played a major part in Slovak political reasoning. It is a fact, however, that the Slovaks did not obtain the fulfillment of a single one of the demands voiced at Liptovský Sväty Mikuláš.[19] Indeed, expectations that the stern and hostile policy of the neo-absolutist regime (1849 to 1859–60) toward prostrate and defeated Magyarism would imply a far-reaching improvement of the Slovak status were to be severely disappointed.[20]

The serious failure of Austrian policy to reorganize the empire on a constitutional and federal basis after the Magyar defeat in 1849 had a particular effect upon the Slovaks. After the brutal treatment they had received from the Magyars in the course of the revolution,[21] they were only too ready to accept a limited national territorial autonomy, guaranteed by the central power of the empire. Such a solution, because of the geographically homogeneous character of the Slovak settlements within Hungary, would have been relatively simple. Centralistic Austrian absolutism, though free from the national chauvinism of the Magyar regime, did not seriously offer any plan of this kind.[22] On the whole, this system—though greatly superior to Magyar rule in administrative efficiency—in many ways only replaced Magyar-national with centralistic-absolutist oppression. The unquestioned difference in the political motivation between the imperial and the Magyar regime had very little effect on the national status and feeling of the Slovak people.

The following period, from the defeat of Austria in the war against Sardinia and France to the Compromise of 1867, often referred to as the era of constitutional experiments, offered another chance for the reform of the Hungarian nationality problems. It was not as comprehensive a chance as that of the previous period of absolutist centralism, when Hungary was reduced to a complete political nonentity, but in a way it was still a favorable one. At this time, under the moderate Liberal Magyar leadership of Deák and entirely free from Kossuth's revolutionary chauvinism, a fairer Magyar approach to the nationality problem could be expected.

A new, though officially unauthorized, Slovak assembly convened at Turč. Sv. Martin in June, 1861. Embittered by previous disappointments, it made more specific and stringent demands than those voiced in 1848. This new program advocated the recognition of the national individuality of the Slovaks and the grant of administrative autonomy for the predominantly Slovak territory in northern Hungary. Slovak was to be the official language here.[23]

The demands contained in this program were somewhat similar to those made by the Serb and the Rumanian nationalities at about the same time, and their failure also was similar. Still, there was hope that a comprehensive Hungarian nationality law, under discussion during that period, would meet the Slovak demands at least partially. However, in the form finally adopted in 1868, the law disappointed Slovak expectations. Though making concessions to the national status of the individual, it rejected the idea of national autonomy for national groups as a whole.

Nevertheless, the gap between the proposals discussed in the Hungarian diet of 1861 and those finally sanctioned in the Hungarian "Law of Nationalities" of 1868,[24] was trifling compared to the discrepancy between this statute and the actual Magyar political practice. After a few years this practice openly flouted the obligations of 1868. As Redlich observed, the entire history of the nineteenth century, the oppression of the Poles by the Russians excepted, offers scarcely another example of equally flagrant disregard of the statutes securing the national rights of the "majority" of a population to match the one committed by the Magyar ruling classes against the Hungarian nationalities after 1867.[25]

Stillborn though the reform plans of the Hungarian Slovaks, the Serbs, and the Rumanians actually were in the 1860s, this era of constitutional experiments compared favorably with Slovak conditions during the following generation.[26] Yet the new era of complete political suppression from the 1870s onward, met a Slovak people far more conscious of nationality than had the Magyar rule in the prerevolutionary era, and national opposition was stiffened accordingly. Political persecution, now rivaling social discrimination in effectiveness and severity, increasingly gained ground in the Magyar administration. Though Slovak national self-confidence could no longer be seriously impaired by Magyar oppression, plans for actual political cooperation between Czechs in Austria and Slovaks in Hungary continued to be of slight practical significance. They could not be compared in impetus with the south Slav unification movement. The first Slovak generation after 1867 still believed that national problems could be settled in Hungary within the framework of the dualistic system. On the other side of the Leitha the political life of the Czechs was still dominated by the issue of the Bohemian *Staatsrecht* and the Czech-German compromise in Bohemia. Thus, there was not even room ideologically for the federal solution of the Austrian problem on an ethnic basis. Such a program grew in strength slowly on the Czech side and was necessarily camouflaged in the program of the Realist party under Masaryk's farsighted leadership.[27]

As for the Slovaks, their cause received some new encouragement from the vague plans for a federal empire reform which, at the turn of the twentieth century, were centered in the sponsor of the new "Greater Austria" schemes—the heir presumptive, Archduke Francis Ferdinand.[28] Yet, these plans were haphazard and contradictory, and no steps could be taken toward their realization during Francis Joseph's reign anyway. According to Milan Hodža, the one Slovak Hungarian leader who was in personal contact with the archduke, various projects to break up the integrity of the Hungarian crownlands and to introduce a Greater Austrian federal solution, either on the ethnic basis of a union between Czechs and Slovaks, or in Aurel Popovici's modification of this concept of separate Czech and Slovak federal member states, or, lastly, in the form of recognition of the old historico-political entities, were blocked by the archduke's deeply rooted hostility to the new Czech policy. According to Hodža, the heir presumptive's sympathy with the concepts of the Bohemian nobles, as, indeed, all his political philosophy, made him hostile to a promotion of the "Hussite" Czech cause which, much as Czech political leaders disagreed on major points of policy, already was in his lifetime irrevocably committed to democracy.[29]

Hodža's interpretation of the archduke's motives may be too simple, but he was correct in stating that Francis Ferdinand was not definitely committed to any of the sweeping empire reform plans, and every evidence points to the fact that at the time of his death, appreciating the extreme difficulty of their final realization, he had receded to far more modest aims.[30] It is likely, however, that one of the first steps of Francis Ferdinand after his accession to the throne would have been the introduction of a new franchise law in Hungary, if necessary by unconstitutional means. Thus, proportional parliamentary representation would have been secured for the Hungarian nationalities. More widespread concessions in the direction of national autonomy might have followed almost of necessity.

On the Slovak side, it is conceivable that such a policy would have blocked the spread of a Czech-Slovak union movement for a considerable time. Whether any internal Hungarian solution of the nationality problem, if possible at all,[31] could have lasted, and whether it might have been only a first step to farther-reaching objectives overstepping the limits of the dualistic frame remain open questions.

But it is not open to question that the center of gravity of the Slovak problem was not in the Slovaks' "first political attempt at cooperation with the Habsburg dynasty [Francis Ferdinand] since 1849."[32] This problem was not in the field of an intra-Hungarian solution initiated by a franchise reform, but in the direction of the ethnic union with the Czechs in an independent state, envisaged and revived by Masaryk.

It is clear, however, that the proposed union in a fully independent state was far more in the foreground of Czech than of Slovak political thinking prior to the outbreak of the war. In fact, well into the latter stages of the First World War, other solutions were widely discussed, such as Slovak autonomy within Hungary, a Czecho-Slovakian or a Slovakian member state in an Austrian federation, or even Slovak independence under a kind of Russian trusteeship.[33] It is, therefore, difficult to judge whether the development heading toward the Czech-Slovak union in a fully sovereign state was merely accelerated by the war, or whether the war only offered the opportunity for its promotion and final realization. Obviously, this question can be discussed only as part of a larger one—whether on the eve of the war and during its progress a peaceful reform of the empire's nationality problem was possible at all.[34]

To be sure, of the claims of the Hungarian nationalities, only those not backed directly by conational majorities in sovereign neighbor states could conceivably have been solved at best within the framework of a defeated Hungary. These conditions did not apply to the cases of the Croats, the Serbs, and the Rumanians. Autonomy within Hungary, however, would have been feasible then in the case of the Carpatho-Ruthenians and the Slovaks.[35]

But the center of gravity of political thinking and action of the Slovaks, as of other national groups, had shifted from native soil to the political emigration abroad. An important difference between the political emigration during the First and the Second World Wars is obvious and of great significance in this connection. Whereas the storms of fascism and bolshevism had swept a major part of the political prewar leadership of European countries into exile before, during and after the Second World War, the far less ruthless and less "efficient" form of Austrian wartime absolutism forced only the most active and daringly anti-Austrian nationality leaders to leave the monarchy. Thus, as previously mentioned in relation to the Czech case, the political concepts of these activists of superior abilities abroad determined the political course of their peoples.

In the Slovak case, this daring type of political leadership in the emigration abroad was represented by men of the type of Milan Štefánik and Stefan Osuský. As did Masaryk and Beneš on the Czech side, they envisaged solutions of their national problems which presumed the dismemberment of the monarchy before these plans became a part of the political strategy of the Entente Powers.[36]

The influence of the emigration abroad does not sufficiently explain, however, the inherent, though long dormant, wish for union of the kindred Czech-Slovak peoples, a wish deeply rooted in ancient ethnic, linguistic, cultural, and political facts. Yet it does help to explain why the union idea, which, after all, might have been realized in a re-formed federal Austrian empire, became increasingly connected with the demands for Austria's break-up.

Unquestionably, the large prewar Czech and Slovak emigration to foreign countries, particularly to the United States, played an important part in shaping the policy of the political exiles. A majority of the hundreds of thousands of American citizens of Czech and Slovak descent cared very little for minor distinctions between their nationalities and did not consider them sufficient reason for further political separation. They were not concerned with the further existence of the Austrian Empire. They, as the only popular force with a voice to back the political exile leaders during the war period, looked for comprehensive solutions of the Czech-Slovak destiny, as documented in the famous Pittsburgh Declaration of June 30, 1918, proclaiming the joint political future of the two peoples in an independent Czecho-Slovak state.[37]

Another point in the history of the union movement was of considerable psychological importance. Among the political leaders of the joint Czech and Slovak movement in exile, the large number of Slovaks was disproportionate to the numerical and political power relations between the two peoples.[38] Of the three major leaders—Masaryk, Štefánik, and Beneš—the first two were of Slovak descent.

Also, the Slovak Stefan Osuský held an important position in the political fight of his people, as he did again during the Second World War.

These facts were no mere accident. During the last decades prior to 1914 national oppression in Hungary had forced Slovakia's intelligentsia to shift its political struggle to the Austrian Czech territories, which were far less hamstrung nationally. Thus, on the eve of the First World War a kind of Slovak political irredenta came into being within the empire itself. Following the fundamental principles of political-emigration psychology, it soon became radically hostile to the empire idea, preceding a similar reaction in the Czech policy. In the eyes of the Czechs this activism of Slovak leadership in exile largely compensated for the fact that the union movement undoubtedly was not as deeply entrenched in Slovak popular feeling as it was in that of the Czechs. Indeed, no political action to this day has been able to erase fully the consequences of the fact that Slovak "unionist" leadership at that time ran far ahead of Slovak public opinion. It did not, however, run against it. In 1918 Slovak public opinion took great pride in the contribution of the influential political emigration to the formation of the Czechoslovak Republic.

Perhaps the analogy of the English-Scottish union, which was so much alleviated by the fact that the head of the smaller of the rival neighboring kingdoms became king of England, is appropriate here. The final Declaration of October 30, 1918, at Turč. Sv. Martin, in which the newly created national council (of the Slovak people) declared the Slovak people "linguistically and culturally-historically a part of the homogeneous Czecho-Slovak nation," [39] was certainly all the more readily accepted by the Slovak people, as their best sons in commanding positions had helped to create and mold the new union. Above all, the great leader Thomas G. Masaryk, a man of Slovak descent, had become "king of England."

# CHAPTER X

# THE SERBS

THIS DISCUSSION of the Serb problem [1] follows the analysis of the Slovak question because the relations of Croats and Serbs in the south [2] are similar to those of Czechs and Slovaks in the north. Yet this analogy applies only up to a point. Czechs and Slovaks are distinguished from each other chiefly by very slight linguistic differences and the obviously diverse historic tradition of an Austrian and a predominantly Hungarian national group. Croat and Serb linguistic affiliation is even closer than that of the two northern Slav peoples, yet the difference between the Latin and the Cyrillic alphabets appears more conspicuous: Also more noticeable and at the same time more deeply rooted are the religious distinctions between the Greek Orthodox Serbs and the Roman Catholic Croats, the former of Eastern Byzantine and the latter of Western Latin tradition. [3]

It could be said that, on the other hand, a closer political relationship exists between the Croats and the Serbs than exists between the Czechs and the Slovaks. The latter two were separated by the isolation of the lands of the Hungarian crown from the rest of the empire and, after 1867, by the deepening cleavage of the compromise, whereas the majority of both Serbs and Croats were subjects of the Hungarian crown. Here, however, the more complex Serb situation becomes evident. A distinction is necessary between the legal and the political status of the Serbs who settled in Hungary proper and those who settled in Croatia. The same holds true for the Serb minorities in Austria proper and, after the occupation of Bosnia-Hercegovina, in 1878, for the relative majority of Serbs there who belonged neither to Austria nor to Hungary, but were equally subordinate to both. Following an estimate of 1911 there were approximately 100,000 Serbs in Dalmatia under Austrian administration, some 650,000 in Croatia-Slavonia (as against almost three times the number of Croats there), about 850,000 in Bosnia-Hercegovina, and nearly 500,000 in Hungary

proper.[4] Thus, the Serbs lived under four different kinds of administration in the empire, the Austrian in Dalmatia, the Hungarian in
Hungary, the autonomous administration in Hungary's dependency,
Croatia-Slavonia, and, finally, in the common Austro-Hungarian territory, Bosnia-Hercegovina.

Although almost the same national administrative dispersion existed
among the Croats, the important difference was that the Croats in the
kingdom of Croatia-Slavonia had a definite and permanent center of
political gravity within the empire. Not so the Serbs. From the days
of the short-lived Great Serbian Empire of the fourteenth century
throughout the nearly five centuries of Turkish domination and the
fight for national liberation of the nineteenth and early twentieth centuries, the great hopes and deeds of Serb political history reached far
beyond the Habsburg borders.

Yet even within the empire, where the Serbs had to put up with the
modest role of a nationality without history, in the sense formulated
in Chapter II, above, the impact of their nationalism shifted from one
regional theater to the other. Those Serbs who in the course of the
Turkish wars since the fifteenth century had been seeking asylum in
Hungary proper enjoyed some kind of national and religious
autonomy in the territories assigned to them between the Tisza
(Theiss) and the Danube—the so-called Voivody (Voivodina). This
autonomy was enhanced notably on the basis of the charter granted
to them by Emperor Leopold I in 1690. Leopold knew how to make
use of the military qualities of this tenacious people in the fight against
continued Ottoman pressure. As the Turkish danger decreased and
the Magyar fortunes began to rise, the government gradually commenced to pierce the protective covering of the obligations of the repeatedly confirmed charter of 1690. But the Serbs preserved at least
a loose form of administrative and religious autonomy until the era
of rapidly developing Magyar nationalism in the early nineteenth
century. At the Hungarian diet of 1791–92 they even secured some extension of their rights in accordance with the partial fulfillment of the
demands raised at the Serb national congress at Temesvár in 1790.[5]
To be sure, the valid duration of some of these special privileges was
brief. The separate chancellery for the regulation of Serb affairs in
Vienna was maintained for scarcely two years. But the Serbs could at
least fall back upon the autonomy in their separate church organization. In connection with it, they enjoyed to some extent a national

educational system of their own. This, however, was gravely impaired by the Magyar language laws passed at the diet of Bratislava (Pressburg) in 1847–48.[6]

Serb linguistic and literary development in the empire during the last half-century prior to the Revolution of 1848, like corresponding movements among the other Slav peoples, rose to a respectable level, and again it was supported by the imperial government. As in the Slovak case, there was a wide rift in the cultural movement on the issue of the language reform, and here again there were weighty political issues behind this conflict. The language reforms of Vuk Stefan Karadžić (1787–1864) were initiated in order to mold the southern Serbian dialect to the literary language of the Serb people. The reform presented in his grammar, published, significantly enough, as early as 1814 in a German translation, was violently opposed by the orthodox clergy, who feared that Serbian national culture and distinctive religious character would be endangered by western influence upon the reformers. Thus, the conflict between the eastern and the western Slav worlds, competing to unite the Slavs spiritually under different religious and cultural ideas, was distinctly reflected in this Serb language conflict.

Only after Karadžić's death did the west carry the day.[7] Of the three major intellectual leaders of the Serb cultural movement of that time, Karadžić, Milutinović, and George Danicić, only the latter was born and reared within the borders of the empire. Yet the education and lifework of all three were inseparably connected with the German and Austrian cultural sphere. It is safe to say that in the period from the Congress of Vienna to the Revolution of 1848 a decisive stage of intellectual development of the entire Serbian nation was centered in Habsburg territories.

At the outbreak of the Hungarian Revolution in 1848, the Serbs within Hungary were reduced to a national status as wretched as that of the other non-Magyar nationalities. Only the Greek Orthodox church still preserved a certain autonomy. In any case, Serbs who had settled in the Military Frontiers under direct imperial control fared better than those in Hungary proper.

The outcome of the Magyar War of Independence of 1848–49 improved the Serb position within Hungary more markedly, though, than that of the other nationalities. The courageous fight of the Serbs during this struggle against the oppressive Magyar and Magyarizing regime [8] was rewarded by the imperial government's extension of Serb autonomy within Hungary.

An autonomous Serbian Voivody (Voivodina) was to be organized, with the seat of government in Temesvar.[9] Obviously, neo-absolutist centralism in Vienna, anxious to weaken defeated revolutionary Hungary without strengthening the Hungarian nationalities too much, was less afraid of Serb autonomism than it was of Croat autonomism. Thus, while almost all the promises made to the Croats in 1848–49 were violated, those made to the Serbs were kept at least halfway—until 1860. To remain on the safe side, however, the boundaries of the Serb Voivody were drawn in such a manner that it included substantial Magyar, Rumanian and German minorities. Serbian autonomous nationalism was to be kept well under control.

At the beginning of the era of constitutional experiments leading to the reconciliation with the Magyars in 1867, Vienna fully sacrificed the Serb national cause to Magyar claims and reincorporated the Voivody into Hungary in 1860. Seton-Watson, in two sentences, neatly summarizes the future fate of the Serbs within Hungary proper, "The history of the Serbs in Hungary since 1860 is one of slow decay. Shut out from all political influence, they found in their church autonomy the sole outlet for the expression of national individuality." [10]

Since that time treatment of the Serbs in Hungary proper followed the familiar pattern of oppressive Magyar nationality policy. However, the still-existing church autonomy, though its influence on denominational elementary education was increasingly curtailed, distinguished the Serb and Rumanian status somewhat from the even more inferior Slovak and Ruthenian position.[11] This complete reversal of imperial nationality policy in Hungary gradually transformed the Serb problem, rather soluble in 1849 and still manageable until 1867, from a Hungarian to a comprehensive empire problem of national irredentism.

Indeed, the Serbs under Austrian administration in Dalmatia were discriminated against, as well as treated as inferior to the Croats and the Italians. This situation improved markedly, however, after the joint Serb-Croat agreement of Zara in 1905, that is, on the initiative of the southern Slav national groups concerned. Yet even prior to that time distinction in the governmental handling of the problems of both nationalities was relatively unimportant, since both of them, at least until 1909, held a position markedly inferior to that of the privileged Italian national minority.[12] In general the Serb position in Austrian Cisleithanian territories was dependent upon events in the main theaters of southern Slav political evolution.

After the era of constitutional experiments, specifically after the Hungarian-Croatian Compromise of 1868, semiautonomous Croatia became an ever more important theater; so did Bosnia-Hercegovina after her formal annexation in 1908. Indeed, during the era of compromise from 1868 to 1918 Croatia remained the only land within the realm of the Crown of St. Stephen where national claims at least had a chance to come into the open. The better part of this period, that is, until about 1905, was dominated by a permanent, bitter, and violent struggle between the Croatian majority and the Serbian minority in Croatia. It has already been mentioned how skillfully the regime in Budapest exploited this conflict between the sister nationalities to enhance its own rule.[13] It should be clear, however, that this policy, frequently expressed by petty administrative favors granted to the Serb minority, did not prove really sucessful, even from the Magyar viewpoint. Hungary's chief agent in Croatian affairs, the *Banus,* Count Khuen-Héderváry, managed, during his administration from 1883 to 1903, to completely alienate the Croats. But in the long run he was unable to gain the support of the rising Serb cause by a policy of granting administrative favors.[14] The reasons were obvious.

The Croat-Serb conflict came to the fore in relatively small local matters, but it was dominated by a conflict involving the fundamental questions of the whole Southern Slav problem. Its issues, the struggle between the Great-Croatian Catholic concept, the Croatian-dominated trialistic idea, and expanding Serb nationalism increasingly gravitating toward the kingdom of Serbia, have been outlined previously. Magyar ambition for power and imperial reticence to stir up the national furor of the Magyar regime could put brakes on the development of this conflict. But, in the last prewar decade these forces could no longer influence its course decisively. It is conceivable that a more liberal governmental approach to the Serb-Croatian problem might have been successful in the first decades after the compromise. Serb national aspirations in the empire before the Congress of Berlin in 1878 could not yet be forcefully supported by a Serbian state just gaining its full independence. Serbia's foreign policy in the 1880s was, indeed, fully submissive to Austria. Yet as it became increasingly obvious from the 1890s on, this did not imply a slackening of Serb nationalism beyond the empire's frontiers. It proved only that the foreign policy of the Obrenović dynasty was out of line with the objectives of Serbian nationalism.[15] The overthrow of the dynasty in 1903 eliminated every shadow of doubt about the further national activism of Serbian policy beyond the frontiers.

Influenced by the growing strength of this Serbian nationalism, an understanding between Croats and Serbs within the empire, based on a common anti-Magyar policy, was in the offing. This understanding, initiated by the Serb and the Croat Liberal elements, was not favored by Greater Croatian Conservatives and adherents of Trialism. And here the Serbs, supported by only a fraction of the Croat people, but by practically all their conationals in the kingdom, assumed political leadership. This meant that southern Slav unionism henceforward was inevitably committed to an anti-Austrian course. Irrespective of previous loyalties of the Hungarian and the Croatian Serbs, no national movement focused on a power beyond the empire's borders could be expected to remain in line with the empire's centripetal forces. The subsequent political development confirmed this fact.

Austrian policy at that time involuntarily furthered even the Serb cause. Croatian nationalists who were still pro-Austrian felt themselves betrayed once more when the emperor in 1903, fettered by the chains of the Compromise of 1867, flatly rejected any kind of intervention by the Croats in Austria and in Dalmatia on behalf of their brethren under Magyar oppression. Any illusions nourished thus far, such as the hope for the imperial government's consent to a union between Croatia and Bosnia, let alone the desired union with Dalmatia, vanished.[16] On the other hand, the younger political generation among the Serbs clearly envisaged that any sporadic support of their claims by the Magyar government was destined to serve only the process of Magyarization, not that of Serb national emancipation.

The result of the mutual Serb-Croat revision of outdated and controversial political doctrines was manifested in the resolution of Fiume on October 4, 1905, and in the resolutions of Zara in Dalmatia on October 16 and November 18 of the same year. At Fiume the Croatian deputies of Croatia and those of the Austrian crownlands of Dalmatia and Istria (as part of the Austrian Littoral) issued a new national program of Serb-Croat conciliation. The Serb deputies of Dalmatia voiced their agreement to it in the first declaration of Zara, and in a final conference in November (second declaration of Zara) the common policy was finally agreed upon in detail in a joint conference of Serb and Croat political leaders.

The decisive feature of these declarations was that here a political program dared to come out publicly, although in its ultimate objectives it defied the legal barriers of the Austro-Hungarian Compromise of 1867 and committed itself to ethnic solutions of the southern Slav national problems. These plans, pointing towards the ethnic union of all the empire's southern Slav peoples, were no longer drafted by scholars, political exiles, or propagandists without public responsibility, but by elected representatives of the peoples. Reformism emerged from the underground and from the study of the scholar into the political battle area. Compared with this main fact, the actual contents of the resolutions are of almost secondary importance.[17] They were not fully abreast of the relatively advanced stage of political nationalism embodied in the union movement already existing among the southern Slav peoples at that time. Still upholding Croatia's union with Hungary, the resolution of Fiume asked for the reincorporation of Dalmatia into Croatia and for the integrity of Croatia's constitutional rights. It vaguely hinted at an extension of the autonomy granted under the Act of 1868. Perhaps most important, the introduction of a really democratic, unrestricted franchise law was demanded.[18]

This rather modest program became more significant because it was solemnly supported by the Serb declaration of Zara on condition that the principle of equality between Serbs and Croats would be recognized. A coalition between the main Croatian and Serb parties of Dalmatia was formed almost immediately, based on the principle "that the Croats and Serbs are one nation," as formulated in the second declaration of Zara.[19] Practically even more important was the formation of a liberal union of Serbs and Croats in the Croatian diet. This coalition soon stood in firm and unqualified opposition against the Magyar *Bani* and gradually superseded the formerly powerful Party of the Pure Right, the bearers of the old Greater Croatian idea.[20]

Serbo-Croatian unity in the empire appeared to be achieved after a generation of bitter strife. Yet no impartial observer could be blind to the fact that this new coalition developed under very different conditions from those in which the Croatian-Serb settlement conceivably might have been reached during the first decades after the conclusion of the Compromise of 1867. During the earlier period Croat-Serb relations were distinctly on a basis of inequality. The Croatians were unwilling to grant Serb claims for equal national recognition in the desired Greater Croatia. Even the south Slav union movement in Croatia, which followed the tradition of "Illyrism," in a way considered the Croats as the leading south Slav national group. The negotiations leading to and immediately following the resolutions of 1905 were still conducted on the basis of this historic assumption which now, however, no longer corresponded to the actual ratio between Croat and Serb political power. The significance of the Serbs' position was no longer determined by their harassed status as an Austro-Hungarian nationality,[21] but by their becoming the vanguard of Serbia's national policy.

Thus, the Serb problem in the monarchy had reached a stage of political development somewhat similar to that reached by the Italians more than a generation earlier. That is to say, no matter how fairly and intelligently the Serb interests might have been handled in the empire, the Serb question could no longer be settled within the empire alone, but only by an understanding with a foreign state, the kingdom of Serbia supported by Russia. The important difference between the Italian and the Serb positions in the empire was based, however, on two essential points. The Serbs, at least in Hungary proper and in Croatia, were in no way treated comparably to the relatively favorable status accorded the Italians in Cisleithanian Austria. Furthermore, as pointed out previously, the Italian question might conceivably have been settled at the price of minor territorial concessions to Italy. Any satisfactory settlement of the Serb problem within the empire would have disclosed the whole southern Slav problem, implying the revision of the Compromise of 1867 and the constitutional transformation of the monarchy. The alternative to such a comprehensive solution apparently was the complete surrender of the imperial southern Slav position to Serbia, a solution unthinkable from the standpoint of Great Power politics.

Still, the comprehensive solution of the southern Slav problem within Austria, following either the trialistic or, with more likelihood, a federal solution, might have had a remote chance of success. The formal annexation, in 1908, of the lands of Bosnia and Hercegovina, which had been occupied since 1878, shattered such possibilities permanently.[22] Thereby, Austria chose the only political course, worse even than the unchanged continuation of the existing state of affairs.

To be sure, in theory the permanent annexation of territories with a relative Serb majority of population did not in itself block the possibility of a more just handling of Serb national interests within the empire. Yet the annexation, in challenging Serbian nationalism beyond the frontiers, transformed the long-run possibility of a showdown with Serbia to what may well be called a short-run probability. Any further planned revisions of the Serb status in the empire thus appeared scarcely to have a chance to mature.

Such reforms, at least within the limited sphere of the joint Austro-Hungarian lands of Bosnia-Hercegovina, the new Serb center in the monarchy, were not entirely lacking. The decreed Bosnian constitution of 1908, concocted largely by the centralistic bureaucracy in Vienna, combined feeble traces of representative democracy with institutions of the old Estates-curia system at its worst. Particularly fearful of irredentist Serb activities, it reduced the representation of popular liberties to practically nil.[23] This mock constitution substituted for national discrimination almost complete and equal political suppression of all Bosnian nationalities. It would have been truly naïve, however, to assume that a more democratic Bosnian constitution could have substantially influenced the course of Serb nationalism at this point in history.

In almost every way—religion, history, tradition, and economy—the Serbs in Bosnia had been much closer to Serbia and the Greater Serbian idea than to their conationals in Croatia, Hungary, and Dalmatia, with their ancient vested interests in the structure of the Habsburg Power. The Bosnian Serbs were firmly resolved to undo their permanent incorporation into the empire and to join politically the independent part of the nation. Thus, they increasingly became the vanguard of the Greater Serbian idea in the empire, and Bosnian territory became its chief center of operations.

The development of the Serb problem in the monarchy from the annexation in 1908 on, throughout the two Balkan wars, the Albanian crisis of 1913, the murder in Sarajevo, and the ensuing outbreak of the First World War, belong in the realm of world history. At no period in the history of the empire was there more heated and prolonged discussion concerning the problem of Trialism or Subtrialism than between 1908 and 1914. But it had never been clearer that a solution of the Austrian south Slav problem, excluding Serbia, had become virtually impossible. In this respect the First World War revealed publicly a political development that had long before been effective. In this sense, the joint Serb-Croat-Slovene declaration of Corfu on July 20, 1917,[24] proclaiming the creation of the united Yugoslav kingdom under the Karageorgevich dynasty, and thereby the triumph of the Greater Serbian idea, was not a revolutionary act. It simply represented the concluding and conclusive chapter in the passing of southern Slav leadership from an internal, imperial Croatian to an external Serbian center.

# CHAPTER XI

# THE SLOVENES

THE POLITICAL fortunes of the Slovene people within the Habsburg lands¹ can be fully understood only if one perceives them as the classic paradigm of a national group without independent national political history, a people which never had a political entity of its own, even in an imperfect form. Yet, as in the somewhat similar case of the Slovaks, this fact does not impair the Slovene contribution to the Slav renaissance movement. On the contrary, it actually makes their contribution even more impressive. We also cannot underestimate the political role which the Slovene people played in Austrian history after 1848.

As early as the sixth century, Slav tribes appeared in the territories inhabited by the Slovenes of today, in southern Styria, Carinthia, Carniola, and the Littoral, the northernmost and westernmost regions inhabited by any of the southern Slav peoples. The end of the eighth century found these territories under German control after a continuous fight against Avares and, later, Bavarians; in the course of the fourteenth and fifteenth centuries they came under Habsburg domination. Throughout their history, from the early medieval ages, these Slav tribes were continually resisting the German drive toward the south and formed the chief bulwark preventing German penetration to the Adriatic and consequent access to the Mediterranean world. The existence of a true ancient Slovene culture is the only satisfactory means of explaining how a poor people, composed of mountain peasants and herdsmen with no political or military achievements, stemmed Germanization southward for a thousand years and survived that period as a national group.

The Slovenes were Christianized as early as the eighth century. Some of the oldest literary monuments in any Slav language, the so-called Freising Manuscripts, written around the year 1000 A.D. though probably composed even earlier, have been transmitted to posterity in a language which some Slovene scholars considered an early form of their language. By others they were held to be the early documents of the old Slavonic church language, the ancient common tie between western and eastern Slavs. These assertions were of great significance for the strength of Slovene cultural tradition.

The great teacher of the Slovene peoples,[2] Bartholomäus Kopitar (1780–1844), first in his Slovene grammar (1808), later and more specifically in his *Glagolita Clocianus* (1836),[3] asserted that the Slovene language was identical with the old church language of the Slavs. This meant to him that the Slovenes formed the base of the whole Slav Christian culture; it meant in particular that Catholicism—the faith of the Slovene people—paved the way for the Christianization of the eastern Slav world; and the final conclusion was that Austria, by the relative majority of her population a Slav empire, should give the Slav world a Catholic center.[4] And at the core of this center Kopitar saw the Slovenes, godfathers of the redemption and the destiny of all Slav peoples, creators of the language of salvation.

Not all the premises of Kopitar's widely acclaimed Austro-Pan-Slav Catholic concept can withstand the scrutiny of modern historical and philological research. Yet, if an ancient Slovene culture had not existed, Kopitar's program could hardly have been successfully propagated. The contribution of the Slovenes to the spread of Christian culture in the Slav world was indeed outstanding. Later, the Slovene translation of the Catechism and the New Testament by Primož Trubar (1508–86) and, above all, the famous translation of the Bible by George Dalmatin (1546?–89), completed in Wittenberg in 1575, were milestones in the spread of the Reformation to the south. They left indelible marks on language and literature, marks which withstood even the Counter-Reformation that reconquered the greater part of the Slovene lands for Catholicism. On the other hand, the fact that among all the Austro-Slav national groups, apart from the Czechs, the Reformation had made the greatest headway among the Slovenes contributed to the strength of the ensuing countermovement in their territories.

Thus, in the seventeenth century the Austro-Slovene lands, with the exception of a small, but culturally not insignificant, Protestant minority, became bulwarks of the Catholic faith in the Slav world, which they have remained ever since. The strength of Slovene political influence in Austria's parliamentary history in the nineteenth and twentieth centuries came largely from the conservative Catholic camp represented by the so-called "Old Slovenes," also known as the Slovene Conservatives or the Slovene People's party, vigorously fighting a Liberal national "Young Slovene" opposition. This dominant Catholic ideology also explains the close political relationship between the Slovenes in Austria and the Croatians in Hungary. Though in the last prewar decades this alliance had to yield to south Slav unionism under the leadership of the Greater Serbian idea, Slovene Catholicism and Slovene conservatism remained strong "centripetal forces" [5] upholding the empire idea and the Habsburg throne.

Slovene national evolution in the era of rising nationalism in the late eighteenth and early nineteenth centuries followed in many ways the already familiar pattern. The linguistic reforms commenced in the late eighteenth century, somewhat earlier than the corresponding development among the other south Slav peoples. In 1797, a Slovene newspaper edited by the poet Valentin Vodnik (1758–1819) appeared in Ljubljana (Laibach). Some translating into Slovene and much grammatical research, though, prior to Kopitar's work, of an elementary character, was undertaken at that time. Slovene cultural nationalism, as the Czech "renaissance" in the pre-March period, benefited from the central government's benevolent tolerance, which saw in this movement a means of fighting the influence of Russian Pan-Slavism. In the case of the Slovenes, however, additional factors explained this tolerance. The government saw no reason to fear the Slovene national group as a potential political movement. The "danger" that a people without political history would ever claim an autonomous national future appeared too remote to merit consideration. Thus, the imperial administration found reassurance in the profound loyalty of the Catholic Austro-Slav ideology as promoted by the Conservative Janez Bleiweis, and above all, by Bartholomäus Kopitar. In his scholarly achievements this powerful personality was thus characterized by Fischel as

one of the most outstanding characters of the Slav renaissance; in the breadth of his knowledge, in his sagacity, critical perspicacity, ideas, and taste in literary presentation he is far superior to [most of] the Czech and Slovak scholars. . . . The southern Slavs owe a tremendous debt to him and Austria knew him as the most ardent representative of the Austro-Slav idea. His German written Grammar of the Slav language in Carniola, Carinthia, and Styria was the pioneer work of the Slovene language. His activities were also of high importance for the creation of the new Serbian literary language.[6]

But Fischel's evaluation still fails to do justice to Kopitar's political concepts. He was, indeed, something like the central figure of the whole scholarly language-renaissance movement, not only of the Slovenes but in a way of all the Slavs in the empire. He was in inspiring contact with practically all the intellectual leaders of the northern, as well as the southern, Slavs as far as the scholarly aspects of the renaissance movement were concerned. Nevertheless, his scholarly merits probably had least influence on the government's attitude toward the Austro-Slav problem in general and the Slovene problem in particular. Kopitar's immediate and direct political influence was based on his concept, so agreeable to the government, of an Austro-Catholic Slavism, loyal to the throne and the empire.[7] True, practically all the great Slav intellectual leaders of that period either were raised in German culture or at least had become well acquainted with it in the course of their education. Yet, the synthesis between the specific form of German culture represented in the political philosophy of German Austrian centralism and the Slav native world was not as complete and as smooth in any of them as it was in Kopitar's life-work.[8]

This tradition was fully upheld by Kopitar's principal Slovene disciples, France Prešeren (1800–47) and Franz von Miklosich (1821–91).[9] The former represented the romantic trend in the Slovene cultural renaissance. He drew chiefly on the national legend and folklore and thereby performed as indispensable and as typical a task as possible in the history of the national evolution of any of the Austrian Slav peoples. He became one of the most ardent and successful promotors of Slovene national culture. Miklosich, the author of the great comparative grammar of the Slav peoples and the compiler of the etymological dictionary of the Slav languages, brought the Slav linguistic renaissance period in regard to important problems to a successful scientific conclusion. Thus the beginning as well as the end of this meaningful chapter in Slav cultural history was marked by the outstanding achievements of two Slovene scholars Kopitar and Miklosich.

The outstanding impression gained from a study of the Slovene national problem under Kopitar's intellectual leadership in the pre-revolutionary era is the almost complete lack of friction either with the government or, as yet, with other nationalities. Three main factors account for this: first, the insignificance of the Slovene national problem in the eyes of the central government, as well as German Austrian nationalism of that era; second, the "loyal" character of Kopitar's ideological concepts; and, third, the fact that the Slovene peoples were mainly settled only in Austria proper and not in Magyar-dominated Hungary, which was far more intolerant nationally.[10] Thereby they could keep out of the three-cornered fight between imperial centralism, Magyar nationalism, and Slav nationalism.

The separation of the Slovenes from the Magyar-Croat conflict in Hungary did not mean, however, that their national destiny in the pre-March period remained unaffected by the struggle of their kin in Hungary. Above all, it must be remembered that the Slovene territories, like those of the Croats, formed part of Napoleon's short-lived Illyrian kingdom from 1809 to 1813. The Slovenes, like the Croats, benefited from the jurisdictional, educational, and agricultural reforms (serf-tenant emancipation) initiated by the French administration. These reforms, in striking contrast to the inactivity of the preceding and following Austrian administrations furthered the spread of the ideas of Illyrism—the future southern Slav union—in Slovene as in Croatian lands. In particular, an important trend of Slovene Illyrism was chiefly represented by the poet, Stanko Vraz (1810–51), who, writing in the Croatian language, promoted the Croat-Slovene cultural union.[11]

Slovene nationalism during the pre-March period was not yet adversely influenced by its future chief adversary, German nationalism. Rather typical in this respect was the attitude of the well-known aristocratic poet from Carniola, Anton Alexander, Count Auersperg (1808–76), a German Liberal known as a man of letters under the pseudonym Anastasius Grün. Auersperg showed a friendly interest in the new works of Slovene literature and even translated Prešern's writings into German. In the Frankfurt Assembly of 1848 he continued to support Slovene national claims. But in his later life he became a bitter foe of their national aspirations and derided Slovene cultural achievements as inferior. Austro-German nationalism prior to 1848 was not aware of a Slovene national problem potentially comparable to that of the Czechs, the Croats, and the Poles. As soon as it became aware of the problem and its political implications for the German position on the road to Trieste, national conflict commenced.[12]

Here, the position of the Slovenes as an ethnic-frontier people was of paramount importance. In a broader sense, of course, all the Austrian nationalities were ethnic-frontier peoples in regard to some language border. However, this term had a specific political significance in the case of the Slovenes. The Slovene ethnic demands clashed with those of the most numerous and powerful Austrian Cisleithanian national group, the Germans, in a geopolitically most important area which covered the roads to the Adriatic. Furthermore, compared to that other chief opponent of specific German national claims, the Czechs, the Slovene geographic position was precarious in a different way. The Czechs, because of their northern, western, and southern geographic frontiers, formed a clear-cut ethnic peninsula within the German orbit, whereas the Slovenes actually were located on a broad, unstable frontier between the German and the Slav worlds.

The outbreak of the revolution in 1848, the clash between southern Slavs and Magyars in Hungary, as well as the Czech uprising in Austria affected the thus far peaceful development of Slovene nationalism profoundly and in a peculiar way. The revolutionary situation confronted a national group which could not base its claim on historic rights and on the other hand did not experience the same degree of political suppression as did other national groups without political history, especially the Slovaks from the Magyars, in Hungary, and the Ruthenians from the Poles, in Galicia. Furthermore, the geographical factor now came into play. The Slovenes, though living in areas which were fairly homogeneous ethnically, were settled in six Austrian crownlands—Carinthia, Styria, Carniola, and the three parts of the Littoral (Gorizia and Gradiska, Istria, and Trieste). In only two of these lands, Carniola and Gorizia, did they represent a majority of the population.[13]

Thus, no Slovene national political concept based on the crownland organization could develop. It was natural, therefore, that from the beginning of its political activities the Slovene national movement based its claims, not on historic rights, but on ethnic facts. The emergence of Slovene political nationalism brought Austria face to face with the first clear-cut federal program established solely on ethnic foundations.[14] As early as April 1, 1848, a Slovene manifesto addressed to the emperor was issued, raising the following points in remarkably succinct form.

"We Slovenes in Styria, Carniola, Carinthia, Istria, in the territories of Gorizia and Trieste, a kindred nation of one and a half millions . . . ask that we be granted the following national claims.

"1. Abolition of the historic crownland frontiers and fusion of our

Slovene territories, following the language frontiers, to one land and . . . to one nation.

"2. Guarantee of our nationality and general equal rights for the Slovene language as for the German language in the German, and the Italian language in the Italian lands. . . . [Specific demands in regard to higher education in Slovene language are added.]

"3. Opportunity for a closer union . . . with our brothers in Croatia, Slavonia, and Dalmatia, by abolition or lowering of tariff duties, a share of institutions of higher learning, and so forth, according to mutual understanding."

4. The manifesto expressed loyalty to the Austrian Empire, but demanded that the Slovene territories be taken out of the German *Bund*.[15]

This program is remarkable not only for its clearly defined ethnic concept of the Slovene national organization but also for the veiled renunciation of south Slav unionism, toned down to the modest demand for cultural and economic cooperation. This cautious display of feeling toward southern Slav unionism has remained characteristic of Slovene nationalism, which during the following two generations continued to be dominated by Kopitar's and Bleiweiss's conservative ideas.

The revolutionary April Manifesto of 1848 did not remain an isolated action in Slovene national policy. Two of the great empire-reform plans submitted at Kremsier—the Palacký plan and the draft submitted by the Slovene, Kaučič—as well as the previous platform of the Slav Congress of May–June, 1848—take up the demands of the manifesto for a Slovene member state in an Austrian federation based on ethnic lines.[16]

Political fortune did not favor the far-reaching political concepts of the revolutionary Slovenes. The benevolent tolerance which Austrian centralism had shown for Slovene cultural nationalism prior to 1848 changed to rejection as soon as definite political demands were presented. Furthermore, German national opposition was aroused. In fact, the government did not even pay lip service to Slovene demands, as it did in 1848 to those of the Czechs and in 1849 to those of the Croats and the Serbs.

This governmental position remained basically unchanged until the collapse of the German neoliberal regime in Austria in 1879 and the beginning of the Taaffe era (1879–93), with its German-Slav balance-of-power policy.[17] Though no comprehensive legislative solution of the Slovene national problem was ever seriously considered

by the government before 1918, since the time of Taaffe at least administrative policies showed a more conciliatory attitude toward
Slovene demands. At least, the most serious wrongs were righted, only
in the ambiguous way of the Conservative Taaffe "machine," which,
bartering for Slovene parliamentary support, changed administrative
practice, but did not alter the Slovene political status.[18]

Subsequently, Slovene language rights received fairly adequate
recognition in Carniola, the "heart land" of the Slovenes, and their
national claims gained at least an improved, though by no means a
satisfactory, status in Styria and Carinthia.

Yet the stubborn resistance of German nationalism to even the
slightest extension of Slovene national rights, particularly in southern
(Slovene) Styria, where the typically tense national-frontier atmosphere prevailed, is well illustrated by the overthrow of the Windischgrätz cabinet in 1895 due to German opposition. The cabinet fell
primarily because it had pledged itself to the setup of a Slovene junior
high school in addition to an already existing German high school of
the same character in the binational town of Cilli (Celje) in southern
Styria. The fact that the majority of the students were of Slovene nationality only strengthened German-national and German-liberal determination to fight in such a way for their *Volkstum*.[19]

Nevertheless, the need for Catholic Conservative parliamentary
support in the long run favorably influenced the Slovene national
position.

Introduction of general equal franchise in Austria in 1907 finally
gave the Slovenes an increased percentage of representation in the
parliament in Vienna. This, together with fear of Italian irredentism
and south Slav political propaganda coming from the Hungarian
lands, prompted the government to improve the status of the south
Slavs in the Littoral, where throughout the nineteenth century Slovenes, as well as Croats, had been greatly discriminated against in
favor of Italians and Germans.[20]

The limited horizon of the Austrian Cisleithanian nationality policy
in general, coupled with the fact that on the level of mere administrative procedure certain ameliorations of the Slovene status could
still be expected, drove Slovene nationalism to what might be called
a "hand to mouth" program. The realization that sweeping reforms
were unobtainable, but that some small-scale success might be achieved
if Slovene policy sided with the Conservative Catholic, anti-Liberal

trend in governmental policy, shaped the course of the Slovene People's party. These conservative forces remained dominant in Slovenian political life until the end of the monarchy.

The analogy of such a policy with that of the Old Czech program, in spite of the latter's entirely different historic approach, and, above all, with the program of the Croatian Party of the Pure Right is obvious. Here a distinct community of interests between the Slovene Conservatives and their Croatian kin turned Slovene political thought increasingly toward a concept of south Slav unionism. However, as a kind of Conservative pro-Croat and politically anti-Serb unionism, it was radically different from the program of the predominantly Liberal Serb-Croat coalition agreed upon at Fiume and Zara in 1905.[21]

This different spirit was evident in the resolution of Ljubljana in October, 1912, carried by Slovene and Croatian deputies of the Slovene People's party and the Croatian Pure Right party. After professing loyalty to the Catholic faith and to the dynasty, the authors of this program stated:

We declare that the Croats and the Slovenes form a national union. For that aim we, the followers of the Croatian and Slovenian Rightist party, shall work in common, following the program of the Party of the Right for the union of the rights and the free development of the Croatian-Slovene people in the frame of the Habsburg monarchy.[22]

A correct interpretation will show that this program endorsed a thinly veiled tripartite (trialist) program following the Greater Croatian concept. It did not recognize the national claims of the Serb people in the monarchy.[23]

This adherence to the tripartite empire organization program was even more distinctly manifested by the Austrian southern Slav deputies, who were under predominant Slovene influence at the reopening of parliament in May, 1917.[24] With this significant step in the direction of a conservative union policy of the three southern Slav peoples within the empire, the limit was reached of Slovene nationalism in Austria before the collapse of 1918.

As far as the contribution of the Slovene World War irredenta to the Yugoslav union movement abroad went, it certainly did not compare in breadth and in intensity to Croat, let alone to Serb, activities. This particularly holds true for the relatively modest Slovene share in the work preparatory to the southern Slav union declaration of Corfu in July, 1917.

However, it would be an all too superficial criticism to charge the Slovene political Right with political opportunism and narrow-mindedness in their pre-World War policy. First, a Conservative-Clerical policy, not only antirevolutionary but antireformist, was undoubtedly in line with the belief of a large proportion of the masses of this peasant people.[25] Furthermore, the Slovenes had good reason to believe not only the general difficulties attendant upon the realization of an ethnic federal program hindered a broader political action program, but that specific German opposition to a program of far-reaching Slovene autonomy was insurmountable. A Slovene member state of an Austrian federation would have split the predominantly German crownlands of Styria and Carinthia. Above all, it would have blocked German access to the Adriatic. To agree to the setup of such a state between the German Alpine lands and Trieste meant a *non possumus* for German nationalists and, for that matter, for German Liberals as well.[26] For two generations official Slovene policy cautiously deferred its demand for autonomy, let alone southern Slav union, and adjusted itself skillfully to the precarious position of an ethnic-frontier people in imperial Austria.

Nevertheless, proposals by the Slovene Left for action on a larger scale were by no means lacking during that period. Here the creation of the southern Slav Socialist party in Ljubljana (Laibach) in 1896, promoting a program for joint action by the three south Slav peoples in the monarchy, was an event of great ideological significance, though not of immediate practicability. The so-called Tivoli resolution of the south Slav Socialist Congress of Laibach in 1907 sponsored an even more sweeping program of south Slav unionism, by including Bulgarians in a wider union of the southern Slav peoples. The fact that a growing party with an obvious political future openly stood for full-fledged southern Slav unionism and strongly renounced the venerable doctrine of Slovene separatism had some ideological influence on the final achievement of the union in 1918—different as its realization was in many ways from the sacred image of three generations of southern Slav Liberals.[27]

In conclusion, it may be said that within the political limits of the Habsburg Empire the Slovenes contributed two major ideas to the evolution of the Austrian nationality problem, first, Kopitar's concept of the Catholic Slav union as a counterbalance to Russian Pan-Slavism and, secondly, the ethnic autonomy program of 1848. Neither of these ideas has been pursued further in the future predominantly conservative history of Slovene nationalism in Austria, but they found repercussions in the development of other national groups of the empire.

Within the history of nationalism in the nineteenth century in general, the Slovene position is even more significant. It represents a great contribution to Slav cultural, particularly to Slav linguistic, renaissance. Above all, it represents the phenomenon of the development and survival of a national culture without the support of a historicopolitical tradition. The Slovene cultural inheritance, most impressive evidence for the indestructible force of nationalism, has been preserved and transmitted to posterity largely through the words and songs of mountain peasants.

# CHAPTER XII

# THE RUMANIANS AND THE NATIONAL
# PROBLEMS OF TRANSYLVANIA

THE STATUS of this geographically peripheric national group has been determined by a strange combination of social and political factors.[1] The Rumanians in the Habsburg lands were a nationality without independent national political history, a national group which technically later than any other received some degree of legal recognition. Indeed, prior to the nineteenth century no form of politically, let alone legally, recognized group life existed among the empire's Rumanian subjects.

This fact appears even more significant because the bulk of the Rumanian nation, separated from its Austrian kin only by the mountain ranges of the Carpathians, had a rich and active national and political history as early as the fifteenth century. Colorful Transylvania, where the majority of the empire's Rumanians had been living continuously for about seven hundred years, was distinguished by its ancient, reputedly workable multinational institutions well into the nineteenth century. Yet the Rumanians did not benefit from these institutions.

Roughly two thirds of this national group lived outside the borders of the empire. Of the remaining third more than 90 percent lived in Hungarian lands, the rest, in Cisleithanian Austria.[2] This statement, however, is technically correct only for the period after the Compromise of 1867. In early modern times, well into the revolutionary era of 1848, Transylvania was a fief of the emperor rather than of the Hungarian crown, Magyar counterclaims notwithstanding. Thus, until 1867 the Rumanians, except for relatively short intervals, were to be viewed as imperial, as Austrian people in the broadest sense, rather than as a Hungarian nationality.

The ethnic feature of the Rumanian problem in the empire was distinctive. The Rumanians asserted that they were a Latin people, like the Italians.[3] Yet, among the Italians a powerful national tradition worked for severance of the ties of the empire long before an independent Italy existed. No comparable movement commenced to become effective among the Austro-Hungarian Rumanians prior to 1859, the birth year of the new Rumania.[4] In fact, before the beginning of the twentieth century the position of the Rumanians in the empire was scarcely influenced decisively by the affiliation with their kinsmen in the Rumanian kingdom across the borders. Until that time the specific ethnic character of the empire's Rumanians was of little influence in cementing ties to the kingdom, yet it contributed much to their isolation from the other national groups in the Habsburg monarchy. Together with the Magyars, their bitterest antagonists, the Rumanians were the national group least connected by historic, cultural, and ethnic ties to the other national groups. This factor was of cardinal importance to their destiny in the empire.

Demands for national domination in the easternmost part of the Danube monarchy, where the majority of the Habsburg Rumanian population had been living, have for centuries centered on the identity of the first settlers. For all practical purposes this bitterly contested issue was seemingly a moot one. Common-sense interpretation may assume that it should have mattered very little whether a Daco-Roman aboriginal population was still living in Transylvanian territory when the Magyars occupied it, possibly as early as the end of the ninth century A.D. It ought to have been irrelevant whether the Magyars settled there a few generations after the Szekels, probably an Avarian tribe which adopted the Magyar language, had settled there. It was certain, however, that the German Saxons called by the kings of Hungary into the land did not settle there before the thirteenth century. When one calls this "order of arrival" a moot question from the standpoint of political priority, it means not only that actual national interests cannot be decided on the basis of the antiquated claims of the medieval past, but further that above all the Rumanians, who by sheer weight of numbers had the major right to these eastern territories, could not benefit from any recognition of their historic priority anyway.

Unlike the Magyars, the Saxons, and the Szekels, the Rumanian population, well into the nineteenth century, was neither socially nor legally recognized as a national group. As stated before, it was definitely a nationality without history in the whole social structure of the empire. This fact stood out all the more clearly, because the term "nationality" had a very definite meaning in the history of Transylvania. From the twelfth to the fifteenth century, when this principality was ruled by Hungarian vassal princes (later called Voivodes), it was divided into three "nations," or, more accurately, three politically and legally recognized privileged or ruling nations.[5] Each of them sent its separate representations to the Estates diet, which dealt with the common affairs of Transylvania and her relations to the empire and to Hungary. The Transylvanian Magyar *Comitats* to the east, separated from Hungary proper by a broad strip of territory settled predominantly by Rumanians, were organized in *populus* and *plebs*.[6] The Szekels in the southeast, established in so-called *sedes*, were ruled by a count who held office from the Hungarian crown. The whole national group consisted only of free men, who were considered altogether as gentry with appropriate recognized privileges—of which the most important was tax exemption. The Saxon political organization was not less original. They, too, lived under a count, the *Sachsengraf*, on their *sedes* in the *fundus regius* (royal soil). They enjoyed far-reaching administrative autonomy, which survived until 1876 under the name "Saxon national university."

The particularly interesting point in regard to this Saxon autonomy was the fact that the Saxons did not live in territories ethnically as homogeneous as those held by the Magyars and the Szekels. They formed a majority in the larger towns of the land and some scattered country districts. Yet, the autonomy granted to them comprised all the domains inhabited by Saxons under one national administration, whether territorially connected or not. In that respect the Saxon autonomy appears a forerunner of a more refined and ingenious concept of personal autonomy, which materialized only locally and gradually well over half a thousand years after the Saxons had received their autonomous status in Transylvania.

To be sure, the idea of personal autonomy, that is, autonomy affixed to the personal status of the individual members of a national group rather than to the territory, cannot be traced back directly to the Transylvanian institutions. Saxon autonomy in Transylvania was still territorial, albeit elaborate and carefully devised.[7] But the existence of institutions of territorial autonomy in areas which were extremely heterogenous nationally (the German settlements in Transylvania are an outstanding example) appears an indispensable pre-condition for the development of autonomous institutions of a higher order in time to come.

In the period of Turkish predominance in eastern central Europe, from the Battle of Mohács in 1526 to the end of the seventeenth cen-tury, the fortunes of Transylvania fared rather well. Transylvania, off the main battle roads of the running fight between empire and Turks, enjoyed in the main an undisturbed development of her quaint institutions under native princes, protected far more than suppressed by Turkish suzerainty. In particular, the great religious struggle be-tween Reformation and Counter Reformation in its most violent form did not spread to a land where Turkish overlords, unconcerned with the religious schisms of the Western world, could readily grant re-ligious freedom and equal standing to the various Christian faiths.

The reconquest of Hungary by imperial arms at the end of the seventeenth century did not immediately affect the relatively more quiet development in this remote eastern corner of central Europe. Emperor Leopold I, in a wise political move, reaffirmed in 1691 the old liberties of the Transylvanian nations, plus the religious free-dom they had enjoyed under the previous Turkish overlordship. It is true that in the early eighteenth century during the Rákóczy rebel-lion Transylvania experienced an aftermath of the national and re-ligious struggle through which central Europe had passed previously.[8] Religious liberties and national privileges now hung in precarious balance. Though speaking in broad terms, Seton-Watson's estimate of the development following the issue of the Leopoldine Diploma of 1691 is correct, ". . . from 1691 right on till 1867 (with a brief inter-lude in 1848) Transylvania enjoyed complete autonomy under Vienna, forming *de jure* an integral part of the Hungarian crown, but *de facto* being linked by a mere personal union and really controlled by the emperor. In 1765 Maria Theresa stressed Transylvania's separate character still further by assuming the title of 'Great Prince' " of that principality.[9] The preservation of this privileged status, hotly con-tested by Magyar political theory and practice,[10] became the major task of Transylvania in her relation to the empire and to Hungary. Her internal policy was dominated by the interrelation between the "three nations."

The autonomy of the three nations temporarily declined in im-portance during the era of the centralistic reforms of Maria Theresa and Joseph II. Yet the basic institutions, including the three separate diets having a common annual general assembly with elected representatives, and also the "regalists" appointed by the sovereign, remained intact.

The suppression of the majority of the population also remained nearly unchanged. Gradual changes in the political status of these "Vlachs," as the Transylvanian Rumanians usually were called prior to the national unification of Wallachia and Moldavia as the principality of Rumania, again followed a typical pattern. Political reform was preceded by a rise in national consciousness, national consciousness was strongly influenced by a religious schismatic development. The split of the Greek Orthodox church in Transylvania in 1698 into the old church and a new Uniat church under the papacy gave a decisive though not immediately recognizable impetus to the rise of Rumanian nationalism, similar to Ruthenian schism a century earlier. As Seton-Watson puts it, the foundation of the new church "was to become the main instrument of kindling submerged national feeling, raising the standards of education . . . introducing a first breath of Western culture and establishing that link with Rome which was to have so memorable a psychological effect upon the whole nation." [11] The dignitaries of the new church, which Transylvania considered an outright Rumanian national church, gradually found some opportunity to raise their voices on behalf of the national claims of their people. Under Joseph II alleviating measures, especially the right to equal citizenship (Concivilität) on the fundus regius, were granted to the Wallachian serfs.[12] Joseph II's reforms on behalf of the mishandled Wallachians were social and humanitarian rather than national, yet they raised the national consciousness of the Wallachians so markedly that under his successor, Leopold II, the demand for recognition as the fourth Transylvanian nation was voiced openly.[13] It still could be blocked, though, by the combined opposition of the three nations, who feared for the maintenance of their privileged position.

Yet, Rumanian nationalism could no longer be frustrated as easily as in the past. A broad cultural movement among the Rumanians of Transylvania, as well as among their kin in the Danube principalities still under Turkish sovereignty, was in the making.[14] The names of three Transylvanian Rumanians, Samuel Klein, George Sincai, and Peter Major, are foremost in connection with this development, which in some ways was similar to the Slav cultural renaissance. Klein and Sincai were the authors of the first Rumanian grammar, the "Elements of the Daco-Roman or Wallach Language," published in 1780. Peter Major, continuing the linguistic work of his predecessors, was the author of a history of the origin of the Rumanians in Dacia. All three had received their training as priests of the Uniat church in Budapest and in Vienna, and they proved how greatly the new church influenced the rise and western orientation of Wallachian nationalism.[15]

In the political sphere, matters came to a head in the events preceding and during the Revolution of 1848. The Hungarian diets from 1840 to 1848, pressing relentlessly for the Magyarization of all the lands of the Hungarian crown, in particular the substitution of Magyar for Latin, were not deterred by the rights and privileges of the three recognized Transylvanian nations. In fact, the Transylvanian Magyars and the Magyar-speaking Szekels welcomed such a move. Only the smallest of the three nations, the Saxons,[16] opposed it publicly, the Rumanian majority having no voice in the affairs of their country. Consequently, the motion of the diet of Pressburg in the spring of 1848 to unite Transylvania and Hungary, solemnly assuring preservation of the autonomy and privileges of Transylvania and her three ruling nations, was accepted by the Magyar-speaking majority of the Transylvanian diet.[17]

During the two months which elapsed between the Magyar "invitation" to the union and Transylvania's acceptance, the Rumanian national group made itself heard. In the assembly of Blaj, on the "field of liberty," as it was later called, protests were raised against a union which did not recognize the Rumanians' rights as equal among the Transylvanian nations. Retraction of this flagrant injustice was demanded.[18] Neither the Transylvanian Estates nor the Hungarian diet paid any attention to these Rumanian demands. Though there were some enlightened Magyar political leaders, such as the Transylvanian baron, Nicolas Wesselényi, who, following Széchenyi's pattern, stood for the granting of the Rumanian request, they had to yield before "Kossuthism's" aggressive national ideology. At a second assembly at Blaj, in September, 1848, the Rumanians again protested unreservedly against the union as representing Magyar oppression. They asked openly—and vainly—for a Transylvania under the protection of an imperial Austrian constitution. Consequently, in the ensuing Magyar revolutionary war of independence, the Saxons and the Rumanians in the Banat and Transylvania, siding with the imperial armies, suffered only a little less from Magyar revenge than the Serbs in the Vojvodina.[19]

The final reward meted out by the imperial government for Rumanian loyalty was even more disappointing. The Austrian neo-absolutist administration, restoring only on the surface Transylvania's former status as a principality directly under the imperial crown, with a Transylvanian court chancellery in Vienna, made short shrift of the privileges of the proud Transylvanian Magyar and Szekel nations. It considerably reduced the limits of the Saxon autonomy by introducing the Austrian administrative district organization. Except for vague and empty promises in regard to the future protection of general Hungarian nationality rights,[20] the only benefit which the Rumanians could possibly derive from this new setup was the meager satisfaction that the Magyars were now practically in the same boat with them. Though the imperial administration exercised in the German language was nationally colorless and socially less unjust than the previous regime, it was little less illiberal in its approach to the Rumanian national cause.[21]

Nevertheless, the effects of the revolutionary and the counterrevolutionary period on Rumanian nationalism were not negligible. The revolution had at least established Rumanian claims for national equality, not only in Transylvania but in the Banat and Bukovina as well.[22] Indeed, Rumanian national consciousness had increased so greatly that as early as 1849 and 1850 Rumanian petitions were submitted to the imperial government asking for the establishment of a Rumanian crownland uniting the Rumanians in Transylvania, the Banat, and other parts of Hungary, in the Military Frontiers, and in the Bukovina.[23]

The era of constitutional experiments finally gave Rumanian national aspiration a long overdue but only temporary recognition. In connection with the October Diploma of 1860 the emperor solemnly announced his intention of having the ancient Transylvanian constitution restored and stated that "claims for appropriate representation of the nationalities previously not sharing political rights . . . should be considered." [24]

Only after long and difficult debates did the new Transylvanian

diet, still convoked on the basis of the three-nation status in 1863, declare the union with Hungary void. At the same time it finally recognized the Rumanians as the fourth Transylvanian nation. The Magyars in protest declined to participate in this reorganized diet, which
was to upset their previous majority. Consequently, for two years a
Rumanian-Saxon [25] "Rump" diet established Rumanian national
equality within the social limits of the Estates order. Only two major
achievements made for the sake of the Rumanian cause during this
period survived during the following era of complete national suppression: the separation of the Rumanian Orthodox church from the
Serbian and its establishment as a national church on an equal footing
with the Uniat church, and the foundation of the "Association for
the Cultivation of Rumanian Language and Literature." [26]

The progress of the Austro-Magyar negotiations leading to the
Compromise of 1867 increasingly impaired the autonomy of Transylvania and in consequence that of the Rumanians. The successful conclusion of these negotiations completely destroyed both. The way in
which this result was brought about presents one of the saddest
chapters in imperial nationality policy. The diet of 1863 was dissolved
and a new assembly, packed with a Magyar "regalist" majority, was
convoked.[27] It fulfilled the task assigned to it by imperial-Magyar
agreement: the reacceptance of the union of 1848 between Hungary
and Transylvania. Thus, the enactment of the compromise formally
ended the status of Transylvania as a historicopolitical entity. It also
led to the abolition of her internal national organization, since Magyars and Magyar-speaking Szekels—the latter also considered part of
the master nationality of politically restored Hungary—were no longer
interested in preserving the old political structure. In 1876 the last
traces of the medieval Saxon autonomy were eliminated, although compared to the Rumanians the German Saxons continued to hold a
relatively favorable position. The Rumanians themselves were returned to the status of a political nonentity which they had held prior
to 1863.

Thus a great opportunity was lost. The national organization of
the Transylvanian Estates system, though socially very backward,
might have been converted to truly democratic autonomous institutions for the whole population. The new order gave free rein to the
exclusive and arbitrary rule of Magyarism and the policy of Magyarization under administrative pressure.

Any hope that the Hungarian nationality law of 1868—drafted by Liberals as sincere and high-spirited as Eötvös and Deák [28]—might alleviate the plight of the Hungarian nationalities was bluntly suppressed under the "liberal" party regime of the elder Tisza.[29]

Under a revised electoral law, during this regime Rumanians were not represented by a single deputy of their own nationality in the parliament in Budapest, only 3.2 percent of the population in Transylvania being enfranchised.[30] When later the Rumanians succeeded in sending a few deputies to Budapest, 50,000 to 60,000 Rumanian inhabitants of Transylvania elected one deputy, while 4,000 to 5,000 voters elected one Magyar-speaking Szekel. The ratio of the number of secondary schools for Rumanians and Magyars followed the same pattern. The university and secondary-school system was almost completely Magyarized. But even in so-called elementary schools of the nationalities, according to a decree of 1902, no less than eighteen hours out of twenty-six had to be devoted to instruction in Magyar. Pressure on individuals to Magyarize themselves was enormous, though of surprisingly slight practical effect. Political prosecutions for treasonable activities of the most ridiculous kind, for instance, "ostentatious" use of the Rumanian language in public, were carried out even against Rumanian deputies in the Hungarian parliament. The extreme antisocial character of the "Magyar "liberal" regime, under which workers up to the age of eighteen could be flogged, and children under the age of fourteen were allowed to work twelve hours and more a day (Agricultural Law of 1907), aggravated the situation still further.[31] Such social standards hurt Magyar labor as well, but the fact that a far higher percentage of Rumanians and members of the other national groups belonged to the lowest social strata made them suffer much more severely from these conditions.

For a long time Rumanian reaction to this kind of treatment was by no means as violent as might have been expected. As far as it went, until early in the First World War period it was almost exclusively directed against Magyar Hungary, and not against the empire as a whole. As in the case of the other nationalities without independent political history in the empire, Austro-Rumanian nationalism, deprived of the stimulating effect of a fight for the restoration of lost historic achievements, was slow to set up a definite and concrete national program of wide popular appeal.

Indeed, ethnic programs, such as that of the Slovaks or the Rumanians, in their initial stages were scarcely carried by the support of the masses. These masses, rather than putting their faith in the theoretical projects drafted by the young national intelligentsia, still widely believed in the notion that the all-embracing empire, symbolized by the person of the sovereign, would do justice to the victims of national oppression by another nationality.

Another factor is important in this connection. Rumanian nationalism in the monarchy did not receive much active encouragement from the Rumanian kingdom until the end of the nineteenth century. Even the later, more intimate relations between Rumanians in the empire and in the kingdom prior to the First World War could not be compared with the dynamic influence of Italy and Serbia on Austro-Serb and Italian irredentism. The reasons for this fact were obvious. Though Rumania had gained unification and complete national independence only a few years later than had Italy, the power of the Balkan state was not of a kind which could have dared to provoke the anger of its great Austrian neighbor by the open support of an irredentist policy. In this respect she was in an even weaker position than small Serbia, which could rely on the sympathies of the Pan-Slav world and above all of powerful Russia.

Furthermore, to nationalism in Rumania the empire represented no hostile force, but rather it was considered a Great Power which before the outbreak of the Crimean war had supported Rumanian national interests against Russia,[32] then clearly a permanent and powerful threat to future Rumanian independence. The additional fact that Russia at the Congress of Berlin, in 1878, had betrayed Rumania's claims to the spoils of the war against Turkey by forcing her to cede Bessarabia was for decades an open sore on the national body. Finally, although Rumania became only a silent annex to the Austro-German-Italian Tripartite alliance in 1883,[33] the Hohenzollern sovereign, King Carol I, ruling over Rumania from 1866 to 1914, tried hard to live up to its commitments. Only after his death did the kingdom follow the inevitable course of war against the empire in 1916.

Aurel C. Popovici, the Austro-Rumanian champion of ethnic federalism in the empire, summarized correctly the international aspects of this problem as it appeared in the period immediately preceding the First World War.

Rumania, based on her urge for self-preservation, has a great interest in the existence of a mighty Austria. This interest excludes a priori any dream,

any thought of an annexation of Austrian territories inhabited by Rumanians. Such annexation would be possible only in the case of an Austrian
debacle, and such a debacle with mathematical certainty would in the
course of a few decades lead to the ruin of Rumania, her destruction in the
Russian sea.[34]

Fear of such a debacle restrained Rumania's policy before 1916. It
was only the imminent Austrian World War debacle itself which
finally shattered the still-existing hopes for a settlement of the Rumanian problem between empire and kingdom.

Within the Habsburg Empire, Rumanian national policy in Transylvania well into the 1870s was characterized by cautious moderation, consistently stressing loyalty to the empire and to the sovereign.
In regard to the Magyars, the policy of the able Orthodox Archbishop
Andrein Saguna, contributed to the strengthening of Rumanian autonomy in ecclesiastical affairs, the nucleus from which at an opportune time a more active nationalism might develop.

After Saguna's death Rumanian national policy took a more active
course. The program of the Rumanian National party in Transylvania, founded in 1881, openly demanded the restoration of Transylvanian autonomy and re-establishment and expansion of Rumanian
national rights to the point of complete equality with the Magyars.
This program still stood publicly for the platform of the Hungarian
constitution and as yet contained no trace of the irredentism of which
it was accused by the Magyar ruling classes. In the last decade of the
nineteenth century an intensification of the oppressive Magyar course
led the Austro-Rumanians to stress more intensively the racial and
cultural relationship to their kin in the Rumanian kingdom—a development advanced even more by the foundation of the Rumanian
Cultural League in Bucharest, in 1891. Austro-Hungarian Rumanian
attempts to appeal directly to the king-emperor in Vienna for the
rectification of their justified demands not only failed but also led
to judicial prosecution of the signers of the petition and, needless to
say, to their conviction by Magyar courts. The dissolution of the Rumanian National party was the next move of the Hungarian government. Lingering hopes of the Rumanians for a redress of their griev-
ances were gravely disappointed by the outcome of the Hungarian
state crisis of 1905–1906, which shattered the hope of the nationalities
for the introduction of general equal franchise in Hungary.[35]

Only then did the Hungarian Rumanian problem gradually begin to assume the irredentist tinge of Pan-Serb and Italian nationalism. However, the immediate Rumanian national program of action was still moderate and, except for increased cooperation with the other suppressed nationalities in Hungary, not markedly different from the state of affairs up to the early 1890s.[36] Violent Rumanian opposition developed only when new school laws, driving the policy of Magyarization still further, were adopted by the Hungarian parliament in 1907. But it was not only fear of Magyar political terror which prevented Rumanian irredentism from coming into the open.

Hopes were widely entertained in the future course of the Hungarian nationality policy of Francis Ferdinand, the heir presumptive. The archduke's contacts with Rumanian political leaders in Hungary in the immediate prewar period, especially with the later prime ministers of Greater Rumania Alexander Vaida-Voevod and Julius Maniu, are well known. Yet no evidence exists of tangible results of these contacts. Though Francis Ferdinand undoubtedly was sympathetic to the Rumanian cause, it is unlikely that he would or could have adopted sweeping reform plans, such as Popovici's comprehensive Austrian federalization project, which provided for a Rumanian member state comprising the Rumanians in Transylvania, the Banat, and Bukovina. It cannot even be definitely established that the archduke would have agreed to Rumanian autonomy within the lands of the Hungarian crown.[37] Yet what chiefly counted in regard to Rumanian public opinion was the fact that the archduke, whose definite plans were unknown to the public, was believed to be strongly sympathetic to either of these projects. Here the demise of the archduke struck "a death-blow to Rumanian hopes, and thenceforth Bucharest inevitably took the place of Vienna in all plans for the future."[38]

In a way, the history of the Rumanian nationality problem in the monarchy ended with the events of June and July, 1914, that is, the assassination of the archduke and the outbreak of the war. The lame attempts to appease Rumanian nationalism during the first two years of the war, before the kingdom joined the ranks of the Allies, were without prospects from the beginning. The invincible intransigence of the Hungarian Tisza government prior to the war and its refusal to make any concessions to Rumanian ethnic claims had to be paid for dearly.[39] Tisza, however, represented only the firm will of the whole Magyar ruling class when he opposed concessions to the Rumanian nationality, though Austrian and German endeavors to appease the Rumanian "ally" beyond the frontiers by such concessions were never lacking. But this "ally" had raised his price tremendously.

Prior to the war it was certainly conceivable that a settlement of the Rumanian question in the empire might have been effected without outside interference, and thus the aggression of Rumanian nationalism might have been eased at least for a time. Such a settlement in the Hungarian Banat and in Transylvania might have followed the national compromise effected in 1910 in Bukovina, where a kind of national autonomous status on the basis of the personality principle was accorded the Rumanians.[40] After 1914 not the empire's Rumanians, but Rumania herself, would have been for all practical purposes a contracting partner in a compromise. Her price for mere neutrality would have been nothing less than the cession of Transylvania and the Bukovina. Cisleithanian Austria might have been willing to pay her share of that price. Magyar Hungary, in this respect united from the Right to Károlyi's radical Left, would have none of it.[41] Thus, open conflict became inevitable.

Yet this is not to say that any attempt to raise the status of the Hungarian- and Hungarian-Transylvanian Rumanians to that of their kin in Bukovina, which was rather fair until 1910 and even more favorable from then until 1918,[42] would have been assured of success. It is, indeed, likely that such reforms would have alleviated the solution of the problem only temporarily and that the monarchy's Rumanian population would then have advanced the farther-reaching demand for the unification of all the Austro-Hungarian Rumanians in a member state of an imperial federation. Yet it is a historic certainty that the Magyar regime, opposed to a change of the Rumanian status even within Hungary, would have been unalterably opposed to such a more radical solution.

Thus, the question whether the Rumanian problem could have been solved within the empire could not be put to the test. Austria had missed the opportunity for federal reform which had presented itself in 1848–49, and with decreasing chance of success again in the 1860s and in 1905. Consequently, it became obvious that the solution by force "from without" had a clear path.

# CHAPTER XIII

# THE RUTHENIANS AND THE NATIONAL ORGANIZATION IN BUKOVINA

THE CONCEPT of a national group without history as defined previously, particularly if the social and economic conditions of such a group are extremely poor, usually conveys the notion that its political and national problems must be simple and elementary.[1] Several of the surveys of nationality problems presented thus far could well be held to refute such a thesis. None, however, disproves it more convincingly than the complexity of the national problem of the empire's socially most backward people, the Ruthenians.

The Ruthenian question again represents the problems of a national group settled in both parts of the empire. The center of gravity of the Ruthenian nationality in regard to population and cultural development, however, undoubtedly was in Cisleithanian-Austria. The fact that there the Ruthenians were settled in two crownlands was more significant than was the spread of other national groups over several crownlands. The status of the Ruthenians in Galicia and those in Bukovina differed from each other historically, politically, and legally just as much as from that of their kin in Hungary, the Carpatho-Ruthenians.[2]

The Ruthenians also belonged to the type of national group of which a part—in the case of the Ruthenians, an overwhelming majority—lived outside the empire, in another state, the Russian Empire. An important difference, however, between the Ruthenian status and that of the other nationalities whose kin likewise lived in other states is that the Ruthenians beyond the border of the Austrian Empire— that is, the 30,000,000 Ukrainians or Little Russians in Russia—were themselves merely a national group of not quite equal standing with the principal national group within Russia, the Great Russians.

At this point one is confronted with a confusing terminology which refers to the same ethnic group as the Ruthenians in Austria and as the Ukrainians in Russia. The clarification of these concepts is essential to an understanding of the Ruthenian problem in Austria, though it largely refers to a course of events which took place beyond Austria's borders in the Ukraine. Yet, Ukrainian history is not easily comprehended. "Not until the seventeenth century did it form a connected chronicle of events, which happened to one people of one culture, language, and religion; it is rather the story of events, which have taken place in the land which is now called the Ukraine." [3] This fact has an important bearing on Ruthenian national development.

The eastern Slav peoples who settled in the vast territories spreading from the Baltic to the Sea of Azov in the period of the Russo-Kievan Empire—that is, from the middle of the ninth to the middle of the fourteenth century—were usually referred to as Ruthenians, the term being a Latinization of the name Russia. This empire was the real fatherland of present-day Ruthenians-Ukrainians. Their racial, cultural, and linguistic differences from the Great Russians were largely determined by the fact that the population was mixed with Tartaric, Normanic, and other tribes. In the course of the fourteenth century changes took place which profoundely affected the history of the "Ruthenians" of modern times. The western, major part of the Kiev domains came under Polish, Lithuanian, and in the Carpathian regions under Magyar rule. In the eastern part the rising Muscovite principality, from which the Russia of today developed, took over in the course of the following centuries. The Muscovite Russians, denying the assertion of the former "Ruthenians" that they were a distinct nationality, called them just "Little Russians," a term which has survived until today. The native population, however, soon enough readily accepted the term "Ukrainia," which means borderland, but in particular the border between Russia and the lands of the Poles and the Tartars. The inhabitants of this borderland—in history and linguistic and minor racial characteristics different from the Great Russians, but associated with them by common adherence to the Greek Orthodox faith—are the ancestors of the Russian Ukrainians, the closest kin of the Austro-Hungarian Ruthenians.

Domination over the western Ruthenians from the middle of the fourteenth to the middle of the sixteenth century was divided between the Lithuanians and the Poles, the former ruling in the eastern and northern parts, the latter in the western parts of the former Kievan Empire until both states were united (Union of Lublin) in a Greater Poland (1569). Of particular importance here is the fact that the Poles took over the so-called principality of Halich, which territory covered the area of what is called eastern Galicia, that is, the focal point of Ruthenian settlements within Austria. This ancient principality of Halich had been at least semi-independent during the period of slow disintegration of the Kievan Empire, and Ruthenian nationalism in the nineteenth century still dwelt on the glory of their former state-hood in the thirteenth and fourteenth centuries.[4]

The era of Polish and Lithuanian, later merely Polish, domination of the western part of the bygone Kievan empire, which lasted until the end of the Polish kingdom at the close of the eighteenth century, greatly influenced the further development of the Ruthenian national problem. Polish domination succeeded in almost completely assimilating the upper classes, particularly the Ruthenian nobility, and this assimilation included their conversion to the Roman Catholic church. This regime did not succeed in assimilating, or more probably did not care to assimilate, the overwhelming majority of the Ruthenian serfs—a historical problem in that respect largely similar to that of Slovene and Slovak nationalism. The impact of Polish culture never-theless left its mark on the Ruthenian peoples. Many of them followed the Poles in their adherence to the Roman church, though they were unable and unwilling to worship in either the Latin or the Ruthenian language. The so-called Union of Brest Litovsk of 1596, uncontested until 1946, brought about a solution of this dilemma. Then and there the papacy consented to the creation of a "Uniat" church under the jurisdiction of Rome, yet it permitted the use of the old Slavonic liturgy, that is, in principle the liturgy of the Greek Orthodox church.

The importance of this event can scarcely be overestimated. The adherence of the Ruthenians of Halich—that is, the Ruthenians of Galicia—to the new Uniat church separated them equally distinctly from their kin in the Russian Ukraine[5] and from their fellow na-tionals in Bukovina. The latter's religious status was not affected by the provisions of the Union of Brest Litovsk. At that time forming a part of the principality of Moldavia, they were already under Turkish suzerainty and remained so until the northernmost part of this prin-cipality, the Bukovina, was incorporated into Austria, in 1775. Conse-quently, the majority of these Ruthenians in the Bukovina remained members of the Greek Orthodox church.

As far as the Ruthenians within Hungary were concerned, the situation was again different. Catholic influence was prevalent in

Hungary, as well as in Poland, though not to exactly the same degree. Still, it was sufficient to lead the Hungarian Ruthenians from the Greek Orthodox church to the new Uniat church under the sway of the Holy See in Rome. Yet, the Ruthenians in the mountainous northeastern *Comitats* of Hungary were firmly cut off from their kin in Galicia and Bukovina by the force of political and geographic conditions. Practically no social and cultural relations existed between these Hungarian Ruthenian groups to the south and those to the north of the Carpathians, either in the empire or beyond its borders in Poland and Russia.

While in regard to the Hungarian Carpatho-Ukrainians the political and geographic factors outweighted the impact of the religious issue, the same certainly did not entirely hold true for the problem of the far more numerous Ruthenians in Galicia and Bukovina, who, until 1849, lived under a joint crownland administration. Yet it was to some extent only nominal religious influence which determined the Ruthenian national attitude to Austrian and Polish Catholicism and to Russian Orthodoxy. To be sure, Austrian centralism and Polish, Russian, and Russo-Ukrainian political concepts considered the Ruthenian problem largely from the aspect of religion. Yet, they did so mainly because the religious approach appeared to them the most appropriate in dealings with the political problems of a people who were culturally and socially still backward. None of these political camps succeeded, however, in concealing behind often merely alleged missionary tendencies their obvious political designs concerning the domination of the Ruthenian people. This helps to explain why the history of the Ruthenian national cause was fused with the religious issue for a longer time and more strongly than was that of other Slav peoples.

Ruthenian history in the era of emerging nationalism, as, indeed, in the whole period from 1848 to 1918, widely supports this assertion. The first reforms of the Ruthenian status in Galicia under Maria Theresa and Joseph II were initiated with the creation of adequate facilities for the training of priests for the Uniat church. In effect—and this applies particularly to later far-reaching reforms of the educational system in Ruthenian Galicia under Joseph II—these measures led to a revival of national consciousness, which had thus far been equally suppressed by Russians and by Poles.[6] A kind of informally implied Russo-Polish agreement on the nonrecognition of a separate Ruthenian nationality, however, had not gone so far as to settle the question of the orbit to which the Ruthenian belonged. The Poles considered the Ruthenians a poorly developed branch of their national culture as frequently as the Russians considered them their kin.

It was obviously in the interest of the Austrian government to fight both theses and to assert the distinctive national character of the Ruthenian peoples. This assertion happened to coincide with historic truth.[7] Fear of Russian imperialism and, particularly in the later part of the pre-March period, fear of Russian-inspired Pan-Slavism as well as a strong dread of Polish revolutionary nationalism were strong motives for the government to uphold the Ruthenian cause in Galicia, at least in a limited way. Still, during the latter part of the reign of Francis I (1792–1835) the government receded somewhat from the concessions made to the Ruthenians under Joseph II,[8] particularly in regard to higher education. This point is easily explained by the fact that the Metternich system was, in general, suspicious of national institutions of higher learning, believing them to be danger centers of revolutionary activities.

Though severely handicapped by the almost complete illiteracy of the peasant population, Ruthenian national ambition did not hesitate to take up the arduous fight for cultural development on a higher level. Considering the abjectly poor social and educational standards of the people, their relative progress compared well with that of other northern and southern Slav peoples. Indeed, the Ruthenian cultural renaissance, which started on a much lower level than that of most of the other Austrian Slav peoples, was in many ways very similar to the Czech, the Slovak, and the southern Slav development.

The purely literary movement which, under the intellectual leadership of Markiyan Shashkevych, T. Vahylarych, and Ya. Holovatz'kyi revived folklore and ancient literary monuments in the pre-March period, has its obvious parallels among the other Slav peoples.[9] So has the even more important fight for the development of a Ruthenian literary language.

The conflict between Serb Cyrillic and Croatian Latin scripture repeated itself in the Ruthenian cultural evolution. In the 1830s a trend, supported by the Polish upper classes, to drop the Cyrillic writing and to adopt the Polish Latin alphabet and orthography gained some support. It might have succeeded if the nationally conscious general vicar of the Archbishopric See of the Uniat Church of Lemberg (Lwów), Gregor von Yakhimovych, supported by the younger

Ruthenian-speaking clergy, had not opposed such a concession to Polish wishes.

But there also existed violent disagreement within the ranks of the clergy itself, that is, between Yakhymovich's young followers and the higher ecclesiastics. The latter stood for the old Slavonic church language, which was similar to that of the Orthodox church and was not understood by the masses. Since the language of the church was that of the principal carriers of literacy, the outcome of this conflict was to decide whether Ruthenian cultural evolution was an achievement of the few or of the masses. In generations to come it was to decide, also, whether the Ruthenians would follow the "Old Ruthenian" conservative concept, with its ultimate affiliations to czarist, conservative Russia, or the—in national questions—more progressive wing of the Uniat church and its Western orientation. In any case, the ascendancy of the national Ruthenian language in the pre-March period had not yet determined the final course of the peoples.

The pre-March support of the Ruthenian cause by the Austrian government as a consequence of its fear of the Polish revolutionary spirit has been referred to in Chapter VI on the Poles. Likewise, the subsequent letdown of the loyal Ruthenians by the government in the Polish insurrection of 1846 will be remembered.[10] Consequently, it was small wonder that the Ruthenians did not enter the revolutionary struggle in 1848 as an "appeased" national group. Their ecclesiastic political leaders were still convinced, though, that the people's welfare depended on the support of the central government in Vienna. In this respect the Ruthenian political position in the spring revolution of 1848 was rather clearly defined in the Petition of the Ruthenians of Eastern Galicia to the Emperor, dated April 19, 1848. Again the bishop of the Uniat church, Gregor von Yakhimovych, subsequently a Ruthenian representative at the *Reichstag* of Kremsier, took a leading part in shaping Ruthenian policy. This policy was still confined to the limited demands for adequate educational facilities in the Ruthenian language of instruction in eastern Galicia and recognition of Ruthenian as an official language of administration on an equal footing with Polish and German. Furthermore, equal rights for the principal religious denominations and, finally, opportunity for Ruthenians to hold public office were demanded. And, indeed, they could be sure of support for their cause by the enlightened governor of Galicia, Austria's future great centralist reformer, Count Francis Stadion.[11]

Accordingly, the answer of the minister of the interior, Pillersdorf, to this petition on May 9, 1848, almost fully agreed to the Ruthenian demands.[12] But in spite of Pillersdorf's good intentions the government in the stormy spring days of 1848 was in no position to do much in regard to reforms, which could not be immediately realized by the stroke of the pen of a high government official.

Consequently, the unsettled Polish-Ruthenian crisis flared up in the Slav Congress of June, 1848, in Prague. Here, inspired by the example of other nationalities, Ruthenian national consciousness made great strides forward. Administrative separation of Galicia into western Polish and eastern Ruthenian parts was openly demanded— an ethnic claim which became a standard issue of Ruthenian policy in the course of the following generations. These demands were not only opposed by the Poles but the majority of the congress itself was not in favor of so radical a solution, which would have adversely affected the interests of the far more renowned Polish cause.[18] A Polish-Ruthenian compromise, which, however, was agreed upon only after difficult negotiations, met the Ruthenian demands at least halfway.

Not by their actual consequences—which must be disregarded as practically nil—but as an ideological contribution to national understanding between two rival national groups, the provisions of this compromise of Prague are of great interest. Poles and Ruthenians were agreed on their demands for a crownland administration in Galicia responsible to the diet, which should include a fair representation of both national groups. The rights of the two nationalities were to be secured by a franchise reform. Equality of language, religious institutions, right to hold public office, and educational facilities were to be granted in accordance with the Ruthenian demands of April 19, 1848. Even in districts in which an overwhelming majority of the population belonged to one national group, the rights of single communities having a different majority and, more than that, of single individuals were to be fully guaranteed by constitutional provisions within the limits of the principles outlined above. The question of administrative partition of Galicia was to be decided by the reformed diet, to be convened as soon as possible.

The psychological effect of Ruthenian emergence as an active national group in Prague was great enough to give even the most forgotten among the forgotten, the Carpatho-Ruthenians in Hungary, a voice. Like the Slovaks, they asked for recognition of their nationality within Hungary, the right to set up a national council to safeguard their rights in regard to national schools, associations, and so forth.

In all likelihood a feeling of solidarity with their Carpatho-Ruthenian kin, who were cut off from the main stem of the national group, prompted the Ruthenians specifically to stress ethnic aspects in their national program. Here the final address of the Slav Congress, containing the specific demands of all the national groups represented, was of great significance. Unlike all the other nationalities, except the Slovenes, the Ruthenians did not ask for the preservation of the old crownland frontiers.[14] While they did not yet dare openly to demand ethnic union with their kin in Hungary, this otherwise significant omission of the crownland frontier issue in their national program implied a distinct leaning in the direction of ethnic-federal union.

The Ruthenian claims, however cautiously formulated, were to be settled neither by the conciliatory attitude of the Polish Liberals at Prague nor by the Ruthenian ecclesiastic representatives. Only after the suppression of the revolution were they handled, and then by the Austrian government alone. Even prior to the triumph of the counter-revolution, the Ruthenians at the *Reichstag* of Kremsier were not able to hold the line taken at the Slav Congress a few months earlier. The great Palacký plan, dividing Austria into eight federal units, provided for the union of Galicia, Bukovina, and the Hungarian Ruthenian territories (the Carpatho-Ukraine of today) into one federal member state. Thus favoring a comprehensive Polish-Ruthenian state, Palacký rejected the idea of a separate Ruthenian unit.[15] Only the Slovene Kaučič, as representative of a national group whose problems were in many ways similar to those of the Ruthenians, recognized the Ruthenian demand for statehood within the framework of a federation based on ethnic principles. Both the official draft of the Kremsier constitution and the decreed Stadion constitution of March, 1849, however, limited themselves to the promotion of national administrative *Kreise* within the existing crownland frontiers.[16]

Nevertheless, the Ruthenians, considered by the government as a potential weapon and check against possibly renewed Polish revolutionary activities, came out of the revolution politically unscathed and in some ways even rewarded for their imperial loyalties. At least in a limited way they benefited from the partial substitution of the rule of governmental bureaucracy for Polish autocracy. In the national sphere this certainly was not a change for the worse, though in the political sphere it did not indicate a change for the better. For a time Galicia, though not actually partitioned, was divided into three administrative units, and the Ruthenians in Bukovina, since 1850 an independent crownland, could anticipate a somewhat brighter future.[17] Formal recognition of national equality was granted to the Ruthenians by an imperial patent of 1850, still inspired by the ideas of the great friend of the Ruthenian cause Count Francis Stadion.[18]

Furthermore, the after-revolutionary era was the one and only period in the history of the monarchy during which measures resembling national recognition were granted to the Ruthenians in Hungary. A Ruthenian, Adolf J. Dobrianskyí, was appointed governor of four Ruthenian mountain *Comitats,* and Ruthenian was introduced as the official language in these districts.[19] However, these concessions were abolished as suddenly and as permanently as similar rights granted to the Slovaks had been voided when, about a decade later, Magyar Austrian affairs entered the stage of negotiation leading finally to the Compromise of 1867.

Though the political status of the Galician Ruthenians never sank as low as that of the Hungarian Carpatho-Ruthenians or Carpatho-Ukrainians after the Compromise, their national position had even previously suffered a setback. In the early 1850s, under the governorship of Count Agenor Goluchowski in Galicia, the Polish aristocracy came to a kind of temporary agreement with the government. It was to be considered a sort of forerunner to the permanent alliance between Polish Conservatives and Austro-centralism of 1868, which lasted until 1918. Illustrative of consequences of this change in policy was the substitution of the Polish for the Latin language in court and, more painful to the Ruthenians, the official elimination of the Cyrillic Orthodox alphabet in Ruthenian writing.[20]

The ensuing development of Ruthenian policy was a reaction consequent to the twofold political disappointment—the frustration of any hopes for liberal political and social reforms on the part of the central government and the delivery of the Ruthenian national cause to the Polish class regime. Nevertheless, in spite of the unfortunate situation in Galicia the constitutional era after 1867 gave the

Ruthenians the chance to move slowly into line with the national development of the other Austro-Slav peoples.

Two main political groups, the Young Ruthenians and the Old Ruthenians, emerged very clearly at the beginning of that period. The latter were the heirs to the ideological program of the Ruthenian clergy, conservative in outlook, still loyal to the imperial government, and asserting the existence of a distinct Austro-Ruthenian national group strictly different from Poles, Russians, and Russo-Ukrainians. On the language question they stood for a national idiom which was derived from the old Slavonic church language and had little popular appeal among the peasants. Yet this political concept still had some chance to establish itself among the Ruthenians as long as the government was ready to steer a middle course between Poles and Ruthenians. As soon as "Vienna" openly sided with the stronger forces of the Poles, this policy rapidly lost ground among the masses. The only way to survive politically rested in joining forces with a strong power. The Old Ruthenians, anxious to preserve their Conservative tenets, were prepared to drop their demands for existence as a separate Austro-Ruthenian nationality and in the late 1860s and 1870s suddenly declared themselves as part of the Russians, that is, the Great Russian people.[21] Austrian centralism thus had to pay for its alliance with the Conservative Poles with the gradual defection of one of the more loyal supporting groups of the Conservative centralist system.

The Young Ruthenians were by no means ready to make up for that defection. As bitter political opponents of the Old Ruthenians, they vigorously denounced the old conservative concept of an Austro-Ruthenian nationality destined to play the role of a permanent minority oppressed by the powers of the church, the central government, and the Polish *Szlachta*. However, they also refused to consider themselves Russians. They sought ideological and, in veiled form, political union with the 30,000,000 Russo-Ukrainians, of whom they felt themselves a part. Yet, at least as much as and probably more than the Ruthenians in Austria, the Ukrainians in Russia were oppressed in their national claims, with the difference, however, that under the czarist regime political oppression was even more accentuated than national oppression.[22] For a time after the late 1870s relatively more liberal conditions in Austria in general made Galicia a "Piedmont" of Ukrainian Liberal irredentist activities. Here again, Austro-centralism had lost the cause. Ruthenians, formerly called "the Tirolese of the east" in recognition of their outstanding loyalty, had now become "the Piedmontese of the east."

Still, Ruthenian national history in Galicia during the last generation of the empire's existence was not altogether unfortunate. It can be considered a slow, but by no means entirely fruitless, process of catching up with the Polish position. The general Austrian franchise reform of 1906–1907 [23] and the Polish-Ruthenian Compromise of 1914 [24] in regard to internal Galician affairs were important steps in that direction.

Through this Compromise, which had been influenced by the earlier Moravian Compromise of 1905 and the national settlement in Bukovina in 1910, the Ruthenian national position was to be substantially improved. On the basis of a curia organization of the voters, general, though by no means equal, franchise was to be introduced in elections to the Galician diet. That is to say, curias representing larger strata of the population were added to those of the great landowners, chambers of commerce, and propertied townspeople, which thus far had almost exclusively represented Polish interests. Furthermore, minority representation, including that of Jewish districts, was to be introduced according to the principle of personal autonomy. Contrary to the provinces of the Moravian Compromise, the national status of the voters was determined, not in a specific national registration, but on the basis of the colloquial language (*Umgangssprache*) used by an individual, as established by the official census.

Far from being a perfect solution, this arrangement guaranteed to the Ruthenians, who formed more than two fifths of the population of Galicia, at least about 27 per cent of the seats in the diet. Obviously, this compromise, which became law in July, 1914, might well have been further improved by eliminating the residues of the old Estates order in the diet and by further expanding the application of the principle of personal autonomy in nationally heterogeneous territories. Yet the outbreak of the war made the application of the compromise impossible even in its then existing form.

Even if the war could have been averted, it is doubtful, whether the orientation of Ruthenian nationalism toward the East could have been checked and whether the Ruthenians could have been led back to the platform of 1848. Neither the Conservative pro-Russian minority nor the pro-Ukrainian Liberal majority, joined in the early twentieth century by a Socialist force, was in the long run prepared to seek national redemption in Austria.

Attempts to that effect certainly were still made.[25] And it is not improbable that if the First World War could have been prevented or at least postponed the Ruthenian problem would not have unleashed a great empire crisis. Polish charges, branding the Ruthenians even in peacetime as an outright traitor nationality to the empire, were largely products of national bias. Yet they became the basis of wartime persecutions as cruel as they were unwise.

But for its still veiled ultimate objectives, Ruthenian national policy in Austria prior to the First World War was neither predominantly irredentist nor obstructionist.[26] The fact that it had strong ties to forces beyond the empire was, within the general setting of the Austrian national problem after 1867, neither extraordinary nor alarming.

From the viewpoint of the government, it was, however, naïve to believe that as soon as the Greater Ukrainian problem was unfolded in a world-wide conflict a solution of the Ruthenian problem was still possible in the narrow crownland frame of Galicia or even of an Austrian-Ruthenian federal member state. The empire had missed the opportunity to unite its Ruthenian peoples in time and to knit them together, with the help of the force of the times, into a politically widely autonomous ethnic-national group. Only thus could the Ruthenians have conceivably resisted the temptation unfurled before them of either a Great Russian or a Great Ukrainian national solution.[27] It is not possible to determine whether a factor strongly extenuating Austria is that, of all the major national problems accrued from the empire's national inheritance, the postwar world failed perhaps most flagrantly in handling the Ruthenian problem.

The particularly poor showing which Austrian statesmanship had made concerning the Ruthenian issue in Galicia after 1867 was, however, somewhat balanced by the fact that the Ruthenian problem was in a limited way rather satisfactorily solved in Bukovina. Here in the nationally most heterogeneous of the Austrian crownlands, a land without absolute national majorities, several ethnic groups fairly equal in standing were united in their rejection of the encroachments of centralism. Here rested the chance for a happier solution of the national problem.[28] Indeed, the influence of these rather favorable basic conditions was effective in the development of the national question in Bukovina long before the crownland's constitutional reforms of 1910. It was traceable practically from Bukovina's severance from Galicia in 1850. Consequently, the national compromise between Ruthenians, Rumanians, Germans, Jews, Poles, and Magyars in Bukovina was not preponderantly the product of ingenuity on the part of any particular reformer. It was largely due to the conditions of a ground far more fertile for the growth of national tolerance.

Here the two relatively strongest nationalities, Ruthenians and Rumanians, both groups without history in Austria, based their national claims, not on the tradition of historically privileged master peoples, but exclusively on ethnic claims. It is true, however, that the Germans had occupied a privileged position in this crownland since the formal acquisition from the Turks in 1777. Yet this German status was to a great extent still based on the administrative and cultural tradition of Maria Theresa and Josephinian centralism. It was influenced relatively slightly by an aggressive German frontier nationalism. Another factor of particular importance in comparison with conditions in neighboring Galicia is well worth noting. Bukovina, though by no means a rich land, was on a higher level than Galicia in regard to agricultural, industrial, and commercial conditions. Above all, her history in modern times was no longer determined to the same degree by the social conflict between a landed national nobility and an overwhelming majority of serf-tenants. Thus, a most important factor generally poisoning national relations was not decisively important here. The politically dominant nationality, the Germans, represented the administration and, with the Jews, chiefly the professional classes, small industrial enterprise, and commerce. They represented neither the landed nobility nor a practically nonexistent big industry. Thus, their national "superiority" at least was not a means of exploitation in the economic sphere. Yet, as has been noted in the review of the Magyar status in Hungary and the Polish position in Austrian Galicia, the concentration of socioeconomic power in the master nationalities contributed more than any other single factor to aggravate national tension.

Thus Bukovina, where these unfavorable factors were relatively insignificant could look back on a tradition of national tolerance well into the pre-March era.[29] Particularly since the complete administrative separation from Galicia in 1849–50, the status of the Ruthenian and the Rumanian languages as official languages of the land in external intercourse was recognized. Still, German remained the primary language of administration and the predominant language in higher education.[30]

Largely due to the influence of the Austrian franchise reform of 1907 on national problems, the non-German nationalities in Bukovina succeeded in 1910 in securing a large sphere of autonomy. This was done by means of a new crownland constitution (*Landesordnung*) and a new franchise law to the diet, both landmarks in the history of Austrian national reforms.

Somewhat similar to provisions of the earlier Moravian Compromise of 1905 and the later Galician Compromise of 1914, yet strictly on the basis of personal autonomy, six national curias of voters were organized for the purpose of sending adequate national representations of every nationality to the diet. The first two curias elected a number of representatives of the Greek Oriental church and the great landowners of every nationality; they were joined also by the Polish representation, elected on the basis of general equal franchise. The third and fourth curias, voting predominantly on the basis of equal franchise, sent the Ruthenian and Rumanian representatives to the diet. In addition to electing the representatives of the chambers of commerce and the rector (president) of the university, the fifth and sixth curias elected in the same way the German and, for the first time in Austrian history, the national Jewish deputies.[31]

Again, this settlement was by no means perfect from the purely democratic viewpoint, since to some extent the corporate Estates idea, represented by church, landed property, industry, and commerce, still prevailed in the diet. But the purely national distribution of diet seats was rather fair, due to an ingenious application of the principle of personal autonomy in mixed districts. A good deal of administrative autonomy was granted to the nationalities, since the *Landesausschuss*, the crownland executive board composed of the representatives of all curias, organized its agenda according to national interests. Thereby, every nationality decisively influenced the administration of its own national institutions and the appointment of conational officials in purely national affairs.[32]

Only a few years were given to·this national Compromise of 1910 to prove its merits. It stood this test, certainly not a sufficiently long one, very well. Thus, in spite of its obvious shortcomings the compromise in Bukovina approximately represented not only a relatively satisfactory solution of the national problem in a limited area but altogether the one most satisfactory solution ever arrived at in Austrian lands. This proved conclusively that it was not the problem of national diversity in itself—which was more complex in Bukovina than in any other territory of the empire—but exclusively the related, but not identical issue of national inequality that presented the chief difficulty in the solution of the national problem. It also proved, however, that the settlement of the purely national issue in a limited area represented a merely academic success. The national problem of every one of the empire's nationalities was not of a limited administrative, but of a comprehensive ethnic, area cutting into different economic, political, and administrative entities. Thus, the political factor could not be eliminated from the national one.

The cause of Ruthenian nationalism in Austria clearly illustrated this fact. Austria was able to cope with the national administrative problem in Bukovina; it failed, as Hungary had in the Carpatho-Ukraine, in the solution of the economic and political problem in predominantly Polish Galicia. It failed above all, to find a comprehensive approach to the ethnic aspect of the whole empire's Ruthenian problem. It became inevitable, therefore, that Ruthenian nationalism, in itself not one of the empire's most dynamic national problems, added fuel when the whole house was set on fire.

# CHAPTER XIV

# NATIONAL CONFLICT AND NATIONAL CONCILIATION

ON THE BASIS of the foregoing review of the status of the empire's nationalities from their full rise to political consciousness until the breakdown in 1918, it is essential to draw some preliminary conclusions concerning the causes, the consequences, and the possible trends toward conciliation of national conflict. To be sure, it is obvious that the unfortunate influence of absolutism, replaced by the equally fatal consequences of the dualistic organization of 1867, was to a large degree responsible for the national crisis and its final turn to disaster. Yet in a way these facts affected only the superstructure of the Austrian political system. Broader and deeper issues become apparent in the history of the Austrian nationality problem.

In reviewing political-national conditions from the pre-March era onwards, it is striking to see how soon the national development of nationalities which were politically, culturally, and historically widely different fell into line. In this respect the rise of nationalism must not be confused with the closely related political and cultural development of these national groups in general. Undoubtedly, nationalities like the Germans and the Magyars benefited for many centuries from a greatly privileged position. In the course of three generations peasant peoples such as Slovenes, Slovaks, and Ruthenians could not fully catch up with the advantages of this privileged position in the social, economic, cultural, and political spheres. Nor did they have the advantage of the earlier political start enjoyed by oppressed nationalities with a rich national history, such as the Czechs, the Croats, and, in a way, the Poles. Still, as far as the conscious development of political nationalism (the formulation and pursuit of a definite national program) goes, in the course of the seventy years from 1848 to 1918 all the dormant nationalities were able to stand up fully to their privileged neighbor nationalities. More than that, by doing so they were able to surge ahead rapidly in their cultural and political development. The differences between developed and undeveloped nationalities, between national groups with and without history in the sense referred to in this study, certainly were negligible in 1918 when compared to such differences in 1848.

If one realizes that at the same time an evolution from humanitarian cultural to integral nationalism took place among most of these national groups, one is inclined to consider this development as a mixed blessing. Still, it was a kind of blessing. That is to say, if those factors which gave an unquestionably beneficial cultural evolution its ominous political tinge could be singled out, it might be possible to control them in future handling of the nationality problem. Thus, mixed blessings might revert to unmixed benefits reaped from the evolution of nationalism.

Which factors, apart from the obvious political ones rooted in the organization and the political ideology of the Austrian Empire, actually influenced the development of nationalism so ominously? In the analysis of the national problem in Bukovina the statement was made that not the problem of national diversity itself, but the related one of national inequality in "internationality relations" aggravates national conflict. One may go even farther and say that the relative national equilibrium in multinational areas, that is, those areas inhabited by more than two national groups, where no group forms an absolute majority, favorably influences these relations. Such ethnic composition, indeed, makes the rule of privileged master nationalities more difficult, as the experience in Bukovina, Istria, and Austrian Silesia proved.

Nevertheless, it would be obviously erroneous to expect from the study of population statistics the definite answer to the question regarding the nature of the principal political factors which cause national inequality to thrive and, consequently, lead to national discrimination. In this respect, demographic proportions between majorities and minorities are only one important factor among others.

After all, the handling of the national problem was definitely the worst in those Hungarian lands in which the Magyars formed no absolute majority, but possessed all the dangerous qualifications of a social, economic, and political master race. To take the example of Galicia, it is true that the dominant position of the Poles—a master people, at least in regard to the Ruthenians—was strengthened by the fact that they formed the majority in the crownland. But in the main their strength rested, not on the appeal to majority rights, but in their monopolistic entrenchment in the upper classes of the social order. Judged by historic experience, this situation would probably have changed only very gradually even if the numerical relation between Poles and Ruthenians had been reversed. In this respect national conditions in Bohemia were particularly illuminating. Until the constitutional era the Germans there were definitely not only a privileged nationality but also the ruling nationality; yet they formed a mere minority of the population. The explanation of this fact is simple, indeed. A majority has great influence in a society where power depends on appeal to the decision of the people, that is, the majority decision of democracy. Where democracy exists to only a very limited degree or not at all, political power in itself is decisive. Such power may be strengthened if supported by the majority of the people, though it does not depend primarily on such a majority. Majority under such conditions abuses already existing inequality, but it does not create it.

Wherever inequality is based primarily on a specific administrative tradition, such as the influence of German centralism in Bukovina, the Littoral, and so forth, conditions can be improved gradually with little difficulty by the displacement of supranational bureaucracy and professional classes with national intelligentsia. On the other hand, wherever national inequality is primarily based on superior socio-economic power, as in Hungary, Galicia, and the Austrian Slovene territories, such reforms are far more difficult. They cut far more deeply into the existing social structure. In particular, it is more difficult to eliminate an ancient feudal agricultural system than economic superiority based on fairly recently established industrial and commercial power. In this sense the Hungarian and northeastern Austrian (Galician) national problems were particularly difficult to tackle.

Yet the cases of the Ruthenians in Galicia and the non-Magyar nationalities in Hungary were striking, but by no means unique, examples. Inequality as a factor accentuating national conflict must be judged not, by absolute, but by relative standards. That is to say, national tension in every field is determined by the discrepancy in the social, political, and cultural status of the privileged and the under-privileged national groups, not by absolute standards of living. In itself, a relatively favorable standard of any national group may exercise a moderating influence on national claims, or it may, on the other hand, only facilitate their technical promotion. Conversely, a low standing may either increase national tension or check a national group in the pursuit of its objectives. Numerous examples could easily be brought forward to implement either alternative. They all prove only that the intensity of national policy and its course for better or for worse cannot be judged by the absolute social, political, cultural, or demographic standing of any national group.

On the other hand, as borne out by ample historic experience, it is predictable that a relatively wide discrepancy in social status between privileged and underprivileged national groups will aggravate the national problem. Thus, the tension between Magyar upper classes and Hungarian nationalities does not rest primarily in the low standards here and the favorable status there, but, compared to the interrelations of other nationalities, in the relatively greater difference in socioeconomic and political status. In other words, not standards of living in themselves, but inequality in these standards appears of vital significance.

In regard to Magyar Hungary another aggravating factor, the national frontier problem, arises. Any national group, in particular a dominant one, will be far more anxious to assert its national rights at its ethnic frontiers rather than in outlying, isolated national-island positions. In the first case the national group will feel that its own territory is endangered. It will, furthermore, perceive opportunities to extend its national frontiers. In the second case such a nationality might be ready to retreat slowly from an untenable position. The fact that the Magyars were surrounded on all sides by peoples of entirely different ethnic stock made them a frontier people in regard to the national problem. This explains to some extent the peculiar intransigence of their nationalism. All the other national groups, except the Italians, at least lived under somewhat different conditions in this respect. Thus, for the Germans the defense and extension of the language frontier to the Slovene south was even more important than their national interests to the north, where they were confronted by only a Czech wedge, not the entire Slav orbit. To the east, disconnected German-language islands in Bukovina, Hungary, and Hungarian Transylvania represented relatively minor issues in the national conflict. Similar sliding scales of importance of national demands can, of course, be applied to other national groups as well.

Ethnic frontiers may coincide with political frontiers, which raises the question of national influence from outside and the question of irredentism (in short, the problem of the nationalities divided from fellow nationals who enjoy independence). A rather superficial view of Austria's national problems makes them seem particularly tense and complex where political-frontier barriers existed between conationals. Actually, without minimizing the problem and the influence of German, Russian, Italian, Rumanian, and Serbian nationalism from outside on the cause of their kin in the empire, such was not necessarily the case. The national problems of the four groups confined exclusively to the territory of the empire, Magyars, Czechs, Croats, and Slovaks, appeared no less serious than those of others. In fact, competent students of the Austrian national problem have widely held the Czech, the Magyar, and the Croat national problems to be the most serious. Anyway, it is certainly true that the power of nationalism is great enough to sustain itself without ideological or material support from a related national cause beyond the frontiers. Such support may influence the solution of a national problem, but the life of national spirit does not depend on it. In other words, while nationalism from outside may easily force the political issue, the purely national spirit is self-supporting.

This leads to the problem of national solidarity. Obviously, such solidarity existed between fellow nationals outside and inside the empire. It is more difficult to ascertain whether such solidarity existed among national groups inside the empire. If so, was it a solidarity based principally on political interests, or was it based on ethnic affiliations? Did it apply primarily to the oppressed peoples, or was it chiefly effective between the master nationalities?

It appears that community of political interests formed a much stronger tie practically, though probably not psychologically, than did ethnic affiliations. As for the latter, it is true that a strong feeling of solidarity swept through the Austrian Slav world. Nevertheless, it was able to sustain itself for a considerable period of time only by ideological affiliation with an external factor, the Russian Pan-Slav idea. For a long time, however, it was not strong enough to break the barrier between ruling and oppressed nationalities as experienced in the Croat-Serb and the Polish-Ruthenian struggle. The ethnic Croat-Serb solidarity was finally able to overcome this impediment only because of the fact that in relation to a third power—the Magyars—the Croats themselves formed an underprivileged national group.

In the case of the Polish-Ruthenian conflict, however, similar motives prompting "inter-nationality" understanding proved to be not quite strong enough. To be sure, the creation of socioeconomic equality might well have helped to foster ethnic solidarity. Yet, on the whole this situation illustrates the point that socioeconomic conflict generally prevented the cooperation of related national groups to a greater extent than ethnic affiliation promoted such cooperation.

As far as political community of interests is concerned, the history of the empire since the Compromise of 1867 was determined by the Germans and the Magyars. Actually, this alliance of two peoples between whom in the socioeconomic sphere no love was lost, was born out of the necessity of preserving privileged national positions. The same held true for the support given to German centralism by the Poles in Cisleithanian Austria. Such a policy of common objectives certainly did not have popular appeal. In regard to the Magyars and the Poles, it could not even be put to the test of public opinion according to democratic principles, since true democracy, even in the limited sphere prevailing in Western Austria, existed neither in Hungary nor in Galicia. Thus it is possible, perhaps even likely, that under politically less stringent conditions ethnic ideological solidarity would have proved stronger than political affiliations of the upper classes of the national groups which were "most favored" in political and economic questions.

It is obvious, though, that group cooperation based exclusively on ethnic national affiliation would not have been altogether desirable from the viewpoint of national conciliation. Judged from the vantage point of present-day experience, such ethnic coalitions might well have proved to be fertile soil for the outbreak of large-scale racial conflagrations. Thus, it was not entirely unfortunate that, on the whole, the social preconditions for group cooperation on an ethnic basis did not exist among the national groups of the empire. The policy of the oppressed and the privileged nationalities alike was predominantly determined by political, including socioeconomic, expediency.

Yet, in the long run a policy of expediency could not be built on solid foundations. This has been shown in the German-Italian, the German-Polish, and, for a time, in the German-Ruthenian and the Magyar-Serb relations. This kind of cooperation, established under specific political conditions, would probably not last after these conditions changed or appeared likely to change. The history of the empire's collapse in the First World War period offers a striking illustration of this fact. The conflict, born out of the national problems, could be appeased but not settled according to the specific mutual interests of the upper classes of several national groups. It is permissible to go even farther. Such conflicts are not subject to short-term solutions, since most of the basic factors underlying the national problem, whether ethnic, geographic, cultural, or psychological in character, are stable and permanent. This does not hold true, however, for the economic factor, which is subject to change by widely predictable human means.

Indeed, an important key to conceivable solutions of the national problem rests in the rational operation of the economic factor. Count Leo Thun, as early as 1849, and since then many others promoted the idea that the true aim of national understanding rests in the destruction of national-bloc interests and their replacement by the common socioeconomic claims of the people which reach beyond narrow national lines. This idea, indeed, represents democracy at its best. If working effectively, it expresses the will of the people on a far broader basis than mere national representation, let alone corporate Estates representation within a national territory.

Except for the limited influence of the Social Democrats and of socially conscious, religiously inspired movements in the last decades preceding the First World War, the empire had almost completely failed to establish that unity of interests reaching across national frontiers. The reasons for this failure are evident. The establishment of strong social solidarity of the Austrian peoples would have meant modification of economic inequality between the upper classes of the privileged national groups and the underprivileged nationalities. Yet, it would be ingenuous to believe that attempts to that effect could have been confined to single national groups. To take a striking example, large-scale agricultural reforms in Galician or Slovak Hungarian territories would have accentuated the sweeping issue of small peasants versus big landed property in the empire as a whole. Evolutionary reforms dealing with this problem would have been feasible only in a thoroughly democratic empire. Yet the comprehensive democratization of the Danube monarchy would have alienated those conservative forces which were the strongest pillars of the Habsburg Empire and its feudal tradition.

Nevertheless, the elimination of economic injustice, whether started within the various national orbits or more comprehensively, would have been the single strongest force in the fight against the empire's national disintegration. A good many of the reform proposals analyzed in Volume II deal with the vain attempts to establish that form of economic-social solidarity of the peoples which never could be brought into line with the medieval Habsburg Empire idea.

Other types of conflict, by no means insignificant in themselves, represented lesser problems in addition to this (in the realm of the Habsburg scepter) insoluble one. Conflicts resulting from the predominance of absolute national majorities within limited areas might well have been eliminated altogether by the comprehensive application of the principle of personal autonomy. Thus, the relatively favorable situation in Bukovina, a land without absolute national majorities, could have served as legal pattern in the whole empire by approximation. Any member of a minority in a given territory could have become a member of the ethnic community of his conationals throughout the empire, vested with appropriate rights for the protection of his interests. In a somewhat similar way, the elimination of the particularly unfavorable atmosphere of national-frontier psychology could have been influenced by combining the principles of federalism and minority protection. Yet it is obvious that such reforms would have been based on the premise of elimination of national inequality. And here again the economic factor came into play.

No positive evidence exists, except the indirect evidence of the example of other countries, that the elimination or modification of economic injustice could at any time have solved the Austrian national problem. Important influences of power politics and national aggressiveness beyond the frontiers, equally important factors of a geographic, cultural, and religious nature within the empire, to mention only a few salient points, complicated the establishment of national reconciliation. These points will have to be duly discussed. Still, neither does negative evidence exist that the national problem was insoluble at all times, unless one considers the destruction of the empire decisive proof.

Yet apart from the fact that the disintegration of the empire was brought about chiefly by external forces, not all of which were directly connected with the national problem, such evidence could never be conclusive. If anything, Austria's fall only proves that the destruction of the unreformed empire was inevitable, but does not answer the question, could reform conceivably have prevented this destruction? If so, the potential structure of such a reformed empire will have to be analyzed; if not, the further question remains, what kind of socio-political organization able to achieve national reconciliation could have replaced it? The tentative answers to these alternatives, brought forward in the course of two generations, will be discussed in the second volume of this study.

# NOTES TO VOLUME I

## I. INTRODUCTION

1. With few exceptions, only plans drafted by Austrians or men employed in the service of the Austrian government have been included in this survey. This policy of selection appears to be one of the safeguards against the tempting danger of digressing into the realm of utopian schemes not directly concerned with the actual political conditions in the empire. Generally, only Austrian contributions could be exposed to the serious test of political attack by the parties interested in the national conflict. Plans of non-Austrians discussed at some length in this study will be found in Chap. XV, below, in the section on the Pole Count Krasiński, and in Chap. XVIII and Chap. XXIV on the Germans Fröbel and Naumann. The inclusion of these three contributions appears justified by their specific significance within the history of the Austrian reform idea. In regard to Naumann's projects a further very real influence on actual political development is obvious.

2. Even then mutual consent and full indemnification of the parties affected by such transfers should be recognized as a matter of principle. Compliance with these demands ought to be secured by plebiscites under international control. It would, however, be naïve to assume that prevailing conditions in eastern central Europe would permit faith in the humane application of such procedure. There the Western world cannot condone population transfers at all.

3. Joseph von Eötvös, *Die Nationalitätenfrage,* trans. by R. W. Seton-Watson (Budapest, 1865), p. 65.

## I. AUSTRIA: THE NAME

1. Victor von Andrian-Werburg, *Österreich und dessen Zukunft* (Hamburg, 1843, 1847), I, 8 ff. See also Karl Möring, *Sybillinische Bücher aus Österreich,* 2 vols. (Hamburg, 1848), p. 25, for a similar statement.

2. The selected bibliography in Volume II below, gives the general literature to this introductory chapter. Specific items are listed particularly in notes 7, 29, and 32.

3. On the concept of the centripetal and centrifugal forces within the Habsburg lands see Oskar Jászi, *The Dissolution of the Habsburg Monarchy* (Chicago, 1929), pp. 133 ff.

4. Ferdinand (1503–64), the brother of Charles V, ruled as German emperor from 1558–64, as Ferdinand I.

5. Strictly speaking, only in 1619 were all the non-Spanish Habsburg lands united for the first time under one—completely undivided—rule, that of Ferdinand (as German emperor, the second of his name). The principle of indivisibility of all the Habsburg lands was first established by him a century before the enactment of the Pragmatic Sanction as common order of succession—in his testament of 1621; but, as with so many principles laid down in Austrian constitutional history, the exceptions to it formed the rule up to the Pragmatic Sanction. Aside from the great partition of the lands of the German and Spanish Habsburgs, all the divisions of the Habsburg dynasty into several ruling lines

throughout the sixteenth and seventeenth centuries refer to the divisions of the hereditary line into Inner Austrian, Styrian, and Tirol lines.

The rule over Hungary, Bohemia, and Croatia, as well as the German imperial crown, usually fell to the chief of the Austrian line. When, with the death of Matthias I, in 1619, the Austrian line became extinct, the Styrian line under Ferdinand II succeeded. The concentration of the main power, with relatively insignificant exceptions, makes it politically permissible to speak of the *de facto* existence of a personal union of all the Habsburg lands even in the sixteenth and seventeenth centuries.

6. The most adequate English translation of this term, "private possessions of a sovereign," still falls short of its exact meaning. Habsburg's *Hausmacht* means, not private property of the sovereign, but countries under permanent hereditary rule of the dynasty, in contrast to their rule as German emperors, which was based on election. Fundamentally, Hungary, Bohemia, or even Upper and Lower Austria, were not, even in the sixteenth century, any more the private property of the Habsburgs than was France of the Valois or England of the Tudors.

The question whether Habsburg rule in Croatia, Hungary, and Bohemia was based primarily on hereditary succession or on election is legally very much open to debate. Still, it is a fact that, politically speaking, from 1526 on, the permanent character of the Habsburg rule over these kingdoms, except for brief intervals, remained virtually unchallenged. It is, therefore, politically justified to link Habsburg rule over these countries with that over the hereditary lands and in contrast to the German imperial Power.

7. On the history of the Pragmatic Sanction see particularly: G. Turba, ed., *Die Pragmatische Sanktion, Authentische Texte samt Erlänterungen* (text), (Vienna, 1913). G. Turba, *Geschichte des Thronfolgerechtes in den habsburgischen Ländern bis zur pragmatischen Sanktion Kaiser Karls VI* (Vienna, 1903), and *Die pragmatische Sanktion mit besonderer Rücksicht auf die Länder der Stephanskrone 1703 bis 1744* (Vienna, 1906).

For a legal political analysis of the empire problem on the basis of the Pragmatic Sanction see: Friedrich Tezner, *Die Wandlungen der österreichisch-ungarischen Reichsidee* (Vienna, 1905), and "Der österreichische Kaisertitel, seine Geschichte und seine politische Bedeutung," *Zeitschrift für das private und öffentliche Recht,* ed. C. Grünhut, XXV (1898), 351–428; further, Richard Zehntbauer, *Gesamtstaat, Dualismus und Pragmatische Sanktion* (Freiburg, 1914).

For a general legal historical survey see further: A. Huber, *Österreichische Reichsgeschichte,* rev. by Alfons Dopsch (2d ed., Vienna, 1901); Arnold Luschin von Ebengreuth, *Österreichische Reichsgeschichte und Grundriss der österreichische Reichsgeschichte* (Bamberg), various editions; and H. J. Bidermann, *Geschichte der österreichischen Gesamtstaatsidee.* 2 vols. (Innsbruck, 1867, 1889); Vol. I covers the period from 1526 to 1740.

In regard to Hungarian legal history see: Heinrich Marczali, *Ungarische Verfassungsgeschichte* (Tübingen, 1910), written from the Magyar standpoint.

On the political aspects of the problem in regard to modern Austrian history see, as outstanding, Josef Redlich, *Das österreichische Staats- und Reichsproblem* (Leipzig, 1920, 1926), particularly Vol. I, part 1, 1 ff., and part 2, 4 ff.; and Louis Eisenmann, *Le Compromis austro-hongrois de 1867, étude sur le dualisme* (Paris, 1904), pp. 17 ff., 21, 29. See also Theodor von Sosnosky, *Die Politik im Habsburgerreich* (Berlin, 1912, 1913), II, 99 ff.

8. Popular historical works frequently perceived the main reason for the promulgation of the Pragmatic Sanction in the fact that the emperor had no male heir and was anxious to have the rights to the throne by female succession recognized. The fact that the first act of the Pragmatic Sanction was issued five years before the birth of Maria Theresa should dispose of this myth.

9. This is succinctly expressed in the Hungarian Pragmatic Sanction, *Gesetzesartikel* II of 1722–23, regarding "the uninterrupted right to succession of the female line of his sacred Imperial and Royal Majesty's most serene House of Austria in regard to the Holy Crown of Hungary and the lands associated with it.

"Art. 7 . . . in accordance with the order of succession established by his sacred Imperial and Royal ruling Majesty for his other kingdoms and lands inside and outside of Germany, which, according to the above-mentioned bill and established order indivisibly united to each other and at the same time united with the kingdom of Hungary, its associated parts, lands, and provinces, are to be held in hereditary possession, to be ruled and to be governed . . . [according to the above-mentioned principles]." From Gustav Steinbach, ed., *Die ungarischen Verfassungsgesetze* (Vienna, 1900).

10. As a matter of fact, the emperor later submitted the Pragmatic Sanction to the Estates of the Erblande and of Bohemia, the Austrian Netherlands, and Lombardy. However, these acts were of a more formal, legalistic nature, and no concessions comparable to those made to Hungary were granted. The formal character of these acts became particularly clear in regard to the Bohemian Estates, which, at that time played only a puppet role; they declared or, rather, had to declare that the emperor's asking for their consent was entirely superfluous. See A. Huber, *Österreichische Reichsgeschichte*, rev. by Dopsch, 2d ed., p. 179.

11. On the theoretical aspects of Personal and Real Union see the analysis in Hans Kelsen, *Allgemeine Staatslehre* (Berlin, 1925), pp. 166 f., 205 f.

12. Charles VI actually considered a far closer kind of union than the one realized, in the form of a Real Union. Such concept was based on the proposals of the Councillor Christian Julius von Schierendorff in Vienna, included in a manuscript of two volumes, "Parerga sive otia," deposited in the *Niederösterreichisches Landesarchiv* in Vienna. Schierendorff contemplated the creation of a permanent general diet of all the Habsburg lands, including Hungary, with authority in financial affairs. As Alfred Fischel puts it, "his ideals are a *'gesamtstaatliche* constitution' [that is, comprising all the Habsburg lands], a moderate degree of liberty, permanent control of the government by a committee of the Estates, and obligation to take an oath to the new constitution protecting the rights of the lower classes too, for administrative agencies." —— *Studien zur österreichischen Reichsgeschichte* (Vienna, 1906), pp. 170 ff., quoted from Redlich, *Das österreichische Staats- und Reichsproblem*, I, pt. 2, 4. Schierendorff may be justly called the forerunner of the idea of Austrian centralism of later generations.

13. Redlich, *Das österreichische Staats- und Reichsproblem*, I, part 1, 4.

14. Interesting at this point is a letter written by Prince Metternich on April 4, 1850, to his old associate, the president of the Court Chamber (Treasury), Baron Kübeck. "Here I call attention to a strange historical phenomenon. The term 'House of Austria' always has taken the place which everywhere else is taken by the name of a political body. The bond between the separate and in themselves heterogeneous bodies represented by the German Empire and the Austrian monarchy was the House, the ruling family, due to electoral law in the German Empire and due to hereditary law, in what was called the Austrian monarchy." *Tagebücher des Karl Freiherrn von Kübeck* (Vienna, 1909), II, 205 f. Metternich, though not too well acquainted with the pattern of legal-institutional German and Austrian history and therefore not too clear in his way of formulating the question, nevertheless conceives the meaning of the term "House of Austria" correctly.

For a fine literary presentation of this unique historical status of the ruling dynasty see Erich von Kahler, *Das Geschlecht Habsburg* (Munich, 1919).

15. For the history of Austrian administration, particularly on the great reforms in the second half of the eighteenth century, see Thomas Fellner, *Die österreichische Zentralverwaltung*, completed by H. Kretschmayr, 3 vols. (Vienna, 1907). Other important works on the subject are: Ignaz Beidtel, *Geschichte der österreichischen Staatsverwaltung (1740–1848)*, 2 vols. (Innsbruck, 1896–97), and Bidermann, *Geschichte der österreichischen Gesamtstaatsidee, 1526–1804* (Innsbruck, 1867, 1889).

The standard work on political history of the reign of Maria Theresa is Alfred von Arneth, *Geschichte Maria Theresias*, 10 vols. (Vienna, 1863–79) . There is no work of equal standing on the history of the reign of Joseph II. A good biography on Joseph II in English is S. K. Padover, *Revolutionary Emperor Joseph II* (London, 1938).

16. Any reference to Maria Theresa, the last scion of the House of Habsburg as

empress, signifies only her status as empress consort of the Roman German emperor, Francis I of the House of Lorraine, whose descendants form the House of Habsburg-Lorraine.

17. Intercourse among the ministers, particularly in the latter half of the century, was mainly through correspondence rather than in common council.

18. See below, Chapter III, sections on "The Austro-German State Concept" and "Centralism and Estates."

19. The term "crownlands" instead of "lands" was introduced into general official use only by the March constitution of 1849. This change of terminology did not, however, change the political administrative concept itself. The authoritative discussion on the crownland (land) institution is to be found in the extensive article "Länder" in Ernst Mischler and Josef Ulbrich, *Österreichisches Staatswörterbuch* (Vienna, 1905–9), Vol. III; see particularly section C., *ibid.*, pp. 406 ff., by L. Spiegel. See also A. Huber, *Österreichische Reichsgeschichte*, rev. by Dopsch, 2d ed., Section VI.

For a critical evaluation of the concept see Karl Renner's pioneer work, *Das Selbstbestimmungsrecht der Nationen*, Part 1, "Nation und Staat" (Vienna, 1918), pp. 79–82. Renner perceives the crownland institutions as the main stumbling block to a reform of the monarchy along ethnical lines. For a less theoretical but also less one-sided analysis of this concept see Carl M. Danzer, ed., *Das neue Österreich, eine politische Rundfrage* (Vienna, 1908), which gives the opinion of a number of parliamentary deputies and political writers of various national and party affiliations on the problem. See also the Chapter II below, section on "Austrian Historicopolitical Entities."

20. Major, though not permanent, exceptions to that statement are: The territorial administrative organization under the reign of Joseph II, the administrative partition of Hungary in 1849, and the establishment of Military Frontier districts (so-called Militärgrenzen) to the south and east of Hungary from the sixteenth century on. On the "Militärgrenzen" see below, Chapter IV, note 28.

21. The terms "constitution" and "constitutional" are used here in the broadest meaning of the term: that is, "constitution" meaning the fundamental system of laws governing a country, and "constitutional," the legal process in conformity with these fundamental laws. Reference to the "constitutional" acts of Charles VI in establishing the Pragmatic Sanction and of Francis I, in proclaiming the empire of Austria, implies in no way whatsoever representation and participation by the people in the establishment or execution of these fundamental laws.

22. Francis (1768–1835) was emperor of the Holy Roman German Empire from 1792 to 1806, emperor of the newly founded Austrian Empire from 1804 to 1835. As German emperor he is correctly referred to as Francis II, as Austrian emperor, as Francis I. In this study he will be referred to as Francis I.

23. Redlich, *Das österreichische Staats- und Reichsproblem*, I, 1, 42.

24. The territories under the Hungarian crown and Galicia, Bukovina, parts of the Austrian Littoral, and Dalmatia were not part of the German Empire and, after 1815, not part of the German *Bund* either.

25. The "German Bund" of 1815.

26. See Edmund Bernatzik, *Österreichische Verfassungsgesetze* (Vienna, 1911). On the Magyar viewpoint, denying a subordination of the Hungarian crown to the empire of 1804, see Count Albert Apponyi, "Die rechtliche Natur der Beziehungen zwischen Österreich und Ungarn," *Österreichische Rundschau*, XXVIII (1911), 165–74, 249–64, 332–44, 407–21.

27. This whole problem is discussed brilliantly and in great detail in Tezner, "Der österreichische Kaisertitel, seine Geschichte und seine politische Bedeutung," *Zeitschrift für das private und öffentliche Recht*, ed. C. Grünhut, XXV (1898), 351–428. Tezner, with ample support of documents relative to the matter, upholds the thesis that Hungary was a part of the Austrian Empire. For the contrary Magyar standpoint see J. H. Schwicker, "Nochmals der österreichische Kaisertitel," *Zeitschrift für das private und öffentliche Recht*, ed. C. Grünhut, XXVI (1899), 465–84, and Tezner's reply in the same vol., pp. 485–718, "Der österreichische Kaisertitel, das ungarische Staatsrecht und ·die

ungarische Publizistik." See further Hermann I. Biedermann, "Die staatsrechtlichen Wirkungen der österreichischen Gesamtstaatsidee," *Zeitschrift für das private und öffentliche Recht,* XXI (1894), 339–427.

28. A constitution, commonly called the "Pillersdorf constitution" for the then Austrian minister of the interior, was already imposed by imperial rescript of April 25, 1848. Yet this constitution, which was put into practice just as little as the succeeding March constitution of 1849, was not intended to apply to all the Habsburg lands. It referred neither to the lands of the Hungarian crown nor to the Lombardo-Venetian kingdom. It is, however, notable that the western part of the Habsburg lands alone—that is, excluding Hungary and the Italian provinces—are, for the first time, legally referred to as "Austria" in this constitution. See Bernatzik, *Österreichische Verfassungsgesetze,* pp. 101 ff. "All the Habsburg lands" under the March constitution of 1849 do not, of course, include the then existing Italian principalities under the rule of younger branches of the dynasty (Tuscany, Modena, Parma). They had political relations, but no legal relations whatsoever, with the imperial lands.

29. The literature on the compromise, legal as well as political, is vast. Only a few selected items, dealing with the broader aspects of the legal problem, are listed here. Further bibliographical references to the political aspects will be found particularly in Chap. XIX, below, sections on "Belcredi," "Opposition to Dualism," and "Fischhof."

All this literature may be divided into two main groups, the Magyar and the non-Magyar, a division which needs some explanation. While the whole of the literature in the Magyar language, with few exceptions, is fervently and consistently pro-Magyar, a common denominator does not exist for the non-Magyar literature, not even for German literature on the subject. A good number of these items, including German Austrian ones, show a marked understanding of the Magyar viewpoint. Many are partial to a German Austrian centralist interpretation. Yet in general the great bulk of this non-Magyar literature, whether written in or outside of the Habsburg lands, is far less biased than—with notable exceptions—Magyar literature on the subject.

*a) Primary sources:* The text of the compromise bills (the Austrian and Magyar version) is, of course, to be found in all official Austro-Hungarian state publications. Convenient editions are in the collection of *Österreichische Verfassungsgesetze,* edited and commented upon by E. Bernatzik, last available edition, Vienna, 1911. (A section of this work, "Das Österreichische Nationalitätenrecht," was published separately in 1917.)

For the Hungarian text (in German), see: Gustav Steinbach, ed., *Die ungarischen Verfassungsgesetze,* part of which is contained in the above-listed Bernatzik edition. Deák's famous parliamentary speeches and the addresses by the Hungarian parliament (drafted by him) on the subject since 1861, are, in their essential parts, published in Redlich, *Das österreichische Staats- und Reichsproblem,* Vol. II.

*b) Non-Magyar literature:* Ivan Zolger, *Der staatsrechtliche Ausgleich zwischen Österreich und Ungarn* (Leipzig, 1911). This elaborate work written by a high government official presents the most detailed and accurate legal interpretation of the compromise; Eisenmann, *Le Compromis austro-hongrois de 1867,* as well as Redlich, *Das österreichische Staats- und Reichsproblem,* Vol. II, are the standard works on the political issue.

See further: T. Dantscher von Kollesberg, *Der monarchische Bundesstaat Österreich-Ungarn* (Vienna, 1880); Josef Ulbrich, *Die rechtliche Natur der österreichisch-ungarischen Monarchie* (Prague, 1879), and *Österreichisches Staatsrecht* (Tübingen, 1909); Alfred von Offermann, *Das Verhältnis Ungarns zu Österreich* (Vienna, 1902); Harold Steinacker, "Zur Frage nach der rechtlichen Natur der Gesamtmonarchie," *Österreichische Rundschau,* XXIII (1910), 241–62, 325–39; Tezner, *Die Wandlungen der österreichisch-ungarischen Reichsidee* and *Ausgleichsrecht und Ausgleichspolitik* (Vienna, 1907).

For further articles by Tezner, Steinacker, and Turba, in *Österreichische Rundschau,* see particularly the volumes from 1907 to 1912.

All these German Austrian works, though otherwise often in serious disagreement, are committed to the theory that a tie closer than a mere Personal Union existed between Austria and Hungary.

c) *Magyar literature:* Julius Andrássy, *Ungarns Ausgleich mit Österreich vom Jahre 1867* (German ed.; Leipzig, 1897). This is a thorough and moderate presentation of the Magyar viewpoint by the last common minister of foreign affairs of the monarchy.

Francis Deák, *Ein Beitrag zum ungarischen Staatsrecht; Bemerkungen zu Lustkandl's ungarisch-österreichisches Staatsrecht* (Pest, 1867). This classic reply written between 1863 and 1867 by the leading Magyar statesman, who worked on the creation of the compromise, to the work by the Viennese professor of law, Wenzel Lustkandl, *Das ungarisch-österreichische Staatsrecht* (Vienna, 1863), is considered to be the representative formulation of the Magyar standpoint. (Deák's work is not available.)

General works on the history of Hungarian constitutional law (translated into Geman) dealing extensively, of course, with the compromise, are: Geza von Ferdinandy, *Staats- und Verwaltungsrecht des Königreiches Ungarn und seiner Nebenländer* (Hanover, 1909); Marczali, *Ungarisches Verfassungsrecht* (Tübingen, 1911), and *Ungarische Verfassungsgeschichte* (Tübingen, 1910).

Wisely more concerned with the effect of their policy on world opinion than were any of the other peoples under Habsburg rule, the Magyars managed to turn out, even before 1914, a considerable number of items in the English language, most of them of a propagandistic nature, written by leading Magyar statesmen and scholars. In this context belongs Count Albert Apponyi, *A Brief Sketch of the Hungarian Constitution and of the Relations between Austria and Hungary* (Budapest, 1908). Anxious to prove the ancient heritage of "Magyar democracy" and to demonstrate its affiliation with Anglo-Saxon political principles, this work is nevertheless a brilliant piece of political dialectics. Written by the "Great Old Man" of Magyar pseudoliberalism, it gives a clear and succinct view of the more radical autonomist trend among the ruling classes of Hungary in the era under discussion.

30. On the history of the idea of the Austro-Hungarian empire division prior to 1867, see particularly Redlich, *Das österreichische Staats- und Reichsproblem*, I, 1, 188 f. In this respect it should be clear that not the restoration of a long-established privileged Hungarian position in the empire, but negation of the empire idea above the dual states, was the basic idea of the compromise.

31. In contemporary literature, particularly books and pamphlets written during the two decades preceding the compromise, however, these two terms are used indiscriminately, and authors frequently refer to a *Personalunion* when they actually mean the *Realunion.*

32. See the following characteristic Hungarian and Austrian interpretations of the character of the compromise. Count Albert Apponyi, as leader of the Magyar Independence party, states the radical Magyar standpoint as follows: "there is no earthly power placed above her [Hungary] entitled to control her, as she is possessed of all the attributes of a sovereign nation. The Austrian Empire which is supposed to include Hungary has no existence, except in false theory and in former oppressive practice; in public law it always was and now in fact is, a nonentity. Even the term "Austro-Hungarian empire" . . . is a false one; and the officially used term "Austro-Hungarian Monarchy" . . . can be accepted only in the sense of their personal union under a monarch physically one, but representing two distinct personalities of public law, the emperor and the King, and of their joint actions in questions of peace and war; but an objectively unified body containing both Hungary and Austria does not exist." Apponyi, *A Brief Sketch of the Hungarian Constitution*, pp. 56 f. See further, *ibid.*, pp. 58 f. "There are no real common institutions between both countries, only common executive organs in regard to the sovereignty of both countries; Hungary has separate international treaty power and in theory a separate army, embedded in Hungarian public law."

Apponyi's assertion of Hungary's international treaty power came true in practice up to a point. In the early twentieth century Magyar insistence resulted in the signing of several international agreements by an Austro-Hungarian, an Austrian, and a Hungarian delegate. But tolerance of a constitutional clause does not mean legal recognition.

*Ibid.*, p. 67: "Mutual dependency of a political kind certainly exists between Hungary and Austria. . . . This does not affect their independent juridical individuality." *Ibid.*, p. 72: "Austria-Hungary does not mean an empire, but the permanent union of two nations for certain international purposes."

In some respects, Apponyi's opinion, which denies the clear fact of common institutions, however, goes beyond the viewpoint held by the majority of Magyar theorists and statesmen. This latter view, though, insisting on Magyar sovereignty and denying the existence of an Austro-Hungarian empire, at least acknowledged the existence of common institutions, that is, of the basic elements of the *Realunion.* This is the viewpoint of Andrássy in his *Ungarns Ausgleich mit Österreich vom Jahre 1867*, p. 26, and of Marczali. The latter observes, "Hungary in essential state affairs co-decides, that is, does not decide alone. *Qui socium habet, dominum habet!* does not apply merely to persons, but to states too." Marczali, *Ungarisches Verfassungsrecht*, p. 226.

*Ibid.*, p. 228: "The compromise has created a total Power [*Gesamtmacht*] and provided it with 'organs.' Each of its provisions is a living protest against even the possibility of a collective state. Hungarian constitutional law does not recognize it, it recognizes only that the sovereignty of Hungary in common affairs is coordinated to the sovereignty of Austria, but never subordinated."

The non-Magyar interpretation, as stated before, is far more diverse in its views. T. Dantscher von Kollesberg is the most extreme representative of the opinion that the relations between Austria and Hungary are even closer than those of a *Realunion.* According to him, Austria and Hungary are the member states of a federal state, namely, the Austro-Hungarian Empire. See his *Der monarchische Bundesstaat Österreich-Ungarn*, particularly pp. 37 ff.

Such an opinion, expressed in oversimplified form, is hardly tenable. It is, however, supported by Bidermann, *Die rechtliche Natur der österreichisch-ungarischen Monarchie* (Vienna, 1907), who modifies it in so far as he conceives the monarchy as a *Staatenstaat*, that is, a state of states, with three state powers, the central power more perfect than the other two. *Ibid.*, pp. 47 f., Bidermann presents an interesting survey of the history of the theory on this question. Similar also is the view of Josef Ulbrich, *Die rechtliche Natur der österreichisch-ungarischen Monarchie.*

Harold Steinacker, "Der Begriff der Realunion und die rechtliche Natur des Reiches," *Österreichische Rundschau*, XXX (1912), 161–70, 249–57, though acknowledging the legal principles of the *Realunion*, still perceives in the actual social and political position of the monarchy the concept of an empire, whose clear recognition in political practice he strongly favors.

For a theoretical legal appraisal of the entire problem see also Steinacker in "Zur Frage nach der rechtlichen Natur der Gesamtmonarchie," in the discussion in *Österreichische Rundschau*, Vol. XXIII (1910).

G. Turba, *Reichseinheit Personalunion Dualismus*, Vol. II (1905), gives a historical legal analysis from the standpoint of a supreme state power above Austria and Hungary.

Of all the Austrian theorists, Gustav Seidler comes closest to the Magyar point of view. He comprehends the relations as a form of alliance of two sovereign states. See G. Seidler, "Die rechtliche Natur der österreichisch-ungarischen Monarchie," *Österreichische Rundschau*, XIII (1907), 235–43.

Most interesting are the views of Eisenmann and Tezner on the issue. On the general assumption of the existence of the *Realunion*, Eisenmann sets out to prove that the basic premise of equality in this union never existed and that the rigidity of the Hungarian constitution, its willful disregard of the nationality problem, and the financial iniquities of the compromise established a distinct and unmistakable privileged position for Hungary. But, beyond this unjustified Magyar claim, there is a politically, though not legally, recognized superdualistic Austrian state power in existence. See Eisenmann, *Le Compromis austro-hongrois de 1867*, pp. 617 ff., 633 ff., 656 f.

Friedrich Tezner comes probably closest to the correct legal interpretation. "The thesis whose correctness will have to be decided is nothing but the sentence, 'L'état c'est moi.' Translated into Austrian that means 'the collective state' [*Gesamtstaat*] which was, is, and always will be the emperor of the House of Austria or the regent of the monarchy (Austria), to which . . . Hungary belongs too. In his person and by his person the two so-called states of the monarchy exist. With his elimination they would vanish and disperse. The emperor of Austria as bearer of the conservative power bestowed on him by the unification of all the lands represents the condition of life not only of the monarchy but of both of its states."—Tezner, "Apponyi's Beweise gegen die Realität der österreichischen Gesamtstaatsidee," *Österreichische Rundschau*, XIX (1911), 438. See also Tezner, *Die Wandlungen der österreichisch-ungarischen Reichsidee*. According to Tezner, there are not only common affairs between Austria and Hungary, but there is also a power superior to the king of Hungary and to the ruler of Austria proper (that is, the kingdoms and lands represented in the *Reichsrat*), namely, a true emperor who holds rights which are due to neither one of the two sovereigns of the dual states. Such rights are, for instance, the determination of the quota regarding common expenses, if no agreement between the two parliaments can be reached, the convocation of the delegations, and, above all, the disposition over the joint armed forces. See, further, Tezner, "Der österreichische Kaisertitel . . . ," *Zeitschrift für das private und öffentliche Recht*, ed. C. Grünhut, XXV (1898), 358 ff., particularly pp. 394 ff.

*Ibid.*, p. 402 f.: "The Austro-Hungarian monarchy means the *Monarchia Austriaca* comprising Hungary and distinctly stressing that the latter forms a specific part of the state territory. The title "emperor of Austria and king of Hungary" explains the old imperial title in the following way: Hungary within the *Monarchia Austriaca* forms a separate state, ruled by the king of Hungary in her separate affairs. Nevertheless, this state together with the other parts of the monarchy stands under the indivisible rule of a sovereign ruling over the whole territory [of the monarchy]. We have to read: Emperor of Austria and king of Hungary, forming a state, but included in Austria. Consequently, the title "emperor of Austria" is the universal one, the title "king of Hungary," the particularist one. The title "emperor of Austria" rises above and overshadows the royal title. The imperial title is the enclosing—the royal title, the enclosed."

33. This emergency measure was necessary on several occasions. Originally, the Austrian share was to be fixed at 70 percent, the Hungarian at 30 percent of common expenditures. By protracted and most difficult negotiations in the course of decades, this proportion was to be revised to one of approximately 2:1. This settlement was arranged by and large according to the relation of tax returns in both countries. Apart from the fact that the adoption of this principle in itself was an important concession to economically less advanced Hungary, the Hungarian share always was below the figure proportionate even to this relation.

34. Rudolph Sieghart, permanent secretary to the Austrian prime minister's office (1902–10) and president of the Austro-Hungarian Compromise Commission, later one of the most influential financiers of the monarchy, says, in his revealing memoirs, "If, instead of the ten years agreement, a permanent customs Union would have been created, the Compromise probably would have become a living reality." Rudolph Sieghart, *Die letzten Jahrzehnte einer Grossmacht* (Berlin, 1931), p. 144.

35. In case of such conflict the Austro-Hungarian delegations could meet together to bring the question at hand to a vote. But even then joint parliamentary discussion was barred. See Eisenmann's criticism of the delegations, *Le Compromis austro-hongrois de 1867*, pp. 633 ff.

36. See below, Chapter XIX, section on Belcredi.

37. See below, Chapter XXIV, section on "The Concepts of Peace Policy."

38. This is to be understood with the major exception of the German minorities in Hungary which, though forming several substantial homogeneous settlement areas, were, to a large extent, scattered among the Magyar, the Rumanian, and the Croatian population of Hungary.

39. That is to say that Hungary and Austria had relatively large nationality groups of the following peoples in common: Germans, Rumanians, Ruthenians, and Croats. The Czech, the Slovene, the Polish, and the Italian nationalities (the Italians in Fiume excepted) were not represented in Hungary in larger numbers and in larger closed settle-

ments. Of the Hungarian nationalities, Magyars were not represented in the same way in Austria proper, Serbs and Slovaks only in relatively insignificant groups. Schüssler sums up this situation rather well: "It is the decisive ethnographic factor of the monarchy that all the Hungarian nationalities—the Rumanians, German Suebes (Schwaben) [that is, the Germans settled in the so-called *Banat* in southern central Hungary] Ruthenians, Serbs, and Croats have their kin in Austria. Consequently, dualism has made two nationality states out of one, by which means all the above-mentioned peoples were cut in half by the course of the frontier." Wilhelm Schüssler, *Das Verfassungsproblem im Habsburgerreich* (Stuttgart, Berlin, 1918), p. 79.

40. See also Redlich, *Das österreichische Staats- und Reichsproblem*, II, 677 ff., on this point.

41. This interpretation corresponds with the opinion of such thorough analysts of the Austrian problem as Oskar Jaszi, Josef Redlich, R. W. Seton-Watson (pseud., Scotus Viator), and others, and, to a limited degree, with Karl Renner.

42. Wilhelm Schüssler conceives the basic political conditions on which the compromise was founded as follows:

1) A centralized constitutional government in each of the two states, under Magyar and German predominance, respectively.

2) Recognition by Hungary of the provisions of the compromise as absolutely binding.

3) Full constitutionalism in Austria as well as in Hungary.

Wilhelm Schüssler, *Österreich und das deutsche Schicksal* (Leipzig, 1925), p. 44. (See also Tezner, *Die Wandlungen der österreichische-ungarischen Reichsidee*, pp. 113 f., on point 3.)

43. Eisenmann's comment in *Le Compromis austro-hongrois de 1867*, pp. 493 f., is appropriate: "In the expression Austria-Hungary the term Austria is not put in juxtaposition to the term Hungary, though it seems to be so to all appearances; but it includes it. Austria, in the official designation of the monarchy, means all the possessions of the house of Austria as understood in the declaration regarding the creation of the dynastic title in 1804; and Austria-Hungary does not stand for Austria and Hungary, but for Austria, whose most notable part is Hungary. The term Austria in the restricted sense has never been officially employed by the non-Hungarian lands. The entity of the non-Hungarian lands has no common name. One calls them by enumeration or, by a summary of such enumerations, the 'kingdoms and lands represented in the *Reichsrat*,' following a formula taken from the February Patent (1861): 'This is an anonymous state, which by custom frequently is called Cisleithania, even more often by a name more harmonious and fuller of meaning, Austria. But one does well not to forget the exact meaning and origin of that term, because it illustrates the situation in Austria Cisleithania, which, until the dualism [that is, the compromise], was nothing but a part of the Austrian monarchy and, apart from that, has no concrete meaning, no distinctive individuality.' "

A further relatively minor, strictly legal, point is involved in the terminological question. The adherence of one crownland, the kingdom of Dalmatia, to the western part of the Union was contested by Hungary, which considered this kingdom historically linked to Croatia as *pars adnexa* of the Hungarian crown, though it had never been under actual Magyar administration. The use of the cumbersome title "the kingdoms and lands represented in the *Reichsrat*" made it possible to avoid the use of conflicting concepts in the determination of the limits of either partner of the Union. (See also note 49.)

44. For a brilliant, though debatable, social analysis of the groups supporting the empire idea and of those opposed to it, see Jaszi, *The Dissolution of the Habsburg Monarchy*.

45. See below, Chap. XXI.

46. Beust, the joint minister of foreign affairs (1866–71), was the only dignitary who ever held the title of *Reichskanzler*. The mere fact of the creation of this title in the year of the compromise, 1867, though it did imply special functions, is a strong indication that the idea of empire restoration, to which the dual states ought to be

subordinated, was not entirely abandoned at that time. See also below, Chap. V, section on "Hohenwart's Federalist Mission."

47. See particularly Apponyi, *A Brief Sketch of the Hungarian Constitution.*

48. See Redlich, *Das österreichische Staats- und Reichsproblem,* I, 1, 82 f.

49. *Oxford Dictionary of the English Language,* III: "An extensive territory (especially an aggregate of many separate states) under the sway of an emperor or sovereign ruler."

Webster, *New International Encyclopedia:* "A group of nations or states united under a single sovereign power . . . A state characterized by having great extent of territories and variety of peoples under one rule."

50. Terms such as Danube monarchy, instead of Austrian-Hungarian monarchy, or Cisleithania and Transleithania, instead of Austria and Hungary, which were frequently used after 1867, are entirely correct verbal substitutes and synonyms for the original legal political terms. Strictly speaking, however, they are merely literary paraphrases of historically established concepts.

The meaning of the term "Hungary" is, theoretically, almost as involved as that of the corresponding term "Austria," though in practical application much simpler. One correctly refers legally to the "lands of the Hungarian crown" or "the Holy Crown of St. Stephen (the first Christian ruler of Hungary)" if the *partes adnexae* (collateral lands) with special administrative autonomy are included, that is, up to 1918 Croatia-Slavonia and, with a lesser degree of autonomy, Fiume. Dalmatia, though, strictly speaking, historically a collateral of Croatia, is also claimed to be a *pars adnexa* of Hungary. Due to the actual administrative and political incorporation of Dalmatia with Austria as a crownland, this claim was of very little practical significance. (See also note 42 on this point.) The claim that Transylvania ever was a *pars adnexa* is hotly contested in Magyar constitutional theory. If she ever had such a status, it was lost for all practical purpose in 1867. See Marczali, *Ungarisches Verfassungsrecht,* pp. 25 ff. Further classification of the Hungarian mainland and collateral lands is purely academic, as neither the concept "lands of the Hungarian crown," which theoretically includes even claims to Bosnia, Serbia, Bulgaria, Galicia, and so on, nor the term "Hungary" touch upon the main issue, that is, the distinction between the ruling Magyar race and the other nationalities. Even the simple term "Hungary," excluding Croatia, still includes the other Hungarian nationalities (Rumanians, Ruthenians, Serbs, Slovaks, Germans). The Magyar language, a characteristic feature in itself, has no word for "Hungarian" aside from "Magyar." It does not recognize that the terms "Hungary" and "Hungarian" comprise a wider concept than the Magyar-ruled kingdom and its Magyar citizens. In other words, the legal existence of non-Magyar Hungarians is ignored. Consequently, the terms "Magyar" and "Hungarian" are very often used interchangeably in non-Magyar literature as well. See here Sosnosky, *Die Politik im Habsburgerreich,* II, 10 f.

In this study it is therefore necessary to use the term "Hungary" for all the lands under Hungarian rule and to indicate in particular cases whether Croatia is to be excluded.

Finally, the designation of the common sovereign must be touched upon. One does not have to take sides here in the dispute whether the emperor of Austria is superior to the king of Hungary, physically the same, but legally a different, person, or whether there is a concept of emperor superior to the rulers either in Austria or in Hungary. In all the literature of non-Hungarian lands dealing with internal affairs, the common ruler over the Habsburg lands has, by accepted practice, always been called the emperor. This holds good not only for the period since the creation of the Austrian imperial title in 1804, but in a way for the entire historical period since Albrecht II was elected emperor of the Holy Roman German Empire in 1438. Since that time, until 1918, there was no Habsburg ruling in Austria, and, since 1804, there was no Habsburg ruling in Hungary who did not bear either the imperial crown of the Holy Roman Empire or the Austrian imperial title, with the exception of the only female ruler, Maria Theresa, who bore the imperial title merely as empress consort. The impact of this historical tradition makes it obvious that the common ruler over the Habsburg lands must be referred to as emperor. The term "king" or "king-emperor" may be substituted only in purely Hungarian affairs.

A further, almost hair-splitting, distinction refers to the use of the terms "imperial" and "royal" since the Compromise of 1867. Yet, legal literature and even official comments and declarations have given it a great deal of attention. If one refers to the sovereign as ruler over both states of the monarchy and to common institutions, the designation Imperial *and* royal Majesty, Imperial *and* royal armed forces, and so forth—meaning Imperial Austrian and Royal Hungarian—are appropriate. The emperor as ruler over the Austrian state alone and exclusively Austrian institutions is spoken of as his Imperial-Royal Majesty, Imperial-Royal ministry of commerce or education, and so forth. In that case the word "royal" does not refer to the Hungarian crown, but to the crownlands, which formerly stood as historicopolitical entities under a royal ruler of their own and still—though only as a gesture—carry the royal crown in their coat of arms (such as the kingdoms of Bohemia, Dalmatia, and so forth). The fact that these outdated royal crowns are subordinated to the imperial crown is indicated by the hyphen between the words "imperial" and "royal," the assertion that the Austrian crown is coordinated with, and not superior to, the Hungarian is indicated by the coordinating word "and" between imperial and royal, if referring to the common Austro-Hungarian sovereign and common institutions.

## II. PATTERN OF THE NATIONAL PROBLEM IN AUSTRIA

1. The following works are of particular importance for the study of the historic ideological concepts of nationalism as touched upon in the first section of this chapter.

Carlton J. H. Hayes, *The Historical Evolution of Modern Nationalism*, and, by the same author, *Essays on Nationalism* (New York, 1926); Frederick Herz, *Nationality in History and Politics* (New York, 1944); Hans Kohn, *The Idea of Nationalism*, Vol. I (New York, 1944); F. J. Neumann, *Volk und Nation* (Leipzig, 1888), one of the best older works on the subject; J. H. Rose, *Nationality in Modern History* (New York, 1916).

The legal institutional aspects of the general problems, particularly in regard to the minority question, are well analyzed in: Arthur von Balogh, *Der Schutz der internationalen Minderheiten* (Munich, 1928); G. H. Erler, *Das Recht der nationalen Minderheiten* (Münster, 1931); O. L. Janowsky, *Nationalities and National Minorities* (New York, 1945); Pablo de Azcarate y Florez, *League of Nations and National Minorities* (Washington, D.C., 1945), see chiefly the first part of this study; C. A. Macartney, *National States and National Minorities* (London, 1934); Hermann Raschhofer, *Hauptprobleme des Nationalitätenrechts* (Stuttgart, 1931); Hugo Wintgens, *Der völkerrechtliche Schutz der nationalen, sprachlichen und religiösen Minderheiten* (Stuttgart, 1930).

On eastern central European minority problems in general see the periodical *Nation und Staat*, Vienna.

An excellent general bibliography on the subject is Jacob Robinson, *Das Minoritätenproblem und seine Literatur* (Berlin, Leipzig, 1928).

See also map on p. 40.

Concerning the specific Austrian aspects of the problem see the sections "National Problem" and "Nationality Law" in the selected bibliography, Appendix 7, below. Particular attention is called to the works by O. Bauer, J. von Eötvös, R. Herrmann von Herrnritt, K. G. Hugelmann, and I. Seipel, mentioned there.

See further A. Kolnai, "The Problem of Austrian Nationhood," *Journal of Central European Affairs*, Vol. II, No. 3 (Oct., 1942), 290 ff.

2. See Kohn, *The Idea of Nationalism*, I, 580. "The word 'nationality' is preferable to 'nation,' as the latter term frequently denotes 'state' in French and English."

See *Oxford Dictionary*, under "nation": "An extensive aggregate of persons, so closely associated with each other by common descent, language or history, as to form a distinct race of people, usually organized as a separate political state and occupying a definite territory." But, on the other hand, also: "A country, kingdom" and "the whole people of a country, frequently in contrast to some smaller or narrower body within it." In German theoretical literature, as compared with English, the connotation of the term is more on the side of people than of state, but the basic dilemma remains the same. "The nation is the people in the natural sense as distinguished from the state people, the population living within the political borders of a state." See Wintgens, *Der völkerrechtliche Schutz der nationalen, sprachlichen und religiösen Minderheiten*, p. 15.

3. Kohn, *The Idea of Nationalism*, I, 13 f.

4. Probably the most notorious contrary view, namely, that of a national concept composed of a definite number of noninterchangeable factors, has been formulated by Joseph Stalin. Obviously not distinguishing between nation and nationality, he states: "A nation is a historically evolved stable community of language, territory, economic life and psychological makeup manifested in a community of culture." See Joseph Stalin, "Marxism and the National Question," in J. Stalin, *Marxism and the National and Colonial Question* (New York, no date). The partial political purpose of this concept, supposedly formulated in Vienna in 1913 with an eye on the Austrian nationality struggle, is obvious. It means where all these factors constituting a nation do not exist at the same time, a legitimate national concept does not exist, and national struggle is unjustified. Consequently, in Austria, where some of them do not exist in regard to the national groups (see particularly the "community of economic life"), the workers should concentrate on the class struggle rather than participate in an [in Stalin's opinion] unwarranted struggle for multinational organization "under the 'national' flag of the bourgeoisie." *Ibid.*, p. 19.

On Stalin's views on Austria's national organization see also below, Chap. XX, section on Otto Bauer. On Stalin's approach to the theory of the national question see also E. Hula, "The Nationalities Policy of the Soviet Union," *Social Research* XI (1944), 168 ff.

5. The fact that people such as the Czechs and others called themselves a nation prior to 1918 does not contradict the use of the term "nationality." Its use in such cases may refer either to a former status of sovereign independence, such as the lands of the Bohemian crown possessed until 1526, or to an aim to re-establish this status. The term "nationality," as used here, refers only to the position of the national groups in their relations to the empire.

The further point could be raised that a term generally referring only to small national groups does not fit the case of some of Austria's nationalities. Yet, with the exception of the relatively small national groups of Czechs, Slovaks, Slovenes, Croats, and Magyars, this study does not refer to the national groups as a whole, but only to those parts of them settled within the borders of the empire.

While the Austro-Germans are often listed together with the other nationalities in Cisleithania, the Magyars in Hungarian affairs are usually not referred to as a nationality. Literature on the nationality question in Hungary refers usually to the issue between the Magyars and the other peoples within Hungary. It is necessary to follow this generally accepted usage. Thus, reference to the national problems of the empire as a whole includes all the peoples, Germans and Magyars as well. Specific reference to the Hungarian nationalities does not include the Magyars who arrogated to themselves exclusive national power.

6. See G. Erler, *Das Recht der nationalen Minderheiten*, pp. 45 f. See also Karl Renner, *Selbstbestimmungsrecht der Nationen*, Part 1, "Nation und Staat" (Vienna, 1918), p. 12.

7. This is not to say that the term "nationality," which is, after all, a foreign word in the German language, was officially used in Austria. The famous Article XIX of the Austrian Fundamental State Law No. 142 of 1867, the basic law on the issue, refers to *Volksstämme*; imperial proclamations usually plainly refer to the "peoples." But political literature in Austria has recognized the term *Stamm* as rather unfortunate, merely expressing ethnic aspects, whereas the word "peoples" is devoid of any clear connotation in regard to national aspects.

Austrian political and legal literature has generally adopted the use of the concept of nationality. See at this point also Karl G. Hugelmann, ed., *Das Nationalitätenrecht des alten Österreich* (Vienna, 1934), pp. 81 ff., in particular pp. 89 ff.

8. See at this point Erler, *Das Recht der nationalen Minderheiten*, pp. 37 f., 47 f.;

Balogh, *Der Schutz der internationalen Minderheiten*, pp. 63 f.; Wintgens, *Der völker-rechtliche Schutz der nationalen, sprachlichen und religiösen Minderheiten*, pp. 15 ff. For an analysis of the concept, see also M. H. Böhm in *Encyclopedia of Social Sciences* under "Minorities," and, more recently, Erich Mair, *Die Psychologie der nationalen Minderheit* (Innsbruck, 1947).

9. If the whole cultural life of such a group is focused on its religious affiliations and activities, it is possible to conceive even religious differentiation alone as the determining factor for the creation of a national minority. See also Erler, *Das Recht der nationalen Minderheiten*, pp. 8 ff., 72 ff.

10. The peace treaties of 1919, 1920, and 1923 and the treaties of the Chief Allied and Associated Powers with the so-called Succession states of Austria-Hungary and with Greece, of 1919, 1920, 1921, and (1924) in general attempted to protect people differing from the majority of the population in regard to the controversial concept of race, language, or religion. See Balogh, *Der Schutz der nationalen Minderheiten*, pp. 63 ff.; Erler, *Das Recht der nationalen Minderheiten*, pp. 127 ff.; Janowsky, *Nationalities and National Minorities*, pp. 110 ff.; Wintgens, *Der völkerrechtliche Schutz der nationalen, sprachlichen und religiösen Minderheiten*, pp. 107 ff.

This, however, does not, of course, contradict the fact that other factors, such as common customs and tradition, contribute to the determination of the character of a national minority.

11. See below, Appendix 1.

The Austrian and the Hungarian nationality censuses were established in a permanent, modern, and, in the case of the Austrians, on the whole reliable form in 1880. However, fairly correct statistical figures exist for the whole empire at least since 1843. Particularly, the various semiofficial publications of Carl von Czörnig, the first director of the Austrian Statistical Service, published between 1849 and 1858, were considered outstanding in their time. (For bibliographical data see below, Appendix I.)

12. On this fact rests one of the basic ethnic differences between the old empire and the Czechoslovakian Republic which, before 1939, due to its mixed national character, has so often been called a small Austria. Though the absolute majority of the Czechs in the republic was contested, there is no doubt that they formed an absolute majority together with the closely affiliated ethnic group of the Slovaks. In this broader sense, at least, Czechoslovakia had a national majority, the empire did not.

On the character of the national minority concept, as outlined in this study, see also Ignas Seipel, *Die geistigen Grundlagen der Minderheitenfrage* (Vienna, 1925).

13. See below, Appendix 1.

14. The Littoral *Küstenland* is conceived as consisting of the three crownlands—Istria, Gorizia and Gradiska, and Trieste.

15. Bukovina, Istria, Austrian Silesia.

16. Namely, in Lower and Upper Austria, Salzburg, and Vorarlberg, the German language; in Dalmatia, Serbo-Croatian; and in Carniola, Slovene; the size of the last-mentioned linguistic majority has sometimes been contested.

17. See also Janowsky, *Nationalities and National Minorities*, p. 166.

18. Janowsky, on J. T. Shotwell's suggestion, has introduced in this connection the appropriate term "national federalism." See *ibid.*, pp. 37 ff., 166 f. Yet the principle of national federalization of the multinational state is only one way to solve its national problems, though, if practicable, very likely the best one. The organization of the multinational state according to the national principle comprises other potential solutions as well.

19. The terminology referring to the stages of development of nationalism has been adapted from Hayes, *The Historical Evolution of Modern Nationalism*.

20. See Ludwig Gumplowicz, *Österreichisches Staatsrecht* (Vienna, 1907), pp. 72 ff.

21. The era from 1859–60 to 1867, during which four large-scale constitutional revisions took place, is frequently referred to as "the era of constitutional experiments." See, for instance, Chap. IX in Josef Redlich's biography, *Kaiser Franz Josef von Österreich* (Berlin, 1928).

22. Quoted from a speech of Count Szécsen in the sixteenth meeting of the *Reichsrat* of 1860, in Eisenmann, *Le Compromis austro-hongrois de 1867*, p. 227. Anton Count Szécsen de Temerin (1819–96), leading moderate Conservative statesman and minister without portfolio, 1860–61, worked on a reconciliation between the empire and Hungary, prior to 1867, along traditional historic lines. The *verstärkte Reichsrat* was the state council of the empire appointed by the emperor and "strengthened" in 1860 by the inclusion of thirty-eight members of the crownland Estates, each of whom was selected by the emperor out of a Terno proposal submitted by the Estates.

See also Redlich, *Das österreichische Staats- und Reichsproblem*, I, part 1, 198 f., and the quotations there from Count Anton Szécsen, *Politische Fragen der Gegenwart* (Vienna, 1851), and below, Chapter XIX, section on Szécsen.

23. Eisenmann, *Le Compromis austro-hongrois de 1867*, pp. 227 f.

24. Quoted from Redlich, *Das österreichische Staats- und Reichsproblem*, I, 1, 536 ff. Similar views were also expressed by the Polish count Wojciech Dzieduszycki, some time Galician minister in the Cisleithanian cabinet after 1867, in *Das Programm der Autónomisten-Partei Österreichs* (Lemberg, 1896). A discussion from the Austro-German Liberal point of view is to be found in the interesting memoirs of the political journalist O. B. Friedmann, *Zehn Jahre österreichischer Politik, 1859–1869*, 2 vols. (Vienna, 1879). Friedmann was editor of the *Wiener Wochenblatt und Neueste Nachrichten* and also wrote for the *Fremdenblatt*, both German Liberal papers. See particularly Friedmann's memoirs, I, 135 f.

The theoretical aspects of the problem are discussed by Redlich, Eisenmann, and, in a most illuminating way, in Rudolf Herrmann von Herrnritt, *Nationalität und Recht, dargestellt nach der österreichischen und ausländischen Gesetzgebung* (Vienna, 1899). See also Steinacker, "Die geschichtlichen Voraussetzungen des österreichischen Nationalitätenproblems und seine Entwicklung bis 1867," in Hugelmann, ed., *Das Nationalitätenrecht des alten Österreich*.

25. Josef von Eötvös, *Die Garantien der Macht und Einheit Österreichs* (Leipzig, 1859), pp. 85 f.

26. *Ibid.*, pp. 57 f.

27. In the case of Bohemia, the kingdom of Bohemia proper as well as the lands of the Bohemian crown were concepts of living and meaningful historic tradition, either of them historicopolitical entities in the full sense of the word. In Hungary, the problem appears somewhat different, since the institutions of the crownlands did not exist there. Croatia and Transylvania, however, certainly were historicopolitical entities.

28. Such terms as racialism, race, and racial, should be used with great restraint in connection with Austrian nationalities. In addition to the general ambiguity of these terms, there is in Austria the specific problem that some of her various nationalities, such as the Serbs and the Croats, the Czechs and the Slovaks, were practically identical "racially." Therefore, any of these terms loses its meaning here, even as a mere distinguishing factor.

Regarding the interrelations of nationality groups ethnically farther apart, the distinctions are far too complex to be confined to physical features. The term "ethnic" groups, which includes cultural and social attributes as well, is, therefore, more appropriate. The terms race, racial, and so forth, will be applied only if it is clearly necessary to use them in the sense of the Fascist racial doctrine, that is, primarily with reference to the Pan German movement in Austria since the last quarter of the nineteenth century. It is further justified to use this concept in regard to the only non-Indo-German nationality in the empire, the Ugro-Finnish Magyar people.

29. Among national groups where national nobility either did not exist or did not survive in the nineteenth century, no claim for the continued existence of a historicopolitical entity was made. See the following section, "Organization of the National Groups."

30. The two basic laws guaranteeing the rights of the various nationalities—Article XIX of the Austrian Basic State Law of December 21, 1867, No. 142, and the Hungarian Law of Nationalities (Act XLIV of the year 1868)—do not enumerate the national groups

benefiting from the nationality rights embodied in these statutes. Nevertheless, legal practice after 1867 has never seriously contested the fact that in principle only the national groups listed in this study were objects of the general nationality legislation in either Austria or Hungary. See, at this point, Karl Hugelmann, "Die rechtliche Stellung der Nationalitäten in Österreich," *Österreichische Zeitschrift für Verwaltung*, annual X (1877), 192 ff.

31. For an enumeration which links Serbs and Croats and Czechs and Slovaks together, see, for instance, Rudolf Springer (pseud. of Karl Renner), *Grundlagen und Entwicklungsziele der österreichisch-ungarischen Monarchie* (Vienna, 1906), p. 185.

32. See at this point the classic decision of the Austrian Administrative Court of January 3, 1881 (quoted in Chap. XXVI, below, Appendix 3), supported by a series of later decisions by the same court of highest authority, which makes the recognition of the nationality status of any individual only partly dependent on his use of a national language. The Jewish language in Austria was never considered officially as a universally recognized language, but as idiom in local use only.

With special reference to the Jewish nationality problem, see also the decision of the Austrian *Reichsgericht* of October 26, 1909. It should be made clear that the problem of the recognition of a Jewish nationality had nothing to do with the civic equality of the Jews as individuals, which was first, though not universally, established in 1848 and which after several reverses was almost generally recognized after 1861. For a broad treatment of the Jewish problem in Austria during the period under discussion, see S. M. Dubnow, *Weltgeschichte des jüdischen Volkes*, Vols. IX, X (Berlin, 1925–30). For an analysis of the Jewish legal status in Hungary, see Robert A. Kann, "Hungarian Jewry during Austria-Hungary's Constitutional Period (1867–1918)," *Jewish Social Studies*, Vol. VII, No. 4 (October, 1945), 360 ff., and, by the same author, "German-speaking Jewry during Austria-Hungary's Constitutional Era (1867–1918)," *Jewish Social Studies*, Vol. X, No. 3 (July, 1948), 239–56. See also below, Appendix 1.

33. See the Chap. I, above, notes 38 and 39.

34. See at this point literature quoted in note 1 to this Chapter, and Otto Bauer, *Die Nationalitätenfrage und die Sozialdemokratie* (Vienna, 1907), pp. 442 f.

35. Ethnographically, the question whether the Rumanians are preponderantly of Slav or Roman stock is debatable; it is a fact, however, that Rumanian nationalism in and outside the monarchy laid great stress on the basically Latin character of the Rumanian people.

36. This applies particularly to the interrelations of some of the northern Slav peoples and those of the Austrian national groups of Latin stock. In spite of the great ideological influence of Pan-Slavism on the Austrian Slav peoples in general, a specific community of interests in the political or cultural field can scarcely be found in Czech-Polish interrelations, and only antagonism in Polish-Ruthenian relations. No specific ties generally bound the Austro-Italians and the Austro-Rumanians to each other. See also Chap. XIV, above.

37. Franz Mehring, ed., *Aus dem literarischen Nachlass von Karl Marx, Friedrich Engels und Ferdinand Lassalle* (Stuttgart, 1902), Vol. III, containing Engels's articles in the *Neue Rheinische Zeitung*, see the articles from 1849 onwards; Karl Kautsky, ed., *Karl Marx: Revolution und Konterrevolution in Deutschland*, 6th ed. (Stuttgart, 1920), containing the collection and translation of articles which Marx wrote as correspondent for the New York *Daily Tribune* in 1851 and 1852 (various English editions); Friedrich Engels, "Gewalt und Ökonomie bei der Herstellung des neuen Deutschen Reiches," in *Die Neue Zeit, Revue des geistigen und öffentlichen Lebens*, Annual 14, Part 1 (Stuttgart, 1896). This essay was written in 1888 and published only after Engels's death. See also below, Chapter XVI.

38. Marx, *Revolution und Konterrevolution in Deutschland*, ed. by Karl Kautsky, pp. 62 f.

39. F. Mehring, ed., *Aus dem literarischen Nachlass von Karl Marx, Friedrich Engels*, III, 236, 241 ff., 244 ff., 256.

40. Otto Bauer, *Die Nationalitätenfrage und die Sozialdemokratie*, pp. 190 f.; see also

Rudolf Schlesinger, *Federalism in Central and Eastern Europe* (London, 1945), pp. 155 ff.

41. Bauer, *Die Nationalitätenfrage und die Sozialdemokratie,* pp. 215 f.; see also Harold Steinacker, "Die geschichtlichen Voraussetzungen des österreichischen Nationalitätenproblems und seine Entwicklung bis 1867," in K. G. Hugelmann, ed., *Das Nationalitätenrecht des alten Österreich,* pp. 64 ff.

42. *Ibid.,* p. 42.

43. This term of autonomy is to be found in Transylvanian history, particularly in regard to the nationality groups of the Saxons (Germans) and Szekels.

44. *Ibid.,* pp. 42, 46, 47.

45. See *ibid.,* p. 52.

The lowest territorial administrative units for the period under discussion were, excluding Hungary, the *politischen Gemeinden.* Above them were the *Bezirke.* The introduction of the still higher unit, the *Kreis,* into the Austrian administrative system was often planned, but never fully realized in the administrative sphere. A fair translation of *politische Gemeinde* is "municipality" (not to be confused with the Hungarian *municipia*). *Bezirk* may be translated as "district," but it is almost impossible to propose an adequate translation of *Kreis.* The concept of the English and American county implies the idea of self-administration, which is not found in the German word. The term "circuit" refers to juridical districts only, and, though such juridical circuits did exist in Austria, they were not identical in size and in organization with the administrative territorial units. It is, therefore, advisable to use the German term. Quite frequently, the terms district and *Kreis* are used indiscriminately in Austrian political literature.

46. *Ibid.,* p. 52. This refers to German Austrian political philosophy from 1848 onward.

47. Obviously, several of the national groups in the Habsburg Empire, some of them "with" and even some "without" history—as qualified in the text—were connected with historic national concepts reaching or even centering beyond the monarchy's borders. This applies to the Serbs, the Rumanians and, in a way, to the Ruthenians, who possessed a strong national political tradition outside the empire, just as much as the historic nationalities of the Germans, the Magyars, the Poles, the Croats, and the Italians. Since this study is solely concerned with the national evolution within the empire, these aspects of the problem cannot be discussed further.

## III. THE GERMANS

1. As observed in the selected general bibliography of this study, below, in Volume II, general Austrian historiography has been written predominantly from a German Austrian viewpoint. Thus, the principal works listed there may well serve as an introduction to the study of the German problem in Austria. This applies particularly to the works by Charmatz, Friedjung, Krones, Mayer, Redlich, Rogge, and Springer. All of them put special emphasis on the German problem; none of them, however, is tinged with a particular nationalist bias.

The following items, all of a more German national approach, may be added: Raimund F. Kaindl, *Österreich, Preussen, Deutschland* (Leipzig, 1926); Paul Molisch, *Briefe zur deutschen Politik in Österreich von 1848–1918* (Leipzig, 1934), a valuable collection of letters, and, by the same author, *Geschichte der deutschnationalen Bewegung in Österreich von ihren Anfängen bis zum Zerfall der Monarchie* (Jena, 1926); Wilhelm Schüssler, *Österreich und das deutsche Schicksal* (Leipzig, 1925), and *Das Verfassungsproblem im Habsburgerreich* (Berlin, 1918).

Far more impartial are two largely documentary works on Cisleithanian Austria, the first dealing with the development of the executive branch, the second with the legislative branch of government: Alois von Czedik, *Zur Geschichte der k. k. österreichischen Ministerien, 1861–1916.* 4 vols. (Teschen, 1917–20); Gustav Kolmer, *Parlament und Verfassung in Österreich, 1848–1904.* 8 vols. (Leipzig, Vienna, 1902–14).

For bibliography see Richard Charmatz, *Wegweisen durch die Literatur der öster-*

*reichischen Geschichte* (Stuttgart, 1912); (Max Gunzenhauser), *Bibliographie zur Geschichte Österreich-Ungarns, 1848–1914* (Stuttgart, 1938); Karl Uhlirz, in Mathilde Uhlirz, ed., *Handbuch zur Geschichte Österreichs* (Graz, 1927–41); Friedrich Dahlmann and Georg Waitz, *Quellenkunde der deutschen Geschichte* (Leipzig, 1911).

2. The following discussion is, of course, confined to the status of national groups within the empire and does not include the problem of their conationals beyond the borders of the empire. As has been pointed out in Chap. II, above, in addition to the Germans, the Poles, the Rumanians, the Italians, the Serbs, and the Ruthenians were national groups, large bodies of whose conationals lived beyond the borders of the empire in neighboring states. In all those cases, for obvious reasons of simplification, the ethnic terms alone, that is, Germans, Poles, Italians, and so on, instead of Austro-Germans, Austro-Poles, Austro-Italians, have been employed. In general, the hyphenated terms have been used only when otherwise some misunderstanding could have arisen as to whether merely an Austrian national group or the whole ethnic body, including the conationals beyond the border, was referred to.

Thus, it should be clear, but, in the particular case of the Austrian Germans, stressed again, that the terminology used in this study does not imply necessarily a more than ethnic relationship between them and the Germans beyond the frontiers. In this particular case another explanation of the term is, however, advisable.

According to the analysis of the concept of Austria in Chapter I, reference to the Austro-Germans could mean either the Germans in the Austro-Hungarian empire as a whole, or exclusively the Germans in Cisleithanian Austria. The term Germans or Austro-Germans, as used in this study, generally refers to the second meaning, since the separate discussion of the German status in Hungary, except for references to the Saxon position in Transylvania (see below, Chap. XI), does not form a part of this study. The reasons for this are obvious. Though forming a substantial minority of around 2,000,000 peoples, the Germans within the lands of the Hungarian crown were never able to pursue a common national policy of their own, nor was their political history in the period under discussion directly influenced by their kin in Cisleithanian Austria. In other words, the isolated German-language islands in Hungary have a mere local national history and mere local national problems. Their problems, with some exceptions, should be seen in a different light than that of the Germans in Cisleithanian Austria and those of the other national groups.

3. The German term here is *Besitzstand*. It is difficult to translate it exactly, since it means not only possession itself, but implies also the status of ownership of possessions.

4. That is, the recognition of German as the official language in the whole of Cisleithania. The character of German as official language was recognized to a wide extent by administrative practice, but not officially introduced in the era under discussion. See particularly, below, Chap. V, sections on "The Institutional Evolution of the National Conflict" and "The Development of the Language Conflict." See also Appendix 2.

5. Friedrich von Wieser, *Über Vergangenheit und Zukunft der österreichischen Verfassung* (Vienna, 1905), pp. 87 f.

6. Redlich, *Das österreichische Staats- und Reichsproblem*, I, part 1, 36 f. See also Alfred Fischel, *Das österreichische Sprachenrecht* (2d. ed., Brünn, 1910). This work is a unique and rather comprehensive collection of documents concerning the Austrian language problem from the fifteenth century on. The use of its source material is indispensable for studies in the field of the Austrian nationality problem. See in this particular context the extensive historical introduction. For the relative liberality with which the language problem was handled even in the times of Francis I of Austria, see Bauer, *Die Nationalitätenfrage und die Sozialdemokratie* (Vienna, 1907), p. 235; Bauer certainly was unsuspected of pro-imperial sympathies.

7. Joseph II, until 1780, was only coregent in Austria. He started his sweeping reforms after the death of his mother, the Empress Maria Theresa, in 1780. He wrote to a Magyar aristocrat objecting to the Germanization of Hungary as laid down in the imperial ordinance of March 6, 1784 as follows: "The German language is the universal language of my empire. Why should I have handled the laws and public affairs of just one province

in the national language? I am emperor of the German Empire; therefore all the other states in my possession are provinces which, united with the whole state, form one body. I am the head of this body. If the Hungarian kingdom were the most important and first of my possessions, I would make its language the main language of my lands. As things actually are, they are different." Quoted from Fischel, *Das österreichische Sprachenrecht*, xlii. Until 1848 the German language was the uncontested state language or, as Emperor Joseph said, "the universal language of the monarchy," or, according to Emperor Francis, "the general language of affairs" [*Geschäftssprache*]. Fischel, *Das österreichische Sprachenrecht*, xvi.

8. Redlich, *Das österreichische Staats- und Reichsproblem*, I, 1, 37 f.

9. Nobility itself, even of high rank, is not a reliable indicator of noble origin in Austria. This was particularly true from the time of Francis I of Austria and, to some extent, even since Maria Theresa's reign. Nobility was ever-increasingly conferred on commoners, officers, civil servants, and, since Francis I, also on financiers. Only two types of nobility, taken as groups, can be considered powerful social factors. One consists of the noble Houses which, until 1804 (the assembly of the *Reichsdeputationshauptschluss*), ruled in the German principalities and whose sovereignty was not restored by the Congress of Vienna in 1814 and 1815. Their privileges as members of former ruling Houses (above all, the right of marriage to the members of the ruling dynasties) were still recognized. The second, numerically far larger group, was the high landed nobility of the Habsburg lands proper, as represented, since 1867, in the Austrian House of Lords and in the ancient House of Magnates in Hungary. Here the stress is decidedly on landed nobility. See Paragraph 3 of the Austrian Fundamental State Law of December 21, 1867, No. 141: "Hereditary members of the house of lords are the heads of the indigenous noble families . . . who are distinguished in the kingdoms and lands represented in the *Reichsrat* by extensive landed property and on whom the emperor bestows the hereditary dignity as members of the *Reichsrat*." Usually, members of the group mentioned first were also members of the second, but not necessarily so, and it is to be noted that members of the hereditary landed nobility, if not belonging to the former ruling German families, did not have the right of connubium with the ruling dynasties. This fact had grave legal consequences with the marriage of the heir presumptive, Francis Ferdinand, to a countess not belonging to a former ruling House as late as 1901. See below, Chap. XXI, section on the heir presumptive. The rank of nobility itself—knight, baron, count, prince, and so on, though indicative of the social position of an individual, has nothing whatever to do with his belonging to either of the above-mentioned groups.

10. For a chart on the German share in the empire's bureaucracy see below, Appendix 5.

11. "One may well say that the governmental system of Joseph II represented the perfection of the Austrian centralized state, but at the same time, involuntarily, the promoting force for new . . . political forces of the non-German nationalities, who were diametrically opposed to this concept of state." Redlich, *Das österreichische Staats- und Reichsproblem*, I, 1, 39.

12. *Ibid.*, I, 1, 83–84.

13. On the specific influence of the Napoleonic era in this respect see the excellent study by W. C. Langsam, *The Napoleonic Wars and German Nationalism in Austria* (New York, 1930).

14. The literature on this problem—from the German as well as from the Czech viewpoint—is tremendous. This is easily explained by the fact that here two peoples, both of the highest standard of civilization, faced each other in open conflict for the better part of three generations. Numerous specific references will be given in the course of this study.

As general introductory references on this point, two publications in the English language may be mentioned, which give a broad picture of the revival of Czech nationalism in its collision with the German position in Bohemia, S. Harrison Thomson, *Czechoslovakia in European History* (Princeton, 1943). See *ibid.*, particularly Chapter VI, also Chapters VII and VIII; more specific, but still serving as a general introduction to the problem, is Elizabeth Wiskemann, *Czechs and Germans; A Study of the Struggle in the Historic Provinces of Bohemia and Moravia* (London, 1938). See *ibid.*, particularly Chapters II and III.

15. T. von Sosnosky, *Die Politik im Habsburgerreich* (Berlin, 1912, 1913), I, 162 f.

16. Standard works on the period from 1835 to 1848 are: Anton Springer, *Geschichte Österreichs seit dem Wiener Frieden, (1809–1848)*, 2 vols. (Leipzig, 1863, 1865), see Vol. I and the first section of Vol. II (moderately liberal, federalist standpoint); Heinrich von Treitschke, *Deutsche Geschichte im 19 Jahrhundert* (Leipzig, 1918–20), Vol. V, covers the era from 1840 to 1848. Treitschke's nationalist bias becomes particularly obvious as soon as Austrian problems are discussed.

Important also is J. A. von Helfert, *Geschichte der österreichischen Revolution im Zusammenhang mit der mitteleuropäischen Bewegung*, 2 vols. (Freiburg, 1907–1909). For the pre-March period see Vol. I (Conservative governmental standpoint). For a contemporary evaluation of Helfert's interpretation see Hans Kudlich, *Rückblicke und Erinnerungen*, 3 vols. (Vienna, 1873), II, 22. See also Heinrich von Srbik, *Metternich*, 2 vols. (Munich, 1925), see Vol. II; Viktor Bibl, *Kaiser Franz und sein Erbe* (Vienna, 1922). On the administrative history of the period see particularly, Ignaz Beidtel, *Geschichte der österreichischen Staatsverwaltung* (1740–1828), Vol. II (Innsbruck, 1897).

Monographs: Bibl, *Die niederösterreichischen Landstände im Vormärz* (Vienna, 1911); Peter Kuranda, *Grossdeutschland und Grossösterreich bei den Hauptvertretern der deutschösterreichischen Literatur, 1830–1848* (Vienna, 1928).

Contemporary works (for reasons of censorship usually published in Germany) referred to in this section are: Victor von Andrian-Werburg, *Österreich und dessen Zukunft*, 2 vols. (Hamburg, 1843, 1847); [Franz Schuselka], *Ist Österreich deutsch?* (Leipzig, 1843), and *Der Fortschritt und das konservative Prinzip in Österreich* (Leipzig, 1844); also by the same author, *Deutsche Worte eines Österreichers* (Hamburg, 1843), and *Österreichische Vor- und Rückschritte* (Hamburg, 1847); A. von Winterstetten, *Ist Österreich deutsch?* (Leipzig, 1843); Anon., *Vier Fragen eines Österreichers* (Leipzig, 1844); Anon., *Guter Rat für Österreich* (Leipzig, 1847), dedicated to Andrian; [Karl Möring], *Sybillininische Bücher aus Österreich*, 2 vols. (Hamburg, 1848); [Karl Möring?], *Des Österreichers richtiger Standpunkt* (Cologne, 1848).

On Möring and Andrian see also: Schüssler, *Die nationale Politik der österreichischen Abgeordneten im Frankfurter Parlament*, "Abhandlungen zur mittleren und neueren Geschichte, Heft 51" (Berlin, Leipzig, 1913); Hans Günther Telle, *Das österreichische Problem im Frankfurter Parlament im Sommer und Herbst 1848* (Marburg, 1933). Both studies give accounts only of Möring's and Andrian's activities in connection with the work of the Frankfurt Assembly. Their characteristics, however, are of general interest.

See also on Andrian: Eisenmann, *Le Compromis austro-hongrois de 1867*, pp. 152, 163; Redlich, *Das österreichische Staats- und Reichsproblem*, I, 1, 77; 265 f.; I, 2, 20, 73, also on Möring, and below, Chapter XIX, section on Andrian.

On Schuselka see the most interesting memoirs of his political friend during the revolutionary period, Kudlich, *Rückblicke und Erinnerungen*. See particularly Vol. II, pp. 64 ff., and the thorough analysis of his activities in Richard Charmatz, "Franz Schuselka," *Österreichische Rundschau*, XXVIII (1911), 264–75. See also below, Chapter XIX, subsection on Unorthodox German Liberalism. For biographical data of this period Konstantin von Wurzbach, *Biographisches Lexikon des Kaisertums Österreich* (Vienna, 1855), is of particular importance.

17. Frequently, particularly if including German affairs in general, historic literature refers to the whole period from the Congress of Vienna to the revolution as the pre-March era. In regard to Austria's internal and, above all, intellectual history, however, decisive trends leading to the revolutionary development came to the fore far later than in Germany, that is, in the 1830s. It is thus appropriate to confine the Austrian "pre-March" era to a more narrow period.

18. For a social interpretation of the Austrian Estates organization as a transitional stage in the development toward the modern state, see Bauer, *Die Nationalitätenfrage und die Sozialdemokratie*, pp. 198 f. For a legal political analysis see: Friedrich Tezner,

*Technik und Geist des ständisch-monarchischen Staatsrechts* (Leipzig, 1901). For a contemporary discussion of the Estates problem in the pre-March period, see A. Springer, *Geschichte Österreichs seit dem Wiener Frieden*, I, 509–49. Summarizing, he asserts, The Estates movement "is neither to be credited with, nor to be blamed for, the earth-shaking events of the following years." Springer identifies the Estates almost fully with the aristocracy, yet he argues that the aristocracy, as such, enjoyed far more public confidence in their direct influence on the state organism than in, by, and through the clumsy and intricate apparatus of the Estates; *Ibid.,* pp. 548 f.

The problem of the Estates is also extensively dealt with in [Count Franz Hartig], *Genesis der Revolution in Österreich im Jahre 1848* (Leipzig, 1850). It has been published in English as the second part of the fourth volume of Coxe's *History of the House of Austria,* continued by W. K. Kelly (London, 1853), under the title *Genesis or Details of the Late Austrian Revolution; by an Officer of State.* On Hartig see below, Chapter XVII, section on Hartig.

19. See also below, Chapter V, section on "Czech Cultural Evolution," and Chapter VII, sections on "Croatia's Problem," "Croatia's Autonomy," and "Croatia and southern Slav Unionism."

20. See Huber, *Österreichische Reichsgeschichte,* rev. by Dopsch (2d ed., Vienna, 1901), pp. 255 ff., 318 ff. The Estates agenda were, by and large, except for the short reign of Leopold II (1790–92), severely curtailed after the administrative reforms of the Maria Theresan era.

21. See Andrian, *Österreich und dessen Zukunft,* II, 55 f. He proposed election of officials of the Estates, right of nomination of the land marshal, that is, the presiding officer, strengthening of the position of the imperial governor, and so forth. The latter official was not to be in any way responsible to the Estates. Thus, an expansion of his function meant in no way a step toward representative government.

22. Andrian, *Österreich und dessen Zukunft,* I, 187–204; II, 41–44.

23. [Karl Möring], *Des Österreichers richtiger Standpunkt,* pp. 11 f. (published anonymously).

24. Andrian, *Österreich und dessen Zukunft,* I, 187–204.

25. See *ibid.,* II, 106 f., 131 f., 207, a few of many similar passages, and [Karl Möring], *Des Österreichers richtiger Standpunkt,* pp. 6 f.

26. The basic regulations of Austrian censorship, in so far as they were in force at the outbreak of the revolution, were, in theory, amazingly liberal. Government (police) practice, however, failed by far to comply with these regulations of 1810, which culminated in the promising words: "No ray of light, wherever it comes from, shall remain unnoticed and unknown in the monarchy, nor shall it be blocked from being used as far as possible." Dissatisfaction of Austrian intellectuals with the system of censorship throughout the entire pre-March period was widespread, permanent, and, in the main, certainly justified. Proof of this rests in the fact that books as moderate as Andrian's and Möring's could not be published in Austria, even though the latter's *Sybillinische Bücher* was dedicated to the Archduchess Sophie, the wife of the then heir apparent, Archduke Francis Charles, and mother of Emperor Francis Joseph. Nevertheless, the rigidity of the police system did not go so far as to impair the civic position of these authors in Austria. See Andrian's own comments on the Austrian system of censorship and his reform proposals in that respect, in *Österreich und dessen Zukunft,* II, 94 ff.

27. Andrian, for instance, was well acquainted with and largely influenced by Tocqueville's ideas. Redlich, *Das österreichische Staats- und Reichsproblem,* I, 2, 73.

28. For such an exception see the discussion on southern Slav "Illyrism" in Chapter VII, below, section on "Croatia and southern Slav Unionism."

29. See Charmatz, "Franz Schuselka," *Österreichische Rundschau,* XXVIII (1911), 264 ff. Schuselka, because of his radical political convictions, was forced to leave Austria in 1845. He returned only after the outbreak of the revolution and, after its collapse again had to spend some years abroad. When he wrote *Österreichs Vor- und Rückschritte* in exile, he thus was far less restricted in expressing his convictions than either Andrian or Möring.

30. Schuselka, *Österreichs Vor- und Rückschritte*, p. 270.

31. *Ibid.*, p. 276.

32. *Ibid.*, p. 265. Here Schuselka obviously uses the word nationality for nationalism.

33. *Ibid.*, p. 268.

34. *Ibid.*, p. 268.

35. Schuselka, *Deutsche Worte eines Österreichers*, pp. 263 f., 268. The similarity of this last thought to those expressed by Bauer two generations later is obvious.

36. *Österreichs Vor- und Rückschritte*, pp. 276, 282.

37. *Ibid.*, p. 217. Galicia and Bukovina formed one administrative unit at that time.

38. See the section in this chapter on the Pan German idea.

39. Anon., *Politische Memorabilien aus Österreichs Neuzeit* (Leipzig, 1844), pp. 179 f.

40. Anon., *Vier Fragen eines Österreichers*, pp. 30 f.

41. *Ibid.*, pp. 31 f.

42. *Ibid.*, pp. 31 f.

43. *Ibid.*, p. 38.

44. *Ibid.*, p. 38.

45. See O. L. Janowsky, *Nationalities and National Minorities* (New York, 1945), pp. 37 ff., 166 f.

46. Literature dealing with the history of the revolution of the various national movements will be listed in subsequent chapters on the national groups. Literature on the constitutional reform movement concerning the national problem will be dealt with below, in Chap. XV. The following items serve as general introduction to the history of the Revolution as a whole.

As listed previously, see: Springer, *Geschichte Österreichs*, Vol. 2; Redlich, *Das österreichische Staats- und Reichsproblem*, Vol. I, part 1, and Vol. I, part 2.

The most important specific works are, Helfert, *Geschichte der österreichischen Revolution im Zusammenhang mit der mitteleuropäischen Bewegung* (narrative goes up to June, 1848); and, by the same author, *Geschichte Österreichs vom Ausgang des Wiener Oktoberaufstandes 1848*, 4 vols. (Prague, 1869–86), up to May, 1849. Both works are written from an extreme Conservative, German centralist viewpoint. See also Ernst Violand, *Soziale Geschichte der Wiener Revolution in Österreich* (Leipzig, 1850); [Franz Count Hartig], *Genesis der Revolution in Österreich* (Conservative); Maximilian Bach, *Geschichte der Wiener Revolution im Jahre 1848* (Vienna, 1892, socialist).

Biographies: The recollections of the two leading statesmen of the first revolutionary period are presented in Alfred von Arneth, *Johann . . . von Wessenberg*, 2 vols. (Vienna, 1897); F. von Pillersdorf, *Rückblicke auf die politische Bewegung in Österreich in den Jahren 1848 und 1849* (Vienna, 1849), and *Handschriftlicher Nachlass* (Vienna, 1863).

Characteristic for the interpretation of radical German liberalism are, Kudlich, *Rückblicke und Erinnerungen*; Schuselka, *Das Revolutionsjahr* (Vienna, 1850), Vol. II of 2d ed. of his "Deutsche Fahrten."

47. Important works on the German-Austrian national problem in connection with Frankfurt proceedings are:

Documents: *Stenographischer Bericht über die Verhandlungen der deutschen konstutierenden Nationalversammlung zu Frankfurt am Main* (Leipzig, Frankfurt, 1848–49). This will be cited in the following as *Sten. Ber.*

Outstanding general presentations of the work of the Frankfurt Assembly are, Heinrich Laube, *Das erste deutsche Parlament*. 3 vols. (Leipzig, 1849); Veit Valentin, *Die erste deutsche Nationalversammlung* (Munich, Berlin, 1919).

Also important in this respect is the same author's standard work, *Die deutsche Revolution von 1848–49*. 2 vols. (Berlin, 1930); and his briefer work in the English language, *1848; Chapters of German History* (London, 1940).

Monographs: Schüssler, *Die nationale Politik*; Telle, *Das österreichische Problem;* see also Redlich, *Das österreichische Staats- und Reichsproblem*, Vol. I, part 1, 141–64; Vol. I, part 2, 33–41.

Contemporary monographs: Bartholomäus Carneri, *Neu Österreich; Ein Wort über echten und falschen Constitutionalismus* (Vienna, 1861); Franz von Sommaruga, *österreichs Zukunft und dessen Stellung zu Deutschland* (Stuttgart, 1848).

Biographies: As representative of a number of memoirs and biographies of 1848 deputies at Frankfurt, the following are of particular significance: Julius Fröbel, *Ein Lebenslauf,* 2 vols. (Stuttgart, 1890, 1891); Franz Krones, *Moritz von Kaiserfeld, sein Leben und Wirken* (Leipzig, 1888); Kudlich, *Rückblicke und Erinnerungen;* Arneth, *Anton von Schmerling* (Vienna, 1895), concludes with the year 1849, and, *Aus meinem Leben,* 2 vols. (Stuttgart, 1883).

48. The use of the German terms in this context needs some explanation. The term *Grossdeutsch* has often been translated into English either as Great or as Greater German, the former translation being more accurate. Yet both translations bear a strong connotation of racial imperialistic Pan-Germanism, which the term *Grossdeutsch* acquired only in the course of later generations and which by no means expresses the rather specific meaning connected with it in the revolutionary period; that is, the idea to join Austria and Germany together in some kind of federal organization of basic German character, but generally implying at the same time the unimpaired preservation of the Austrian Empire as part of such union. The term *Kleindeutsch,* very inadequately translated into English as small or little German, conceives a German solution leaving the Austrian Power outside of the German union. Such a concept, however, does not preclude the existence of an Austro-German alliance such as that concluded in 1879. In contradiction to *Grossdeutsch* and *Kleindeutsch,* the term *Alldeutsch* of later days of integral nationalism can be perfectly translated as "Pan-German," which carries exactly those connotations which so often are erroneously connected with the *Grossdeutsch* of 1848.

Concerning the terminology *Grossdeutsch-Kleindeutsch* used in 1848 in connection with the Austrian problem (and originally these terms had no other connection) see Telle, *Das österreichische Problem,* pp. 19, 20.

49. For an analysis of the Austrian vote on these articles, see Schüssler, *Die nationale Politik,* pp. 34 ff. Reference to German and Austrian deputies in the course of this discussion means German non-Austrian and German Austrian deputies.

50. Redlich, *Das österreichische Staats- und Reichsproblem,* I, 1, 143. See also Schüssler, *Die nationale Politik,* pp. 19 ff.

51. *Ibid.,* p. 23.

52. *Ibid.,* pp. 19 ff. Throughout the following the terms confederation and federation are used in the same sense at the Frankfurt Convention; that is, basically in line with the doctrines of modern theory of constitutional law. Confederation is to be understood as that form of union of states in which the sovereignty of each member state in regard to international law is preserved; federation, as the closer form of union, in which the autonomy of the member states is restricted to more or less wide functions of internal administration; its member states do not possess any sovereignty in terms of international law. The German terms *Staatenbund* and *Bundesstaat,* as frequently used in Frankfurt, correspond to the English confederation and federation.

Particularly in regard to quotations, it should be remembered, however, that the terms federation and confederation frequently have been used indiscriminately even in recent literature.

53. On Palacký's policy toward the German confederation plan see particularly below, Chapter V, section on "The Czechs and the German Confederation."

54. Victor von Andrian-Werburg, vice chairman of the important constitutional committee of the assembly, was one of the outstanding promoters of this "German soil" tolerance. See Schuselka, *Das Revolutionsjahr,* p. 107; quoted from Schüssler, *Die nationale Politik,* pp. 24 ff.

The text of the Marek motion read as follows: Germany declares through her representatives:

"1. That she will never contribute to the suppression of any nationality.

"2. That all those citizens of a state allied with Germany should share the rights of all German citizens. The preservation and observation of this nationality should be guaranteed to them.

"3. The German language is the state language, but in those *Kreisen* where the majority speaks a non-German language, this other language will be introduced in communal and educational matters and as language in court." *Sten. Ber.*, p. 118; quoted in Schüssler, *Die nationale Politik*, pp. 25 ff. See also Redlich, *Das österreichische Staats- und Reichsproblem*, I, 1, 154 f.; Telle, *Das österreichische Problem*, pp. 63 f., 66 f.

55. See Redlich, *Das österreichische Staats- und Reichsproblem*, I, 1, 146 f.; I, 2, 34–39; also Helfert, *Geschichte Österreichs*, IV, 1; see also Friedjung, *Österreich von 1848 bis 1860*, I, 166–200, particularly pp. 184 ff., 193 ff. For an analysis of Schwarzenberg's German policy in connection with the imperialist concept of "Middle Europe" see below, Chapter XVIII, section on Schwarzenberg.

56. The study by Carneri, *Neu Österreich; Ein Wort über echten und falschen Constitutionalismus*, pp. 26 ff., conceives of five principal approaches to these problems. Apart from the fact that one of these schemes attempts to establish a union of the small and medium-sized German states as a balancing force between Austria and Prussia, these proposals only qualify the above analysis. The notion to boost up the position of the smaller states as the third Power in a confederation was frequently discussed from 1848 until the dissolution of the German *Bund* in 1866. It never materialized for two main reasons: Prussian and Austrian claims for exclusive hegemony, and the potential and actual inferior strength of the smaller states, which made them unable to compete, even combined with one of the two Great German Powers.

57. Telle, however, rightly points to the inconsistency that the Frankfurt Left supported the incorporation of the Czechs into Germany and the Croatians into Hungary. Telle, *Das österreichische Problem*, pp. 8 ff.

58. The following analysis is largely based on Schüssler, to some extent on Telle and Redlich, and on Sommaruga's writings. It is solely concerned with the views of Austrian deputies in Frankfurt.

59. Schüssler, *Die nationale Politik*, pp. 26, 58 ff. *Sten. Ber. 2885.* See also Chapter XIX, below, note 167.

60. Quoted from Unterrichter, *Ein paar Worte über die österreichische Frage*, in Schüssler, *Die nationale Politik*, p. 26. Unterrichter's treatise is not available.

61. Schüssler, *Die nationale Politik*, pp. 62 f. See also Andrian, *Österreich und dessen Zukunft*, 1, 162 ff.

62. Count F. X. Deym, *Drei Denkschriften*, pp. 22, 25, quoted in Schüssler, *Die nationale Politik*, pp. 21 f., 61 f.; see also Deym, *Friedrich Graf Deym und die österreichische Frage in der Paulskirche*, quoted in Schüssler, *Die nationale Politik*, but not available, and Deym, *Sten. Ber. 2882, 3783*, quoted in *ibid.*

63. See Redlich, *Das österreichische Staats- und Reichsproblem*, I, 1, 159; Schüssler, *Die nationale Politik*, pp. 61 ff.

64. Schmerling was minister of the interior, later prime minister of the Frankfurt shadow cabinet. Though for all practical purposes the representative of the Austrian government in Frankfurt, he joined the Schwarzenberg cabinet as minister of justice only in 1849. Although Schmerling's Austrian governmental mission curtailed his freedom of action even more severely than that of any other Austrian Frankfurt deputy, he was not fully subservient to the wishes of the Schwarzenberg cabinet and certainly less so to the preceding less autocratic Wessenberg ministry.

65. The obvious contradictory example is, seemingly, the tragic fate of the Frankfurt leftist deputy Robert Blum, who, for his participation in the October Revolution in Vienna, was court martialed and executed by Windischgrätz's military dictatorship. But although parliamentary immunity for Frankfurt deputies was openly flouted by Blum's execution, it cannot be said that Blum's conviction was directly connected with his activities at the Frankfurt Convention.

66. On Möring, see Schüssler, *Die nationale Politik*, p. 22, and the literature quoted there; Telle, *Das österreichische Problem*, pp. 64, 48 f.

67. On Schmerling in regard to Frankfurt see Friedjung, *Österreich von 1848 bis 1860*, I, 121 ff., 184 ff., 193 ff.; Redlich, *Das österreichische Staats- und Reichsproblem*, I, 1, 159, I, 2, 34 ff.; Schüssler, *Die nationale Politik*, pp. 54 ff.; Arneth, *Anton von Schmerling*,

II, 305. On Schmerling's after-revolutionary activities see below, Chapter XIX, section on "Return to German Centralism."

68. On Giskra, see Schüssler, *Die nationale Politik,* pp. 22, 49 f.; *Sten. Ber. 1203, 4656, 4661,* quoted there.

69. On Berger, see Schüssler, *Die nationale Politik,* pp. 23, 31, 56 f.; *Sten. Ber. 675, 2817, 5887,* quoted there. On Perthaler, see Schüssler, *Die nationale Politik,* p. 30; Red-lich, *Das österreichische Staats- und Reichsproblem,* I, 1, 715 ff., and below, Chapter XIX, section on "Return to German Centralism."

70. See Sommaruga, *Österreichs Zukunft und dessen Stellung zu Deutschland,* and, by the same author, *Der Ausgleich mit Ungarn* (Vienna, 1867); also Redlich, *Das öster-reichische Staats- und Reichsproblem,* I, 1, 160 ff., I, 2, 40 f.; Schüssler, *Die nationale Politik,* pp. 26 ff.; and Telle, *Das österreichische Problem,* pp. 64, 120.

71. Sommaruga, *Österreichs Zukunft,* p. 27.

72. *Ibid.,* pp. 36 ff. A plan similar in this respect was submitted to the assembly by Giskra two months after the publication of Sommaruga's work. See Schüssler, *Die nationale Politik,* pp. 49 f.

73. Sommaruga, *Österreichs Zukunft,* p. 16.

74. On Belcredi's project see below, Chapter XIX, section on Belcredi; on Jaszi's, see below, Chapter IV, section on "The First World War."

75. For similar plans regarding Galicia promoted by the Pan-Germans of the next generation, see section on the Pan-German idea, in this chapter.

76. See Rudolf Springer (pseud. of Karl Renner), *Grundlagen und Entwicklungsziele der österreichisch-ungarischen Monarchie* (Vienna, Leipzig, 1906), pp. 240–47.

77. Redlich, *Das österreichische Staats- und Reichsproblem,* I, 1, p. 161; see also pp. 162 f.

78. Yet even the draft of the German confederate constitution at Frankfurt did not disregard the national problem entirely, when in Article 188 it established a kind of minority protection for non-German nationalities within the confederation. See also in this respect the bill submitted by the Styrian deputy Mareck.

79. Redlich, *Das österreichische Staats- und Reichsproblem,* I, 1, p. 163.

80. Basic works for the study of the German problem in Austria from 1849 to 1860 are: Heinrich Friedjung, *Österreich von 1848–1860,* 2 vols. (Stuttgart, 1908, 1912), to which the first volume of the same author's *Der Kampf um die Vorherrschaft in Deutsch-land* (Stuttgart, 1897), forms a kind of continuation, though only as far as political history is concerned. See also Redlich, *Das österreichische Staats- und Reichsproblem,* and the previously mentioned works, Helfert, *Geschichte Österreichs;* Charmatz, *Öster-reichs innere Geschichte* (Leipzig, 1911), Vol. I; Bibl, *Von Revolution zu Revolution* (Vienna, 1922–24); Kolmer, *Parlament und Verfassung in Österreich,* Vol. 1; Czedik, *Zur Geschichte der österreichischen Ministerien,* Vol. 1; Walter Rogge, *Österreich von Vilagos bis zur Gegenwart* (Leipzig, 1872–73).

See further, Heinrich von Srbik, ed., *Quellen zur deutschen Politik Österreichs 1859–66,* 5 vols. in 6 (Berlin, 1934–38). This important collection of source material is primarily concerned with the history of the Austro-Prussian political conflict. It also contributes much significant information on the German Austrian internal problem.

Of particular significance for the understanding of the German national ideology and the rising German Austrian political party movements, though not confined to the period up to 1867, are, Schüssler, *Österreich und das deutsche Schicksal* (German national interpretation); Molisch, *Briefe zur deutschen Politik in Österreich von 1848–1918,* and *Geschichte der deutschnationalen Bewegung in Österreich.* Both of these studies, com-piled by a historian of strictly German national viewpoint, present important source material. See, further, the following contemporary pamphlets as significant examples of German ideology prevailing in the fifties and sixties of the nineteenth century: *Gesamt-petition der Völker Österreichs an seine Majestät den Kaiser* (Leipzig, 1861); B. Carneri, *Neu Österreich;* N. H., *Zur Einigung Österreichs* (Vienna, 1862); Poinz (pseud.), *Staat oder Nationalität?* (Leipzig, 1867). For literature on the representative German statesmen and political thinkers concerning the national reform movement, see the more comprehensive bibliographical notes to Chapters XVII–XIX, below.

81. The frequently used term "Bach regime" usually refers to the period from 1852–59, that is, when Alexander Back, after the death of Schwarzenberg, was the leading minister, though never technically prime minister. Bach was a member of the cabinet from 1849 on. The term "Bach Hussars" was a widely used, strongly derogatory term for the police force. However, in non-German territories, particularly in Hungary, the whole centralistic bureaucracy, police, and military forces functioning there were referred to by this name. On Bach's political concepts, see below, Chapter XVIII, section on Bach.

82. See Friedjung, Österreich von 1848–1860, I, 469–73, and the contemporary literature on Bach quoted there.

83. A brief and unpretentious study submitting the constitutional changes in Austria's internal organization giving the basic data on the subject is Bernhard Weisz, Die Verfassungen Österreichs seit 1848 und ihre unitaristischen und föderalistischen Elemente (Innsbruck, 1937). On this period see also below, Chapter XIX, sections on "Return to German Centralism" and "Belcredi," and the literature quoted there.

84. According to the Austrian-Cisleithanian December constitution a separate Austrian prime minister (Prince Carlos Auersperg) was appointed, however, in December, 1867.

85. For literature on the German problem from 1867 to 1918 see the basic works by Charmatz, Czedik, Kolmer, Molisch, and Schüssler, listed in note 80 of this chapter; these are relevant also for the period since 1867. The following items should be added: Bibl, Geschichte Österreichs im XX. Jahrhundert (Vienna, 1933); Rogge, Österreich seit der Katastrophe Hohenwart-Beust. 2 vols. (Leipzig, 1879), German Liberal standpoint, covering the period 1871–78. See also Fischel, Das österreichische Sprachenrecht (Brünn, 1901), and, by the same author, Materialien zur Sprachenfrage in Österreich (Brünn, 1910). These two last mentioned reference works of paramount importance for the study of the history of the Austrian nationality problem in general are a particularly fertile source of information for the understanding of the German national movement.

Monographs and biographies: Charmatz, Deutsch-österreichische Politik; Studien über den Liberalismus und die auswärtige Politik Österreichs (Leipzig, 1907); Heinrich Rauchberg, Die Bedeutung der Deutschen in Österreich (Dresden, 1908); Alexander von Peez, Die Aufgaben der Deutschen in Österreich (Vienna, 1907); Herman von Tinti, In letzter Stunde (Vienna, 1904); [Crown Prince Rudolph of Austria], Der Adel und der Konservatismus in Österreich (Vienna, 1879); Oskar von Mitis, Das Leben des Kronprinzen Rudolf (Leipzig, 1928).

The following works are representative of German liberalism from the early constitutional era on: Ernst von Plener, Reden (1873–1910). 3 vols. (Stuttgart, 1911) and, by the same author, Erinnerungen. 3 vols. (Stuttgart, 1911–21). The Liberal leader's speeches and memoirs are highly informative and characteristic of the rigid German Liberal-centralistic viewpoint, particularly in the later constitutional era.

See also Rudolph Sieghart, "Ernst von Plener; Zu seinem siebzigsten Geburtstag," Österreichische Rundschau, XXIX (1911), 95 ff.; Victor von Hochenburger, Neu-Babylon (Vienna, 1899), German national interpretation; Monsignor Joseph Scheicher, Erlebnisse und Erinnerungen. 6 vols. (Vienna, 1908–11), Catholic, Christian Social interpretation. Gustav Pollatschek, ed., Viktor Adler's Aufsätze, Reden und Briefe, with an introduction by Otto Bauer (Vienna, 1922–29), is a voluminous collection of essays, speeches, and letters of the founder and leader of the Austrian, and particularly the German Austrian, Social Democratic party, comprising a wealth of material and a running commentary on Austria's internal history from the 1880s to 1918, from a strictly Socialist viewpoint (see particularly sections VI, VIII, X). Renner, Der deutsche Arbeiter und der Nationalismus (Vienna, 1910), Socialist interpretation. Further literature on the principal German political party movements will be cited in the following sections.

86. See Charmatz, Österreichs innere Geschichte, I, 76 f. Hugelmann, Das Nationalitätenrecht des alten Österreich, pp. 98 f. Actually, the parliament consisted of 203 mem-

bers, elected from the diets. The exact proportion of Germans and non-Germans in the assembly as a whole cannot be given here, particularly since many of the members delegated from the big landowner's curias of the diets represented no distinct national affiliation. In any case, the Germans, then comprising little more than a third of the Cisleithanian population, held an absolute majority in the lower house. Furthermore, they held absolute majorities even in such crownland diets with large non-German majorities (of population) as Bohemia, Moravia, Carniola, Bukovina, and Silesia.

87. On Liberal party politics, in addition to the previously mentioned works, among them especially the works of Plener and Molisch, see also Eduard Suess, *Erinnerungen* (Vienna, 1915). The eminent geologian Suess was from the 1860s to the 1890s a leading German Liberal parliamentarian.

88. Ludwig Gumplowicz, *Österreichisches Staatsrecht* (Vienna, 1907), p. 72. According to Gumplowicz, the disloyalty to the constitution of 1867 consists in the fact that in 1873 the German Liberal parliamentary majority changed the electoral law against the Federalists' opposition to the effect that deputies henceforth were not to be delegates of the diets, but elected directly as members of central parliament. This implied, undoubtedly, a big further step toward centralism, but it is certainly incorrect to call this reform a disloyalty to the constitution.

Reference to the disintegration of the party in the 1880s means the rise of the radical German National (Pan-German) and Christian Social movements and their secession, or, rather, first the secession of their founders, from the Liberal party. Attempts to stem the rapidly growing disintegration of the German Liberal parliamentary organization, particularly after the 1890s, into radical nationals, Catholic Conservatives, increasingly Christian Socials and last and now least orthodox Liberals led to the foundation of the parliamentary "shelter" organization called *Deutscher Nationalverband* (German National Association), in 1910. This loose organization included all German parties except the Pan-Germans and the Socialists. The exact position of the true Liberals (in the Western sense) in that organization was highly ambiguous. The German Progressives, the official—and in competition with other affiliated groups, increasingly nationalist— remainder of the Liberal splendor in the seventies, had to bar Jews, with few exceptions, from their ranks, this as a price for their acceptance in the German *Nationalverband*. On the other hand, the very few, chiefly German-Jewish, Liberal deputies outside of the *Verband* could hardly claim to be representative of the once flourishing Liberal movement. Thus, actually even before the First World War, German liberalism as a parliamentary force was dead. See Molisch, *Geschichte der deutschnationalen Bewegung in Österreich*, pp. 218 f., 227 f.

89. English studies on modern Austrian history frequently translate *Christlichsoziale* as "Christian Socialists." This translation gives an erroneous impression of the character of this consistently anti-Socialists party. The correct translation is "Christian Socials," that is, a Christian, socially minded party.

90. According to the convention concluded at the Congress of Berlin, it was technically still a mere "occupation." The formal annexation followed only in 1908.

91. See below, Chapter V, section on "Hohenwart's Federalist Mission."

92. Typical manifestations of the old Liberal party spirit, upright, sincere, but incapable of understanding the social and national questions, are Ernst von Plener's long-winded explanations, frequently in brilliant dialectics, promoting the claim of the German state language, fighting the Bohemian *Staatsrecht*, defending the idea of the centralistic state against the federalized nationality state, and so forth. See particularly Plener, *Erinnerungen*, II, 253 f., 311 f., 385 f.; III, 451 ff., and so forth. See further, Molisch, *Briefe zur deutschen Politik in Österreich*, p. 209, the letter of February 11, 1879, written by the Clerical Conservative Count Falkenhayn to Count Richard Belcredi, on the imminent downfall of the Liberal regime and the reasons for this downfall. See also *ibid.*, p. 258, the notes of the deputy of the German Constitutional party (Liberal), Dr. Weeber, of December 13, 1879, on the alleged supranational character of the party. Also *ibid.*, pp. 266 ff., the letter by the elder Plener (Ignaz), former minister of finance

in the Liberal era, to his son, Ernst, December 15, 1886, on the German-Czech problem.

93. See also at this point Otto von Bismarck, *Gedanken und Erinnerungen* (Stuttgart), Vol. II, Chap. XXIX, on the conclusion and premises of the alliance.

94. On Count Taaffe see A. Skedl and E. Weiss, eds., *Der politische Nachlass des Grafen Eduard Taaffe* (Vienna, 1922), a well-interpreted collection of personal documents; R. Charmatz, "Der 'Kaiserminister' Graf Eduard Taaffe," in *Lebensbilder aus der Geschichte Österreichs*, Vienna, 1947, pp. 124 ff.; see further Czedik, *Zur Geschichte der k. k. österreichischen Ministerien*, Vol. I, particularly pp. 339 f., on the political character of Taaffe; pp. 390–391, on the handling of nationality and language questions under the Taaffe regime. See G. Pollatschek, ed., *Viktor Adler's Aufsätze*, Section X, and, in O. Bauer, *Österreichische Revolution* (Vienna, 1923), p. 21, an evaluation of the political balance of power in Austria which is particularly appropriate for the Taaffe era. "From 1860 to 1890 political life in Austria was dominated by the conflict between centralistic great bourgeoisie on the one hand, federalist feudal nobility on the other. The centralistic great bourgeoisie was represented by the German liberal parties, the federalist feudal nobility united under its leadership the German clericals with the Old Czechs [Czech bourgeois conservatives] and the southern Slavs. It was not a national conflict because Germans stood on either side." See also *ibid.*, p. 22, "Parallel with the German national movement against the liberal great bourgeoisie, the Young Czechs' opposition against the Old Czech followers of the feudal regime developed. In the elections to the Bohemian diet of 1890 the Old Czechs were swept away by the Young Czechs. Thereby Czech bourgeoisie had liberated itself from feudal leadership. The 'Iron Ring,' which had united the federalist parties under feudal leadership, was broken."

See also the following contemporary studies defending Taaffe's policy: *Graf Taaffe, 1879–1889; Eine innerpolitische Studie aus Österreich* (Leipzig, 1889), and Justus Austriacus (pseud.), *Zum 60. Gebertstag des Grafen Eduard Taaffe, 27 Februar 1883* (Vienna, 1883).

95. On Pan-Germanism in Austria see: Georges Weil, *Le Pangermanism en Autriche* (Paris, 1904); for the Pan-German and German-national viewpoint see Otto Hornung, *Neu Österreich* (Zürich, 1890); Herweg [Eduard Pichl], *Georg Schönerer und die Entwicklung des Alldeutschtums in der Ostmark*, 5 vols. (Vienna, 1921–35); Hochenburger, *Neu Babylon* (Vienna, 1899); Deutscher Verein in Wien, *Politisches Wörterbuch für die Deutschen in Österreich* (Vienna, 1885); Julius A. von Zeysig, *Die ungarische Krise und die Hohenzollern* (Berlin, 1905); *Österreichs Zusammenbruch und Wiederaufbau* (Munich, 1899).

See also Pollatschek, ed., *Viktor Adler's Aufsätze*, VIII, 390 ff. (Socialist interpretation). For a critical appraisal of important aspects of the Austrian Pan-German movement in English see Oscar Karbach, "The Founder of Modern Political Antisemitism: George von Schönerer," *Jewish Social Studies*, Vol. VII, No. 1 (January, 1945), 3–30; see further R. Charmatz, "Nationalismus als Phrase: Georg Ritter von Schönerer," pp. 141 ff. in his *Lebensbilder aus der Geschichte Österreichs* (Vienna, 1947).

Pan-German and German national literature on the World War development: E. V. Zenker, *Die nationale Organisation Österreichs* (Berlin [1915?]); Franz Jesser, "Organisation und Partikularismus in Österreich," *Österreichische Rundschau*, III (1917), 6 ff.; Munin (pseud.), *Österreich nach dem Kriege* (Jena, 1915); Friedrich G. Kleinwächter, *Der Untergang der österreichisch-ungarischen Monarchie* (Leipzig, 1920), Austro-German national interpretation.

Literature dealing specifically with the German-Czech conflict is generally referred to in Chapter V, below, sections on "The Institutional Evolution of the National Conflict" and "The Development of the Language Conflict."

Literature on Naumann and the revised central Europe concept, and so forth, is referred to below, in Chapter XXIV, section on "Mid-Europe."

96. Regarding the program of Linz see Sieghart, *Die letzten Jahrzehnte einer Grossmacht* (Berlin, 1932), pp. 305 f.; Plener, *Erinnerungen*, II, 233; Charmatz, *Österreichs*

*innere Geschichte,* II, 28; Fischel, *Materialien zur Sprachenfrage in Österreich;* Herweg [E. Pichl], *Georg von Schönerer,* Vol. 1.

97. See particularly Adolf Hitler, *Mein Kampf* (New York, Reynal and Hitchcock, 1941), pp. 125 ff., 158.

98. As used here, the term Pan-German movement refers to the Pan-German (*Alldeutsche*) idea as well as to the various radical German national organizations into which the movement was broken up in Austria as early as 1902, namely, first into Pan-Germans (Schönerer's immediate followers), and, secondly, into so-called Eastern Germans, under K. H. Wolf's leadership. Georg von Schönerer himself, the most powerful personality ever active in the movement until 1918, could not win a parliamentary seat after 1901.

To be sure, the Pan-German ideology was by no means confined to Schönerer's party, which decreased rapidly after 1902. It dominated ideologically all the radical German national groups and, to a large extent, the over-all organization of the German parties, the previously mentioned *Deutscher Nationalverband,* of 1910. In a new Pan-German party split in 1907, fourteen deputies formed the German Radical party under K. H. Wolf, only three deputies remaining faithful to Schönerer. In the elections of 1911, the last ones held in imperial Austria, the German Radicals gained seventeen seats, the Pan-Germans (Schönerer's followers), four. At that time, the German *Nationalverband* had nearly 100 parliamentary members. It is further necessary to keep in mind that the Pan-German movement in Austria was a kind of sectarian movement. Far more strongly than in loose parliamentary-party organizations was its spirit expressed in huge cultural organizations such as the German school association (*Deutscher Schulverein*), the *Südmark* (South-March), athletic organizations (*Deutscher Turnerbund*), and so on. On the early organization and tactics of the Pan-Germans in the wider meaning of the term, see Kolmer, *Parlament und Verfassung in Österreich,* Vols. III, IV. See also Theodor von Sosnosky, *Die Politik im Habsburgerreich,* 2 vols. (Berlin, 1912, 1913). II, 189 ff.

99. These repeatedly advanced proposals for the transformation of the Austrian Real Union with Hungary into a mere Personal Union, resting solely on the tenuous tie of a common sovereign must not be confused with the generally voiced criticism of the principles of the dualistic system. However unfortunate dualism admittedly was in the constitutional forms of 1867, its replacement by the Personal Union meant nothing but the last step toward the break-up of the empire. Promotion of this concept in this connection, clearly aiming at the monarchy's disintegration, had nothing in common with proposals to change the dualistic into a federal empire.

100. Typical of the national program of the official Pan-German party line was the following bill, introduced by Schönerer on April 23, 1901, in the Austrian parliament: "*The illustrious House should resolve:* that the Imperial, Royal government be asked to introduce bills

"1. Concerning the demarcation of territorial jurisdiction between the lands previously comprised in the German Bund (German-Austria) on the one hand, and Galicia and Bukowina on the other.

"2. Concerning the actual incorporation of Dalmatia into the lands of the Hungarian crown.

"3. Concerning the preservation of the German official language for the former lands of the German *Bund* (German Austria). . . ." Fischel, *Materialien zur Sprachenfrage in Österreich,* No. 12, p. 47.

Thus, the Austrian lands of the bygone German *Bund,* including Bohemia, Moravia, Carniola, Gorizia, and so forth, were still here actually considered German lands. In Schönerer's own words, they formed German Austria. See also Herweg, *Georg von Schönerer,* particularly Vol. I on the various party programs, particularly on plans for the conversion of the Real Union with Hungary into a mere Personal Union. For the demand concerning a customs union with Germany see *Politisches Wörterbuch für die Deutschen in Österreich,* edited by several members of the German national association (Vienna, 1885), article: "Zollunion," pp. 156 f., "The customs union between Austria and Germany is one of the most important points in the program of the German national party in Austria."

See Hochenburger, *Neu Babylon*. The author likewise comes out for the Personal Union with Hungary, for recognition of German as the official language, for and preservation of Austrian centralism in the German interest. Hochenburger, minister of justice in the Conservative centralistic Stürgkh cabinet from 1911–16, was not a Pan-German by party affiliation, but a representative member of the radical national wing of the *Nationalverband*.

In regard to the German-language question, see, as representative, the motion by the German national deputy, Bareuther, introduced in parliament on June 17, 1902, concerning the recognition of German as the official language. The use of a non-German language on the part of the non-German population in this respect was only permissible on the lower administrative levels—in the district administration—and even then only if the majority of the district's population was non-German and did not command the German language. This bill was not intended to be applied to Galicia, Bukovina, and Dalmatia. See Fischel, *Materialien zur Sprachenfrage in Österreich*, pp. 343 f.

See, further, the so-called "Osterbegehrschrift," 1915 (Easter petition) which advocated a strengthening of the alliance with Germany, including customs union, German official language in Austria, partition of Bohemia in national districts, and so on. Instigated by the chairman of the Pan-German Association in Germany, Dr. Class, it was drafted by the members of the parliamentary German *Nationalverband* as well as by the executives of the numerous German national academic institutions in Austria and executives of German associations and clubs, and so forth. This early program of the First World War is, therefore, far more representative for the spirit of the Pan-German movement than mere parliamentary motions. In the essential points this program was backed by the German *Nationalverband*. See Arthur von Polzer-Hoditz, *Kaiser Karl* (Vienna, 1929), pp. 389 f. (available in English); see also below, Chapter XXIV, section on "German Centralism's Final Course."

Concerning the huge, unofficial, Pan-German party literature see as characteristic examples:

"Austria must be rebuilt on German foundations as a part of Germany. Semi-German Austria must become a full German member of a new German Peoples house." *Österreichs Zusammenbruch und Wiederaufbau*, p. 4.

The aim must be the union of the central European German language territory in one state and the securing of an access to the Adriatic. *Ibid.*, p. 5. Silesia and Moravia ought to go to Prussia, Saxony to Bohemia, the Littoral and southern Dalmatia ought to be German bases in the Adriatic. Galicia and Bukovina should go to Hungary, Rumania or Russia, depending on the attitude of each of these countries, toward Germany. Full citizenship in this Great German Empire, which should include two kingdoms cut out of Austria, Ostmark and Südmark, was to be granted only to those who commanded the German language completely. The rest of the population was to be considered as "protective companions" [*Schutzgenossen*] who were not to be inducted into the army. Instead, they had to pay a special defense tax [*Wehrgeld*]. Their freedom of movement was to be restricted and no franchise was to be granted to them.

"Enforcement of the reincorporation of the Ostmark into the German Empire would be a worthy price of victory for the sacrifices made by Germany for three decades for her army. Only on this broader basis could Germany, with the support of her navy, attempt to gain the position in world economics which she needed for her preservation in coming centuries. 'Our future rests on the sea' [the famous saying of the 'Kaiser' (William II of Germany)]—but our presence lies between the Adriatic and the Baltic, between the Memel [river] and the channel." *Ibid.*, p. 14.

Zeysig, *Die ungarische Krise und die Hohenzollern*, pp. 33 f., likewise proposes the *Anschluss* of German Austria, including Bohemia, Silesia, Moravia, Carniola, German access to the Adriatic, and so forth. Hungary should be considerably enlarged by way of the incorporation of Galicia, Dalmatia, and Bosnia, and should be ruled by a younger son of the Hohenzollern dynasty.

See further as at least somewhat saner examples of the radical national program: Hornung, *Neu Österreich* (Zurich, 1890), particularly opposed to Taaffe's policy; Munin (pseud.), *Österreich nach dem Kriege*. The author was a moderate supporter of the old Schönerer program and proposes a partition of Austria into four parts:

1. The lands once belonging to the German *Bund*, plus Istria and Trieste (again, these "German" lands were to include the best part of Austria's Czech, Slovene, and Italian populations).

2. Croatia-Slavonia, Bosnia and Hercegovina, Dalmatia and Serbia.

3. Hungary minus Croatia-Slavonia.

4. Eastern Galicia and Bukovina plus a slice of Russian Poland, but not western Galicia, which might go to a Polish Vassal State or, as Munin frankly calls it, "Province," Poland. The German part of an Austria thus divided was to be administered on a strictly German centralistic basis. The franchise law had to guarantee to the German population in particular a parliamentary two thirds majority. Language rights of non-Germans were generally and in a limited way recognized only on the lowest administrative level of the district administration.

Kleinwächter, *Der Untergang der österreichisch-ungarischen Monarchie*, pp. 325 ff., refers to a program supported by many German deputies printed under the title, *Forderungen der Deutschen Österreichs zur Neuordnung nach dem Kriege* (date unascertainable). This program has much in common with the Pan-German "Eastern claims of 1915." It proclaims again the elimination of Dalmatia, Galicia, and Bukovina from the Austrian Empire organization proper. However, this program is less reticent than others regarding the future destiny of Dalmatia and the two Trans-Carpathian crownlands. They should be placed under military administration. The empire of Austria, minus these newly created military frontiers, was to be ruled in a truly German way. Customs union with Germany was advocated, likewise "reexamination" of the constitutional relations with Hungary. Territorial expansionism by way of access to the Aegean Sea—which necessarily implied, in some form, the incorporation of Serbia—was demanded. Kleinwächter adds, "At the time, when propaganda for this program was made, the outcome of the war was not any more in doubt for a clearly seeing observer." *Ibid.*, p. 326.

101. The most important document on the relatively moderate German national policy drafted by the last pre-World War generation was the so-called *Pfingstprogramm* (Whitsuntide program) of May, 1899, drafted by the German opposition in the Austrian parliament—except the Pan-Germans and the German Socialists—that is, the German Peoples Party, the German Progressives, the so-called Association of the large Estate owners faithful to the constitution (a kind of enlightened Conservative group), the Christian Social Association, and the Free German association. (See Fischel, *Materialien zur Sprachenfrage im Österreich*, No. 11, pp. 33 ff. for the text of this lengthy document.) The program pledged its allegiance to the constitution and in particular to the centralistic state (*Einheitsstaat*). It asked for the official designation of the name "Austria" for the Cisleithanian part of the monarchy program (*ibid.*, I, 3). The old demand for Galicia's exclusion reappears in a rather diluted form, asking for a guarantee that Austro-German national life should remain uninfluenced by the Polish parliamentary representation, (*ibid.*, I, 6). This referred, of course, to the Polish parliamentary alliance with the Conservative, allegedly anti-German, cabinets of Taaffe and his successors. Austrian relations with Hungary should be revised in the spirit of mutual equality, which had, since 1867, been practically shifted to Hungary's advantage (*ibid.*, I, 7).

The alliance with the German *Reich* was to be strengthened, particularly in regard to economic and cultural relations (*ibid.*, I, 8). Regarding the language question, the program formally deviated slightly from previous German platforms asking for the recognition of the German state language in Austria. Presently, only the recognition of German as the general and official language of mediation (*Vermittlungssprache*) among the various nationalities was demanded. German was to be the official language of all branches of the central government, including its intercourse with the crownland administrations. German was further to be the official language in government agencies in the crownlands, except in the Polish and Italian territories and in the Czech districts of Bohemia. The official language of intercourse between government and public was only in unilingual territories the language of those territories. In bilingual territories, German was to be used as second language of equal rights.

Concerning specific areas, the program practically advocated, in regard to the nationally most contested crownland,—Bohemia, full administrative partition along national lines. The Czechs were, of course, firmly and unalterably opposed to this proposal.

National curias were to be organized for the election of representatives for parliament, diets, townships, and so forth. Each national group had to set up a separate budget for educational purposes. Official intercourse of state agencies, even on the local level, was to be (exceptions provided, but not yet determined) in German alone. Bilingual organization was to take place in the crownland's capital of Prague, though the overwhelming Czech majority of population there was actually uncontested. (*Ibid.*, III, B).

Similar provisions were drafted for other bilingual crownlands, relatively the most liberal ones for the Italian part of Tirol, the most presumptuous demands being raised in regard to Carniola and Styria. In regard to Carniola, a crownland of homogeneous Slovene population (except for the scattered German-language communities), recognition of a general, bilingual German-Slovene character was claimed. The same demand was raised for southern Styria which was predominantly Slovene. Here, the outrageous claim was made that the language of instruction in all secondary schools in Slovene districts should be German and that all entries in public registers should be made in German. Similar demands were made in regard to Carinthia and her Slovene border territories, and Silesia with her trilingual German, Czech, and Polish population (*ibid.*, III, E-H).

102. On the Christian Social party movement see Kolmer, *Parlament und Verfassung in Österreich*, Vols. IV–VIII; for the Christian-social viewpoint see Franz Stauracz, *Dr. Karl Lueger* (Vienna, 1907); Rudolph Kuppe, *Karl Lueger und seine Zeit* (Vienna, 1933), and, by the same author, a briefer study, *Dr. Karl Lueger, Persönlichkeit und Wirken* (Vienna, 1947); Richard von Kralik, *Lueger und der christliche Sozialismus* ([Vienna?], 1923). As general background reading see the previously listed memoirs by J. Scheicher, and R. von Kralik, *Österreichische Geschichte* (Vienna, 1919), Catholic viewpoint.

For criticism of Christian Social policies from the German Austrian Liberal viewpoint see G. Kolmer, *Parlament und Verfassung in Österreich*, Vols. IV–VIII; for criticism from the Austrian Socialist viewpoint see Gustav Pollatschek, ed., *Viktor Adler's Aufsätze*, in particular VIII, 373 ff., XI, 62 ff., 106 ff.

103. The Christian Social movement emerged technically from the same national associations as the Pan-German movement, that is, the German National Association, the Reform Association, and others. In 1887, the Christian Social Association, the forerunner of the party organization, was founded. In the elections of 1888, the Pan-Germans and the Christian Socials still campaigned on a common platform. The leader of the new party, Lueger, as Schönerer, had previously been a mandatary of the Liberal party.

It would not do, though, to draw any precipitate conclusions from these facts in regard to the intellectual foundations of the Christian Social party. If one realizes that, until the early 1880s the Liberals held a practical monopoly of all German political activities except those of the Socialists, Lueger's Liberal background carries no great weight as evidence of a supposed basic Liberal element in the Christian Social movement. Neither does the fact that the German opposition breaking away from the Liberals did not immediately, but only after a few years' time, split into a Catholic and a National movement, lead to the conclusion that a particularly strong tie existed between the Catholic and the Radical Nationalist movements.

The Christian Social movement, though technically in a way an offspring of the Liberals and the Pan-German nationalists as well, was basically built on a doctrine entirely of its own, a fact which would have appeared more obvious but for the violent anti-Semitic current in the early history of the party. See Charmatz, *Österreichs innere Geschichte*, II, 27 ff.; Kolmer, *Parlament und Verfassung in Österreich*, Vols. III–V.

Concerning the history of the party, it should be made clear that the Christian Social movement must in no way, not even in its intellectual foundations, be confused with the German Clerical Conservatives, who were prominent in Tirol, yet with the rise of the Christian Social party decreased rapidly in political significance. These groups represented entirely different, generally higher, social strata than the Christian Socials. There was a touch of a Conservative-Federalist policy in their concepts which gave them a position somewhat closer to that of Conservative Czech and Polish party groups. See, for instance, Wieser, *Über Vergangenheit und Zukunft der österreichischen Verfassung*, p. 90; Molisch, ed., *Briefe zur deutschen Politik in Österreich*, pp. 116 ff., 139, quoting political letters on the possible cooperation between Tirolese Clerical Conservatives and Old Czechs in 1870 and 1871.

104. In this respect of great ideological importance in the history of the Christian Social party was the Social reform movement under Carl von Vogelsang's (1819–90) intellectual leadership which—opposed to Manchester liberalism and Jewish economic influence—moved in the direction of Christian corporate concepts. On Vogelsang see Wiard Klopp, ed., *Die sozialen Lehren des Freiherrn Karl v. Vogelsang* (St. Pölten, 1894); R. Charmatz, "Ein konservativer Sozialpolitiker: Karl Freiherr von Vogelsang," in *Lebensbilder aus der Geschichte Österreichs* (Vienna, 1947), pp. 112 ff.; R. Charmatz, *Österreichs innere Geschichte*, I, 126 f.; G. Kolmer, *Parlament und Verfassung in Österreich*, III, 362 f.; R. Kann, "German-speaking Jewry during Austria-Hungary's Constitutional Era (1867–1918)," *Jewish Social Studies*, Vol. X, No. 3 (1948), 39–56.

105. For Hitler's evaluation of the Christian Social party organization as superior to that of the Pan-Germans and on his estimate of Lueger as "the greatest German mayor of all times," see *Mein Kampf* (Reynal and Hitchcock ed.), particularly pp. 71 f., 88, 125–29, 158. (Lueger became mayor of Vienna in 1897).

106. See below, Chapter XXI.

107. See, for instance, Seton-Watson, *Racial Problems in Hungary* (London, 1908), p. 184. Also his *The Southern Slav Question and the Habsburg Monarchy* (London, 1911), pp. 295, 340.

108. One of the most interesting of the few such proposals is the Utopian essay of the Christian Social deputy, Monsignore Dr. Joseph Scheicher, *Traum aus dem Jahre 1920*, written before the outbreak of the First World War. It foresees in 1920 an Austria converted into a federal empire, the "United Eastern States." Scheicher conceives this federal empire, organized along ethnic lines, foremost as a bulwark against Pan-Germanism. He promotes an extension toward the east by incorporating the Serbs and the Rumanians beyond the borders in southern Slav and Rumanian member states of the new Austrian federation. Far-reaching political and social reforms (curtailments of the rights of the crown, socialization of heavy industry, and so on) are part of Scheicher's interesting proposals which, of course, did not meet with the approval of official Austria. See Rudolf Wolkan, *Der österreichische Staatsgedanke im Zeitalter Franz Josephs*, "Mitteilungen des österreichischen Institutes für Geschichtsforschung, Suppl. Vol. XI" (Innsbruck, 1929), pp. 834 ff.; Scheicher, *Erlebnisse und Erinnerungen*, 6 vols. (Vienna, 1898–1911).

109. See below, Chapter XXIII.

110. On the Social Democratic party see Kolmer, *Parlament und Verfassung in Österreich*, Vols. IV–VIII.

Socialist literature: Ludwig Brügel, *Geschichte der österreichischen Sozialdemokratie*, 5 vols. (Vienna, 1925), the standard work in the field; Julius Deutsch, *Geschichte der österreichischen Gewerkschaftsbewegung* (Vienna, 1908); Pollatschek, ed., *Viktor Adler's Aufsätze* (on the party organization and history see particularly sections VI, XI). See also Engelhart Pernerstorfer, *Zeitfragen* (Vienna, 1917); Bauer, *Die Nationalitätenfrage und die Sozialdemokratie* (1st ed., Vienna, 1907; 2d ed. with a new introduction, 1924). See further, *Protokoll der Verhandlungen der österreichischen Sozialdemokratischen Parteitage* (Vienna). See particularly year 1888/89, on the foundation of the party; 1897, 1899, and 1917, on the national question. The Socialist periodical *Der Kampf* contains many very interesting studies in this field.

Non-Socialist literature: Karl Reinold, *Die österreichische Sozialdemokratie und der*

*Nationalismus* (Vienna, 1910), which criticises the Socialist nationality program from the German national viewpoint; see also Anon., "Sozialdemokratische Politik," *Österreichische Rundschau*, XXI (1909), 81–88 (Conservative viewpoint). The principal works by Karl Renner and O. Bauer dealing with the Austrian nationality problem are listed below in Chapter XX. See this chapter for more detailed bibliographical information. In English see the comprehensive study of Charles A. Gulick, *Austria from Habsburg to Hitler* (Berkeley, Los Angeles, 1948), Vol. I, Chap. II.

111. See above, Chapter II, and below, Chapter XVI.

112. See R. Charmatz, "Gärung vor Klärung in der Arbeiterbewegung: Heinrich Oberwinder," pp. 95 ff. in his *Lebensbilder aus der Geschichte Österreichs* (Vienna, 1947).

113. Claims to supranational organization of their party systems were, however, made by other parties as well, so for a time by the German Liberals. Yet they were never seriously put into political practice. See Molisch, *Briefe zur deutschen Politik in Österreich*, p. 258. It is true, however, that the great landowners at one time or another formed parliamentary supranational associations. However, these groups, favored by the curia francisc system, represented such an infinitesimal part of the population that they could scarcely be called parties in a truly democratic sense. Several major parties in Austrian parliamentary history were organized on the basis of religious affiliation, but practically always combined with the principle of national organization as well.

114. See Rudolf Springer (pseud. of Karl Renner), *Grundlagen und Entwicklungsziele der österreichisch-ungarischen Monarchie*, pp. 238–39. Engelbert Pernerstorfer, in his polemic with Hermann Bahr in the latter's *Schwarzgelb* (Berlin, 1916), p. 205, states, "You are a fanatical Austrian with soul and body. I am an Austrian with my brain: in my heart I am and remain a German." See also Pernerstorfer, *Zeitfragen*, pp. 20 ff., and the declaration of Otto Bauer, as secretary for foreign affairs of the young Austrian Republic in parliament on June 7, 1919, published also in *Unser Friede!*, "Flugblätter für deutsch-österreichisches Recht," No. 35 (Vienna, 1919).

115. See Brügel, *Geschichte der österreichischen Sozialdemokratie*, V, 77 ff., Pollatschek, ed., *Viktor Adler's Aufsätze*, VIII, 81 ff., *Protokoll des Parteitages 1917*; Reinold, *Die österreichische Sozialdemokratie und der Nationalismus*, pp. 40 ff., 277 ff., in regard to the southern Slav opposition, 100 ff.

116. See particularly below, Chapter XX, section on Bauer.

117. The fact that the peace treaty of St. Germain between the Allied and Associated Powers and Austria was to bar the *Anschluss* was not foreseen by the Austrian National Assembly, which voted for the union with Germany in the autumn of 1918.

118. See below, Chap. XVI.

119. See Polzer-Hoditz, *Kaiser Karl*, pp. 551 f.; see also below, Chapter XXIV, sections on "German Centralism's Final Course" and "The Concepts of Peace Policy."

## IV. THE MAGYARS

1. The following works may serve as a general introduction to the problems of the Magyar-dominated Hungarian kingdom. A greater part of this literature than that on any other national group of the empire has been written in English. It is, however, of very unequal value. Part of it has been inspired by Magyar propaganda, yet a very substantial remainder represents outstanding contributions in the field. Specific literature will be listed in later sections of this chapter. For literature on the non-Magyar Hungarian nationalities see the following chapters on Croats, Slovaks, Serbs, Rumanians, and Ruthenians. For literature on the Hungarian constitutional problem see primarily Chapter I, above.

1) Magyar history. All items in this group represent a definite Magyar national viewpoint.

*a*) General background: Bálint Hóman and Julius Szekfü, *Magyar Történet* [History of Hungary], 5 vols. (Budapest, 1935–36), the modern, standard history of Hungary; László von Szalay, *Geschichte Ungarns*, 3 vols. (Pest, 1866–75), up to the beginning of the eighteenth century; Michael Horvath, *Geschichte der Ungarn bis zum Jahre 1825*, 3 vols. (Pest, 1873). See also, by the same author, *Kurzgefasste Geschichte Ungarns*, 2 vols. (Pest, 1863), to 1848.

*b*) General history and history of the nineteenth and twentieth centuries: Dominic G. Kosáry, *A History of Hungary* (Cleveland, New York, 1921), contains a good bibliography; Julius Szekfü, *Der Staat Ungarn* (Stuttgart, 1918), excellent short presentation; Rustem Vámbéry, *Hungary—To Be or Not To Be* (New York, 1946), radical-progressive approach; Count Paul Teleki, *The Evolution of Hungary and Its Place in European History* (New York, 1923), excellent bibliography, much material on socioeconomic problems, but biased.

*c*) Magyar Hungarian history since 1848: Albert Berzeviczy, *Az abszolutizmus kora Magyarországon* [The era of absolutism in Hungary], 3 vols. (Budapest, 1922); Gustav Gratz, *A dualizmus kora* [The era of dualism], *1867–1918*, 2 vols. (Budapest, 1934).

2) Non-Magyar historical literature: C. M. Knatchbull-Hugessen, *The Political Evolution of the Hungarian Nation*, 2 vols. (London, 1908); C. A. Macartney, *Hungary* (London, 1934), excellent work.

3) Nationality problem: Julius Szekfü, *État et nation* (Paris, 1945), authoritative modern Magyar study on the problem; Oscar Jászi, *The Dissolution of the Habsburg Monarchy* (Chicago, 1929), excellent work; Ernst Flachbarth, *Histoire des minorités* (Paris, 1944); Scotus Viator (pseud. of R. W. Seton-Watson), *Racial Problems in Hungary* (London, 1908); R. W. Seton-Watson, *The Southern Slav Question and the Habsburg Monarchy* (London, 1911). Both of Seton-Watson's works are standard works on the Hungarian nationality problem. They are strongly critical of the Magyar nationality policy. See also Raimund F. Kaindl, *Geschichte der Deutschen in Ungarn* (Gotha, 1912). The more radical Magyar viewpoint on the nationality problem is presented in the polemics against Seton-Watson in Count Joseph Mailáth, *A Vindication of Hungary* (London, 1908), in the above-quoted work by Teleki, and in the items listed under 5, below.

4) Constitutional problems: See particularly the previously listed works, written from the Magyar viewpoint, that is, Heinrich Marczali, *Ungarisches Verfassungsrecht;* Julius Andrássy, *Ungarns Ausgleich mit Österreich vom Jahre 1867;* Albert Apponyi, "Die rechtliche Natur der Beziehungen zwischen Österreich und Ungarn." See the following works giving a non-Magyar interpretation: Louis Eisenmann, *Le Compromis austro-hongrois de 1867;* Ivan Zolger, *Der staatliche Ausgleich zwischen Österreich und Ungarn;* [A. Fischhof and S. Unger], *Zur Lösung der ungarischen Frage* (Vienna, 1861). See also Josef Redlich, *Das österreichische Staats- und Reichsproblem.*

5) Economics: Alexander von Matlekovits, *Das Königreich Ungarn*, 2 vols. (Leipzig, 1900), standard work.

6) General (collected works on Magyar history, politics, law, economics, culture, and so forth): Joseph von Jekelfalussy, ed., *The Millennium of Hungary and Its People* (Budapest, 1897); A. von Berzeviczy, ed., *Ungarn* (Budapest, 1917). Both works contain some excellent contributions by Magyar experts in various fields.

Bibliography: *Történeti Szemle* [Historical Review] (Budapest, 1912–   ); Géza Petrik and Sándor Kiszlingstein, eds., *Bibliographia Hungarica*, 7 vols. (Budapest, 1885–1903); *Bibliographica Hungariae, in non-Magyar language, 1861–1921* (Berlin, 1923). See also Karl Uhlirz (Mathilde Uhlirz, ed.), *Handbuch der Geschichte Österreichs* (Graz, 1927–41).

2. Count Stephen Széchenyi (1791–1860) on November 27, 1842, in the Hungarian Academy of Sciences, founded by him. Quoted by Arthur von Polzer-Hoditz, *Kaiser Karl* (Vienna, 1929), p. 45.

3. Rudolf Springer (pseud. of Karl Renner), "Warum uns die ungarische Verfassung imponiert?", *Österreichische Rundschau* (II), 1905, 189–204. See also Scotus Viator (pseud. of R. W. Seton-Watson), *Ungarische Wahlen* (Leipzig, 1912).

4. There were also forty Croatian deputies in the Hungarian parliament whose status, according to the Hungaro-Croatian Compromise of 1868, was, however, not comparable to the position of the other nationality representatives, in so far as they participated in

parliamentary activities as delegates of the Croatian diet (*Sabor*), but only in regard to common affairs of Croatia and Hungary.

5. The above and following data are taken from the official *Annuaire statistique hongroise* (Budapest), Matlekovits, *Das Königreich Ungarn*, Vol. 1, and particularly from Jaszi, *The Dissolution of the Habsburg Monarchy* (Chicago, 1929), pp. 271 ff. See below, Appendix 1. On the peculiarities of Hungarian nationality statistics see also Seton-Watson, *Racial Problems in Hungary*.

6. See Julius Bunzel, *Ungarn und wir* (Berlin, 1918), on the agricultural distribution of land in Hungary. In the First World War period, 46 percent of the Hungarian land was still held by farms comprising more than 1,000 Hungarian *Joch* (roughly about 1,100 acres), 94 families held about 15.5 millions of *Joch* and their landed property had substantially increased in the period after 1867. *Ibid.*, pp. 77 f.

See further, Jászi, *Revolution and Counter-Revolution in Hungary* (London, 1924), pp. 6 f., referring to the situation as of early autumn, 1918: "There is hardly any other country with so lamentable a system of land distribution as Hungary, where a comparatively diminutive proportion of the land is in the possession of the peasant farmers and a relatively enormous proportion in the hands of the large landowners. Frequently a single owner holds domains of immense size. Apart from pasture and forest land, which are naturally the predominant type among the large estates, the cultivable area in Hungary is roughly 24,000,000 hectares divided into about 2,800,000 agricultural holdings. Of these 2,400,000 small estates (up to 20 yokes) account for barely 7,600,000 hectares, while 3,977 large estates of over 1,000 yokes account for 7,452,640 hectares. The contrast is still more striking if we include pasturage and forest lands, which are mainly in private hands, and if we remember that in Hungary estates of 20,000 yokes are nothing unusual, and in many cases belong to a single owner.

"The situation is rendered still worse by the large extent of entailed property: including meadows and forest lands, the area of entailed property totals 15,680,000 yokes (without Croatia and Slavonia). . . .

"A hectare is 2.47 acres. The Austrian *joch* ("yoke") is 0.575 hectares, or about 1.42 acres."

See Louis Eisenmann, *Cambridge Modern History*, XII, 205 f., for a succinct statement of the Magyar franchise in force until 1918: "The electoral system of Hungary is even worse than that of Schmerling [see below, Chapter XIX, section on "Return to German Centralism"]; its extreme complexity—there are thirty-six electoral qualifications—gives clear evidence of the intention to confine the electoral franchise almost exclusively to the Magyars, and, amongst these, to a few privileged classes. The electoral arrangements give to the Magyars a representation which may be twelve times as great in proportion to their numbers as that of the Roumanians, for instance. The procedure for deciding upon electoral qualifications allows the Minister presiding over the offices in which the lists of voters are drawn up to exclude practically all the electors of whom he disapproves from the exercise of their rights. The proportion of the electors to the population, which has been steadily decreasing for some time, has now sunk to 52.5 per mile. One-fourth of the electors are officials or employees of the state. Under these conditions and in consequence of historic tradition, the political and parliamentary staff is chosen almost exclusively from one caste, that of the lesser nobility."

See also Rudolf Springer (pseud. of Karl Renner), "Warum die ungarische Verfassung uns imponiert?"

7. Dominic G. Kosáry, an ardent Magyar nationalist, has this to say on the Magyar Liberal party, in *A History of Hungary*, p. 311, "Everyone was proud of the admittedly great strides forward made possible by recent liberal reforms [the period from 1867 to 1905]. But a historian cannot fail to recognize the lack of consideration for social and national issues." And further, "During the ascendancy of the liberal party there was no serious interest in social problems, simply because not a single member's election depended on the ballot of workers. The policy and social outlook of the party were decided by its members and these were mostly of that party of the old, well-to-do stock of educated noblemen that had retained its wealth. . . . The Liberal Party was char-

acterized by conservative Liberalism, professing the principle that no development was to be interfered with beyond the granting of equality before the law. It refused to interfere even where this would have meant positive assistance and protection for the lower classes. It allowed free passage for the sudden growth of capitalism, but for a long time it left agricultural and industrial laborers to their fate." *Ibid.*, pp. 313 f. See also on this point R. A. Kann, "Hungarian Jewry during Austria-Hungary's Constitutional Period (1867–1918)," *Jewish Social Studies*, Vol. VII, No. 4 (Oct., 1945), 357–86.

8. In the course of the second half of the nineteenth century, substantial industrial enterprises developed in the non-Magyar territories, but, with the exception of Croatia, they were predominantly Magyar-owned.

The fact that the Hungarian nationalities had no upper classes comparable in their social structure to the Magyar nobility has been hotly contested by Kossuth. "This constitution, which we transferred in 1848 from the narrow ground of privileges to the broad basis of popular liberty, was not founded on the rule of one race, but of one class. The privileges of nobility, which entitled them to all constitutional benefits, were never exclusively preserved for the Magyar race, every other race in the country had their equal share in them. Altogether the racial question had nothing to do with the limits of constitutional rights. While thousands of non-Magyars held privileges of nobility, more than five millions of true Magyars were excluded from the benefit of constitutional rights." L. Kossuth, *Meine Schriften aus der Emigration* (Pressburg, Leipzig, 1880–82), II, 149, quoted from Julius Szekfü, *Der Staat Ungarn.*

This assertion is based on the demagogical abuse of distorted half-truth. It is true, of course, that there existed legal discrimination against the overwhelming majority of the Magyar population, but Kossuth remains absolutely silent on the discrimination against the non-Magyars, which certainly is not contradicted by the fact that a few thousands of non-Magyars as compared to more than 700,000 Magyars (!) enjoyed the privileges of nobility (Kosáry, *A History of Hungary*, p. 188). Even these few thousands, with the exception of a negligibly small group of landed aristocrats in Croatia, belonged largely to the nobility "by letter," a group of insignificant economic influence.

9. The only European peoples racially closely related to the Magyars are the Finns and the Estonians.

10. From Michael Vörösmarty, *Szózat* (a summons) (1936), translated by W. Kirkconnel, in *The Magyar Muse* (Winnipeg, 1933).

11. Friedrich von Wieser, *Über Vergangenheit und Zukunft der österreichischen Verfassung* (Vienna, 1905), p. 29.

12. Friedrich Tezner, *Die Wandlungen der österreichisch-ungarischen Reichsidee* (Vienna, 1905), pp. 112 f. Tezner and Wieser, in referring to the Hungarians, actually mean only the Magyars.

13. Wieser, *Über Vergangenheit und Zukunft der österreichisch-ungarischen Verfassung*, p. 131.

14. The impact of the Magyar national tradition was so powerful that Emperor Francis, before issuing the imperial declaration of 1804, considered whether he ought not call himself emperor of Hungary and make Hungary the pivot of the monarchy. This concept of Hungarian, that meant Magyar, leadership in the empire was advanced again after 1867, and particularly during the First World War period, though in a very different context. See Redlich, *Das österreichische Staats- und Reichsproblem*, I, part 2, 46. See further Wilhelm Schüssler, *Das Verfassungsproblem im Habsburgerreich* (Stuttgart, Berlin, 1918), p. 223 f.; Polzer-Hoditz, *Kaiser Karl*, pp. 87 f. See also note 86 in this chapter and below, Chapter XXIV, sections on "German Centralism's Final Course," "Mid-Europe," and "The Concepts of Peace Policy."

15. The close connections between the Magna Charta and the Bulla Aurea have been stressed in D. Kosáry, *A History of Hungary*, pp. 33 f. See also Elemer Hantos, *The Magna Carta of the English and of the Hungarian Constitution* (London, 1944). Actually, the Magyar Bulla Aurea of 1222, as the Magna Charta, regulated primarily the relations between crown and nobility. Yet, unlike the history of the British document, later in-

terpretation of the Bulla Aurea did not conceive it, to the same extent, as the foundation of a broad system of civic liberties.

16. "Nomine autem et appellatione populi hoc in loco intellige solummodo dominos praelatos, barones et alios magnatos, atque quoslibet nobiles, sed non ignobiles. . . . Plebis autem nomine soli ignobiles intelliguntur." See *Tripartitum*, Werböczi, p. II, title VI, quoted by Eisenmann, *Le Compromis austro-hongrois de 1867*, pp. 546, 529 f. The tripartitum was considered the statute book still in force until 1848. See Marczali, *Ungarisches Verfassungsrecht*, pp. 8 f.

17. Rudolf Springer (pseud. of Karl Renner), "Warum uns die ungarische Verfassung imponiert?"

18. See also below, Chapter XVII, section on Stadion, and Chapter XIX, section on "Return to German Centralism."

19. Alexander Dárday, "The Administration," p. 262 in Jekelfalussy, ed., *The Millennium of Hungary and Its People;* Marczali, *Ungarisches Verfassungsrecht*, pp. 123 ff. Hungary, including Croatia, comprised, in 1910, ninety-nine *Comitats*, respectively municipal townships invested with a limited administrative autonomy.

20. See Rudolf Springer (pseud. of Karl Renner), "Warum uns die ungarische Verfassung imponiert?" While Renner is sharply critical of the undemocratic administrative procedure in the *Comitat* system, he recognizes the potentialities for comprehensive empire reform entailed in this system. On the *Kreis* system see particularly below, Chapter XV, section on "The *Reichstag* of Kremsier," and Chapter XVII, section on Stadion; see also above, Chapter II, note 45.

21. *a)* Contemporary Literature on the Reform Period: Michael Horváth, *25 Jahre aus der Geschichte Ungarns von 1823–1848*, 2 vols. (Leipzig, 1867); Count Georges Andrássyi, *Umrisse einer möglichen Reform in Ungarn im Geiste des juste milieu* (London, 1833); Alexius Fényes, *Ungarn im Vormärz* (Leipzig, 1851); Josef von Eötvös, *Die Reform in Ungarn* (Leipzig, 1846), not available; L. Kossuth, *Ungarns Anschluss an den deutschen Zollverband* (Leipzig, 1842).

See also the following anonymous pamphlets: *Stimmen aus Ungarn angeregt durch den bevorstehenden Landtag, mit besonderer Berücksichigung der jüngst erscheinenen Schrift "Österreich und dessen Zukunft"* (Erlangen, 1843); *Guter Rat für Österreich, mit Bezugnahme auf das Programm der liberalen Partei in Ungarn* (Leipzig, 1844); N. M., *Slawen und Magyaren* (Leipzig, 1844); N. M., *Ungarische Wirren und Zerwürfnisse* (Leipzig, 1846).

*b)* Modern literature: Hans Platz, *Das historische Recht und das österreichisch-ungarische Ausgleichsproblem von 1849–1862* (Leipzig, 1930); Hanns Schlitter, *Aus Österreichs Vormärz*, Vol. III, "Ungarn" (Vienna, 1920).

*c)* Biographies: Aurel von Kecskeméthy, *Graf Stephan Széchenyi's staatsmännische Laufbahn* (Budapest,. 1866); Francis Pulszky, *Meine Zeit, mein Leben*, 4 vols. (Pressburg, Leipzig, 1880), see Vols. 1 and 2; Eduard Somogyi, *Ludwig Kossuth* (Leipzig, 1894); J. B. Moore, *Kossuth* (New York, 1895); Dominik Kosáry, *Kossuth Lajos a reformkorban* (Budapest, 1946). Széchenyi's main works have not been translated from the Magyar.

22. Central governmental agencies concerned with Hungarian affairs were, at that time: the War Council, the Court Chamber (entrusted with the administration of finances), and the Crown Council, which actually was the imperial cabinet under Metternich's and Kolowrat's direction, responsible to the emperor alone. Consequently, the central government still had wide authority in Hungarian affairs. See Friedrich Tezner, "Der österreichische Kaisertitel, seine Geschichte und seine politische Bedeutung," *Zeitschrift für das private und öffentliche Recht*, ed. C. Grünhut (XXV), 363.

23. In fact, the central government after 1840 was not absolutely unwillingly to cooperate with some of the moderate reformers, such as Count Dessewffy, Szécsen and Apponyi, Baron Jósika, and Széchenyi himself, in regard to Hungarian constitutional reforms, at least in the direction of wider powers for the Estates. Particularly Metternich was not personally opposed to such a policy, though the speed of the revolutionary events made all previous tentative reform attempts in this direction appear, soon enough,

as academic. See Redlich, *Das österreichische Staats- und Reichsproblem*, I, 2, 22 f., 47 f., Kosáry, *A History of Hungary*, pp. 200 f. He was much in sympathy with the aims of Magyar nationalism led by the nobility in the limited sphere of the ancient "historic rights," whereas the state minister, Count Kolowrat, representative for the claims of the Bohemian nobility, sided to a very limited degree with the interests of national movements of the Slav nationalities in Hungary. See, as examples of contemporary, moderate Conservative views on the Hungarian reforms, *Stimmen aus Ungarn angeregt durch den bevorstehenden Landtag*. This anonymous study advances reform plans for Hungary in line with those promoted by Andrian for Austria. See also A. [Count Georges Andrássy ], *Umrisse einer möglichen Reform in Ungarn im Geiste des juste milieu.*

24. See Kossuth, *Ungarns Anschluss an den deutschen Zollverband*, pp. 45, 57 (taken from Kossuth's editorials in the *Pesti Hirlap*). Kossuth originally was not opposed to a common tariff policy with the Austrian lands. Under the impact of Friedrich List's central European customs union plans, expressed in his "Das nationale System der politischen Ökonomie" (1841), he completely reversed his standpoint and promoted the nationalist idea of a completely independent Hungarian customs system with the professed aim of protecting a still insignificant Hungarian industry. At that time, a preferential tariff between Austria and Hungary was in existence. The complete customs union with Austria was favored by Széchenyi. See also Marczali, *Ungarisches Verfassungsrecht*, p. 21, and Anton Springer, *Geschichte Österreichs seit dem Wiener Frieden 1809* (Leipzig, 1863-65); M. Horvath, *Fünfundzwanzig Jahre aus der Geschichte Ungarns von 1823–1848* (Leipzig, 1867), II, 341-49.

25. See N. M., *Ungarische Wirren und Zerwürfnisse*. This pamphlet opposes the ruthless Magyarization policy directed against the Slavs. The intolerant Magyar viewpoint, directed chiefly against Magyar leaders such as Deák and Széchenyi, moderate in national questions, is upheld in N. M., *Slawen und Magyaren*. See also Helfert, *Geschichte der österreichischen Revolution*, 2 vols. (Freiburg, 1907-9).

26. See also Kosáry, *A History of Hungary*, pp. 217 f., Szekfü, *État et nation*, pp. 36, 46 f.

27. Michael Károlyi, *Fighting the World: the Struggle for Peace* (New York, 1925), p. 37. See also Milan Hodža, *Federation in Central Europe* (London, 1941), p. 71. Hodža was the last Czechoslovakian prime minister before the Munich crisis and a Slovakian deputy in the Hungarian parliament before 1914. See below, Chapter XIX, section on Kossuth.

28. Kossuth, *Meine Schriften aus der Emigration* (Pressburg, Leipzig, 1881, 3 vol. ed., authorized German translation), II, 148 ff., 157. These quotations are taken from a lecture, "Essay about Hungary," delivered by Kossuth in 1858.

29. M. Hodža, *Federation in Central Europe*, pp. 20 f., Helfert, *Geschichte der österreichischen Revolution*, I, 443; Springer, *Geschichte Österreichs seit dem Wiener Frieden 1809*, II, 131 f.

30. E. Glaise-Horstenau, *The Collapse of the Austro-Hungarian Empire* (London, 1930), pp. 194 f.

31. On the negotiations of the diet in Bratislava, see Springer, *Geschichte Österreichs seit dem Wiener Frieden 1809*, II, 124 f.; Helfert, *Geschichte der österreichischen Revolution*, I, 87 ff., 154 ff., 431 ff., Horvath, *Kurzgefasste Geschichte Ungarns*, II, 436 ff.

32. On the well-planned constitutional development in Hungary compared to the precipitate events in Austria in the early revolutionary period, see Friedjung, *Österreich von 1848–1860*, I, 36 ff. See further Redlich, *Das österreichische Staats- und Reichsproblem*, I, 1, 84, on the admiration of German Liberals for Hungarian reformism.

See also the Austro-German Liberal pamphlet, *Guter Rat für Österreich. Mit Bezugnahme auf das Programm der liberalen Partei in Ungarn*, (Leipzig, 1847) on the Hungarian reform policy. "On whatever points our conditions are superior to those in Hungary, higher standard of general education, greater prosperity, all that is counterbalanced and supplemented by the freer political institutions in Hungary, the greater freedom of speech and resolution, the perfect parliamentary training. We have the structure, they the superstructure; we have the basis of a free and strong constitution, they have the constitution itself." *Ibid.*, p. 36.

33. See Marczali, *Ungarisches Verfassungsrecht*, pp. 22 f.; Friedjung, *Österreich von 1848 bis 1860*, I, 46 f. The reform laws with an introductory interpretation by E. Bernatzik have been published in German. E. Bernatzik, ed., *Österreichische Verfassungsgesetze* (Vienna, 1911), pp. 78 ff. The influence of the Belgian constitution of 1831 on the Hungarian April laws of 1848 is generally recognized.

34. The Military Frontiers, the administrative districts along the southern boundary of Hungary, chiefly but not exclusively settled by Croatians and Serbs, were social and administrative institutions of a very original character. Created in the late sixteenth century and endowed with privileges during the following centuries, they were completely incorporated into Hungary proper and Croatia only in the last quarter of the nineteenth century.

Originally, they were founded as a kind of buffer territory, as bulwarks against dreaded Turkish drives towards the west and north. The settlers there received land as hereditary fiefs with the obligation of taking up arms against attacks from the east. The frontiersmen and their families, under the supreme administration of the imperial army, lived in strictly regulated semimilitary communities of a primitive, half-communist character. Perthaler says they lived under a constitution of military-patriarchic character. See H. L. Perthaler, *Österreichische Desorganisation und Reorganisation* (Vienna, 1861), pp. 97–99.

The standard work on the Military Frontiers is Johann H. Schwicker, *Geschichte der österreichischen Militärgrenze*, 4 vols. (Teschen, 1883). See also the imperial manifesto of June 10, 1848, on the subordination of the Military Frontiers under the Hungarian ministry and the guarantee of noninterference with the nationality, language, and religion of the frontier population, published in Franz von Hartig, *Genesis der Revolution in Österreich* (Leipzig, 1850), pp. 367 ff.

35. Magyar literature usually refers to the Hungarian parliamentary institutions prior to 1848 in the sense of royal assembly, *Reichstag*, German literature merely as "diet," (*Landtag*). Only since 1867 is reference usually made to the Hungarian "parliament."

36. On the language conflict see particularly below, Chapter VII, section on "Croatia's Autonomy within Hungary."

37. The only exception was the concession to the Italian communities in the Hungarian Littoral—above all Fiume—which were permitted the use of Italian during this transition period.

38. See A. C. Popovici, *Die vereinigten Staaten von Gross-Österreich* (Leipzig, 1906), p. 151; see also Helfert, *Geschichte der österreichischen Revolution*, I, 154 ff.; Springer, *Geschichte Österreichs seit dem Wiener Frieden 1809*, II, 131 f.; Szekfü, *État et nation*, Part 1, 11–103.

39. One of the best of the briefer surveys, imperial in viewpoint, yet by no means anti-Magyar, is the first volume of H. Friedjung, *Österreich von 1848–1860*, 2 vols. (Stuttgart, 1908, 1912). J. A. von Helfert, *Der ungarische Winterfeldzug und die oktroyierte Verfassung, 1848–1849* (Prague, 1886), German centralistic viewpoint.

Magyar presentations, all of them written from a strictly national viewpoint, include the following: Michael Horvath, *Geschichte des Unabhängigkeitskrieges in Ungarn, 1848–1849* (Pest, 1872), in Magyar and German; Julian Chownitz, *Geschichte der ungarischen Revolution in den Jahren 1848 und 1849*, 2 vols. (Stuttgart, 1849); Nikolaus Jósika, *Zur Geschichte des ungarischen Freiheitskampfes*, 2 vols. (Leipzig, 1851). Memoirs of Magyar leaders during the war: Francis Pulszki, *Meine Zeit, mein Leben* (see particularly Vol. II); Arthur Görgey, *Mein Leben und Wirken in Ungarn in den Jahren 1848 und 1849*, 2 vols. (Leipzig, 1852). G. Klapka, *Aus meinen Erinnerungen* (Zürich, Vienna, 1887). On Kossuth during the revolution see, A. Frey, *Ludwig Kossuth*, 3 vols. (Mannheim, 1849); P. C. Headley, *The Life of Louis Kossuth* (Auburn, 1852).

40. Magyar historiography often distinguishes between the revolution in the non-Hungarian Habsburg lands from March, 1848, onward and the War of Independence from Jelačić's invasion of Hungary in September, 1848, to the capitulation of Világos in August, 1849. Undoubtedly, from a military point of view, the actions which took place from the fall of 1848 to August, 1849, had the character of a full-fledged war. From the

imperial Austrian viewpoint, the warlike character of the conflict was politically established only with the Hungarian Declaration of Independence on April 14, 1849. It is, thus, correct to consider the entire conflict from March, 1848, to August, 1849, as the Revolution, of which the War of Independence forms a part.

41. See Friedjung, *Österreich von 1848–1860,* I, 64 ff.

42. See *ibid.,* pp. 59 ff.; Seton-Watson, *Racial Problems in Hungary,* pp. 32 ff.; H. Wendel, *Der Kampf der Südslawen* (Frankfurt, 1925), pp. 269 ff.

43. See also below, Chapter VII, section on "The Greater Croatian Idea."

44. Typical of these pro-Magyar revolutionary sentiments are Friedrich Engels's articles in the *Rheinische Zeitung,* written in 1849. See *Aus dem literarischen Nachlass von Karl Marx, Friedrich Engels und Ferdinand Lassalle,* ed. Franz Mehring, Vol. III (Stuttgart, 1902). See particularly pp. 233–45.

Particularly western European, and also British and American, public opinion was thoroughly sympathetic with the cause of the Magyar Revolution, but any active intervention was, of course, never seriously considered. See Charles Sproxton, *Palmerston and the Hungarian Revolution* (Cambridge, 1929); M. E. Curt, *Austria and the United States, 1848–52* (Northampton, 1926); Kosáry, *A History of Hungary,* chapters VIII and IX.

45. See Seton-Watson, *The Southern Slav Question,* p. 35: "Then at the eleventh hour, when ruin stared him in the face, Kossuth laid before the revolutionary diet at Szeged a law guaranteeing the free development of all nationalities upon Hungarian soil. Here at length were genuine linguistic concessions on paper, paper which was worthless. A law, which if voted in March 1848, might perhaps have rallied the whole of Hungary in support of Magyar pretensions, was worse than useless in July 1849 . . . when overwhelming masses of Russian troops were closing in on every side. . . . The Szegedin concessions contain no allusion to Croatia; and in any case it can hardly be doubted that at that moment nothing short of complete independence under the Habsburg crown would have satisfied Jelačić and his countrymen."

Actually, there existed an earlier draft of another nationality law favorably reported by a committee of the Hungarian *Reichstag* of 1848, which never became a statute. According to J. Ludvigh, a former Liberal member of the revolutionary parliament and later a fellow exile of Kossuth, this bill, drafted on Kossuth's insistence, was more liberal to the nationalities than the subsequent law of Szegedin. See Janos Ludvigh, *L'Autriche despotique et la Hongrie constitutionelle* (Brussels, 1861), pp. 119 ff. For the text of this draft, see *Ibid.,* pp. 117 ff. Its authenticity is not clearly established, yet the influence of the bill on the Hungarian nationality law of 1868 cannot be excluded.

Of particular interest are the following points:

INTRODUCTORY REMARKS

". . . The equality of the nationalities formulated by Kossuth. . . .

"What will happen in the interest of the nationalities? Will the inhabitants divide the state territory according to their language?

"This is, in fact, impossible because the nationalities are intermingled or, at least, it is politically impossible without exposing the state to dissolution and without prejudicing the rights and security of the citizens of the other nationalities.

". . . The inhabitants of a state who speak different languages in the interest . . . of developing their nationality will associate with one another (like members of the same church).

"The community of language is of the same social significance as the community of religion. It has to be developed by means of association within the state and not by placing it above the state, which would mean the dissolution of the state. . . .

"This association has nothing in common with the state and the state has nothing in common with it. . . .

THE DRAFT OF THE DIET'S COMMISSION ON THE OFFICIAL USE OF LANGUAGES
..........................

"1. All the Hungarian citizens, whatever language they speak, are politically only one nation, the one and indivisible Hungarian (Hongroise) nation, according to the historic concept of the Hungarian state.

"2. All races which inhabit the country, such as Magyars, Slavonians, Roumanians, Germans, Serbs, Ruthenians, enjoy equal rights as nationalities and, within the limits of the political unity of the kingdom and on the basis of association and individual liberty, can look after their specific national interests without restrictions.

...........................

*A. Individuals and corporations*

"Article 1. Every citizen is free to use his mother tongue in all actions which he addresses to the community, to his comitat and to the central authorities.

"Article 3. In the communal assemblies everyone can use his maternal idiom.

"Article 4. Each communal assembly decides for itself which will be its official language; it is up to the minority to use its own idiom in the discussion.

"Article 5. The communal authorities, in their official relations with those whom they govern, shall use the language of the latter.

"Article 6. The religious communities freely regulate all their particular affairs and especially what idiom should be used in the official registers and in elementary education.

"Article 7. Each denomination and each nationality has the same right of asking the state to support those communities which are unable to maintain [services of] worship and instruction themselves.

"Article 8. Each denomination and each nationality is free to establish secondary schools and universities. The decision what should be the language of instruction . . . lies with the individual or the corporation which establishes it—some right of inspection by the state is to be reserved.

"Article 9. In the state schools the ministry of public education decides on the language of instruction; . . . it has to take into consideration the idioms used in the respective parts of the country.

"Article 10. Special chairs of language and literature will be set up at the university for each idiom used in the country.

*B. The Comitats*

"Article 11. In the reunions of the comitats, all those who have the right to speak are free to use their maternal idiom.

"Article 12. The general assembly of the comitat decides the language to be used in the minutes and in the official files. However, each nationality represented in the comitat has the right to ask, in addition, that its minutes be written in its own language.

"Article 13. In all cases where the official language of the minutes is not Magyar, it will be written, in addition, in Magyar, in the interest of the right, of control on the part of the central (Hungarian) authorities.

"Article 14. The judicial officials of the district are obliged to use the idiom of the communities and citizens of the comitat when dealing with them. . . .

"Article 15. The comitats correspond with each other in the Magyar language. However, those comitats which speak the same official non-Magyar language may also use this idiom in their mutual relations. . . .

"Article 17. The comitats have their correspondence with the central authorities in the Magyar language.

*C. The central authorities*

"Article 18. The Hungarian (Magyar) language is the official language of the central authorities.

"Article 19. The state employees and the dignitaries are selected according to merit and individual capacity without any regard to nationality.

"Article 20. The ministers [of state] have to watch that the different nationalities are represented in the central administrations by a sufficient number of individuals capable of handling the cases coming in from authorities or individuals in the mixed districts. . . .

*D. The Diet*

"Article 21. The Magyar language is used in the deliberations and the actions of the Diet.

"Article 22. The laws are published in all idioms used in the country; the translation is done officially under the direction of the Diet.

"Article 23. All laws contrary to the preceding provisions are null and void.

"Article 24. The rights assured in this way to all nationalities existing in the country are declared fundamental laws and placed under the safeguard of national honor."

On the obvious relationship of this bill which never materialized to the notions of personal autonomy developed by Kossuth in exile, see below, Chapter XIX, section on Kossuth.

46. The previously mentioned main works of Eisenmann, Redlich, Friedjung, and, from the Magyar viewpoint, Kosáry, are important on the period from 1849 to 1868.

The modern Magyar standard work on the neo-absolutist era in Hungary is Albert Berzeviczy, *The Era of Absolutism in Hungary*, 3 vols. (Budapest, 1922); the Magyar viewpoint is further represented in C. M. Knatchbull-Hugessen, *The Political Evolution of the Hungarian Nation*, Vol. II; Bartholomew de Szemere, *Hungary from 1848 to 1860* (London, 1860), Conservative Magyar viewpoint; and E. von Wertheimer, *Graf Julius Andrássy*, Vol. I (Stuttgart, 1910).

Contemporary Magyar works: Except for the writings of the political exiles abroad (see below, Chapter XIX, section on Kossuth), this literature is chiefly represented here by Conservatives, who were the only political group in Hungary not fully restricted in their writings. See in this respect Count Coloman von Mailáth, *Fünf Brücken zum Staate* (Leipzig, 1860), and *Ungarn und die Centralisation* (Leipzig, 1850); Paul von Somssich, *Das legitime Recht Ungarns und seines Königs* (Vienna, 1850); [Paul von Somssich?], *Patriotische Wünsche eines Ungarn für Gesamt-Österreich* (2d ed., Nördlingen, 1860); *Eine Adresse der ersten politischen Notabilitäten Ungarns vom Jahre 1857* (Leipzig, 1861), Address signed by Count Emil Dessewffy, Josef von Eötvös, Counts George Apponyi, George Mailath, Jr., Anton Szécsen, Sámuel Jósika, etc.; Anon., *Die Conservativen in Ungarn und die Zentralisation* (2d ed., Leipzig, 1850); Anon., *Die Lebensfrage Österreichs* (Brunswick, 1860); Anon., *Zur ungarischen Frage; Eine Denkschrift von einem ungarischen Patrioten* (Leipzig, 1859).

For the German Austrian Liberal viewpoint see O. B. Friedmann, *Zehn Jahre österreichischer Politik 1859–1869*, 2 vols. (Vienna, 1879); and Anon., *Betrachtungen eines Österreichers über das kaiserliche Handschreiben vom 9. September 1857* (Leitomischl, 1860).

On Deák and the constitutional conflict preceding the conclusion of the Compromise of 1867 see particularly: Francis Deák, *Ein Beitrag zum ungarischen Staatsrecht; Bemerkungen über Lustkandl's ungarisch-österreichisches Staatsrecht* (Pest, 1867). This famous exposition of the Magyar constitutional viewpoint, preceding the conclusion of the compromise, represents the answer to Wenzel Lustkandl, *Das ungarisch-österreichische Staatsrecht* (Vienna, 1863), Austrian centralist viewpoint; [Francis Deák], *Drei Jahre Verfassungsstreit* (Leipzig, 1864). See also Franz Schuselka, *An Franz Deák* (Vienna, 1861), Austro-German traditional Federalist viewpoint; E. Warren, *Über Deák's Rede* (Vienna, 1861); Franz Schmitt, *Die Rechtsverhältnisse Ungarns zu den übrigen Ländern der österreichischen Monarchie* (Vienna, 1861). The treatises of Lustkandl, Warren, Schmitt, and Schuselka represent diverse Austrian reactions to the ideas of this founding father of dualism. Count Coloman von Mailath, *An Franz Schuselka* (Pest, 1861), reasserts the Deákist Magyar viewpoint.

Biographies: J. A. Forster, *Francis Deák* (London, 1860); Francis von Pulszky, *Franz Deák* (Leipzig, 1876); Anton Csengery, *Franz Deák* (Leipzig, 1877). The two last-mentioned works are written from a strictly Magyar viewpoint. See also Gustav Steinbach, *Franz Deák* (Vienna, 1888).

Redlich, *Das österreichische Staats- und Reichsproblem*, Vol. II, contains a good bit of documentary material on Deák's policy, in German translation. On the constitutional problems see further the literature on the dualistic concept in Chapter I, above, and below, Chapter XIX, sections on Belcredi and "Opposition to Dualism." See also below, Chapter XIX, sections on Eötvös and Kossuth, for literature on Eötvös and Kossuth in the postrevolutionary period.

47. Friedjung, *Österreich von 1848 bis 1860*, I, 381.

48. For the text of the constitution, see Redlich, *Das österreichische Staats- und Reichsproblem*, I, 2, 215 ff.; for comment, *ibid.*, I, 1, 355 ff.; for text and interpretation see E. Bernatzik, ed., *Österreichische Verfassungsgesetze* (Vienna, 1911), pp. 146 ff.; see also Eisenmann, *Le Compromis austro-hongrois de 1867*, 156 ff., and Seton-Watson, *The Southern Slav Question*, pp. 52–64, and below Chapter XVII, "the transition to absolutism" section on Stadion.

The fact that, from the revolution *de jure* until the Magyar-Croatian Compromise of 1868, the ties between Hungary and Croatia-Slavonia and—until the Austro-Hungarian Compromise of 1867—those between Hungary and Transylvania were severed was a consequence, not of the never-enforced March constitution of 1849, but of specific imperial ordinances. Neither the status of Croatia-Slavonia nor that of Transylvania (the first largely, the latter almost wholly, subject to the rule of German centralism) during that period corresponded to the promises of the paper constitution of 1849. Only the first part of the imperial promise—independence from Hungary—but not its second—autonomous position within the empire—was thus fulfilled.

49. See also the imperial edict of November 18, 1849, setting up the autonomous Serb Voivodina and the Banat of Temesvar, by separating the administration of these territories, for all practical purposes, from Hungary.

50. See particularly Friedjung, *Österreich von 1848–1860*, I, 350 ff., 378 ff., 387 ff. A whole new territorial organization of the court system, with the cooperation of eminent Magyar lawyers considerably accelerating the course of justice, was introduced by Schmerling, then imperial minister of justice. Registers of landed property were introduced. The abolition of personal agricultural services in Austria proper (except Galicia) generally took place between 1848 and 1853. Somewhat similar, though less sweeping, reforms were put through in Hungary by the Bach regime. The materialization of such reforms as also instigated in Hungary's revolutionary era in 1848 would scarcely have been feasible under the ruling Magyar regime prior to 1848 and after 1867. See at this point the great compendium of Magyar national history: G. Beksics, in Alexander Szilagyi, ed., *A Magyar Nemzet története* [History of the Hungarian Nation], X, 445, quoted from Friedjung, *Österreich von 1848 bis 1860*, I, 352.

51. See *ibid.*, pp. 388 f., and the literature quoted there.

52. That is, primarily, announcement of ordinances in the various languages of the land, instead of in Magyar alone, and the permission for everybody to approach the government authorities in his own language. *Ibid.*, pp. 377, 409.

53. Kosáry, *A History of Hungary*, pp. 255 f.

54. See above, Chapter XIX, section on Kossuth.

55. Quoted in Friedjung, *Österreich von 1848 bis 1860*, I, 371; see also pp. 373 f., 391 f.

56. *Ibid.*, pp. 394 ff.

57. On this split within the nobility see Redlich, *Das österreichische Staats- und Reichsproblem*, I, 1, 325 ff.; on Windischgrätz's plans for a revised Estates order and the restoration of the prerevolutionary Hungarian constitution see *ibid.*, pp. 351 ff. See also Friedjung, *Österreich von 1848–1860*, I, 144 ff., and 373, 445; and Schlitter, *Aus Österreichs Vormärz*, Vol. III, "Ungarn," on the sympathies of the retired chancellor, Prince Metternich, for the viewpoint of the Magyar Conservatives. See also Herman Kriebel, *Feldmarschall Fürst Windischgrätz* (Innsbruck, 1929), and Paul Müller, *Feldmarschall Fürst Windischgrätz, Revolution und Gegenrevolution in Österreich* (Vienna, 1934). See also below, Chapter V, sections from "Czech Cultural Evolution" through "The Czechs from the Revolution to the Hohenwart Regime." See also Chapter XVII, section on Windischgrätz, Chapter XVIII, section on Schwarzenberg, and Chapter XIX, section on Szécsen.

58. See Anon. (probably Somssich), *Patriotische Wünsche eines Ungarn für Gesamt-Österreich;* Somssich, *Das legitime Recht Ungarns und seines Königs*, particularly pp. 127 f.; see also Redlich, *Das österreichische Staats- und Reichsproblem*, I, 2, 180 f.; Friedjung, *Österreich von 1848–1860*, I, 397 ff.; Eisenmann, *Le Compromis austro-hongrois de 1867*, pp. 152, 180 f.

59. Kemény's main political works are *Forradalom után* [after the revolution] (1850), and *Még egy szó forradalom a után* [another word after the revolution] (1851). See also Eisenmann, *Le Compromis austro-hongrois de 1867*, pp. 153 f., Friedjung, *Österreich von 1848-1860*, I, 53 ff., 400.

60. See below, Chapter XIX, section on Eötvös.

61. For the preliminary history of the compromise after 1859 and 1860 see Redlich, *Das österreichische Staats- und Reichsproblem*, I, 1, 464 ff., and practically all of Vol. II. Redlich also presents the most important parts of Deák's drafts of the Hungarian diets' addresses to the emperor in 1861. See also Eisenmann, *Le Compromis austro-hongrois de 1867*, pp. 205-400; Platz, *Das historische Recht und das österreichisch-ungarische Ausgleichsproblem von 1849-1862;* Friedjung, *Der Ausgleich mit Ungarn* (2d ed., Leipzig, 1877).

Further selected items on the history of the compromise, stressing historicopolitical rather than legal aspects—the latter having been listed in Chapter I—are: O. B. Friedmann, *Zur Einigung Österreichs* (Vienna, 1862), containing a German Liberal proposal for a dualistic empire constitution under Magyar-German leadership. The national problem should be settled within the existing historic and political boundaries. Austria should quit the German *Bund* and conclude an alliance with the German lands, the nucleus of future Germany. These proposals come remarkably close to the ideas promoted by Deák.

Josef von Helfert, *Revision des ungarischen Ausgleiches* (Vienna, 1876), written from an imperial centralist viewpoint, promotes an expansion of the functions common to Austria and Hungary. See further Alexander von Spitzmüller (common minister of finance in the First World War period), "Franz Joseph und der Dualismus," pp. 103 ff., in E. von Steinitz, ed., *Erinnerungen an Franz Joseph* (Berlin, 1931), written from an Austro-German centralist viewpoint. See also above, Chapter I, and below, Chapter XIX, sections on Szécsen, "Return to German Centralism," Belcredi, and "Opposition to Dualism."

62. See Redlich, *Das österreichische Staats- und Reichsproblem*, II, 268 ff.

63. See particularly, *ibid.*, pp. 270 ff., and 258 ff., with particular reference to the reunion with Transylvania. See also Seton-Watson, *The Southern Slav Question*, pp. 55 f. Seton-Watson attributes the Magyar-Croatian Compromise largely to the Croatian confidence in Deák's loyalty in contrast to the vacillating policy of the Austrian government. Though none of the other non-Magyar Hungarian nationalities had a legal chance to participate in the political decisions of 1867, Deák was not unmindful of the state of public opinion among the national groups.

64. See Seton-Watson, *Racial Problems in Hungary*, p. 160; Redlich, *Das österreichische Staats- und Reichsproblem*, I, 286.

65. See Seton-Watson, *Racial Problems in Hungary*, pp. 140 ff.; Redlich, *Das österreichische Staats- und Reichsproblem*, II, 230 ff., 272 ff., and Chap. XII.

66. See Seton-Watson, *The Southern Slav Question*, pp. 52 ff.; for the background history see also Redlich, *Das österreichische Staats- und Reichsproblem*, II, 203 ff. See in Seton-Watson particularly appendices III and IV, pp. 350 ff., containing the address of the Croatian diet of June, 1848, to the emperor on the severance of constitutional ties with Hungary. See also the diets' declaration of 1861 concerning the recognition of the Personal Union with Hungary and the Croatian willingness to enter a new constitutional bond with Hungary on the basis of complete autonomy and equal state rights. See [Francis Deák] *Franz von Deák's Denkschrift über das Verhältnis zwischen Ungarn und Kroatien* (Vienna, 1861). See also below, Chapter VII, section on "The Greater Croatian Idea."

67. For text and interpretation of the Hungarian-Croatian Compromise see E. Bernatzik, *Österreichische Verfassungsgesetze*, pp. 733 ff.; in English see, for the text, Seton-Watson, *The Southern Slav Question*, pp. 361 ff., and, for an analysis of its terms, *ibid.*, pp. 65 ff. Heinrich Marczaly, *Ungarisches Verfassungsrecht*, pp. 154 ff., representing the Magyar standpoint, does not recognize a Croatian state, but merely a separate territory endowed with specific autonomous rights, that is, in Magyar legal terminology, a *corpus*

*adnexum* of the Hungarian crown. See also below, Chapter VI, sections on "Croatia's Autonomy" and "The Greater Croatian Idea."

68. See Paragraph 59 of the Hungaro-Croatian Compromise.

69. On the compromise in the light of continued administrative practice see Seton-Watson, *The Southern Slav Question*, pp. 85 ff.

70. For the text of the law see Gustav Steinbach, ed., *Die ungarischen Verfassungsgesetze* (Vienna, 1900), published in English in Seton-Watson, *Racial Problems in Hungary*, pp. 429 ff.; see also *ibid.*, pp. 147 ff., and Jaszi, *The Dissolution of the Habsburg Monarchy*, pp. 314 ff. For the background history of the law see Redlich, *Das österreichische Staats- und Reichsproblem*, II, 286 ff.; Eisenmann, *Le compromis austrohongrois de 1867*, pp. 549 ff. See also H. I. Bidermann, "La loi hongroise sur les nationalités," *Revue de Droit International*, I (1869), II (1870); Szekfü, *État et nation*, pp. 84 f.

71. That is, the concept of territorial autonomy to be discussed below, in Chapter V, section on "The Institutional Evolution of the National Conflict."

72. See this draft in Seton-Watson, *Racial Problems in Hungary*, pp. 421 ff.; Redlich, *Das österreichische Staats- und Reichsproblem*, II, 286 ff.

73. Jaszi, *The Dissolution of the Habsburg Monarchy*, pp. 315 f. To mention only a few points, the law in its final adopted form proclaimed Magyar as the official language of the state in the broadest meaning of the term. Provisions were made, however, that in county assemblies a second language might be used, if desired by at least one fifth of the members. In official intercourse with individuals, the latter's language was to be applied "as far as possible" (Paragraph 6), a provision which, probably against the intentions of the sponsors of the law, was skillfully employed to put the protective measures out of operation. (See Seton-Watson, *Racial Problems in Hungary*, pp. 151, 159). The same clause was affixed to Paragraph 27 on the right of the nationalities to fill civil service positions. The right of each individual to use his own language in court and also church autonomy were granted. Elementary and secondary education in the languages of the nationalities was to be secured (Paragraph 17).

Furthermore, a separate Education Act of 1868, drafted under Eötvös's direct sponsorship, determined in a very liberal spirit the principles of the nationality law in matters of education. Yet, unlike the nationality law itself, which *at pompam et ostentationem* remained unchanged on the Statute book, the Education Act was subject to several revisions. A law of 1879, by the simple means of making the appointment of a teacher dependent upon the testimonial of a state inspector of schools certifying his ability to teach in Magyar in an elementary school, made it possible to deny the teaching qualification of any non-Magyar by the arbitrary decision of one Magyar nationalist official. Subsequent laws of 1891, 1893, and particularly of 1907 frequently made the operation of schools in a non-Magyar language of instruction well-nigh impossible. This was largely a consequence of governmental demands for instruction in Magyar covering an increasingly great part of the curriculum, scarcely veiled discrimination against non-Magyar teachers, and, in regard to higher education, against students as well. See Jaszi, *The Dissolution of the Habsburg Monarchy*, pp. 315 f.; Seton-Watson, *Racial Problems in Hungary*, pp. 205–33, Kosáry, *A History of Hungary*, pp. 334 ff. See also Scotus-Viator (pseud. of R. W. Seton-Watson), "Die ungarische Unterrichtsgesetzgebung und die Nationalitäten," *Österreichische Rundschau*, XVII (1908), 242 ff.

74. See Seton-Watson, *Racial Problems in Hungary*, pp. 148 ff., pointing out that this ambiguous version of the law was probably intended by Deák as a concession to the extreme nationalists in parliament, who otherwise might have prevented the passage of the bill.

75. See particularly Jaszi, *The Dissolution of the Habsburg Monarchy*, pp. 316 f., and Eisenmann, *Le Compromis austro-hongrois de 1867*, pp. 552 f.

76. Deák, during the last years of his life, was obviously aware of this new nationalist trend. See his moving speech of January 23, 1872, in the Hungarian parliament warning that intolerance of the Hungarian nationalities would endanger the Magyars themselves. See Seton-Watson, *Racial Problems in Hungary*, pp. 162 f.

77. Jaszi, *The Dissolution of the Habsburg Monarchy*, pp. 318 f.

78. *a*) General works dealing with the era of Magyar "liberalism": Gratz, *A dualizmus kora* [the era of dualism]; Szekfü, *Három Nemzedék* [three generations] (Budapest, 1935).

*b*) Biographies: Wertheimer, *Graf Julius Andrássy*, 3 vols. (Stuttgart, 1910–13); Apponyi, *Lebenserinnerungen* (Vienna, 1912), and *Emlékiratai* [memoirs], (Budapest, 1934).

*c*) Monographs: Leopold von Chlumecky, "Graf Julius Andrássy und die Einheit der Armee," *Österreichische Rundschau*, XXVI (1911), 87 ff.; J. György, *Der Bund der Donau- und Balkanstaaten* (Kolozsvár, 1910) [A dunai és a balkáni államok szövetsége]; Lutz Korodi, "Das allgemeine Wahlrecht in Ungarn und die Nichtmagyaren," *Österreichische Rundschau*, V (1905), 461–68; Joseph von Kristóffy, "Der Wahlrechtskampf in Ungarn," *Österreichische Rundschau*, XXII (1910), 243 ff. (pro-Austrian viewpoint); Rudolf Springer (pseud. of Karl Renner), "Warum uns die ungarische Verfassung imponiert?" *Österreichische Rundschau*, IV (1905), 189 ff.; Friedrich Tezner, *Ausgleichsrecht und Ausgleichspolitik* (Vienna, 1907); E. Treumund, "Baron Deszider Bánffy," *Österreichische Rundschau*, XXVII (1911), 437 ff.; Arthur B. Yolland, *The Hungarian Diet of 1905* (Budapest, 1905), containing chiefly documents, and, by the same author, *The Constitutional Struggle of the Magyars* (London, 1907).

79. It is interesting to review at this point remarks by the most eminent Hungarian prime ministers of the period after the compromise concerning the nationality problem. Kálmán von Tisza, prime minister from 1875 to 1890, declared that the nationalities must follow the Magyar proverb " 'Be silent and pay' . . . the non-Magyars could not boast of any such thing as 'a national history.' " Seton-Watson, *Racial Problems in Hungary*, pp. 211 f.

Baron Deszider Bánffy, prime minister from 1895 to 1899, "Hungary can become a legal state (*Rechtsstaat*) only when it becomes a homogeneous national state." Treumund, "Baron Deszider Bánffy," *Österreichische Rundschau*, XXVII (1911), 437 ff.; see also Seton-Watson, *Racial Problems in Hungary*, pp. 197 f. On another occasion Baron Deszider Bánffy also said, "Without chauvinism it is impossible to found the unitary Magyar national state." *Ibid.*, p. 182.

Kálmán Széll, prime minister from 1899 to 1903, "We have only one single categorical imperative, the Magyar state-idea and we must demand that every citizen should acknowledge it and subject himself unconditionally to it. From this point of view we, all politicians of Hungary, are intransigent . . . I shall tell why. Because Hungary has its age-old, holy and legitimate rights to strengthen the idea of such state. The Magyars have conquered this country for the Magyars and not for others. The supremacy and the hegemony of the Magyars is fully justified." Jaszi, *The Dissolution of the Habsburg Monarchy*, p. 321.

Count Stephen Tisza, prime minister from 1903 to 1905, and from 1913 to 1917, "Our citizens of non-Magyar tongue must, in the first place, become accustomed to the fact that they belong to the community of a nation state, of a state which is not a conglomerate of various races." *Ibid.*, p. 321.

80. Actually, these parties demanded the abolition of the common German language of command for the armed forces of the whole empire. This practically implied the disintegration of a joint army. It is clear that insistence upon the maintenance of the German language of command on the part of the emperor was an issue standing entirely on its own merits and in no way connected with the claims of German nationalism. The German language of command was based on a century-old army tradition, its abolition would have opened the way for similar demands on the part of the other nationalities and would have led to the destruction of the army as a homogeneous and effective force. See the imperial order of September 13, 1903, to the army, defending its supranational character. A. von Czedik, *Zur Geschichte der k. k. österreichischen Ministerien, 1861–1918*, 4 vols. (Teschen, 1917–20), II, 353. G. Kolmer, *Parlament und Verfassung in Österreich, 1848–1904*, 8 vols. (Leipzig, Vienna, 1902–14), VIII, 491 ff.

81. See Charmatz, *Österreichs innere Geschichte von 1848 bis 1907*, II, 161 f.

82. Eisenmann in *Cambridge Modern History*, XII, 204 ff.; Jaszi, *The Dissolution of the Habsburg Monarchy*, p. 372; Kosáry, *A History of Hungary*, pp. 309 ff.

83. The mere introduction of a general franchise bill in Hungary was one of the most powerful incentives for the parallel movement in Austria to gain general equal franchise, and in Austria, indeed, it succeeded in 1906–1907. Consequently, the first elections held in Austria on the basis of general equal franchise, in 1907, led to a radical shift to the socially progressive forces of the Social Democrats and the Christian Socials. However, Austria's franchise, at least after the Taaffe era (1879–93), had not been as narrow as Hungary's. The social evolution following the triumph of general franchise in 1907 was gradual, in Austria, from a regime relatively far more enlightened in social and national questions, even prior to 1907, than the Hungarian regime. The ruling system in Austria could, after all, put up with the social evolutionary development after 1907, but similar changes in feudal Hungary might easily have taken a revolutionary turn.

See below, Chapter XXIII, and Pollatschek, ed., *Viktor Adler's Aufsätze*, VIII, 254 ff., on the effect of the Hungarian crisis on the franchise issue in Austria.

84. That is, most of those powers which Jaszi in *The Dissolution of the Habsburg Monarchy* calls the centripetal forces within the empire. This study, however, does not accept unreservedly his concept of centrifugal and centripetal forces.

85. For discussions of the First World War and the October Revolution of 1918 see Count Albert Apponyi, *Erlebnisse und Ergebnisse* (Berlin, 1933), semi-Liberal, actually national-Conservative viewpoint; Paul von Fazekas, *Das Staatsrecht des Weltkrieges* (Warnsdorf, 1917), produalistic interpretation; Roland von Hegedüs, *Ungarn nach dem Kriege* (Warnsdorf, 1916), Magyar imperialist viewpoint; Oskar Jaszi, *Der Zusammenbruch des Dualismus und die Zukunft der Donaustaaten* (Vienna, 1918), and *Revolution and Counter-Revolution in Hungary* (London, 1924); in German, [*Magyariens Schuld, Ungarns Sühne*] (Berlin, 1923); Count Michael Károlyi, *Fighting the World*. (Jaszi's and Károlyi's works are written from a socially radical, antinationalist viewpoint.) Joseph Szterény, *Wirtschaftliche Verbindung mit Deutschland* (Warnsdorf, 1915), Magyar "liberal" plea for Naumann's Middle-Europe project; J. von Szilassy, *Der Untergang der Donau-Monarchie* (Berlin, 1921), one of the moderate Conservative Magyar studies on the First World War period, largely on foreign politics; Prince Ludwig Windischgrätz, *My Memoirs* (London, 1921), in German, *Vom roten zum schwarzen Prinzen* (Berlin, 1920), revealing memoirs by a leader of the aristocratic *fronde* against the Tisza regime.

86. See Schüssler, *Das Verfassungsproblem im Habsburgerreich*, pp. 222 ff.

As to the various proposals concerning Hungarian aggrandizement as a counterbalance to a union of Greater Poland with Austria see, for instance, Otto Bauer, *Österreichische Revolution* (Vienna, 1923), pp. 39 ff.; Schüssler, *Das Verfassungsproblem im Habsburgerreich*, pp. 221 ff.; O. von Glaise-Horstenau, *Die Katastrophe* (Vienna, 1929), pp. 70 ff.; Count O. Czernin, *Im Weltkrieg* (Berlin, 1919), pp. 273 ff., gives an authentic account of his negotiations, as foreign minister, with Tisza on the Polish and Rumanian question. See also below, Chapter XXIV, section on "The Concepts of Peace Policy."

Plans to make Hungary the center of gravity of the empire have been advanced from time to time since the days of Francis I, though hardly of as radical a nature as those discussed by Schüssler. See also Redlich, *Das österreichische Staats- und Reichsproblem*, I, 2, 46 ff., referring to Francis I's doubt whether he should proclaim himself emperor of Hungary and Bohemia rather than of Austria. See further Polzer-Hoditz, *Kaiser Karl*, pp. 87 f. Arthur, Count Polzer-Hoditz, one-time chief of cabinet of the Emperor Charles and Austro-German centralist by conviction, narrates in his memoirs a discussion with the then heir apparent, Archduke Charles, on March 6, 1915, in which he raised the same issue: "But I considered it well possible to persuade the Magyars to the grant of national autonomy, if a Greater Hungarian imperial idea were to be substituted for a Great Austrian imperial idea. Only in that way would it be possible to gain the political force of Hungary for the empire. Soon afterwards I handed a memorandum to the heir apparent . . . in which I explained the advantages if a predominant position were granted to Hungary, if the center of gravity were shifted to Budapest. I actually promoted the idea of a federation in which the rights of the presiding Power would be granted to the crown of Hungary. I considered the chief advantage of such constitutional construc-

# 392 NOTES TO PAGES 142–147

tion the fact that the Magyars, as the only people of the Austro-Hungarian monarchy, were not represented in a state abroad. Consequently, they would concentrate all their endeavors and forces on the interior problems of the empire. I considered the federalization of the empire and the grant of national autonomy in the individual lands absolutely necessary. . . . If this aim could not be achieved against Hungary's intention, it was possible perhaps to achieve it with concessions to Hungary."

Obviously, only political desperation led an Austrian centralist statesman and sworn enemy of overweaning Magyar ambitions to the consideration of such odd projects.

See also footnote 88 in the chapter and below, Chapter XXIV, sections on "German Centralism's Final Course," "Mid-Europe," and "The Concepts of Peace Policy."

87. Friedrich Naumann, *Central Europe* (London, New York, 1917), pp. 91 ff., see particularly p. 96, trans. from his *Mitteleuropa* (Berlin, 1915). For Magyar literature favoring this scheme see Sztereny (several times royal minister of commerce), *Wirtschaftliche Verbindung mit Deutschland* (Berlin, 1915); Hegedüs, *Ungarn nach dem Krieg;* Fazekas, *Das Staatsrecht des Weltkrieges.* Fazekas and Hegedüs held important positions in Hungarian economic life. See also below, Chapter XXIV, section on "Mid-Europe."

88. Polzer-Hoditz, *Kaiser Karl,* pp. 171 f.; Th. von Sosnosky, *Der Erzherzog-Thronfolger* (Munich, Berlin, 1929), pp. 71 ff. See also below, Chapter XXI, and Chapter XXIV, sections on "The Change of Sovereigns" and "The Concepts of Peace Policy."

89. Tisza had even rejected a proposal for franchise extension to grant the right to vote to every veteran who had seen action.

90. Szilassy, *Der Untergang der Donau-Monarchie;* for the first memorandum of November 9, 1917, see pp. 379 f., 391 ff., for the second, of September 9, 1918, submitted on September 13, see pp. 409 ff.

91. Windischgrätz, *My Memoirs,* p. 207.

92. *Ibid.,* pp. 176 ff.

93. Jaszi, *Revolution and Counter-Revolution in Hungary,* p. 16.

94. *Ibid.* See Jaszi's own very skeptic analysis of the political forces behind the revolution, pp. 21 ff.

95. Bauer, *Österreichische Revolution,* p. 86. The Kurucok were the Magyar rebels against the Habsburgs in the seventeenth and eighteenth centuries.

Actually, severance of the Real Union with Austria, based on Austria's alleged violation of the compromise, was declared a few days before Károlyi came to power. On October 16, 1918, the prime minister, Wekerle, declared the Real Union void, due to the fact that the Imperial October proclamation promising Cisleithanian Austria's conversion into a federation ran counter to the premises of the compromise, that is, the continued existence of a centralized Cisleithanian Austria based on the Austrian constitutional laws of December, 1867. This legal argumentation was highly questionable. The Austrian manifesto—and this was actually its chief political shortcoming—stated expressly that its provisions did not intend to affect political relations in and with Hungary.

Wekerle's declaration, of course, merely represented the Magyar viewpoint, since the non-Magyar nationalities altogether rejected the idea of the monarchical system under the Habsburg dynasty and the further existence of a Hungarian state in its prewar structure and territorial extent. See below, Chapter XXIV, section on "The Concepts of Peace Policy."

96. Michael Hodža, *Federation in Central Europe* (London, 1942), pp. 72 f., 76. The word "traitor" represents the way the old Magyar ruling classes referred to the aristocratic renegade Károlyi.

97. On Kossuth's national program developed in exile see below, Chapter XIX, section on Kossuth; on Károlyi's basic adherence to it, see Jaszi, *Revolution and Counter-Revolution in Hungary,* pp. 3 f.; Károlyi, *Fighting the World,* p. 336.

Károlyi's political record on these issues was, to say the least, not entirely consistent. To be sure, prior to the revolution he favored a Western orientation of Austria, opposed the German alliance and the Dualistic Compromise, and supported a democratization of Hungary, implying a more liberal nationality policy. In his parliamentary speeches during the war, as well as in general as head of the Magyar Hungarian government, he attempted to preserve the territorial integrity of Hungary, qualified, however, by the offer of far-reaching concessions to the nationalities.

Beneš, *Der Aufstand der Nationen* (Berlin, 1936), pp. 674 ff., considered Károlyi's endeavors to uphold Magyar territorial integrity thus, "Prime Minister Károlyi . . . had understood that the preservation of an undivided Hungar could be possible only under certain conditions. He did consciously everything to this effect in his power, not differently though perhaps more skillfully than Tisza, Apponyi, Andrássy or Wekerle would have done."

See Czernin, *Im Weltkrieg*, pp. 36, 354, on Károlyi's national Magyar attitude at the time of Rumania's entry into the war.

Károlyi's memoirs, *Fighting the World*, published after the war, present a conflicting picture; on page 65, he champions the cause of an imperial federation on an ethnic basis; on pages 224 ff., he promoted Slovak and Rumanian (Transylvanian) autonomy within Hungary; on page 336, he considers Kossuth's Danube confederation plans (that means exclusive of German-Austria) as feasible; on page 372, he agrees to southern Slav independence, but intends to preserve Fiume for Hungary, on pages 398 ff., he comes out for self-determination of the non-Hungarian nationalities within Hungary "in the conviction that these principles not only do not endanger the territorial integrity of the country, but on the contrary, . . . establish it on a firm foundation . . ." (Program of the national Council).

Jászi, in *Revolution and Counter-Revolution in Hungary*, pp. 37 f., relates that neither he nor Károlyi and their partisans "did . . . deceive ourselves for a moment with thoughts of preserving the territorial integrity of Hungary in the geographical sense . . . Károlyi frequently made it clear that he was concerned with territorial integrity in an economic sense."

98. See particularly Jászi, *The Evolution of the National States and the Nationality Problem* (Budapest, 1912). This important work has, unfortunately, never been translated from the Magyar into any major Western language.

99. See Jászi, *Revolution and Counter-Revolution in Hungary*, pp. 37 f., 57 f.; Károlyi, *Fighting the World*, p. 333; on the concepts of national autonomy see below, Chapter V, section on "The Institutional Evolution of the National Conflict."

100. Jászi, *Revolution and Counter-Revolution in Hungary*, pp. 57, 38.

101. *Ibid.*, p. 38.

102. See *ibid.*, pp. 2 f., and below, Chapter XXIV, section on "Mid-Europe."

103. Jászi, *Der Zusammenbruch des Dualismus und die Zukunft der Donaustaaten*, pp. 32 f., 39 ff., 62 f. This study was written prior to the empire's breakdown. On the Belcredi plan see below, Chapter XIX, section on Belcredi.

104. Jászi, *Revolution and Counter-Revolution in Hungary*, pp. 58 f.

## V. THE CZECHS

1. Principal sources of the Czech peoples' history which serve as an introduction to their position in Austria are the following.

Czech viewpoint: Ernest Denis, *La Bohême depuis la Montagne Blanche*, 2 vols. (Paris, 1903), decidedly representative of the older Liberal Czech standpoint; Václav Novotný and Rudolf Urbánek, *České dějiny*, 9 vols. (Prague, 1912–), standard work; Kamil Krofta (last foreign minister of the republic before the Munich crisis in 1938), *A Short History of Czechoslovakia* (New York, 1934), and, by the same author, *Das Deutschtum in der tschechoslowakischen Geschichte* (Prague, 1936), and *Dějiny Československé* (Prague, 1946); Zdeněk Tobolka, *Politické dějiny československého národa od 1848 až po dnešní doby*, 5 vols. (Prague, 1932–37).

German viewpoint: Succinctly presented in Raimund F. Kaindl, *Böhmen, zur Einführung in die böhmische Frage* (Leipzig, 1919); Alfred Schmidtmayer, *Geschichte der Sudetendeutschen* (Karlovy Vary, 1936); and, more comprehensively, in Hugo Hassinger, *Die Tschechoslowakei* (Vienna, 1925), and Bertold Bretholz, *Geschichte Böhmens und*

*Mährens*, 4 vols. (Reichenberg, 1924). See also Alfred Fischel, *Das tschechische Volk* (Breslau, 1928).

The best presentations in English are R. W. Seton-Watson, *A History of the Czechs and Slovaks* (London, 1943), and S. Harrison Thomson, *Czechoslovakia in European History* (Princeton, 1943); Robert J. Kerner, ed., *Czechoslovakia*, Part 1 (Berkeley, Los Angeles, 1945). See also Count Francis Lützow, *Bohemia* (London, 1909).

On the general historical background to this section see Robert J. Kerner, *Bohemia in the Eighteenth Century* (New York, 1932), and, by the same author, Chapter II in *Czechoslovakia*, published under his editorship. The ideas of the cultural renaissance period in the early nineteenth century are well expressed in Edvard Beneš, *Le Problème autrichien et la question tchèque*, "Études sur les luttes politiques des nationalités Slaves en Autriche" (Paris, 1908). The conclusions of this excellent, entirely pro-Austrian, presentation of the main political ideologies in modern Czech history do not correspond with the views of the author expressed since the outbreak of the First World War. See also Beneš, "Die Politik als Wissenschaft und Kunst," *Gedanke und Tat* (Prague, 1937), Vol. I; Alfred Fischel, *Der Panslawismus bis zum Weltkrieg* (Stuttgart, 1919), an informative work, German Liberal interpretation; and Hans Raupach, *Der tschechische Frühnationalismus* (Essen, 1939), German nationalist interpretation.

On the political history of the pre-March period see Hanns Schlitter, *Aus Österreichs Vormärz*, Vol. II (Böhmen, Vienna, 1920).

On legal institutional implications see Hugo Toman, *Böhmisches Staatsrecht und die Entwicklung der österreichischen Reichsidee, 1527–1848* (Prague, 1872). For further general and specific works on Czech history after the revolution of 1848 see the following sections in this chapter. See also the bibliographies on Czech history in *Česky časopis historický* (Prague, 1895–), Z. Tobolka ed., *Česká bibliografie* (Prague, 1903–), *Jahresberichte der Geschichtswissenschaft* (Berlin, 1878–1913), and Karl Uhlirz (Mathilde Uhlirz, ed.), *Handbuch zur Geschichte Österreichs* (Graz, 1927–41).

2. Otto Bauer, *Österreichische Revolution* (Vienna, 1923), pp. 36 f. Of the two famous statements by the great Czech leader the first was made in Palacký's letter to the Committee of Fifty in the national assembly in Frankfurt, signed as of April 11, 1848. It says, literally, "Indeed, if the Austrian Empire had not been in existence long ago, one would have to hurry in the interest of Europe, in the interest of humanity, to create it." The second statement was made in Palacký's book, *Österreichische Staatsidee* (Prague, 1866), p. 77.

3. Friedrich G. Kleinwächter, *Der Untergang der österreichische-ungarischen Monarchie* (Leipzig, 1920), p. 136. Kleinwächter's admission is all the more significant as he, of definite German Austrian national sympathies, certainly cannot be charged with pro-Czech bias.

4. Redlich, *Das österreichische Staats- und Reichsproblem*, I, part 1, 183.

5. Theodor Veiter, "Die Sudetenländer," in Karl G. Hugelmann, ed., *Das Nationalitätenrecht des alten Österreichs* (Vienna, 1934), pp. 322 f., quoting from Charles Kramář, *Das böhmische Staatsrecht* (Vienna, 1896), p. 34.

The three lands to which this definition refers are the ancient lands of the Bohemian crown, Bohemia, Moravia, and Silesia, and, after the Silesian wars ending in 1763, Austro-Silesia. No serious claim has ever been made to uphold the rights of the Bohemian crown to the territories lost to Saxony and Prussia in the course of the seventeenth and eighteenth centuries, that is, Upper Lusatia and Prussian Silesia.

The literal translation of "Bohemian *Staatsrecht*" would, of course, be "Bohemian constitutional law." Yet, the Czechs gave this term a connotation which cannot be brought out either in the German term *Staatsrecht* or in the English "constitutional law." They conceived the Bohemian *Staatsrecht* not only as the constitutional law or charter of the lands of the Bohemian crown, but as the designation for these lands themselves. The term frequently stands for the union of the lands of Bohemia, Moravia and (Austrian) Silesia itself.

The terms "Bohemia" and "Bohemian" need some clarification, too. Geographical Bohemia stands simply for the land or kingdom of Bohemia (without its *partes adnexae,*

Silesia and Moravia). A Bohemian, therefore, is an inhabitant of this crownland, irrespective of his Czech or German nationality. Generally, until the middle of the nineteenth century and occasionally even later, Czech authors when writing in German frequently used the term "Bohemian" to refer only to the Czech population of Bohemia in contradistinction to the Germans. Reference will have to be made in cases in which the meaning seems to be equivocal.

6. For a discussion of the administrative setup of the lands of the Bohemian crown since 1620 see A. Huber, *Österreichische Reichsgeschichte,* rev. by Alfons Dopsch (2d ed., Vienna, 1901), pp. 286 ff., 305 f.

7. See Fischel, *Der Panslawismus bis zum Weltkrieg.*

8. Charles Sealsfield, *Österreich wie es ist* (Vienna, 1934), pp. 63 f., 87 f., 148 f. (first published in 1826) obviously includes only the Czechs under the term "Bohemians."

9. Kleinwächter, *Der Untergang der österreichisch-ungarischen Monarchie,* pp. 131 f., admits the connection between the appeal of Czech nationalism and its intrinsic democratic tradition.

10. Andrian-Werburg, *Österreich und dessen Zukunft* (Hamburg, 1843), I, 173. Nevertheless, Andrian at the same time believes that Bohemia needs a close affiliation with Germany, but not vice versa. See Victor von Andrian-Werburg, *Österreichs innere Politik mit Beziehung auf die Verfassungsfrage* (Stuttgart, 1848), pp. 308 ff.

11. See, for instance, Alfred von Skene, *Entstehen und Entwicklung der slawisch-nationalen Bewegung in Böhmen und Mähren im 19. Jahrhundert* (Vienna, 1893), pp. V f.

"Rarely indeed will it be possible to find a political movement in history which can be traced back so little to the influence of the broader strata of the population than that which was created by the awakening of the Slav-national spirit in Bohemia and Moravia at the end of the eighteenth century.

"The national movement was first stimulated by the Bohemian Estates. It was favored by external influences, but in the main it was developed by the activity of a relatively small number of Slav scholars and writers."

12. See Eisenmann, *Le Compromis austro-hongrois de 1867,* pp. 225 ff.: "The German Austrian aristocracy is 'catholic and dynastic' but not 'national.' The Bohemian nobility is provincial. If it allies itself to the Czechs, it does so with cool reasoning, but by no means for any sentimental considerations. It dreams of exercising a lucrative mediation between the two national groups of the land, Czechs and Germans. Neither is the idea of the Bohemia historicopolitical entity national in character. For the Czechs this entity is the entity of the Bohemian state." Obviously, this last conclusion goes too far. Whether originally national or not, the concept of the historicopolitical entity of the lands of the Bohemian crown carried for centuries the idea of Czech nationalism. See also Jaszi, *The Dissolution of the Habsburg Monarchy,* pp. 149 ff.

13. In general the split between territorial and court aristocracy was by no means of a national character. Very commonly, the head of a noble house, as heir to its entailed Estates, belonged to the territorial nobility while cadets of the same family joined the court nobility.

14. Kleinwächter, *Der Untergang der österreichisch-ungarischen Monarchie,* pp. 131 f.

15. See Bauer, *Die Nationalitätenfrage und die Sozialdemokratie* (Vienna, 1907), pp. 290 f.

16. See also Rudolf Springer (pseud. of Karl Renner), *Grundlagen und Entwicklungsziele der österreichische-ungarischen Monarchie* (Vienna, 1906), p. 195, and Eisenmann, *Le Compromis austro-hongrois de 1867,* pp. 225 ff.

17. Albert Eberhard Schäffle, *Aus meinem Leben,* 2 vols. (Berlin, 1905), I, 173 f. See also section on "Hohenwart's Federalist Mission," in this chapter. On the state of the Czech language in its influence on the political course of the Czech leaders see Richard Zehntbauer, *Verfassungswandlungen im neueren Österreich* (Heidelberg, 1911), p. 78.

"Count Leo Thun, who stood for the Czech movement at the end of the pre-March period, gives an instructive picture . . . 'Among all . . . who have enjoyed education in school, only very few are able to command fully [the Czech language]. Those few, even if they were a few hundred in number, thereby have gained an influence which they would not wield fully without this monopoly. . . . Not everybody knows how to use this influence properly.' "

See also Harold Steinacker, "Die geschichtlichen Voraussetzungen des österreichischen Nationalitätenproblems," in Karl G. Hugelmann, ed., *Das Nationalitätenrecht des alten Österreich*, p. 28.

18. On the history of the literary movement in its political aspects see Denis, *La Bohême depuis la Montagne Blanche*, Vol. II, Chap. III; Fischel, *Der Panslawismus bis zum Weltkrieg*, Chap. II. See also Tomson, *Czechoslovakia in European History*, pp. 158 ff.

Some of the most influential works of the pioneers of the Czech cultural renaissance are Joseph Dobrovský, *Das Lehrgebäude der böhmischen Sprache* (Prague, 1819); Institutiones linguae Slavicae (Vienna, 1822); *Geschichte der böhmischen Sprache und älteren Literatur* (Prague, 1818); and a periodical on Czech folklore with the significant title *Slavin: Botschaft aus Böhmen an alle slawischen Völker oder Beiträge zu ihrer Charakteristik, zur Kenntnis ihrer Mythologie, ihrer Geschichte und Altertümer, ihrer Literatur und ihrer Sprachkunde nach allen Mundarten* (Prague, 1806).

Joseph Jakub Jungmann (1773–1847) *Historie literatury ceské* (Prague 1849) ; *Slovník česko-německý*, 5 vols. (Prague, 1835–39), Czech-German dictionary.

Pavel Josef Šafařík (1795–1861), *Slawische Altertümer* (first published in Czech, 1837). Jointly with Palacký, *Die ältesten Denkmäler der böhmischen Sprache; Anfangsgründe der alttschechischen Grammatik* (1845); *Slawische Ethnographie* (1848). Šafařík was ethnically a Slovak, though his lifework was focused primarily on the history of the Czech language.

Francis Palacký, *Geschichte Böhmens* (until 1526), 5 vols. (Prague, 1864–67).

This list is informative in regard to the question of language. Significantly enough, the earliest of these scholars, the Abbé Dobrovský, wrote only in Latin and German: all the others wrote at least a good part of their literary work in German. All of them had received German education. See also Fischel, *Der Panslawismus bis zum Weltkrieg*, pp. 59, 75 f.; see also Miloš Weingart, "Joseph Dobrovský, The Patriarch of Slavonic Studies," *Slavonic (and East European) Review*, VII (London, 1928–29), 663–75.

If the works of the scholarly rejuvenators of Czech were to be selected, not according to their scientific merits, but according to the publicity they received in the contemporary learned world of Europe, Václav Hanka's (1791–1861) edition of the Königshof and Grünberg manuscripts in 1818 would undoubtedly have to be placed at the top of the list. These manuscripts, written in an "old" Czech language and alleging the existence of a highly cultured Czech nation in the pre-Christian era, were supported by Goethe's enthusiastic interest and acclaimed by literary Europe. It took two generations of scientific and, in the end, political struggle, above all Thomas G. Masaryk's unflinching courage, to expose definitely this already contested "scientific discovery" as forgery and to destroy a myth which meanwhile had become dear to the Czech people. Whoever uses this romantic transgression of an abounding nationalism to draw deprecatory conclusions on the honesty of the Czech renaissance movement in general should not forget the rather unique fact that it was Czech scholarship and political courage which finally repudiated it.

19. Fischel, *Der Panslawismus bis zum Weltkrieg*, pp. 56 ff.

20. Count Sedlnitzky, the president of the Austrian police administration and one of the most influential officials under the Emperor Francis's regime after 1815, recommended the support of Dobrovský's endeavors for the restoration of the Czech written language in a report to the emperor of April 26, 1820 in the following way: "It will serve weighty interests of the Austrian state that the tie of the non-Uniate Slavs [meaning the Greek Orthodox Slavs as against the Uniate Catholic Slav churches] with Russia will be weakened, a tie which has so far been kept by means of the Russian Slav church books. Such [weakening] is to be expected, particularly if, following the instruction of this grammar [namely, Dobrovský's] these church books will be revised for the use of the imperial royal subjects as speedily as possible."—From the archives of the Imperial

Royal Ministry of the Interior, quoted by Fischel, *Der Panslawismus bis zum Weltkrieg*, pp. 57 f.

21. Beneš, "Die Politik als Wissenschaft und Kunst," pp. 104 f., on Kollár, in particular pp. 89 f.

Kollár's scientific main work, *Über die literarische Wechselseitigkeit zwischen den verschiedenen Stämmen und Mundarten der slawischen Nation* (Leipzig, 1837), was first published in German. It presumes the existence of one great Slav mother nation divided into various tribes of different dialects. It is the basic work in western Slav literature, on which these concepts of cultural romantic Pan-Slavism have been founded. See also Fischel, *Der Panslawismus bis zum Weltkrieg*, pp. 102–18. On Kollár's position regarding the development of Slovak nationalism see Chapter X, below.

Any reference to Kollár's mystic romanticism must first consider his strange collection of sonnets, "Slavy scera" [daughter of Slava], 1824 (rev. 1832). It pictures the divine Slava in the center of the world; it dreams of a giant, Russia forms his head, Poland the chest, Bohemia the arms, Serbia the legs, and so forth. Europa—naturally—would tremble before it. The effect of this work on the Czech literary public was tremendous, not the least due to the fact that it was considered of violent anti-German character.

See also "Jan Kollár and Literary Panslavism," and, by Albert Pražák, "The Slovak Sources of Jan Kollár's Pan Slavism," *Slavonic (and East European) Review*, VI (London, 1927–28), 336–43, 579–92.

On the Russian-inspired Pan-Slav concept see Rostislav A. Fadičev, *Opinion on the Eastern Question* (London, 1876). See also Count Valerian Krasiński, *Pan-Slavism and Germanism* (London, 1848).

22. Beneš, "Die Politik als Wissenschaft und Kunst," pp. 89, 104 f.

23. See also Fischel, *Der Panslawismus bis zum Weltkrieg*, pp. 182 ff.

24. See below, Chapter XV, section on "The Reform Plans at Kremsier," and Chapter XIX, section on "Palacký in His Old Age."

25. On Thun see A. von Helfert, *Fürst Alfred Windischgrätz und Graf Leo Thun in den Prager Junitagen* (Munich, 1886). This study deals largely with the repercussions of the Slav Congress in Prague. See also Salomon Frankfurter, *Graf Leo Thun-Hohenstein, Franz Exner und Hermann Bonitz* (Vienna, 1893); and numerous references in Helfert, *Geschichte der österreichischen Revolution im Zusammenhauge mit der mitteleuropäischen Bewegung* (Freiburg im Breisgau, 1907–9), Redlich, *Das österreichische Staats- und Reichsproblem*, and Eisenmann, *Le Compromis austro-hongrois de 1867*.

26. See Chapter IX, below.

27. Thun, *Über den gegenwärtigen Stand der böhmischen Literatur und ihre Bedeutung* (Prague, 1841), pp. 88 f. The term "Bohemian" literature refers here to "Czech" literature.

28. Thun, *Betrachtungen über die Zeitverhältnisse insbesondere im Hinblick auf Böhmen* (Prague, 1849). This study was first published in Czech, as Thun states, with assistance required because of his limited knowledge of the language. See particularly *ibid.*, pp. 35 f., 59 f. The above-outlined features of Thun's ideas on the language problem belie the criticism brought forward by an anonymous contemporary that Thun, in his survey on the status of Bohemian literature, had promoted the transformation of Austria into a Slav empire. See [Koch], *Österreichs innere Politik mit Bezug auf die Verfassungsfrage* (Stuttgart, 1847), p. 336.

29. Thun, *Betrachtungen über die Zeitverhältnisse*, pp. 93 ff.

30. See section in this chapter on "The Development of the Language Conflict."

31. During practically all the history of the Austrian Empire—the reign of Joseph II not excluded—the use of German as the language of official intercourse was based primarily on customs legally recognized by imperial ordinances. Statutes in this respect were generally confined to individual crownlands and specific subject matters. There never was a basic law which recognized German as the official state language of the Habsburg lands. It is therefore, correct in this context to speak of the language of official business rather than of the official language. See Fischel, *Das österreichische Sprachen-*

*recht* (2d ed., Brünn, 1910), vii ff. See also the sections in this chapter on "The Institutional Evolution of the National Conflict" and "The Development of the Language Conflict, 1871–1909."

32. Thun, *Betrachtungen über die Zeitverhältnisse,* pp. 93 f. See also Thun, *Nachtrag zum offenen Schreiben an Herrn Johann Slavik in Betreff der Ereignisse der Pfingstwoche 1848* (Prague, 1849).

33. Thomson, *Czechoslovakia in European History,* p. 157.

34. The standard work on Havlíček is Thomas G. Masaryk, *Karel Havlíček* (Prague, 1904). This important biography has not yet been translated from the Czech into any major Western language. In German Austrian literature, Havlíček's activities are usually treated far too sketchily; Friedjung and Redlich give relatively the best accounts available.

35. Beneš, *Le Problème autrichien et la question tchèque,* pp. 141 ff. Havlíček's comment is taken from Masaryk's biography of Havlíček, as quoted by Beneš.

36. Masaryk, *Karel Havlíček,* pp. 107 ff., quoted from Redlich, *Das österreichische Staats- und Reichsproblem,* I, 2, 42 ff. In particular, Havlíček cited the struggle of the Irish Catholics, under O'Connell, against the union with England as analogous to the Austrian-Czech struggle during the years 1846–48. See also Masaryk, *Palacký's Idee des böhmischen Volkes* [Palackého idea národa českého], (Prague, 1912), and Redlich, *Das österreichische Staats- und Reichsproblem,* I, 1, 109 f.; Helfert, *Geschichte der österreichischen Revolution,* I, 62.

37. Redlich, *Das österreichische Staats- und Reichsproblem,* I, 1, 167 f.

38. See below, Chapter XV, section on "The *Reichstag* of Kremsier," and Chapter XIX, section on Palacký.

39. See Thomson, *Czechoslovakia in European History,* pp. 306 f.; H. Steinacker, "Die geschichtlichen Voraussetzungen des österreichischen Nationalitätenproblems und seine Entwicklung bis 1867," in K. G. Hugelmann, ed., *Das Nationalitätenrecht des alten Österreich,* pp. 44 f. See also Friedjung, *Österreich von 1848 bis 1860,* I, 276 f. As will be shown in the following section, Havlíček, again following Palacký's lead, for a time reversed his views on this point and supported the idea of complete German-Czech separation.

40. See also Bauer, *Die Nationalitätenfrage und die Sozialdemokratie,* pp. 235 f. Havlíček, banished to German Tirol from 1851 to his death in 1856, wrote a violently anticlerical and antifeudal epic, the *Tiroler Elegien.* Obviously, he was adversely influenced by his surroundings in Tirol, which of all the Austrian crownlands preserved most faithfully the medieval state and church traditions.

41. For the German share in the cultural liberal movement in Bohemia see Friedjung, *Österreich von 1848 bis 1860,* I, 281–84, and Krofta, *Das Deutschtum in der tschechoslowakischen Geschichte* (see particularly pp. 134 f.).

42. Helfert, *Geschichte der österreichischen Revolution,* I, 236 f., 422; Zehntbauer, *Verfassungswandlungen im neueren Österreich,* pp. 83 ff.

43. From Fischel, *Materialien zur Sprachenfrage in Österreich* (Brünn, 1902). "Bohemian" in this address stands for Czech.

44. It is perfectly true that among the then politically unknown Bohemian leaders rallied at St. Wenzelsbad—Faster, Trojan, Gabler, Pinkas, Count Deym, and others—there was a fair proportion of sincere German Liberals. Yet within a period of a few weeks these German Liberals in Bohemia, as everywhere else in Austria, joined their political fortune to the cause of German liberalism fought beyond the borders in Frankfurt. As a result, the revolution in Bohemia as a binational movement came to an abrupt end. It is, therefore, only fair to consider the Liberal revolution in Bohemia, as far as it is confined to the problems of the Bohemian lands, primarily a Czech movement.

45. In addition to the works previously mentioned, such as those by Novotný and Urbánek, S. H. Thomson, Seton-Watson, Brethholz, Kolmer, Zehntbauer, and others, the following specific items deal in some detail with the revolution of 1848 and the period from 1848 to 1871. However, apart from Zeithammer's comprehensive work, none of them is solely confined to the period under discussion.

Karel Kazbunda, *České hnuti roku 1848,* (Prague, 1929) ; Otokar Zeithammer, *Zur*

*Geschichte der böhmischen Ausgleichsversuche, 1865–71*, 2 vols. (Prague, 1912–13), Czech viewpoint; Raimund F. Kaindl, *Der Völkerkampf und Sprachenstreit in Böhmen im Spiegel der zeitgenössischen Quellen* (Vienna, 1927), German national viewpoint; Rudolph Sieghart, *Die letzten Jahrzehnte einer Grossmacht* (Berlin, 1932); Alfred von Skene, *Entstehen und Entwicklung der slawischen nationalen Bewegung in Böhmen und Mähren im 19. Jahrhundert* (Vienna, 1893); Elisabeth Wiskemann, *Czechs and Germans, A Study of the Struggle in the Historic Provinces of Bohemia and Moravia* (London, 1938).

Of outstanding significance in the field are, in addition, the three works by A. Fischel, *Das österreichische Sprachenrecht, Materialien zur Sprachenfrage in Österreich*, and *Der Panslawismus bis zum Weltkrieg*, Friedjung, *Österreich von 1848 bis 1860*, Vol. I, Redlich, *Das österreichische Staats- und Reichsproblem*, G. Kolmer, *Parlament und Verfassung in Österreich*, Vols. I and II, and A. von Czedik, *Zur Geschichte der k. k. österreichischen Ministerien*, Vol. I. For literature and on Palacký and the Slav Congress see below, Chapter XV, sections on "The Slav Congress" and "The Reform Plans at Kremsier"; and Chapter XIX, section on Palacký.

46. See also Redlich, *Das österreichische Staats- und Reichsproblem*, I, 2, 45.

47. The petition declared as follows, ". . . The renovation of the inseparable union between all the lands belonging to the crown of Bohemia . . . by way of a general Bohemian-Moravian-Silesian national assembly, separate central governmental agencies, under a separate, responsible ministry of the interior appears as a measure which, due to the pragmatic, historic, national, and geographic union of these lands, will safeguard the constitutional throne of your Majesty as well as the integrity of the Austrian Empire as a whole." See Fischel, *Materialien zur Sprachenfrage in Österreich*, No. 15, p. 51; see also "Erläuterungen der Prager Abgeordneten zu der zweiten Petition," *ibid.*, No. 16, pp. 52 f. See further Redlich, *Das österreichische Staats- und Reichsproblem*, I, 1, 110 ff.; Zehntbauer, *Verfassungswandlungen im neueren Österreich*, pp. 116 ff. Regarding the dilatory and equivocal handling of the petition of March 11 by the central government see Helfert, *Geschichte der österreichischen Revolution* (Freiburg, 1907–1909), I, 423.

48. See Zehntbauer, *Verfassungswandlungen im neuren Österreich*, pp. 73 ff. (text of document); Redlich, *Das österreichische Staats- und Reichsproblem*, I, 1, 115 f., I, 2, 45; E. Denis, *La Bohême depuis la Montagne Blanche*, II, 254 f.; A. von Helfert, *Geschichte der österreichischen Revolution*, I, 425 f. See also the elaboration of the principles laid down in the imperial "rescript" of April 8, in the "leading principles for the draft of a constitution for the kingdom of Bohemia," issued by the Bohemian National Committee on May 30. According to this draft, the Bohemian diet should consist of two houses, the lower elected by direct suffrage, the senate consisting of a selected group of sixty members originally elected to the lower house. Army, foreign affairs, including commercial treaties, public debts, currency, tariff regulations, matters of communication, and legislation concerning civil and criminal law, and so forth, were to be left to the central government in Vienna. The text of this draft has been published in Zehntbauer, *Verfassungswandlungen im neueren Österreich*, pp. 177 f.; Redlich, *Das österreichische Staats- und Reichsproblem*, I, 1, 117 f. See also *ibid.*, I, 2, 32.

A provisional ministry (*Regierungsrat*) including, besides several Feudal Conservatives, men such as Palacký and Rieger, was appointed by the imperial governor of Bohemia, Count Leo Thun. Scarcely two weeks later, Windischgrätz's military intervention wrecked this theoretically not unpromising attempt to conciliate centralistic and federalist claims.

49. A Czech university in Prague was established only in 1882, i.e., the medieval university of 1348 was divided into Czech and German institutions.

50. See Fischel, *Materialien zur Sprachenfrage in Österreich*, No. 19, pp. 58 f.; Redlich, *Das österreichische Staats- und Reichsproblem*, I, 1, 185 f., 1, 2, 45 f.

51. See Helfert, *Geschichte der österreichischen Revolution*, I, 424; on the increasing influence of the Bohemian nobility in the provisional government in Prague see *ibid.*, II, 278 f. The support of the revolutionary cause on the part of the Bohemian high

nobility was dependent on an increased representation of the interests of the owners of landed property in Bohemian representative institutions.

52. See Denis, *La Bohême depuis la Montagne Blanche*, II, 310 ff., Friedjung, *Österreich von 1848 bis 1860*, I, 56 ff.; Seton-Watson, *A History of the Czechs and Slovaks*, p. 188, and particularly p. 317. For a centralistic-conservative interpretation see Helfert, *Fürst Alfred Windischgrätz und Graf Leo Thun in den Prager Junitagen*.

53. See Friedjung, *Österreich von 1848 bis 1860*, I, 57 f. "Thereupon the governor and the general [that is, Thun and Windischgrätz] drafted the ingenious plan of convoking the Bohemian diet, of rallying all the antiradical elements, particularly among the Czechs, and of giving the Slavs a welcome national target for their attack; it was intended to turn jointly against German-democratic Vienna. This ought to have given the Slavs the opportunity to break centralism, whereas the absolutists wanted to end the revolution. It was the first attempt of the Bohemian nobility to exploit national conflicts for the sake of their own rule. Count Thun went a step farther in these proceedings by establishing a kind of provisional government in the Bohemian capital as a counterbalance against the Liberal ministry in Vienna. Yet reaction had attacked too soon. The Liberal ideology in Vienna, which was centralistic at the same time, was strong enough to obviate the design. . . . It belonged to the decisive results of the revolution that the center of gravity of the state remained in Vienna and that the central parliament preserved its precedence. The leading Czech party (including Palacký and Rieger) agreed to Thun's plans."

See also Springer, *Geschichte Österreichs seit dem Wienen Frieden 1809*, II, 349 f., stressing the great significance of the split of the Slav movement into revolutionary and Austro-Slav forces, which was furthered by Windischgrätz's action.

54. The sudden change from the pre-March atmosphere of cooperation between Czech and German intellectuals, who put their liberal convictions above their national claims, to the reversed after-revolutionary situation, in which nationalism increasingly dominated political liberalism, is well expressed by Seton-Watson: "Czechs and Germans fell apart rapidly, and in place of the cordial relations of the forties, in which writers like Meissner or Hartmann celebrated Žižka or Hus, there is soon open hostility, based on the desire of the Germans to retain the artificial majority which they owed to a narrow franchise, and of the Czechs to regain all the ground lost in two centuries of subjection, and if possible augment it still further. It was a situation such as lent itself to friction, and there was never any lack of agitators on both sides to aggravate the quarrel." Seton-Watson, *A History of the Czechs and Slovaks* (London, 1943), p. 186.

55. Translated from the text published in Palacký, *Gedenkblätter* (Prague, 1874), pp. 149 ff. The text has also been partly translated into English in Thomson, *Czechoslovakia in European History*, pp. 44 f., 165 f. See also Redlich, *Das österreichische Staats- und Reichsproblem*, I, 1, 148 ff., 165 ff.; Seton-Watson, *A History of the Czechs and Slovaks*, pp. 186 f.; Denis, *La Bohême depuis la Montagne Blanche*, II, 261 f.; Eisenmann, *Le Compromis austro-hongrois de 1867*, pp. 95 ff., and Otokar Odložilík, "A Czech plan for a Danube Federation in 1848," *Journal of Central European Affairs*, I (1941), 253 ff.

56. Redlich, *Das österreichische Staats- und Reichsproblem*, I, 1, 184 f.; I, 2, 45 f., and Wiskemann, *Czechs and Germans*, pp. 37 f.; see also sections of this chapter on "The Institutional Evolution of the National Conflict" and "The Development of the Language Conflict."

57. See Friedjung, *Österreich von 1848 bis 1860*, I, 272–91, particularly pp. 286–91; Fischel, *Das österreichische Sprachenrecht*, pp. lxv f.

58. On Clam-Martinič's views expressed in the meetings of the strengthened *Reichsrat* see Redlich, *Das österreichische Staats- und Reichsproblem*, I, 1, 536 ff.; on Thun's views voiced in the councils of the semifederalist Rechberg-Goluchowski cabinet in 1860 see *ibid.*, particuarly I, 583–99.

See also the "memorandum of the nine very noble lords" of July, 1860, signed by princes Schwarzenberg, Salm, Colloredo-Mannsfeld, Auersperg, the two counts Wolkenstein, further, counts Nostitz, A. A. Auersperg (Anastasius Grün), and Count H. Clam-Martinic, the probable editor of the document. Most of the signers of this memorandum, which promoted a program of moderate Conservative federalism on the basis of the historicopolitical entities, were Bohemian lords. See *ibid.*, I, 638 ff.; see also Eisenmann, *Le Compromis austro-hongrois de 1867*, pp. 223 ff., 251 f.

59. Among 241 members of the Bohemian diet, the great landowners, with the exception of the representatives of some ecclesiastic institutions who were largely members of the high nobility, obtained seventy seats, all the peasants together, seventy-nine. Concerning the national distribution of the diets' seats and the considerably lower number of popular votes required to elect a German deputy rather than a Czech deputy, see also Charmatz, *Österreichs innere Geschichte von 1848 bis 1907*, I, 51.

60. On Rieger's policy see Richard Charmatz, *Adolf Fischhof* (Stuttgart, 1910), pp. 260 ff.

61. On the congress see Fischel, *Der Panslawismus bis zum Weltkrieg*, pp. 381 ff., and J. Klaczko, *Le Congres de Moscovie et la propaganda panslaviste, Revue des deux Mondes*, LXXI (Paris, 1867), 132–87.

62. An interesting contribution to the parliamentary activities of that era was the motion in the Bohemian diet by the deputy Seidl in 1861 for the demarcation of German, Czech, and mixed-language territories. According to Seidl, the language character of a district was to depend upon the language in which sermons from the pulpits were traditionally delivered. Czech demands for strict demarcation of language territories were later taken up by the Germans against stiff Czech opposition.

The Czech policy of passive resistance during that period unfortunately led to the abolition of one of the most intelligent laws of the Belcredi cabinet (1865–67), the so-called *Sprachenzwangsgesetz* (language-compulsion law), which compelled Czech and German students in secondary schools to learn the other national language. At the time when higher education in Bohemia was still predominantly in German hands this law, contributing to mutual understanding between the two peoples in Bohemia, decidedly worked in favor of the Czechs. Yet Czech abstention from the diet made it possible for the Germans to remove it from the statute book. Sieghart, *Die letzten Jahrzehnte einer Grossmacht* (Berlin, 1932), pp. 404 ff.

On the official standpoint of Czech policy in the period between 1860 and 1870, see Rieger's letter of March 1, 1869, to Count Taaffe protesting the nonrecognition of the autonomy of the lands of the Bohemian crown on the basis of the *Staatsrecht*. A. Skedl and E. Weiss, *Der politische Nachlass des Grafen Eduard Taaffe* (Vienna, 1922), pp. 148 ff. See also *ibid.*, pp. 175 ff.; the report about a conference with Rieger, in which the Old Czech leader formulated the Czech viewpoint as follows: "In the constitutional question it is impossible for the Czechs to recognize an equal German position concerning the Bohemian crown. In the kingdom of Bohemia proper, the Czechs form three fifths of the population, in Moravia three quarters of the whole population. It must be recognized that the solution of the constitutional question definitely must be organized in regard to the majority of the population. Yet, in national matters the Czechs are willing to give the Germans ample guarantees in regard to national equality in a nationality law."

Representative of the German Liberal centralistic point of view are Ignaz von Plener's letters to his son, written between 1869–71, Paul Molisch, *Briefe zur deutschen Politik in Österreich von 1848–1918* (Leipzig, 1934), pp. 49 f., 54, 62, and particularly the letter (pp. 74 f.) of April, 1871. Plener objects to the Bohemian *Staatsrecht* not so much from the centralistic angle as from the viewpoint of German superiority. "It would easily be possible to fulfill Galicia's wishes with respect to the Poles and to sacrifice the Ruthenians. . . . One could sacrifice the Slavs and Rumanians in Hungary to the Magyars. One can colonize and Magyarize Ruthenians and Slovaks very well, but one cannot make Germans into Czechs. The Germans in Bohemia are so outstanding in number and significance (property, industry, and intelligentsia), they are in such close intercourse and have such intimate relations with the Germans in Austria and even in Germany, that to ignore their feelings would be identical with delivering the German population of Austria to the neighboring German empire."

It should be noted that this was the viewpoint of a very moderate, German Liberal centralist.

63. Charmatz, *Österreichs innere Geschichte von 1848 bis 1907*, I, 100 ff.; Sieghart, *Die letzten Jahrzehnte einer Grossmacht*, pp. 390 f.

64. Most illuminating on the subject of Hohenwart's federalist mission are the outstanding biographies of the chief actors in that historical interlude in the Austrian national struggle—Albert E. Schäffle, Hohenwart's chief collaborator, Julius, Count Andrássy, then Hungarian prime minister and shortly after common minister of foreign affairs, and Friedrich, Count Beust, imperial chancellor and minister of foreign affairs: Schäffle, *Aus meinem Leben,* see particularly Vol. I; Eduard von Wertheimer, *Graf Julius Andrássy* (Stuttgart, 1910–13), see particularly Vol. I; Friedrich, Count Beust, *Aus Drei Viertel Jahrhunderten (1809–1885)*, 2 vols. (Stuttgart, 1887), see particularly Vol. II (in English, *Memoirs of Frederick F. Count von Beust*, London, 1887); F. W. Ebeling, *F. W. Graf von Beust*, 2 vols. (Leipzig, 1870–72); Zeithammer, *Zur Geschichte der böhmischen Ausgleichsversuche, 1865–71*, Czech viewpoint; Eric Fischer, "New Lights on German-Czech Relations in 1871," *Journal of Modern History*, XIV (1942), 177 ff., and, by the same author, "The Negotiations for a National *Ausgleich* in Austria in 1871," *Journal of Central European Affairs*, II, (1942), 134 ff. Other important sources on the subject are J. A. von Helfert, *Ausgleich und "Verfassungstreue"* (Leipzig, 1873); Josef Penížek, "Von einem toten Ausgleich," *Österreichische Rundschau*, XXXIII (1912), 252 ff.; Kolmer, *Parlament und Verfassung in Österreich*, Vol. II; Czedik, *Zur Geschichte der k. k. österreichischen Ministerien*, Vol. I, and Molisch, *Briefe zur deutschen Politik in Österreich von 1848–1918*.

65. See, for instance, Hohenwart's letter to Prince Alexander Dietrichstein-Mensdorff of June 26, 1870, Molisch, *Brief zur deutschen Politik*, pp. 148 ff.

66. Even before he tackled the Bohemian question, Hohenwart had attempted to put Galicia's administrative privileged position, granted in 1868–69, on a firmer legal basis. See Kolmer, *Parlament und Verfassung in Österreich*, II, 135 ff.

Concerning the standpoint of the Bohemian aristocracy on the Compromise of 1867 and the concept of the Bohemian *Staatsrecht* see the correspondence between Hohenwart, Count Leo Thun, Prince George Lobkowitz, Prince Schwarzenberg, and Prince Dietrichstein-Mensdorff, between 1870 and 1879. Molisch, *Briefe zur deutschen Politik in Österreich*, pp. 159, 180, 181, 194, 205. See also Charmatz, *Adolf Fischhof*.

67. Schäffle, *Aus meinem Leben*, II, 76. The term *Territorienreich*, the aim of Conservative Austrian federalism rejected by Schäffle, meant the concept of a federation based on the old historicopolitical entities and the old crownland Estates orders.

Schäffle's *Kapital und Socialismus* was first published in 1870. Werner Sombart considers Schäffle an outstanding representative of that form of "national socialism" from Plato through Thomas Morus, Campanella, and Fichte to Goethe which was significantly represented in nineteenth-century Germany by men such as Lorenz von Stein, Ferdinand Lassale, Adolf Wagner, Adolf Stöcker, and Friedrich Nietzsche. See Werner Sombart, *A New Social Philosophy* (Princeton, 1937).

68. Schäffle, *Aus meinem Leben*, I, 200 ff.

69. *Ibid.* See also the earlier analysis in Count Leo Thun's *Über den gegenwärtigen Stand der böhmischen Literatur* on the problem of party organization in the section of this chapter on "Czech Political Evolution."

70. Schäffle, *Aus meinem Leben*, I, 200 ff.; see also *ibid.*, II, 3 ff.

71. See, for instance, *ibid.*, I, 173 f., as quoted on pages 157 f. of this chapter.

72. These documents are published in Bernatzik, *Österreichische Verfassungsgesetze* (Vienna, 1911), pp. 1091 ff., and Fischel, *Materialien zur Sprachenfrage in Österreich*, pp. 72 f.

73. See Bernatzik, *Österreichische Verfassungsgesetze*, p. 1109. See also Beneš, *Le Problème autrichien et la question tchèque*, pp. 258 ff. "The political situation abroad changed and, in the interior, the old coalition against the Slavs started a bitter fight against them. In this situation it would have been wise for them to limit and, above all, to simplify their claims. But, blindly obstinate, the Czechs refused to make the least formal concessions."

74. See Heinrich Rauchberg, *Die Bedeutung der Deutschen in Österreich* (Dresden,

1908). According to Rauchberg, of each 1,000 crowns of taxes paid in Austria-Cisleithania, Germans paid 634 crowns, Czechs 192, Poles 70, Ruthenians 37, Slovenes 29, Serbs and Croats 8, Italians 27, and Rumanians 3. Considering the fact that in Austria the ratio of Germans to Czechs was about 3 to 2, this still meant a more than 100 percent greater German taxation per capita.

75. Hohenwart's franchise-reform plans for election to the diets also implied parliamentary franchise reform. Until 1873, members of parliament were not elected directly by the people, but by the diets, from the assemblies to which they were delegated. The chief objective of the government—to replace centralistic, Liberal bourgeois majorities in the diets by Conservative, Clerical-Federalist ones—was to be achieved by a reorganization of constituencies. This reform was to favor rural communities and great landowners. On the other hand, it was intended to eliminate representation of chambers of commerce. The government further ordered a lowering of the property qualifications. Thereby the urban, generally antiliberal lower middle classes were to be enfranchised. Thus, the franchise policy which some twenty years later facilitated the rapid rise of the Christian Social party was actually initiated by Hohenwart. On the franchise reform plans, see Kolmer, *Parlament und Verfassung in Österreich*, II, 168 ff., Charmatz, *Österreichs innere Geschichte von 1848 bis 1907*, I, 110 ff.

76. See Bernatzik, *Österreichische Verfassungsgesetze*, p. 1109. The draft of an imperial rescript in the main acknowledging specific claims of the Bohemian crown was already prepared at that time. See Skedl and Weiss, *Der politische Nachlass des Grafen Eduard Taaffe*, pp. 198 ff.; also *ibid.*, p. 70, a letter by Prince Dietrichstein-Mensdorff, governor of Bohemia, dated August 26, 1870, warning against privileged treatment of one specific crownland as impairing the unity of the empire.

77. See Wertheimer, *Graf Julius Andrássy*, I, 554–611, particularly pp. 590 ff.; Wilhelm Schüssler, *Österreich und das deutsche Schicksal* (Leipzig, 1925), pp. 96 ff.; Schäffle, *Aus meinem leben*, II, 33 ff., 44 ff.; Sieghart, *Die letzten Jahrzehnte einer Grossmacht*, pp. 394 f.

78. See paragraph 2 of the Hungarian Article XII of August 31, 1867.

79. See Molisch, *Briefe zur deutschen Politik in Österreich*. I. von Plener to his son Ernest, February 16, 1871, pp. 65 f.

80. Beust, *Aus Drei Viertel Jahrbunderten*, II, 501 ff., see particularly pp. 506 f.

81. See *ibid.*, pp. 480 f., and particularly pp. 493 f.

82. Molisch, *Briefe zur deutschen Politik in Österreich*. I. von Plener to his son Ernest, February 24, 1869, and August 22, 1870, pp. 49 f., and 62.

83. See Penížek, "Von einem toten Ausgleich." See Rieger's letter to Count Taaffe after the fall of the Hohenwart cabinet, in which from the opposite standpoint he came to the same conclusions as Beust and Plener, that is, the existence of a danger of German intervention in Bohemia. To Rieger, very naturally, not a German-Centralist, but a Slav-Federalist course appeared to be the only possible means to avert this danger. Skedl and Weiss, *Der politische Nachlass des Grafen Eduard Taaffe*, pp. 207 ff.

84. In *Österreich und das deutsche Schicksal*, pp. 96 ff., it is Schüssler's well-founded thesis that Bismarck relied on Andrássy's successful veto of the Hohenwart program, which enabled him to show his hand not too openly. See also Wertheimer, *Graf Julius Andrássy*, I, 562 f., 565 f., and the diplomatic correspondence between Bismarck and the German ambassador in Vienna, von Schweinitz, quoted there.

See *Denkwürdigkeiten des Botschafters, General von Schweinitz*, 2 vols. (Berlin, 1927); *Briefwechsel des Botschafters, General von Schweinitz*, 2 vols. (Berlin, 1928); see also Otto von Bismarck, *Gedanken und Erinnerungen* (Stuttgart), II, Chaps. XX and XXIX; on Bismarck's policy toward the nationality conflicts in Austria in later years, see also Theodor von Sosnosky, *Die Politik im Habsburgerreich*, 2 vols. (Berlin, 1912, 1913), II, 208 f.

85. Sieghart, *Die letzten Jahrzehnte einer Grossmacht*, p. 394. See also Charmatz, *Österreichs innere Geschichte von 1848 bis 1907*, I, 113, E. Fischer, "New Lights on German-Czech Relations in 1871," *Journal of Modern History*, XIV (1942), 189 f.

86. For general historic surveys on Czech history from 1871 to 1918 see the previously

mentioned works by Denis, Novotný and Urbánek, Seton-Watson, and S. H. Thomson. For information on the problem of ethnic distribution of population in Bohemia and Moravia see *Jahrbuch des tschechoslowakischen Republik* (Prague), annual in Czech language, and *Statistisches Handbuch der Tschechoslowakei* (Prague, 1920–25). See also Hugo Hassinger, *Die Tschechoslowakei* (Vienna, 1925). The previously mentioned works by Fischel, Kolmer, Czedik, Sieghart, Zeithammer, and Wiskemann are indispensable for studies on the language conflict.

Further works on the institutional evolution of the national conflict in general and of specific importance on the development of the language conflict in Bohemia, particularly from 1867 on, are:

Czech viewpoint: Karel Kramář, *Anmerkungen zur böhmischen Politik* (Vienna, 1906), and *Das böhmische Staatsrecht* (Vienna, 1896); Beneš, *Le Problème autrichien et la question tchèque;* Bohuslav Rieger, "Kreisverfassung in Böhmen," *Österreichisches Staatswörterbuch,* Vol. III. Masaryk's viewpoint on the language problem before 1914 is treated in Czedik, *Zur Geschichte der k. k. österreichischen Ministerien, 1861–1916,* Vols. II, III, and IV. For further literature on Masaryk and Beneš see the following sections of this chapter.

German viewpoint: Veiter, "Die Sudetenländer," pp. 288–458, in Karl G. Hugelmann, ed., *Das Nationalitätenrecht des alten Österreich,* strongly German-national; Max Menger, *Der böhmische Ausgleich* (Stuttgart, 1891); Herman von Tinti, *In letzter Stunde* (Vienna, 1904); Joseph Turnwald, "Zur Frage der administrativen Zweiteilung Böhmens," *Österreichische Rundschau,* XVII (1908), 410 ff.; R. F. Kaindl, *Der Völkerkampf und Sprachenstreit in Böhmen, Im Spiegel der zeitgenössischen Quellen* (Vienna, 1921); Wilhelm Kosch, *Die Deutschen in Österreich und ihr Ausgleich mit den Tschechen* (Leipzig, 1909); Ferdinand von Trautmannsdorff-Weinsberg, "Zur Sprachenfrage," *Österreichische Rundschau,* XVIII (1909), 341 ff.; Joseph M. Bärnreither, *Zur böhmischen Frage* (Vienna, 1910); Franz Jesser, *Das Wesen des nationalen Kampfes in den Sudentenländern* (Vienna, 1912); Ernst von Plener, *Reden (1873–1910),* 3 vols. (Stuttgart, 1911, and *Die Kreiseinteilung für Böhmen* (Vienna, 1903).

Supranational viewpoint: Heinrich Rauchberg, *Der nationale Besitzstand in Böhmen* (Leipzig, 1905); Alfred von Skene, *Der nationale Ausgleich in Mähren, 1905* (Vienna, 1910); Rudolf Springer (pseud. of Karl Renner), *Grundlagen und Entwicklungsziele der österreichisch-ungarischen Monarchie* (Vienna, 1906); Wenzel Frind, *Das sprachliche und sprachlich-nationale Recht* (Vienna, 1899), (Catholic viewpoint).

87. Succinctly expressed in Kramář, *Anmerkungen zur böhmischen Politik,* p. 114.

88. See, for instance, Redlich, *Das österreichische Staats- und Reichsproblem,* I, part 1, 184 f.

89. See M. H. Böhm on "Autonomy" in *Encyclopedia of the Social Sciences.* For a survey of the most common definitions on the subject, with particular reference to the national problem, see Theodor Veiter, *Nationale Autonomie; Rechtstheorie und Verwirklichung im positiven Recht* (Vienna, Leipzig, 1938). See also Sieghart, *Die letzten Jahrzehnte einer Grossmacht,* pp. 386 f., 430, 433 ff.

Ernst von Körber in *Studien über die Reform der inneren Verwaltung* (Vienna, 1905), distinguishes in Austria between the political autonomy of the crownlands, the autonomy granted to the communities, and the right of self-administration in general. See also below, Chapter XV, section on "The *Reichstag* of Kremsier," and Chapter XX.

90. Redlich, *Das österreichische Staats- und Reichsproblem,* I, 1, 261 f., see also I, 301 f. Sieghart, *Die letzten Jahrzehnte einer Grossmacht,* pp. 430, 313 f.

91. Renner, *Das Selbstbestimmungsrecht der Nationen,* pp. 75 ff., 71 ff. For the contrary view see Sieghart, *Die letzten Jahrzehnte einer Grossmacht,* pp. 413 f. Concerning the juxtaposition of territorial and personal autonomy see Renner, *Das Selbstbestimmungsrecht der Nationen,* particularly pp. 71–85; Bauer, *Die Nationalitätenfrage und die Sozialdemokratie,* pp. 317 f., 326 f., 353 f. See, further, Paul Samassa, *Völkerstreit im Habsburger Staat* (Leipzig, 1910), pp. 162 f.; Veiter, *Nationale Autonomie,* pp. 50 ff.; Otto Lang, *Die Verfassung als die Quelle des Nationalitätenhaders in Österreich,* pp. 41 ff.; Sieghart, *Die letzten Jahrzehnte einer Grossmacht,* pp. 313 f.; Bernatzik, *Über nationale*

*Matrikeln* (Vienna, 1910). For a more specific analysis of the autonomy concepts see Chapter XX below.

92. Renner, *Das Selbstbestimmungsrecht der Nationen,* pp. 74 ff.

93. For a brief discussion of the practical aspects of the application of either principle in national affairs in Bohemia and Moravia, see J. M. Baernreither's speech in the Austrian house of Lords, December 29, 1909, in Czedik, *Zur Geschichte der k. k. österreichischen Ministerien,* IV, 265 ff.

94. Sieghart, *Die letzten Jahrzehnte einer Grossmacht,* p. 413.

95. See Article XIX, basic state law No. 142 of 1867: "All the nationalities [*Volksstämme*] of the state have equal rights; each nationality has an inviolable right to preserve and cultivate its nationality and language.

"The equal rights of all languages customarily spoken in the lands in the schools, government offices, and public life are recognized by the state.

"In lands inhabited by more than one nationality, public educational institutions should be organized in such a way that, without the compulsion of learning a second language of the land, any of the nationalities [in these crownlands] "ought to get the necessary funds for the cultivation of its language."

Regarding the interpretation of the terms *Landessprache* and *landesübliche Sprache* see particularly Hugelmann, *Das Nationalitätenrecht des alten Österreich,* pp. 94 f., 124 ff., 139 ff., 313 ff. The whole section from p. 81 to p. 286 discusses the development of the interpretation of the language problem and its terminology since 1867. See further, Rudolf Hermann von Herrnritt, *Nationalität und Recht* (Vienna, 1899), pp. 84 ff.; Wenzel Frind, *Das sprachliche und sprachlich-nationale Recht,* pp. 208 ff., 279 ff.; Fischel, "Nationalitäten," in *Österreichisches Staatswörterbuch,* and his *Das österreichische Sprachenrecht.* See also above, Chapter III, section on "The Pan-German Idea."

96. See below, Appendices 1 and 2.

97. See the German Whitsuntide program 1899, published in Fischel, *Materialien zur Sprachenfrage in Österreich,* pp. 33 ff. See also the declaration of the German people's councils of Styria, Carinthia, Carniola, and the Littoral of September 4, 1917, in Schüssler, *Das Verfassungsproblem im Habsburgerreich* (Stuttgart, Berlin, 1918), pp. 199 ff.; P. Hofmann von Wellenhof, *Der Kampf um das Deutschtum, Steiermark Kärnten, Krain, und das Küstenland* (Munich, 1899). See also above, Chapter III, section on "The Pan-German Idea," and below, Chapter XXIV, section on "The Concepts of Peace Policy," and Appendices 1 and 2.

98. See Hugelmann, *Das Nationalitätenrecht des alten Österreich,* pp. 164 ff. The Czech and German sections of these boards were united in a general assembly dealing with matters of common interest to both nationalities. A somewhat similar arrangement of national organization was effected at that time in the highest Bohemian court of appeal.

99. See Sieghart, *Die letzten Jahrzehnte einer Grossmacht,* p. 399. Renner, *Das Selbstbestimmungsrecht der Nationen,* pp. 62 ff.

100. See Fischel, *Das österreichische Sprachenrecht,* pp. xlii–xcviii ff.

101. See section in this chapter on "Czech Political Evolution."

102. For a concise historical presentation of the problem see Fischel, *Das österreichische Sprachenrecht* (particularly the brilliant historical introduction) and Count F. Trautmannsdorff-Weinsberg, "Zur Sprachenfrage," *Österreichische Rundschau* XVIII (1909), 341 ff. See also below, Appendix 2.

103. Slav deputies in parliament blocked the motion by the deputies Count Wurmbrandt (1884) and Baron Scharschmidt (1886) for the introduction of German as the official state language with some consideration for the requirements of non-German nationalities concerning the external official language. A move by the Liberal leader Herbst for the administrative partition of Bohemia was rejected in 1886. Representative of the standpoint of the Slav opposition (this time including the Poles) was the opinion of the Polish deputy Stanislaus von Madeyski, elaborated in his *Die deutsche Staatssprache oder Österreich ein deutscher Staat* (Vienna, 1884). According to Madeyski, the principle of the national state and the principle of national liberty were incompatible in Austria. The principle of the national state language would presuppose the existence

of a common German state-nation in Austria. Actually, he said, Austria is composed of several nations, and therefore there could not be one state language. See Charmatz, *Österreichs innere Geschichte,* II, 37 ff., 42. The Stremayr ordinance in regard to court procedure was slightly modified in favor of the Czechs in 1886. See *ibid.* Fischel, *Materialien zur Sprachenfrage in Österreich,* pp. 10 ff. For this period see also the correspondence between the German Liberal leader Dr. Schmeykal and the Old Czech leader Dr. Rieger on the mutual party viewpoints. *Ibid.,* No. 36.

104. See Chapter III, above, sections on "The Liberal Inheritance," "The Pan-German Idea," "The Christian Socials," and "The Social Democrats."

105. See Fischel, *Materialien zur Sprachenfrage in Österreich,* for the text of the entire agreement; see further A. Skedl and E. Weiss, eds., *Der politische Nachlass des Grafen Taaffe,* pp. 419 ff.; G. Kolmer, *Parlament und Verfassung in Österreich,* IV, 397 ff., 406 ff.; Ernst von Plener, *Erinnerungen,* II, 396 ff.; Max Menger, *Der böhmische Ausgleich,* pp. 12 f.; see Beneš, *Le Problème autrichien et la question tchèque,* pp. 279 ff., commenting rather favorably on the provisions of the proposed compromise.

106. On the Badeni crisis see specifically Kolmer, *Parlament und Verfassung in Österreich,* Vol. VI; Czedik, *Zur Geschichte der k. k. österreichischen Ministerien, 1861–1916,* Vol. II; Sosnosky, *Die Politik im Habsburgerreiche,* II, 172 ff.; Molisch, *Briefe zur deutschen Politik in Österreich von 1848–1918,* pp. 315 ff., 352 ff.; Fischel, *Das österreichische Sprachenrecht,* pp. 208 ff.; G. Pollatschek ed., *Viktor Adlers Aufsätze,* VIII, 178 ff., XI, 111 ff.

107. The Young Czechs, however, though a party of the Left, supported Badeni. Yet the chief pillar of strength of his cabinet was the support of the Polish Conservative *Szlachta,* augmented by the Federalist-Conservatives of all nationalities, including the German Clerical-Conservative Right.

As Hohenwart, Badeni introduced a rather limited electoral reform. A fifth curia of voters, not subject to property qualifications, was organized. This curia, however, only elected approximately one sixth of all parliamentary seats. Due to the Young Czech support, this reform did not impair the parliamentary majority of the government. See Charmatz, *Österreichs innere Geschichte,* II, 102 ff.; Kolmer, *Parlament und Verfassung in Österreich,* Vol. VI.

108. Sieghart, *Die letzten Jahrzehnte einer Grossmacht,* pp. 413 f. Sieghart defends the unilingual inner-language system in official intercourse, as follows: "In the intercourse between government authorities and parties, the party has to understand the authorities and has to be understood by them. The authorities cannot expect the citizen to learn their language, but the state can expect it from its officials. In the inner government service . . . it is primarily the task of the state itself to arrange things most practically. The question of equality is here confined to the problem of proportional admission to office of members of each nationality."

*Ibid.,* p. 414: "As long as the Czechs were not even able to fill the government posts in their own closed-language territory, they themselves stood for the demarcation of Czech, German, and mixed territories. See the draft of the Fundamental Articles. . . . Actual development outran their program. Industry and commerce as well as the liberal professions attracted the young German generation chiefly between 1870 and 1880 and decreased their demands for government positions. Czech economy, on the other hand, was not yet equally developed, and Czech aspirants sought government service. The young Czech generation understood German, it was bilingual, the rising German generation unfortunately repulsed the idea of learning the second language of the land."

See also, at this point, Renner, *Das Selbstbestimmungsrecht der Nationen,* p. 64; Fischel, *Das österreichische Sprachenrecht* lxxxvii f., xcii f., 346 ff.; Friedrich von Wieser, *Über Vergangenheit und Zukunft der österreichischen Verfassung* (Vienna, 1905), pp. 76 ff.; Pollatschek, ed., *Viktor Adler's Aufsätze,* VIII, 224 ff. On Körber see R. Charmatz, "Ein Moderner Ministerpräsident: Dr. Ernst von Körber," pp. 165 ff. in his *Lebensbilder aus der Geschichte Österreichs* (Vienna, 1947).

109. On the language ordinances of the ministries of Taaffe, Badeni, Gautsch, Clary, Körber, and Bienerth see A. Fischel, *Das österreichische Sprachenrecht,* lxxxiv ff.

110. At least in regard to the language problem, a comprehensive solution was proposed in parliament by the Ruthenian Dr. Lewicky in 1908:

"1. The whole state territory is to be divided into homogeneous national districts on the basis of the ethnographic position of the population.

"2. Simultaneously . . . the existing organization of administrative and court districts touching the so-called language borders is to be changed accordingly and to be adjusted to the borders of the language territory.

"3. Official language in internal intercourse of the government authorities is the language of the language territory in the fields of administration and jurisdiction. In external intercourse with the parties, all languages customary in the territory are recognized by the authorities and considered as of equal right. In any district a language is considered customary if spoken by more than 15 percent of the population. . . .

"5. The law applies to all government authorities of first and second *Instanz* ["instance" of appeal]. Boards of appeal comprising several language territories are compelled, in all affairs of the language territories subordinated to them, to use as official the one language which, according to the previously mentioned regulations, is considered as the official language in the language territory." Fischel, *Das österreichische Sprachenrecht*, pp. 344 f.; Czedik, *Zur Geschichte der k. k. österreichischen Ministerien, 1861–1916*, II, appendix 10. For further German language proposals see the motion of the German deputy Schauer in the Bohemian diet in 1908. Fischel, *Das österreichische Sprachenrecht*, pp. 356 ff.

The Pan-German proclamation of 1901 asked for a Bohemia "Pure German, Pan German and undivided [sic]." Kaindl, *Der Völkerkampf und Sprachenstreit in Böhmen*. The German national eastern petition of 1916 demanded a division of Bohemia into districts of German and mixed, but not of Czech nationality, that is, German was to be the official language of the whole land. Czech was to be admitted as the second language only in the so-called mixed districts. *Ibid.*, pp. 67 ff.

On the Czech part see the proposal by the deputy to the Bohemian diet Trojan for the adoption of Czech as inner official language, Hugelmann ed., *Das Nationalitätenrecht des alten Österreich*, p. 158; Sieghart, *Die letzten Jahrzehnte einer Grossmacht*, p. 409. See also the Pacák-Herold proposal in parliament in 1906 for a constitutional reform based on the principle of national autonomy as developed in Kremsier; see Czedik, *Zur Geschichte der k. k. österreichischen Ministerien 1861–1914*, Vol. III.

111. The Polish-Ruthenian Compromise, concluded in 1914 in Galicia but never put into practice because of the outbreak of the First World War, was influenced by the Moravian regulation as well.

112. Concerning the Moravian Compromise see Theodor Veiter, "Die Sudetenländer," in K. G. Hugelmann, ed., *Das Nationalitätenrecht des alten Österreich*, pp. 383 ff., particularly pp. 390 f. See also K. G. Hugelmann, *ibid.*, pp. 226 ff.; Fischel, *Das österreichische Sprachenrecht*, pp. 14 ff., 276 f.; Bernatzik, *Österreichische Verfassungsgesetze;* Herrnritt, "Die mährischen Ausgleichgesetze und das Nationalitätenrecht," *Österreichische Rundschau*, VI (1906), 169 ff.; Bauer, *Die Nationalitätenfrage und die Sozialdemokratie*, pp. 354 ff.

113. See G. Erler, *Das Recht der nationalen Minderheiten* (Münster, 1931), p. 109.

114. The procedure of national registration employed in Moravia represented a compromise between two divergent theories. One promoted the determination of the national status of the individual on the basis of his own declaration, the other stood for administrative or court decision on the basis of objective criteria (language, place of birth and residence, education, ancestry, and so forth). See Bernatzik, *Über nationale Matrikeln;* A. Fischel, *National Kurien* (Vienna, 1908), historical survey. On the general theory, see further, H. Wintgens, *Der völkerrechtliche Schutz der nationalen, sprachlichen und religiösen Minderheiten* (Stuttgart, 1930), and Erler, *Das Recht der nationalen Minderheiten,* and the literature quoted in these two works.

115. See, for instance, Masaryk's parliamentary speech of December 17, 1908, in Czedik, *Zur Geschichte der k. k. österreichischen Ministerien,* IV, 162 ff., which comprises an expressed declaration of loyalty not only to the empire but to the dynasty as well.

See also J. M. Baernreither, *Fragments of a Political Diary* (London, 1930), pp. 145 ff., 219, on Masaryk's endeavors for an understanding between Austria-Hungary and Serbia. See Kramář, *Anmerkungen zur böhmischen Staatsrecht*, particularly pp. 97 ff., 107 ff.; see also his thoroughly "Austrian" parliamentary speech of October 29, 1909, for Czech-German understanding on the basis of a national compromise, Czedik, *Zur Geschichte der k. k. österreichischen Ministerien*, IV, 198; Beneš, *Le Problème autrichien et la question tchèque*, pp. 305 ff.

On Joseph Kaizl's activities, particularly as minister of finance, 1898–99 see Kolmer, *Parlament und Verfassung in Österreich*, Vol. VII; Czedik, *Zur Geschichte der k. k. österreichischen Ministerien*, Vol. II.

116. On Masaryk in the prewar period see particularly *ibid.*, Vols. II–IV; R. Sieghart, *Die letzten Jahrzehnte einer Grossmacht*.

See the following works by Masaryk: *Der Agramer Hochverratsprozess und die Annexion von Bosnien und Herzegowina* (Vienna, 1909), *The Making of a State* (London, 1927), published in German under the title *Die Weltrevolution* (Berlin, 1925) (the English edition listed above has been slightly abbreviated); *Das neue Europa; Der slawische Standpunkt* (Berlin, 1922), shortened English version under the title *The New Europe; The Slav Standpoint* (London, 1918); "The Future Status of Bohemia," in the periodical *The New Europe*, Vol. II, No. 19 (February 22, 1917); and *The Problem of the Small Nations in the European Crisis* (London, 1915).

See also R. W. Seton-Watson, *Masaryk in England* (Cambridge, 1943); Kramář, *Anmerkungen zur böhmischen Politik*, and *Das böhmische Staatsrecht*; Beneš (prewar period), *Le Problème autrichien et la question tchèque* (Paris, 1908).

On the war and immediate postwar period see J. O. Novotný, *Vzkříšení samostatnosti československé, kronika let 1914–1918*, 2 vols. (Prague, 1932), covers First World War period; Beneš, *Der Aufstand der Nationen. Der Weltkrieg und die tschechoslovakische Revolution* (Berlin, 1936), in the Czech edition *Světová válka a naše revoluce* (Prague, 1935), abridged English edition *My War Memoirs* (New York, 1928), and *Gedanke und Tat*, 3 vols. (Prague, 1937); see also E. von Glaise-Horstenau, *Die Katastrophe* (Zürich, Vienna, 1929); see, further, Jan Opočensky, *The Collapse of the Austro-Hungarian Monarchy and the Rise of the Czechoslovak State* (Prague, 1928), in the Czech edition *Konec monarchic rakousko-uherské* (Prague, 1928).

117. Masaryk, *The Making of a State*, p. 47 (see *Weltrevolution*, pp. 30 f.). On Masaryk's prewar standpoint see also Seton-Watson, *Masaryk in England*, p. 20, "He distrusted the Habsburgs and all their ways, but he did not despair of an evolution in a federal direction of what was often called a monarchical Switzerland, in which all the many nationalities of Austria-Hungary would attain equal rights. But that seemed to him possible only on a democratic basis." See also Seton-Watson, *A History of the Czechs and Slovaks*, pp. 285 f.

118. The party never comprised more than three parliamentary members. See *ibid.*, pp. 245 f.

119. Masaryk, *The Making of a State*, p. 47 (see note 117).

120. In *Neue Freie Presse* (leading Liberal daily in Vienna) of December 24, 1907, quoted from Czedik. *Zur Geschichte der k. k. österreichischen Ministerien*, IV, 226 ff.

121. *Ibid.*, II, 108.

122. Masaryk on the Bohemian Compromise and the Bohemian question in *Neue Freie Presse*, December 24, 1907, published in *ibid.*, IV, 226–34. In this letter to *Neue Freie Presse*, Masaryk, referring to the Czech abandonment of the demand that every Bohemian official must command both languages, frankly admits: "Since the Germans themselves have voiced the slogan 'learn Czech,' the claim for bilingualism appears to us Czechs in a new light. I always remember very vividly the advice which Prince Bismarck gave to the German national delegates from Austria 'Learn Czech if you want to rule the Czechs.'"

Enlightened and moderate German Austrian politicians such as Renner repeatedly made the suggestion that Germans in Bohemia and Moravia learn Czech for the double purpose of reconciling Czech and German differences and of increasing German influence in Bohemia and Moravia. German nationalists, who previously had firmly refused to learn a Slav language, finally accepted this idea as a means of increasing German influence. This led to a strange reversal of Czech and German national policy. The Czechs, adverse to Czech-speaking German officials, began to put up with the idea of unilingual officials. The Germans increasingly attempted to look for Czech-speaking German national officials in the crownland administrations. This whole problem proved again that measures of bilingual language requirements, though sound in themselves, defeat their purpose if they are introduced too late; in this case when they were already permeated with the spirit of integral nationalism.

For further observations of Masaryk on the Czech-German conflict see his parliamentary speech on February 4, 1909, Czedik, *Zur Geschichte der k. k. österreichischen Ministerien*, IV, 175 ff. On the ethnic-federal solution of the southern Slav problem see his speech of December 1908, *ibid.*, pp. 162 ff.

123. Beneš, *Le Problème autrichien et la question tchèque*, pp. 141 ff.

124. *Ibid.*

125. *Ibid.*, p. 258. Written with particular regard to the Old Czech demands to recognize the equal status of the Bohemian lands and Hungary after 1867.

126. *Ibid.*, p. 270.

127. *Ibid.*, pp. 279 ff.

128. *Ibid.*

129. For an evaluation of Kramář's personality see Sieghart, *Die letzten Jahrzehnte einer Grossmacht*, p. 330; see also Seton-Watson, *A History of the Czechs and Slovaks*, pp. 244 f.; Thomson, *Czechoslovakia in European History*, pp. 190 f., 307 f.

130. Beneš, *Le Problème autrichien et la question tchèque*, pp. 279 ff. Kramář's national program was definitely more radical than the Young Czech program of the 1880s and 1890s. This was largely obscured by his decidedly pro- (Czarist) Russian views on foreign policy. On this aspect of Kramář's prewar program see particularly Fischel, *Der Panslawismus bis zum Weltkrieg*, pp. 484 ff., 512 ff., 518 ff., 526 f., 553 f., 557 ff., 561 f.; Wiskemann, *Czechs and Germans*, pp. 46 f.

Regarding the internal German-Czech conflict, Kramář's policy prior to the First World War was by no means intransigent. While steadfastly adhering to the idea of the Bohemian *Staatsrecht*, he was little concerned with the problem of German infiltration in Bohemia. He took a far graver view of the dominating German influence all over the empire. Specifically, Kramář advocated the administrative indivisibility of Bohemia, supporting a *Kreisorganization* on an economic, but not a national, basis of organization. He demanded the complete bilingualism of the whole administration, but, as in the case of Masaryk, he did not claim the bilingual character of every official. He agreed, however, to the separation of the Czech and German school systems.

"If we get back the internal official language and a Bohemian university in Moravia, then there is no serious obstacle to cooperation with the Germans in matters of economic and even cultural interests," he asserted. Kramář, *Anmerkungen zur böhmischen Politik*, pp. 129 f. See also *ibid.*, pp. 24 f., 41, 64, 93, 97, 107 ff., 113 ff., 121 ff. See also his *Böhmisches Staatsrecht*, pp. 56, 69.

131. Technically, the Czech Socialist organization became a politically completely independent party within the Austrian Socialist movement only in 1912.

132. Beneš, *Le Problème autrichien et la question tchèque*, pp. 279 ff. See also the reference to an analogous situation between great Polish landowners and Ruthenian peasants.

133. See also Kramář, *Anmerkungen zur böhmischen Politik*, pp. 121 ff., on the same point. For a contrary view see below, Chap. XX, on Bauer's and Renner's ideas. Both considered personal autonomy fairer than territorial autonomy from the social and economic angle.

134. Beneš, *Le Problème autrichien et la question tchèque*, pp. 279 ff.

135. Masaryk, *Das neue Europa*, pp. 65 f. See also above, Chapter III, section on "The Pan-German Idea"; below, Chapter XVIII, sections on Schwarzenberg, Bruck, and Fröbel; Chapter XX; and Chapter XXIV, section on "Mid-Europe."

136. Here Beneš refers, of course, to the organization of nationally homogeneous *Kreise*. He himself recommends the setup of nationally mixed *Kreise,* with adequate protection for either nationality, wherever necessary, as well. *Le Problème autrichien et la question tchèque*, pp. 279 ff.

137. *Ibid.*

138. Beneš, *Der Aufstand der Nationen*, p. 5.

139. See below, Chapter XXIV, section on "The Concepts of Peace Policy," for a general evaluation of the problems of empire disintegration. See *ibid.* and below, Appendix 6, for a chronology of events.

140. Particularly Seton-Watson's testimonial—besides Wickham Steed, foreign editor and prewar Austrian correspondent of the London *Times,* Masaryk's earliest supporter in England, gives full witness to this fact. See particularly Seton-Watson's *Masaryk in England,* on his discussions with Masaryk in October, 1914, in Rotterdam, concerning the setup of an independent Czechoslovakia. See also *ibid.,* pp. 117 ff., 125 ff., on Masaryk's memorandum of April, 1915, concerning her prospective frontiers. See also the text of this memorandum in K. F. Nowak, *Chaos* (Munich, 1923), pp. 313 ff.

Masaryk's early war program was based on the historic state rights of the Bohemian crown due to the difficulty of drawing "a tenable frontier on a basis of ethnography. If, however, the arguments in favor of an ethnographic frontier should prevail at the [peace] settlement," he believed that "concessions should be made in the southwest of Bohemia toward Austro-German Upper Austria and in Silesia, the German portion of which could be united to German Silesia," while the part of the crownland chiefly inhabited by Poles should be apportioned to a new autonomous Russian Poland: the Carpatho-Ukraine (that is, the Ruthenian part of Hungary) was to be incorporated into Russia. "Northern Bohemia, however," he argues, "is essential to the existence and prosperity of the new Czechoslovakia, both from the economic standpoint and in the interest of the Czech racial minorities." Seton-Watson, *Masaryk in England,* pp. 43 ff., 47, 19.

Masaryk stated further in 1917, "In so far as the German minority is concerned, I should not be opposed to a rectification of the political frontier; parts of Bohemia and Moravia, where there are only a few Czechs, might be ceded to German Austria. In that way the German minority could perhaps be reduced by one million." Masaryk, "The Future Status of Bohemia," *New Europe,* Vol. II, No. 19 (Feb. 22, 1917).

Masaryk also stressed the desirability of a common frontier between the prospective Czechoslovakia and the new southern Slav states. See Seton-Watson, *Masaryk in England,* pp. 117 f.; Masaryk, *The Making of a State,* p. 28. It is further notable that, according to Masaryk, the Carpatho-Ukraine was to be incorporated into Russia. Seton-Watson, *Masaryk in England,* pp. 19 f.

141. Masaryk relates that, shortly before he left Austria for good (in late fall, 1914), he had a conversation with the fairly liberal former prime minister, von Körber, to whom he put squarely the question whether a victorious Austria would be likely to introduce the necessary reforms. Körber replied, "No! Victory would strengthen the old system, and a new system under the young heir-apparent, the Archduke Charles . . . would not be better than the old. The soldiers would have the upper hand after a victorious war and they would centralize and Germanize. It would be absolutism with parliamentary embellishments." "What about Berlin," Masaryk asked, "Will Germany be wise enough to make her ally adopt reforms?" "Hardly," was Körber's reply. Masaryk, *The Making of a State,* pp. 43 f. Masaryk implies that Körber's views helped to prompt him to early action.

142. Kramář himself, prior to his arrest and indictment on the charge of high treason in 1915, also supported the official introduction of the Orthodox church in Czech territory. Even after the fall of czarism, until 1918 he still stood for a monarchical solution, under the cadet of a Western dynasty. See Masaryk, *The Making of a State,* pp. 44, 66, 106, 153; Beneš, *Aufstand der Nationen,* p. 613. See also Seton-Watson, *A History of the Czechs and Slovaks,* pp. 285 f.

143. Very naturally, these considerations could only be implied in Masaryk's postwar

writings, since as president of the republic he did not want to take part in political arguments reflecting on still active politicians and, in substance though not in name, on still active party organizations as well. Beneš' criticism of Czech political activism in Austria was less hampered by these considerations. See Masaryk, *The Making of a State*, pp. 23 ff., and particularly pp. 129 ff.; Beneš, *Aufstand der Nationen*, pp. 11 ff., 31 ff., 252 ff., 443 ff.

144. Masaryk, *The Making of a State*, pp. 129 ff., 336 ff.; Beneš, *Aufstand der Nationen*, pp. 270 ff., 441. Masaryk's and Beneš' criticism refers particularly to the declaration of loyalty to Austria by the "Czech [semiparliamentary] Association" in November, 1916. It refers also to the Czech Catholic party's renunciation of Entente support for the cause of Czech-Slovak independence (December 21, 1916).

145. See, for instance, Seton-Watson, *A History of the Czechs and Slovaks*, pp. 292 ff.

146. The Czech declaration of May 30, 1917, asked for a transformation of the empire into a federation of free and equal member states, national self-determination, union between Czechs and Slovaks, and recognition of the Czech historic rights, that is, a federal combination of the historic traditional and the ethnic program. See Czedik, *Zur Geschichte der k. k. österreichischen Ministerien*, II, xxiv ff. The counterdeclaration of the German National Association and the Christian Social deputies expressly protested against the recognition of the Bohemian *Staatrecht* in any form. Schüssler, *Das Verfassungsproblem im Habsburgerreich*, pp. 194 f.

147. See Beneš, *Aufstand der Nationen*, p. 447: "Today I won't conceal the fear which has haunted us since we first read the news concerning the imminent amnesty and, in connection with it, the attempts for a parliamentarization of the cabinet." This refers to the unsuccessful attempts of the government to set up a cabinet representing the various nationalities with a strong parliamentary majority; in short, a Slav-German parliamentary coalition. Beneš continues, "The Czech club had previously made its cooperation with the government chiefly dependent upon the amnesty. . . . To us the persecutions at home, up to then, were a weighty argument; the amnesty had robbed us of it. If, in addition to it, the political course [in Austria] had changed, it would have meant a severe blow to our action."

See also, Masaryk, *The Making of a State*, pp. 129 f., 250 ff., 271, 274.

Even if the ill-fated imperial manifesto of October 16, 1918, announcing the transformation of Cisleithanian-Austria into a federation, was bound to failure right from the start by the exclusion of Hungary in the reform, it aroused Masaryk's fear. "His [Emperor Charles's] idea was dangerous and it was necessary to forestall the effect which the manifesto might have in quarters that still retained considerable sympathy with Austria." Masaryk, *The Making of a State*, p. 270. See also below, Chapter XXIV, section on "The Concepts of Peace Policy."

148. Text in Schüssler, *Das Verfassungsproblem im Habsburgerreich*, pp. 184 ff. See also Masaryk, *The Making of a State*, pp. 205 f.; Beneš, *Aufstand der Nationen*, pp. 453 f.

149. According to Masaryk, the two legally most important acts in the gradual process of Czechoslovakia's recognition as an independent state are the letter of recognition by the United States (through Secretary of State Lansing) of October 18, 1918, and the French recognition of October 15, 1918, the latter date being, according to Masaryk, the legal and technical birthday of the Czechoslovak Republic. (Masaryk, *Weltrevolution*, p. 403; *The Making of a State*, pp. 272, 343 f.) October 28, however, has been traditionally celebrated as Independence Day of the Republic, in commemoration of the day when the National Committee in Prague proclaimed itself the government.

## VI. THE POLES

1. Literature on the Polish problem in Austria, as far as general presentations are concerned, does not compare in fullness to the literature on Czech, Magyar, German Austrian, or southern Slav problems. The best surveys on the subject are undoubtedly

to be found in general Polish histories, which, however, generally treat the Austro-Polish question as a mere historic side show.

Numerous important references are, of course, to be found in general works on the Austrian state and national problem, such as those by Bauer, Fischel, Kleinwächter, Renner, Sosnosky, and others. References to monographs will be given at the appropriate places.

General references: *Austrian-Poland*, British Foreign Office Handbook, No. 46 (London, 1920); Samuel König, "Geographic and Ethnic Characteristics of Galicia," *Journal of Central European Affairs*, Vol. I, No. 1 (April, 1941), 55 ff. General presentations, particularly on the period from 1848 to 1914; W. F. Reddaway, J. H. Penson, O. Halecki, R. Dyboski, eds., *The Cambridge History of Poland* (Cambridge, 1941), Vol. II, covering the period from 1697 to 1935, contains significant sections on the Austrian administration in Galicia until 1918 (to be cited hereafter as Reddaway); Oskar Halecki, *A History of Poland* (New York, 1943); Wilhelm Feldman, *Geschichte der polnischen Idee in Polen seit dessen Teilung, 1795–1914* (Munich, Berlin, 1917); Raimund F. Kaindl, *Polen* (Leipzig, 1917), German national viewpoint.

Pre-March period and Revolution of 1848: Józef Feldman, *Sprawa Polska w roku 1848* (Cracow, 1933); Hanns Schlitter, *Aus Österreichs Vormärz*, Vol. I, "Galizien und Krakau" (Vienna, 1920), excellent study; Johann Loserth, "Zur vormärzlichen Polenpolitik in Österreich," *Preussische Jahrbücher*, Vol. 112 (1903); von Ostrow, *Der Bauernkrieg vom Jahre 1846 in Galizien* (Vienna, 1869); Moritz von Sala, *Geschichte des polnischen Aufstandes von 1846* (Vienna, 1867); Ludwig von Mises, *Die Entwicklung des gutsherrlich-bäuerlichen Verhältnisses in Galizien, 1772–1848* (Vienna, 1902).

On the Polish problem during the Revolution of 1848 see Valerian, Count Krasiński, *Panslavism and Germanism* (London, 1848).

On the Polish situation during and immediately preceding the First World War: Walter Schücking, *Das Nationalitätenproblem; eine politische Studie über die Polenfrage und die Zukunft Österreich Ungarns* (Dresden, 1908); Julia Swift Orvis and B. E. Schmitt, in Bernadotte E. Schmitt, ed., *Poland* (Berkeley, Los Angeles, 1945), see Part II, Chapters 5 and 6; G. Gothein, *Das selbständige Polen als Nationalitätenstaat* (Stuttgart, 1917); for the Magyar viewpoint see Count Julius Andrássy, *Diplomacy and War* (London, 1921), and for the Socialist viewpoint see Friedrich Austerlitz, "Die Austro-polnische Lösung," *Kampf* (Oct., 1918), 649 ff.

For a biography of Francis Smolka, the great man of Austro-Polish liberalism in the revolutionary period and after, see K. Widman, *Franz Smolka* (Vienna, 1886).

On the legal development of the nationality problem in Galicia and Bukovina see Richard Wenedikter, "Die Karpathenländer," in K. G. Hugelmann, ed., *Das Nationalitätenrecht des alten Österreich* (Vienna, 1934), pp. 685–738.

On socioeconomic conditions as a basis for political development see also Max Rosenfeld, *Die polnische Judenfrage* (Vienna, 1918). Though the conclusions of this interesting study are concerned only with the Jewish problems, the broad treatment of the general background gives much insight into the apparatus of Austro-Polish politics.

On the Polish-Ruthenian question see Stanislaus Smolka, *Die Ruthenen und ihre Gönner in Berlin* (Vienna, 1902), Polish viewpoint; in answer to it see Julian Romanchuk, *Die Ruthenen und ihre Gegner in Galizien* (Vienna, 1902), and Roman Sembratovych, *Polonia irredenta* (Frankfurt, 1907), both written from the Ruthenian viewpoint.

Bibliography: K. T. Estreicher, *Bibliografia polska,* 27 vols. (Cracow, 1870–1929); L. Finkel, *Bibliografia historyi polskiej* (Cracow, 1891—1914), 1 vol. in 3 separate parts and supplements.

2. To be sure, Bosnia and Hercegovina came under Austrian domination more than a full century later (occupation in 1878 after the Congress of Berlin). Yet with the occupation and, later on, the annexation of these lands, no new nationality group heretofore not represented in Austria joined the monarchy. Ruthenians, on the other hand, had been settled for generations on the southern slopes of the Carpathian Mountains in Hungary, at the time when Galicia and Bukovina were joined to the empire, in 1772 and 1776, respectively.

3. Galicia, as acquired by Austria in 1772, was in territory and in social structure different from the crownland in its extent after 1849. In fact, none of the other Austrian crownlands has ever changed its boundaries as radically and as frequently as Galicia between 1772 and 1849. Galicia, as compared with the status of 1772, was considerably enlarged by the acquisition of territory to the north in the partition of 1795 and by the incorporation of the province of Bukovina—occupied in 1774—in 1777. Yet, in the Peace of Vienna in 1809, Austria was forced to cede all this newly gained territory to the north, plus a part of eastern Galicia and, most important from the Polish point of view, the old city of Cracow, the shrine of Polish national culture. At the Congress of Vienna, Austria regained approximately all of Galicia in its extent at the time of the first partition of Poland in 1772. However, it did not regain possession of Cracow, which became a city republic under a joint Austrian, Prussian, and Russian protectorate. This city republic of Cracow was to become the "Turin" of the Polish national movement. It was closely tied up with the great Russo-Polish insurrection of 1830 as well as with the later activities of the Polish national movement. After a temporary occupation of Cracow by the three protecting powers in 1836, the Galician peasant insurrection of 1846 gave the Metternich government in Vienna a pretext for permanent occupancy of the city with the consent of the other protecting powers. Cracow was incorporated into Galicia in 1849, while Bukovina was at the same time organized as an independent crownland.

Much of the Polish attitude toward Austria before the Compromise of 1867 becomes clearer if it is realized that in the course of seventy-seven years, from 1772 to 1849, the extent and administrative organization of Galicia was radically changed six times (in 1772, 1776, 1795, 1809, 1815, and 1849) and that the residuary symbol of Polish freedom—Cracow—was robbed of its semi-independence only two years before the Revolution of 1848.

The boundaries of Galicia after 1849 corresponded roughly to those of 1772.

4. On the socioeconomic status of Galicia after 1815, see J. Feldman, "The Polish Provinces of Austria and Prussia after 1815," in Reddaway, pp. 337 ff.; see also Schlitter, "Galizien und Krakau," pp. 7 ff.

5. Economically at that time the Prussian administration was undoubtedly most advanced in its Polish eastern provinces. Even politically the Prussian government, while exercising pressure in the direction of Germanization of the Polish people, could not help but take into consideration the great sympathies among German Liberals for the romantic Polish revolutionary cause.

See Feldman in Reddaway, pp. 344–64 f., on the important economic reforms performed in the Polish Prussian provinces during the pre-March period. On the influence of German Liberal public opinion on the handling of the Polish question in Prussia see particularly *ibid.*, pp. 355 f.

Even in Russia, the Polish position was not unfavorable as compared to other parts of the Czarist Empire. Russian Poland was the only part of the Russian Empire which was granted a constitution in 1815 and enjoyed a status of relatively wide, though gradually curtailed, autonomy until 1830. Russian policy under Alexander I intended to have Russian Poland appear as the "Piedmont" of the Polish nation. Within the frame of the empire it was at some opportune time to be joined by its oppressed sons in Austria and Prussia. This policy was reversed with the accession to the throne of Nicholas I in 1825, and Polish aspirations for national resurrection in the framework of the Russian Empire were downed in the ruthless suppression of the Revolution of 1830.

Still, the economic situation in Russian Poland as a whole, and this holds good for the Russian administration in Poland from 1815 to 1918, compared rather favorably to conditions in Galicia, in spite of the shortcomings of the Russian social and economic system in general. In Prussia as well as in Austria the Polish provinces were the remotest, the least industrialized, and culturally the most backward territories. In Russia it was quite the reverse. Russian Poland, the westernmost part of Russia and in closest cultural contact with the Western world, ranked culturally, industrially, and even agriculturally among the most advanced parts of the empire. On the Russian administration in Poland see M. Handelsman, B. Pawlowski, and A. P. Coleman in Reddaway, pp. 275–95, 295–

310, 365–408. See also Schlitter, "Galizien und Krakau," pp. 10, 75, and Otto Bauer, *Österreichische Revolution* (Vienna, 1923), p. 39: "Though Galicia enjoyed far more national and political freedom than the two other parts of Poland [that is, Prussian and Russian Poland] it remained economically and socially far behind them. It did not possess a strong peasant organization as existed in the Prussian part of Poland; it did not possess a developing industrial bourgeoisie as in the Russian part. Here, up to 1914, the power in the country and the leadership of the nation remained in the hands of the nobility." Though Bauer here refers only to the after-revolutionary situation, his remarks on the comparative socioeconomic status of Austrian Poland are entirely correct even for the prerevolutionary period.

In conclusion, economically speaking, the Prussian administration was more progressive and more efficient than the Austrian; the Russian administration, at least basically, worked under more favorable conditions. Politically speaking, Austria's handling of the Poles before 1830 was definitely more intolerant than that of either Prussia or Russia; after 1830, Russia certainly caught up in this respect with Austria. Only after 1867 was the political status of the Austro-Poles definitely superior to that of either of their conationals in Russia and in Prussia.

6. J. Feldman in Reddaway, p. 338. Schlitter, "Galizien und Krakau," pp. 62, 123 f.

7. J. Feldman in Reddaway, pp. 338 ff.

8. Schlitter, "Galizien und Krakau," pp. 10 ff.; J. Feldman in Reddaway, p. 341.

9. *Ibid.*, p. 339; in regard to the language question in court procedure, see Schlitter, "Galizien und Krakau," p. 10.

10. A. Huber and A. Dopsch, *Österreichische Reichsgeschichte*, pp. 255, 321; J. Feldman, in Reddaway, p. 339.

11. "Since the gentry was the only class in Polish society whose national conscience was fully awake, Austria tried to create a gulf between the manor and the cottage. The gentry was burdened with functions hated by the peasants, such as the police jurisdiction in local cases, the collecting of taxes and the enlistment of recruits. . . . The peasant, facing the class-egotism of the gentry and its indifference to his fate, saw in the Austrian official his protector and learned to stress that he was not Polish, but imperial." See Feldman in Reddaway, pp. 339 f.

As to the structure of the *Szlachta* see Rosenfeld, *Die polnische Judenfrage,* and also Schlitter, "Galizien und Krakau," pp. 7 f. The *Szlachta* was by no means devoid of fellow travelers from the small-bourgeois middle class, yet in the preparliamentary era it nevertheless had the rather distinct character of a social-group organization of the nobility. In the parliamentary period after 1867, when it more and more assumed the character of a political-party organization, commoners played an increasing role in it.

12. "The Galician peasant population did not know . . . any kind of patriotism, it had never formed a political part of the nation. . . . It was loyal to the government, to whom it owed the abolition of serfdom in 1781." This refers only to the grant of personal freedom, not to the abolition of the "robot" (agricultural serfdom) system, which still existed at that time. "In the main, the nation was represented by the *Szlachta.* . . . Apart from few exceptions, only the *Szlachta,* including their numerous servant clientele, supported the national cause and the revolution." Schlitter, "Galizien und Krakau," pp. 7 f.

Considering the fact that the bourgeois middle class then scarcely counted numerically and that the gentry by far outnumbered the aristocracy, there is some point in Schlitter's allegation that the *Szlachta* represented the middle class of the nation.

13. See J. Feldman in Reddaway, pp. 339 f., as typical of the Polish standpoint on this problem; the governmental point of view is represented in J. A. von Helfert, *Geschichte der österreichischen Revolution,* 2 vols. (Freiburg, 1907–1909), I, 23 ff.; on the proposed administrative partition see Schlitter, "Galizien und Krakau," pp. 61 ff., 123 ff.

Count Francis Stadion, the famous originator of the March constitution of 1849, succeded his brother Rudolph as governor of Galicia only in 1847. He had, however, previously served in the crownland administration. See also H. Friedjung, *Österreich von 1848 bis 1860,* 2 vols. (Stuttgart, 1908, 1912), I, 263 ff.

14. See Helfert, *Geschichte der österreichischen Revolution,* I, 26. Schlitter, "Galizien und Krakau," p. 61. See also Chapter XIII, below, on the Ruthenians.

15. The Ruthenians, as part of the Ukrainian or Little Russian peoples, are, as is well known, a branch of the Russian ethnic family and, as such, possibly of purer ethnic stock than the Great Russians. See, for instance, *The Ukraine,* British Foreign Office Handbook, No. 52 (London, 1920), pp. 9 f. Isaiah Bowman, *The New World,* (4th ed., Yonkers, 1928), pp. 422 f.; Michael Hrushevsky, *A History of Ukraine* (New Haven, 1941), pp. 20 ff.

16. Future parliamentary leaders in the period of Polish home rule in Austria—Francis Smolka (1811–99), later president of the Austrian parliament of long standing, and F. Ziemialkowski—were already showing their hands in this movement.

17. See Schlitter, "Galizien und Krakau," pp. 14 ff., 80, and J. Feldman in Reddaway, pp. 346 ff., on the history of the insurrection of 1846.

18. See Helfert, *Geschichte der österreichischen Revolution,* I, 25. Later research has disproved the statement that the Austrian government was taken by surprise and was unprepared for this revolt.

19. It has been repeatedly charged in contemporary as well as in more recent literature that the Austrian government had openly supported the peasant insurrection and had even promised a head tax for every killed Polish nobleman. These charges are, in the main, unsubstantiated. The truth is most probably that the government, relying on a passive resistance of the peasants against the revolutionary movement, was itself surprised by the active, violent, semi-communist character of the peasant uprising and, after a few days of observation, crushed it abruptly as soon as it went out of bounds. It is fair to assume that the government not only for political reasons opposed, though mildly, the outrageous social conditions in Galicia. Interesting in this respect is a letter written by Metternich on the second of March, 1846—that is, after the peasant revolt—to the Prussian minister Canitz, "The large majority of the preachers of freedom are peasant sweaters [*Bauernschinder*] at home." See Schlitter, "Galizien und Krakau," pp. 79 ff.

20. For a typical, conservative, Polish nationalist interpretation of the question of responsibility for the uprising see, Krasiński, *Panslavism and Germanism,* pp. 201 f.

"The persecution in consequence of the Polish efforts which had hitherto been considered as solely inflicted by Russia, came now from the quarter where a short time before our hopes were placed, and with the addition of two new deadly weapons suspended over our heads, namely the flail of the instigated peasants and the daggers of the new Polish demagogues, generated by the rank suppuration of the cruelly irritated wound of the national body . . .

"This alludes to the massacre of the Polish nobles by the peasants in Galicia, who instead of being punished, were rewarded by the Austrian government. Many Poles, bewildered by the sufferings of their country, fell into the evils of communism and actively spread it amongst the peasantry of Galicia. The Austrian government saw it and permitted that mischievous propaganda to go on unmolested in order to create a dissension between landowners and peasants, exciting the latter against the former, but we do not think that there was any instance of Polish demagogic emissaries attempting the life of their countrymen or even of having had such intentions." See also *ibid.,* p. 193.

From the viewpoint of Austria's foreign policy see Bismarck's interesting comment on the revolution of 1846 and Austria's Polish-Ruthenian policy in general. Otto von Bismarck, *Gedanken und Erinnerungen,* Vol. II, Chap. XXIX, 2.

21. The government introduced some, though extremely limited, measures for reform of the robot system in the period from 1846–48, at least in so far as it took control of arbitrary abuse of the bondsmen by the lords. The "patrimonial" jurisdiction and administration of the lords was restricted, and the government now exercised the major part of the former administrative and jurisdictional functions of the lords. Nothing, however, came of the long-planned administrative division of Galicia and, all in all, the final result of the "reform period" was equally disappointing to both the Polish and the Ruthenian peasants. It turned out to be, not a victory of the peasants over the lords, but merely a victory of Austro-German centralism over Polish feudal separatism. On

the record of the Polish aristocratic mismanagement and viewed from the standpoint of the peasants it is, however, only fair to say that the lesser evil had succeeded. On the reform schemes and plans from 1846 to 1848 see Schlitter, "Galizien und Krakau," pp. 38–61.

22. On this point see also Springer, *Geschichte Österreichs seit dem Wiener Frieden 1809*, I, 233 f. On Polish claims for autonomy during the revolution see A. Fischel, *Materialien zur Sprachenfrage in Österreich*, Nos. 73 and 75.

23. See G. Kolmer, *Parlament und Verfassung in Österreich, 1848–1904*, 8 vols. (Leipzig, Vienna, 1902–14), I, 351 ff., 366 ff., 397 f.; Redlich, *Das österreichische Staats- und Reichsproblem*, II, 619 ff. See A. Skedl and E. Weiss, eds. *Der politische Nachlass des Grafen Eduard Taaffe* (Vienna 1922), pp. 230 ff.

24. F. G. Kleinwächter, *Der Untergang der österreichisch-ungarischen Monarchie* (Leipzig, 1920), p. 116. See also Friedrich von Wieser, *Über Vergangenheit und Zukunft der österreichischen Verfassung* (Vienna, 1905), p. 89.

The Social Democrats were not members of the *Polenklub*.

The Polish autonomy rested, not on statutes, but on imperial administrative ordinances. Nevertheless, the imperial government always adhered to it strictly, and it was not subjected to the frequent changes conforming to parliamentary conditions, as the Czech position in Bohemia.

According to the ordinance of June 5, 1869, functions under the jurisdiction of the ministries of the interior, finances, agriculture, and commerce, affairs of public security and defense (in Austria Cisleithania, to be sure), education, and justice were in internal intercourse, but for eastern Galicia for all practical purposes administered exclusively in the Polish language. In the last prewar decades the Ruthenian language obtained equal status with Polish in eastern Galicia.

Legally existing German language rights were practically not exercised any longer.

Actually, the Galician autonomy was by no means confined to the privileged status of the Polish language. The whole crownland administration was thoroughly Polish. Even the control functions of the imperial ministries were reduced to an absolute minimum. For all practical purposes the imperial governor of Galicia, generally a Polish aristocrat, and the Galician diet had free rein in the administration, a status unparalleled in any other crownland.

See A. Fischel, *Das österreichische Sprachenrecht*, xciii ff., 122 f., 179 f., 207 f.

An even farther-reaching autonomy was promised to the Austro-Poles in principle in November, 1918, at the time when the Central Powers proclaimed the restoration of a (Russian) Polish puppet kingdom. See E. von Glaise-Horstenau, *The Collapse of the Austro-Hungarian Empire* (London, 1930), pp. 6 ff.

25. In fact, the immediate cause of the withdrawal of Polish support from the government was the forced cession of a part of eastern Galicia to the new Ukrainian Republic in the peace treaty of Brest Litovsk in February, 1918, which Austria agreed to only under extreme German pressure and in the most urgent need of imports of grain from the Ukrainian Republic. See Glaise-Horstenau, *The Collapse of the Austro-Hungarian Empire*, pp. 76 ff.

The fact that the proclamation of the Polish kingdom by the Central Powers in November, 1916, exclusive of the Austrian (Galician) and Prussian Polish territories, did not lead directly to the severance of the expedient alliance between government and "Polish club," proved the strength of this relationship. It proved further how little the *Szlachta* understood the national feelings of the Polish masses. The development of the Polish independence movement in former Russian Poland during the First World War was finally chiefly responsible for the Polish secession from Austria. Its history, however, does not form a part of this study.

## VII. THE CROATS

1. It is scarcely possible to draw a bibliographically definite line between literature on the southern Slav problem in the empire in general and the Croatian problem in

particular. Almost any work on the southern Slav question is largely devoted to a discussion of the Croatian problem. Likewise, any informative work on the Croatian question must give close attention to the southern Slav problem as a whole.

Thus, general works in this field should also be consulted in connection with the chapters on the Slovene and the Serb national groups. Conversely, discussions on the Slovene and the Serb national problems have an important bearing on the Croatian question.

History of southern Slav nationalism and Croatian nationalism in particular: Bartholomäus Kopitar, *Grammatik der slavischen Sprache in Krain, Kärnten und Steyermark* (Laibach, 1808), pp. III–XLVIII. Directly concerned with the rise of Slovene literary nationalism, Kopitar's introduction also gives an illuminating picture of the ideological foundations of Croatian nationalism within the southern Slav problem.

Alfred Fischel, *Der Panslawismus bis zum Weltkrieg* (Stuttgart, 1919); Nikola Andrič, "Kroatische Literaturgeschichte," in *Die österreichisch-ungarische Monarchie in Wort und Bild,*" Vol. "Kroatien," pp. 125 ff. I. R. Thim, "Die Gründungsversuche Jugoslawiens 1848–49," *Ungarische Jahrbücher* (Berlin, 1921), I, 22 ff.

History of the Croats: Ferdo Šišić, *Pregled povijesti hrvatskoga naroda* (Zagreb, 1916), Croatian history until 1873; Josip Horvat, *Politička povijest Hrvatske* (Zagreb, 1936), with introduction by F. Šišić, covers Croatian history since 1832.

Theodor von Sosnosky, *Die Balkanpolitik Österreich-Ungarns seit 1866,* 2 vols. (Stuttgart, Berlin, 1913–14), Austrian imperial viewpoint, particularly informative on the interrelations between the domestic and foreign political aspects of the Southern Slav question; R. W. Seton-Watson, *The Southern Slav Question and the Habsburg Monarchy* (London, 1911), sharply critical of Magyar policy, but optimistic in regarding a solution of the "question" within the empire; contains documents and a good bibliography.

G. de Montbel, *La Condition politique de la Croatie-Slavonie dans la monarchie austro-hongroise* (Toulon, 1909), conservative approach; Hermann Wendel, *Der Kampf der Südslawen um Freiheit und Einheit* (Frankfurt, 1925), good bibliography, and *Die Habsburger und die Südslawenfrage* (Belgrade, Leipzig, 1924). Wendel largely follows Otto Bauer's ideas and is equally sharply opposed to the imperial and to the Magyar policy.

J. M. Baernreither (several times minister in Austria), *Fragmente eines politisches Tagebuches. Die südslawische Frage und Österreich-Ungarn vor dem Weltkrieg,* ed. by J. Redlich (Berlin, 1928). In English, *Fragments of a Political Diary* (London, 1930), particularly informative on the Austrian south Slav problem in relation to Serbia, also on the Croatian-Serb problem in Austria, written from a conciliatory imperial Austrian viewpoint.

L. von Südland (Ivo Pilar), *Die südslawische Frage und der Weltkrieg* (Vienna, 1918), a conservative pendant to Wendel's work; though inferior in presentation, it is useful for its broad historic outline and its excellent bibliography; J. H. Schwicker, *Geschichte der österreichischen Militärgrenze,* 4 vols. (Teschen, 1883), regional-institutional approach; Peter Matković, *Kroatien und Slavonien* (Zagreb, 1873), legal political approach; T. G. Masaryk, *Der Agramer Hochverratsprozess und die Annexion von Bosnien und Herzegowina* (Vienna, 1909), an important source on the stand of south Slav unionism at the time of the beginning Balkan crisis.

On the same period see also R. W. Seton-Watson, *Absolutism in Croatia* (London, 1912), in German, *Absolutismus in Kroatien* (Vienna, 1909); Bogumil Vošnjak, *A Dying Empire* (London, 1918).

Constitutional problems: Joseph Pliverić, *Beiträge zum ungarisch-kroatischen Bundesrechte* (Zagreb, 1886); [Stephan Pejaković], *Aktenstücke zur Geschichte des kroatisch-slavonischen Landtages* (Vienna, 1861), a collection of documents; J. Krišnjavi, on "Die politischen Verhältnisse Kroatiens" (titles vary), *Österreichische Rundschau,* Vols. V–XXIII (1905–1910), a series of articles from the imperial standpoint; Edmund von Polner, "Das Staatsrecht des Königreiches Ungarn und seiner Mitländer," in A. von Berzeviczy, ed., *Ungarn* (Budapest, 1917), pp. 214 ff., Magyar standpoint; see also Heinrich Marczali, *Ungarisches Verfassungsrecht* (Magyar viewpoint), J. Szekfü, *État et nation* (Paris, 1945), and, for a comprehensive and impartial discussion, J. Redlich, *Das österreichische Staats- und Reichsproblem* (Leipzig, 1920, 1926).

Bibliography: Franjo Rački, *Nacrt hrvatske historiografije* (Zagreb, 1908); Josip Mal, "Neuere kroatische Historiographie," *Zeitschrift für osteuropäische Geschichte*, Vol. IV, No. 2 (Berlin, 1913). For further references see Chapter XI, below, on the Slovenes, Chapter X, on the Serbs, and Chapter IV above, on the Magyars, particularly the section on the Magyar-Croatian Compromise of 1868, in Chapter IV.

2. On the legal character of this "Real Union" of constitutionally unequal partners, roughly corresponding to that of Finland to czarist Russia in the nineteenth century, Poland to Russia between 1815 and 1830, and Iceland to Denmark until the end of the Second World War, see E. Bernatzik, *Österreichische Verfassungsgesetze* (Vienna, 1911), pp. 733 ff. See also above, Chapter IV, section, "From Suppression to Full Restoration."

3. The term "Serb-Croatian" refers here to Serb-Coratian interrelations and interests of two different national groups, in distinction to the term "Serbo-Croatian," frequently used in literature on the southern Slav problem to designate an assumed common ethnic *and* political group consisting of Serbs and Croats. As pointed out previously in Chapter II, above, in the section on "The Organization of the National Groups," in spite of the ethnic and linguistic identity of Serbs and Croats, this study perceives both groups as culturally and politically different entities. Concerning this terminological question see particularly L. von Südland [Pilar], *Die südslawische Frage und der Weltkrieg*, pp. 585 f. See also Chapter XI, below.

4. *Ibid.*

5. From a strict ethnic viewpoint the term "southern Slav peoples" comprises the Balkan peoples not represented in the empire as well, namely, the ethnically mixed Bulgarian, Macedonian, and Albanian peoples. Austrian history and, in a sense, general European history prior to 1914 regarded the southern Slav problem as primarily that of the southern Slav groups who were represented (though not solely represented) in the empire—Croats, Slovenes, and Serbs. This is the sense in which the term "southern Slavs" is used in this study.

6. See above, Chapter II, section on "The Organization of the National Groups."

7. The autonomy of Serbia within the orbit of the Ottoman Empire was first established in 1812, lost in the following year, and re-established and gradually expanded in 1814, 1830, and 1856. During this whole period important fortified places in Serbia, above all Belgrade, were still garrisoned by Turkish troops. Only in 1878 was the unrestricted sovereignty of Serbia recognized by the Great Powers. Great as the influence of Serbia's political sovereignty became on the development of southern Slav nationalism within the empire with the Austrian occupation of Bosnia in 1878, Serb political influence from outside prior to that time was relatively negligible. The stream of national feeling prior to 1878 flowed from the empire to Serbia rather than in the opposite direction. The political foundations of these facts in their historic setting are well analyzed in Sosnosky, *Die Balkanpolitik*, I, 1–68.

8. On the differences and similarities in the cultural tradition of Croats and Slovenes see Vošnjak, *A Dying Empire*, pp. 66 f. See also, by the same author, *A Bulwark against Germany; the Fight of the Slovenes, the Western Branch of the Yugo-Slavs, for National Existence* (London, 1917), pp. 29 ff.

9. The royal city of Fiume, Croatia's ancient Adriatic port, became in 1868 a *corpus separatum* of the Hungarian crown.

10. On the Dalmatian problem see Karl G. Hugelmann, ed., *Nationalitätenrecht des alten Österreich* (Vienna, 1934), pp. 150 ff., and Alfred Manussi-Montesole, "Dalmatien," *ibid.*, pp. 632–83. See also *Dalmatia*, British Foreign Office Handbook, No. 11 (London, 1920).

The Magyar standpoint in this question, which concurs largely with Croatian claims, is presented in Marczali, *Ungarisches Verfassungsrecht*, pp. 50 ff. See also Marczali, "Übersicht der Geschichte Ungarns," in A. von Berzeviczy, ed., *Ungarn* (Budapest, 1917), 129 ff., and *ibid.*, E. von Polner, "Das Staatsrecht des Königreichs Ungarns und seiner

Mitländer," pp. 225 ff. (hereafter cited as Polner, in *Ungarn*); J. Ludvigh, *L'Autriche despotique et la Hongrie constitutionelle* (Brussels, 1861), pp. 139 ff.

11. The Hungarian government, in particular, managed to prevent the construction of a direct railway connection between Dalmatia and the bulk of the Austrian lands, since this line would have had to cross Hungarian territory.

12. On the legal history of the term "Slavonia" see Marczali, *Ungarisches Verfassungsrecht*, pp. 30–34; Polner, in *Ungarn*, pp. 227–29; Ernest Denis, *La grande Serbie* (Paris, 1915), pp. 145–47.

13. That is, for a time during the latter part of the reign of Maria Theresa (1767–77), during the Napoleonic Wars from 1809–13, and in the period from 1848 to 1868, the union was severed.

14. Croatia, on the other hand, thought of the constitutional relations of the Triune kingdom to Hungary as those of *regna socia,* that is, allied or associated countries.

15. The national aspects of this conflict, however, could become more apparent only during the last part of the reign of Francis I, since the Hungarian *Reichstag* was not called into session by the king-emperor before 1823. The Croatian Estates themselves were convoked only in 1825.

16. On the history of the language conflict and particularly, also, of the Hungarian *Reichstag* proceedings of 1790–91, 1825–29, 1840, 1843, and 1847–48, where the language question was thoroughly discussed, see Fischel, *Das österreichische Sprachenrecht*, pp. 66 ff.; also Helfert, *Geschichte der österreichischen Revolution*, I, 38 f., 154 ff., 445 ff.; Redlich, *Das österreichische Staats- und Reichsproblem*, II, 207 ff.; Eisenmann, *Le Compromis austro-hongrois de 1867*, pp. 62 f.; Seton-Watson, *The Southern Slav Question*, pp. 28 ff. See also above, Chapter IV, section on "The National Concept of Magyarism."

17. Farther-reaching and broader national reaction became apparent in the Croatian Estates of October, 1847, when for the first time the use of the national language in school and government office was proclaimed. See Seton-Watson, *The Southern Slav Question*, pp. 25 ff., 30 ff., and *Racial Problems in Hungary* (London, 1908), pp. 42 f.; Wendel, *Der Kampf der Südslawen*, pp. 189 ff.

18. The Hungarian *Reichstage* of 1790–91 and 1847 dealt specifically with these questions. See Marczali, *Ungarisches Verfassungsrecht*, pp. 21 ff., and Seton-Watson, *The Southern Slav Question*, pp. 25 ff., and the literature quoted there.

19. The terms "Illyria" and "Illyrians" are of great significance in the history of southern Slav nationalism. Illyricum was the name of the Roman province on the eastern shores of the Adriatic whose native population were the Celtic peoples of the "Illyrians." In early modern times the Greek Orthodox Serbs and the Bulgarians were often designated by this name. Yet the sometimes rather artificial historic traditionalism, which in a way is so characteristic of the national movement in Europe from the Congress of Vienna to the Revolution of 1848, gave the term a different connotation. It comprehended "Illyrism" as the movement striving for the national unification of all the southern Slav peoples, the so-called "Illyrians." See Seton-Watson, *The Southern Slav Question*, pp. 15 f., 25 f., 29 f., and Fischel, *Der Panslawismus bis zum Weltkrieg*, pp. 138 f.

20. For a discussion of the character and consequences of the French administration see particularly Wendel, *Der Kampf der Südslawen*, pp. 113–39. See also Vošnjak, *A Bulwark against Germany*, pp. 55 ff., and E. C. Black, "Fonché in Illyria: 1813," *Journal of Central European Affairs*, Vol. II, No. 4 (Jan., 1943), 356 ff.

21. See Kopitar, *Grammatik*, pp. iv ff.

22. The technically, though by no means ideologically, artificial character of this Illyrian language movement notwithstanding, actually an Italo-Illyrian and a French-Illyrian dictionary were compiled.

23. Wendel, *Der Kampf der Südslawen*, p. 214. See also Fischel, *Der Panslawismus bis zum Weltkrieg*, particularly pp. 55, 247, on Goethe's and Jakob Grimm's interest in Serbo-Croatian literature and language, available soon in German translation. Indeed, the interest of German romanticists in "Illyrian" literature was even greater than their attachment to Czech literary excavations. Southern Slav literature was even further off

the main tracks of western European literature, and therefore appeared still more romantic and politically more innocent.

24. The previous Austrian crownland system was fully restored only in 1849, and remained territorially unchanged until 1918.

25. Wendel, *Der Kampf der Südslawen*, pp. 137 f.

26. *Ibid.*, p. 134.

27. It must be remembered that in the period of absolutism, in spite of Croatia's constitutional connection with Hungary, the king-emperor was able to exercise a very real influence on Croatian affairs through the imperial cabinet of Vienna. Only after 1867 was the crown strictly prevented from communicating with Croatia through any other agent but the royal Hungarian government. Previously, imperial Austria's support of the Illyrian movement was not restricted to the Austrian Slovene lands, the Littoral, and Dalmatia, but extended as well to Croatia and other territories under the Hungarian crown. See also above, Chapter IV, sections on "The National Concept of Magyarism" and "The Reform Period in Magyar Hungary."

28. This greater linguistic affinity is based (in broad principles) on the common historic church language of the Slav Orthodox and the Greek Uniat churches. Old Slavonic was also the literary language of Catholic Croatia until early modern times.

29. On Gaj in connection with the rise of Illyrism see particularly, Fischel, *Der Panslawismus bis zum Weltkrieg*, pp. 130 ff.; Wendel, *Der Kampf der Südslawen*, pp. 196 ff.; Helfert, *Geschichte der österreichischen Revolution*, I, 36 f., 41 ff.; Denis, *La grande Serbie*, pp. 150 f.; Seton-Watson, *The Southern Slav Question*, pp. 27, 29 ff., 136 f.

30. Fischel, *Der Panslawismus bis zum Weltkrieg*, p. 130.

31. The fact that Gaj's Illyrian movement was strongly and ably supported by a Croatian aristocrat, Count Janko Drašković, and continued after the revolution by the great champion of cultural nationalism, the colorful bishop of Djakovo, Josip Strossmayer, forms rather the exception to the general policy of nobles and high clergy. The overwhelming majority of them either remained autonomists in the old sense or submitted to Magyar national or German centralist-imperial demands.

On Drašković see *ibid.*, pp. 131, 136 f.; Wendel, *Der Kampf der Südslawen*, see particularly pp. 203, 210 f. See *ibid.*, on Strossmayer, pp. 398 ff., 377 ff., and Seton-Watson, *The Southern Slav Question*, pp. 52 ff., 60 ff., 118 ff., 416 ff.

32. The difficulties involved in this task went far beyond Kollár's and Gaj's expectations. For the understanding of some of the problems involved, it is illuminating to turn to Fischel: "The Slavonians and Bosnians . . . as well as the Croats considered themselves as nationalities of their own. In these territories, if one leaves the Old or Church Slavs aside, there existed the following literatures: the vulgar Serbian, the Schocaztcic (literature of the Catholic Serbians—in Slavonia), the specific Dalmatian, the Glagolitic (in Istria and Dalmatia), the Croatian,"—Fischel, *Der Panslawismus bis zum Weltkrieg*, pp. 132 f. The spelling in these various languages, which were only a part of those then in existence in south Slav territories, was altogether different.

33. *Ibid.*, p. 134.

34. Particularly in the literary supplement to the Illyrian national newspaper, *Danica* (Morning Star), and in the periodical *Kolo*, established in 1842.

35. See particularly Dragutin Seljan, *Zemljopis pokraina ilirskih* (Geography of the Illyrian lands), 1843, which according to modern terminology stressed the "geopolitical" significance of this relationship to Russia. It considered the Slavs the most numerous people on earth. A map in this book marked the frontier of the coming Greater Illyria, which was to comprise all the lands between the Adriatic and the Black seas, including Serbia, Albania, Macedonia, Thracia, and so forth. See Fischel, *Der Panslawismus bis zum Weltkrieg*, pp. 140 f. See also in Kopitar, *Grammatik*, III, references to the Slavs as the largest ethnic family of peoples on earth.

36. Typical in this respect are Kossuth's postrevolutionary statements defending his prerevolutionary and revolutionary southern Slav policy as not directed against Croatian autonomy, but against Pan-Slav activities, allegedly supported by Metternich. See L. Kos-

suth, *L'Europe, L'Autriche, et la Hongrie* (3d ed., Brussels, 1859), pp. 19–27; see particularly pp. 21 ff.; see also below, Chapter XIX, section on Kossuth.

37. See Wendel, *Der Kampf der Südslawen*, pp. 206 f. Charges that Gaj's conservatism was due to the fact that the Illyrian leader was actually a secret agent of Metternich, as brought forward chiefly by his Magyar opponents, are unsubstantiated. See Fischel, *Der Panslawismus bis zum Weltkrieg*, pp. 146 f. It would be more appropriate to call the conservative Illyrian leader just a "politician" in his dealings with the Metternich government.

38. On the Austrian government's southern Slav language policy see particularly *ibid.*, pp. 234 ff.

39. On Kopitar, in this connection, see *ibid.*, pp. 233 ff.; Wendel, *Der Kampf der Südslawen*, pp. 32, 131 ff., 181 ff., 221 ff.; Seton-Watson, *The Southern Slav Question*, pp. 134 f. Kopitar's specific contribution to the evolution of Slovene nationalism is discussed in Chapter XI, below.

40. See Kopitar, *Grammatik* (Laibach, 1808), XIX, later elaborated in his *Glagolita Clozianus* (Vienna, 1836). See also Fischel, *Der Panslawismus bis zum Weltkrieg*, pp. 234 ff.

41. In theory, the trialistic state concept referred not only to the southern Slav problem, but also to any form of tripartite empire organization. In a way, Hohenwart's plan of 1871, aiming at the recognition of the Bohemian *Staatsrecht,* represented such a trialistic concept, as did various World War plans to join a Greater Poland to the monarchy.

What distinguished these and other trialistic schemes from the southern Slav trialistic problem is the fact that, as trialistic concepts, they were only intermittently under serious political discussion. The southern Slav trialistic program, on the other hand, was in the forefront of reform plans during most of the last two generations of the empire's existence. Political reality thus primarily connects the southern Slav concept with the idea of trialism. But this southern Slav program does not necessarily imply the union of all three Austro-Hungarian southern Slav peoples. Frequently, in its more conservative forms, the Austrian Slovenes are not included.

42. See particularly, in this respect, the following state documents: Baron Jelačić proclaiming his appointment as *Banus* of Croatia, March, 1848, in [Pejaković], *Aktenstücke*, pp. 1 ff. Address of the Croatian diet to the emperor asking for the reincorporation of Dalmatia, June, 1848, *ibid.*, pp. 77 ff. (translated into English in Seton-Watson, *The Southern Slav Question*, pp. 350 ff.). Memorandum of the Croatian Banal assembly of December 31, 1848, proclaiming the direct relationship of a Croatian, Slovene, Serb federation with the empire. This memorandum, however, does not directly demand the incorporation of Slavonia into Greater Croatia; [Pejaković], *Aktenstücke*, pp. 148 ff. See also the address of the Croatian diet committee of April 25, 1849, to the emperor, *ibid.*, pp. 199 ff., and the declaration of the Croatian diet on the severance of the union with Hungary in 1861, in Seton-Watson, *The Southern Slav Question*, pp. 357 f.

43. See below, Appendix I, on the proportional relation of the southern Slavs to the other national groups.

44. For a discussion of Croat-Magyar relations with particular regard to the Compromise of 1868 and the revival of Magyar liberalism, see Chap. IV, above.

45. Wendel, *Der Kampf der Südslawen*, pp. 582 f.

46. Hodža, *Federation in Central Europe* (London, 1942), p. 32.

47. See below, Appendix 1.

48. On Antony Starčević and the Party of Right see Seton-Watson, *The Southern Slav Question*, pp. 52 ff., 99, 101 ff. On Josip Frank, his political successor as leader of the new Party of Pure Right, see *ibid.*, pp. 110 ff., 146 ff., 161 ff. See the party program of the Party of Pure Right, *ibid.*, pp. 392 f. The term "Right" stands not for conservative leanings, but for the avowed righteousness of the claims for the erection of a Greater Croatia including the Slovene territories. Josip Frank's political concepts are well expressed in his article "Die Eingliederung Bosniens und der Hercegovina," *Österreichische Rundschau*, XVII (1908), 160–63.

49. See Paul Samassa, *Der Völkerstreit im Habsburger Staat* (Leipzig, 1910), pp. 170 ff. See also Chap. XXI, below.

50. See Seton-Watson, *The Southern Slav Question,* pp. 99 ff.

51. See Baernreither, *Fragments of a Political Diary,* pp. 115 f. E. von Glaise-Horstenau, *Die Katastrophe* (Vienna, 1929), p. 69. This offer had been communicated directly to Baernreither, who, however, at that time occupied no official position in the empire. Similar plans were conveyed to Baernreither by private sources in 1910, *ibid.,* pp. 94 f.

On the history of Austrian-Serbian relations at the time of Serbia's political dependency on Austria-Hungary in the 1880s see A. F. Pribram, *The Secret Treaties of Austria-Hungary, 1879–1914* (Cambridge, Mass., 1920, 1921), I, 50 ff. See also Sosnosky, *Die Balkanpolitik,* Vol. I.

52. Thus, Südland [Pilar] in his *Die südslawische Frage und der Weltkrieg,* see particularly pp. 716 ff., perceived a southern Slav state as a prospective Austro-Hungarian condominium. General Stephan von Sarcotić, the last governor of Bosnia-Hercegovina, proposed to join the future southern Slav state to Hungary. See Sarcotič, "Meine letzten Audienzen beim Kaiser," in E. von Steinitz, ed., *Kaiser Franz Joseph* (Berlin, 1931), pp. 349 f. This scheme was promoted during the First World War in the form of a double subdualistic solution which as compensation envisaged the affiliation of a Greater Poland to Austria. For a time such projects were favorably considered by the then leading Magyar statesman, Count Stephan Tisza. See Julius, Count Andrássy, *Diplomacy and the War* (London, 1921), p. 147 (in German, *Diplomatie und Weltkrieg,* Berlin, 1920). On the loyal pro-Austrian trialistic ideology, see particularly the articles by J. Kršnjavi, "Die politischen Verhältnisse Kroatiens," *Osterreichische Rundschau,* Vols. V–VIII (1905, 1906, 1907).

53. See Seton-Watson, *The Southern Slav Question,* pp. 336 ff.

54. *Ibid.,* pp. 337, 338.

55. Seton-Watson, *The Future of Austria-Hungary and the Attitude of the Great Powers* (London, 1907), p. 61; *The Southern Slav Question,* p. 2.

56. See above, Chapter V, section on "Hohenwart's Federalist Mission."

## VIII. THE ITALIANS

1. Grave aspects of foreign policy permanently involved in the problem of Italian irredentism in Austria explain the fullness of the literature on the Austro-Italian problem. The small selection listed here does not include a discussion of national conflict in Lombardy and Venetia, which does not form a part of this study.

Italian presentations: L'Adriatico, *Studio geografico, storico e politico* (Milan, 1915), Cesare Battisti (the World War martyr of Italian irredentism in the Trentino), *Il Trentino, Illustrazione statistico-economica* (Milan, 1915). There are various political pamphlets by C. Battisti on the political claims of Italian south Tirol. G. Borghetti, *Trento Italiano* (Florence, 1903), Gualtiero Castellini, *Trente e Trieste, l'Irredentismo e il problema Adriatico* (Milan, 1915); Giulio Caprin, *L'ora di Trieste* (Florence, 1915).

Non-Italian presentations: Hermann I. Bidermann, *Die Italiener im Tiroler Provinzverbande* (Innsbruck, 1874); Eduard Reut-Nicolussi, *Das altösterreichische Nationalitätenrecht in Welschtirol* (Innsbruck, 1930), German national standpoint; Michael Mayr, *Der italienische Irredentismus* (2d ed., Innsbruck, 1917), German Catholic viewpoint; Georg Pockels, "Tirol," in Karl G. Hugelmann, ed., *Das Nationalitätenrecht des alten Österreich,* pp. 545–68; Alfred Manussi-Montesole, "Die Adrialänder," *ibid.,* pp. 569–631. Both of the above-mentioned sections in Hugelmann's collective work present a definitely pro-German viewpoint. Montanus (pseud.), *Die nationale Entwicklung Tirols in den letzten Jahrzehnten* (Vienna, 1918).

See also A. Skedl and E. Weiss, eds., *De politische Nachlass des Grafen Eduard Taaffe* (Vienna, 1922), dealing with plans for autonomous organization of the Italian part of South Tirol; Paul Molisch, *Briefe zur deutschen Politik in Österreich von 1848–1918* (Vienna, 1934), German national; William K. Wallace, *Greater Italy* (London, 1917); Whitney Warren, *The Just Claims of Italy; the Question of the Trentino, of Trieste, and of the Adriatic* (New York?, 1917); Theodor von Sosnosky, *Die Politik im Habsburger-reich*, 2 vols. (Berlin, 1912, 1913).

The Italian problem in the history of the Austrian Revolution of 1848 is discussed in Paula Geist-Lanyi, *Das Nationalitätenproblem auf dem Reichstag zu Kremsier 1848–1849* (Munich, 1920).

Bibliography: *Anuario bibliografico della storia d'Italia* (Pavia, 1902–).

2. This refers to wars of 1848 and 1859 against Piedmont-Sardinia and of 1866 and 1915–18 against the kingdom of Italy. The Austro-Prussian War against Denmark of 1864, the only war during that period of Austrian history in which Italy was not involved, can scarcely be called a major conflagration.

3. Empire reform plans from 1848 onward generally ignored the problems of Lombardy and Venetia as reaching beyond the empire's jurisdiction.

4. See A. Huber and A. Dopsch, *Österreichische Reichsgeschichte*, pp. 310, 320. Austria, after she had regained her Italian possessions at the Congress of Vienna, organized Lombardy and Venetia in one administrative unit under the "unhistoric" designation of Lombardo-Venetian Kingdom.

5. See A. von Helfert, *Kaiser Franz I und die Stiftung des lombardo-venetianischen Königreiches* (Innsbruck, 1901), and also Ludwig von Simonyi, *Geschichte des lombar-disch-venezianischen Königreiches*, 2 vols. (Milan, 1846–47) (see Vol. II).

6. For the best part of the era from 1848 to 1918 Fiume, as *corpus separatum* of the Hungarian crown, with an overwhelmingly Italian population, enjoyed a relatively far-reaching autonomous status, which secured local self-administration in the Italian language to the district. From 1848 to 1918, in marked contrast to postwar development, the problem of Fiume was not one of national conflict between southern Slavs (Croats) and Italians, but of political conflicts between Magyars and Croats. The local problems of the Italian population never led to serious complications during that period. For a discussion of the legal status of Fiume see Heinrich Marczali, *Ungarisches Verfassungsrecht*, pp. 34, 167–72. See also R. W. Seton-Watson, *The Southern Slav Question and the Habsburg Monarchy* (London, 1911), pp. 81 ff.

7. The Austrian Littoral (Küstenland), though under the supreme administration of an imperial governor for the whole territory, was actually composed of three crownlands, with separate diets and local administrations of their own. They were Gorizia and Gradiska to the north and the city-state of Trieste (since 1849 under at least semi-autonomous administration) and Istria to the south. Only in the smallest of these three units, Trieste, did the Italians form an absolute majority, followed by a substantial Slovene and a small German minority. In the land of Gorizia (not to be confused with its capital of the same name), the Slovenes outnumbered the Italians by almost two to one. In Istria, the Croatians held the first rank, followed by Italians and Slovenes. In 1913 the population of the whole Littoral was estimated as about 900,000: 20 percent Slovene, 32.5 percent Croatian, 3.5 percent German, and 43 percent Italian, disregarding insignificant Friaulian and Rumanian minorities. See Manussi-Montesole, "Die Adrialänder," in Hugelmann, pp. 570 ff. (This estimate corresponds roughly with the Austrian official statistics of 1910.)

Four languages—German, Italian, Serbo-Croatian, and Slovene—were officially recognized in the Littoral in 1849. Yet not until the last prewar decades did the Slav languages actually gain equal standing with German and Italian.

The Italians in Dalmatia formed only some 3 percent of the total population of about 650,000 in 1910 (against more than 96 percent Croatians). Manussi, "Die Adrialänder," in Hugelmann, p. 636. Nevertheless, until 1867 the Italian language enjoyed a privileged, and until 1907 at least an equal, standing with the Croatian language. The some 380,000 Italians in Tirol, forming about 42 percent of the population (census of 1910), lived in a nationally almost wholly homogeneous area, the so-called "Trentino."

8. See below, Chapter XIV.

9. See Geist-Lanyi, *Das Nationalitätenproblem auf dem Reichstag zu Kremsier*, pp. 35 ff., on the history of the prerevolutionary national movement among the Austro-Italians.

10. See below, Chapter XV, section on "The *Reichstag* of Kremsier."

11. On the history of Tirol see J. Egger, *Geschichte Tirols* (Innsbruck, 1872-80).

12. Traces of the special privileges and statutes for Tirol existed until the German occupation of Austria in 1938. They included the so-called "liberty of arms," the right of every male Tirolese citizen to carry a gun without special license.

13. It is assumed that, in a peaceful settlement of Italian demands, Austria would have ceded Italian territory only to the limits of the German-Italian language frontier in Tirol, that is, as far as Salurn (Salorno) to the south, not as far as the Brenner Pass. Thus what commonly is called German-speaking South Tirol, Alto Adige, or Upper Etsch, would still have remained Austrian territory.

14. Regarding the consequences of the Treaty of London see Georges de Manteyer, ed., *Austria's Peace Offer, 1916-17* (London, 1921); Richard Fester, *Die Politik Kaiser Karls und der Wendepunkt des Weltkrieges* (Munich, 1926); H. W. Temperly, *A History of the Peace Conference of Paris*, Vols. III-VI London, 1921). In regard to the fact that the United States was not informed properly on the provisions of this treaty before President Wilson's arrival at the Peace conference, see *ibid.*, particularly III, 71, and IV, 296. See also below, Chapter XXIV, section on "The Concepts of Peace Policy."

15. The question whether the high cultural standard of the Italian people was a further factor determining the government's conciliatory policy is difficult to answer. But it is true that, for instance in the field of higher education, the government introduced compulsory instruction in Italian in German Tirolese secondary schools, in exchange for German instruction in Italian schools, while similar beneficial arrangements of a German-Slav language "exchange" usually met stiff German opposition. (See Pockels, "Tirol," in Hugelmann, pp. 546, 560 f.) In principle, however, recognition of the high cultural standard of any national group just as often led the government to exactly the opposite course: stricter enforcement of the German centralistic policy. The reason, fear of the growing strength of the national movements, was obvious.

16. Typical of the demands for administrative autonomy are the bills introduced by Italian deputies in the Tirolian diet in 1900. See E. Bernatzik, *Österreichische Verfassungsgesetze* (Vienna, 1911), pp. 1117 ff. See also Skedl and Weiss, eds., *Der politische Nachlass des Grafen Eduard Taaffe*, pp. 698 ff.

17. See Manussi-Montesole, "Die Adrialänder," in Hugelmann pp. 615 ff., for the elaborate national statistics in regard to educational institutions, which prove this preferential treatment. The author himself supports and consistently defends, however, the German Italian position against justified Slav demands for equal treatment (see pp. 575 f.) even in regard to Dalmatia, with her insignificant Italian minority (pp. 632 ff.).

It is true, though, that during the three decades preceding the First World War, as in other crownlands, the Slavs in the Littoral and Dalmatia largely, but not fully, caught up with the privileged German and Italian position.

18. *Parliamentary seat per capita*

| | |
|---|---|
| 38,000 Italians | 52,000 Poles |
| 40,000 Germans | 55,000 Croats |
| 46,000 Rumanians | 55,000 Czechs |
| 50,000 Slovenes | 102,000 Ruthenians |

These figures are from E. Bernatzik, *Österreichische Verfassungsgesetze*, pp. 879 ff., quoted from Heinrich Rauchberg, *Statistische Grundlagen der österreichischen Wahlreform* (Brünn, 1907). See also Sieghart, *Die letzten Jahrzehnte einer Grossmacht*, pp. 87 f.; Hugelmann, *Das Nationalitätenrecht des alten Österreich*, pp. 238 ff.; Charmatz, *Österreichs innere Geschichte von 1848 bis 1907*, II, 169 f. The general implications of this franchise reform are discussed in Chapter XXIII, below.

19. See Pockels, "Tirol," in Hugelmann, pp. 566 f., on Italian parliamentary and administrative collaboration in Austria. The author makes a point of the fact that only the upper classes in general and the town population in particular supported the Italian national movement, whereas the rural population in the main was not interested in the national question. This is probably a fair observation. Yet the national indifference of the latter part of the population in no way indicated the existence of active pro-Austrian

sentiments, which possibly might have influenced the political orientation of the Austro-Italians.

In regard to the Austrian administrative policy as evidence of the relatively rich cultural facilities of the Italian population and their status of relative economic prosperity see the following figures, collected by Rauchberg and quoted by Bernatzik, in *Österreichische Verfassungsgesetze*, pp. 879 ff. (Figures on the basis of the census of 1900.)

| | In percentage of Austrian Cisleithanian population | Percentage of direct-tax contribution | Percentage of Austrian secondary schools |
|---|---|---|---|
| Italians (and Ladinians) | 2.83 | 10.4 | 9.20 |

## IX. THE SLOVAKS

1. Slovak political literature in any of the great Western languages is necessarily limited, due to the stringent restrictions placed on Slovak national life until 1918. Yet it contains a number of excellent works, some of them in English.

*General presentations:* Julius Botto, *Slováci, vývin ich národného povedomia* [Slovaks, the evolution of their national consciousness], 2 vols. (Turčiansky Svätý Martin, 1906–10); Peter Yurchak, *The Slovaks; their history and tradition* (Whiting, 1947).

The chapter on the Slovaks in S. Harrison Thomson's *Czechoslovakia in European History* (Princeton, 1943), gives an excellent historical introduction, particularly good on the interrelations between Czech and Slovak national history. Thomas Čapek, *The Slovaks of Hungary; Slavs and Panslavism* (New York, 1906) is illuminating on the history of Slovak cultural nationalism in the nineteenth century. R. W. Seton-Watson, *Racial Problems in Hungary* (London, 1908), with a good annotated bibliography, is probably the most important work on the Slovak political and cultural status and the Hungarian misadministration in the late nineteenth and early twentieth centuries. Facts on this point were made known for the first time to the Western world in this, perhaps the most important of Seton-Watson's numerous works on central and eastern European national problems. See R. W. Seton-Watson, ed., *Slovakia Then and Now* (London, 1931), a collected work on Slovakia's cultural, political, and national development, including the history of the Slovaks in the new republic of Czechoslovakia. Of particular interest is the chapter by Milan Hodža, "The Political Evolution of Slovakia," pp. 65–91. Milan Hodža, *Federation in Central Europe* (London, 1942), is particularly informative on the reform plans concerning the Hungarian nationalities centered around the heir presumptive, Archduke Francis Ferdinand. Ernest Denis, *La Question d'Autriche; les Slovaques* (Paris, 1917), deals largely with the First World War situation, which is also covered in R. W. Seton-Watson, *Masaryk in England* (Cambridge, 1943), and in the World War reminiscences of Masaryk and Beneš. See further Alexander Szana, *Die Geschichte der Slovakei* (Bratislava, 1930), and, by the same author, *Zum ewigen Frieden* (Bratislava, 1931); see also Albert Mamabey, *The Situation in Austria-Hungary* (National Slovak League of America, 1915), and A. Fischel, *Der Panslawismus bis zum Weltkrieg* (Stuttgart, 1919), and Jan Opočenský, *The Collapse of the Austro-Hungarian Monarchy and the Rise of the Czechoslovak State* (Prague, 1928).

Magyar presentations: Louis Steirer, *A tót nemzetiségi mozgalom* [The Slovak Nationalist Movement] (Budapest, 1912); Bela Grünwald, *A Felvidék* [The Highlands] (Budapest, 1878), extreme chauvinist viewpoint; J. Szekfü, *État et nation* (Paris, 1945).

The Slovak question until 1849: See, above all, M. M. Hodža, *Der Slowak* (Prague, 1848), and L'udovít Štúr, *Das XIX. Jahrhundert und der Magyarismus* (Leipzig, 1845), both Slovak interpretations; Leo, Count Thun, *Die Stellung der Slovaken in Ungarn* (Prague, 1843). The latter work contains the very informative correspondence between Thun as defender of Slovakia's national claims and the Magyar standpoint, represented by Francis Pulszky, one of Kossuth's most loyal lieutenants, who denied the existence of a Slovak nationality. See also Nikolaus von Wesselényi, *Eine Stimme über die un-*

*garische und slavische Nationalität* (Leipzig, 1844), Magyar interpretation, and, as a contemporary contribution, Th. J. C. Lochner, *Die nationale Differenzierung und Integrierung der Slowaken und Tschechen in ihren geschichtlichen Verlanf bis 1848* (Harleem, 1931). The representative modern Magyar work on the Slovak question in the Revolution of 1848-49 is Louis Steirer, *A tót nemzetiségi kérdés, 1848-49-ben* [The Slovak nationality question in 1848-49] 2 vols. (Budapest, 1938).

Bibliography: L'udovít V. Rizner, *Bibliografia písomníctva slovenského*, 6 vols. (Turčiansky Svätý Martin, 1929-34), covers literature until 1900. See also *Český Časopis Historický* (Prague, 1895-).

2. According to the official Hungarian statistics of 1910, there were some 2,030,000 Slovaks settled in Hungary. Even taking into account the tendency of Hungarian statistics to cut down the figures of the Hungarian non-Magyar nationalities, it is still fair to assume that in the whole monarchy there certainly never were, at the highest estimate, more than two and a half million Slovaks, which estimate includes the Slovaks living in the Austrian crownland of Moravia whose nationality was listed by the Austrian official census as Czech.

3. The Slav population, particularly the eastern Slav population of the Great Moravian Empire, is unquestionably the historic ancestor of the Slovaks of today, though by no means ethnically identical with them. Thus, on the basis of this relationship, the Slovaks can scarcely be called a national group with history in the sense used in Chapter II. On the Great Moravian Empire see particularly Thomson, *Czechoslovakia in European History*, pp. 10 ff., 196 ff.

4. See particularly Seton-Watson, *Racial Problems in Hungary*, pp. 392 ff.

5. Thomson, *Czechoslovakia in European History*, p. 215.

6. Heinrich Marczali, *Hungary in the Eighteenth Century* (Cambridge, 1910), see particularly p. 34, which refers to the existence of a Slovak noble class. Yet a continued Magyarization of the nobility reduced their significance as a national force to almost nil. The slight influence of mere ethnic factors severed completely from environmental loyalties is well illustrated by the fact that Louis Kossuth and the great Magyar poet, Petöfi, were of Slovak descent. On Kossuth's express denial of the existence of Slovak nationality see Seton-Watson, *Racial Problems in Hungary*, p. 393.

7. The term "Slovakia," as used here and in the following material, refers until 1918 not to a recognized political concept, but merely to the former Hungarian *Comitats* predominantly settled by Slovaks.

8. On the Slovak religious problem see Thomson, *Czechoslovakia in European History*, pp. 207 ff.; Seton-Watson, *Racial Problems in Hungary*, pp. 27 ff.; Fischel, *Der Panslawismus bis zum Weltkrieg*, pp. 95, 119 f., 122 f.; and Borbis, *Die evangelisch-lutherische Kirche Ungarns* (Nördlingen, 1861), and also, by the same author, *Die Märtyrer Kirche der evangelisch-lutherischen Slovaken* (Erlangen, 1863).

9. See particularly Čapek, *The Slovaks of Hungary*, pp. 105 ff.; Fischel, *Der Panslawismus bis zum Weltkrieg*, p. 95.

10. See Thomson, *Czechoslovakia in European History*, p. 216; Čapek, *The Slovaks of Hungary*, pp. 126 ff.

11. See particularly *ibid.*, pp. 102 ff., 120 ff.; Fischel, *Der Panslawismus bis zum Weltkrieg*, pp. 117 ff.; Seton-Watson, *Racial Problems in Hungary*, pp. 77 ff.

12. Kollár's collection of Slovak folksongs was edited from 1823 to 1827. On Kollár see also above, Chapter V, section on "Czech Cultural Evolution."

13. See particularly the chapter, "Language and Literature," in Čapek, *The Slovaks of Hungary*, pp. 102 ff.

14. This controversy has been published in Thun, *Die Stellung der Slovaken in Ungarn.*

15. See also Pulszky's references to this corespondence in his interesting memoirs, *Meine Zeit, mein Leben* (Pressburg, Leipzig, 1880) I, 247 f.

16. See, for instance, Fischel, *Der Panslawismus bis zum Weltkrieg*, pp. 123 f.

17. See below, Chapter XV, section on "The *Reichstag* of Kremsier."

18. For the revolutionary and postrevolutionary development of the Compromise of 1867 see Redlich, *Das österreichische Staats- und Reichsproblem*, II, 274 ff.; Seton-Watson, *Racial Problems in Hungary*, pp. 99 f. On the Slav Congress see particularly Čapek, *The Slovaks of Hungary*, pp. 39 ff.; Fischel, *Der Panslawismus bis zum Weltkrieg*, p. 276; Seton-Watson, *Racial Problems in Hungary*, p. 99; and Albert Pražák, "The Slavonic Congress of 1848 and the Slovaks," *Slavonic (and East European) Review*, VII (London, 1928–29), 141–59. See also below, Chapter XV, section on "The Slav Congress."

19. Seton-Watson, *Racial Problems in Hungary*, pp. 96 ff.

20. See particularly *ibid.*, pp. 108 ff.

21. *Ibid.*, pp. 90 ff.

22. *Ibid.*, pp. 108 ff., 234 ff. It is true that in 1849 the Austrian government had started to negotiate with the Slovak refugee leaders who had fled from Hungary concerning their claim for Slovak autonomous institutions. These negotiations came off without any result. The decreed imperial March constitution of 1849, but for its general references to protection of nationality rights in Hungary (Article 71), ignored the Slovak problem altogether.

23. For a summary of this program see Seton-Watson, *Racial Problems in Hungary*, pp. 120 f.; see also Redlich, *Das österreichische Staats- und Reichsproblem*, II, 282 f.

24. On the "Law of Nationalities" see Chapter IV, section 4, the literature quoted there. See also *ibid.*

25. *Ibid.*, p. 290. Redlich's reference to a non-Magyar majority of the Hungarian population is correct, if Croatia-Slavonia is included.

26. At that earlier period, under the conciliatory spirit of the Deák era, there were a few Slovak secondary schools and a Slovak literary society which were dissolved in the 1870s. See Seton-Watson, *Racial Problems in Hungary*, pp. 117 ff.

27. An authoritative contemporary account of the national program of the Realist party with its demands for "natural," not historic, rights is given in Eduard Beneš, *Le Problème autrichien et la question tchèque* (Paris, 1908), pp. 279 ff. See also above, Chapter V, section, "From Masaryk to the Collapse."

28. See below, Chapter XXI.

29. On the archduke's position regarding the greater Austrian programs, with particular reference to the Czech and Slovak problems, see Hodža, "The Political Evolution of Slovakia," in Seton-Watson, ed., *Slovakia*, pp. 77 f.; Hodža, *Federation in Central Europe*, pp. 37 f., 45 f. See also Seton-Watson, *Masaryk in England*, p. 19; Fieldmarshal F. Conrad von Hötzendorf, *Aus meiner Dienstzeit*, 5 vols. (Vienna, 1921–25), III, 97; and Carl von Bardolff, *Soldat im alten Österreich* (Jena, 1938), p. 157. According to this former chief of the archduke's military cabinet, the archduke was opposed to Czech-Slovak union plans. See further R. Sieghart, *Die letzten Jahrzehnte einer Grossmacht*, pp. 239 ff. The author largely concurs with Hodža and refers to the archduke's aversion to the Czech "Hussite" liberal ideology. His account of Francis Ferdinand's unwillingness to compromise with Czech demands is supported by the publication of a letter by the archduke to the then Austrian prime minister, von Körber, pp. 462 f. See also Chapter XXI, below.

30. *Ibid.*, section on "The Heir Presumptive."

31. Since of all the non-Magyar Hungarian nationalities the Slovaks alone were almost exclusively confined to Hungarian territories, a Hungarian solution of the Slovak problem was not inconceivable in theory. It certainly would have found the support of a part of the Slovak population opposed to the union with the Czechs. Yet, prewar Magyar opposition to reforms in general as dangerous precedents for future farther-reaching demands, could well make the specific point here that Slovak autonomy could not be brought into line with the different national aspirations of Serbs, Croats, Ruthenians, and Rumanians, whose national interests beyond the Hungarian borders demanded different solutions.

32. Hodža, "The Political Evolution of Slovakia," in Seton-Watson, ed., *Slovakia*, pp. 77 f.

33. See Seton-Watson, *Racial Problems in Hungary*, pp. 399 ff.; Thomas G. Masaryk, *The Making of a State* (London, 1927), pp. 208 ff.; Hodža, "The Political Evolution of Slovakia," in Seton-Watson, ed., *Slovakia*, pp. 77 f.

34. See below, Chapter XXIII, and Chapter XXIV, section on "The Concepts of Peace Policy."

35. See, for instance, Michael Károlyi, *Fighting the World; the Struggle for Peace* (New York, 1925), pp. 222 ff., 333, 336, 344, on his and Jaszi's endeavors in October, 1918 to secure a settlement of the Slovak demands within the limits of autonomy in Hungary. See also above, Chapter IV, section on the Magyars in "The First World War and the October Revolution of 1918."

36. See *ibid.*, Chapter V, subsection on the Czechs in "The First World War" and below, Chapter XXIV, section on "The concepts of Peace Policy."

37. On Slovak political activities in the United States see particularly Mamabey, *The Situation in Austria Hungary*. On the Pittsburgh Declaration, which actually was a resolution made by citizens of another nation, namely, the representatives of the American Czech and Slovak societies of United States citizenship, see Masaryk, *The Making of a State*, pp. 208 ff., and Thomson, *Czechoslovakia in European History*, pp. 272 f.

38. Besides Masaryk's *The Making of a State* and Beneš *The Revolt of the Nations* (*Aufstand der Nationen*), Seton-Watson's *Masaryk in England* is an important source from which to ascertain the early history of the Czecho-Slovak union movement during the war. See particularly pp. 47 f. and 52 ff. According to Seton-Watson, Ernest Denis, as early as October, 1914, proposed the union of the Sudeten provinces and Slovakia *within* an Austrian federation. Masaryk's confidential memorandum of April, 1915, already perceived an independent Czecho-Slovak state, *ibid.*, pp. 116 ff.

39. The entire declaration is published in Beneš, *Der Aufstand der Nationen* (Berlin, 1936), pp. 645 f.

# X. THE SERBS

1. General references: *The Yugoslav Movement*, British Foreign Office Handbook, No. 14 (London, 1920).

*a) General presentations:* Stanoje Stanojević, *Istorija srbskoga naroda* (Beograd, 1910) (standard work), and, by the same author, *Histoire nationale succincte des Serbes, Croates et de Slovénes* (Paris, 1918); Lazarovich-Hrbelianovich, *The Serbian People,* 2 vols. (London, 1910); Felix P. Kanitz, *Das Königreich Serbien,* 2 vols. (Leipzig, 1904–1909); R. W. Seton-Watson, *The Rise of Nationality in the Balkans* (London, 1917); Harold Temperly, *History of Serbia* (London, 1917). These works, though not primarily concerned with the history of the Hungarian Serbs, give important information on many aspects of the problem.

The same holds true for two older works: Leopold von Ranke, *A History of Servia* (London, 1853), translated from the German; Count Valerian Krašinski, *Montenegro and the Slovenians of Turkey* (London, 1853).

*b) The Greater Serbian Idea:* Ernest Denis, *La grande Serbie* (Paris, 1915), Serb viewpoint, important on the development of the Greater Serbian idea; Wladan Georgewitsch, *Die serbische Frage* (Stuttgart, 1909), pro-Serb; Benjamin Kallay, *Geschichte der Serben* (Budapest, 1878), Magyar viewpoint; Vojislav M. Petrovič, *Serbia; Her People, History, and Aspirations* (New York, 1915); Stanoje Stanojević, *Le Role des Serbes de Hongrie* (Paris, 1919), Serb viewpoint.

*c) Serbs in Austria-Hungary:* See the bibliography to Chapter VII, above, particularly the previously mentioned works by Baernreither, Seton-Watson, Südland [Pilar], Wendel, and Szekfü.

*The Serbs in Hungary and Croatia:* For earlier history see Jovan Radonić, *Histoire des Serbes de Hongrie* (Paris, 1919) on the development up to 1700. This work also contains a selection of documents pertaining to events until 1849 (Serb viewpoint). A. von Helfert, "Geschichte der südungarischen Bewegungen und Kämpfe gegen die

Zumutungen des Pan Magyarismus," *Österreichisches Jahrbuch, 1907–1908,* imperial viewpoint; Anon., *Österreich, Ungarn und die Woiwodina von einem Saxo-Magyaren* (Vienna, 1850); Eugen Horváth, *Hungary and Servia; the Fate of Southern Hungary* (Budapest, 1919); Dénes Jánossy, *Die Territorialfrage der serbischen Woiwodschaft in Ungarn* (Vienna, 1933), Magyar viewpoint; Matthias Murko, "Kroaten und Serben," *Österreichische Rundschau,* IX (1906), 235 ff., on the differences between the Croatian and Serb national groups; Emile Picot, *Les Serbes de Hongrie* (Prague, Paris, 1873); Yovan Radonić, *The Banat and the Serbo-Roumanian Frontier* (Paris, 1919); see also, by the same author, *La Batchka* (Paris, 1919), and *Le Banat* (Paris, 1919). All three of Radonić's studies are written from a Serb viewpoint. See also Johann Heinrich Schwicker, *Politische Geschichte der Serben in Ungarn* (Budapest, 1880), imperial viewpoint; A. Stojacsovics, *Über die staatsrechtlichen Verhältnisse der Serben in der Wojwodina und überhaupt in den Ländern der ungarischen Krone* (Temesvar, 1860), pro-Serb.

The Serbs in Dalmatia: *Dalmatia,* British Foreign Office Handbook, No. 11 (London. 1920); A. Manussi-Montesole on Dalmatien in Hugelmann, *Das Nationalitätenrecht des alten Österreich,* pp. 632 ff.

The Serbs in Bosnia-Hercegovina: On the national problem in Bosnia-Hercegovina, with particular regard to the Serb question see: *Bosnia and Hercegovina,* British Foreign Office Handbook, No. 12 (London, 1920); J. M. Baernreither, *Bosnische Eindrücke* (Vienna, 1908); Thomas G. Masaryk, *Der Agramer Hochverratsprozess und die Annexion von Bosnien und Hercegovina* (Vienna, 1909), important on the national problem; Ferdinand Schmid, *Bosnien und die Hercegovina unter der Verwaltung Österreich-Ungarns* (Leipzig, 1914), comprehensive work. On the Bosnian constitution of 1908 see E. Bernatzik, *Österreichische Verfassungsgesetze* (Vienna, 1911), and Gustav Steinbach, "Die bosnische Verfassung," *Jahrbuch des öffentlichen Rechtes,* IV (1910), pp. 479–95. With particular regard to aspects of foreign policy see Theodor von Sosnosky, *Die Balkanpolitik Österreich-Ungarns seit 1866,* 2 vols. (Stuttgart, Berlin, 1913–14), Bernadotte E. Schmitt, *The Annexation of Bosnia* (Cambridge, 1937); Seton-Watson, *The Role of Bosnia in International Politics, 1875–1914* (London, 1932).

Bibliography: Royal Serbian Academy, *Spomenik* [Memoirs] (Belgrad, 1890–); Ivan, Ivanić, *Essai de bibliografie française, anglaise, et allemande sur la Serbie et les Serbes* (London, 1907).

2. See above, Chapter II, section on "The Organization of the National Groups."

3. See also Murko, "Kroaten und Serben," *Österreichische Rundschau,* IX (1906), 235 ff.

4. See below, Appendix 1. Austrian Cisleithanian statistics listed Serbs and Croats together, as Serbo-Croats. Political practice, however, considered the Serbs a separate nationality, particularly in Dalmatia, where the Serbs formed a separate party club in the diet. The figure of 100,000 Serbs in Austria (Dalmatia) is based on estimates. See Seton-Watson, *The Southern Slav Question and the Habsburg Monarchy* (London, 1911), pp. 1 ff.; on the Serb status in Dalmatia, see also Manussi-Montesole on Dalmatien in Hugelmann, *Das Nationalitätenrecht des alten Österreich,* pp. 632 ff.

In regard to Bosnia-Hercegovina, the national affiliation, Serb or Croat, was directly connected with religious affiliation. The Greek Orthodox population considered itself by and large as Serb, the Roman Catholic as Croat, and the Mohammedans, ethnically in no way different from either of the two other groups, called themselves "Bosnians," which, of course, they were no more nor less than the Croats and Serbs were in Bosnia.

Supplementary figures of the Serbs outside of the empire may be given as follows, representing the status immediately preceding the Balkan wars: 2,600,000 Serbs in the kingdom of Serbia and about 400,000 in Turkey.

Sometimes a verbal distinction is made in English between the Serbs and the Serbians or Servians. The first term refers to the ethnic group as a whole, as well as to its members outside the kingdom of Serbia or Servia, the second refers to the citizens of the kingdom. In German and Magyar, the Serbs within the empire until the early nineteenth century were frequently referred to as Raczen or Raitzen. Neither of these distinctions is generally used in this study, except in quotations.

5. See Seton-Watson, *The Southern Slav Question,* p. 45; J. Radonić (Radonitch),

*Historire des Serbes de Hongrie*, p. 250, and Fischel, *Der Panslawismus bis zum Weltkrieg*, pp. 149 f., particularly on the Illyrian National Congress of Temesvar in 1790 and the Serb demands raised there.

6. See above, Chapter VII, section on "Croatian Autonomy within Hungary."

7. On Karadžič's reforms and the cultural national reform movement among the Serbs, see Fischel, *Der Panslavismus bis zum Weltkrieg*, pp. 151 ff., Seton-Watson, *The Southern Slav Question*, pp. 134 ff.

The basic idea of Karadžič's reforms was to assimilate the spoken and written language as far as possible and to simplify the latter accordingly. This idea, which was intended to make the understanding of the written language accessible to the broad strata of the population, was opposed by the church as profanization of church language. It is not too much to say that, without the success of Karadžič's basic ideas and the consequent adoption of language reforms, the political union of the Croat and the Serb peoples would never have been feasible.

The merits of this remarkable man were, however, not confined to the linguistic issue. Together with Simon Milutinović (1791–1847), he was the first great collector of Serbian fairy tales, folk songs, and ballads, which aroused enthusiasm in the German literary and learned world. Jakob Grimm, one of the most famous champions of the historic philology of the age, actively supported the work of Karadžič and Milutinović. He wrote the introductions to the German edition of Karadžič's *Kleine serbische Grammatik* (Berlin, Leipzig, 1814), as well as to his collection of "Volksmärchen der Serben" (Berlin, 1854). Goethe's interest in Serb folklore and in Karadžič's activities is likewise well known.

8. The immediate cause of the Magyar government's military action against the Serbs rested in its nonrecognition of the Serb attempt to constitute an autonomous national group within Hungary. This claim was made at the Serb national assembly of Carlowitz in May, 1848. The Serbs demanded, also, the union of the Voivody with the Triune kingdom as a recognized autonomous unit. See Seton-Watson, *The Southern Slav Question*, pp. 47 f. See also H. L. Perthaler, *Österreichische Desorganisation und Reorganisation* (Vienna, 1861), pp. 55 ff., and above, Chapter IV, section on "The Magyars in the Revolutionary Period."

9. See Radonić, *Histoire des Serbes de Hongrie*, pp. 253 ff., on the text of the imperial manifesto of November, 1849, setting up the Voivody of Serbia in former Hungarian territory. The emperor himself accepted the title of Great Voivode of the Voivody of Serbia.

In regard to the limits of the autonomy of the Voivody from the very beginning, the following sentences from the manifesto are significant, "We preserve for ourselves the right to determine by special ordinance the [popular] representation in this territory as well as the participation of the inhabitants in an assembly of the empire, analogous to the institutions of other crownlands according to the principles of the imperial constitution."

This refers to the decreed March constitution of 1849, drafted by Stadion but never put into practice. The imperial reservation is illuminating in so far as it clearly indicates that even then the intention was not immediately to grant to the Serbs the benefits of popular representation, as provided in the constitution.

See further, "Concerning the union of the Serbian Voivody with any other crownland [it] will be decided in accordance with Paragraph 72 of the constitution of the empire after having heard the opinion of the *Kreis* representations." Obviously, this clause referred to a possible union of the Voivody with Croatia. A union with Hungary was, of course, not contemplated at that time. Article 72 of the constitution, in its second paragraph, refers to such a potential union in almost the same words.

The first paragraph of Article 72 (March constitution of 1849) runs as follows, "The Voivody of Serbia will be assured of such institutions which, for the preservation of its church community and nationality, are based on older charters and imperial declarations of recent times." The autonomy of the Voivody established by Leopold I was confirmed by Joseph I, Charles VI, and Maria Theresa. See also the imperial declaration of December 15, 1848, concerning Serb religious autonomy and restoration of the offices of Voivode, Radonić, *Histoire des Serbes de Hongrie*, pp. 251 ff.

10. Seton-Watson, *The Southern Slav Question*, p. 51.

11. See Seton-Watson, *Racial Problems in Hungary*, pp. 224 ff., and above, Chapter IV, sections "From Suppression to Full Restoration" and "Magyar Liberalism in Power."

12. On the Serbs in Dalmatia see A. Manussi-Montesole "Dalmatia" in Hugelmann, pp. 632 ff., and Chapter VIII, above. On the status of the Serbs in Hungary proper since the 1860s see the previously listed monographs by Radonić, *Le Banat* and *La Batchka*.

13. See above, Chapter VII, section on "The Greater Croatian Idea."

14. On Khuen Héderváry's policy see Seton-Watson, *The Southern Slav Question*, pp. 100 ff.; H. Wendel, *Der Kampf der Südslawen um Freiheit und Einheit* (Frankfurt, 1925), pp. 462 ff. See above, Chapter VII, section on "The Greater Croatian Idea."

15. See A. F. Pribram, *The Secret Treaties of Austria-Hungary, 1879–1914*, 2 vols. (Cambridge, Mass., 1920, 1921) see I, 50 ff. translated from the German, *Die politischen Geheimverträge Österreich-Ungarns, 1879–1914* (Vienna, 1920). See also Theodor von Sosnosky, *Die Balkanpolitik Österreich-Ungarns seit 1866*, Vol. I, Section III, Vol. II, Section I–III. See also above, Chapter VII, section on "The Greater Croatian Idea."

16. Seton-Watson, *The Southern Slav Question*, p. 114, considers this attitude of the emperor—which was legally correct—the turning point for the worse in southern Slav-Habsburg relations.

17. The text of these resolutions has been translated into English by Seton-Watson, *ibid.*, pp. 392 ff. For political comment see *ibid.*, pp. 142 ff. See also Wendel, *Der Kampf der Südslawen*, pp. 525 ff.; Sieghart, *Die letzten Jahrzehnte einer Grossmacht*, pp. 343 ff.; *The Yugoslav Movement*, II, British Foreign Office Handbook, No. 14, p. 17; and, most detailed L. von Südland, *Die Südslawische Frage und der Weltkrieg* (Vienna, 1918), pp. 638 ff.

The resolutions clearly proclaimed the principle of ethnic national self-determination. Beyond the demand for incorporation of Dalmatia into Croatia they were, however, vague in regard to their merely implied concern for the interest of the Austrian Cisleithanian southern Slavs, that is, primarily the Slovenes.

18. See *The Yugoslav Movement*, British Foreign Office Handbook, No. 14, p. 17. It would be erroneous to assume that the repeated references in these manifestoes welcoming cooperation and understanding with Magyar-Hungary were merely the product of necessary political caution or opportunism. The resolutions of Fiume and Zara coincided with the culmination of the great Hungarian parliamentary crisis, when plans for a loosening or even severance of the Real Union with Austria on the one hand, and the introduction of universal suffrage in Hungary on the other, hung in the balance. During that brief period, hopes for understanding with Hungary ran high and were supported in part by the Magyar Independence party. Disillusionment soon followed.

19. Somewhat strangely from the viewpoint of logic, the declaration stated "that the Croats and Serbs are, one nation that enjoys equal rights with the other." [sic]. Obviously the second clause contradicted the first. Clearly, the passage refers exclusively to the desired political union.

20. A kind of counterpart to the resolutions of Zara and Fiume was the memorandum submitted to the emperor by fifty-five deputies of the Frank party, as representatives of the Croatian, Bosnian, Austrian, and Dalmatian diets, asking for the establishment of Greater Croatian trialism. Yet at this time the popular support for the Greater Croatian idea was rapidly vanishing. See Wendel, *Der Kampf der Südslawen*, p. 558. See also above, Chapter VII, section on "The Greater Croatian Idea."

21. The fact that official Austria, Hungary, and Croatia took account of the changed position of the Serbs chiefly by a wave of political persecution is evidenced by the sordid history of the high treason trials against fifty-eight Serbs in Agram and the subsequent action of slander preferred by the defendants against their accuser, the famous historian H. Friedjung, in 1909. The latter, though in good faith, had testified to the authenticity of treasonable Austro-Serb documents which turned out to be forgeries produced at the instigation of high officials in the imperial and royal foreign office. The breakdown of the treason charges against the Serb leaders did not dispose of the fact that anti-Austrian political activities were actually going on among the Serbs in the empire. However, the

trials exposed the unwise administrative policy of dealing with a political movement in highly objectionable legal proceedings. On the history of these trials see Seton-Watson, *The Southern Slav Question*, pp. 174-302; Masaryk, *Der Agramer Hochverratsprozess;* and J. M. Baernreither, *Fragments of a Political Diary* (London, 1930), pp. 96 ff.

22. Concerning futile endeavors for an understanding between Austria-Hungary and Serbia even after 1908 see above, Chapter VII, section on "The Greater Croatian Idea."

23. The Bosnian constitution of 1908 combined features of a social, national, and denominational curia system of a most complex character. Yet, unlike similar outdated institutions in the old Austrian crownland constitutions, it was not even based on a specific Bosnian tradition. The diet, on the basis of a restricted franchise law, was to be composed of elected deputies, as well as members *"ex officio"* (so-called *Virilisten*). As to the former, representation in three curias was based on religious Orthodox (chiefly Serb), Roman Catholic (chiefly Croat), Mohammedan, and Jewish affiliation. This arrangement gave the Serbs, in rather fair proportion to their numbers, thirty-one out of seventy-two elected representatives.

As to the appointed high ecclesiastic and secular officials—*ex officio* members—only five out of twenty seats were guaranteed to the Serbs.

Peculiarities of Bosnian "democratic" institutions were the following: The presiding officials of the diet were not elected, but appointed by the emperor, and the right to question the government in the diet had to be previously approved by the very same government. Bills adopted by the diet were subject to the approval of the parliaments in Vienna and Budapest as well as of the joint Austro-Hungarian ministry of finance, the supreme administrative agency in Bosnian affairs. Altogether, this constitution, comparable in some of its basic institutions to the contemporary, new crownland charters in Moravia (1906) and Bukovina (1910), was much inferior to either of them as far as the rights of the legislative branch were concerned.

For the text of the Bosnian constitution see E. Bernatzik, *Die österreichischen Verfassungsgesetze*, pp. 1037 ff.; see also *Bosnia and Hercegovina*, British Foreign Office Handbook, No. 12, p. 28; Wendel, *Die Habsburger und die Südslawenfrage* (Belgrade, Leipzig, 1924), pp. 18 f., and *Kampf der Südslawen*, pp. 581 f. On the Mohammedan ("Bosnian") national position, see note 4 in this chapter.

24. For the text of the declaration of Corfu see *The Yugoslav Movement*, British Foreign Office Handbook, No. 14, pp. 35 ff.; see also *ibid.*, pp. 27 f.


## XI. THE SLOVENES

1. Monographic literature on the Slovene problem is not as extensive as that on the other Austrian southern Slav national groups and has to be supplemented by a number of general works on the southern Slav problem.

*a) General reference: The Slovenes*, British Foreign Office Handbook, No. 13 (London, 1920); *Carniola, Carinthia and Styria*, British Foreign Office Handbook, No. 9 (London, 1920); A. E. Moodiz, "Slovenia—a Zone of Strain," *Journal of Central European Affairs*, III, No. 1 (April, 1943), 65 ff.

*b) Slovene viewpoint:* Josip Gruden, *Zgodovina, slovenskega naroda*, 2 vols. (Celovec, 1912-28); Janez Krek, *Les Slovenes* (Paris, 1917); Dragotin Lončar, *The Slovenes, a Social History from the Earliest Times to 1910* (Cleveland, 1939); Bogumil Vošnjak, *A Bulwark against Germany* (London, 1917), and *A Dying Empire* (London, 1918), particularly informative on Slovene-Croat relations. On this point *see also* A. Milčinivić and J. Krek, *Kroaten und Slovenen* (Jena, 1916).

*c) German viewpoint:* Oskar Lobmeyr-Hohenleiten, "Steiermark, Kärnten, Krain," in Karl G. Hugelmann, ed., *Das Nationalitätenrecht des alten Österreich* (Vienna, 1934), pp. 459 ff.; Alfred Manussi-Montesole, "Die Adrialänder," in *ibid.*, pp. 569 ff.; Paul Hofmann von Wellenhof, *Steiermark, Kärnten, Krain und Küstenland* (Munich, 1899); R. Pfaundler, "Die nationale Frage in Steiermark," *Österreichische Rundschau*, XI (1907),

394 ff., and Hugo Suette, *Der Nationale Kampf in der Steiermark von 1867 bis 1897*, Munich, 1936. Anne Heidrich, *Der völkische Kampf im steirischen Unterland vor dem Weltkrieg*, Brünn, 1944, (both nationalist interpretations).

d) *Slovene language history:* Since knowledge of the language development is particularly important for the understanding of Slovene nationalism, the following works are of interest: Bartholomäus Kopitar, *Grammatik der slawischen Sprache in Krain, Kärnten und Steiermark* (Laibach, 1808); an important source on the history of Slovene nationalism, see pp. III–XLVIII; Franz von Miklosich, *Ethymologisches Wörterbuch der slawischen Sprachen* (Vienna, 1886), and *Vergleichende Grammatik der slawischen Sprachen*, 4 vols. (Vienna, 1868–79).

Bibliography: Fran Simonič, *Slovenska bibliografija* (Ljubljana, 1903–1905); *Zbornik Slovenske Matice* [Magazine of Slovene Foundation] (Ljubljana, 1899 ff.).

2. On Kopitar see also above, Chapter VII, section on "The Greater Croatian Idea."

3. Glagolita is the Old Slav scripture as probably drafted by the apostle Cyrillus in the ninth century.

4. See Alfred Fischel, *Der Panslawismus bis zum Weltkrieg* (Stuttgart, 1919), pp. 234 f.

5. See Oskar Jaszi, *The Dissolution of the Habsburg Monarchy* (Chicago, 1929), pp. 133 f.

6. Fischel, *Der Panslawismus bis zum Weltkrieg*, p. 126; see also on Kopitar, *ibid.*, pp. 56 f., 59 ff., 96, 152 f., 233 ff.; Wendel, *Der Kampf der Südslawen* (Frankfurt, 1925), pp. 131 ff., 181 ff., 200 ff. On Bleiweis, from 1843 editor of the Slovene journal *Novice*, see Fischel, *Der Panslawismus bis zum Weltkrieg*, pp. 129 f.; Vosnjak, *A Bulwark against Germany*, pp. 71, 80, 231; Wendel, *Der Kampf der Südslawen*, pp. 222 f., 232, 282, 371.

7. See above, Chapter VII, section on "The Greater Croatian Idea."

8. This is proven even by the external facts of Kopitar's life. He was librarian at the *Hofbibliothek* (imperial library) in Vienna, censor on Slav literature, and also for a time editor of the then leading German Austrian periodical on belleslettres, the *Wiener Jahrbücher für Literatur*. Its editors were greatly interested in the revival of outstanding monuments of Slav literature. Kopitar's course ran smoothly, except for the controversies with romantic Slav leaders of pro-Russian, Pan-Slav tinge. Many of his far-reaching projects and undertakings for the mutual assimilation of the Slav written languages had been only partly successful, and other proposals, such as those for the cultivation of the Slav church language and the foundation of a central Slav academy in Vienna, failed altogether. But this certainly did not alter the fact that under his and his followers' intellectual guidance the remodeled Slovene literary language took deeper and deeper root in Slovene cultural life, without notable opposition from any side.

9. On Slovene literary activities in the pre-March era see Fischel, *Die Panslawismus bis zum Weltkrieg*, pp. 127 ff.; Vošnjak, *A Bulwark against Germany*, pp. 66 ff.; on Miklosich in the postrevolutionary era see also Wendel, *Der Kampf der Südslawen*, p. 373, Vošnjak, *A Bulwark against Germany*, p. 232; on Presern, see *ibid.*, pp. 71 f.

10. See below, Appendix 1.

11. On the French administration in Slovene territories see *ibid.*, pp. 55 ff.; on Vraz see Wendel, *Der Kampf der Südslawen*, pp. 201, 208, 212, 214, 246. See also above, Chapter VII, section on "Croatia and Southern Slav Unionism."

12. On Anastasius Grün, in his attitude toward Slovene nationalism, see Fischel, *Der Panslawismus bis zum Weltkrieg*, pp. 56, 129; Wendel, *Der Kampf der Südslawen*, pp. 281, 364, 369.

13. See below, Appendix 1.

14. See D. Lončar, "The political program of the Slovenes could be based of necessity only on natural rights, for the Slovenes could not point to any historic development, on whose basis they could cooperate as a nation. . . . The fight between the Slovenian peasants and the German-Italian bourgeoisie could therefore only be cultural and economic, and not constitutional in the sense of historic-political individualism." Loncar, *The Slovenes*, pp. 60, 61.

15. "Unter den Slovenen Innerösterreichs im April, 1848, verbreitete Petition," *Grazer*

*Zeitung*, Vol. I (April, 1848), quoted from Fischel, *Materialien zur Sprachenfrage in Österreich*, No. 102, pp. 331 f.

16. See below, Chapter XV, sections on "The Slav Congress" and "The Reform Plans at Kremsier"; see also Fischel, *Der Panslawismus bis zum Weltkrieg*, pp. 288 ff.

17. On the administration of Taaffe (1879–93), the longest ever experienced by Austria since the days of Metternich, see above, Chapter III, section on "The Liberal Inheritance."

18. To give one striking example: the Slovenes, though forming more than nine tenths of the population of Carniola, until 1883 held only one third of the diet's seats, against a two-thirds German majority, since the curia of the great landowners, having no more than 120 voters, played the decisive part in the elections. This curia was composed of either Germans or supporters of German centralism. The Taaffe regime did not change this outrageous franchise law, but used its influence to swing the big Estate vote to the Slovene cause. Thus, only by devious methods was the rightful Slovene majority seated in the diet in 1883 and maintained ever since. See particularly Lobmeyr-Hohenleiten, "Steiermark, Kärnten, Krain," in Hugelmann, *Das Nationalitätenrecht des alten Österreich*, pp. 514 ff., and Vošnjak, *A Bulwark against Germany*, pp. 98 f.

19. See O. Lobmeyr-Hohenleiten, "Steiermark, Kärnten, Krain," in Hugelmann, *Das Nationalitätenrecht des alten Österreich*, pp. 467 ff.; Richard Charmatz, *Österreichs innere Geschichte von 1848 bis 1907*, II, 92 ff.; Gustav Kolmer, *Parlament und Verfassung in Österreich, 1848–1904*, 8 vols. (Leipzig, Vienna, 1902–14), V, 511 ff.

20. For a survey of the status of Slovene nationality rights in regard to languages see below, Appendix 2, based on Fischel, *Materialien zur Sprachenfrage in Österreich*, pp. xciii–cxiii. See further the article "Nationalitäten," by Fischel, in *Österreichische Staatswörterbuch*, Vol. III, which also gives a brief historic survey on the question and Oskar Lobmeyr-Hohenleiten and Alfred Manussi-Montesole in Hugelmann, *Das Nationalitätenrecht des alten Österreichs*, pp. 459–543, 569–684.

21. See Chapter X above.

22. See A. von Czedik, *Zur Geschichte der k. k. österreichischen Ministerien, 1861–1916*, 4 vols. (Teschen, 1917–20), IV, 380 ff.; Wendel, *Der Kampf der Südslawen*, pp. 715 f.

23. On the violent anti-Serb feelings among Slovenes at the beginning of the First World War, see *ibid.*, p. 699.

24. Anton Korošec, the Slovene peasant leader and chairman of the Southern Slav Club, read the declaration in the Austrian parliament when it reassembled for the first time during the First World War. See Czedik, *Zur Geschichte der k. k. österreichischen Ministerien*, IV, xxiv; Wendel, *Der Kampf der Südslawen*, pp. 736 f. Though this declaration was sponsored by the parliamentary representation of all the southern Slav groups, predominant Slovene influence was largely based on the fact that in Austria-Cisleithania the Slovenes outnumbered the combined Serb-Croat groups by about three to two.

25. See Lončar, *The Slovenes*, p. 60, who perceives the Slovenes' national policy to be a product of their social structure, which is essentially that of a people without history within the meaning discussed in Chapter II, below.

26. See the so-called Whitsuntide program of the German parties (the Socialists excepted) in political opposition to the government, of 1899, published in Fischel, *Materialien zur Sprachenfrage in Österreich*, pp. 33 ff. See further the declaration of the German peoples' councils of Styria, Carinthia, Carniola, and the Littoral of September 4, 1917, protesting strongly against Slovene claims for national autonomy. See Wilhelm Schüssler, *Das Verfassungsproblem im Habsburgerreich* (Stuttgart, Berlin, 1918), pp. 199 ff. See also above, Chapter III, section on "The Germans in the Constitutional Era," and below, Chapter XXIV, sections on "German Centralism's Final Course" and "The Concepts of Peace Policy."

27. On the Socialist Southern Slav program see Wendel, *Der Kampf der Südslawen*, pp. 504 f., 564 f., 738 f., and, by the same author, "Marxism and the Southern Slav Question," *Slavonic Review*, II (1923), 289–307. See also Otto Bauer, *Österreichische Revolution* (Vienna, 1923), pp. 13 ff.

## XII. THE RUMANIANS

1. Literature on the Rumanian question in the monarchy is ample, and part of it is on a high level. This certainly is not due to the fact that the Rumanian problem received particular attention in the empire, since rather the opposite is true, at least until the middle of the nineteenth century. Yet, the romantic land of Transylvania and its history continuously attracted great interest. This led indirectly to some information on the Rumanian problem. After the end of the First World War, the problem of the Magyar minority in Transylvania, one of the most intricate of the central and eastern European minority problems, aroused new interest in the history of Magyar-Rumanian relations. For general reference see *Roumania,* British Foreign Office Handbook, No. 23 (London, 1920); *Transylvania and the Banat,* British Foreign Office Handbook, No. 6 (London, 1920).

*History of the Rumanian People in General:* Nicolas Jorga, *A History of Roumania* (London, 1925), standard work; Alexandru D. Xénopol, *Istoria Rominilor din Dacia Traiană* (Jassi, 1888–93), 6 vols., older standard work; R. W. Seton-Watson, *A History of the Roumanians* (Cambridge, 1934). Seton-Watson's comprehensive works put far more stress than Jorga's on the empire's Rumanian question. See also R. W. Seton-Watson, *Roumania and the Great War* (London, 1915); Charles Upton Clark, *Greater Roumania* (New York, 1922), a portrait of postwar Rumania, with an interesting comparative analysis of the previous Austro-Hungarian administration; Marcu Beza, *The Roumanian Church* (London, 1943); Adrian Fortescue, *The Orthodox Eastern Church* (London, 1911).

*Rumanians in Hungary, Particularly in Transylvania and the Banat:* Gusztáv Beksics, *La Question roumaine et la lutte des races en Orient* (Paris, 1895); Sándor de Bertha, *Magyars et Roumains devant l'histoire* (Paris, 1899); Nicolas Jorga, *Histoire des Romains de Transylvanie et de Hongrie,* 2 vols. (Bucharest, 1915, 1916), German ed., 1905, a standard work; Eugen Brote, *Die rumänische Frage in Siebenbürgen* (Berlin, 1895), an analysis from the viewpoint of the non-Magyar-speaking Transylvanian nationalities; Sylvius Dragomir, *The ethnic minorities in Transylvania* (Geneva, 1927), Rumanian anti-Magyar viewpoint; Ladislas Makkai, *Histoire de Transylvanie* (Paris, 1946); Dimitrie Draghiéscu, *La Transylvanie* (Paris, 1918), Greater Rumanian viewpoint; Paul Hunfalvy, *Die Rumänen und ihre Ansprüche* (Vienna, Teschen, 1883), a well-known, extremely nationalistic Magyar work; David Mitrany, *Greater Roumania* (London, 1917); Aurel C. Popovici, *La Question roumaine en Transylvanie·et en Hongrie* (Paris, 1918), a masterful piece of political propaganda by the author of the *Vereinigten Staaten von Gross-Österreich;* J. M. Schwicker, *Die national politischen Ansprüche der Rumänen in Ungarn* (Leipzig, 1894), from the Austro-centralistic viewpoint; Mircea R. Sirianu, *La Question de Transylvanie et l'unité politique roumaine* (Paris, 1916), from the Greater Rumanian standpoint; Joan Slavici, *Die Rumänen in Ungarn, Siebenbürgen und der Bukowina* (Vienna, 1881).

c) *Other Nationality Problems in Transylvania and the Banat:* J. H. Schwicker, *Geschichte des Temesvarer Banats* (Pest, 1872); Eugen von Friedenfels, *Joseph Bedeus von Scharberg, Beiträge zur Zeitgeschichte Siebenbürgens,* 2 vols. (Hermannstadt, 1877–85), a standard work with an Austro-German centralist slant; Balint Hóman, "Der Ursprung der Siebenbürger Szekler," *Ungarische Jahrbücher* (Berlin, Leipzig, 1922), II, 9 ff.; Julius Szekfü, *Etat et nation,* Part III, "Historiographie des Saxons de Transilvanie" (Paris, 1945); R. F. Kaindl, *Geschichte der Deutschen in Ungarn* (Gotha, 1912). For German national interpretation see F. G. Schultheiss, *Magyaren und Sachsen, 1848–1911* (Leipzig, 1912). See also Friedrich Teutsch and G. D. Teutsch, *Geschichte der Siebenbürgener Sachsen,* 3 vols. (Hermannstadt, 1899–1908).

For numerous problems on the history of Transylvania and her national problems, see *Revue de Transylvanie,* Clui, (1936–).

*Rumanians in Bukovina:* Raimund F. Kaindl, *Geschichte der Bukowina* (Czernowitz, 1888), and *Geschichte der Deutschen in den Karpathenländern,* 2 vols. (Gotha, 1907), also on Transylvania; D. Drăghicescu, *Les Problèmes nationaux de l'Autriche-Hongrie, les Roumanis (Transylvanie, Bucovine, Banat)*, (Paris, 1918); Richard Wenedikter, "Die Karpathenländer," in Karl G. Hugelmann, ed., *Das Nationalitätenrecht des alten Österreich* (Vienna, 1934); Adrian Văleanu "The Question of Bukovina—Then and Now," *Journal of Central European Affairs*, Vol. IV, No. 4 (Jan., 1945), 372 ff.

Bibliography: *Academia Romînă, Analele* [Annals]. (Bucuresci, 1867–); *Revue historique* (Paris, 1867–). I. Crăciun, Bibliographie de la Transylvanie Roumaine, *Revue de Transylvanie*, Vol. III, No. 4 (in Rumanian and French).

2. Approximate number of Rumanians in the empire in 1849, 2,680,000; in 1910, 3,200,000. Approximate number of Rumanians in Hungary in 1910, 2,950,000. Of all those in Hungary there were in Transylvania approximately 1,470,000; in Banat, 850,000. Rumanians in Austria (in Bukovina) in 1910, approximately 275,000. Insignificant Rumanian minorities in the Littoral are disregarded here.

National Composition in Transylvania and the Banat (1910)

|  | Transylvania | Banat |
|---|---|---|
| Rumanians | c.1,470,000 | c.850,000 |
| Magyars and Szekels (The Szekels, of the same language as the Magyars but probably of different racial background, comprised more than 50 percent of this figure) | 970,000 | 475,000 |
| Germans, referred to as "Saxons" | c.234,000 | 427,000 |
| Serbs |  | c.290,000 |

The religious census of Transylvania corresponded closely to the national composition: Orthodox, c.800,000; Uniats, 750,000; Calvinists, 400,000; Roman Catholics, 375,000; Lutherans, 230,000.

Practically all the Rumanian population belonged either to the Greek Orthodox or the Greek Uniat church (under the jurisdiction of the Holy See). Most of the Germans (Saxons) were Lutherans, the Magyars and the Szekels being either Roman Catholics, Calvinists, or Unitarians. The religious composition of the Banat, nationally even more complex, does not run parallel to the national census to the same degree.

3. The psychologically deeply rooted trend for closer affiliation with Western European culture among the Eastern European nationalities in the nineteenth century largely explains the fact that Rumanians used to stress the predominant Latin character of their race and language. Yet, their strong mixture with Slav elements is a universally recognized fact, though often minimized in Rumanian historiography. In any case the alleged Rumanian Latin tradition was strong enough all through the nineteenth century to restrain Pan-Slav-Russian influence, which appealed to the Slav element in the Rumanian national character and to the community of interests between the Russians and the Orthodox part of the Rumanian population. Concerning the ethnic problem see Popovici, *La Question roumaine en Transylvanie et en Hongrie*, pp. 40 ff., and Jorga, *A History of Roumania*, pp. 11 ff.

4. In 1859 Alexander Cuza became prince of the two then separate Rumanian principalities, Moldavia and Walachia. In 1866 the hereditary monarchichal constitution under the Hohenzollerns was established in Rumania. Rumania's complete independence from Turkey was proclaimed only in 1877. In 1881 Rumania was raised to the status of a kingdom. Yet the decisive step toward the gradual development of full independence, the union of Moldavia and Walachia, was already established under Cuza's rule.

5. See Seton-Watson, *A History of the Roumanians*, pp. 20 ff.

6. "Populus" stands here for nobility.

7. On the institutions of autonomy see above, Chapter V, section on "The Institutional Evolution of the National Conflict: Autonomy."

8. What could well be called the first Hungarian national revolution—a revolution of the nobility, to be sure—might have succeeded due to the support given Racoczi's cause by Louis XIV during the War of the Spanish Succession. Yet—a fact not without historic irony—Rákóczi's first general, Alexis Károlyi, the ancestor of Count Michael Károly, defeated Louis XIV in 1711 and thereby saved Hungary and Transylvania for the emperor.

9. Seton-Watson, *A History of the Roumanians*, p. 121.

10. See Heinrich Marczali, *Ungarisches Verfassungsrecht*, p. 30. The author believes that Transylvania had always been a dependency of the Hungarian crown, even though the crown rights could not be exercised at times.

11. Seton-Watson, *A History of the Roumanians*, p. 176.

12. These measures did not imply, however, recognition of a fourth Rumanian nation in Transylvania.

13. These demands were raised in the so-called *Supplex Libellus Valachorum;* see Jorga, *A History of Roumania*, pp. 209 ff.

14. Jorga actually speaks of a renaissance movement. Yet the term is not fully appropriate, at least for the empire's Rumanians. The Walachians in Transylvania and in the Banat did not share the national life of their kin in the principalities under Turkish domination. Neither did a national autonomous Walachian culture have any chance of rising on imperial soil prior to the late eighteenth century. The Rumanian cultural movement of the late eighteenth and the early nineteenth century in Transylvania and the Banat generally did not represent the revival of a destroyed culture. It was in many respects thoroughly original. The recognition of this fact actually does more justice to the remarkable cultural achievements of the Rumanians of that time than a nationalist interpretation, which perceives Rumanian culture in the late eighteenth century as a revival of the bygone colonization achievements of the emperor Trajan among the Dacians in the second century A.D. See Jorga, *A History of Roumania*, pp. 213 ff., and also J. C. Campbell, "The Influence of Western Political Thought in the Roumanian Principalities, 1821–1848: The Generation of 1848," *Journal of Central European Affairs*, Vol. IV, No. 3 (Oct., 1944), 263 ff.

15. Jorga, *A History of Roumania*, pp. 207 ff.; Seton-Watson, *A History of the Roumanians*, pp. 271 ff.

16. It is important at this point to compare the opinions of two celebrated Magyar statesmen expressing the idea of Magyarism toward the nationalities separated from each other by the course of seven decades, but joined together by a remarkable unity of spirit. When in September, 1848, at the outbreak of the revolutionary war the Saxon deputies withdrew from the Hungarian parliament, chiefly because the Magyar government had failed to make good its lavish promises to the nationalities in newly incorporated Transylvania, Kossuth declared, "We may go under, but I swear by God we shall not be the last, but shall sink into the grave under the corpses of traitors." Seton-Watson, *A History of the Roumanians*, p. 284.

At the end of September, 1918, in a no less critical situation for Hungary, when, on the insistence of the emperor, Count Stephan Tisza went to Sarajevo to discuss with Serb political leaders the Yugoslav question, he ended these parleys by pounding the table with his fist and shouting, "It may be that we shall be ruined, but before then we shall still have the power to crush you." E. von Glaise-Horstenau, *The Collapse of the Austro-Hungarian Empire* (London, 1930), p. 195.

17. See Popovici, *La Question roumaine en Transylvanie et en Hongrie*, pp. 77 ff. The Magyar address, signed by the members of the Magyar government, Batthiányi, Deák, Kossuth, Eötvös, Széchenyi, and others, welcoming the acceptance of union by the Transylvanian diet in the most enthusiastic terms, is published in Francis, Count Hartig's *Genesis der Revolution in Österreich im Jahre 1848* (Leipzig, 1850), pp. 369 ff. This Magyar eulogy of Transylvania's liberties makes interesting reading, if only in contrast to the actual handling of Transylvania's affairs as soon as the union was perfected and thereafter.

18. A good account of the attitude of the Rumanians at that time has been given in H. L. Perthaler's *Österreichs Desorganisation und Reorganisation*, Part 1 (Vienna, 1861), pp. 47 ff. It proves the well-reasoned sympathies of German Austrian centralism for the oppressed nationalities in Hungary and Transylvania.

19. The conflict between Rumanians and Magyars in the beginning of the revolutionary war had the character of a social far more than of a national revolution. The rising of the Rumanian peasants against the Magyar nobles represents a striking parallel

to the Ruthenian revolt against the Polish lords in 1846. See H. Friedjung, *Österreich von 1846 bis 1860*, 2 vols. (Stuttgart, 1908, 1912), I, 128.

20. See articles 71–74 of the decreed March constitution of 1849, the text of which is published in E. Bernatzik, *Österreichische Verfassungsgesetze* (Vienna, 1911). Only the preliminary draft of article 71 (36) referred also to the protection of Rumanian language rights. See Josef Redlich, *Das österreichische Staats- und Reichsproblem* (Leipzig, 1920, 1926), I, 2, 93 f.

The final text of the constitution refers expressly only to Croat, Serb, and Saxon (German) nationality rights in Hungarian lands. See also below, Chapter XVII, section on Stadion.

21. For an account of the imperial administration in Rumania in the 1850s see Friedjung, *Österreich von 1848 bis 1860*, I, 413 ff. See also on this period J. C. Campbell, "The Transylvania Problem in 1849," *Journal of Central European Affairs*, Vol. II, No. 2 (April, 1942), 20 ff.

22. In regard to Rumanian national claims in the Banat after 1848 see Friedjung, *Österreich von 1848 bis 1860*, I, 422; regarding Rumanian demands in Bukovina for separation from Galicia in June, 1848, see Fischel, "Rumänen," *Österreichisches Staatswörterbuch*, Vol. III.

23. Specifically, the following demands were raised: (1) Union of all the Rumanians of the Austrian states in one independent nation under the Austrian scepter as . . . part of the empire. (2) Independent national administration in political and ecclesiastical matters. (3) Speedy opening of a general congress of the whole nation. (4) A proportional Rumanian representation in the common imperial parliament. (5) The Rumanian nation asks for a representative of its own in the imperial ministry.

24. Imperial missive of October 20, 1860, to the prime minister, Count Rechberg; see Bernatzik, *Österreichische Verfassungsgesetze*, pp. 311 f. The influence of German Austrian centralism on the Rumanian movement during this period as well as the still modest range of its program becomes very obvious in the pseudonymous pamphlet *Die Sprachen- und Nationalitätenfrage in Österreich, von einem Rumänen* (Vienna, 1860). This pamphlet stands for a limited autonomy for the various nationalities within the framework of a centralistic empire organization.

From A. C. Popovici, *Die Vereinigten Staaten von Gross-Österreich* (Leipzig, 1906), p. 244, quoting Nicolae Popea, *Memorialul archiepiscopului si metropolitului Andreiu Baron de Saguna, sau luptele nationale-politice a le Romanilor 1846–71* (Sibiu, Institutul Tipografic, 1889), Part I, p. 249. See also Friedjung, *Österreich von 1848 bis 1860*, I, 417 f. The work by Trebonian Laureanu, an Austro-Rumanian leader, *Die Romanen der österreichischen Monarchie* (Vienna, 1851), which contains the documents pertinent to these claims, was not available.

25. The Saxons were also the only Transleithanian deputies who participated in the so-called *erweiterte Reichsrat* in Vienna in 1863, thereby supporting the government pretense that a representative assembly of the whole monarchy was actually in existence.

26. Seton-Watson, *A History of the Roumanians*, p. 298.

27. That is, a majority appointed by the sovereign; *ibid.*, pp. 297 ff. See above, Chapter IV, sections "From Suppression to Full Restoration" and "Magyar Liberalism in Power."

28. See Deák's reference to a just solution of the Transylvanian national problem in his famous address of May 13, 1861; Redlich, *Das österreichische Staats- und Reichsproblem*, II, 255 ff.; see above, Chapter IV, sections, "From Suppression to Full Restoration" and "Magyar Liberalism in Power."

29. Kálmán von Tisza, the father of Count Stephan Tisza, was prime minister from 1875 to 1890.

30. See Seton-Watson, *A History of the Roumanians*, Chap. XIII, "Transylvania under the Dual System," pp. 390 ff.; see also Popovici, *La Question roumaine en Transylvanie et en Hongrie*, pp. 82 ff.; Draghiéscu, *La Transylvanie*, pp. 51 ff.

31. Seton-Watson, *A History of the Roumanians*, p. 429.

32. It is a matter of conjecture how much importance should be attributed to the fact that Rumanian leaders several times wanted to join Rumania to the lands of the emperor.

In 1600, presumably for the first time, Michael the Brave of Moldavia proposed such a union. As late as 1848 the Rumanian chargé d'affaires at Frankfurt, Jon Majorescu, proposed the incorporation of a Rumanian state comprising the Danube principalities as well as Transylvania, Bukovina, and the Rumanian parts of Hungary into a federalized empire. Similar ideas have been discussed in Rumanian journals much later, and the point has been stressed that the incorporation of a Rumanian member state into the empire would give Rumania true protection. See Popovici, *Die Vereinigten Staaten von Gross-Österreich*, p. 414, and the Rumanian literature quoted there. As a matter of fact, as late as the period between 1911 and 1914 Austrian and Rumanian statesmen had discussed a new scheme to such effect. At the time it appeared pretty obvious, though, that the Magyar regime would never consent to such plans, which would impair the Dualistic Compromise of 1867. See Seton-Watson, *A History of the Roumanians*, pp. 466 ff., and the literature quoted there. See also Friedrich G. Kleinwächter, *Der Untergang der österreichisch-ungarischen Monarchie* (Leipzig, 1920), pp. 168 f.

33. Technically, Rumania was only a partner to the Austro-German alliance. This alliance had to be kept secret because it would have been opposed by public opinion in the kingdom.

34. Popovici, *Die Vereinigten Staaten von Gross-Österreich*, p. 418. Similar ideas were expressed by an officially more responsible author, the Rumanian parliamentary leader in the Hungarian parliament, Alexander Vaida-Voevod, "Slaven, Deutsche, Magyaren und Rumänen," *Österreichische Rundschau*, XXIV (Jan., 1913), 8–12.

35. See above, Chapter IV, section on "Magyar Liberalism in Power."

36. See the Rumanian national program of 1905 asking for a recognition of a Rumanian national group, a fight against the Magyarization of the army, and in an implied form for revision of the Compromise of 1867, in Popovici, *Die Vereinigten Staaten von Gross-Österreich*, p. 56. See also below, Chapter XXI, section on Popovici.

37. On these problems see below, Chapter XXI, the sections on the Heir Presumptive and particularly on Popovici.

38. Seton-Watson, *A History of the Roumanians*, p. 431. See also *ibid.*, on the archduke's attitude toward the Rumanian problem, his intercourse with Rumanian leaders, and the Popovici program, pp. 425–31, 447 f., 467 f., 470 f., 487. See further the account of Milan Hodža, partly a direct participant in some of the archduke's negotiations, *Federation in Central Europe* (London, 1942), p. 40, 52, 63; Leopold von Chlumecky, *Erzherzog Franz Ferdinand Wirken und Wollen* (Berlin, 1929); Arthur von Polzer-Hoditz, *Kaiser Karl* (Vienna, 1929), p. 75.

39. Count Stephan Tisza, undoubtedly the strongest personality among the Magyar statesmen in the twentieth century, was prime minister from 1903 to 1905, and from 1913 to 1917. See, for instance, E. Treumund, "Tisza und die Rumänen," *Österreichische Rundschau*, XXXVIII (1914), 205 ff., analyzing the Hungarian prime minister's immediate prewar Rumanian policy. See also Count O. Czernin (Austria's First World War foreign minister and minister to Rumania 1913–16), *Im Weltkrieg* (Berlin, 1919), pp. 139 ff.

40. On the national compromise in the Bukovina see Chapter XIII, below.

41. Czernin, *Im Weltkrieg*, pp. 138 ff., 36, 354. Czernin relates further (pp. 107 f.) that the Rumanian Conservative politician Nicolai Filipescu proposed to him—probably in 1913 or 1914—that Rumania should incorporate Transylvania and then as "Greater Rumania" join Austria-Hungary in a legal political relation comparable to that between Germany and Bavaria. According to Czernin, the plan came to naught because Count Tisza, backed by Emperor Francis Joseph, was opposed to it. Yet, even if the empire had taken up the discussion of such a proposal it is open to most serious doubt whether it was submitted in good faith and, if so, whether public opinion in Rumania could have supported it.

42. See Wenedikter, "Die Karpathenländer," in Hugelmann, *Das Nationalitätenrecht des alten Österreich*, pp. 724 ff.; Seton-Watson, *A History of the Roumanians*, pp. 556 ff.; Bernatzik, *Österreichische Verfassungsgesetze*, pp. 937 ff. For a discussion of the national setup in Bukovina see Chapter XIII, below.

## XIII. THE RUTHENIANS

1. Literature on the Ruthenian problem in Austria-Hungary written by Ruthenians is scarce. Hungarian and Polish historians have, of course, reflected on this national group, yet their approach is very often dictated by their own nationalist tinge. However, during and shortly after the First World War a considerable literature developed on the Ukrainian problem in general and the Russo-Ukrainian problem in particular. Though rarely unbiased, this literature contributes much-needed additional data on the national history of the Ruthenians in the empire.

*Ruthenians in Austria-Hungary:* Alexander Barwinski, "Die Bedeutung des ruthenischen Volksstammes für Österreich-Ungarn," *Österreichische Rundschau*, XXXI (1912), 161 ff., Volodymyr Gnatjŭk, *The National Renaissance of the Austro-Hungarian Ukrainians, 1772–1880* (Vienna, 1916), in Ukrainian, both written from a Ruthenian viewpoint.

*Ruthenians in Galicia:* K. Levitsky, *History of the Political Ideas of the Galician Ukrainians from 1848–1914* (Lwów 1929) in Ukrainian. Gregorii Kupchanko, *Das Schicksal der Ruthenen* (Leipzig, 1887) ; Volodymyr Kushnir, *Der Neopanslavismus* (Vienna, 1908) , deals largely with the Russo-Ruthenian problem; Julian Romanchuk, *Die Ruthenen und ihre Gegner in Galizien* (Vienna, 1902), Ruthenian viewpoint; Stanislaus Smolka, *Die Ruthenen und ihre Gönner in Berlin* (Vienna, 1902), Polish viewpoint; Max Rosenfeld, *Die polnische Judenfrage* (Vienna, 1918), a discriminating approach to the Polish Ruthenian conflict in Galicia from the Jewish national viewpoint; Richard Wenedikter, "Die Karpathenländer" in Karl G. Hugelmann, ed., *Das Nationalitätenrecht des alten Österreich* (Vienna, 1934), pp. 685–737, deals also with the situation in Bukovina, particularly informative on the development in the twentieth century (German viewpoint).

*Ruthenians in Bukovina:* Omelyan Popovych, *The Renaissance of Bukovina* (Lwów, 1933), in Ukrainian; Raimund F. Kaindl, *Geschichte der Bukowina* (Czernowitz, 1888), German national viewpoint; see also, by the same author, *Die Ruthenen in der Bukowina* (Czernowitz, 1889), and *Geschichte der Deutschen in den Karpathenländern*, 2 vols. (Gotha, 1907); Adrian Valeanu, "The Question of Bukovina—Then and Now," *Journal of Central European Affairs*, Vol. IV, No. 1 (Jan., 1945), 372 ff. See also R. Wenedikter, in Hugelmann, pp. 724 ff.

*Ruthenians in Hungary: Hungarian Ruthenia*, British Foreign Office Handbook, No. 7 (London, 1920); Hermann I. Bidermann, *Die ungarischen Ruthenen* (Innsbruck, 1862); Alexander Bonkáló, "Die ungarländischen Ruthenen," *Ungarische Jahrbücher* (Berlin, Leipzig, 1921), I, 215 ff., 313 ff.; R. W. Seton-Watson, *Racial Problems in Hungary* (London, 1908).

*The Ukrainian Problem in Relation to the Austro-Ruthenian Question: The Ukraine*, British Foreign Office Handbook, No. 52 (London, 1920). One of the best-known works on Ukrainian history has been published and brought up to date in revised form in English; Michael Hrushevsky, *A History of Ukraine* (New Haven, 1941). Though its references on the Austro-Ruthenian question are scarce, it is an important contribution to the historical background of the problem. See also, by the same author, *Die ukrainische Frage in ihrer historischen Entwicklung* (Vienna, 1915), and *The Historical Evolution of the Ukrainian Problem* (London, 1915) . See, further, Dimitri Markov, *Die russische und ukrainische Idee in Österreich* (Vienna, 1908). Stefan Rudnitzky, *The Ukraine and the Ukrainians* (Jersey City, Ukrainian National Council, 1915), and, by the same author, *Ukraina, Land und Volk* (Vienna, 1916). Typical of the German Austrian World War literature on the subject is *Die Ukraine*, essays by A. Barwinski, Paul Eugen Lewicky, Falk, Schaupp (Berlin, 1916).

On Ruthenian church history see Yuliyan Pelesh, *Geschichte der Union der ruthenischen Kirche mit Rom*, 2 vols. (Vienna, 1878—81) , and Stanislaus Smolka, *Les Ruthenes et les problèmes religieux du monde russe* (Berne, 1917) , Polish viewpoint.

Bibliography: Michael Hrushevsky, *The Traditional Scheme of Russian History and the Problem of a National Organization of the Eastern Slavs* (St. Petersburg, 1904), in

Ukrainian; D. Bahalij, *Outline of Ukrainian Historiography* (Kiev, 1923–25), 2 vols., in Ukrainian.

2. There were roughly about 3,150,000 Ruthenians in the empire in 1880 and about 4,000,000 in 1910. Their percental share in the population of the empire as a whole was remarkably stable, their relative increase of population being the smallest among all Austrian nationalities.

*a) Galicia*

In particular, in 1910 there were in Galicia 4,672,500 Poles (58.6 percent) and 3,208,092 Ruthenians (40.2 percent). The Poles formed the overwhelming majority in western Galicia up to the San River and a majority in Lemberg, the capital, situated in the central part of the crownland. The Ruthenians formed about 64 percent of the population in central and eastern Galicia.

For an understanding of the precarious national equilibrium in Galicia, it is necessary at this point to touch upon the Jewish problem in Galicia. Throughout the nineteenth century the Jews in Galicia, as everywhere else in the empire, not being recognized as a separate national group, usually declared themselves in the official census as Poles and voted for the Polish parliamentary candidates. Growing national consciousness among eastern Jewry after the last decade of the nineteenth century encouraged a large part of that group increasingly to assert its claim for national recognition. These claims were violently opposed by the Poles, who badly needed Jewish support to secure their precarious majority in many districts of the crownlands. On the other hand, Jewish demands in this respect were, quite naturally, supported more and more by the Ruthenians. Consequently, and particularly because of the growing recognition that Jewish economic and social interests were similar to those of the underprivileged Ruthenian national group, the Jews were led increasingly to change their national affiliation from Polish to Ruthenian. The choice of declaring themselves of Jewish nationality was not granted to them by Austrian legislation and jurisdiction. This change in Jewish national policy was a significant factor in the rise of the Ruthenian political status in Galicia during the decades preceding the First World War. Indeed, if it were not for the outbreak of the war itself, a continued trend in that direction might have unseated the Polish majority in Galicia altogether. (See Rosenfeld, *Die polnische Judenfrage,* and below, Appendix 1.)

Regarding the distribution of national cultural institutions in Galicia, the Poles, constituting 58.6 percent of the population in 1911–12, a time when the Ruthenian national status had already improved markedly, possessed 296 secondary and trade schools, while the Ruthenians had twelve; the Poles had two universities—only one of them, the university in Lwów, having some Ruthenian chairs—and three other institutions of equal rank; the Ruthenian had none. See Wenedikter, "Die Karpathenländer," in Hugelmann, pp. 732 ff.

The inferior Ruthenian economic status is illustrated by the fact that the Poles held 40 percent of the land in the predominantly Ruthenian territories and that the Ruthenians, though forming more than two fifths of the population, were able to raise only 18 percent of the whole crownland taxes, that is, per capita less than a third of the average Polish tax contributions. See *ibid.,* p. 695.

Regarding parliamentary representation in Vienna, Poles outnumbered Ruthenians by a ratio declining gradually from 19:1 (1879) to about 2.35:1 after the introduction of general equal franchise in 1907. Even then, however, a Ruthenian deputy was elected by 102,000 votes as against a Polish one by 52,000, a German one by 40,000 and an Italian deputy by 38,000 votes. See E. Bernatzik, *Österreichische Verfassungsgesetze* (Vienna, 1911), pp. 879 ff., and below, Chap. XXIII.

Likewise in the Galician diet the Poles held an undue, though varying, disproportionate majorty (4:1 in 1867). A fairer proportion was to be established, however, in the Galician diet reform of 1914 which due to the outbreak of the war could not be materialized.

*b) Bukovina*

In the Bukovina in 1910 there were 305,000 Ruthenians (38.4 percent of the population), 273,000 Rumanians (34.4 percent), 36,000 Poles (4.6 percent), and about 10,000

Magyars (1.3 percent). There were, furthermore, 169,000 persons speaking the German language (21.4 percent), the best part of them Jews. The Jews, about 13 percent of the population of the crownland, in their overwhelming German language affiliation technically formed a part of the German representation. From 1910 they had been recognized in internal crownland affairs as a nationality of their own.

Prior to 1910 the German diet and parliamentary representation exceeded by far its percental share in the crownland population. After that time the Germans' privileged position was confined to cultural affairs (German university system). No discrimination comparable to the Galician situation existed against the Ruthenians in Bukovina.

*c) Hungary*

There were 473,000 Ruthenians in Hungary in 1910 (Hungarian census of 1910). The economic position of these Hungarian- or Carpatho-Ruthenians was scarcely better than that of their kin in Galicia; their political status—except for approximately the first decade after 1848—was even worse. Ruthenians were represented neither in the Hungarian parliament nor in the *Comitat* representations. No Ruthenian secondary school with Ruthenian as the language of instruction existed in Hungary, and the relatively few elementary schools, with few exceptions, had only one teacher.

3. *The Ukraine*, British Foreign Office Handbook, No. 52, p. 15.

4. A purely legalistic approach which intends to stretch a point thus could defend the thesis that the Ruthenians would technically come under the category of the national groups with independent national political history. Such an argument is not accepted here. The independence of the principality of Halich is contested. It emerged in an area where the state concept was altogether far looser and more fleeting than it was in western and western central Europe, and it by no means played as lasting or as important a role as the Polish, the Bohemian, or the Hungarian state in medieval times. Above all, the eastern Galician territories did not possess for any length of time the social structure which is attributed to the nationalities with history.

5. Those Ukrainians who in the course of the partitions of Poland in the eighteenth century came under Russian domination, returned, often under pressure, to the fold of the Greek Orthodox church.

6. See Wenedikter, "Die Karpathenländer," in Hugelmann, pp. 688 f.

7. From the ethnic and ethnic-linguistic viewpoints, there is, of course, no doubt that the Ruthenians are much closer to the Russians than they are to the Poles. Yet, the Ruthenians in Galicia passed to Austrian rule in 1772, after more than four centuries of Polish domination, and this long-lasting Polish rule had strongly penetrated Ruthenian national culture. Thus, during the first decades after the first and second partitions of Poland, the ethnic position of the Ruthenians appeared obscured by the facts of political history.

8. See also Chapter VI, above.

9. See Alfred Fischel, *Der Panslawismus bis zum Weltkrieg* (Stuttgart, 1919), pp. 156 ff.

10. See Chapter VI, above.

11. On Stadion see Chapter VI, above, and particularly below, Chapter XVII, section on "Stadion and the March constitution of 1849."

12. Both documents have been published in Fischel, *Materialien zur Sprachenfrage in Österreich*, Nos. 74 and 76.

13. On the Slav Congress see below, Chapter XV, section on "The Slav Congress."

14. On the Ruthenian problem on the Slav Congress see Fischel, *Der Panslawismus bis zum Weltkrieg*, pp. 273, 276 f., 285 ff., 289.

15. The Ruthenian policy at Kremsier, predominantly influenced by the able Clerical leaders Yakhimovych and Shashkevych put full confidence in the emperor. Though it wished for partition of Galicia, it was ready to cooperate with the Polish peasants, particularly in questions of agricultural reforms. See Paula Geist-Lanyi, *Das Nationalitätenproblem auf dem Reichstag zu Kremsier 1848–1849* (Munich, 1920), pp. 41 ff., 84 ff., 163 f., 171 ff. See also the Ruthenian declaration of October 26 made by a revolutionary assembly at Lwów asking for the partition of Galicia, Fischel, *Materialien zur Sprachen-*

*frage in Österreich,* No. 79. See also below, Chapter XV, section on "The *Reichstag* of Kremsier," and the literature and sources quoted there.

16. See below, Chapter XV, section on "The Reform plans at Kremsier," and Chapter XVII, section on Stadion.

17. The Galician crownland constitution of September 29, 1850, established a tripartition of Galicia into a Polish western part with Cracow as capital and two Ruthenian parts with the administrative centers of Lwów and Stanislawów. This crownland constitution was abolished by the Sylvester Patent of 1851. Each of these three parts were to be represented in a different curia of the diet. See Michael Losynskyi, *Die Schaffung einer ukrainischen Provinz in Österreich* (Berlin, 1915), pp. 14 ff.

Actually, a partition of Galicia into a western and an eastern Galician part was already under serious consideration in 1847; yet it was not materialized before the revolution. See the history of this administrative reform plan in Hanns Schlitter, *Aus Österreichs Vormärz,* Vol. I, "Galizien und Krakau" (Vienna, 1920), pp. 61 ff.

18. At that time the incurably ill Stadion, minister of the interior from spring, 1848, to summer, 1849, had already withdrawn from public office.

19. Fischel, *Der Panslawismus bis zum Weltkrieg,* pp. 311 f.

20. The Cyrillic alphabet was, however, gradually reintroduced under the Schmerling cabinet in various ordinances from 1860 to 1862. See Wenedikter, "Die Karpathenländer," in Hugelmann, pp. 690 f. See also the Ruthenian memorandum, submitted to the government by two high functionaries of the Ruthenian clergy, for reintroduction of the Cyrillic alphabet and for practical recognition of equal Ruthenian language rights in 1861. Fischel, *Materialien zum österreichischen Sprachenrecht,* No. 82.

21. The ideological influence of Michael Pogodin, the Russian historian of strong Pan-Slav convictions, was here particularly significant. See Seton-Watson, *Racial Problems in Hungary,* p. 57; Fischel, *Der Panslawismus bis zum Weltkrieg,* pp. 158 f., 185 ff., 310 f., 332, 360, 390 f.

22. See Rudnitzky, *The Ukraine and the Ukrainians,* pp. 26 f.; *The Ukraine,* British Foreign Office Handbook, No. 52, pp. 25 ff.; Fischel, *Der Panslawismus bis zum Weltkrieg,* pp. 358 ff.

23. On the Austrian-Cisleithanian franchise reform of 1906–1907 and its favorable influence on the Ruthenian position see below, Chapter XXIII.

24. On the Galician Compromise of 1914 see Wenedikter, "Die Karpathenländer," in Hugelmann, pp. 714 ff.

25. See, for instance, the Popovici plan for the federalization of the empire, which envisaged the creation of a Ruthenian member state comprising the Ruthenians in Galicia, Bukovina, and Hungary. Aurel C. Popovici, *Die Vereinigten Staaten von Gross-Österreich* (Leipzig, 1906). See also below, Chapter XXI, section on Aurel C. Popovici.

26. The fact that Ruthenian national policy, in spite of its basically increasing anti-Austrian course, was by no means entirely negative in its day-to-day policy is well illustrated by the comprehensive language bill of 1908, presented by the Ruthenian deputy Dr. Eugen Lewicky, one of the most valuable parliamentary contributions to that problem. For its basic ideas see Chapter V, section 8, footnote 98.

27. Certainly no such temptation was seen by the Ruthenians in the naïve World War attempts by the German and Austrian governments to set up a Ukrainian puppet state which, except for the small Cholm district, was not to include any part of eastern Galicia.

28. See Chap. XIV, below.

29. For a short survey of the socioeconomic conditions in Bukovina, see *Bukovina,* British Foreign Office Handbook, No. 5, and Eugen Ehrlich, *Die Aufgaben der Sozialpolitik im österreichischen Osten* (Munich, 1916).

30. On the history of the nationality legislation in the Bukovina see Wenedikter, "Die Karpathenländer," in Hugelmann, pp. 724 ff. On national statistics of educational institutions in the crownland see *ibid.,* p. 733.

31. Except for the practically meaningless representation in the Bosnian paper constitution of the same year. See Chapter X, above.

32. On the Compromise of 1910 see Bernatzik, *Österreichische Verfassungsgesetze*, pp. 937 ff.; Wenedikter, "Die Karpathenländer," in Hugelmann, pp. 728 ff.

The system of proportions of nationalities in the franchise order was applied in the elections of deputies to the central parliament in Vienna as well.

The Jewish representation in the crownland diet had to form a second German curia in a merely formal sense, since general Austrian administrative and judicial practice did not recognize the Jews as a separate nationality. Practically, however, within the crownland administration the Jews were recognized as a full-fledged national group having equal rights with the other nationalities. In this instance the recognition of Jewish national rights was supported equally by German and by Jewish demands. Since a very large percentage of the German-speaking population was Jewish, the Germans might otherwise have been represented exclusively by Jewish deputies or, possibly, the Jews largely by German Gentile representatives. In the era of tense national consciousness in this frontierland, and in line with obvious trends of the period, such a possibility appeared almost equally unacceptable to Germans and Jews. But for the outbreak of the war, this national recognition of the Jews might well have influenced the development of the Jewish problem in the empire as a whole, particularly in Galicia, where a rapidly increasing part of Jewry likewise demanded national recognition. However, no national movement of comparable strength yet existed among the Jews in Magyar Hungarian territories and western Austria. Nevertheless, the gradual rise of similar trends could be clearly observed there. See below, Appendices 1 and 3. Solomon Kassner, *Die Juden in der Bukowina* (Vienna, 1917); O. L. Janowsky, *The Jews and Minority Rights* (New York, 1933); Max Rosenfeld, *Die polnische Judenfrage* (Vienna, 1918); Saul Landau, *Der Polenklub und seine Hausjuden* (Vienna, 1907).

## DATE DUE

| | | | |
|---|---|---|---|
| FEB 22 '67 | | | |
| MAR 9 '67 | | | |
| APR 0 '67 | | | |
| APR 2 4 '67 | | | |
| AUG 2 '67 | | | |
| APR 2 0 '68 | | | |
| OCT 21 '68 | | | |
| MAR 24 '70 | | | |
| MAY 1 '70 | | | |
| JUN 18 '71 | | | |
| FEB 25 '72 | | | |
| AP 5 '79 | | | |
| MR 25 '82 | | | |
| | | | |
| | | | |
| | | | |
| | | | |
| GAYLORD | | | PRINTED IN U.S.A. |